BRIEF REVIEW

Physics

BERNADINE HLADIK COOK
Greater Johnstown
School District
Johnstown, New York

SAMUEL A. MARANTZ
formerly of
James Madison High School
New York City

ORDER INFORMATION

Send orders to:

PRENTICE HALL SCHOOL DIVISION
CUSTOMER SERVICE CENTER
4350 Equity Drive
P.O. Box 2649
Columbus, OH 43272

or

CALL TOLL-FREE: 1-800-848-9500
(8:00 AM–4:30 PM)

- Orders processed with your call. Please include the ISBN number on the back cover when ordering.
- **Your price includes all shipping and handling.**

PRENTICE HALL Textbook Programs that help you meet the requirements of the Regents:

Biology: The Study of Life
Biology by Miller and Levine
Chemistry: The Study of Matter
Chemistry: Connections to Our Changing World
Physics: Its Methods and Meanings
Earth Science: A Study of a Changing Planet

Prentice Hall

Needham, Massachusetts   Upper Saddle River, New Jersey

ABOUT THIS BOOK

General Description

Brief Review in Physics is a concise text designed to help you prepare for the New York State Regents examination in physics. This edition, which has been completely revised, provides explanations of all fundamental concepts included in the *new* physics syllabus and follows the sequence of topics in that syllabus. The text

- has all of the fundamental formulas of introductory physics;
- stresses the proper use of appropriate units for all quantities;
- gives numerous examples illustrating the basic types of calculations encountered in high school physics;
- contains hundreds of Regents-type practice questions interspersed throughout the text to illustrate preceding content;
- has two appendixes that review basic mathematical skills and problem-solving procedures required for solving physics problems;
- contains the Reference Tables for Physics used in the Regents course and Regents examination;
- includes the most recent Regents examinations; and
- has a section that helps you prepare for the College Board Achievement Test in Physics.

A separately bound Answer Key that has answers for all the questions in the text is available from the publisher.

Special Features

The text has three special features:

- Can You Explain This?
- Practical Applications
- Problem Solving

The first feature, Can You Explain This?, presents specific instances of the types of discrepancies listed in the physics syllabus. The discrepancies in this feature usually are related to a difference between what one expects to happen and what actually does happen, yet other types of discrepancies are also presented. For example, some events may seem inconsistent simply because of a lack of specific knowledge of the events. Or, an inconsistency may be the result of a difference between what is regarded as a fact and an observation that seems to contradict that fact. While the explanations of these discrepancies need not be memorized, questions about them may appear on the Regents examination.

The second special feature, Practical Applications, gives examples of the application of physics concepts to common phenomena, and thus enhances understanding by relating physics to everyday life. References to practical applications and questions about practical applications may appear on the Regents examination.

The third special feature, Problem Solving, is a section that appears at the end of each of the first five units (the five core units). Each "Problem Solving" section contains a sample problem that is followed by free-response problems for you to solve on your own. You will need to use a variety of techniques to solve these problems, including constructing a vector diagram, drawing a ray diagram, making and interpreting a graph, and comparing and contrasting two situations. Working these problems will help you prepare for the free-response portion of the Regents examination.

CONTENTS

Measurement

Because the science of physics is based on observations and measurements of the physical world, scientists have adopted standard conventions for describing natural phenomena. It is helpful to start with a review of these conventions.

SI UNITS

A **unit** is a standard quantity with which other similar quantities can be compared. All measurements must be made with respect to some standard quantity. It would not make sense to say that the length of a car is 4.3. The length would have to be stated in terms of a standard unit. For example, its length might be 4.3 meters. The International System of Units (*SI*) was established in 1960 to provide standardized units for scientific measurements. All quantities measured by physicists can be expressed in terms of the seven **fundamental units** indicated in Table 1. **Derived units** are combinations of two or more of the fundamental units and are used to simplify notation.

Analyzing units can help you in solving problems. The units on the left side of an equation must always be equivalent to the units on the right side of the equation. This can be used to check whether your answers are reasonable.

Table 1. The International System of Units *(SI)*.

	Quantity Being Measured	Name of Unit	Symbol
Fundamental units:	length	meter	m
	mass	kilogram	kg
	time	second	s
	electric current	ampere	A
	temperature	kelvin	K
	amount of substance	mole	mol
	luminous intensity	candela	c
Derived units:	frequency	hertz	Hz
	force	newton	N
	energy, work	joule	J
	quantity of electric charge	coulomb	C
	electric potential, potential difference	volt	V
	power	watt	W
	magnetic flux	weber	Wb
	electric resistance	ohm	Ω

Symbols for Units and Quantities

Symbols for *SI* units are printed in normal type. For example, m is the symbol for meters, and s is the symbol for seconds. Letter symbols are also used for the names of quantities in equations. These symbols are printed in *italic* type. For example, m is the symbol for mass, and s is the symbol for distance. Be careful not to confuse these different meanings of the same letter.

SCALAR AND VECTOR QUANTITIES

Physical quantities can be categorized as either scalar or vector quantities. As physical quantities are introduced in this text, their scalar or vector nature will be indicated.

A **scalar** quantity has only magnitude, without a direction being specified. Temperature and mass are examples of scalar quantities. For example, 30 degrees Celsius and 45 kilograms are scalar quantities. The measurement of a scalar quantity is indicated by a number with appropriate units. Scalar quantities are added and subtracted according to the rules of arithmetic.

A **vector** quantity has magnitude and direction. For example, velocity is a vector quantity because it must be described not only by a number with appropriate units but also by a specific direction. For example, the velocity of a car might be described as 30 meters per second, due north. Vector quantities are added and subtracted using geometric or algebraic methods; these methods will be illustrated later in the text.

UNIT 1   MECHANICS

I. KINEMATICS

Mechanics is the study of forces and motion. A mathematical description of motion itself without regard to the forces that produce it is called **kinematics.**

Distance and Displacement

When an object moves from one point to another, its change in position may be described by either distance or displacement. **Distance** is the total length of the path the object travels; **displacement** is a vector that extends in a straight line from the starting point to the ending point. In either case, the **meter**—the *SI* unit of length—is used; it is a fundamental unit and is represented by the symbol m.

If a baseball player runs the 27.4 meters from home plate to first base, then overruns 3.0 meters and finally returns to first base, the *distance* that he has traveled is 33.4 meters. However, the player's *displacement* from the starting point, home plate, is 27.4 meters directed along the first-base line. Distance is a scalar quantity having only magnitude. Displacement is a vector quantity having magnitude and direction. Total displacement is a *vector sum,* as illustrated in the following examples.

EXAMPLE

A student walks 5.0 meters due east and then 12.0 meters due north. Find the magnitude and direction of the student's resultant displacement, *R*.

Solution
Make a sketch of the situation.

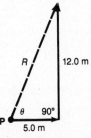

By the Pythagorean Theorem, in a right triangle,

$$c^2 = a^2 + b^2$$

3

Therefore,
$$R^2 = (5.0 \text{ m})^2 + (12.0 \text{ m})^2 = 25 \text{ m}^2 + 144 \text{ m}^2 = 169 \text{ m}^2$$
$$R = 13 \text{ m}$$
and
$$\sin \theta = {}^{12}\!/_{13} = 0.92$$
$$\theta = 67°$$

The resultant displacement is 13 m at 67° north of east

If, in the previous example, the student had walked 5.0 meters east and then 12.0 meters east, the resultant would have been 17.0 meters east. If the successive displacements had been 5.0 meters east and 12.0 meters west, the resultant would have been 7.0 meters west.

A more involved problem can be solved graphically using a scale drawing made with a metric ruler and protractor.

EXAMPLE

A person walks 5.0 meters due east and 12.0 meters at 60.° north of east. Find the magnitude and direction of the person's resultant displacement.

Solution

Construct a scale drawing. In the accompanying drawing, 1.0 cm represents 4.0 m.

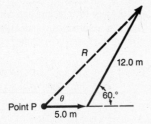

Scale: 1 cm = 4 m

Using a ruler, R measures 3.75 cm on the drawing. Therefore,

$$R = (3.75 \text{ cm})(4.0 \text{ m/cm}) = 15 \text{ m}$$

Using a protractor, θ measures 43°. Thus the resultant is 15 m at 43° north of east.

PRACTICAL APPLICATION ====

When traveling from city A to city B, a car's odometer records the distance traveled. The displacement is given by the direction and length of the straight line between the two cities. ■

Speed and Velocity

As an object moves, its position in space changes with time. The distance that a body moves in a unit of time is called its **speed;** speed is a scalar quantity. If s_i is the initial position of the body at time t_i, and s_f is the final position at time t_f, the change in position, or distance moved, is

$$\Delta s = s_f - s_i$$

and the change in time, or time taken for the motion, is

$$\Delta t = t_f - t_i$$

The average speed, $\bar{v}$, of the body is

$$\bar{v} = \frac{\Delta s}{\Delta t} \qquad \textbf{(Eq. 1-1)}$$

If the speed is constant during the entire time interval, the body is said to be in **uniform motion,** and $\bar{v}$ is its constant speed. If the speed is not constant, the motion is non-uniform. The average speed, $\bar{v}$, is the constant speed that would result in the same change in position, Δs, that resulted from the actual motion during the time interval, Δt. Equation 1-1 also shows that

$$\Delta s = \bar{v}\Delta t \qquad \text{(Eq. 1-1a)}$$

The **second,** s, is the *SI* unit of time; it is a fundamental unit. You can see from Equation 1-1 that the *SI* unit of speed is the meter/second, m/s. It is a derived unit.

When the speed of a body is associated with a direction, the result is the **velocity** of the body, a vector quantity. The speed of a body is the magnitude of its velocity. The velocity changes when the direction of motion changes, even if the speed remains the same. For example, if a body moves uniformly 150 m north in 10. s, its velocity is 150 m/10. s north = 15 m/s north. If it then moves 150 m east in 10. s, its velocity is 15 m/s east. Although its velocity changes, its *speed* is the same, 15 m/s, in both cases.

CAN YOU EXPLAIN THIS? ====

Two cars moving at 88 km/h in opposite directions have different velocities.

A scalar quantity, such as speed, has only magnitude. A vector quantity, such as velocity, has both magnitude and direction. Speed is the magnitude of velocity. The two cars have the same speed, but their velocities differ because their direction of travel is not the same. In physics, the terms speed and velocity may not be used interchangeably.

The distinction between speed and velocity is important chiefly in discussions of motion along curved paths. This unit covers motions that occur only along a straight path. On a straight path, there are only two possible directions for the velocity. One of these is called positive, and the other, for motion in the opposite direction, is called negative. Likewise, changes in displacement, or distance, are also positive or negative, depending on the direction of the motion. When discussing motion along a straight path, this book uses the symbol v for both velocity and speed, and it uses the symbol s for both displacement and distance.

Various kinds of straight-line motion can be described by means of graphs in which time (the independent variable) is measured along the horizontal axis and distance is measured along the vertical axis. Figure 1-1 shows several examples. A sloping straight-line graph indicates that the speed or velocity is constant. The magnitude of the slope of the graph line equals the speed, and the algebraic sign of the slope indicates whether the velocity is in the positive or negative (opposite) direction. A horizontal graph line indicates that the object is at rest (speed = 0). If the distance-time graph is a curved line, the speed is not constant. The slope of the tangent to the curve at any point is called the **instantaneous speed** of the body at that time. The steeper the slope, the greater the instantaneous speed.

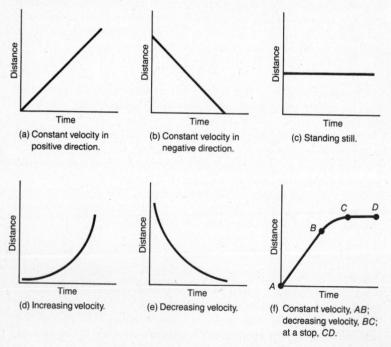

(a) Constant velocity in positive direction.

(b) Constant velocity in negative direction.

(c) Standing still.

(d) Increasing velocity.

(e) Decreasing velocity.

(f) Constant velocity, *AB*; decreasing velocity, *BC*; at a stop, *CD*.

Figure 1-1.   Graphs of linear motion.

Acceleration

The time-rate of change of velocity is **acceleration,** a vector quantity. The average acceleration, $\bar{a}$, over a period of time equals the change in velocity divided by the change in time:

$$\bar{a} = \frac{\Delta v}{\Delta t} \qquad \text{(Eq. 1-2)}$$

where $\Delta v = v_f - v_i$, and $\Delta t = t_f - t_i$. The *SI* unit of velocity is the meter per second, so it follows that the *SI* unit of acceleration is the meter per second squared, m/s^2.

If the acceleration is constant, or uniform, it may be represented by the symbol a, without the bar. This unit of the book covers only uniform accelerations.

You can use the change in velocity and the elapsed time to find uniform acceleration. For example, the velocity of a child coasting downhill on roller skates may increase from 4 m/s to 10. m/s in 3 s. The change in velocity, Δv, found by subtracting the initial velocity, v_i, from the final velocity, v_f, is 6 m/s downhill. The elapsed time, Δt, is 3 s. The acceleration, a, of the child may be found using Equation 1-2:

$$a = \frac{6 \text{ m/s}}{3 \text{ } s} = 2 \text{ m/s}^2, \text{ downhill}$$

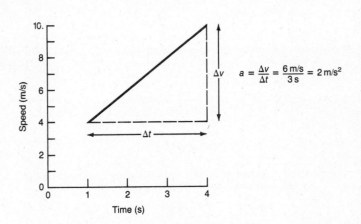

Figure 1-2. Graph on speed-time axes of a child accelerating at 2 m/s² for 3 s. Note that the slope of a speed-time graph gives the acceleration, a.

The acceleration of the child is shown graphically in Figure 1-2, where speed, or the magnitude of velocity, is plotted against time. The slope of the speed-time graph is the magnitude of the acceleration.

Accelerated motion of various kinds along straight paths can be shown on speed-time graphs (see Figure 1-3). For example, a horizontal line shows constant speed (no acceleration); a line with positive slope shows increasing speed (acceleration); and one with negative slope shows decreasing speed (negative acceleration or deceleration). A line that crosses the time axis is interpreted as a change of direction: the speed in one direction decreases to zero at the time the graph line crosses the time axis, and then the speed increases in the opposite direction. A curved speed-time line indicates that the acceleration is not constant.

  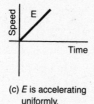

(a) Both *A* and *B* are moving at constant speed; acceleration is zero; *A* is traveling faster than *B*.

(b) *C* and *D* have zero acceleration, constant speed. *D* is moving faster than *C*, but in the opposite direction.

(c) *E* is accelerating uniformly.

(d) The speed of *F* is decreasing uniformly.

(e) *G* is decreasing speed from (1) to (2), is motionless at (2), and increases speed in the opposite direction from (2) to (3). Slope and acceleration are negative at all times. (An object thrown upward would have this curve.)

(f) *H* is at rest up to time (1), and has nonuniform acceleration after that time.

Figure 1-3.   Graphs of various types of motion in a straight path, drawn on speed-time axes.

QUESTIONS

1. **Which graph represents the motion of an object moving with a constant speed?**

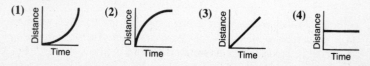

2. Which is a vector quantity? (1) speed (2) time (3) velocity (4) distance

3–7. Base your answers to Questions 3 through 7 on the graph at right, which represents the motion of a cart traveling for 12 seconds along a straight line.

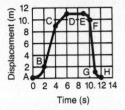

3. The cart was at rest during the interval (1) *AB* (2) *BC* (3) *DE* (4) *GH*
4. The total distance covered by the cart in 12 seconds was (1) 6 m (2) 11 m (3) 12 m (4) 22 m
5. The average speed of the cart during interval *CD* was (1) 1 m/s (2) 2 m/s (3) 10. m/s (4) 11 m/s
6. An interval during which the cart was moving with constant velocity is (1) *AB* (2) *BC* (3) *EF* (4) *GH*
7. A part of the trip during which the cart's velocity was not constant is represented by the line (1) *AB* (2) *BC* (3) *DE* (4) *FG*

Final Velocity and Distance Traveled During Constant Acceleration

The average speed, $\bar{v}$, of a body that accelerates uniformly from an initial speed, v_i, to a final speed, v_f, can be written as

$$\bar{v} = \frac{v_f + v_i}{2} \qquad \text{(Eq. 1-3)}$$

By rearranging Equation 1-2 (page 7), you can see that $\Delta v = a\Delta t$. Into this formula you can substitute $v_f - v_i$ for Δv, which gives

$$v_f - v_i = a\Delta t$$

$$v_f = v_i + a\Delta t$$

Substituting this value of v_f into Equation 1-3 gives

$$\bar{v} = \frac{(v_i + a\Delta t) + v_i}{2} = v_i + \tfrac{1}{2}a\Delta t$$

Substituting this formula for $\bar{v}$ in Equation 1-1a

$$\Delta s = \bar{v}\Delta t \qquad \text{(Eq. 1-1a)}$$

gives

$$\Delta s = (v_i + \tfrac{1}{2}a\Delta t)\Delta t$$

$$\Delta s = v_i\Delta t + \tfrac{1}{2}a(\Delta t)^2 \qquad \text{(Eq. 1-4)}$$

From Equation 1-2, $\Delta t = (v_f - v_i)/a$. Substituting this value of Δt into Equation 1-4, gives

$$\Delta s = \frac{v_i(v_f - v_i)}{a} + \frac{\frac{1}{2}a(v_f - v_i)^2}{a^2}$$

$$a\Delta s = v_i v_f - v_i^2 + \frac{1}{2}(v_f^2 - 2v_i v_f + v_i^2)$$

$$a\Delta s = v_i v_f - v_i^2 + \frac{1}{2}v_f^2 - v_i v_f + \frac{1}{2}v_i^2$$

$$a\Delta s = \frac{1}{2}v_f^2 - \frac{1}{2}v_i^2$$

$$v_f^2 = v_i^2 + 2a\Delta s \qquad \textbf{(Eq. 1-5)}$$

In many problems involving motion, the initial speed, v_i, is zero. In such cases, some of the equations given above can be simplified to the following useful forms:

$$a = \frac{v_f}{\Delta t} \qquad \text{(Eq. 1-2a)}$$

$$\bar{v} = \frac{v_f}{2} \qquad \text{(Eq. 1-3a)}$$

$$\Delta s = \frac{1}{2}a(\Delta t)^2 \qquad \text{(Eq. 1-4a)}$$

$$v_f^2 = 2a\Delta s \qquad \text{(Eq. 1-5a)}$$

where v_f is the speed at the end of time Δt, and the acceleration, a, is uniform, or constant. The symbol for the final velocity, v_f, is often written simply as v. This practice is followed in this text. There are four quantities in these equations that may be given in a problem involving motion starting from rest: a, v, Δs, and Δt. If any two of these quantities are given, the equations can be used to find the other two.

EXAMPLE

A plane increases its speed uniformly, starting from rest and reaching a speed of 50. meters/second after 10. seconds. Find (a) the average speed of the airplane, (b) the acceleration, and (c) the distance traveled during these 10. seconds.

Solution

The given quantities are $v = 50.$ m/s and $\Delta t = 10.$ s.

(a) From Equation 1-3a,

$$\bar{v} = \frac{v}{2} = \frac{50. \text{ m/s}}{2} = 25 \text{ m/s}$$

(b) From Equation 1-2a,

$$a = \frac{v}{\Delta t} = \frac{50. \text{ m/s}}{10. \text{ s}} = 5.0 \text{ m/s}^2$$

(c) From Equation 1-4a,

$$\Delta s = \tfrac{1}{2}a(\Delta t)^2 = \tfrac{1}{2}(5.0 \text{ m/s}^2)(10. \text{ s})^2 = 250 \text{ m}$$

The motion of the airplane can be represented by a speed-time graph, as shown in Figure 1-4. The quantities in the example above can be found from the graph. The average speed equals one-half the final speed (Figure 1-4a). The slope of the graph equals the acceleration (Figure 1-4b). The distance equals the area of the right triangle under the graph line (shaded area in Figure 1-4c). To understand why the distance equals the area of the triangle, look at the small rectangle $ABCD$ in Figure 1-4d. The area of this rectangle equals $v_t\Delta t$. This is also equal to the distance traveled at speed v_t during the small time interval Δt. The entire triangle can be divided into small rectangles, each equal to a part of the total distance. Adding all of these areas gives both the total distance and the total area.

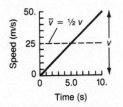

(a) The average velocity, $\bar{v}$, equals $\tfrac{1}{2}$ of the final velocity, v.

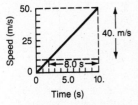

(b) On a speed-time graph, the slope of the line equals the acceleration:

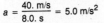

$$a = \frac{40. \text{ m/s}}{8.0. \text{ s}} = 5.0 \text{ m/s}^2$$

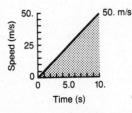

(c) The distance traveled by the plane equals the area under the graph (shaded area). This area is $\tfrac{1}{2}$ of the base of the triangle (10. s) multiplied by the altitude of the triangle (50. m/s):

Distance = $\tfrac{1}{2}$ (10. s)(50. m/s) = 250 m/s

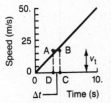

(d) The area of the small dashed rectangle $ABCD$ is $v_t\Delta t$. See the text for an explanation of the use of this rectangle.

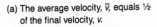

Figure 1-4.   The meaning of a speed-time graph.

Figure 1-5 indicates how distances traveled at various speeds may be calculated and compared.

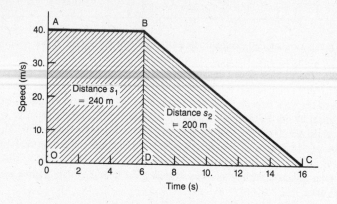

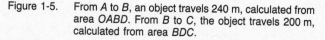

Figure 1-5.   From A to B, an object travels 240 m, calculated from
               area OABD. From B to C, the object travels 200 m,
               calculated from area BDC.

From $t = 0.0$ s to $t = 6.0$ s, the object traveled at a constant speed of 40. m/s. Therefore,

$$\Delta s = v\Delta t = (40.\text{ m/s})(6.0\text{ s}) = 240\text{ m}$$

Between $t = 6.0$ s and $t = 16$ s, the average speed was 20. m/s, so the distance traveled was

$$\Delta s = \bar{v}\Delta t = (20.\text{ m/s})(10.\text{ s}) = 200\text{ m}$$

Thus, the total distance traveled was 440 m.

PRACTICAL APPLICATION

The equation $v_f^2 = v_i^2 + 2a\Delta s$ (Equation 1-5) can be used to calculate the stopping distance of a car if the acceleration and initial velocity are known. For example, suppose a driver traveling at 30. m/s applies the brakes to decelerate at $-10.$ m/s^2. The final velocity will be 0. m/s. From Equation 1-5,

$$2a\Delta s = v_f^2 - v_i^2$$

$$\Delta s = \frac{v_f^2 - v_i^2}{2a} = \frac{0^2 - (30.\text{ m/s}^2)^2}{2(-10.\text{ m/s}^2)}$$

$$\Delta s = \frac{-900\text{ m}^2/\text{s}^2}{-20.\text{ m/s}^2} = 45\text{ m}$$

If the initial velocity were doubled to 60. m/s, the stopping distance would quadruple:

$$\Delta s = \frac{-3600 \text{ m}^2/\text{s}^2}{-20. \text{ m/s}^2} = 180 \text{ m}$$

Thus, at higher speeds drivers need to leave much more distance between cars to allow for the longer stopping distance. ∎

Freely Falling Objects

Near the surface of the earth, an object falling freely has a constant acceleration due to the force of gravity. Neglecting air friction, this acceleration due to gravity, g, is 9.8 m/s^2. The speed of a body falling from rest and the distance it falls during time Δt can be found using Equations 1-2a and 1-4a. In this case, the acceleration a equals g:

$$v = g\Delta t$$

$$\Delta s = \tfrac{1}{2}g(\Delta t)^2$$

The following table shows the changes in distance and speed of an object, initially at rest, during its first five seconds of free fall, assuming negligible air friction.

Table 1-1. Free fall of an object starting at rest.

Time of fall (s)	0.00	1.00	2.00	3.00	4.00	5.00
Speed (m/s)	0.0	9.8	19.6	29.4	39.2	49.0
Distance traveled (m)	0.0	4.9	19.6	44.1	78.4	123.0

CAN YOU EXPLAIN THIS? ═══════════════════

Although the acceleration due to gravity of any freely falling object near the surface of the earth is 9.8 m/s^2, a coin will hit the ground before a feather dropped from the same height at the same time.

The actual acceleration of the feather is less than that of the coin because the shape and exposed area of the feather result in greater air resistance. If the air is removed from a tall tube, the coin and the feather will fall with the same acceleration inside the tube. Astronaut David Scott simultaneously dropped a hammer and a feather on the moon and both objects fell with the same acceleration to the surface, because the moon has no atmosphere, and thus, no air resistance.

PRACTICAL APPLICATION

Examples of free fall include amusement park rides such as the roller coaster and sports such as sky diving (assuming negligible air resistance). ∎

QUESTIONS

1. The graph at right shows the speed of an object plotted against time. The total distance traveled by the object during the first 4.0 seconds is (1) 0.50 m (2) 2.0 m (3) 8.0 m (4) 4.0 m

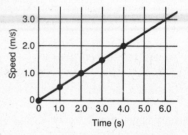

2. How far will a freely falling object, initially at rest, fall in 2.4 seconds? (1) 6.0 m (2) 12 m (3) 23 m (4) 28 m

3. An object originally at rest is uniformly accelerated along a straight-line path to a speed of 8.0 meters/second in 2.00 seconds. The acceleration of the object is (1) 0.25 m/s² (2) 10. m/s² (3) 16 m/s² (4) 4.0 m/s²

4. The time-rate of change of displacement is (1) acceleration (2) distance (3) velocity (4) speed

5. A body falls freely from rest near the surface of the earth. The distance the body falls in 2.00 seconds is (1) 2.3 m (2) 7.1 m (3) 12 m (4) 20. m

6. Which graph represents the motion of a freely falling object near the surface of the earth?

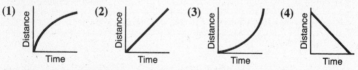

7. To change the velocity of an object, there *must* be (1) an increase in its speed (2) a decrease in its speed (3) a change in either its speed or direction (4) a change in both its speed and direction

8. The motions of cars A, B, and C in a straight path are represented by the graph at right. During the time interval from t_1 to t_2, the three cars travel (1) the same distance (2) with the same speed only (3) with the same acceleration only (4) with both the same speed and the same acceleration

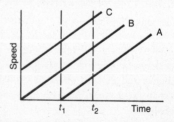

9. An object is accelerated uniformly from rest to a speed of 25 meters per second in 10. seconds. The acceleration of the object is (1) 1.0 m/s² (2) 2.0 m/s² (3) 1.5 m/s² (4) 2.5 m/s²

10. **Starting from rest, how far can a 2.00-kilogram mass fall freely in 1.00 second?** (1) 4.90 m (2) 2.00 m (3) 9.80 m (4) 19.6 m

11. **As the time required to accelerate an object from rest to a speed of 4 meters per second decreases, the acceleration of the object** (1) decreases (2) increases (3) remains the same

12. **As an object falls freely near the earth, its acceleration** (1) decreases (2) increases (3) remains the same

13. **The velocity-time graph at right represents the motion of a ball released vertically upward at $t =$ 0. During the time interval 1.0 second to 2.0 seconds, the displacement of the ball from the point where it was released** (1) decreases (2) increases (3) remains the same

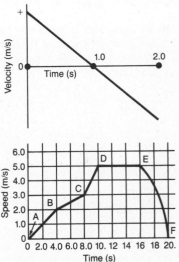

14–18. Base your answers to Questions 14 through 18 on the graph at right, which represents the changing speed of a cart during an interval of 20. seconds.

14. **What is the distance traveled by the cart during interval AB?** (1) 1.0 m (2) 2.0 m (3) 8.0 m (4) 4.0 m

15. **In which of the following intervals is the magnitude of the cart's acceleration greatest?** (1) AB (2) BC (3) CD (4) DE

16. **During interval BC, the magnitude of the cart's acceleration is** (1) 1.0 m/s^2 (2) 0.25 m/s^2 (3) 0.50 m/s^2 (4) 4.0 m/s^2

17. **The average speed of the cart during interval CD is** (1) 15 m/s (2) 2.0 m/s (3) 7.5 m/s (4) 4.0 m/s

18. **The cart's acceleration is changing during interval** (1) BC (2) CD (3) DE (4) EF

19–23. Base your answers to Questions 19 through 23 on the velocity-time graph at right.

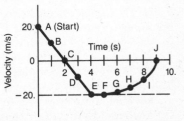

19. **During which interval is the magnitude of the object's acceleration greatest?** (1) EF (2) FG (3) GH (4) IJ

20. The acceleration of the object at point D on the curve is (1) 0 m/s^2 (2) 5 m/s^2 (3) -10 m/s^2 (4) -20 m/s^2

21. During what interval does the object have zero acceleration? (1) BC (2) EF (3) GH (4) HI

22. At what point is the object's displacement from the start equal to zero? (1) C (2) E (3) F (4) J

23. At what point is the object's displacement from the start a minimum? (1) C (2) E (3) G (4) J

24–28. Base your answers to Questions 24 through 28 on the speed-time graph at right representing the motion of a cart.

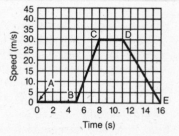

24. The cart travels the shortest distance in interval (1) AB (2) BC (3) CD (4) DE

25. The cart's average speed is greatest during interval (1) AB (2) BC (3) CD (4) DE

26. The cart travels the greatest distance during interval (1) AB (2) BC (3) CD (4) DE

27. The magnitude of the cart's acceleration is greatest during interval (1) AB (2) BC (3) CD (4) DE

28. During how many intervals is the cart's acceleration equal to zero? (1) 1 (2) 2 (3) 3 (4) 4

29. A cart initially traveling at 10. meters per second north accelerates uniformly at 3.0 meters per second squared to the north for 4.0 seconds. The displacement of the cart from its initial position at the end of this 4.0 seconds is (1) 40. m north (2) 64 m north (3) 88 m north (4) 180 m north

30. A cart initially traveling at 10. meters per second to the right and accelerating uniformly at 2.0 meters per second squared to the right is displaced 11 meters. The final velocity of the cart is (1) 2.0 m/s right (2) 2.0 m/s left (3) 12 m/s right (4) 12 m/s left

31. An object initially traveling at 20. meters per second west decelerates uniformly at 4.0 meters per second squared for 2.0 seconds. The displacement of the object during these 2.0 seconds is (1) 32 m east (2) 32 m west (3) 48 m east (4) 48 m west

32. An object initially traveling at 20. meters per second south decelerates uniformly at 6.0 meters per second squared and is displaced 25 meters. The final velocity of the object is (1) 26 m/s north (2) 26 m/s south (3) 10. m/s north (4) 10. m/s south

II. STATICS

The division of mechanics that studies the relation between forces acting on an object at rest is called **statics.**

Concurrent Forces

Any push or pull is a **force.** Force is a vector quantity because it is always associated with a direction. In the *SI* system, the magnitude of a push or pull is expressed in newtons, N, a derived unit. (Force and the derivation of the newton will be further explained in Section III, Dynamics.)

Two or more forces that act on the same body at the same time are called **concurrent forces.** The single force that is equivalent to the combined effect of these concurrent forces is called the **resultant.**

If two concurrent forces act in the same direction (at an angle of 0° to each other), their resultant is simply the sum of their magnitudes, acting in the same direction as the two forces. This is the largest resultant that two forces can have. If the two forces act in the same line, but in opposite directions (at an angle of 180° to each other), their resultant is the *difference* of their magnitudes, acting in the direction of the larger force. This is the smallest possible resultant of the two forces. Figure 1-6 illustrates these facts for a force of 8.0 N acting concurrently with a force of 6.0 N. The resultant for an angle of 0° is 14.0 N; for an angle of 180°, it is 2.0 N in the direction of the 8.0-N force.

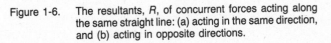

(a) Vectors acting in the same direction

Adding the vectors (head-to-tail method)

$F_1 = 8.0$ N

$F_2 = 6.0$ N

head-to-tail

$F_1 = 8.0$ N $F_2 = 6.0$ N

$R = 14$ N

(b) Vectors acting in opposite directions

$F_1 = 8.0$ N $F_2 = 6.0$ N

Adding the vectors (head-to-tail method)

$F_1 = 8.0$ N

$F_2 = 6.0$ N $R = 2.0$ N

head-to-tail

Figure 1-6.   The resultants, R, of concurrent forces acting along the same straight line: (a) acting in the same direction, and (b) acting in opposite directions.

Triangle Method of Adding Concurrent Forces. The resultant of two concurrent forces acting at an angle between 0° and 180° can be found by the triangle method of vector addition. In this method, each force is represented by a vector arrow drawn to scale, with its length corresponding to the magnitude of the force and its direction corresponding to the direction of the force. To add the two vectors, the tail of the second vector is placed at the head of the first vector.

The resultant is the vector drawn from the tail of the first vector to the head of the second vector, as shown in Figure 1-7. If the two vectors are drawn accurately, the magnitude of the resultant can be found by measuring the vector length, and its direction can be found with a protractor. Note that in Figure 1-7a, the magnitude of the resultant is greater than either force. In Figure 1-7b, it is smaller than either force. Figure 1-7c shows that the resultant of any number of concurrent forces acting on a body can be found by adding their vectors head to tail. The final resultant is the **net force** acting on the body.

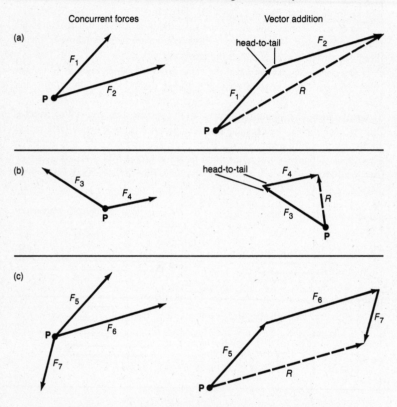

Figure 1-7. Adding force vectors by the triangle method.

If two concurrent forces act at right angles (90°) to each other, their resultant can be calculated from the Pythagorean theorem for right triangles, $c^2 = a^2 + b^2$, as well as graphically by vector addition. Figure 1-8 illustrates this method for a force of 8.0 N acting east and a force of 6.0 N acting north (at right angles to the 8.0-N force). The magnitude of the resultant is the square root of the sum $(8.0 \text{ N})^2 + (6.0 \text{ N})^2$. The square root of this sum is 10. N. The direction can be found from the sine of the angle (6.0/10. = 0.60). From a table of sines, the angle is found to be 37°. The direction of the resultant is therefore 37° north of east. These results will agree with measurements of an accurately drawn vector diagram.

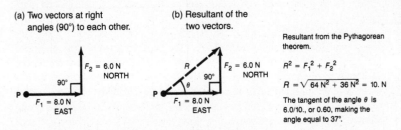

Figure 1-8.   Finding the resultant of two concurrent forces acting at right angles (90°) to each other.

Parallelogram Method of Adding Concurrent Forces. An alternate method of graphical addition of two concurrent forces is the parallelogram method illustrated in Figure 1-9. In this method, the two vectors are drawn from the same point. A parallelogram is then constructed with these vectors as adjacent sides. The diagonal of the parallelogram drawn from the vertex of the two vector tails is the resultant. Since opposite sides of a parallelogram are equal and parallel, this method is seen to be equivalent to the triangle method.

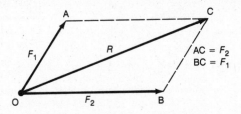

Figure 1-9.   Finding the resultant of two concurrent forces at any angle to each other by the parallelogram method.

These methods also can be used to find the resultant (or net force) of more than two concurrent forces. First the resultant of any two of the forces is found. This force is then added to a third force, and the process is repeated until all the forces are accounted for.

Resolution of Forces

A single force can be considered to be the resultant of two concurrent forces, called **components** of the force. Any force can have an unlimited number of components, but forces are usually divided, or resolved, into two components that are positioned at right angles to each other. The process of finding the magnitude and direction of component forces is called **resolution of forces.** It is the reverse of the process of vector addition that you have just finished reading about.

The component forces are generally given directions to match the x and y axes of a graph. These directions might be east-west and north-south, perpendicular and parallel to the ground, or perpendicular and parallel to an incline. The method of resolution of a force is illustrated in Figure 1-10, which shows a force of 50. N at 37° north of east that has been graphically resolved into two component forces at an angle of 90.° to each other. One force, F_1, is along the north-south axis, and the other force, F_2, is along the east-west axis. The magnitude of each force is found by drawing perpendiculars to each axis from the head end of the given vector. The line drawn from the origin, O, to each intersection with the axes will determine the magnitude of each vector. The components are thus found to be: $F_1 = 30$. N north, $F_2 = 40$. N east. Note that the vector sum of the components is equal to the original force, F.

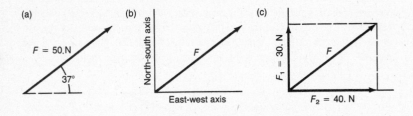

Figure 1-10   Resolution of a force into two components at right angles (90.°) to each other. (a) The vector to be resolved is a force vector, F, of 50. N directed at 37° north of east. (b) Horizontal (east-west) and vertical (north-south) axes are constructed at the tail of the vector. (c) Dashed lines that start at the head of vector F and extend perpendicularly to the axes define two new vectors, F_1 and F_2, that are the vertical and horizontal components of the original force vector, F. To the scale of the drawing, F_1 measures 30. N north and F_2 measures 40. N east.

Sometimes it is necessary to find components of a force along directions, or axes, that are *not* at right angles to each other. In that case, the reverse of the parallelogram method of adding vectors is used, as illustrated in Figure 1-11. Each component of the force is found by drawing a line that is parallel to an axis and that extends from the head of the vector to the point at which the line intersects the other axis. It can be seen that the resultant of the two components is the original force.

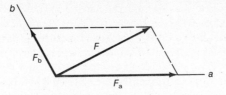

Figure 1-11.   Finding the components of a force, F, along two axes
a and b at any angle to each other.

PRACTICAL APPLICATION

When pulling a suitcase along the ground by a strap, the force that needs to be
exerted depends on the angle of the strap with the ground. The force that moves
the suitcase is the component of the applied force parallel to the ground. This
component is a smaller fraction of the applied force when the angle with the
ground is larger. Therefore, a larger force must be applied to move the suitcase
as the angle of the strap becomes larger. ∎

Equilibrium

As illustrated in Figure 1-8 (page 19), the resultant of a force of 8.0 N east
and 6.0 N north is a force of 10. N acting at 37° north of east. If a third force of
10. N acting 37° south of west were applied, the net force would be zero. Such a
force, which is equal in magnitude and opposite in direction to the resultant of
concurrent forces, is called the **equilibrant** of those forces.

If the vector sum of the concurrent forces, or net force, acting on a body is
zero, the body is in **static equilibrium.** An object in static equilibrium is at rest.
Figure 1-12a shows a sign hanging from the side of a building. Since the sign is
at rest, it is in static equilibrium, and the net force on it must be zero. There are
three forces acting on the sign: its weight, acting downward; the force exerted by
the cable, pulling in the direction of the cable toward the building; and the
outward push of the horizontal rod.

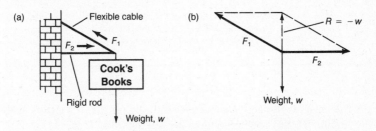

Figure 1-12.   (a) A sign supported by a flexible cable and a rigid
rod. (b) A free-body diagram showing the relationships among the forces on the sign while it is in static
equilibrium.

Figure 1-12b is a free-body diagram for the sign. A **free-body diagram** shows all the forces acting on an object. The weight of the sign must be the equilibrant of the forces exerted by the cable and the rod. That is, the weight is equal in magnitude and opposite in direction to the resultant of those two forces. Therefore, if we know the weight of the sign, we can draw the resultant of the two other forces. We can then resolve the resultant into two components, one acting along the direction of the cable, the other along the direction of the rod. The free-body diagram allows us to determine the forces exerted by the rigid rod and the flexible cable.

PRACTICAL APPLICATION

The free-body diagram in Figure 1-12b can be used to determine how strong the cable must be. Because F_1 in this scale drawing is twice the length of w, the cable must be able to support a force twice as great as the weight of the sign. ■

CAN YOU EXPLAIN THIS?

A child whose mass is 30 kilograms can outpull two football linemen, each of whose mass is 90 kilograms.

The diagram shows two linemen and a child pulling on an object. The resultant of the pulls of the linemen is quite small. The child can easily exert enough force to overcome this resultant and make the object move toward her.

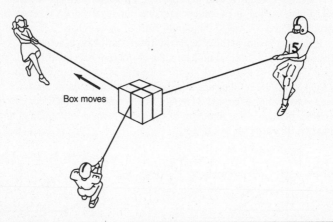

Box moves

QUESTIONS

1. An object is displaced 3.0 meters to the west and then 4.0 meters to the south. Which vector represents the resultant displacement?

(1) | 37°   (2) | 55°   (3) 37° | (4) 55° |

2. Four forces act concurrently on a point as shown at the right. The resultant of the four forces is (1) 0.0 N (2) 5.0 N (3) 14 N (4) 20. N

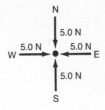

3. A 5-newton force directed north and a 5-newton force directed west both act on the same point. The resultant of these two forces is approximately (1) 5 N northwest (2) 7 N northwest (3) 5 N southwest (4) 7 N southwest

4. The resultant of a 12-newton force and a 7-newton force has a magnitude of 5 newtons. The angle between the original forces is (1) 0° (2) 45° (3) 90.° (4) 180.°

5. Two concurrent forces of 30. newtons act to produce a resultant whose magnitude is 60. newtons. The angle between the two original forces must be (1) 0° (2) 60.° (3) 90.° (4) 120.°

6. Concurrent forces of 10. newtons east and 10. newtons south act on an object. The resultant force is (1) 0.0 N (2) 5.0 N southeast (3) 14 N southeast (4) 20. N southeast

7. Which pair of concurrent forces may produce a resultant of 20. newtons? (1) 5.0 N and 10. N (2) 20. N and 20. N (3) 20. N and 50. N (4) 30. N and 5.0 N

8. The magnitude of the resultant force produced by a 9.0-newton force acting west and a 12.0-newton force acting south concurrently on a point is (1) 30. N (2) 25 N (3) 3.0 N (4) 15 N

9. Which vector best represents the resultant of forces F_1 and F_2 acting on point P?

(1) 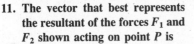 (2) (3) (4)

10. The resultant of two forces acting on the same point is a maximum when the angle between the two forces is (1) 0° (2) 45° (3) 90° (4) 180°

11. The vector that best represents the resultant of the forces F_1 and F_2 shown acting on point P is

(1)  (2) (3) (4)

12. What is the magnitude of the vertical or y-component of vector *OB* in the diagram? (1) 9 (2) 6 (3) 3 (4) 0

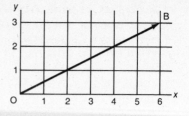

13. Which force could act concurrently with force *A* to produce force *B* as a resultant?

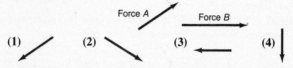

14. Three forces act concurrently on an object in equilibrium. These forces are 10. newtons, 8 newtons, and 6 newtons. The resultant of the 6-newton and 8-newton forces has a magnitude of (1) 0.0 N (2) between 0.0 and 10. N (3) 10. N (4) more than 10. N

15. As the angle between two concurrent forces increases, the magnitude of their resultant (1) decreases (2) increases (3) remains the same

16. As the angle between two concurrent forces is increased from 15 degrees to 75 degrees, the magnitude of their equilibrant (1) decreases (2) increases (3) remains the same

III. DYNAMICS

The study of how the forces acting on an object affect its motion is the subject matter of **dynamics.** The fundamental laws and principles of dynamics were established by Isaac Newton about 300 years ago.

The Relationship Between Force and Motion

Newton's First Law of Motion. As stated previously, when the resultant of all the forces acting on an object is zero, that is, all the forces are balanced, the object is in a state of equilibrium. Newton's first law of motion, the law of inertia, states that an object in a state of equilibrium will remain at rest or, if in motion, will maintain a uniform (constant, straight-line) velocity, unless it is acted upon by an unbalanced force. In effect, this laws says that an unbalanced force will always produce a *change* in velocity—an acceleration—by changing the speed of the object, its direction of motion, or both.

For example, a car parked on a level road (velocity = 0) will not start moving (accelerating) unless an unbalanced force is applied to it by the motor or by other means. Although there *are* forces acting on the car (gravity and the upward push of the ground), the forces are balanced. The same is true of an airplane moving at constant speed in one direction (moving with constant velocity). Its velocity will not change unless an unbalanced force acts upon it.

This resistance of an object to a change in its state of motion is called **inertia.** The inertia of an object is directly proportional to its **mass,** the amount of matter the object contains. The **kilogram,** kg, is the *SI* unit of mass. It is a fundamental unit.

CAN YOU EXPLAIN THIS?

A space probe continues moving after the engines are shut off.

According to Newton's first law of motion, an object remains at rest or moves with a constant velocity unless acted upon by an unbalanced force. The space probe, experiencing no unbalanced force such as air resistance, continues to move at constant speed in a straight line.

PRACTICAL APPLICATION

If a car hits an obstruction, the force of the collision may cause a rapid deceleration of the car. This force, however, does not act on the occupants of the car. They therefore continue to move forward at the same speed as before the collision, until they are decelerated by colliding with some part of the car, such as the dashboard or front window. A seat belt fastens the occupants to the car, allowing them to decelerate at the same rate as the car. This prevents the serious injury that might result from unrestrained forward motion during a collision. ∎

Newton's Second Law of Motion. When an unbalanced net force acts on an object, the object is accelerated in the direction in which the force acts. For a given object, the larger the unbalanced force, the greater the resulting acceleration. Acceleration is therefore directly proportional to force. Experience also shows that the greater the mass of an object, the less a given force will accelerate it. For example, the same force will give less acceleration to a loaded cart than to an empty cart. Acceleration is therefore inversely proportional to mass. Combining these proportionalities gives Newton's second law, which states that the unbalanced force, F, applied to an object is equal to its mass, m, multiplied by the acceleration, a, produced by the force. In equation form,

$$F = ma \qquad \text{(Eq. 1-6)}$$

The force that gives an acceleration of one meter per second squared to a one-kilogram mass is one **newton.** As stated earlier, the newton, N, is the *SI* unit of force. It is a derived unit equal to one kilogram · meter per second squared. That is,

$$1 \text{ N} = 1 \text{ kg} \cdot \text{m/s}^2$$

Written in the form $a = F/m$, the equation shows that the acceleration is directly proportional to the force and inversely proportional to the mass. In the form $m = F/a$, the equation defines the mass of an object as the ratio between the force acting on it and the resulting acceleration. That is, the slope of a force-acceleration graph is the mass of the object. In Figure 1-13, the mass of the body is 2.5 kg.

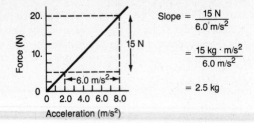

Figure 1-13.   The slope of the line on a force-acceleration graph
               gives the mass of the object being accelerated. Note
               in the calculation that the newton, N, is equivalent to
               a kilogram-meter per second squared.

EXAMPLE

A 10.-newton force gives a mass, m_1, an acceleration a. A 20.-newton force
gives another mass, m_2, the same acceleration. How large is m_1 compared
to m_2?

Solution

If $F = ma$ (Newton's second law), then $m = F/a$. Therefore,

$$m_1 = 10. \ \text{N}/a \qquad \qquad \text{(Eq. A)}$$

Applying the same equation, $m = F/a$, to m_2:

$$m_2 = 20. \ \text{N}/a \qquad \qquad \text{(Eq. B)}$$

To compare m_1 and m_2, divide Equation A by Equation B:

$$\frac{m_1}{m_2} = \frac{10. \ \text{N}/a}{20. \ \text{N}/a}, \quad \text{or}$$

$$m_1 = \tfrac{1}{2} m_2$$

Newton's Third Law of Motion. According to Newton's third law of motion, whenever one object exerts a force on a second object, the second object
exerts an equal force on the first object, but in the opposite direction. The two
equal and opposing forces are often referred to as "action" and "reaction," and
the third law then states that to every action there is always an equal and opposite reaction. One of the most important consequences of Newton's third law of
motion is that a single force cannot be produced in nature; when one force is
generated, another force of equal magnitude and opposite direction must also be
generated.

For example, if a bat exerts a 50.-newton force on a baseball, the bat at the
same time receives a 50.-newton force from the ball, but in the opposite direction. Each member of the pair of forces acts on a different object: one force acts
on the ball and the other on the bat. If no other forces are present, the objects
will be accelerated in opposite directions as long as the forces are applied.

CAN YOU EXPLAIN THIS?

A wall can push.

You can push as hard as you wish against a wall, because the wall "pushes back." If the wall did not exert a reaction force equal and opposite to your push, you could not exert the push in the first place.

QUESTIONS

1. The unbalanced force required to accelerate a 2.0-kilogram mass at 4.0 meters per second squared is (1) 6.0 N (2) 2.0 N (3) 8.0 N (4) 16 N

2. A force of 10. newtons applied to a given mass accelerates it at 1.0 meter per second squared. The same force applied to a mass one-half as great would produce an acceleration of (1) 1.0 m/s^2 (2) 2.0 m/s^2 (3) 0.50 m/s^2 (4) 4.0 m/s^2

3. Which is a derived unit? (1) second (2) meter (3) kilogram (4) newton

4. An unbalanced force of 2.0 newtons acts on a 3.0-kilogram object for 6.0 seconds. The magnitude of the object's change in velocity is (1) 18 m/s (2) 2.0 m/s (3) 36 m/s (4) 4.0 m/s

5. If an unbalanced force of 50. newtons accelerates an object 20. meters per second squared, the mass of the object is (1) 0.40 kg (2) 2.5 kg (3) 70. kg (4) 1,000 kg

6. What unbalanced force must be applied to a 2.0-kilogram mass moving at 5.0 meters per second to give it an acceleration of 5.0 meters per second squared? (1) 0.40 N (2) 2.5 N (3) 10. N (4) 20. N

7. A 30.-kilogram child exerts a force of 100 newtons on a 50.-kilogram object. The force the object exerts on the child is (1) 0.0 N (2) 100 N (3) 980 N (4) 1,500 N

8. A car whose mass is 2,000 kilograms is accelerated uniformly from rest to a speed of 15 meters per second in 10. seconds on a level highway. The net force accelerating the car is (1) 2,000 N (2) 3,000 N (3) 20,000 N (4) 30,000 N

9. A certain net force causes a 10.-kilogram mass to accelerate at 20. meters per second squared. The same force will cause a 5.0-kilogram mass to accelerate at (1) 9.8 m/s^2 (2) 10. m/s^2 (3) 25 m/s^2 (4) 40. m/s^2

10. A car traveling at 15 meters per second on a level highway is brought to a stop in 10. seconds by a braking force of 3,000 newtons. The mass of the car is (1) 1,500 kg (2) 2,000 kg (3) 2,500 kg (4) 3,000 kg

11. The graph at the right represents the relationship between the unbalanced force applied to a body and its acceleration. The mass of the body is (1) 1.0 kg (2) 2.0 kg (3) 0.5 kg (4) 8.0 kg

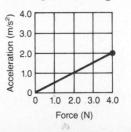

12. Which graph best represents the motion of an object on which the net force is zero?

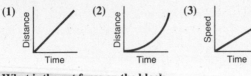

(1) Distance / Time (2) Distance / Time (3) Speed / Time (4) Speed / Time

13. What is the net force on the block shown at the right? (1) 0.0 N (2) 9.8 N (3) 10. N (4) 20. N

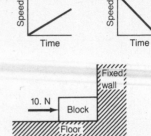

14. If the net force applied in the direction of motion to a certain object on a horizontal frictionless surface is doubled, the acceleration of the object is (1) halved (2) doubled (3) unchanged (4) quadrupled

15. A 10.-kilogram object is at rest on a horizontal frictionless table. What is the unbalanced force that must be applied to that object to give it a speed of 20. meters per second after 4.0 seconds? (1) 40. N (2) 50. N (3) 200 N (4) 800 N

16. If the mass of an object is decreased, its inertia (1) decreases (2) increases (3) remains the same

17. If the sum of all the forces acting on a car is zero, the car (1) *must* be at rest (2) *may* be at rest (3) *must* be moving at constant speed (4) *must* be accelerating

18. As a constant unbalanced force acts on an object in the direction of motion, the object's speed (1) decreases (2) increases (3) remains the same

19. As the vector sum of all the forces acting on an object decreases, the acceleration of the object (1) decreases (2) increases (3) remains the same

20–24. Base your answers to Questions 20 through 24 on the graph at the right, which depicts the motion of a 2-kilogram mass that initially starts to move to the right along a straight-line path.

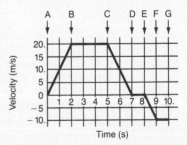

20. The mass has an acceleration of +10. meters per second squared during interval (1) *AB* (2) *BC* (3) *CD* (4) *EF*

21. How far does the 2-kilogram mass travel in the interval *AB*? (1) 10 m (2) 20 m (3) 30 m (4) 40 m

22. **The net force on the 2-kilogram mass is zero during the interval (1)** *AB* **(2)** *BC* **(3)** *CD* **(4)** *EF*
23. **The 2-kilogram mass is at rest during interval (1)** *AB* **(2)** *BC* **(3)** *DE* **(4)** *EFG*
24. **There is a net force toward the left on the 2-kilogram mass for the time interval (1)** *AB* **(2)** *BC* **(3)** *CD* **(4)** *FG*

Newton's Universal Law of Gravitation

All objects exert a force of attraction on each other, even when separated by large distances. This force is called **gravitation,** and it is assumed to act throughout the universe. Newton stated that any two masses attract one another with a force that is directly proportional to the product of their masses and inversely proportional to the square of the distance between them. In mathematical form, this **universal law of gravitation** is:

$$F = \frac{Gm_1m_2}{r^2}$$ **(Eq. 1-7)**

where F is the gravitational force in newtons between two objects, m_1 and m_2 are the masses of the objects in kilograms, r is the distance of separation in meters, and G is a proportionality constant equal to 6.67×10^{-11} N · m²/kg². The law holds for "point" masses, that is, masses whose sizes are small compared to the distance between them, and for spherical masses that are of uniform density. For spheres, the separation distance, r, is measured from the centers of the spheres.

Since r^2 appears in the denominator, the force of attraction between the masses decreases rapidly as the distance of separation increases. For example, if the distance of separation for two given masses is doubled, the force of attraction is quartered.

On the other hand, the force is directly proportional to the masses m_1 and m_2. If either mass is doubled, with distance remaining constant, the force is only doubled. If one mass is doubled and the other is tripled, the force will become six times the original force of attraction.

EXAMPLE

An object of 3.0 kilograms mass is located 1.0×10^4 meters from the center of an object of 2.0×10^9 kilogram mass in interstellar space. What is the gravitational force of attraction between the objects?

Solution
The force of attraction is given by Newton's law of gravitation:

$$F = \frac{Gm_1m_2}{r^2}$$

Substituting the given values and recalling that

$$G = 6.67 \times 10^{-11} \text{ N} \cdot \text{m}^2/\text{kg}^2$$

yields

$$F = \frac{(6.67 \times 10^{-11} \text{ N} \cdot \text{m}^2/\text{kg}^2)(2.0 \times 10^9 \text{ kg})(3.0 \text{ kg})}{(1.0 \times 10^4 \text{ m})^2}$$

$$F = \frac{(6.67 \times 10^{-11} \text{ N} \cdot \text{m}^2/\text{kg}^2)(6.0 \times 10^9 \text{ kg}^2)}{1.0 \times 10^8 \text{ m}^2}$$

$$F = 4.0 \times 10^{-9} \text{ N}$$

PRACTICAL APPLICATION

Newton's universal law of gravitation can be used to explain the tides. As shown in Figure 1-14, the two high tides per day are a result of differences in the gravitational pull of the Moon on the opposite sides of the Earth.

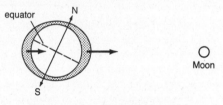

Figure 1-14. The cause of tides.

Gravitational attraction decreases with increasing distance of separation. Thus, the water nearest the moon has the greatest attraction for the moon and bulges to form a high tide. The Earth is attracted to the Moon with a greater force than the water on the opposite side and is pulled away from the water, thereby creating a second high tide. The water in between the high tides recedes to form the low tides. When the Sun *and* Moon are on the same or opposite sides of the Earth, the high tides are their highest, and low tides their lowest, due to the added gravitational pull of the Sun. ∎

Gravitational Field Strength. In physics, the region in which some condition exists is called the **field** of that condition. For example, the region in which a force is observed to act is called the field of that force. Around every mass there exists a gravitational field in which **gravitational force** acts on other objects. The interaction of an object with the gravitational field produced by another object results in their mutual attraction. The gravitational field that results from some object, for example the earth, can be mapped using a "unit test mass." In Figure 1-15a, the test mass, placed at various locations, is acted on by a force attracting it to the earth. As shown in the illustration, the magnitude of the force increases as the distance from the earth becomes smaller. In Figure 1-15b, the force vectors have been joined to form lines of gravitational force.

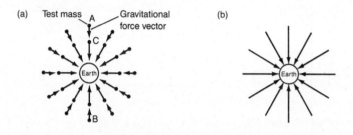

Figure 1-15.   The gravitational field around the earth. (a) When the test mass is at points *A* or *B*, the gravitational force is the same because both points are the same distance from the center of the earth. At point *C* the gravitational force is greater than at *A* or *B* because *C* is closer to the center of the earth. (b) The force vectors have been joined to form lines of gravitational force.

Lines of force in any force field show the direction of the force at any point in the field. The concentration of the lines of force show the strength, or magnitude, of the force in any region of the field. For example, in Figure 1-15 the lines of gravitational force are closer together (more concentrated) near the earth than far away. Thus the **gravitational field strength** increases as the distance from the earth decreases. Remember that field strength is a vector quantity, with both magnitude and direction.

The direction of the earth's gravitational field is always toward the center of the earth. The magnitude of the field (the field strength) at any point in the field equals the force per unit mass at that point. The gravitational field strength of the earth is represented by the symbol g, and is given by the equation

$$g = \frac{F}{m}$$

where F is the force in newtons on a mass, m, in kilograms, and g is the gravitational field strength in newtons per kilogram. Since

$$1 \text{ newton} = 1 \text{ kilogram} \cdot \text{meter/second}^2$$

then

$$1\frac{\text{newton}}{\text{kilogram}} = 1\frac{\text{kilogram} \cdot \text{meter/second}^2}{\text{kilogram}} = 1 \text{ meter/second}^2$$

Thus, a closer look at the unit of gravitational field strength, N/kg, shows that it is actually a unit of acceleration, m/s^2. Another way to see this is to recognize from Equation 1-6 ($a = F/m$) that F/m is an acceleration. In other words, g is the acceleration produced on a mass, m, by the gravitational force, F. For this reason, the gravitational field strength, g, is also called the acceleration due to gravity. For short distances above the earth's surface, g is the same for all masses:

g (gravitational field strength) = 9.8 N/kg, and
g (acceleration due to gravity) = 9.8 m/s^2

CAN YOU EXPLAIN THIS?

An object can push or pull you without touching you.

If you were to jump off a diving board above a pool of water, for a period of time you would not be in physical contact with the earth. Nevertheless, the earth would pull you toward the water.

Weight

The gravitational force acting on an object near the earth is called the **weight** of the object. If M is the mass of the earth, m is the mass of the object, and r is the distance from the center of the earth, it can be seen from Equation 1-7 that the weight, w, of the body at the earth's surface is directly proportional to its mass, m, since all the other quantities are constant. Weight and mass, however, are different quantities and are measured in different units. Weight is a force measured in newtons; mass is measured in kilograms. Also, the weight of a body will decrease if its distance from the center of the earth, r, increases, because the magnitude of the gravitational field varies with location. The mass of the body will not change.

The acceleration of a freely falling body is the result of the force of gravitation acting on it. This force is the object's weight, w. As noted previously, the acceleration near the earth's surface is g, a constant with a value of 9.8 meters per second squared. Substituting the weight, w, for F and the acceleration, g, for a in Equation 1-6 (Newton's second law) yields

$$w = mg \qquad \text{(Eq. 1-8)}$$

In this equation, the weight, w, is a force expressed in newtons, the mass, m, is in kilograms, and the acceleration, g, is 9.8 meters per second squared near the surface of the earth. Therefore, the weight of any object in newtons near the earth's surface is 9.8 times its mass in kilograms.

PRACTICAL APPLICATION

Weight, a vector quantity, is always directed vertically downward. If an object is on an inclined surface, its weight can be resolved into two components, one parallel to the inclined surface and the other perpendicular to the surface. The component perpendicular to the surface has no effect on the motion of the body, since the body cannot move in the direction of that force. Only the component parallel to the surface tends to accelerate the body down the incline. As the angle of the incline increases, the component of the weight parallel to the surface increases, and the acceleration down the incline also increases. (Acceleration down the incline is opposed by the force of friction between the body and the surface. As explained later in this unit, the force of friction depends on the component of the weight pressing the body against the surface. As the angle of the incline increases, the component of the weight perpendicular to the incline decreases, and the friction force also decreases.) ■

Although the term *weight* usually refers to the force of the earth's gravity, it can also be used for the force of gravity exerted by other large bodies, such as the moon. The mass of a body is the same on the earth and on the moon, but its weight on the moon would be less than on the earth. This is because the mass of the moon is very much smaller than that of the earth, so the moon exerts a smaller gravitational pull on the body. On the earth and on the moon, the weight of any object is proportional to its mass (Equation 1-8). A graph of weight versus mass is a straight line whose slope equals g. The graph for the moon has a smaller slope than the graph for the earth has, because g on the moon is smaller than g on the earth.

CAN YOU EXPLAIN THIS?

If a person stands on a scale in an elevator, the reading of the scale will increase when the elevator begins to rise.

When the elevator is at rest, the scale registers the downward force of the person's weight. The elevator floor exerts an upward force that balances the weight. When the elevator starts to rise, it must exert an additional upward force to accelerate the person's mass. By Newton's third law, the person's body must exert an equal reaction force downward, in addition to its weight. Thus the scale registers an increased total force. When the elevator stops accelerating and starts rising at a constant speed, there is no additional upward force, and the scale reading returns to the person's weight alone.

QUESTIONS

1. If the distance between two masses is tripled, the gravitational force between them becomes (1) ⅑ as great (2) ⅓ as great (3) 3 times as great (4) 9 times as great
2. A rocket weighs 10,000 newtons at the earth's surface. If the rocket rises to a height equal to the earth's radius above the earth's surface, its weight will be (1) 2,500 N (2) 5,000 N (3) 10,000 N (4) 40,000 N
3. If the distance between two objects of constant mass is doubled, the gravitational force of attraction between them is (1) halved (2) doubled (3) quartered (4) quadrupled

4. If the mass of an object were doubled, its weight would be (1) halved (2) doubled (3) unchanged (4) quadrupled

5. An object weighing 20.0 newtons at the earth's surface is moved to an altitude where its weight is 10.0 newtons. The acceleration due to gravity at this altitude is (1) 2.45 m/s^2 (2) 4.90 m/s^2 (3) 9.80 m/s^2 (4) 19.6 m/s^2

6. If the weight of an object of mass m is mg, then the weight of an object of mass $3m$ is (1) $mg/3$ (2) mg (3) $3mg$ (4) $9mg$

7. A block with a mass of 2.00 kilograms rests on a horizontal table. The force exerted by the table upon the mass is (1) 0.00 N (2) 2.00 N (3) 9.80 N (4) 19.6 N

8. A block with a mass of 2.00 kilograms rests on a horizontal table. The horizontal component of the block's weight is (1) 0.00 N (2) 2.00 N (3) 9.80 N (4) 19.6 N

9. A 10.-kilogram iron ball and a 5.00-kilogram iron ball have the same acceleration when dropped from rest from the same height because (1) action equals reaction (2) both are made of iron (3) the ratio of the gravitational force to mass is the same for both (4) the gravitational force is the same for both

10. As the distance between two masses increases, the gravitational force of attraction between them (1) decreases (2) increases (3) remains the same

11. As a satellite moves farther away from the earth, the weight of the satellite with respect to the earth (1) decreases (2) increases (3) remains the same

12. Three spheres, A, B, and C, of equal mass are arranged as shown in the diagram at the right. If the gravitational force between A and B is 3.0 newtons, then the gravitational force between A and C is (1) 1.0 N (2) 9.0 N (3) 3.0 N (4) 27 N

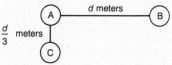

13. A student whose weight is 600 newtons is standing in an elevator. If the elevator rises with an acceleration of 9.8 meters per second squared, the force the elevator exerts on the student is (1) 300 N (2) 600 N (3) 1,200 N (4) 1,500 N

14. An object weighing 16 newtons at the earth's surface is moved above the earth a distance equal to the earth's radius. The gravitational field strength at this new position is (1) 2.5 N/kg (2) 4.9 N/kg (3) 9.8 N/kg (4) 4.0 N/kg

15. A block weighing 10. newtons is held motionless on a frictionless inclined plane that makes an angle of 30. degrees with the horizontal. The force parallel to the incline needed to hold the block in position is (1) 0.0 N (2) 5.0 N (3) 10. N (4) 20. N

16. A 10.-kilogram rocket fragment falling toward the earth has a net downward acceleration of 5.0 meters per second squared. The net downward force acting on the fragment is (1) 5.0 N (2) 10. N (3) 50. N (4) 98 N

17. A block with a mass of 2.00 kilograms rests on a horizontal table. The vertical component of the block's weight is (1) 0.0 N (2) 2.00 N (3) 9.80 N (4) 19.6 N

18. A box rests on a plank that is inclined to the horizontal. As the angle between the plank and the horizontal increases, the component of the weight of the box parallel to the plank (1) decreases (2) increases (3) remains the same

19. As an object moves away from the earth's surface, its inertia (1) decreases (2) increases (3) remains the same

20. Object A with a mass of 2 kilograms and object B with a mass of 4 kilograms are dropped simultaneously from rest near the surface of the earth. At the end of 3 seconds, what is the ratio of the speed of object A to that of object B? (Neglect air resistance.) (1) 1/1 (2) 2/1 (3) 1/2 (4) 1/4

Friction

The motion of one object in contact with another is opposed by a force called **friction,** which acts parallel to the surfaces in contact. The force of friction between two bodies depends on the magnitude of the forces acting perpendicular to the surfaces in contact. This perpendicular force is called the **normal force,** and it is the force pressing the two surfaces together. For any two given surfaces in contact, the frictional force is proportional to the normal force. The ratio of the frictional force to the normal force is the **coefficient of friction.** For example, if a normal force of 100. N causes a frictional force of 25 N, the coefficient of friction is 25 N/100 N = 0.25.

There are several types of friction. The friction between two solid bodies at rest with respect to each other is **static friction.** Static friction prevents the motion of one body relative to the other until the applied force is greater than the maximum static friction between them. This minimum force needed to start motion is called the **starting friction.** Once motion starts, the friction between the bodies decreases. This friction of motion is called **kinetic** or **sliding friction.** The coefficient of static friction is usually greater than the coefficient of sliding friction.

Coefficients of friction vary greatly, depending on the materials in contact. For example, the coefficient of friction between a rubber tire and concrete is about 1.0. Between a waxed ski and dry snow, it is about 0.04. The high coefficient of friction for rubber tires is desirable to prevent slipping as a car accelerates or brakes. On the other hand, ease of sliding and, hence, a low coefficient of friction are desirable for skiing.

When a body is at rest or sliding on a horizontal surface, the normal force is the weight of the body. The magnitude of sliding friction depends only on the coefficient of friction. It is independent of both the area in contact and the speed of motion. For example, if a rectangular block of wood sliding across a horizontal surface has dimensions of 4.0 cm × 6.0 cm × 10. cm, the frictional force depends only on the weight of the block. It makes no difference which face of the block is in contact with the surface (24 cm^2, 40. cm^2, or 60. cm^2), since the normal force (the weight of the block) is the same in each case.

When a round object, such as a cylinder, rolls over a surface, the frictional force is usually much less than when the object slides across the surface. The friction of a rolling object is called **rolling friction.** Wheels and ball bearings reduce friction between moving objects in contact by replacing sliding friction with rolling friction.

The friction on an object moving through a fluid, such as water or air, is **fluid friction.** Unlike sliding friction, fluid friction varies with the speed of motion and with the shape and area of the surface in contact with the fluid. Airplanes are streamlined (given a special tapered shape) to reduce air friction, or "drag." Reducing fluid friction is also a consideration in the design of automobiles, boats, and other vehicles.

CAN YOU EXPLAIN THIS?

The sliding friction between two extremely smooth glass plates is very large.

Usually, sliding friction is increased by roughness of the surfaces in contact. If the surfaces are extremely smooth, however, friction is increased by the phenomenon of adhesion. The molecules on either side of the contact surface are so close together that they attract one another by the same kind of intermolecular forces that hold solids together. It is as though the two surfaces have been joined.

QUESTIONS

1. If a cart is moving to the north at constant velocity, the force of kinetic friction on the cart is directed toward the (1) north (2) south (3) east (4) west

2. As an object initially at rest on a horizontal surface is set into motion, the force of friction between them (1) decreases (2) increases (3) remains the same

3. In a classroom, a steel ball and a sheet of paper are dropped to the floor from the same height at the same time. The ball hits the floor before the sheet of paper because of the effects of (1) static friction (2) kinetic friction (3) rolling friction (4) fluid friction

4. An *empty* wooden crate is slid across a warehouse floor. If the crate were *filled*, the *coefficient* of kinetic friction between the crate and the floor would (1) decrease (2) increase (3) remain the same

5. An *empty* wooden crate is slid across a warehouse floor. If the crate were *filled*, the *force* of kinetic friction between the crate and the floor would (1) decrease (2) increase (3) remain the same

6. A wooden block is at rest on a wooden inclined plane. As the angle the plane makes with the horizontal increases, the *coefficient* of static friction between the block and the plane (1) decreases (2) increases (3) remains the same

7. A wooden block is at rest on a wooden inclined plane. As the angle the plane makes with the horizontal increases, the *force* of static friction between the block and the plane (1) decreases (2) increases (3) remains the same

Momentum

The product of the mass and the velocity of an object is a vector quantity called **momentum.** An object's momentum is in the same direction as its velocity and is given by the formula

$$p = mv \qquad \text{(Eq. 1-9)}$$

where m is mass in kilograms, v is velocity in meters per second, and p is momentum in kilogram · meters per second. The *SI* unit for momentum is the kilogram · meter per second, kg · m/s.

CAN YOU EXPLAIN THIS?

An automobile moving at 30 m/s has more momentum than a bullet moving at 500 m/s.

The magnitude of the momentum of an object is equal to the product of its mass and velocity. A car having a mass of 1,100 kg and traveling at 30. m/s has a momentum of 33,000 kg · m/s, whereas a 0.0050-kg bullet traveling at 500 m/s has a momentum of only 2.5 kg · m/s.

Impulse and Change in Momentum

If a force is applied to an object, the product of the force and the time during which the force is applied is called the **impulse.** Impulse, a vector quantity having the same direction as the force applied to the object, is given by the formula

$$J = F\Delta t \qquad \text{(Eq. 1-10)}$$

where F is the average force in newtons, Δt is the time during which the force acts, and J is the impulse in newton · seconds. The newton · second, N · s, is the *SI* unit for impulse. When an unbalanced force acts on a body, its velocity changes and therefore its momentum changes. The relationship between an impulse, $F\Delta t$, applied to a mass, m, and the resulting change in its momentum, $m\Delta v$, can be derived from Newton's second law of motion, $F = ma$ (Equation 1-6). Recall from Equation 1-2 that $a = \Delta v/\Delta t$. Therefore,

$$F = ma = \frac{m\Delta v}{\Delta t}, \quad \text{or}$$

$$F\Delta t = m\Delta v \qquad \text{(Eq. 1-11)}$$

Since $F\Delta t$ equals the impulse, and $m\Delta v$ equals the change in momentum, Equation 1-11 states that when an unbalanced force F acts on a mass, m, the impulse, $F\Delta t$, applied to the body equals the change in its momentum, $m\Delta v$. Remember that impulse and momentum are both vector quantities. The direction of the impulse is the same as the direction of the change in momentum it produces.

PRACTICAL APPLICATION

A baseball batter and a golfer "follow through" when hitting the ball, that is, they try to keep the bat or golf club in contact with the ball as long as possible. The longer the time during which the force of impact acts on the ball, the larger the impulse given to it, and therefore the greater its final momentum and distance of travel. A catcher catching a fast ball, or a fielder catching a line drive, will try to prolong the time of slowing the ball by moving the gloved hand back in the direction of the ball's motion. By increasing the time during which the glove acts on the ball to reduce its momentum to zero, the force needed to produce the necessary impulse is reduced. This action minimizes the "sting" of stopping the ball. ∎

EXAMPLE

An object that has a mass of 5.0 kilograms is moving east with a velocity v_i that is equal to 8.0 meters per second. An unbalanced force acting on the mass for 3.0 seconds reduces the velocity of the object to 2.0 meters per second east. What are the magnitude and the direction of the force?

Solution

Let east be the positive direction, so west will be the negative direction. The change in momentum of the mass is

$$\Delta p = mv_f - mv_i$$

$$\Delta p = (5.0 \text{ kg})(2.0 \text{ m/s}) - (5.0 \text{ kg})(8.0 \text{ m/s})$$

$$\Delta p = 10. \text{ kg} \cdot \text{m/s} - 40. \text{ kg} \cdot \text{m/s}$$

$$\Delta p = -30. \text{ kg} \cdot \text{m/s}$$

The impulse must be equal to this change in momentum. Therefore,

$$F\Delta t = -30. \text{ kg} \cdot \text{m/s}$$

$$F = \frac{-30. \text{ kg} \cdot \text{m/s}}{\Delta t} = \frac{-30. \text{ kg} \cdot \text{m/s}}{3.0 \text{ s}}$$

$$F = -10. \text{ kg} \cdot \text{m/s}^2$$

$$F = -10. \text{ N}$$

The force is 10. N directed to the west.

Conservation of Momentum

Any group of objects not acted on by any external force is called an **isolated system.** Within an isolated system, the objects may exert forces upon one another. For example, a mass, m_1, may exert a force, F, on another mass, m_2. By Newton's third law of motion, mass m_2 must exert an equal force on m_1, but in the opposite direction. Since the force, F, acts on both bodies for exactly the same time interval, the magnitude of the impulse is the same for both bodies, and therefore the magnitude of the change in momentum must be the same for both. The directions of the change in momentum are opposite, however, so if one change is positive, the other is negative. We can thus write

$$m_1 \Delta v_1 = -m_2 \Delta v_2, \quad \text{or}$$
$$m_1 \Delta v_1 + m_2 \Delta v_2 = 0$$

The total change in momentum resulting from the interaction of the two bodies is zero. The same reasoning can be applied to any of the forces acting between any pair of bodies in the system. It follows that nothing that happens inside an isolated system can change its total momentum. The total momentum of the bodies in an isolated system is constant. This principle is called the **law of conservation of momentum.**

EXAMPLE

Cart A, of mass $m_1 = 1.0$ kilogram, is at rest ($v_i = 0.0$ m/s) on a frictionless air track. It is struck by cart B, of mass $m_2 = 0.20$ kilogram, moving to the right at $v_2 = 10.$ m/s. After the collision, cart A is moving to the right at $v_1' = 3.0$ m/s. What is the velocity v_2' of cart B after the collision?

Solution

Let velocity to the right be positive.

$$m_1 = 1.0 \text{ kg} \qquad v_1 = 0.0 \text{ m/s} \qquad v_1' = 3.0 \text{ m/s}$$
$$m_2 = 0.20 \text{ kg} \qquad v_2 = 10. \text{ m/s} \qquad v_2' = ?$$

The total momentum after the collision must be equal to the total before the collision.

$$m_2 v_2' + m_1 v_1' = m_2 v_2 + m_1 v_1$$

$$(0.20 \text{ kg})v_2' + (1.0 \text{ kg})(3.0 \text{ m/s}) = (0.20 \text{ kg})(10. \text{ m/s}) + (1.0 \text{ kg})(0.0 \text{ m/s})$$

$$(0.20 \text{ kg})v_2' = 2.0 \text{ kg} \cdot \text{m/s} - 3.0 \text{ kg} \cdot \text{m/s}$$
$$(0.20 \text{ kg})v_2' = -1.0 \text{ kg} \cdot \text{m/s}$$
$$v_2' = -5.0 \text{ m/s}$$

The velocity of cart B after the collision is 5.0 m/s to the left.

QUESTIONS

1. A 10.-kilogram mass moving at a speed of 5.0 meters per second on a frictionless surface collides with a stationary 10.-kilogram mass. If the two masses remain joined after the collision, their speed will be (1) 0.0 m/s (2) 2.5 m/s (3) 5.0 m/s (4) 10. m/s

2. A 1.0-kilogram object falls freely from rest. The magnitude of its momentum after 1.0 second of fall is (1) 1.0 kg · m/s (2) 4.9 kg · m/s (3) 9.8 kg · m/s (4) 20. kg · m/s

3. A 10-kilogram gun recoils with a speed of 0.1 meter per second as it fires a 0.001-kilogram bullet. Neglecting friction, what is the speed of the bullet as it leaves the gun? (1) 10 m/s (2) 100 m/s (3) 1,000 m/s (4) 10,000 m/s

4. Which is a scalar quantity? (1) speed (2) displacement (3) force (4) momentum

5. A mass having a momentum of 40. kilogram · meters per second receives an impulse of 20. newton · seconds in the direction of motion. The final momentum of the mass is (1) 2.0 kg · m/s (2) 20. kg · m/s (3) 60. kg · m/s (4) 800 kg · m/s

6. A mass of 2.0 kilograms that experiences a momentum change of 50. kilogram · meters per second must have received an impulse of (1) 25 N · s (2) 2.0 N · s (3) 50. N · s (4) 100 N · s

7. A mass experiences a change of momentum of 35 kilogram · meters per second in 10. seconds. What is the magnitude of the average force causing this change? (1) 3.5 N (2) 35 N (3) 45 N (4) 350 N

8. If a 2.0-kilogram mass moves with a constant speed of 20. meters per second, the magnitude of its momentum is (1) 8.0 kg · m/s (2) 10. kg · m/s (3) 40. kg · m/s (4) 160 kg · m/s

9. A 1-kilogram ball of putty traveling at 5 meters per second hits a wall perpendicularly and sticks to it. The ball experiences a change of momentum of (1) 1 kg · m/s (2) 5 kg · m/s (3) 10 kg · m/s (4) 0 kg · m/s

10. A 1-kilogram ball hits a surface perpendicularly with a speed of 3 meters per second and bounces back with a speed of 2 meters per second. The ball undergoes a change in momentum of (1) 1 kg · m/s (2) 5 kg · m/s (3) 3 kg · m/s (4) 6 kg · m/s

11. An average unbalanced force of 30. newtons acts on a 2.0-kilogram object for 3.0 seconds. The object's change in momentum is (1) 10. kg · m/s (2) 15 kg · m/s (3) 6.0 kg · m/s (4) 90. kg · m/s

12. As an object falls freely toward the earth, the momentum of the object-earth system (1) decreases (2) increases (3) remains the same

13. As the momentum of a moving mass increases, the magnitude of the impulse required to stop the mass (1) decreases (2) increases (3) remains the same

14. When two stationary objects are suddenly pushed apart by a compressed spring between them, and no friction acts on the objects, the total momentum of the system (1) increases (2) decreases (3) remains the same

15. As a freely falling object approaches the earth's surface, the impulse required to stop the object (1) decreases (2) increases (3) remains the same

16–19. Base your answers to Questions 16 through 19 on the following information and the diagram at the right.

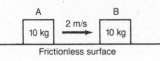

Block *A* moves with a velocity of 2 meters per second to the right and then collides with block *B*, which is at rest. After the collision, block *A* stops moving, and block *B* moves to the right.

16. What is the magnitude of the combined momentum of blocks *A* and *B* before the collision? (1) 0 kg · m/s (2) 10 kg · m/s (3) 20 kg · m/s (4) 40 kg · m/s

17. What is the total change in momentum of blocks *A* and *B* during the collision? (1) 0 kg · m/s (2) 20 kg : m/s (3) 40 kg · m/s (4) 200 kg · m/s

18. If block *A* is stopped in 0.1 second, the magnitude of the average force acting on block *A* is (1) 50 N (2) 100 N (3) 200 N (4) 400 N

19. If the blocks had remained together after collision, the magnitude of their velocity would have been (1) 1 m/s (2) 2 m/s (3) 0 m/s (4) 0.5 m/s

20–23. Base your answers to Questions 20 through 23 on the following information.

A horizontal force is applied to a 5.0-kilogram object resting on a horizontal surface. The force is always applied in the same direction, but its magnitude varies with time according to the graph. (Neglect friction.)

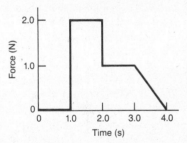

20. What is the acceleration of the object at time $t = 2.5$ seconds? (1) 1.0 m/s² (2) 0.20 m/s² (3) 5.0 m/s² (4) 9.8 m/s²

21. During which time interval did the object have a constant velocity? (1) 0.0 s to 1.0 s (2) 1.0 s to 2.0 s (3) 2.0 s to 3.0 s (4) 3.0 s to 4.0 s

22. The greatest change in momentum of the object occurred during the time interval from (1) 0.0 s to 1.0 s (2) 1.0s to 2.0 s (3) 2.0 s to 3.0 s (4) 3.0 s to 4.0 s

23. If a 5.0-kilogram mass is added to the original mass at the time t = 2.5 seconds, the acceleration of the object will (1) decrease (2) increase (3) remain the same

24–28. Base your answers to Questions 24 through 28 on the following information.

A compressed spring is "exploded" between two carts that

are initially at rest, as shown. The mass of cart B is twice that of cart A. The magnitude of the impulse applied to cart B is 8.0 newton · seconds. (Neglect friction.)

24. The magnitude of the impulse applied to cart A is (1) 8.0 N · s (2) 2.0 N · s (3) 16 N · s (4) 4 N · s

25. If the time for the spring to explode is 0.1 second, the average force on cart B is (1) 0.8 N (2) 8 N (3) 40 N (4) 80 N

26. If the total momentum of the carts before the explosion is 0.0 kg · m/s, the total momentum after the explosion is
    (1) 0.0 kg · m/s   (3) 16 kg · m/s
    (2) 8.0 kg · m/s   (4) 4.0 kg · m/s

27. The ratio of the magnitude of the change in the momentum of cart A to the magnitude of the change in momentum of cart B is (1) 1/1 (2) 1/2 (3) 2/1 (4) 8/1

28. A constant unbalanced force acts on an object initially at rest. As the time the force acts increases, the momentum of the object (1) decreases (2) increases (3) remains the same

29–31. Base your answers to Questions 29 through 31 on the graph at right, which shows the speed of a 1,500-kilogram car during a 20.-second time interval.

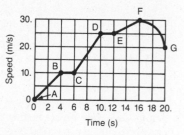

29. The acceleration of the car during time interval AB is (1) 0.40 m/s^2 (2) 2.5 m/s^2 (3) 10. m/s^2 (4) 40. m/s^2

30. During time interval CD, the average speed of the car is (1) 7.5 m/s (2) 17.5 m/s (3) 15 m/s (4) 35 m/s

31. The impulse applied to the car during time interval AB is
    (1) 9.0 × 10^2 N · s   (3) 6.0 × 10^3 N · s
    (2) 4.5 × 10^3 N · s   (4) 1.5 × 10^4 N · s

Solving problems in mechanics often involves many steps, such as determining the unknown(s) to be solved for, drawing vector diagrams, choosing appropriate equations, or graphing results. The following sample problem is representative of problems you will encounter in Part III of the Regents exam.

Sample Problem

A block weighing 100. newtons is positioned on an incline that makes an angle of 30. degrees with the horizontal, as shown in Figure A. The friction force between the block and the incline is 10. newtons. A force of 120. newtons is applied by pulling on the rope, which makes an angle of 30. degrees with the incline, as shown.

(a) Draw a free-body diagram, and provide labels for weight, friction, and the tension in the rope.
(b) Determine the components of the car's weight relative to the incline.
(c) Give the magnitude and direction of the component of the tension that is useful in moving the block up the incline.
(d) Determine the magnitude and direction of the block's acceleration.

Figure A.

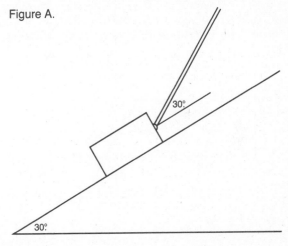

Solution

(a) There are four forces acting on the block on the incline, as shown in Figure B on the following page: weight, friction, the pull (or tension) of the rope, and the normal force of the incline. The normal force is always perpendicular to the two surfaces in contact. The normal force is directed opposite to the weight only when the surfaces in contact are horizontal.

(b) The block's weight is directed perpendicular to the horizontal (level ground). The weight can be resolved into one component parallel to the incline and one component perpendicular to it. Select an appropriate scale and, using a

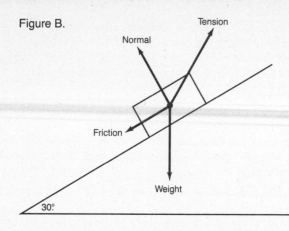

Figure B.

protractor and ruler, draw the vector representing the block's weight. Resolve the weight into its two components by constructing the parallelogram of forces as shown in Figure C. (Because of space limitations, the scale of the drawing here is too small for reasonable precision. You would make your drawing to a larger scale, such as 1.0 cm = 10. N.) Measure the sides of the resulting rectangle and multiply by the scale factor to determine the magnitude of the components.

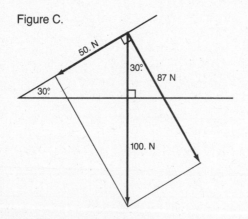

Figure C.

The problem can also be solved mathematically by using a table of trigonometric functions. The component of the weight parallel to the incline is:

$$100. \text{ N} \times \sin 30.° = 50. \text{ N}$$

The perpendicular component is:

$$100. \text{ N} \times \cos 30.° = 87 \text{ N}$$

(c) Like the weight of the block, the tension in the rope can be resolved into a component parallel to the incline and one perpendicular to it. The perpendicular component has no effect on motion along the incline. Only the parallel component is effective in this direction. As with the weight, the components can be found by drawing a parallelogram (rectangle) to scale, in which the tension is a diagonal, as shown in Figure D. The measured component is 104 N. The component can also be calculated:

$$120. \text{ N} \times \cos 30.° = 120. \text{ N} \times 0.866 = 104 \text{ N}$$

Figure D.

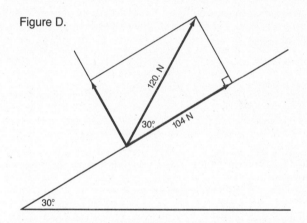

(d) The forces acting on the block parallel to the incline are:

component of tension:	+104 N
component of weight of block:	−50. N
friction:	−10. N

There is a net unbalanced force of 44 N on the block directed up the incline. This force will cause the block to accelerate up the incline. The acceleration can be calculated using the formula $F = ma$, but first the mass of the block must be determined using $w = mg$:

$$w = mg, \text{ and } m = w/g$$

$$m = (100. \text{ N})/(9.80 \text{ m/s}^2) = 10.2. \text{ kg}$$

The acceleration is then

$$a = F/m = (44 \text{ N})/(10.2 \text{ kg}) = 4.3 \text{ m/s}^2, \text{ up the incline}$$

In solving this problem, you would have used the following skills: applying mathematics, identifying/selecting alternatives, making drawings to scale, using measurement tools, and verifying results by alternative methods. Now try the following practice problems on your own.

PROBLEM SOLVING

Practice Problems

1. Explain each of the following on the basis of physical principles.
   (a) A rocket is propelled by its exhaust gases.
   (b) A car accelerates as it travels at a constant speed around a traffic circle.
   (c) You throw a raw egg as hard as you can against a bedsheet backdrop. The egg does not break when it hits the sheet, but the egg does break when it hits the floor below.

2. Describe a laboratory experiment to show that the resultant of two non-parallel forces acting concurrently upon a point is equal in magnitude and opposite in direction to the equilibrant. Make a diagram and label the forces.

3. A person is hanging a picture that weighs 100. newtons by a cord attached as shown in Figure E.

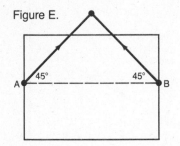

Figure E.

A 45°   45° B

(a) If the picture is hung from a single hook at the center of the cord, what is the tension (pull) in the cord if the cord makes an angle of 45° with the horizontal? (Note: the tension in a cord is the same throughout its length. The pull at A equals the pull at B and equals the tension in the cord.)

(b) The person wants to hang the picture so that the hook will not show. This can be done in two ways: (1) Use two hooks as shown in Figure F. (2) Shorten the cord as shown in Figure G. Calculate the tension in the cord for each method.

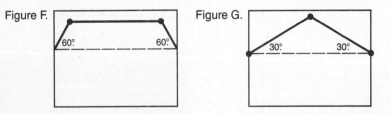

Figure F.

60°   60°

Figure G.

30°   30°

(c) If the breaking strength of the cord is 500 newtons, what is the smallest angle that the cord may make with the horizontal when the picture is hung from a single hook?

4. A block of wood is sliding at constant speed down a wooden incline that makes an angle of 25° with the horizontal.
    (a) If the weight of the block is 50 newtons, what is the force of sliding friction between the block and the incline?
    (b) The sliding surfaces are lubricated so that the friction force is reduced to 10.0 newtons. Describe the motion of the block that will now occur.

5. A student throws a stone with an initial velocity of 20. meters per second straight upward from the edge of a cliff 100. meters above a canyon floor. If the stone just misses the cliff's edge on its way down, determine each of the following for the stone:
    (a) time to reach maximum height
    (b) maximum height relative to the top of the cliff
    (c) time required to return to the level of the student
    (d) velocity upon returning to the student's level
    (e) velocity 6.0 seconds after release time
    (f) position after 6.0 seconds
    (Show all work and label units correctly.)

6. Using the information obtained in Question 5, make a graph of
    (a) velocity vs. time
    (b) speed vs. time
    (Label axes and select an appropriate scale.)

UNIT 2   ENERGY

I. WORK AND ENERGY

Every body or system of bodies has a quantity called energy associated with it. Energy can be defined as the capacity to do work. In every system, energy is present in various forms. When work is done on or by a system, energy is needed to do the work, and the total energy of the system is changed. The meaning of the terms *energy* and *work* will become clearer as you proceed through this unit of study.

Work

When a force applied to a body causes the body to move in the direction of the force, **work** is done on the body. Work is a scalar quantity. The amount of work done, W, is equal to the product of the force, F, and the displacement, Δs:

$$W = F\Delta s \qquad \text{(Eq. 2-1)}$$

The *SI* unit of work is the **joule,** J. One joule is the amount of work done when a force of one newton causes a displacement of one meter. In the equation above, if F is in newtons and Δs is in meters, the work, W, is in joules. For example, suppose a 10.-N force causes a body to move 5.0 m in the direction of the force. The work done is

$$W = F\Delta s = (10.\ \text{N})(5.0\ \text{m}) = 50.\ \text{N} \cdot \text{m} = 50.\ \text{J}$$

The joule is a derived unit:

$$1\ \text{joule} = 1\ \text{newton} \cdot \text{meter}$$

Since 1 newton = 1 kilogram · meter/second^2, in fundamental units

$$1\ \text{joule} = \frac{1\ \text{kilogram} \cdot \text{meter}}{\text{second}^2} \cdot \text{meter} = \frac{1\ \text{kilogram} \cdot \text{meter}^2}{\text{second}^2}$$

When a force is applied to a mass, but the mass does not move, no work is done. If a student were to hold an object, however heavy it might be, at a constant height above the ground, no work would be done, regardless of the effort expended by the student.

CAN YOU EXPLAIN THIS?

It is less work for a short person to lift 1,400 N overhead from the ground than it is for a tall person.

Work is equal to the product of the force acting on an object and its resultant displacement in the direction of the force. Both persons would need to exert the

48

same force, 1,400 N, in lifting the object overhead. The displacement of the object for the short person, however, would be less than that for the tall person. Thus, the product of force and displacement is less for the short person and that person does less work.

Power

The work done by a force depends only on the product of the force and the displacement, regardless of the time required to do the work. The *rate* at which work is done is called **power.** Power, P, a scalar quantity, is given by the equation

$$P = \frac{W}{\Delta t}$$

where W is the work done in the time Δt. Since $W = F\Delta s$ (Equation 2-1), and $\bar{v} = \Delta s/\Delta t$ (Equation 1-1), these values may be substituted into the above equation for power as follows:

$$P = \frac{W}{\Delta t} = \frac{F\Delta s}{\Delta t} = F\bar{v} \qquad \text{(Eq. 2-2)}$$

where F is the force applied to an object that causes it to move with an average speed, $\bar{v}$.

The *SI* unit of power is the **watt,** W. One watt of power equals one joule of work done per second. In Equation 2-2, if W is in joules and t is in seconds, then power, P, is in watts. (Do not confuse the symbol W for work with the abbreviation W for watt. See the note about symbols for quantities and units on page 2.)

The watt is a derived unit:

$$1 \text{ watt} = 1 \frac{\text{joule}}{\text{second}}$$

Because, in fundamental units, 1 joule = 1 kilogram $\cdot$ meter^2/second^2,

$$1 \text{ watt} = \frac{1 \text{ kilogram} \cdot \text{meter}^2}{\text{second}^2} \cdot \frac{1}{\text{second}} = \frac{1 \text{ kilogram} \cdot \text{meter}^2}{\text{second}^3}$$

Since power is inversely proportional to time, the less time required to do a given amount of work, the greater the power developed. Thus, as the length of time it takes a student to swim 25 meters decreases, the power developed by the student increases.

EXAMPLE

(a) If 50. joules of work is done in 5.0 seconds, how much power is used?
(b) If the time required to do the work increases to 10. seconds, what is the power?

Solution

(a) $\qquad P = \dfrac{W}{\Delta t} = \dfrac{50.\ \text{J}}{5.0\ \text{s}} = 10.\ \text{J/s} = 10.\ \text{W}$

(b) $\qquad P = \dfrac{W}{\Delta t} = \dfrac{50.\ \text{J}}{10.\ \text{s}} = 5.0\ \text{J/s} = 5.0\ \text{W}$

EXAMPLE

In order to overcome friction, a force of 40. newtons must be applied to a mass to keep it moving at a constant speed of 5.0 meters per second. What power is used to keep the mass moving?

Solution

$P = F\overline{v} = (40.\ \text{N})(5.0\ \text{m/s}) = 200\ \text{N} \cdot \text{m/s} = 200\ \text{J/s} = 200\ \text{W}$

Energy

When one system can do work on another system, we say that the first system has **energy** relative to the second system. When one system does work on another, the second system gains an amount of energy equal to the amount of work done on it. This process is called transfer of energy.

Energy, a scalar quantity, has many different forms, including mechanical, thermal, chemical, nuclear, sound, and electrical energy. Whatever its form, energy is measured by the amount of work it can do. The *SI* unit for energy is therefore the same as the unit for work—the joule.

Because $P = W/\Delta t$,

$$W = P\Delta t$$

This equation indicates that one watt of power used for one second transfers one joule of energy or does one joule of work. One joule is equivalent to one watt · second, and energy can be measured in watt · seconds.

CAN YOU EXPLAIN THIS?

A power company (electric utility company) really sells energy.

Power is the time-rate of doing work. A power company is always ready to supply electrical power to its customers, but unless the power is used, no work is done. Because energy = power × time, a 60-watt lamp operating for 2 seconds consumes twice as much energy as the same lamp operated for 1 second. The power company therefore charges its customers for watt · seconds of energy or kilowatt · hours of energy rather than for watts of power. (One kilowatt · hour is equal to 1,000 watts × 3,600 seconds, or 3,600,000 watt · seconds.) The kilowatt · hour meter found in the home, office, and factory records the total energy used by the consumer.

Potential Energy. If the energy possessed by an object is due to its position or condition, it is said to possess **potential energy.** Provided there is no energy lost to friction, the work done to bring the object to that position or condition from its original position or condition is equal to the change in potential energy of the object.

For example, when an object is moved from the earth's surface to a position at some height above it, work is done against gravitational force. The work done gives the object **gravitational potential energy** relative to the earth's surface. In fact, the work done is equal to the gravitational potential energy acquired by the object. If the object falls, work is done by gravity on the object, and the object gives up gravitational potential energy. The work done by gravity on the object causes the object's energy of motion (kinetic energy) to increase as the object increases in speed during its fall. This energy can do work. Thus, falling water can turn water wheels to run machinery and do other kinds of work.

The amount of work that may be performed is

$$W = F\Delta s$$

In this expression, F, which is the weight of the water, is equal to mg—the mass, m, of the water multiplied by the acceleration of gravity, g. Also, Δs is the height, Δh, through which the water falls. Furthermore, W is equal to the loss in potential energy, ΔPE, of the water during its fall. Substituting these quantities for W, F, and Δs gives

$$\Delta PE = mg\Delta h \qquad \text{(Eq. 2-3)}$$

That is, the change in gravitational potential energy of an object equals the product of its weight and the vertical change in its height. It should be noted that this formula is valid only for displacements that are small compared to the radius of the earth—that is, for regions in which g can be considered to be constant.

EXAMPLE

If 1,000 kilograms of water is held at a height of 2.00 meters above ground level, what is the water's potential energy relative to the ground?

Solution

$$PE = mgh = (1{,}000 \text{ kg})\left(9.8 \ \frac{\text{m}}{\text{s}^2}\right)(2.00 \text{ m})$$

$$PE = 19{,}600 \text{ N} \cdot \text{m} = 2.0 \times 10^4 \text{ J}$$

PRACTICAL APPLICATION

A pile driver forces a pile, or post, into the ground by repeatedly dropping a heavy object onto the pile. When the object hits the pile, the work done on the pile equals the product of the force applied to the pile and the distance the pile moves. This work equals the potential energy that the object had at the top of its fall. A greater displacement of the pile at each stroke can be achieved by increasing the weight of the object, the height of its drop, or both. ∎

The energy stored in a spring when work is done in compressing or stretching it is called **elastic potential energy.** The amount that a spring is stretched is directly proportional to the force applied to it. This relationship is called Hooke's Law and is given by the equation

$$F = kx \qquad \text{(Eq. 2-4)}$$

where k is the constant of proportionality between the applied force, F, and the elongation, x, of the spring. The constant k is called the **spring constant.** If F is in newtons and x is in meters, then k is in newtons/meter. The newton/meter, N/m, is the SI unit for the spring constant. If a graph of F versus x is plotted for a given spring, the slope of the graph equals the spring constant, k. A stiff spring has a larger value of k than a weak spring has.

EXAMPLE

The data in the table below were recorded as the force on a spring was varied and the resulting elongation measured. Graph the data and determine the spring constant.

Force (N)	0.0	1.0	2.0	3.0	4.0	5.0
Elongation (m)	0.00	0.04	0.08	0.12	0.16	0.20

Solution

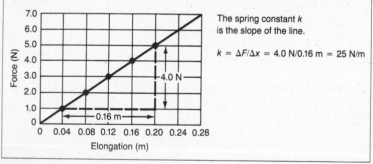

The spring constant k is the slope of the line.

$$k = \Delta F / \Delta x = 4.0 \text{ N}/0.16 \text{ m} = 25 \text{ N/m}$$

When the force, F, applied to a spring is zero, the elongation, x, is also zero. As F increases, x also increases according to Equation 2-4, $F = kx$. Since F increases uniformly from 0 to kx, the average force applied equals $\frac{1}{2}kx$. The work done in stretching the spring is equal to the average force multiplied by the elongation, x:

$$W = \frac{1}{2}kx \cdot x = \frac{1}{2}kx^2$$

The work done on the spring equals its elastic potential energy, PE_s. Hence, the elastic potential energy stored in a spring is also

$$PE_s = \frac{1}{2}kx^2 \qquad\qquad \textbf{(Eq. 2-5)}$$

where the spring constant, k, is in newtons/meter, the elongation, x, is in meters, and the elastic potential energy, PE_s, is in newton · meters, or joules.

EXAMPLE

Determine the potential energy stored in the spring in the previous example when a force of 2.5 newtons is applied to it.

Solution

Using the equation $x = F/k$, find the elongation, x, when a force of 2.5 newtons is applied to the spring. Because $k = 25$ N/m,

$$x = \frac{F}{k} = \frac{2.5 \text{ N}}{25 \text{ N/m}} = 0.10 \text{ m}$$

$$PE_s = \frac{1}{2}kx^2$$

$$PE_s = \frac{1}{2}(25 \text{ N/m})(0.10 \text{ m})^2$$

$$PE_s = 0.13 \text{ J}$$

Kinetic Energy. A moving object can do work on other objects and therefore has energy. The energy of a body due to its motion is called **kinetic energy**, KE. If a mass, m, has a velocity, v, its kinetic energy, a scalar quantity, is given by the equation

$$KE = \frac{1}{2}mv^2 \qquad\qquad \textbf{(Eq. 2-6)}$$

This equation can be derived from the definition of work, $W = F\Delta s$, and Newton's second law, $F = ma$. When a force acting on a mass accelerates it, the mass acquires kinetic energy equivalent to the work done by the force. Since $W = F\Delta s$, and $F = ma$,

$$W = ma\Delta s$$

Recall from Equations 1-1, 1-2a, and 1-3a that for a mass accelerating uniformly from rest to velocity, v,

$$\Delta s = \bar{v}\Delta t, \quad a = v/\Delta t, \quad \text{and} \quad \bar{v} = v/2$$

If we substitute these values of a and Δs in the above equation for the value of W, we get

$$W = ma\Delta s = m \cdot \frac{v}{\Delta t} \cdot \bar{v}\Delta t = m \cdot \frac{v}{\Delta t} \cdot \frac{v}{2} \cdot \Delta t = \frac{1}{2}mv^2$$

Work-Energy Relationship

If a body is lifted to a new height without friction, all the work done is changed to an equivalent amount of potential energy. The change in potential energy depends only on the change in height; it does not depend on the path taken. For example, the work done in lifting a 10.-kg box from the floor to a table top 1.0 m high equals the change in gravitational potential energy, or $mg\Delta h$:

$$W = \Delta PE = mg\Delta h = (10.\text{ kg})(9.8\text{ N/kg})(1.0\text{ m}) = 98\text{ J}$$

As Figure 2-1 shows, the work is the same whether path A, B, C, or any other is taken. When work done against a force does not depend on the path taken, the force is said to be a **conservative force.** Gravitation is an example of a conservative force. Potential energy has meaning only in relation to work done against conservative forces.

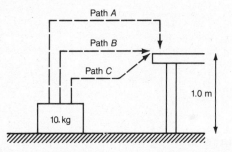

Figure 2-1.   Because gravitation is a conservative force, the same amount of work is done when raising the box from the floor to the table top regardless of which path is followed.

Friction is an example of a non-conservative force. The work done against a non-conservative force does depend on the path taken. For example, the box could be moved to the table top by sliding it up inclined plane A in Figure 2-2. In this case, work would have to be done against friction in addition to the work needed to change the potential energy of the box. The total work will be greater than 98 J.

If inclined plane B is used to move the box to the top of the table, the work done against friction will be even greater even though planes A and B have the same coefficient of friction. This is true because the force of friction is greater when a plane is inclined at a smaller angle. Furthermore, the frictional force acts over a greater distance on incline B. Because friction is a non-conservative force, the work required to raise the box from the floor to the top of the table on incline B is greater than the work to raise it on incline A.

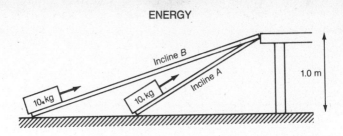

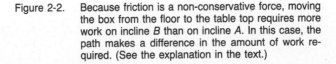

Figure 2-2. Because friction is a non-conservative force, moving the box from the floor to the table top requires more work on incline *B* than on incline *A*. In this case, the path makes a difference in the amount of work required. (See the explanation in the text.)

Conservation of Energy

All observations of energy transfer in a closed system lead to the conclusion that the sum of the energies (potential, kinetic, and internal) in a closed system is always constant. In a closed system there are no external forces doing work on the system, no external work being done by the system, and no transfer of energy into or out of the system. The energy in the system may take various forms and may be interchanged among the components of the system, but there is never any net gain or net loss of energy by the system as a whole. This conclusion is called the **law of conservation of energy.**

For example, an object of mass, m, at a height, h, above the ground has potential energy $PE = mgh$. If the object falls, its potential energy decreases. As it falls, its velocity increases, so its kinetic energy ($KE = \frac{1}{2}mv^2$) also increases. By the law of conservation of energy, the sum of the potential energy and the kinetic energy must remain the same. It follows that the sum of the *changes* in potential and kinetic energy must equal zero:

$$\Delta PE + \Delta KE = 0, \quad \text{or} \quad \Delta KE = -\Delta PE$$

As the body falls, $\Delta PE = -mgh$. If the body falls from rest, the change in its kinetic energy is $\Delta KE = \frac{1}{2}mv^2$. Since the sum of these two changes is zero,

$$\frac{1}{2}mv^2 - mgh = 0, \quad \text{or} \quad \frac{1}{2}mv^2 = mgh$$

Dividing by m,

$$\frac{1}{2}v^2 = gh, \quad \text{or} \quad v^2 = 2gh$$

Because g is a constant, this equation can be used to determine the speed of a mass falling from rest from a known height. Likewise, if the speed is known, the equation can be used to calculate the height from which the mass has fallen.

Similarly, if friction is neglected, the sum of the changes in kinetic energy and potential energy is equal to zero for a pendulum. The relationship between potential and kinetic energy for an ideal pendulum is shown in Figure 2-3. The sum of the kinetic and potential energies is called the total **mechanical energy.**

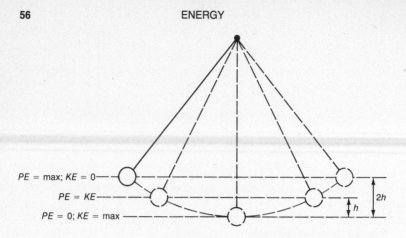

Figure 2-3.   The relationship between potential and kinetic energy
for an ideal pendulum.

The preceding discussion assumes that there is no friction or other non-conservative force acting. In reality, two objects in contact and moving relative to one another experience frictional force opposing the motion. The direction of the frictional force is always opposite to the direction of motion of the moving object.

The effect of this force is to convert some or all of the kinetic energy of the moving object into potential or kinetic energy of the component particles of the object. The energy of these particles is called the **internal energy** of the object. The increase of internal energy usually appears as an increase in temperature of the objects in contact. Since friction does work on objects in motion, tending to increase their internal energy at the expense of their kinetic energy, this amount of work must be taken into account in applying the law of conservation of energy.

PRACTICAL APPLICATION
A space vehicle reentering the atmosphere is slowed for landing by air friction. Some of the kinetic energy of the vehicle is changed to work done against the air friction, and this work is converted to heat. The vehicle must have a heat-resistant surface or shield to protect it against destruction by the high temperatures that result. ■

QUESTIONS

1. **The work required to raise a 10.-kilogram box from the surface of the earth to a height of 5.0 meters is (1) 50. J (2) 100 J (3) 200 J (4) 490 J**
2. **The work done in accelerating an object along a frictionless horizontal surface is equal to the object's change in (1) momentum (2) velocity (3) potential energy (4) kinetic energy**

3. Two objects unequal in mass falling freely from the same point above the earth's surface will experience the same (1) acceleration (2) decrease in potential energy (3) increase in kinetic energy (4) increase in momentum

4. A 20.-kilogram object is moved a distance of 6.0 meters by a net force of 50. newtons. The total work done is (1) 120 J (2) 300 J (3) 420 J (4) 1,000 J

5. A 2-kilogram object is thrown vertically upward with an initial kinetic energy of 400 joules. The object will rise to a height of approximately (1) 10 m (2) 20 m (3) 400 m (4) 800 m

6. Which is a scalar quantity? (1) acceleration (2) momentum (3) force (4) energy

7. A simple pendulum whose mass is 1.00 kilogram swings to a maximum height of 0.200 meter above its lowest point. Neglecting friction, the kinetic energy of the pendulum bob at the lowest point in its swing is (1) 0.980 J (2) 1.96 J (3) 9.80 J (4) 19.6 J

8. A box is sliding down an inclined plane as shown. The force of friction is directed toward point
   (1) A
   (2) B
   (3) C
   (4) D

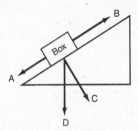

9. A bullet fired from a rifle emerges with a kinetic energy of 2,400 joules. Neglecting friction, if the barrel of the rifle is 0.50 meter long, the average force on the bullet in the barrel is approximately (1) 600 N (2) 1,200 N (3) 2,400 N (4) 4,800 N

10. Which is a vector quantity? (1) power (2) weight (3) energy (4) mass

11. The work required to lift a 50.-newton box a vertical distance of 5.0 meters is (1) 10. J (2) 45 J (3) 55 J (4) 250 J

12. If an object weighing 1.00 newton falls a vertical distance of 4.00 meters, the object's loss in potential energy is (1) 1.00 J (2) 9.80 J (3) 39.2 J (4) 4.00 J

13. What is the amount of work done when a force of 5 newtons moves a 10-kilogram mass a horizontal distance of 4 meters? (1) 5 J (2) 20 J (3) 40 J (4) 50 J

14. A 2.00-kilogram mass that is 15.0 meters above the ground has a potential energy of 294 joules. After falling 5.0 meters, the potential energy of the mass, with respect to the ground, will be (1) 49.0 J (2) 98.0 J (3) 196 J (4) 245 J

15. Which is a unit of power?

(1) joule   (2) $\dfrac{\text{joule}}{\text{second}}$ (3) $\dfrac{\text{kilogram} \cdot \text{meter}}{\text{second}}$ (4) $\dfrac{\text{newton} \cdot \text{meter}^2}{\text{second}}$

16. At a height of 10. meters above the earth's surface, the potential energy of a 2.0-kilogram mass is 196 joules. After the mass, which starts from rest, has fallen 5.0 meters, its kinetic energy will be approximately (1) 200 J (2) 150 J (3) 100 J (4) 50 J

17. If the kinetic energy of an object is 16 joules when its speed is 4.0 meters per second, then the mass of the object is (1) 0.50 kg (2) 2.0 kg (3) 8.0 kg (4) 4.0 kg

18. A 10.-kilogram mass rests on a horizontal frictionless table. How much energy is needed to accelerate the mass from rest to a speed of 5.0 meters per second? (1) 25 J (2) 125 J (3) 3,125 J (4) 6,250 J

19. A force of 10 newtons is required to keep an object moving at a constant speed of 5 meters per second. The power used is (1) 0.5 W (2) 2 W (3) 5 W (4) 50 W

20. Which of these is a vector quantity? (1) velocity (2) speed (3) time (4) work

21. A net force of 9.0 newtons acts on an object through a distance of 3.0 meters. The work done on the object is (1) 27 J (2) 81 J (3) 98 J (4) 120 J

22. A 5.0-kilogram mass is raised 2.0 meters above a laboratory table. The potential energy of the mass with respect to the table is (1) 10. J (2) 50. J (3) 98 J (4) 120 J

23. A mass of 2.0 kilograms dropped from a height of 10. meters will strike the ground with a kinetic energy of approximately (1) 1.0×10^1 J (2) 2.0×10^1 J (3) 1.0×10^2 J (4) 2.0×10^2 J

24. As a stone thrown vertically upward rises, there is an increase in the stone's (1) weight (2) kinetic energy (3) potential energy (4) total energy

25. A wooden box is dragged along a horizontal floor toward the east. The direction of friction on the box is (1) up (2) down (3) east (4) west

26. One kilogram · meter squared per second squared is equivalent to one (1) newton (2) joule (3) watt (4) ampere

27. A box whose mass is 2 kilograms is pushed across a frictionless horizontal floor a distance of 3 meters with a force of 10 newtons. The increase in the potential energy of the box is (1) 0 J (2) 2 J (3) 30 J (4) 60 J

28. An elevator weighing 2.5×10^4 newtons is raised to a height of 10. meters. Neglecting friction, the work done on the elevator is (1) 2.5×10^4 J (2) 2.5×10^5 J (3) 2.5×10^3 J (4) 7.5×10^4 J

29. As a ball falls freely toward the earth, its kinetic energy (1) decreases (2) increases (3) remains the same

30. As the time required for a person to run up a flight of stairs increases, the power developed by the person (1) decreases (2) increases (3) remains the same

31. As a satellite in orbit moves from a distance of 300 kilometers to a distance of 160 kilometers above the earth, the kinetic energy of the satellite (1) decreases (2) increases (3) remains the same

32. A pendulum is set into motion to oscillate freely. As the pendulum's displacement from its rest position increases, its potential energy with respect to the earth (1) decreases (2) increases (3) remains the same

33. As a bullet shot vertically upward rises, its kinetic energy (1) decreases (2) increases (3) remains the same

34. As the time required to lift a 60-kilogram object 6 meters increases, the work required to lift the object (1) decreases (2) increases (3) remains the same

35. As a ball thrown vertically upward rises, its total energy (neglecting friction) (1) decreases (2) increases (3) remains the same

36. As the kinetic energy of a bullet in a rifle barrel increases, its momentum (1) decreases (2) increases (3) remains the same

37. As the time required for accomplishing a given amount of work decreases, the rate at which energy is expended (1) decreases (2) increases (3) remains the same

38. As a mass falls freely in a uniform gravitational field, the total mechanical energy of the mass (1) decreases (2) increases (3) remains the same

39–43. Base your answers to Questions 39 through 43 on the following information.

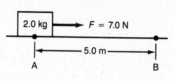

As shown in the diagram, a 2.0-kilogram mass is moved at a constant speed from point A to point B on a horizontal surface. The distance from A to B is 5.0 meters. The applied force, F, is 7.0 newtons.

39. The force of friction acting on the mass is (1) 0.0 N (2) 1.4 N (3) 7.0 N (4) 35 N

40. When the mass moves from A to B, its increase in kinetic energy is (1) 0.0 J (2) 10. J (3) 14 J (4) 35 J

41. If energy is transferred at the rate of 15 watts, the work done during 1.0 second is (1) 7.5 J (2) 15 J (3) 30. J (4) 35 J

42. While being moved from point A to point B, the kinetic energy of the mass (1) increases (2) decreases (3) remains the same

43. If the surface were frictionless, the 7.0-newton force would cause the block to accelerate at (1) 2.5 m/s² (2) 3.5 m/s² (3) 10. m/s² (4) 14 m/s²

44–48. Base your answers to Questions 44 through 48 on the following information.

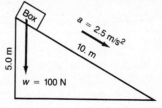

An inclined plane 10. meters long is elevated 5.0 meters at one end as shown in the diagram. Starting from rest at the top of the incline, a box weighing 100 newtons accelerates at a rate of 2.5 meters per second squared along the plane.

44. The potential energy of the box at the top of the incline was (1) 1,000 J (2) 500 J (3) 50 J (4) 0 J

45. How long will it take the box to reach the bottom of the incline? (1) 2.8 s (2) 2.0 s (3) 4.6 s (4) 4.0 s

46. What is the approximate mass of the box? (1) 400 kg (2) 100 kg (3) 40 kg (4) 10 kg

47. If there is no friction as the box slides down the incline, the sum of its potential and kinetic energies will (1) decrease (2) increase (3) remain the same

48. As the box slides down the incline, its momentum will (1) decrease (2) increase (3) remain the same

49–53. Base your answers to Questions 49 through 53 on the following information.

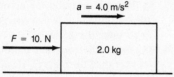

A horizontal force of 10. newtons accelerates a 2.0-kilogram block from rest along a level table as shown, at a rate of 4.0 meters per second squared.

49. The work done in moving the block 8.0 meters is (1) 8.0 J (2) 20. J (3) 80. J (4) 800 J

50. When the speed of the block is 8.0 meters per second, its kinetic energy is (1) 8.0 J (2) 16 J (3) 64 J (4) 80. J

51. The time required for the block to attain a speed of 20. meters per second is (1) 1.0 s (2) 2.0 s (3) 5.0 s (4) 4.0 s

52. What is the frictional force retarding the forward motion of the block? (1) 8.0 N (2) 2.0 N (3) 10. N (4) 12 N

53. If there were no friction between the block and the table, the acceleration of the block would be (1) 20. m/s^2 (2) 9.8 m/s^2 (3) 5.0 m/s^2 (4) 4.0 m/s^2

54–58. Base your answers to Questions 54 through 58 on the information below.

A 6.0-kilogram object falls freely from rest for 5.0 meters and strikes the ground.

54. Which graph best describes the motion of the falling object?

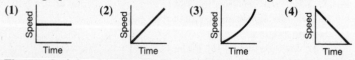

55. The speed of the object just before it strikes the ground is closest to (1) 140 m/s (2) 30. m/s (3) 10. m/s (4) 5.0 m/s

56. The time for the object to fall is closest to (1) 0.10 s (2) 1.0 s (3) 10. s (4) 15 s

57. The kinetic energy of the mass just before it strikes the ground is closest to (1) 1.0 J (2) 30. J (3) 50. J (4) 300 J

58. The weight of the object is closest to (1) 1.0 N (2) 6.0 N (3) 30. N (4) 60. N

59–63. Base your answers to Questions 59 through 63 on the statement below.

A 2.00-kilogram rock, which originally rested on the edge of a cliff 100. meters high, fell to the base of the cliff.

59. Before falling, the rock's potential energy with respect to the base of the cliff was (1) 50.0 J (2) 980. J (3) 1,960 J (4) 6,400 J

60. What is the kinetic energy of the falling rock 50. meters above the base of the cliff? (1) 25 J (2) 490 J (3) 980 J (4) 3,200 J

61. What is the momentum of the rock when its speed is 10.0 meters per second? (1) 10.0 kg · m/s (2) 20.0 kg · m/s (3) 50.0 kg · m/s (4) 100. kg · m/s

62. The speed of the rock an instant before it hits the base of the cliff is approximately (1) 22 m/s (2) 31 m/s (3) 44 m/s (4) 62 m/s

63. Neglecting air resistance, the total mechanical energy of the rock at any time during its fall is equal to which of the following? (1) its potential energy minus its kinetic energy (2) its kinetic energy minus its potential energy (3) zero (4) the sum of its potential and kinetic energies

64–66. Base your answers to Questions 64 through 66 on the diagram at the right, which shows a 1.0-kilogram aluminum sphere and a 3.0-kilogram brass sphere. Each of the spheres has the same diameter, and each is 19.6 meters above the ground. Both spheres are allowed to fall freely. (Neglect the effects of air resistance.)

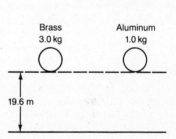

64. Both spheres are released at the same instant. They will reach the ground at (1) the same time, but with different speeds (2) the same time and with the same speeds (3) different times, but with the same speeds (4) different times and with different speeds

65. If the spheres are 19.6 meters above the ground, the time required for the aluminum sphere to reach the ground is (1) 1.0 s (2) 2.0 s (3) 8.0 s (4) 4.0 s

66. Which graph shows the relationship between the potential energy and height above the ground for each sphere?

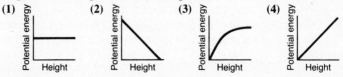

67–71. Base your answers to Questions 67 through 71 on the following information.

As shown in the diagrams, object *A* has a mass of 5.0 kilograms and a speed of 10. meters per second at the foot of a frictionless hill. Object *B* has a mass of 10. kilograms and a speed of 5.0 meters per second at the foot of an identical hill.

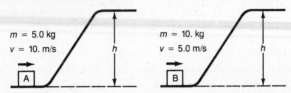

67. In the positions shown in the diagrams, how does the kinetic energy of object *A* compare with the kinetic energy of object *B*? (1) It is one-fourth as great. (2) It is one-half as great. (3) It is the same. (4) It is twice as great.
68. In the positions shown in the diagrams, how does the momentum of object *A* compare with the momentum of object *B*? (1) It is one-fourth as great. (2) It is one-half as great. (3) It is the same. (4) It is twice as great.
69. Which graph best represents the relationship between height up the hill and kinetic energy for each of the masses?

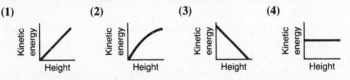

70. At the top of the hill, the force of gravity on *A*, compared with that on *B*, will be (1) less (2) greater (3) the same
71. At the top of the hill, the potential energy of *A*, compared with that of *B*, will be (1) less (2) greater (3) the same

72–77. Base your answers to Questions 72 through 77 on the following information.

A pendulum with a 10.-kilogram bob is released at point *A* and allowed to swing without friction, as shown in the diagram at the right.

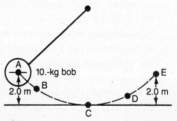

72. What is the weight of the bob? (1) 0.10 N (2) 0.98 N (3) 10. N (4) 98 N
73. The force of the string on the bob is greatest at point (1) *A* (2) *B* (3) *C* (4) *D*

74. What is the velocity of the bob at point E? (1) 0.0 m/s (2) 2.0 m/s (3) 6.3 m/s (4) 9.8 m/s

75. The potential energy of the bob at point A compared to its potential energy at point C is approximately (1) 20 J (2) 40 J (3) 200 J (4) 400 J

76. In moving from point A to point B, the bob's total mechanical energy (1) decreases (2) increases (3) remains the same

77. As the bob moves from point C to point D, the kinetic energy of the bob (1) decreases (2) increases (3) remains the same

78–80. Base your answers to Questions 78 through 80 on the following information and the diagram at the right.

A toy figure is situated on top of a spring attached to a suction cup. The spring is compressed 0.020 meter by a force of 0.30 newton.

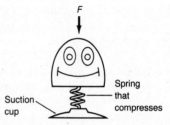

78. What is the spring constant for this spring? (1) 0.0060 N/m (2) 9.8 N/m (3) 15 N/m (4) 750 N/m

79. The work done in compressing the spring is approximately (1) 3.0×10^{-3} J (2) 2.0×10^{-1} J (3) 3.0 J (4) 1.5×10^{1} J

80. The potential energy stored in the compressed spring is approximately (1) 3.0×10^{-3} J (2) 2.0×10^{-1} J (3) 3.0 J (4) 1.5×10^{1} J

81. A force is applied to a given spring causing it to stretch a distance x. If the applied force is halved, the elongation of the spring will be (1) halved (2) doubled (3) quartered (4) quadrupled

82. A force is applied to a spring causing it to stretch. If the applied force is doubled, and the elasticity of the spring is not exceeded, the potential energy stored in the spring will be (1) halved (2) doubled (3) quartered (4) quadrupled

83. A spring having a spring constant k is cut in half. Each of the newly formed springs has a spring constant that is equal to (1) $k/2$ (2) $2k$ (3) k (4) $4k$

84. If the distance a spring is stretched is doubled, and the elastic limit is not exceeded, the potential energy stored in the spring is (1) halved (2) doubled (3) quartered (4) quadrupled

85. A 0.10-kilogram ball that is dropped to the floor from a height of 2.0 meters then rebounds to a height of 1.8 meters. The increase in internal energy for the system is approximately (1) 1.8 J (2) 2.0 J (3) 0.10 J (4) 0.20 J

86. A 2.00-kilogram mass suspended from a spring causes the spring to elongate 1.00×10^{-1} meter. The spring constant of the spring is (1) 0.200 N/m (2) 1.96 N/m (3) 49.0 N/m (4) 196 N/m

87. A given spring has a spring constant of 400 newtons per meter. How much work is done in stretching the spring a distance of 0.020 meter from its equilibrium position?

    (1) 8.0 J (2) 8.0×10^{-1} J (3) 8.0×10^{-2} J (4) 8.0×10^{-3} J

88. A spring having a spring constant of 400 newtons per meter is stretched to a distance of 0.020 meter from its equilibrium position. How much work is done to stretch the spring an additional 0.020 meter? (1) 0.080 J (2) 0.16 J (3) 0.24 J (4) 0.32 J

89–93. Base your answers to Questions 89 through 93 on the information given below.

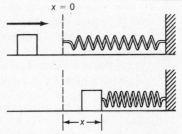

A block that is sliding on a frictionless horizontal surface collides with a spring, as is illustrated in the diagram at the right.

89. During the interval of collision, the speed of the block (1) decreases (2) increases (3) remains the same

90. During the interval of collision, the potential energy of the spring (1) decreases (2) increases (3) remains the same

91. As the block compresses the spring, the spring constant for the spring (1) decreases (2) increases (3) remains the same

92. As the block compresses the spring, the total mechanical energy of the system (1) decreases (2) increases (3) remains the same

93. If the initial speed of the block had been greater, the maximum compression of the spring would have been (1) less (2) greater (3) the same

Sample Problem

Cart A of 1.0-kilogram mass and cart B of 2.0-kilogram mass are placed on a frictionless table as shown in the diagram below. A spring of negligible mass is compressed between the two carts until the spring's potential energy is 12 joules. When the cord is cut the spring will force the carts apart.

(a) Compare the following quantities while the spring is pushing the carts apart:
    (1) The forces acting on the two carts.
    (2) The change in momentum of the two carts.
    (3) The total initial momentum and final momentum of the two carts.
    (4) The acceleration of the two carts.
(b) Calculate the final velocity of cart A.
(c) Determine the ratio of the maximum kinetic energy of cart A to that of cart B.

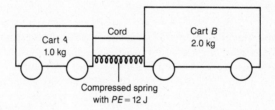

Cart A
1.0 kg   Cord   Cart B
2.0 kg

Compressed spring
with $PE = 12$ J

Solution

(a) (1) The forces are equal in magnitude and opposite in direction.
    (2) The change in momentum is equal in magnitude and opposite in direction for the two carts at all times.
    (3) The total momentum is zero at all times.
    (4) The acceleration of cart A will be twice that of cart B (because the forces are equal and the mass of A is ½ that of B) and opposite in direction.
(b) From the conservation of momentum, the initial momentum of the system must equal the final momentum of the system. Because the carts are initially at rest, their initial momentum is zero. Therefore, their total momentum must remain zero:

$$m_A v_A + m_B v_B = 0$$

$$m_B v_B = -m_A v_A$$

$$v_B = -\frac{m_A v_A}{m_B}$$

$$v_B = -\frac{(1.0 \text{ kg}) v_A}{2.0 \text{ kg}} = -\tfrac{1}{2} v_A$$

PROBLEM SOLVING

From the conservation of energy, the final kinetic energy of the carts must equal the initial potential energy of the spring, since the initial kinetic energy is zero and the final potential energy is zero.

$$12 \text{ J} = \tfrac{1}{2}m_A v_A^2 + \tfrac{1}{2}m_B v_B^2 = \tfrac{1}{2}(1.0 \text{ kg})(v_A^2) + \tfrac{1}{2}(2.0 \text{ kg})(v_B^2)$$

Substituting the value of v_B:

$$12 \text{ J} = \tfrac{1}{2}(1.0 \text{ kg})(v_A^2) + \tfrac{1}{2}(2.0 \text{ kg})\left(-\frac{v_A}{2}\right)^2$$

$$12 \text{ J} = (0.50 \text{ kg})(v_A^2) + (1.0 \text{ kg})(\tfrac{1}{4})v_A^2$$

$$12 \text{ J} = (0.75 \text{ kg})v_A^2$$

$$v_A^2 = 16 \text{ J/kg}$$

Because $1 \text{ J} = 1 \text{ kg} \cdot \text{m}^2/\text{s}^2$,

$$v_A = 4.0 \text{ m/s}$$

(c) Kinetic energy is given by the formula $KE = \tfrac{1}{2}mv^2$. Because it has already been determined that the speed of cart B is one-half that of cart A, it follows that the speed of cart B must be 2.0 meters per second. Therefore,

$$\frac{KE_A}{KE_B} = \frac{\tfrac{1}{2}m_A v_A^2}{\tfrac{1}{2}m_B v_B^2} = \frac{\tfrac{1}{2}(1.0 \text{ kg})(4.0 \text{ m/s})^2}{\tfrac{1}{2}(2.0 \text{ kg})(2.0 \text{ m/s})^2} = \frac{8.0 \text{ J}}{4.0 \text{ J}} = \frac{2}{1}$$

Some skills used in solving this problem are identifying variables in a physical situation, communicating information, and applying mathematics to new situations.

Practice Problems

1. A cart of mass m starts at point A with speed v_i and travels along the track shown in the diagram below. The height of hills A and B is h, the height of hill C is $h/2$, and the distance from point D to E is s.
   (a) What will be the speed of the cart at point B?
   (b) What will be the speed of the cart at point C?
   (c) What will be the momentum of the cart at point D?
   (d) What constant deceleration is required to stop at point E if the brakes are applied at point D?

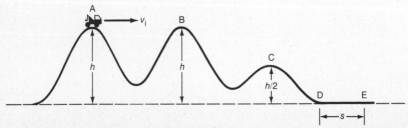

2. A 60.-kilogram girl and a 70.0-kilogram boy swing together on a rope 5.0 meters long attached to a tree over a swimming hole. At the start of the swing, the end of the rope is 10. meters above the surface of the water. At the bottom of the arc, the girl lets go and drops into the water. The boy remains on the rope. How high does the end of the rope rise at the top of its swing with the boy alone?

3. A student on skis starts from rest at the top of a hill and reaches the bottom of a hill going 20.0 meters per second. The mass of the student is 60.0 kilograms.
   (a) What is the student's momentum at the bottom of the hill?
   (b) If the student strikes a snowdrift and stops in 3.0 seconds, what average force does the snowdrift exert?
   (c) How far does the student penetrate the snow drift?
   (d) If friction is neglected, what is the difference in height between the top and bottom of the hill?

4. A 1,200-kilogram car accelerates uniformly from rest to a speed of 16 meters per second in 8.0 seconds.
   (a) What is the acceleration of the car?
   (b) What distance does the car travel in this 8.0 seconds?

5. The car in Question 4 climbs a hill 30. meters high at a uniform speed of 16 meters per second in 30. seconds.
   (a) What is the potential energy of the car at the top of the hill relative to the bottom of the hill?
   (b) What is the change in kinetic energy of the car while it is climbing the hill? Explain your answer in a complete sentence.
   (c) What is the power developed by the car in climbing the hill?

6. Explain each of the following on the basis of physical principles.
   (a) It requires more work to stop a ferry boat than a canoe if both are originally traveling with the same velocity.
   (b) A 20.-kilogram ball is used as the bob of a pendulum suspended from the ceiling of a classroom. The bob is drawn from its equilibrium position and released from the tip of a student's nose. If the student does not move, there is no danger of being struck by the ball on its return swing.
   (c) A 700-newton physics teacher runs at a constant speed up a flight of stairs rising 6.0 meters in 7.0 seconds. The teacher is billed as being "more powerful than five 100-watt light bulbs."

UNIT 3   ELECTRICITY AND MAGNETISM

I. STATIC ELECTRICITY

Electrically charged objects exert forces upon each other that depend on the quantity of charge, on the distance between charges, and on whether the objects are at rest relative to each other. The study of these forces between charges *at rest* is the subject matter of the topic **static electricity.** Note that the term "at rest" means that there is no net transfer of charge in any direction, although charged parts of a given object may be in motion relative to each other.

CAN YOU EXPLAIN THIS?

Dancing on a nylon carpet can cause sparks to fly.

On a dry day, a person dancing on a nylon carpet may become electrically charged as friction transfers electrons between the person and the carpet. The resulting electric force may be sufficient to ionize air molecules, causing charge flow and sparking, when the person touches another person or a metal surface.

Microstructure of Matter

The following review of atomic structure is given to aid the study of electricity.

The matter in the universe is composed of various combinations of about 100 different elements, with each element consisting of one kind of atom. Although the atom is the unit of molecular structure, it consists basically of three particles. The least massive particle, the **electron,** carries a **negative** (−) **charge.** The **proton,** which is 1,836 times as massive as the electron, carries a **positive** (+) **charge** equal in magnitude to that of the negative electron. These **elementary units of charge** are the smallest that have ever been isolated. The third particle is the **neutron.** It bears no charge and is of approximately the same mass as the proton. The electron and proton are among the class of particles called charge carriers.

Protons and neutrons are found only in the central core, the **nucleus,** of the atom. The electrons are in motion outside the nucleus and possess specific levels of energy. Atoms as a whole are electrically neutral because the number of protons in the nucleus is the same as the number of electrons outside it. Energy applied to atoms in the form of friction, heat, and light, for example, may remove some of the electrons, but neither protons nor neutrons can be separated from atoms by ordinary means. This means that, in general, objects become charged only by gaining or losing electrons (elementary units of negative charge).

Charged Objects

When electrons are lost or gained by a neutral atom, the resulting particle is electrically charged and is called an **ion**. The charge of an ion depends on the nature and quantity of the excess elementary charges. For example, an atom with 11 protons and 11 electrons is neutral, but if one electron (one elementary unit of negative charge) is removed from this atom, leaving 11 protons and 10 electrons, the resulting ion will have a single elementary unit of net *positive* charge. Similarly, an ion with 16 protons and 18 electrons has a net *negative* charge of 2 elementary units.

When two charged bodies of *like* sign are brought near one another, they are *repelled* by an electrical force acting on each in opposite directions. When the bodies carry charge of *opposite* sign, they are *attracted* to one another by an electrical force acting on each, also in opposite directions. An electroscope is a device that has a pair of conducting vanes that are hinged so that they can move apart, as shown in Figure 3-1. When the electroscope is given a charge, the like charges on the two vanes cause them to repel each other and move apart against the pull of gravity. If a charged object with the same charge is brought near the electroscope, additional charge of the same sign is repelled into the vanes and causes them to separate farther. If the object has an opposite charge, it will attract charge away from the vanes. The force of repulsion between the vanes will then be smaller, and the vanes will fall closer together. In this way, an electroscope can detect the presence and sign of a charge on an object.

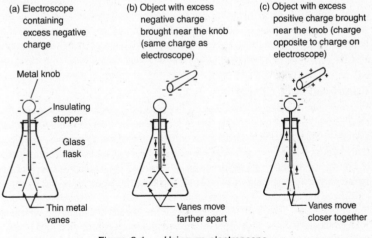

(a) Electroscope containing excess negative charge

Metal knob
Insulating stopper
Glass flask
Thin metal vanes

(b) Object with excess negative charge brought near the knob (same charge as electroscope)

Vanes move farther apart

(c) Object with excess positive charge brought near the knob (charge opposite to charge on electroscope)

Vanes move closer together

Figure 3-1.   Using an electroscope.

CAN YOU EXPLAIN THIS?

During the summer months, static cling in clothes is generally not a problem.

Static cling is caused by the force of attraction that exists between surfaces that have opposite net charge. In summer, moist air causes a tiny film of water to condense on surfaces, making them conductive. Consequently, static charges quickly "leak" between the surface and air and there is no substantial net accumulation of charge.

Transfer of Charge. A system consisting of neutral objects will have a total net charge equal to zero. Objects within the system may exchange electrons, becoming charged relative to each other, but the system as a whole will remain neutral. This can occur if the objects are in contact, especially when they rub against each other. If one object loses electrons, becoming positively charged, the object in contact with it will acquire the electrons, becoming negatively charged.

Grounding. The earth or some other large conductor can act as an **electrical ground** capable of accepting or donating large numbers of electrons without significantly affecting its own electrical state. Grounding an object neutralizes its charge by adding electrons to it (if it is positively charged) or removing electrons from it (if it is negatively charged). The process of removing the charge from an object is called *discharging*.

PRACTICAL APPLICATION

A practical application of grounding is the lightning rod, a pointed metal rod attached to the top of a building and connected by a wire to another metal rod in the earth. A lightning stroke is a discharge of electric charge from a cloud. Often the discharge occurs between the cloud and the earth or an object attached to the ground. A metal lightning rod is a better conductor of charge than the wood or stone of which houses are built. If a lightning discharge occurs near a house protected by a lightning rod projecting above the roof, the charge carriers will flow through the metal rod to the ground rather than through the house. ∎

Conservation of Charge

In a system isolated so that electric charge carriers cannot enter or leave, the total net charge is constant. This means that whatever changes occur within the system as charge carriers are transferred from one object to another, the algebraic sum of all positive and negative charges never changes. This observation is known as the **law of conservation of charge.** For example, consider an isolated system consisting of two identical conducting spheres, A and B, separated by some distance. If A possesses a net charge of -16 elementary units and B possesses a net charge of $+4$ elementary units, the net charge of the system is -12 elementary units. If the spheres are brought into contact, electrons from A will move to B until each sphere possesses -6 elementary units of charge. The net charge of the system remains at -12 units and is evenly distributed between the two objects.

Quantity of Charge

The smallest isolated charge observed to exist in nature is that of the electron (or of its equivalent, in terms of charge magnitude, the proton). This elementary charge, symbolized as $-e$ (or $+e$ for a positive charge) is extremely small compared to those dealt with in ordinary experience. The *SI* unit of charge is the **coulomb,** C. The coulomb is a derived unit and is defined in terms of the ampere, a unit of electric current to be discussed later. The coulomb is a quantity of charge much larger than the elementary charge. One coulomb equals 6.25×10^{18} elementary charges. The charge on an electron is thus equal to -1.6×10^{-19} coulomb, and the charge on a proton is $+1.6 \times 10^{-19}$ coulomb. The net charge on any larger object depends on its excess or deficiency of electrons and is always an *integral multiple* of e. Thus, a body can have a charge of $2e$ (3.2×10^{-19} C) or $3e$ (4.8×10^{-19} C), but it can never have a charge of $2\frac{1}{2}e$ (4.0×10^{-19} C).

Coulomb's Law

Experiments have shown that the magnitude of the force between charged objects at rest is directly proportional to the product of the charges carried by the objects. Thus, if all other conditions are the same, the force between an object carrying a charge of $+4e$ and one carrying a charge of $+3e$ is of the same magnitude as the force between two objects carrying charges of $+2e$ and $+6e$, respectively. Experiments also show that the force between fixed charges varies inversely with the square of the distance separating them. Combining these two proportionalities yields the relationship called **Coulomb's Law.** This law is given by the equation

$$F = k\frac{q_1 q_2}{r^2} \qquad \text{(Eq. 3-1)}$$

where the force, F, is in newtons, the charges q_1 and q_2 are in coulombs, and the separation of the charges, r, is in meters. The electrostatic force is directed along the line joining the charges and is equal in magnitude and opposite in direction for the two objects. The proportionality constant, k, has been found to be approximately equal to 9.0×10^9 newton $\cdot$ meter squared per coulomb squared in a vacuum or in air. Notice that, just as Newton's law of gravitational force is exact only for "point" masses, Coulomb's law is exact only for "point" charges—that is, charged objects whose dimensions are insignificant compared to the distance between them—and for charged spherical objects if r is the distance between their centers.

EXAMPLE

What is the force between two relatively small charged objects that carry charges of $+0.20$ coulomb and -0.30 coulomb, respectively, if the distance between them is 1,000 meters?

Solution

$$F = \frac{kq_1 q_2}{r^2} = \frac{\left(9.0 \times 10^9 \dfrac{\text{N} \cdot \text{m}^2}{\text{C}^2}\right)(0.20 \text{ C})(-0.30 \text{ C})}{(1.0 \times 10^3 \text{ m})^2}$$

$$F = \frac{\left(9.0 \times 10^9 \frac{N \cdot m^2}{C^2}\right)(-6.0 \times 10^{-2} \ C^2)}{1.0 \times 10^6 \ m^2}$$

$$F = -5.4 \times 10^2 \ N$$

The negative sign indicates a force of attraction.

Electric Fields

The region in which electrical force acts on a charge is called an **electric field.** By definition, the direction of a field at a given point is the direction in which force acts on a small *positive* test charge. For example, if electric force acts on a positive charge in a northerly direction, then the electric field direction is north. At the same point in the field, a small *negative* charge would experience a force directed to the *south*. An electric **field line** is the line along which a charged particle would move as a result of its interaction with the electric field. The direction of a field line is the direction of the force exerted on a positively charged particle located on the field line.

The strength of the field at any point is called the **field intensity** or **field strength,** E. The field intensity or field strength is equal to the force exerted on a unit of charge at that point in the field. The equation for determining electric field strength is

$$E = \frac{F}{q} \qquad \text{(Eq. 3-2)}$$

where F is the force on a charge q. If F is measured in newtons, and q in coulombs, then E is in *newtons per coulomb,* N/C, the *SI* unit for electric field intensity or strength. For example, if an object carrying a charge of 2×10^{-6} C is acted upon by an electric force of 0.06 N, the magnitude of the electric field intensity at that point is

$$E = \frac{6 \times 10^{-2} \ N}{2 \times 10^{-6} \ C} = 3 \times 10^4 \ N/C$$

Electric field intensity, E, must be designated both in magnitude and direction because it is a vector quantity. When two fields interact, the net field must be obtained by vector methods.

Field Around a "Point" (or Spherical) Charge. The origin of an electric field is a charged object. An electric field exists around every charged object. For any charged object on which charge can spread uniformly (a charged conductor), the electric field lines are normal to the surface. Around a "point" charge, the electric field is directed *radially* away from the charge if it is positive and toward the charge if it is negative. As indicated by Coulomb's Law, the intensity of the field around a point charge decreases inversely as the square of the distance from the charge. This is also true of the field around a charged conducting sphere. The field acts as if it were the result of a point charge located at the center of the sphere. Within a charged conducting sphere itself, however, the field intensity is zero; that is, no force will be observed on a charge inside a hollow charged conducting sphere.

Field Between Parallel Charged Plates. The electric field that exists in the region between two oppositely charged parallel plates is essentially uniform if the distance between the plates is small relative to their area. This means that the field strength is the same at each point between the plates. A unit charge within this region of uniform field will experience the same force in the same direction, wherever it is placed. The fields surrounding charged objects are shown in Figure 3-2.

Field lines

(a) "Point" charge

(b) Spherical charged object

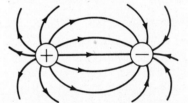

(c) Field between opposite charges

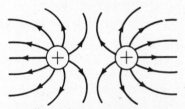

(d) Field between two positive charges

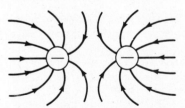

(e) Field between two negative charges

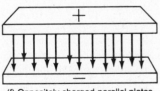

(f) Oppositely charged parallel plates

Figure 3-2.   Fields surrounding charged objects.

Electric Potential

If the direction of an electric field is such that it opposes the motion of a charged particle, work must be done to move the particle in that direction. The work needed to move a particle with one unit of positive charge from an infinite distance to any given point in an electric field is called the electric potential of that point. Like work and energy, electric potential is a scalar quantity. If work must be done to move a positively charged particle from point A to point B in an electric field, point B has a higher (more positive) potential than point A. If the positively charged particle is allowed to "fall" from point B to point A, the same amount of work will be done on the particle by the field. These work relationships are exactly the opposite for a *negatively* charged particle. Work must be done to move a negatively charged particle from higher to lower potential, but a negatively charged particle will fall freely from lower potential to higher.

Potential Difference. The **potential difference,** or **potential drop,** between two points in an electric field is the change in potential energy (or the work done) per unit charge as a charged particle is moved between the points. The potential difference is given by the formula

$$V = \frac{W}{q} \qquad \text{(Eq. 3-3)}$$

where W is the work in joules, q is the charge in coulombs, and V is the electric potential difference in joules/coulomb. If one joule of work is done against an electric field to transfer one coulomb of charge between two points in the field, a potential difference of one **volt** is said to exist between the two points. That is,

$$1 \text{ joule/coulomb} = 1 \text{ volt}$$

The volt, V, is the derived *SI* unit of electric potential and potential difference. Because the volt is a measure of the electric potential difference between points in an electric field, it can be used to calculate the energy required to transfer a given charge between these points. For example, to move 2 coulombs of charge across a potential difference of 3 volts, the work required is:

$$W = Vq = (3 \text{ V})(2 \text{ C}) = 6 \text{ J}$$

For example, an electric toaster connected to two points at a potential difference of 120 volts will receive 120 joules of energy for each coulomb of charge that passes through the toaster. On the other hand, when a 12-volt storage battery is charged from some external energy source, for every coulomb of charge transferred from one terminal of the battery to the other, 12 joules of energy are expended by the outside source.

The Electronvolt. If an elementary charge (the charge on an electron) is moved against an electric field through a potential difference of one volt, the work done on the charge is given by

$$W = Vq = (1.0 \text{ V})(1.6 \times 10^{-19} \text{ C}) = 1.6 \times 10^{-19} \text{ J}$$

This amount of work, or gain in potential energy, is called the **electronvolt,** eV. That is,

$$1 \text{ eV} = 1.6 \times 10^{-19} \text{ J}$$

(Do not confuse the italic symbol V, electric potential difference, with V, the *SI* unit for measuring the amount of electric potential difference.) The electronvolt is extremely small in comparison with the joule, but its size is convenient for expressing the energy commonly involved in chemical reactions between atoms and ions. For example, the energy needed to ionize (remove the electron from) a hydrogen atom when the electron is in its lowest possible energy level is 13.6 eV.

Relationship of Field Intensity to Field Potential. The electric field intensity of a uniform field is the rate at which electric potential changes with position. That is,

$$E = \frac{V}{d} \qquad \text{(Eq. 3-4)}$$

where V is potential in volts, d is change in position in meters, and E is the electric field intensity expressed in units of **volts/meter,** V/m. The volt/meter is identical with the unit newton/coulomb for E in Equation 3-2:

$$\frac{\text{volt}}{\text{meter}} = \frac{\text{joule/coulomb}}{\text{meter}} = \frac{\text{joule}}{\text{coulomb} \cdot \text{meter}} = \frac{\text{newton} \cdot \text{meter}}{\text{coulomb} \cdot \text{meter}} = \frac{\text{newton}}{\text{coulomb}}$$

QUESTIONS

1. **A metal (conducting) sphere with an excess charge of +11 elementary charges touches an identical sphere with an excess charge of +15 elementary charges. After the spheres touch, the excess of elementary charges on the first sphere is (1) +13 (2) +26 (3) −4 (4) +4**

2. **How much work is required to transfer 10. coulombs of charge between two points having a potential difference of 120 volts? (1) 0.083 J (2) 12 J (3) 600 J (4) 1,200 J**

3. **If a positively charged rod is brought near the knob of an uncharged electroscope without touching it, the leaves will diverge because**
   (1) negative charges are transferred from the electroscope to the rod
   (2) negative charges are attracted to the knob of the electroscope
   (3) positive charges are repelled to the leaves of the electroscope
   (4) positive charges are transferred from the rod to the electroscope

4. **An electron may be placed at positions A, B, or C between the two parallel charged metal plates shown. The electric force on the electron will be (1) greatest at A (2) greatest at B (3) greatest at C (4) the same at all three positions**

5. Which graph best represents the relationship between electrostatic force and distance of separation for two point charges?

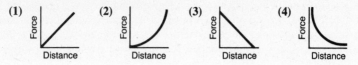

6. When a positively charged body touches a neutral body, the neutral body will (1) gain protons (2) lose protons (3) gain electrons (4) lose electrons

7. Two point charges that are separated by a distance of 1.0 meter repel each other with a force equal to 9.0 newtons. What is the force of repulsion when these two charges are 3.0 meters apart? (1) 1.0 N (2) 27 N (3) 3.0 N (4) 81 N

8. An electron gains 2 electronvolts of energy as it is transferred from point A to point B. The potential difference between points A and B is (1) 3.2×10^{-19} V (2) 2.0 V (3) 32 V (4) 1.3×10^{19} V

9. Two parallel metal plates have a potential difference of 50. volts. How much work is done in moving a charge of 4.0×10^{-5} coulomb from one plate to the other? (1) 8.0×10^{-7} J (2) 1.6×10^{-3} J (3) 2.0×10^{-3} J (4) 1.3×10^6 J

10. One metallic sphere has a charge of +16 units and a second, identical sphere has a charge of −4 units. After the two spheres touch, the charge on each sphere is (1) +6 units (2) +12 units (3) +20 units (4) −20 units

11. If object A becomes positively charged when rubbed with object B, then object B has (1) gained electrons (2) lost electrons (3) gained protons (4) lost protons

12. The main purpose of an electroscope is to (1) neutralize a charge (2) produce a charge (3) measure a charge (4) find the sign of a charge

13. If the distance between 2 protons is tripled, then the force they exert on each other, compared with the original force, will be (1) one-ninth as great (2) one-third as great (3) three times as great (4) nine times as great

14. Why does a neutral hard rubber rod become negatively charged when rubbed with wool? (1) The rod loses protons. (2) The rod loses electrons. (3) The wool loses protons. (4) The wool loses electrons.

15. An energy of 2.0×10^4 electronvolts is equal to (1) 1.6×10^{-19} J (2) 3.2×10^{-19} J (3) 3.2×10^{-15} J (4) 5.0×10^{-5} J

16. A and B are two identical uncharged metal spheres. Sphere A is given an electrical charge of $+q$, touched to sphere B, and then removed. The charge on sphere A after separation is (1) $+q$ (2) $-q$ (3) $+q/2$ (4) $-q/2$

17. Three electric charges are arranged as shown. Which vector best represents the resultant force that charges q_2 and q_3 exert on charge q_1?

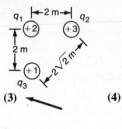

(1) ◄━━━━ (2) ↘ (3) ↖ (4) ↑

18. The work required to move 1.0 coulomb of charge through a potential difference of 2.0 volts is (1) 0.50 J (2) 2.0 J (3) 3.0 J (4) 4.0 J

19. An electron moves through a potential difference of 3.00 volts. The energy acquired by the charge is (1) 5.33×10^{-19} J (2) 1.60×10^{-19} J (3) 4.80×10^{-19} J (4) 3.00 J

20. A and B are two points in an electric field. If 6.0 joules of work are done in transferring 2.0 coulombs of electric charge from point A to point B, then the potential difference between points A and B is (1) 0.0 V (2) 1.5 V (3) 3.0 V (4) 12 V

21. A neutral object can become positively charged by (1) gaining electrons (2) losing electrons (3) gaining protons (4) losing protons

22. When two objects are rubbed together, which particle is most likely to be transferred? (1) nucleus (2) electron (3) proton (4) neutron

23. The electronvolt is a unit of (1) current (2) power (3) resistance (4) energy

24. If the charge on one of two positively charged spheres is doubled, the electrostatic force of repulsion between the spheres will be (1) halved (2) doubled (3) quartered (4) quadrupled

25. The electric force between two charged spheres is 18 newtons. If the distance between the centers of the spheres is tripled, the resulting electric force will be (1) 6.0 N (2) 2.0 N (3) 3.0 N (4) 54 N

26. The electric force between two charged spheres is 64 newtons. If the distance between the centers of the spheres is quadrupled the resulting electric force will be (1) 8.0 N (2) 2.0 N (3) 16 N (4) 4.0 N

27. In general, solid materials become electrically charged because of transfer of (1) positrons (2) electrons (3) protons (4) neutrons

28. As an electron approaches a proton, electrostatic force acts on (1) the electron only (2) the proton only (3) both the electron and the proton (4) neither the electron nor the proton

29. The energy of an electron may be increased by 8×10^{-17} joule if it is moved through a potential difference of (1) 0.002 V (2) 200 V (3) 500 V (4) 5,000 V

30. If the distance between two point sources of equal charge is halved, the electrical force between the sources will be (1) halved (2) doubled (3) quartered (4) quadrupled

31. A charge of 8.0×10^{-5} coulomb is moved by a force of 2.0×10^{-2} newton between two points 0.10 meter apart in a uniform electric field. The potential difference between the two points is (1) 25 V (2) 40. V (3) 75 V (4) 160 V

32. An electron is projected from D toward B between two parallel charged plates as shown in the illustration. The electric force acting on the electron is directed toward (1) A (2) B (3) C (4) D

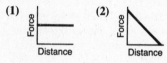

33. A battery of constant potential is connected to two parallel metal plates. Which graph best represents the relationship between the force on an electron between the plates and the distance between the plates?

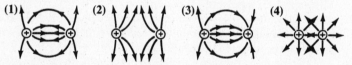

34. Four electric charges, A, B, C, and D, are arranged as shown. The electric force will be least between charges (1) A and B (2) A and C (3) A and D (4) B and D

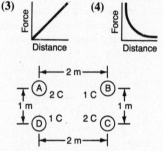

35. Which diagram best represents the electric field surrounding two positively charged spheres?

36. Which graph best illustrates the relationship between electrostatic force and the charge on two positive point charges that are always equal to each other in magnitude?

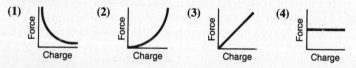

37. As the amount of charge held on an object increases, the potential difference required to add additional charges of the same sign to it (1) decreases (2) increases (3) remains the same

38. As a charged object located between two oppositely charged parallel plates is moved parallel to the surfaces of the plates, the electric force on the object (1) decreases (2) increases (3) remains the same

39. As the electric charge on the surface of a hollow metal sphere increases, the electric field intensity inside the sphere (1) decreases (2) increases (3) remains the same

40. As an electron moves toward a positively charged body, the electron's kinetic energy (1) decreases (2) increases (3) remains the same

41. As an electron approaches a proton, the electrical force between them (1) decreases (2) increases (3) remains the same

42. As charged body A charges neutral body B by direct contact, the quantity of charge on body A (1) is decreased (2) is increased (3) remains the same

43. As a negatively charged rod is moved toward the tip of a positively charged electroscope, the number of electrons in the tip of the electroscope (1) decreases (2) increases (3) remains the same

44. A battery of constant potential difference is connected to two parallel metal plates. As the distance between the plates is increased, the electric field intensity between the plates (1) decreases (2) increases (3) remains the same

45–49. Base your answers to Questions 45 through 49 on the drawing and the following information.

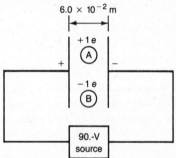

Two particles, A and B, are placed between two parallel plates 6.0×10^{-2} meter apart in a vacuum. The potential difference across the plates is 90. volts. The charge on A is +1 elementary charge and that on B is −1 elementary charge. The mass of A is 4 times the mass of B.

45. What is the increase in the kinetic energy of particle A as it moves from the positive to the negative plate? (1) 1.44×10^{-17} eV (2) 1.60×10^{-19} eV (3) 90 eV (4) 360 eV

46. What is the increase in the kinetic energy of particle B as it moves from the negative to the positive plate? (1) 1.44×10^{-17} J (2) 1.60×10^{-19} J (3) 22.5 J (4) 90 J

47. The ratio of the increase in the kinetic energy of particle A to the increase in the kinetic energy of particle B is (1) 1/1 (2) 2/1 (3) 1/2 (4) 4/1

48. What is the electric field intensity between the two plates? (1) 5.4 N/C (2) 1.5×10^3 N/C (3) 6.7×10^{-2} N/C (4) 2.4×10^{-16} N/C

49. If the distance between the plates is decreased while other factors remain the same, there will be no change in the (1) charge on the plates (2) force on an electron between the plates (3) electric field between the plates (4) potential difference across the plates

50–54. Base your answers to Questions 50 through 54 on the following information and the illustration at the right.

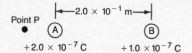

Two identical metal spheres, A and B, are given charges of $+2.0 \times 10^{-7}$ coulomb and $+1.0 \times 10^{-7}$ coulomb, respectively. The separation between their centers is 2.0×10^{-1} meter.

50. The electric force exerted on B by A will be directed (1) to the left (2) to the right (3) toward the top of the page (4) into the page

51. If the magnitude of the electric force on B is equal to F, the magnitude of the electric force on A will be equal to (1) F (2) $2F$ (3) $F/2$ (4) $4F$

52. The magnitude of the electric force exerted on B is equal to (1) 9.0×10^3 N (2) 9.0×10^{-4} N (3) 4.5×10^4 N (4) 4.5×10^{-3} N

53. A positive charge of 1.0×10^{-10} coulomb at a point P near sphere A is acted upon by a force of 2.0×10^{-15} newton. What is the intensity of the electrical field at point P? (1) 2.0×10^{-15} N/C (2) 2.0×10^{-5} N/C (3) 2.0×10^5 N/C (4) 5.0×10^{-6} N/C

54. If A and B are brought into contact, which will gain electrons? (1) A only (2) B only (3) both A and B (4) neither A nor B

55–59. Base your answers to Questions 55 through 59 on the following information.

A metal sphere, A, has a charge of $-q$ coulombs. An identical metal sphere, B, has a charge of $+2q$ coulombs. The magnitude of the electric force on B due to A is F newtons.

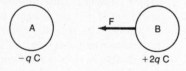

55. The magnitude of the electric force on A due to B, in newtons, is (1) F (2) $2F$ (3) $F/2$ (4) $4F$

56. If the distance between the centers of the spheres is halved, the magnitude of the force on B due to A, in newtons, will be (1) F (2) $2F$ (3) $F/2$ (4) $4F$

57. If an electron were placed midway between A and B, the resultant electric force on the electron would be (1) toward A (2) toward B (3) up (4) down

58. If A and B are connected by a copper wire whose surface is negligible compared with that of the spheres, charge will flow through the connecting wire until the charge on B in coulombs becomes (1) 0 C (2) $+q/2$ C (3) $+q$ C (4) $-q$ C

59. The current in the wire consists of a flow of (1) protons from A to B (2) protons from B to A (3) electrons from B to A (4) electrons from A to B

60–63. Base your answers to Questions 60 through 63 on the diagram, which represents two large parallel metal plates with a small charged sphere between them.

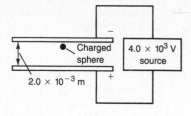

60. The energy gained by the charged sphere as it moves from the negative plate to the positive plate can be measured in (1) electronvolts (2) volt · meters (3) coulombs/volt (4) volts/meter

61. What is the intensity of the electric field between the two charged plates? (1) 5.0×10^{-17} m/V (2) 2.0×10^{6} V/m (3) 1.6×10^{-16} C/m (4) 8.0 V · m

62. If the distance between the plates were increased, the field intensity would (1) decrease (2) increase (3) remain the same

63. As the sphere moves from the negative plate to the positive plate, the force on the sphere (1) decreases (2) increases (3) remains the same

64–66. Base your answers to Questions 64 through 66 on the following information.

Charge $+q$ is located a distance r from charge $+Q$. Each charge is 1.0 coulomb.

64. The electric field due to charge $+Q$ at distance r is equal to

(1) $\dfrac{kQ}{F}$ (2) $\dfrac{kQq}{r}$ (3) $\dfrac{Q}{r^2}$ (4) $\dfrac{kQ}{r^2}$

65. If 200 joules of work is required to move $+q$ through distance r to $+Q$, the potential difference between the two charges is (1) 100 V (2) 200 V (3) 800 V (4) 50 V

66. If distance r is doubled, then the force that $+Q$ exerts on $+q$ is (1) halved (2) doubled (3) unchanged (4) quartered

67–71. Base your answers to Questions 67 through 71 on the following information.

An electron is projected into the vacuum space between two charged parallel plates, as shown. The plates are 0.030 meter apart. The potential difference between the plates is 300 volts.

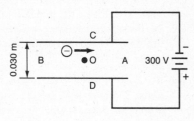

67. The direction of the electric field at point O between the plates is toward (1) A (2) B (3) C (4) D

68. The magnitude of the electric field at point O between the plates is
(1) 1.0×10^4 N/C (2) 1.5×10^{-3} N/C (3) 9.0×10^{-3} N/C
(4) 6.7×10^{-11} N/C

69. An electron moving from B toward A between the plates will be acted upon by an electric force that is always directed (1) toward the positive plate (2) toward the negative plate (3) parallel to the plate surfaces (4) at right angles to the instantaneous velocity of the electron

70. As the electron moves between the plates, its kinetic energy (1) decreases (2) increases (3) remains the same

71. If the distance between the plates is increased, the intensity of the electric field between them (1) decreases (2) increases (3) remains the same

72–76. Base your answers to Questions 72 through 76 on the following information.

A proton (represented by ⊕) is placed between the two parallel plates, A and B, as shown. The plates are 0.20 meter apart and connected to a 90.-volt battery. The proton has a force exerted on it toward A.

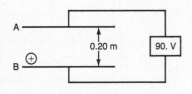

72. The direction of the electric field between the two plates is from (1) positive plate A to negative plate B (2) negative plate A to positive plate B (3) positive plate B to negative plate A (4) negative plate B to positive plate A

73. The magnitude of the electric field intensity between the two plates is (1) 18 N/C (2) 45 N/C (3) 180 N/C (4) 450 N/C

74. The kinetic energy gained by the proton in moving from plate B to plate A is (1) 1.4×10^{-21} J (2) 1.8×10^{-21} J (3) 1.4×10^{-17} J (4) 1.8×10^{-17} J

75. If the proton is now moved back toward plate B, its potential energy will (1) decrease (2) increase (3) remain the same

76. As the separation between plates A and B is increased, the electric field intensity between the plates will (1) decrease (2) increase (3) remain the same

77–81. Base your answers to Questions 77 through 81 on the diagram, in which circular lines are drawn at 60. volts, 30. volts, and 20. volts about electric charge $+q$.

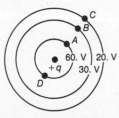

77. The total work done in moving 1.0 coulomb of charge from A to D is (1) 0.0 J (2) 40. J (3) 60. J (4) 80. J

78. The total work done in moving 2.0 coulombs of positive charge from position C to position A is (1) 0.0 J (2) 40. J (3) 60. J (4) 80. J

79. If 5.0 coulombs of charge moves from position A to position B, the energy expended will be (1) 5.0 J (2) 6.0 J (3) 30. J (4) 150 J

80. Compared with A, the magnitude of the electric field intensity at B is (1) less (2) greater (3) the same

81. If $+q$ is increased to $+2q$, the potential at B (1) decreases (2) increases (3) remains the same

82–86. Base your answers to Questions 82 through 86 on the following information.

There is a potential difference of 50. volts across parallel plates A and B. A positive charge is located as shown.

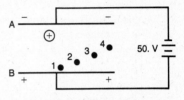

82. If the separation of the plates is 1.0×10^{-1} meter, then the electric field intensity between them is (1) 8.0×10^{-16} V/m (2) 5.0×10^2 V/m (3) 5.0×10^{-1} V/m (4) 3.1×10^{18} V/m

83. How much work would be required to move $+2.0$ coulombs of charge from plate A to plate B? (1) 5.0×10^1 J (2) 2.0×10^1 J (3) 1.0×10^2 J (4) 6.25×10^{18} J

84. The greatest amount of work would be required to move the positive charge from its present position to point (1) 1 (2) 2 (3) 3 (4) 4

85. An electron moving freely from plate A to plate B would acquire a maximum kinetic energy of
(1) 4.5×10^{-3} eV (2) 2.5 eV (3) 5.0×10^1 eV (4) 1.0×10^2 eV

86. The electrical potential energy of the positive charge is greatest if the charge is located at position (1) 1 (2) 2 (3) 3 (4) 4

87–91. Base your answers to Questions 87 through 91 on the following information.

The diagram represents two equal negative point charges, A and B, that are a distance d apart.

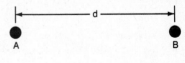

87. Which diagram best represents the electric field between the two charges?

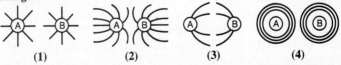

(1)　　　　(2)　　　　(3)　　　　(4)

88. **Where would the electric field intensity of the two charges be minimum?** (1) one-quarter of the way between *A* and *B* (2) midway between *A* and *B* (3) on the surface of *B* (4) on the surface of *A*

89. **Which graph expresses the relationship of the distance between the charges and the force between them?**

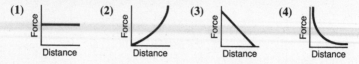

90. **If charge *A* is doubled, the force between *A* and *B* will be** (1) halved (2) doubled (3) quartered (4) quadrupled

91. **If *A* has an excess of 2.5×10^{19} electrons, its net charge is** (1) -1.6 C (2) -2.5 C (3) -6.5 C (4) -4.0 C

II. ELECTRIC CURRENT

The Unit of Current

A flow of electric charge is an **electric current.** The rate at which charge passes a given point in an electric circuit is the quantity called **current,** represented by the symbol *I*. The *SI* unit of current is the **ampere,** A. The ampere is a fundamental unit. The **coulomb,** C, the unit of charge, is a derived unit. It is defined as the charge that passes a point when a current of 1 ampere flows for 1 second. This relationship can be expressed as follows:

$$I = \frac{\Delta q}{\Delta t} \qquad \text{(Eq. 3-5)}$$

where *I* is current in amperes, *q* is charge in coulombs, and *t* is time in seconds. An **ammeter** is a device used to measure current. The symbol for an ammeter is shown in Figure 3-3.

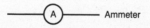

Figure 3-3. The symbol for an ammeter.

Conditions Necessary for an Electric Current

A closed path along which charged particles move is called an **electric circuit.** In order to maintain this movement, a difference in potential must exist between two points in the circuit. The potential difference in a circuit (also called *voltage*) may be supplied by a single **electric cell** or by two or more cells connected to form a **battery.** The potential difference of a circuit can be measured with a **voltmeter.** These devices are represented in an electric-circuit diagram by the symbols shown in Figure 3-4.

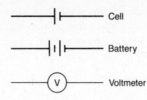

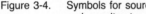

Figure 3-4.   Symbols for sources of potential difference (voltage) and a voltmeter for measuring potential difference.

Recall that positive charges tend to move from points of higher potential to points of lower potential, or from positive potential to negative potential. Negative charges tend to flow in the opposite direction. The *direction* of a current in an electric circuit can be defined as either of these directions. In certain mathematical treatments of electrical phenomena, it is convenient to treat the current as flowing from positive to negative. This is called the "conventional" current flow. However, because most currents in practice consists of electrons (negative charges) in motion, it is more natural to choose the electron flow as the direction of a current. This is the definition adopted in this book.

Conductivity in Solids

For electric current to exist in a circuit, the circuit must consist of materials through which charge (usually electrons) can move. The conductivity of a material depends on the number of free charges per unit volume and on their mobility. That is, it depends on the availability of charges that are relatively free to move under the influence of an electric field. In pure metals, there are many electrons that are not bound, or that are only loosely bound, to any particular atom within the material. These electrons move readily. The presence of this large number of free electrons makes metals good **conductors.** In nonmetallic elements and in most compounds, all the charged particles are tightly bound to fixed positions. There are few or no free electrons. Such materials are called **insulators.** They are poor conductors and are often used as insulating materials.

Resistance

The current that can be produced in a conductor by a given potential difference is determined by a property of the conductor called its **resistance,** R. The resistance of a conductor is the ratio of the potential difference applied to its ends and the current that flows through it:

$$R = \frac{V}{I} \tag{Eq. 3-6}$$

If V is expressed in volts, and I in amperes, the resistance R is in *SI* units called **ohms,** Ω, a derived unit. One ohm equals one volt/ampere.

Suppose the potential difference (the voltage) across a metallic conductor and the resulting current through the conductor are measured while the temperature is constant. If the measurements are plotted on a graph of potential difference versus current, the graph will be a straight line going through the origin. This result shows that the resistance of the conductor, which is equal to the slope of the graph line, is constant as the potential difference and current vary.

EXAMPLE

A current of 0.10 ampere was found to flow through a lamp in a 12-volt circuit. What was the resistance of the lamp?

Solution

$$R = \frac{V}{I} = \frac{12 \ V}{0.10 \ A} = 120 \ \Omega$$

The relation between resistance, potential difference, and current given in Equation 3-6 is called **Ohm's Law.** It can be written in three forms:

$$R = \frac{V}{I} \qquad V = IR \qquad I = \frac{V}{R}$$

These equations are true for entire circuits or for any portion of a circuit, provided that the temperature does not change.

If a conductor, such as a wire, is of uniform cross-sectional area and uniform composition, its resistance varies directly as its length and inversely as its cross-sectional area. For example, if two wires have the same composition and length, but one is double the diameter of the other, the thicker wire will have 4 times the cross-sectional area, and therefore one-quarter the resistance, of the thinner one. If the length of either wire were doubled, its resistance would also be doubled. This relationship is expressed by the formula:

$$R = \frac{kL}{A}$$

where R is resistance, L is length, A is area, and k is a constant depending on the material and on the temperature. As the temperature of a *metal* conductor increases, its resistance also increases. The resistance of *nonmetals*, however, generally *decreases* with an increase in temperature. A portion of an electric circuit that has resistance, called a *resistor,* is represented in electric-circuit diagrams by the symbol in Figure 3-5.

Figure 3-5.   The symbol for a resistor (a portion of a circuit with resistance).

CAN YOU EXPLAIN THIS?

Short, thick, cold wires are better conductors than long, thin, hot wires.

Resistance increases with increasing length of the wire because electrons encounter and collide with an increasing number of atoms. As the thickness of a wire decreases, there are fewer spaces between atoms in the cross section through which electrons can travel in a given period of time. In addition, increasing the temperature of a conductor increases the amplitude of the vibrations of its atoms and the speeds of its electrons, resulting in an increased number of collisions between electrons and atoms. These collisions : etard the forward motion of the electrons, increasing resistance.

Types of Electric Circuits

The simplest type of electric circuit consists of a *source* of electrical energy, connecting wires, and a *circuit element,* or component, which is a device that converts the electrical energy to some other form. The source may be a battery; the circuit element may be a resistor—a device that converts electrical energy to heat energy. The current in the circuit depends on two factors. One is the potential difference, V, established by the battery at the ends of the resistor. The other is the resistance, R, of the resistor. These quantities are related to each other according to Ohm's Law (Equation 3-6). For example, the current across a 2.0-ohm resistor in a 12-volt circuit is 6.0 amperes, as shown in Figure 3-6. When there are two or more resistors in a circuit, they are differentiated by subscripts, for example, R_1, R_2, R_3. The current through R_1 is then denoted by I_1, and the potential drop across R_1 is denoted by V_1.

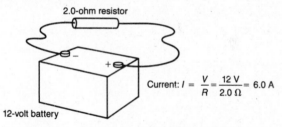

Current: $I = \dfrac{V}{R} = \dfrac{12\ V}{2.0\ \Omega} = 6.0\ A$

Figure 3-6.   Resistance in a simple circuit.

Series Circuits. When more than one resistor is present in a circuit, there are two basic methods of connecting them. The first is called the **series circuit,** shown in Figure 3-7, in which there is only one current path.

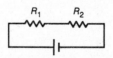

Figure 3-7.   Resistors in a series circuit.

The same current exists in each resistor in such a case. Therefore, for resistors in series, the current is given by

$$I_t = I_1 = I_2 = I_3 = \ldots \qquad \text{(Eq. 3-7)}$$

On the other hand, the total potential difference, V, at the terminals must equal the sum of the separate potential differences across the resistors:

$$V_t = V_1 + V_2 + V_3 + \ldots \qquad \text{(Eq. 3-8)}$$

By Ohm's law, $V_t = I_t R_t$, where R_t is the total resistance of the entire circuit, so

$$I_t R_t = I_1 R_1 + I_2 R_2 + I_3 R_3 + \ldots$$

But I_1, I_2, I_3, and so on are all equal to I_t:

$$I_t R_t = I_t R_1 + I_t R_2 + I_t R_3 + \ldots$$

Dividing by I_t, we have

$$R_t = R_1 + R_2 + R_3 + \ldots \qquad \text{(Eq. 3-9)}$$

Equations 3-7, 3-8, and 3-9 are true only for *series circuits*.

EXAMPLE

Resistors of 4.0, 6.0, and 8.0 ohms are connected in series to an applied potential difference of 36 volts. Calculate (a) total resistance, (b) current through each resistor, and (c) potential drop across each resistor.

Solution

(a) $\qquad R_1 = 4.0\ \Omega \qquad R_2 = 6.0\ \Omega \qquad R_3 = 8.0\ \Omega$

$\qquad R_t = R_1 + R_2 + R_3 = 4.0\ \Omega + 6.0\ \Omega + 8.0\ \Omega = 18.0\ \Omega$

(b) $\qquad I_t = \dfrac{V_t}{R_t} = \dfrac{36\ \text{V}}{18.0\ \Omega} = 2.0\ \text{A}$

In a series circuit, the current is the same in all parts of the circuit:

$$I_t = I_1 = I_2 = I_3 = 2.0\ \text{A}$$

(c) $\qquad V_1 = I_1 R_1 = (2.0\ \text{A})(4.0\ \Omega) = 8.0\ \text{V}$

$\qquad V_2 = I_2 R_2 = (2.0\ \text{A})(6.0\ \Omega) = 12\ \text{V}$

$\qquad V_3 = I_3 R_3 = (2.0\ \text{A})(8.0\ \Omega) = 16\ \text{V}$

Note that in a circuit having resistors in series, the sum of the potential differences across the individual resistors is equal to the applied potential difference (36 V):

$$V_{\text{applied}} = V_1 + V_2 + V_3 = 8.0\ \text{V} + 12\ \text{V} + 16\ \text{V} = 36\ \text{V}$$

Parallel Circuits. The second method of connecting two resistors to form an electric circuit is known as a **parallel circuit,** which is one in which there is more than one current path. In this circuit, current is divided among the branches of the circuit, as shown in Figure 3-8.

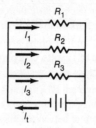

Figure 3-8.   Currents in a parallel circuit. The total current, I_t, divides among the three branches: $I_t = I_1 + I_2 + I_3$

In a parallel circuit, the sum of the currents in the branches is equal to the total current from the source:

$$I_t = I_1 + I_2 + I_3 + \ldots \qquad \text{(Eq. 3-10)}$$

Note, however, that the same potential difference exists across each resistor, so that

$$V_t = V_1 = V_2 = V_3 = \ldots \qquad \text{(Eq. 3-11)}$$

According to Ohm's Law, $I = V/R$ for each branch of the circuit. Since $V = V_t$ for each branch, we can substitute V_t/R for each I on the right side of Equation 3-10:

$$I_t = \frac{V_t}{R_1} + \frac{V_t}{R_2} + \frac{V_t}{R_3} + \ldots$$

By Ohm's law,

$$I_t = \frac{V_t}{R_t}$$

Therefore,

$$\frac{V_t}{R_t} = \frac{V_t}{R_1} + \frac{V_t}{R_2} + \frac{V_t}{R_3} + \ldots$$

Dividing by V_t, we have

$$\frac{1}{R_t} = \frac{1}{R_1} + \frac{1}{R_2} + \frac{1}{R_3} + \ldots \qquad \text{(Eq. 3-12)}$$

a current of 8 amperes must flow down toward junction Q. If 6 amperes is known to be flowing away from Q toward the left, then 2 amperes must be flowing away to the right, since the total current leaving Q must equal the total entering Q, or 8 amperes.

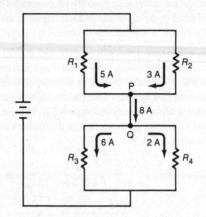

Figure 3-10.   Circuit illustrating the law of currents in a complex circuit.

Potential Drops Around a Circuit. A potential difference, or potential drop, across any part of a circuit represents a change in electric energy between the two ends of that part of the circuit. If we measure (or calculate) the potential drops from one end to the other of a complete circuit, their total must equal the total potential difference applied to the entire circuit. In Figure 3-11, a 24-V battery is connected to a complex circuit. If the potential drops across R_1 and R_2 are 8 V and 12 V, respectively, the potential drops across R_3 and R_4 must be 4 V, to make the total equal to 24 V.

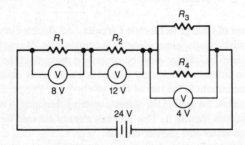

Figure 3-11.   Circuit illustrating the law of potential differences (potential drops) in a complex circuit. The sum of potential drops equals the total potential difference applied to the entire circuit.

Electric Power

In electricity, as in mechanics, the time rate of transfer or use of energy is power. That is, $P = W/\Delta t$ (Equation 2-2), where work, W, is in joules, time, t, is in seconds, and power, P, is in watts. As stated previously, the watt, W, is the derived *SI* unit of power. Both electric and mechanical power are scalar quantities.

In electric circuits, the power equals the product of potential difference and current:

$$P = VI \qquad \text{(Eq. 3-13)}$$

where power, P, is in watts, potential difference, V, is in volts, and current, I, is in amperes. To see why this relation is true, recall that 1 volt = 1 joule/coulomb, and 1 ampere = 1 coulomb/second. Therefore,

$$1 \text{ volt} \cdot 1 \text{ ampere} = \left(1 \frac{\text{joule}}{\text{coulomb}}\right)\left(1 \frac{\text{coulomb}}{\text{second}}\right) = 1 \frac{\text{joule}}{\text{second}} = 1 \text{ watt}$$

Because $V = IR$ (Ohm's Law), we can substitute IR for V in Equation 3-13:

$$P = (IR)I, \text{ or } P = I^2R \qquad \text{(Eq. 3-13a)}$$

Also, because $I = V/R$, we can substitute V/R for I in Equation 3-13:

$$P = V\left(\frac{V}{R}\right), \quad \text{or} \quad P = \frac{V^2}{R} \qquad \text{(Eq. 3-13b)}$$

CAN YOU EXPLAIN THIS?

A 30-watt light bulb can be more powerful than a 60-watt light bulb.

At normal operating temperatures, a "30-watt" lamp has twice the resistance of a 60-watt lamp, which has a thicker filament. When operated in parallel, where each lamp experiences the same applied potential difference, the 30-watt lamp has only one-half as much current as the 60-watt lamp. Since power is the product of potential difference and current, the 30-watt lamp is only half as powerful as the 60-watt lamp when connected in parallel.

When connected in *series,* the lamps will have the same *current,* but the potential drop across the 30-watt lamp will be greater than that across the 60-watt lamp, because the former has a greater resistance (not necessarily twice as much, because the temperatures will now be different). Since power equals *VI,* and *I* is the same for both lamps, *VI* will be greater for the 30-watt lamp. That is, the power used by the 30-watt lamp will be greater. The lamps consume 30 watts and 60 watts of power, respectively, only when operated, as designed, in parallel at 120 volts in a household circuit.

Electrical Energy

The total electrical energy consumed (that is, converted to other forms) in a circuit can be obtained by multiplying the power consumption, P, of the circuit by the time of charge flow, t. Thus, the energy, W, consumed is a scalar quantity given by

$$W = Pt = VIt = I^2Rt \qquad \text{(Eq. 3-14)}$$

The joule, J, is the *SI* unit for electrical energy, as it is for all forms of energy. It is a derived unit equal to one watt · second, or, in fundamental units, to one kilogram · meter squared per second squared.

EXAMPLE

The current measured in a 10.-ohm resistor is 4.0 amperes. How much energy is used by the resistor in 10. seconds?

Solution

$$W = I^2RT = (4.0 \text{ A})^2 \, (10. \text{ } \Omega)(10. \text{ s}) = 1,600 \text{ J}$$

PRACTICAL APPLICATION

Household appliances are commonly labeled with their power requirements. For example, an electric hot-water heater may be rated at 4,500 watts, whereas a color television may be only 100 watts. Thus, over a period of one hour, the hot-water heater is 45 times more costly to operate than the television, because the heater uses 45 times the energy of the television. ■

QUESTIONS

1. If three resistors of 3 ohms, 6 ohms, and 9 ohms are connected in parallel, the combined resistance will be (1) greater than 9 Ω (2) between 6 Ω and 9 Ω (3) between 3 Ω and 6 Ω (4) less than 3 Ω

2. How much electrical energy is used when a 120-volt appliance operates at 2.0 amperes for 1.0 second? (1) 60. J (2) 240 J (3) 480 J (4) 30,000 J

3. Which is a unit of electric power? (1) watt (2) volt (3) ampere (4) kilowatt · hour

4. To reduce the resistance of a metal conductor, one should (1) cool the conductor to a low temperature (2) heat the conductor to a high temperature (3) coat the conductor with an insulator (4) wire the conductor in series with another resistor

5. Two copper wires have the same length, but the cross-sectional area of wire A is twice that of wire B. Compared to the resistance of wire B, the resistance of wire A is (1) one-half as great (2) twice as great (3) one-quarter as great (4) four times as great

6. A 6.0-ohm resistor is connected in series with a 12-ohm resistor in an operating circuit. If the current in the 12-ohm resistor is 3.0 amperes, the potential drop across the 6.0-ohm resistor is (1) 1.5 V (2) 18 V (3) 3.0 V (4) 36 V

7. A resistor carries a current of 0.10 ampere when the potential difference across it is 5.0 volts. The resistance of the resistor is (1) 0.020 Ω (2) 0.50 Ω (3) 5.0 Ω (4) 50. Ω

8. An electric motor lifts a 10.-kilogram mass 100. meters in 10. seconds. The power developed by the motor is (1) 9.8 W (2) 98 W (3) 980 W (4) 9,800 W

9. Compared to the current in the 10-ohm resistor, the current in the 5-ohm resistor, in the circuit shown, will be (1) the same (2) twice as great (3) one-half as great (4) one-third as great

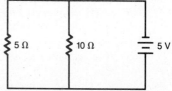

10. If energy is used at a rate of 20. joules per second in an electric circuit, the power developed is (1) 5.0 W (2) 20. W (3) 25 W (4) 100 W

11. One ampere is equivalent to one (1) coulomb per second (2) joule per coulomb (3) electronvolt (4) newton per coulomb

12. Energy is being consumed at the greatest rate in an appliance drawing (1) 5.0 A at 110 V (2) 5.0 A at 220 V (3) 10. A at 110 V (4) 10. A at 220 V

13. If three resistors, each having a resistance of R ohms, are connected in parallel, their equivalent resistance is (1) R ohms (2) $2R$ ohms (3) $3R$ ohms (4) $R/3$ ohms

14. A 5-ohm resistor and a 10-ohm resistor are connected in series. If the current in the 5-ohm resistor is 2 amperes, then the current in the 10.-ohm resistor is (1) 1 A (2) 2 A (3) 0.5 A (4) 4 A

15. If the voltage across a 4-ohm resistor is 2 volts, the current through the resistor is (1) 1 A (2) 2 A (3) 0.5 A (4) 8 A

16. Three ammeters are located near junction P in an electric circuit as shown. If A_1 reads 8.0 amperes and A_2 reads 2.0 amperes, then the reading of ammeter A_3 could be (1) 16 A (2) 6.0 A (3) 5.0 A (4) 4.0 A

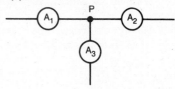

17. What potential difference must be applied to cause a current of 0.50 ampere in a circuit having a resistance of 24 ohms? (1) 6.0 V (2) 12 V (3) 24 V (4) 48 V

18. What is the current in a circuit if 15 coulombs of electric charge move past a given point in 3.0 seconds? (1) 5.0 A (2) 12 A (3) 18 A (4) 45 A

19. A series circuit contains a 4-ohm and a 2-ohm resistor connected to a 110-volt source. Compared to the energy dissipated in the 2-ohm resistor, the energy dissipated in the 4-ohm resistor during the same time is (1) one-half as great (2) twice as great (3) the same (4) four times as great

20. Assuming total conversion of electrical energy to heat energy, how much heat is produced by a 20.-watt heating unit in 5.0 seconds? (1) 100 J (2) 25 J (3) 24 J (4) 4.0 J

21. A series circuit carries a current of 4.0 amperes for 8.0 seconds. The amount of electric charge passing any point in the circuit in 8.0 seconds is (1) 32 C (2) 2.0 C (3) 8.0 C (4) 4.0 C

22. The ratio of the potential difference across a conductor to the current in it is (1) voltage (2) energy (3) power (4) resistance

23. An operating lamp draws a current that is equal to 2.0 amperes at 6.0 volts. The resistance of the lamp is (1) 1.5 Ω (2) 6.0 Ω (3) 3.0 Ω (4) 12 Ω

24. Electric charge Q_1 is transferred through a conductor in time t. The ratio Q_1/t determines average (1) current (2) potential (3) power (4) resistance

25. In the diagram, ammeter A reads 5.0 amperes and ammeter B reads 2.0 amperes, as shown. The reading of ammeter C is (1) 1.4 A (2) 5.0 A (3) 3.0 A (4) 7.0 A

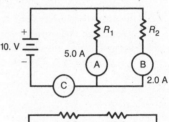

26. What is the current in ammeter A in the circuit shown at the right? (1) 200 A (2) 100 A (3) 25 A (4) 4.0 A

27. The electrical energy consumed by a 20.-ohm resistor carrying a current of 2.0 amperes for 1.0 second is (1) 5.0 W (2) 40. W (3) 40. J (4) 80. J

28. In the diagram, the current through ammeter A is 1 ampere. Resistor B has a resistance of (1) 9 Ω (2) 6 Ω (3) 3 Ω (4) 0.3 Ω

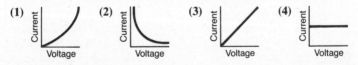

29. Which graph best represents the relationship between current and voltage in a series circuit of constant resistance?

30. A circuit is supplied with a constant voltage. As the resistance of the circuit decreases, the power dissipated by the circuit (1) decreases (2) increases (3) remains the same

31. If the length and the cross-sectional area of a wire are both halved, the resistance of the wire will (1) decrease (2) increase (3) remain the same

32. As additional resistors are connected in parallel to a source of constant voltage, the current supplied by the source (1) decreases (2) increases (3) remains the same

33. Two lamps of different resistances are connected in series to a battery. As electrons flow from the lamp of higher resistance through the lamp of lower resistance, the rate of electron flow (1) decreases (2) increases (3) remains the same

34. A light bulb is connected in series with a rheostat (variable resistance) and a fixed voltage is applied across the total circuit. As the resistance of the rheostat decreases, the brightness of the bulb (1) decreases (2) increases (3) remains the same

35. As the temperature of a metal conductor increases, the electrical resistance of the conductor usually (1) decreases (2) increases (3) remains the same

36. As resistors are added in series to a circuit, the current in the circuit (1) decreases (2) increases (3) remains the same

37. A 6-volt battery is connected to a 3-ohm resistor. As additional resistors are connected in series, the potential difference across each resistor (1) decreases (2) increases (3) remains the same

38. A constant potential difference is applied to a variable resistance. As the value of the resistance increases, the current through it (1) decreases (2) increases (3) remains the same

39–43. Base your answers to Questions 39 through 43 on the diagram, which shows a 3-ohm metal wire resistor connected to a 6-volt battery. (Neglect the resistance of the source and connecting wires.)

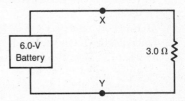

39. The amount of charge passing point X in 1.0 second is (1) 6.0 C (2) 2.0 C (3) 12 C (4) 18 C

40. The amount of energy lost by a coulomb of charge each second in moving from X to Y through the resistor is (1) 6.0 J (2) 2.0 J (3) 12 J (4) 18 J

41. In this circuit, electrical energy is converted to heat at the rate of (1) 6.0 V (2) 2.0 A (3) 12 W (4) 18 J

42. If 1.0 coulomb of charge passes point X during a given time interval, the amount of charge that passes point Y in the same time interval is (1) less than 1.0 C (2) more than 1.0 C (3) 1.0 C

43. As the temperature of the resistor increases, the current in the circuit (1) decreases (2) increases (3) remains the same

44–47. Base your answers to Questions 44 through 47 on the diagram.

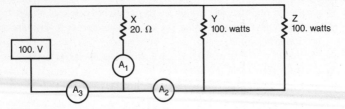

44. The current in resistor Y is (1) 1.0 A (2) 2.0 A (3) 0.5 A (4) 5.0 A
45. The reading of ammeter A_2 is equal to (1) 1.0 A (2) 2.0 A (3) 3.0 A
    (4) 0.50 A
46. The reading of ammeter A_3 is equal to (1) 1.0 A (2) 2.0 A (3) 6.0 A
    (4) 7.0 A
47. The power dissipated in resistor X is (1) 100 W (2) 200 W (3) 220 W
    (4) 500 W

48–52. Base your answers to Questions 48 through 52 on the information given in the diagram.

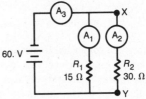

48. The equivalent resistance of R_1 and R_2 is (1) 10. Ω (2) 20. Ω (3) 25 Ω
    (4) 45 Ω
49. Ammeter A_1 reads (1) 1.0 A (2) 2.0 A (3) 8.0 A (4) 4.0 A
50. The reading of ammeter A_3 is (1) 1.3 A (2) 6.0 A (3) 8.0 A (4) 4.0 A
51. At what rate does the battery supply energy to the circuit? (1) 360 W
    (2) 66 W (3) 54 W (4) 10. W
52. The potential difference between points X and Y is
    (1) 60. J/C (2) 40. J/C (3) 30. J/C (4) 15 J/C

53–57. Base your answers to Questions 53 through 57 on the diagram, which shows a 0.50-ohm resistor, R, and a light bulb connected in series to a 6.0-volt battery. The current in resistor R is 4.0 amperes.

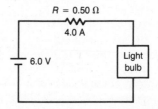

53. The potential difference between the two ends of the resistor is
    (1) 0.13 V (2) 2.0 V (3) 6.0 V (4) 8.0 V
54. The electric current through the light bulb is (1) 0.67 A (2) 2.0 A
    (3) 6.0 A (4) 4.0 A
55. How much electrical energy will the battery supply in 10. seconds?
    (1) 24 J (2) 240 J (3) 360 J (4) 600 J

56. The resistance of the light bulb is (1) 1.0 Ω (2) 0.5 Ω (3) 0.17 Ω (4) 23.5 Ω

57. Energy is being dissipated in resistor R at the rate of (1) 8.0 J/s (2) 16 J/s (3) 3.0 J/s (4) 24 J/s

58–62. Base your answers to Questions 58 through 62 on the information given in the diagram at the right.

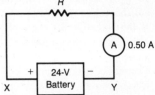

58. What is the resistance of resistor R? (1) 0.020 Ω (2) 12 Ω (3) 48 Ω (4) 100 Ω

59. How much charge moves past point X in 10. seconds? (1) 0.50 C (2) 5.0 C (3) 12 C (4) 48 C

60. Energy is being dissipated in resistor R at a rate of (1) 6.0 W (2) 12 W (3) 24 W (4) 48 W

61. Another resistor with the same value as resistor R is placed in series with resistor R. The reading of ammeter A will be (1) halved (2) doubled (3) unchanged (4) quadrupled

62. Compared with the original circuit, the power dissipated by the circuit in Question 61 is (1) halved (2) doubled (3) quartered (4) quadrupled

63–67. Base your answers to Questions 63 through 67 on the diagram, which represents a motor connected in series with a 12-volt battery, a resistance, R, and an ammeter, A. Mass M is suspended from a pulley that is attached to the shaft of the motor.

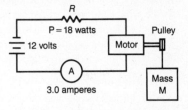

63. What is the resistance of resistor R? (1) 8.0 Ω (2) 2.0 Ω (3) 3.0 Ω (4) 6.0 Ω

64. What is the potential difference across resistor R? (1) 0 V (2) 12 V (3) 6.0 V (4) 4.0 V

65. What is the rate at which the motor uses electrical energy? (1) 0 W (2) 18 W (3) 36 W (4) 4.0 W

66. What is the total charge that will pass through the motor in 5.0 seconds? (1) 0.60 C (2) 15 C (3) 3.0 C (4) 4.0 C

67. If the operating motor were 100 percent efficient, in 10. seconds the gravitational potential energy of mass M would increase (1) 9.8 J (2) 12 J (3) 18 J (4) 180 J

68–71. Base your answers to Questions 68 through 71 on the diagram at right.

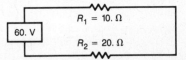

68. **What is the total resistance of the circuit?** (1) 6.6 Ω (2) 10. Ω (3) 20. Ω (4) 30. Ω

69. **If the potential difference across R_1 is V volts, the potential difference in volts across R_2 would equal** (1) V (2) $\frac{1}{2}(60 - V)$ (3) $(60 - V)$ (4) $(60 + V)$

70. **If the potential difference of the source were decreased, the total heat developed in the circuit would** (1) decrease (2) increase (3) remain the same

71. **Compared to the current in R_1, the current in R_2 is** (1) less (2) greater (3) the same

III. MAGNETISM

Objects called magnets exert **magnetic forces** on each other and on certain materials, such as iron, that are called **ferromagnetic materials.** A magnet has two regions, called **poles,** where the magnetic force is strongest. One of these poles is called a **north magnetic pole,** or N-pole. The other is a **south magnetic pole,** or S-pole. Like poles of two magnets repel each other, and unlike poles attract each other.

The earth is a large magnet with an S-pole near the geographic North Pole (the northern end of its axis of rotation), and an N-pole near the geographic South Pole. If a magnet in the shape of a needle or bar is free to rotate, its N-pole will be attracted toward the earth's S-pole (geographic North Pole) and its S-pole will be attracted toward the earth's N-pole (geographic South Pole). A magnetic compass is a magnetized needle mounted so that it can turn and orient itself in a north-south direction in the manner just described.

Magnetic Force

When current is switched on in a conductor, a nearby compass needle will move. The magnetic force acting on the needle is assumed to be the result of movement of charge in the conductor because the needle will return to its original position when the current is switched off. This observation, supported by all experimental evidence, has led to the conclusion that all magnetic force is due to the motion of charged objects relative to each other. That is, magnetic force is a force that exists between currents. The magnetism of a magnet is due to the nonsymmetrical motion of electrons in the atoms of the magnetic material. Even magnets at rest relative to each other will therefore exert magnetic forces because the electrons within them are in motion.

Magnetic Field

Just as a gravitational field surrounds a mass, and an electric field surrounds a charged object, a magnetic field surrounds a charged object *in motion.* The moving charged object may be a proton, an ion, an electron moving within an atom, or an electron current in a conducting material. In each case, a magnetic field exists in the vicinity of the charged particle in motion.

A magnetic field exerts a force on any charge *in motion* and can be detected and measured by this effect. The standard test object for a magnetic field, called a *current element,* consists of a wire of length *l* carrying a current *I*. The unit current element is defined as a wire 1 meter long carrying a current of 1 ampere. In a magnetic field, a current element will be acted upon by a force that is perpendicular to both the magnetic field and the direction of the current. The direction of the magnetic field is defined as the direction in which the N-pole of a compass would point in the field. When the field lines are curved, the direction of the field is determined by the direction of the N-pole of a compass placed along the tangent to the field line at that point. The direction of the force exerted on a current element in a magnetic field can be determined by means of a *hand rule,* such as the one shown in Figure 3-12.

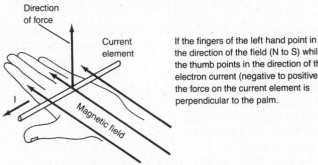

Figure 3-12.   Left-hand rule for force on a current element in a magnetic field.

Magnetic Flux. The **field strength,** *B,* of a magnetic field is measured by the force it exerts on a current element in the field. A magnetic field can be represented by lines of magnetic force drawn in the direction of the field in every region of the field. The concentration of the lines of force can represent the field strength in that region. The lines of force are called **magnetic flux lines.** Flux lines are imaginary, but they are a convenient means of visualizing both the magnitude (strength) and the direction of a magnetic field. The pattern of flux lines resembles that made by sprinkling iron filings on a card held in the field. Magnetic flux lines always form closed loops, and they never cross or intersect. The field strength is greatest where the flux lines are closest together.

Flux Density and Field Strength. One way of expressing the strength of a magnetic field is in terms of the concentration of flux lines. The unit for measuring the number of flux lines in a region is the **weber,** Wb, which is a derived unit. The number of flux lines per unit of area passing through a plane perpendicular to the direction of the lines is called the **flux density.** Flux density, which is a vector quantity, is measured in webers per square meter (Wb/m^2). The **tesla,** T, which is a derived unit, is the *SI* unit of flux density and is equal to 1 weber/meter^2.

The tesla, the unit of flux density or magnetic field strength, is related to the force on a current element in the field. If the force on a unit current element (1 ampere in a conductor 1 meter long) is 1 newton, then the field strength is 1 newton per ampere · meter (1 N/A · m). By definition, the flux density in such a field is 1 tesla. In other words, a flux density of 1 weber/meter^2 is the same as a field strength of 1 newton/ampere · meter:

$$1 \text{ T} = 1 \text{ Wb/m}^2 = 1 \text{ N/A} \cdot \text{m}$$

The magnetic field strength B is analogous to the electric field strength E and the gravitational field strength g (all of these field strengths are vector quantities):

> Gravitational field strength = force per unit mass
> Electric field strength = force per unit charge
> Magnetic field strength = force per unit current element

Field Around a Straight Conductor. When a current flows in a straight conductor, its magnetic field has the form of concentric circles around the conductor, in planes perpendicular to the conductor. The strength of the field decreases with increasing distance from the conductor and increases with an increase in current. The direction of the field around a straight conductor can be determined by a hand rule, as in Figure 3-13a.

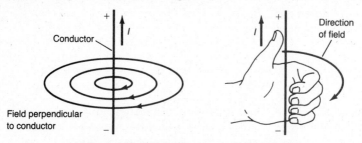

(a) Hand rule for field direction around a straight conductor

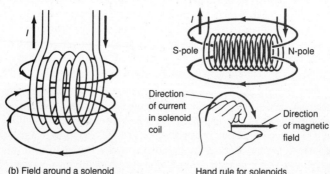

(b) Field around a solenoid   Hand rule for solenoids

Figure 3-13.   Hand rules for determining magnetic field direction around conductors.

Field Around a Solenoid. If a wire is wound as a **solenoid** (a coil with many parallel turns of the same diameter), its magnetic field resembles that of a bar magnet. The lines of magnetic flux emerge from the N-pole at one end of the solenoid and curve around to reenter the S-pole at the other end. Inside the solenoid, near the center, the lines of flux are practically parallel to one another and to the coil axis, and the flux density is a maximum. The strength of the field increases as the number of turns is increased, and as the current in the coil is increased. A hand rule can be used to determine the polarity of the magnetic field of a solenoid, as shown in Figure 3-13b. A solenoid with a core made of iron or other ferromagnetic material is called an **electromagnet.**

Magnets

According to current theory, permanent magnets owe their properties to the motions of electrons within atoms. Whenever there is relative motion between any two charged particles, the particles exert a force on each other. Such a force is called a magnetic force. Atoms of all elements can be classified according to the kind of magnetic property they possess. In *diamagnetic* substances, these properties combine to *reduce* the flux density of an applied magnetic field. In *paramagnetic* substances, the flux density of an applied field is *increased*. In *ferromagnetic* substances, such as iron, nickel, and cobalt, the electron currents tend to align the atoms in clusters called *domains*. Within a domain the magnetic fields of the aligned atoms add to produce a relatively strong field, but, normally, the axes of the domains are randomly arranged so that the fields cancel. In a magnet, however, some domains are enlarged relative to others, producing a net field.

When a permanent magnet is in the shape of a bar with poles at the ends, the overall effect of the atomic current elements is the same as that of a current-carrying solenoid wound around the bar. Concentrated lines of flux emerge from one end of the bar, which is called the N-pole. They enter the other end, which is called the S-pole, after curving around outside the bar to produce the external field. Figure 3-14, which appears on the following page, shows the locations of the lines of magnetic flux around some bar magnets and around a horseshoe magnet.

Force on a Charged Particle Moving in a Magnetic Field

The force acting on a charged particle (or charge carrier) moving in a magnetic field depends upon the field strength B, the charge q on the particle, and the speed v and direction of motion of the particle. The direction of the force is perpendicular to both the direction of the field and the direction of motion of the particle and may be found by using the hand rule in Figure 3-12. If the charge is moving along a flux line, that is, at an angle of 0° to the field, the force on the particle is zero. If the particle is moving perpendicularly to the field, that is, at 90° to it, the force is a maximum. When the charge moves at an angle between 0° and 90° to the field, the force varies between zero and maximum, depending on the magnitude of the velocity component perpendicular to the field. The magnitude of the force is also proportional to the speed of the particle.

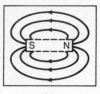

(a)

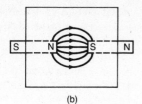

(b)

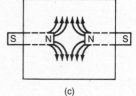

(c)

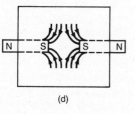

(d)

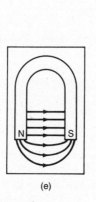

(e)

Figure 3-14.   Lines of magnetic flux around some bar magnets and a horseshoe magnet.

CAN YOU EXPLAIN THIS?

Iron fences become magnetic after standing in the same place for many years.

An iron fence becomes magnetized by the earth's magnetic field. In iron and other ferromagnetic materials, such as nickel, electrons in the atoms spin on their axis and circulate about the nucleus in such a way as to produce tiny "atomic magnets," just as an electric current flowing in a circular circuit produces a magnetic field. Over time, a sufficient number of the "atomic magnets" in the iron fence align with each other under the influence of the earth's magnetic field, and the fence becomes a magnet.

Electromagnetic Induction

If a straight conductor is moved through a magnetic field in such a way as to cut across the lines of flux, the electrons in the conductor will be acted upon by a magnetic force, just as they would if they were moving freely in the field. This force will tend to move the electrons along the conductor from one end toward the other. Since the electrons are free to move in the conductor, they will do so, causing an excess of negative charge at one end of the wire and shortage at the other end. As a result, there will be a potential difference between the ends of the conductor.

The potential difference along the conductor is said to be *induced* by the change in the field relative to the conductor, and the process is called **electromagnetic induction.** The induced potential difference depends upon the rate at which the flux surrounding, or linked by, the conductor is changing. The change in flux may be due to motion of the conductor relative to the field or to a change in the field strength.

Electromagnetic Radiation. Oscillating or accelerating electric charges produce changing electric and magnetic fields that radiate outward into the surrounding space in the form of waves. Such a combined electric and magnetic wave is called an **electromagnetic wave.**

QUESTIONS

1. **In the diagram, the direction of the magnetic field at point** P **is toward point**
   (1) A (3) C
   (2) B (4) D

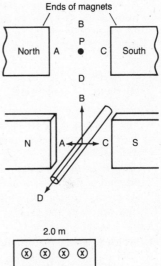

2. **An electric potential difference will be induced between the ends of the conductor shown in the diagram when the conductor moves in direction**
   (1) A (3) C
   (2) B (4) D

3. **The diagram represents magnetic flux intersecting a plane at right angles. If the magnitude of the flux is 16 webers, the average flux density intersecting the plane is**
   (1) 64 T   (3) 8.0 T
   (2) 16 T   (4) 4.0 T

4. **An electron moving parallel to a magnetic field as shown in the diagram will experience (1) no magnetic force (2) a magnetic downward force (3) a magnetic force out of the page (4) a magnetic force into the page**

Magnetic field

5. If the electrons in the wire shown are flowing eastward, in which direction will the needle of a compass held above the wire point?
   (1) north   (3) east
   (2) south   (4) west

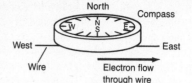

6. The north pole of the solenoid shown would be located at point
   (1) A   (3) C
   (2) B   (4) D

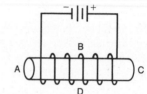

7. A beam of electrons is moving from north to south as shown. The direction of the magnetic field above the beam is toward the
   (1) north   (3) east
   (2) south   (4) west

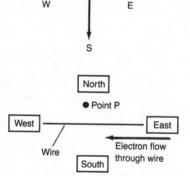

8. The direction of the electron flow in a conductor is from east to west as shown.
   What is the direction of the magnetic field at point P?
   (1) north (2) south (3) into the page (4) out of the page

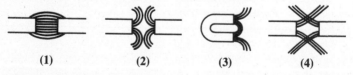

9. Which magnetic-field configuration is not possible?

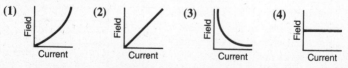

      (1)   (2)   (3)   (4)

10. Which graph best represents the relationship between current in a straight conductor and magnetic field strength at a point near the conductor?

11. An iron core is placed inside a solenoid connected to a voltage source. Which of the following properties of the solenoid will change? (1) magnetic field strength (2) current (3) resistance (4) magnetic polarity

12. Which diagram best represents the magnetic field around a current-carrying conductor? (The x indicates that the field is into the page; the • indicates that the field is out of the page.)

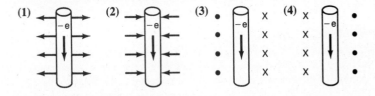

13. Magnetic flux density may be measured in (1) newtons (2) teslas (3) hertz (4) webers

14. As an electron passes between the poles of a horseshoe magnet in the direction shown by the arrow in the illustration, the direction of the magnetic force acting on the electron is (1) to the left (2) to the right (3) upward (4) downward

15. At point X above the current-carrying wire, the direction of the magnetic lines of force is (1) into the page (2) out of the page (3) to the left (4) to the right

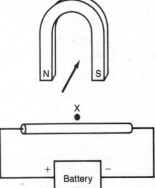

16. As the difference in potential across the terminals of a solenoid increases, its magnetic flux density (1) decreases (2) increases (3) remains the same

17. If an iron rod is inserted into a solenoid parallel to the coil axes, the flux density (1) decreases (2) increases (3) remains the same

18. Given the diagram at right, at the moment when switch S_1 is closed, the force of the magnet on the soft iron core (1) decreases (2) increases (3) remains the same

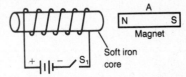

19. As the current in a circular loop of wire increases, the magnetic field strength at the center of the loop (1) decreases (2) increases (3) remains the same

20. As the current in a conductor is increased, the strength of the magnetic field at a point near the wire (1) decreases (2) increases (3) remains the same

PROBLEM SOLVING

Sample Problem

(a) Compare and contrast Newton's Law of Universal Gravitation with Coulomb's Law, using complete sentences.

(b) Determine the ratio of electric force to gravitational force by the proton and electron in a hydrogen atom, if the average separation of the particles is 5.3×10^{-11} meter.

Solution

(a) Newton's Law of Universal Gravitation states that any two bodies in the universe are attracted toward each other by a force that is proportional to the product of their *masses* and inversely proportional to the square of the distance between them. Coulomb's Law states that the force between two *charged* bodies is directly proportional to the product of the *charges* and, like the gravitational force, is inversely proportional to the square of the distance between them. In both cases, the force is directed along the line connecting the centers of the bodies. The gravitational force, however, is always a force of attraction, whereas the electrostatic force may be either an attraction or a repulsion. Furthermore, whereas the gravitational force exists between *any* two bodies, the electrostatic force exists only between *charged* bodies.

(b)

$$F_e = \frac{kq_1q_2}{r^2} = \frac{\left(9.0 \times 10^9 \frac{N \cdot m^2}{C^2}\right)(+1.6 \times 10^{-19} \text{ C})(-1.6 \times 10^{-19} \text{ C})}{(5.3 \times 10^{-11} \text{ m})^2}$$

$$F_e = \frac{\left(9.0 \times 10^9 \frac{N \cdot m^2}{C^2}\right)(-2.6 \times 10^{-38} \text{ C}^2)}{2.8 \times 10^{-21} \text{ m}^2}$$

$$F_e = -8.2 \times 10^{-8} \text{ N} \quad \text{(electrostatic attraction)}$$

$$F_g = \frac{Gm_1m_2}{r^2} = \frac{\left(6.7 \times 10^{-11} \frac{N \cdot m^2}{kg^2}\right)(1.7 \times 10^{-27} \text{ kg})(9.1 \times 10^{-31} \text{ kg})}{(5.3 \times 10^{-11} \text{ m})^2}$$

$$F_g = \frac{\left(6.7 \times 10^{-11} \frac{N \cdot m^2}{kg^2}\right)(1.5 \times 10^{-57} \text{ kg}^2)}{2.8 \times 10^{-21} \text{ m}^2}$$

$$F_g = 3.7 \times 10^{-47} \text{ N} \quad \text{(gravitational attraction)}$$

Therefore,

$$\frac{F_e}{F_g} = \frac{8.2 \times 10^{-8} \text{ N}}{3.7 \times 10^{-47} \text{ N}} = 2.2 \times 10^{39}$$

Practice Problems

1. An electric broiler is rated at 1,440 watts and 120 volts. The broiler is connected to a 120-volt line.
   (a) Draw a diagram of the circuit, showing a voltmeter and an ammeter properly connected to determine the actual power (wattage) of the broiler.
   (b) Find the resistance of the heating coil, if the broiler is operating at its rated power.
   (c) Assuming that all of the electrical energy used is converted to heat energy, determine the heat energy it produces in 10 minutes.
   (d) The line is protected by a 15-ampere fuse. How much additional current can be drawn from the line before the fuse blows?

2. Two resistors of 3.0 and 6.0 ohms are connected in parallel to an applied potential of 12 volts.
   (a) Draw a labeled circuit diagram.
   (b) Determine the current in the 6.0-ohm resistor.
   (c) Find the potential drop across the 3.0-ohm resistor.
   (d) Calculate the power developed in the circuit.
   (e) If an additional 2.0-ohm resistor is connected in parallel in the circuit, determine the resistance of the circuit.

3. Determine the maximum speed of an electron as it travels in a vacuum between two oppositely charged, parallel metal plates connected to a 100-volt power supply.

4. Explain each of the following, using physical principles.
   (a) A magnet brought near the picture tube of a television causes distortion of the picture.
   (b) A charged rod can attract a neutral object.
   (c) An ordinary bar magnet is weakened if it is dropped to the floor.
   (d) It would be highly impractical to have household circuits wired in series.
   (e) An electron appears to defy gravity as it accelerates upward between two charged parallel metal plates.

5. A student is to make an electromagnet from the following components:

   Batteries: 6-volt, 12-volt
   Cores: copper, iron, nickel
   Insulated coils: 50 turns of copper wire having a 0.002-meter diameter
                        50 turns of copper wire having a 0.004-meter diameter
                       100 turns of copper wire having a 0.002-meter diameter
                       100 turns of copper wire having a 0.004-meter diameter

   (a) If the student may use only one battery, one core, and one insulated coil (along with the needed connecting wires), which combination of components will make the strongest electromagnet?
   (b) Explain why the components chosen make the electromagnet stronger than any other that can be made with the same materials.

UNIT 4   WAVE PHENOMENA

I. INTRODUCTION TO WAVES

If a particle is moving back and forth about its average position, it is said to be *vibrating,* or oscillating. If other particles nearby are set into vibration by the first one, the vibrations are said to be transferred, or *propagated.* The propagation of vibration from one particle to another, or from one point to another, is called *wave motion.* A **wave** is a vibratory disturbance that propagates through a medium. The medium may be a body of matter or may consist of empty space (a vacuum).

Waves and Energy Transfer

Waves transfer energy from one place to another by means of repeated small motions (vibrations) of particles or by repeated small changes in the strength of a field. The first kind are called waves in a *material medium;* the second kind are called waves in *space.* Although the vibrating source itself moves back and forth, there is no actual transfer of mass from the source to the distant point. Sound waves are examples of waves in a material medium. Light waves are examples of waves in an electromagnetic field; an electromagnetic field can be completely empty of matter.

CAN YOU EXPLAIN THIS?

Sound from a rifle could trigger an avalanche.

Sound, a form of mechanical energy, is produced by vibrating matter. The sound from a rifle is easily transmitted through the air. In a mountainous area, the vibrations from the sound are transmitted to the surrounding land masses. If the rock or snow on the sides of mountains rests in an unstable position, it can become dislodged. Then gravity will produce rockfalls or avalanches on steep slopes.

Pulses and Periodic Waves

A wave may be classified as either a pulse or a periodic wave. A **pulse** is a single short disturbance that moves from one position to another. For example, a pulse produced on a stretched rope moves *horizontally* along the rope, as shown in Figure 4-1 on the following page. Successive parts of the rope take the wave's characteristic shape, moving *vertically* (up and down) from their rest position. The pulse consists of this single vertical disturbance that is transmitted horizontally.

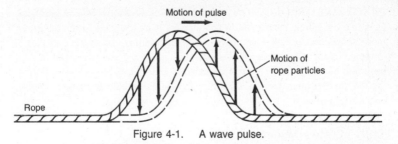

Figure 4-1. A wave pulse.

The speed of a pulse is defined as the time it takes the pulse to move a unit distance through the medium. The speed of a pulse depends upon the type and properties of the medium. Pulse speed is constant if the medium is a uniform material with the same properties throughout. If the pulse reaches the boundary of a new medium, part of the pulse is absorbed, part is reflected back to the source, and part is transmitted through the new medium.

If the original medium ends in a fixed unyielding body, then a pulse will be completely reflected—none of the wave energy will be absorbed or transmitted. The reflected wave, however, will be inverted, as shown in Figure 4-2. This inversion can be explained by Newton's third law. When the pulse in Figure 4-2 arrives at the unyielding body, the pulse exerts an upward force on the unyielding body. Because the unyielding body does not move, it exerts an equal force on the rope in the opposite direction—the downward direction. This reaction force inverts the pulse just before it is reflected back through the original medium.

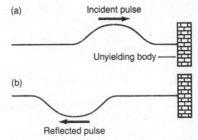

Figure 4-2. (a) A wave pulse traveling to the right along a rope attached to a brick wall. (b) When the pulse reaches the wall, it is reflected back toward the left in an inverted position.

If the initial disturbance causing a pulse is repeated regularly without interruption or change, then the result is a series of regular (evenly timed) disturbances in the medium. This series of regularly repeated disturbances is called a **periodic wave.** It is also referred to as a *wave train*.

PRACTICAL APPLICATION ════════════════════════

Ceiling tile is porous, and sound waves striking it are reflected within the irregularly shaped air pockets. Each reflection results in a loss of sound energy that is absorbed by the material and converted to heat energy. Some sound is reflected back into the room, but the reflected sound is greatly reduced by absorption in the tile. In a similar manner, draperies and carpeting help to minimize noise levels in a room. ■

Types of Wave Motion

Longitudinal Waves. A wave in which the motion of the vibratory disturbance is *parallel* to the direction of propagation (travel) of the wave through the medium is a **longitudinal wave.** Sound waves and compression waves in springs are examples of longitudinal waves.

Transverse Waves. A wave in which the motion of the vibratory disturbance is *perpendicular* (at right angles) to the direction of travel of the wave is a **transverse wave.** For example, a transverse wave is produced in a rope if the end is moved up and down or side to side (see Figure 4-3). In the first case, the wave is in a vertical plane; in the second, it is in a horizontal plane. In both cases, the oscillation, or vibratory disturbance, of the rope is perpendicular to the direction of wave travel.

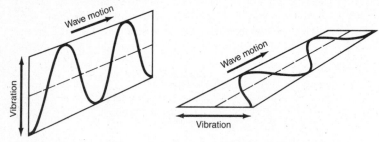

Wave in a vertical plane   Wave in a horizontal plane

Figure 4-3.   Transverse waves with the same direction of travel but in different planes.

II. CHARACTERISTICS OF PERIODIC WAVES

Frequency

The complete series of changes at one point in a medium as a wave passes is called a **cycle.** The number of cycles, or complete vibrations, each point experiences per unit time is called the **frequency,** f, of the wave. For example, if a point in a medium completes 10. cycles, representing the passage of 10. complete waves, in 1.0 second, the frequency of the wave is 10. cycles per second, or simply 10. per second. A frequency of 1 cycle per second is called 1 **hertz.**

The hertz, Hz, is the derived *SI* unit of frequency. Therefore, a frequency of 10. cycles per second is a frequency of 10. Hz. In fundamental units, 1 Hz equals 1/s, or s^{-1}, and can be stated as *per second*.

PRACTICAL APPLICATION

The frequency of a sound wave determines its pitch, whereas the frequency of a light wave determines its color. The human ear can detect frequencies in the range of 20 to 20,000 hertz, and the eyes perceive frequencies of approximately 4.3×10^{14} to 7.5×10^{14} hertz. Other organisms are sensitive to different ranges of sound and light frequencies. A dog, for example, will respond to a high-pitched whistle that a human cannot hear. ■

Period

Another way of describing the rate of wave motion is to state the time required for an entire wave cycle to pass a given point of the medium. This is the time taken for completion of a single vibration, and is called the **period,** T. Because a wave with a frequency of 10. hertz takes 0.10 second to complete one cycle, its period is 0.10 second. Period is inversely proportional to frequency:

$$T = \frac{1}{f}, \quad \text{or} \quad f = \frac{1}{T} \qquad \text{(Eq. 4-1)}$$

where T is the period in seconds and f is the frequency per second (hertz). The second, s, is the *SI* unit for period.

Amplitude

The graph of the displacement of a wave versus time is called the wave's *waveform*. The discussion that follows will deal only with the relatively simple waveform called a sine wave, which, as its name suggests, has the shape of a sine curve. All complex waveforms may be analyzed in terms of the interactions of many different sine waves.

The maximum change in position (displacement) of a particle of the medium from its rest position during one wave cycle is called the amplitude of the wave. This term is also used for waves in a field, where it refers to the maximum change in the field strength from its normal value during one wave cycle.

In a *transverse* wave, the position of maximum displacement of a particle of the medium in the positive direction (for example, upward) is called a wave *crest*. The position of maximum displacement in the negative direction (downward) is called a wave *trough*. The greater the amplitude of the wave, the higher the crests and the lower the troughs (see Figure 4-4 on the following page). In a *longitudinal* wave, the periodic displacements of the particles of the medium produce regions of maximum compression (called *condensations*) alternating with regions of maximum expansion (called *rarefactions*). The greater the amplitude of the wave, the greater the compression of the particles in the condensations and the greater the separation of the particles in the rarefactions.

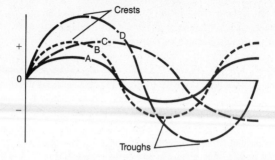

Figure 4-4.   Waves *A* and *B* have the same frequency but different amplitudes. Waves *B* and *C* have the same amplitude but different frequencies. Wave *D* has the greatest amplitude of the four waves shown.

The amplitude of a wave is related to the amount of energy being transmitted by it. The greater the amplitude of a sound wave, the louder is the sound; the greater the amplitude of a light wave, the greater is the intensity (brightness) of the light.

Phase

Points on successive wave cycles of a periodic wave that are displaced from their rest positions by the same amount in the same direction, and are moving in the same direction (away from or toward their rest positions), are said to have the same **phase,** or to be *in phase* with each other. For example, in a transverse wave, all the wave crests are in phase. In Figure 4-5, points *A* and *E* are in phase, *B* and *F* are in phase, and *C* and *G* are in phase.

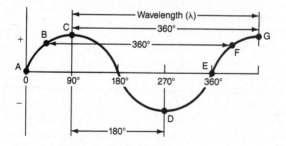

Figure 4-5.   Phase relations in a wave.

Since there are 360° in a complete circle, one complete cycle of a periodic wave is often represented as equal to 360°. One half-cycle is then 180°. Points on a wave that are 180° apart are said to be *out of phase*. In Figure 4-5, Points *C* and *D* are out of phase.

Wavelength

The distance between any two successive points in phase with one another in a periodic wave is called the **wavelength** of the wave. Wavelength is represented by the symbol λ and is measured in meters. Two points that are 180° out of phase on the same cycle of a waveform are therefore separated by ½ wavelength, or ½λ. For convenience, wavelength is often measured between successive crests or troughs of a given wave, as shown in Figure 4-5, but any points in phase on the wave may be chosen.

Speed of Waves

The speed of a wave is equal to the product of its wavelength and frequency. That is,

$$v = f\lambda \qquad \text{(Eq. 4-2)}$$

where frequency, f, is in hertz, wavelength, λ, is in meters, and speed, v, is in meters per second. This relation is true for all waves in all media.

CAN YOU EXPLAIN THIS?

To begin a race, you look for the flash of the starting pistol instead of listening for the sound.

The bat is seen hitting the ball before the crack is heard.

Light travels at nearly 3.00×10^8 meters per second in air, whereas sound travels at a mere 346 meters per second in air at 25°C. The light from the flash of the pistol or from the bat hitting the ball reaches your eyes before the sound reaches your ears.

Wave Fronts

When a pebble is dropped into a quiet pond, waves spread as a series of concentric circles from the source of the disturbance. In a similar fashion, circular waves spread, or *radiate,* from any point source of a vibratory disturbance. In a three-dimensional medium, such as space, the waves radiate as spheres around the point as a center. All points on the wave that are in phase make up what is called a **wave front.** For example, in the waves on the pond, all points on the crest of one of the circular waves make up one of the wave fronts of the wave. Successive wave fronts that are in phase with each other are one wavelength apart. Thus two successive crests are one wavelength apart.

Doppler Effect

When a source and an observer (receiver) of waves are moving relative to each other, the *observed* frequency will be different from the frequency of the vibrating source. This change in observed, or apparent, frequency due to relative motion of source and observer is called the **Doppler effect,** after Christian Doppler, the physicist who first studied it and explained it in 1842.

If the source is approaching the observer or the observer is approaching the source, the frequency appears to increase. If the source is receding from the observer or the observer is receding from the source, the frequency appears to decrease. Because the speed of the waves in the medium is not affected by the Doppler effect, by Equation 4-2 the change in apparent *wavelength* will be inversely proportional to the change in apparent frequency.

The wave-front diagrams in Figure 4-6 illustrate the changes in apparent frequency and wavelength caused by the Doppler effect. In Figure 4-6a, the source is stationary, and the four successive wave fronts (1, 2, 3, and 4) are equally spaced circles in all directions. The observed wavelength and frequency are the same for all stationary observers. In Figure 4-6b, the source is moving from right to left. Each successive wave front has a different center. To a stationary observer at the left, the wavelength appears shorter and the frequency higher; to an observer at the right, the effect is the opposite.

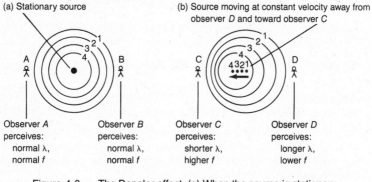

(a) Stationary source

(b) Source moving at constant velocity away from observer D and toward observer C

Observer A perceives: normal λ, normal f

Observer B perceives: normal λ, normal f

Observer C perceives: shorter λ, higher f

Observer D perceives: longer λ, lower f

Figure 4-6. The Doppler effect. (a) When the source is stationary, the wave fronts are equally spaced in all directions. (b) When the source is moving, the wave fronts are closer together in the direction in which the source is moving.

The Doppler effect can cause changes in the apparent pitch of a sound wave, since the ear perceives a sound wave of higher frequency as a sound of higher pitch. Thus the pitch of an approaching sound source is higher than its pitch when the source is stationary, and it drops lower as the source passes the observer and begins to recede.

Visible light waves are subject to a similar effect. The human eye perceives light waves of different frequencies as differences in color. Light waves of the lowest frequency (longest wavelength) that the eye can detect are seen as red, while those of highest frequency (shortest wavelength) are seen as blue-violet, with other colors distributed between these extremes in the *visible spectrum*. Because of the Doppler effect, the apparent color of an approaching light source will be shifted toward the blue-violet end of the spectrum, while that of a receding source will be shifted toward the red end. If the light source is a mixture of many frequencies, such as the light from a star, its light will appear slightly bluer if it is approaching us, or slightly redder if it is receding, than it would appear if it were not moving relative to us.

If an object is a source of waves (sound or light) of known frequency, the Doppler effect can be used to measure the speed at which the object is moving toward or away from the observer.

PRACTICAL APPLICATION

The speed of a car can be determined by a computerized radar system. If a car is at rest and a beam of radio waves is directed at the car from a stationary source, the incident and reflected waves have the same frequency. If the car is moving toward the source of radar, however, the reflected waves have a higher frequency than the waves emitted by the source have. The greater the car's speed toward the radar source, the greater the Doppler shift in frequency. In a similar manner, if the car is moving away from the source of radar, the frequency of the reflected waves decreases by an amount that depends upon the speed of the car. Thus, equipped with a radar "gun," a law-enforcement officer can detect speed-limit violators "coming or going." ∎

QUESTIONS

1. The maximum displacement of a particle from its rest position due to wave motion is called (1) amplitude (2) frequency (3) period (4) wavelength

2. A periodic wave that has a frequency of 5.0 hertz and a speed of 10. meters per second has a wavelength of (1) 50. m (2) 2.0 m (3) 0.50 m (4) 0.20 m

3. A point source vibrating up and down on the surface of a container of water produces a periodic surface wave. The wave fronts are (1) straight (2) vertical (3) spherical (4) circular

4. On the wave train shown at the right, which point is in phase with point A?

   (1) E   (3) C
   (2) B   (4) D

   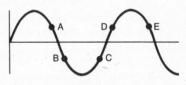

5. A wave has a frequency of 50 hertz. The period of the wave is (1) 0.02 s (2) 0.2 s (3) 2 s (4) 20 s

6. Compared to observations made when both the source and the observer are stationary, when the source of a periodic wave is receding from an observer, there is an apparent increase in the wave's (1) speed (2) frequency (3) wavelength (4) amplitude

7. In the diagram at the right, which two points are in phase? (1) A and E (2) A and F (3) B and E (4) E and F

   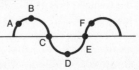

8. What generally occurs when a pulse reaches a boundary between two different media? (1) The entire pulse is reflected. (2) The entire pulse is absorbed. (3) The entire pulse is transmitted. (4) Part of the pulse is transmitted, part reflected, and part absorbed.

9. A periodic wave has a frequency of 10 hertz. The period of the wave is (1) 1 s (2) 0.1 s (3) 0.01 s (4) 0.001 s

10. A train of waves is moving along a string at 3.0 meters per second, as shown at the right. The wavelength is (1) 6.0 m (2) 2.0 m (3) 1.5 m (4) 0.75 m

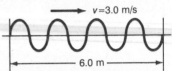

11. As an ambulance with siren blaring approaches and then passes a stationary observer, the frequency of the sound heard by the observer (1) increases, then decreases (2) decreases, then increases (3) continually increases (4) continually decreases

12. In a transverse wave, the maximum displacement of the medium from its rest position is the wave's (1) amplitude (2) frequency (3) wavelength (4) velocity

13. What is the frequency of a water wave that has a speed of 0.4 meter per second and a wavelength of 0.02 meter? (1) 10 Hz (2) 20 Hz (3) 0.008 Hz (4) 0.05 Hz

14. In the diagram shown at the right, which point is in phase with point X?
(1) A   (3) C
(2) B   (4) D

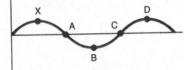

15. If the energy in a longitudinal wave travels from south to north, the particles of the medium move (1) from north to south only (2) both north and south (3) from east to west only (4) both east and west

16. A wave x meters long passes through a medium and has a speed of y meters per second. The frequency of the wave could be expressed as
(1) $\frac{y}{x}$ Hz   (2) $\frac{x}{y}$ Hz   (3) xy Hz   (4) $(x + y)$ Hz

17. If the frequency of a train of waves is 25 hertz, then the period of the wave is (1) 0.040 s (2) 0.25 s (3) 0.40 s (4) 25 s

18. A pulse traveling in a spring transmits (1) energy only (2) mass only (3) both energy and mass (4) neither energy nor mass

19. If the water wave shown is moving toward the right, in which direction are the particles A and B moving? (1) Both A and B are moving upward. (2) Both A and B are moving downward. (3) A is moving upward and B is moving downward. (4) A is moving downward and B is moving upward.

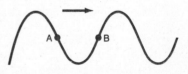

20. The frequency of a water wave is 6.0 hertz. If the wave's wavelength is 2.0 meters, then the speed of the wave is (1) 0.33 m/s (2) 2.0 m/s (3) 6.0 m/s (4) 12 m/s

21. As the frequency of a vibrating spring increases, its period of vibration (1) decreases (2) increases (3) remains the same

22. As the amplitude of a wave increases, the energy transported by the wave (1) decreases (2) increases (3) remains the same

23. As a wave travels into a medium in which its speed increases, its wavelength (1) decreases (2) increases (3) remains the same

24. As a pulse travels through a uniform medium, the speed of the pulse (1) decreases (2) increases (3) remains the same

25–29. Base your answers to Questions 25 through 29 on the diagram, which represents a wave traveling to the right along a horizontal material medium. The horizontal distance from *b* to *f* is 0.08 meter. The vertical distance from *x* to *y* is 0.06 meter.

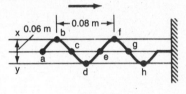

25. If the crest at *b* takes 2.0 seconds to move from *b* to *f*, the speed of the wave is (1) 0.03 m/s (2) 0.04 m/s (3) 0.05 m/s (4) 0.06 m/s

26. If the period of the wave is 2.0 seconds, its frequency is (1) 0.50 Hz (2) 2.0 Hz (3) 5.0 Hz (4) 4.0 Hz

27. The wave's amplitude is (1) 0.03 m (2) 0.04 m (3) 0.05 m (4) 0.06 m

28. As the wave moves to the right from its present position, in which direction will the medium at point *e* first move? (1) down (2) up (3) to the right (4) to the left

29. If the velocity of the wave remains constant, while the frequency is doubled, the wavelength is (1) halved (2) doubled (3) unchanged (4) quartered

30–33. Base your answers to Questions 30 through 33 on the following information.

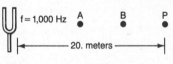

The speed in air of the sound waves produced by the tuning fork in the diagram at the right is 340 meters per second.

30. The time required for the waves to travel from the tuning fork to point *P* is (1) 0.020 s (2) 0.059 s (3) 0.59 s (4) 2.9 s

31. The wavelength of the sound waves produced by the tuning fork is (1) 0.29 m (2) 0.34 m (3) 0.43 m (4) 2.9 m

32. If the waves are in phase at points *A* and *B*, then the minimum distance between points *A* and *B* is (1) 1 wavelength (2) 2 wavelengths (3) ¼ wavelength (4) ½ wavelength

33. If the vibrating tuning fork is accelerated toward point *P*, the pitch observed at point *P* will (1) decrease (2) increase (3) remain the same

III. PERIODIC WAVE PHENOMENA

Interference

The effect produced by two or more waves passing simultaneously through the same region of a medium is called **interference.** The resultant displacement at any point is the algebraic sum of the displacements due to the individual waves. The process of constructing the new wave by finding this algebraic sum, point by point, for two or more waves is called **superposition.** At points where the two waves are in the same phase, as when two crests appear at the same

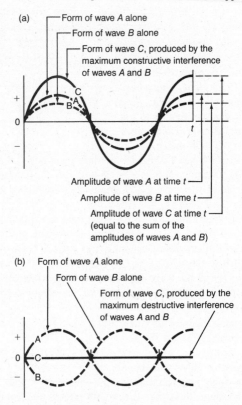

Figure 4-7.   (a) Waves A and B have the same frequency and a phase difference of 0°. As a result, they show maximum constructive interference, producing wave C. Note that the amplitudes of A and B always add up to the amplitude of C at every instant of time. This is demonstrated for the time t at the extreme right of the graph. (b) Waves A and B have the same frequency and the same amplitude, but a phase difference of 180°. As a result, they show maximum destructive interference. (Waves A and B cancel each other.)

point, maximum **constructive interference** occurs. This type of interference thus occurs when the phase difference is equal to 0° (see Figure 4-7a). When two waves of equal frequency and amplitude whose phase difference is 180° meet at a point (for example, crest to trough), there is maximum **destructive interference** (see Figure 4-7b). Maximum destructive interference results in the formation of **nodal points** and **nodal lines,** which are regions of zero displacement of the medium. Intermediate degrees of interference occur between the regions of maximum constructive interference and maximum destructive interference.

CAN YOU EXPLAIN THIS? ═══════════

Two waves can be less disturbing than one.

It is possible for two periodic waves traveling in the same medium to experience total destructive interference. This can occur if the waves have the same frequency and the same amplitude and have a phase difference of 180°, as shown in Figure 4-7.

PRACTICAL APPLICATION ═══════════

Beats are produced by the interference of two notes of slightly different frequencies that are heard simultaneously. The resulting sound has a loudness that rises and falls because the waves reinforce each other at one instant and partially cancel each other at the next. ■

Two Sources in Phase in the Same Medium. When two point sources in phase generate waves in the same medium, the pattern of nodes and antinodes (maximum destructive and constructive interference, respectively) spreads out to form a symmetrical **interference pattern.** The path distance from any point of destructive interference (that is, any point on a nodal line) to the two sources differs by an *odd* number of half-wavelengths. Such a difference results in a phase difference of 180°.

Regions of constructive interference, called antinodal lines, form where the path distances differ by an even number of half-wavelengths, in which case the phase difference is 0° (or 360°). Figure 4-8 on the next page illustrates the formation of antinodal lines by two point sources of waves that have the same frequency and are 4 wavelengths apart. The difference in path length from A and B to every point on an antinodal line is an even number of half-wavelengths. For example, the path length from A to point C is 7 half-wavelengths, and the path length from B to C is 5 half-wavelengths, giving a difference of 2 half-wavelengths. The difference in path length is 2 half-wavelengths for every point along antinodal line A. Nodal lines—that is, lines made up of points of maximum destructive interference—occur midway between the antinodal lines. The same pattern appears on the left, but reversed. This half of the pattern has been omitted from the diagram for the sake of clarity.

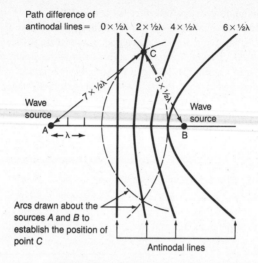

Figure 4-8. Antinodal lines (regions of maximum constructive interference) generated by two point sources of waves with the same frequency. The sources are four wavelengths apart. The difference in path length from A and B to every point along an antinodal line is an even number of half-wavelengths, as shown at the top of the drawing. The pattern is repeated in reverse on the left side of the vertical antinodal line (this half of the pattern has been omitted for clarity).

Standing Waves. The antinodal lines between the two sources in Figure 4-8 represent wave crests that remain in the same place and do not move through the medium. Any pattern of wave crests and troughs that remains stationary in a medium is called a **standing wave.** Standing waves form when two waves of the same frequency and amplitude travel through a medium in opposite directions. Standing waves often appear in a stretched string that is fixed at both ends. Wave trains traveling along the string are reflected at the ends and travel back with the same frequency and amplitude. Figure 4-9 illustrates several possible kinds of standing waves in a string.

Resonance. Every elastic body has a particular **natural frequency** at which it will vibrate if disturbed. If a body receives a series of wave pulses at its natural frequency, it will absorb energy from the pulses and vibrate at that frequency with increasing amplitude. The vibration of an object at its natural frequency caused by a vibrating source of the same frequency is called **resonance,** or *sympathetic vibration.* As an example, consider two tuning forks that are not vibrating and that have the same natural frequency placed near each other. If one tuning fork is made to vibrate, the other tuning fork will vibrate in resonance as energy from the first tuning fork is transferred to it.

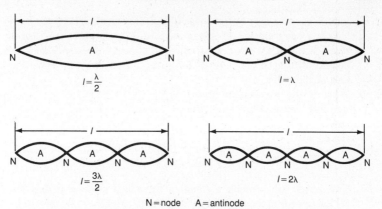

Figure 4-9. Standing waves of different wavelengths along a string.

PRACTICAL APPLICATION

An example of resonance occurs when an opera singer shatters a glass by maintaining a note with a frequency equal to the natural frequency of the glass. The transfer of energy by resonance increases the amplitude of vibrations in the glass until its structural strength is exceeded.

Probably the most dramatic example of resonance was the collapse of the Tacoma Narrows Bridge in the state of Washington. Gale winds caused the bridge to vibrate in a torsional (twisting) mode for an hour, increasing the amplitude of vibrations by resonance. To prevent a recurrence, the collapsed bridge was replaced with one that was more structurally sound and that had a higher natural frequency. ■

QUESTIONS

1. **A student blows air across the top of a soda bottle and produces a note. This is an example of (1) refraction (2) interference (3) diffraction (4) resonance**

2. **Relative to the radio signals sent by a spacecraft headed away from the earth, the signals that are received on the earth have (1) lower frequency (2) higher frequency (3) lower speed (4) higher speed**

3. **Total destructive interference of two periodic waves traveling in the same medium can occur if the waves have a phase difference of 180° and have (1) equal amplitudes and different frequencies (2) different amplitudes and equal frequencies (3) equal amplitudes and equal frequencies (4) different amplitudes and different frequencies**

4. **The particles in a standing wave that do not move appreciably are located at the (1) crests (2) troughs (3) antinodes (4) nodes**

5. Standing waves may be produced in the same medium if (1) the wavelength of one wave is half that of the other (2) two waves travel in the same direction (3) two waves travel in opposite directions and then back toward each other (4) the frequency of one wave is three times that of the other

6. What is the wavelength of the standing wave shown at the right?

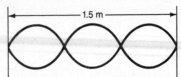

   (1) **1.0 m**   (3) **3.0 m**
   (2) **0.5 m**   (4) **1.5 m**

7. Two waves will produce a standing wave in a medium if they have (1) the same frequency, different amplitudes, and the same direction of travel (2) the same frequency, the same amplitude, and the same direction of travel (3) the same frequency, the same amplitude, and opposite directions of travel (4) different frequencies, the same amplitude, and the same direction of travel

8. When two waves pass each other in a medium, maximum constructive interference will occur in places where the phase difference between the two waves is (1) 0° (2) 45° (3) 90° (4) 180°

9. A vibrator is used to produce standing waves in a stretched string. As the frequency of the vibrator increases, the number of nodes in the string (1) decreases (2) increases (3) remains the same

10. As a periodic wave passes into a different medium in which the speed of the wave decreases, the frequency of the wave (1) decreases (2) increases (3) remains the same

IV. LIGHT

What we usually refer to as light is actually an electromagnetic disturbance that gives rise to the sensation of sight. The complete electromagnetic spectrum, which consists of a broad range of such disturbances (of which visible light is only an extremely small portion), will be discussed in detail at a later point in this unit.

Speed of Light

Accurate measurements of the speed of light to more than 2 or 3 significant figures could not be made until about 100 years ago because the speed is so great: 3.00×10^8 meters per second in a vacuum or in air. (If the speed is given to more than three digits, the speed of light in air is revealed to be slightly less than it is in a vacuum.) The speed of light in a vacuum is represented by the symbol c, which is an important physical constant. It has been found that c has the same value for all observers, regardless of their own speed. For example, if an observer traveling in the same direction as a light wave measures its speed relative to the observer, the observer will obtain exactly the same result as an observer moving in the opposite direction. This experimental observation, although contrary to common sense (it is not true for sound waves, for example), is accepted by all scientists and is the basis of Einstein's Theory of Relativity.

The speed of light in a vacuum is the upper limit for the speed of any material body. No object can travel faster than c. The speed of light in a material medium is always less than c. Equation 4-2 applies to light waves, so that

$$c = f\lambda \qquad f = c/\lambda \qquad \lambda = c/f$$

where f is the frequency of a light wave in a vacuum, and λ is the wavelength.

CAN YOU EXPLAIN THIS?

You see the flash of lightning before you hear the clap of thunder.

A single bolt of lightning may develop 3.75×10^{12} watts of power, but the lightning lasts only a fraction of a second. About 75% of the energy produced is dissipated as heat that raises the temperature of air in a lightning channel to about 15,000°C. This forces the air to expand quickly. The movement creates sound waves that can be heard as thunder for distances up to 30 kilometers. Because light travels at 3.00×10^8 m/s in air and sound travels at only 3.3×10^2 m/s in air at standard temperature and pressure, an observer sees the lightning before hearing the thunder.

Reflection

In studying light phenomena, such as reflection, it is often helpful to draw diagrams. A straight line indicating the direction of wave travel is called a **ray.** A ray that originates in one medium and reaches the surface of a second medium is called an **incident ray.** A ray that has rebounded from the surface of the second medium is called a **reflected ray.** A line perpendicular to the reflection surface is called a **normal.** The angle between the normal and the incident ray is called the **angle of incidence,** θ_i, and the angle between the normal and the reflected ray is called the **angle of reflection,** θ_r.

The **law of reflection** that describes the behavior of light waves also applies to other types of waves. This law states that the angle of incidence equals the angle of reflection ($\theta_i = \theta_r$) and that the incident ray, the normal, and the reflected ray all lie in one plane (see Figure 4-10).

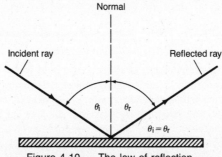

Figure 4-10. The law of reflection.

If a beam of parallel light rays strikes a smooth plane surface, such as a sheet of glass or polished metal, all the reflected rays will also be parallel, because the normals to the surface all point in the same direction. Reflection of this kind is called **regular reflection** (see Figure 4-11a). When the eye receives light from an object by regular reflection, the brain forms an *image* of the object, just as though the rays had traveled directly to the eye. The image produced by regular reflection is called a **mirror image.**

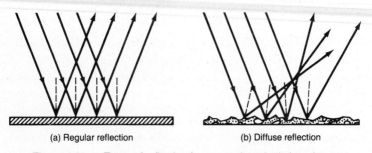

(a) Regular reflection   (b) Diffuse reflection

Figure 4-11.   Types of reflection from smooth and rough surfaces.

When a beam of parallel light rays strikes an irregular surface, such as the surface of a sheet of paper, the reflected rays are scattered in all directions. Although each individual ray obeys the laws of reflection, the surface irregularities produce nonparallel normals, so that the reflected rays are not parallel (see Figure 4-10b). This prevents image formation. Such reflection is known as **diffuse reflection.**

Refraction

When a wave strikes a boundary, it may be transmitted in modified form through the second medium. Since the velocity of the wave in this new medium will, in general, be different from that in the original medium, waves incident at an angle other than 90° to the boundary (that is, waves that strike the boundary obliquely) will be bent from their original direction. This change in direction of a wave due to a change in velocity is called **refraction.** The ray is said to have been *refracted*. Only if the incident ray lies along the normal will there be no refraction.

CAN YOU EXPLAIN THIS?

You can see the sun when it is below the horizon.

Since the density of the earth's atmosphere increases gradually as the earth's surface is approached from space, sunlight entering the atmosphere obliquely is gradually refracted to produce a curved path, as shown in Figure 4-12. Since our brain has learned to assume that light entering our eyes has been traveling in straight lines, at sunset we "see" the sun higher in the sky than it actually is. When we "see" it on the horizon, it has already set.

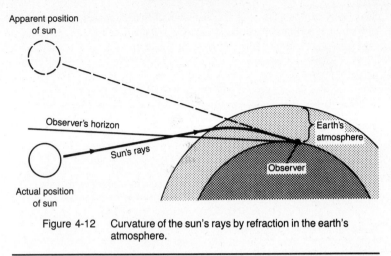

Figure 4-12   Curvature of the sun's rays by refraction in the earth's atmosphere.

Speed of Light and Refraction. When a wave obliquely enters a medium in which it is slowed, it will always be bent (refracted) toward the normal extended into the second medium. Such is the case when light rays pass from air into water, as shown in Figure 4-13a. When the wave enters a medium in which the speed is greater than the speed in the first medium, the wave is bent away from the normal, as shown in Figure 4-13b.

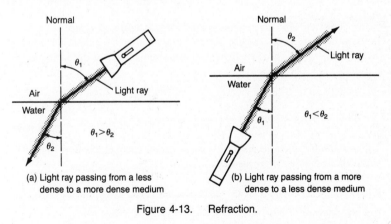

(a) Light ray passing from a less dense to a more dense medium

(b) Light ray passing from a more dense to a less dense medium

Figure 4-13.   Refraction.

PRACTICAL APPLICATION

Refraction of light in the atmosphere can produce a mirage. In the summer, when a road is very hot, a warm layer of air near it is less dense than the cooler air above. Light travels faster through the warm, less dense air than it travels through the cool air. As a result, light rays directed toward the ground at a small angle to it will be gradually refracted away from the ground and will travel upward as if reflected from the ground (see Figure 4-14).

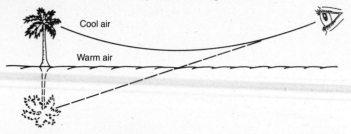

Cool air

Warm air

Figure 4-14.   The formation of a mirage by refraction of light through a layer of warm air near the ground.

A distant observer may seem to see an object, such as a tree, upside down as though reflected from a pool of water. The surface of a road may also seem to have wet spots because of similar effects of refraction of light rays at small angles to the surface. ■

Absolute Index of Refraction. The **absolute index of refraction,** n, of a medium is the ratio of the speed of light in a vacuum, c, to its speed in the medium, v:

$$n = \frac{c}{v} \qquad \text{(Eq. 4-3)}$$

Since c and v are both given in meters per second, the absolute index of refraction has no units. The absolute index of refraction of a medium is inversely proportional to the speed of light in the medium. For two different media,

$$\frac{n_1}{n_2} = \frac{v_2}{v_1}, \quad \text{or}$$

$$n_1 v_1 = n_2 v_2 \qquad \text{(Eq. 4-4)}$$

The medium in which the speed of light is slower and n is therefore greater is called the *optically denser* medium.

CAN YOU EXPLAIN THIS?

A straw appears to bend when placed in a glass of water.

A straw placed in the glass of water seems bent upward where it enters the water. That is, the straw's submerged portion appears to be closer to the surface than it actually is. Light from the submerged tip of the straw is bent away from the normal upon entering the less-dense air (see Figure 4-15). To an observer, who interprets what is seen in terms of light traveling in a straight line, the submerged tip of the straw seems closer to the surface than it actually is.

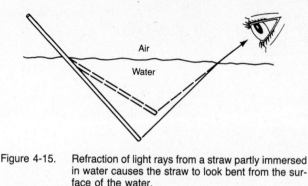

Figure 4-15.   Refraction of light rays from a straw partly immersed in water causes the straw to look bent from the surface of the water.

Snell's Law. When a ray of light passes from one medium to another, the angle formed by the ray and the normal to the surface in the first medium is called the *angle of incidence*. The angle formed by the ray and the normal in the second, or refractive, medium is called the **angle of refraction.** It can be shown mathematically or by experiment that the relation between the angles of incidence and refraction is given by the following equation:

$$\frac{\sin \theta_1}{\sin \theta_2} = \frac{n_2}{n_1}, \quad \text{or}$$

$$n_1 \sin \theta_1 = n_2 \sin \theta_2 \qquad \text{(Eq. 4-5)}$$

where θ_1 and θ_2 are the angles of incidence and refraction, respectively, and n_1 and n_2 are the absolute indices of refraction of the incident and refractive media, respectively. This relation is called **Snell's Law.**

From Equation 4-4, we know that

$$\frac{n_2}{n_1} = \frac{v_1}{v_2}$$

It is also true that the frequency of a wave is not changed by refraction; the frequency is the same in both media. Because the speeds in the two media are different, however, the wavelengths will be different. By Equation 4-2,

$$v_1 = f\lambda_1 \quad \text{and} \quad v_2 = f\lambda_2$$

Therefore, dividing the first equation by the second gives

$$\frac{v_1}{v_2} = \frac{\lambda_1}{\lambda_2}$$

Substituting in Equation 4-5, we have

$$\frac{\sin \theta_1}{\sin \theta_2} = \frac{n_2}{n_1} = \frac{v_1}{v_2} = \frac{\lambda_1}{\lambda_2}$$

EXAMPLE

The absolute index of refraction of a medium is 1.6. How fast will light travel in the medium? The speed of light in a vacuum, c, is equal to 3.0×10^8 m/s.

Solution

Equation 4-3 shows the relationship between the speed of light in a vacuum, c, the absolute index of refraction of a medium, n, and the speed of light in that medium, v:

$$n = \frac{c}{v} \text{ or } v = \frac{c}{n}$$

$$v = \frac{3.0 \times 10^8 \text{ m/s}}{1.6}$$

$$v = 1.9 \times 10^8 \text{ m/s}$$

Critical Angle. When a ray of light passes from an optically denser medium into an optically less dense medium, the angle of refraction is always larger than the angle of incidence. Thus, as the angle of incidence increases, the angle of refraction will eventually become equal to 90.°, and the refracted ray will then graze the surface between the two media. If the less dense refractive medium is air or a vacuum, the angle of incidence that produces an angle of refraction of 90.° is called the **critical angle**, θ_c, for the denser medium. Since the index of refraction for air (or a vacuum) is equal to 1, using Equation 4-5 we can write

$$\frac{\sin \theta_c}{\sin 90.°} = \frac{1}{u}$$

where θ_c is the critical incidence in the denser medium, 90.° is the angle of refraction, 1 is the index of refraction of air, and n is the absolute index of refraction of the denser medium. Since $\sin 90.° = 1$,

$$\sin \theta_c = \frac{1}{n} \tag{Eq. 4-6}$$

Total Internal Reflection. Recall that if a wave strikes the boundary between two different media, some of the wave energy is always absorbed, and some is always reflected. Some of the incident wave energy may be transmitted and refracted, but this does not necessarily occur. At angles of incidence in a denser medium greater than the critical angle, no refraction into the less dense medium can occur. All incident rays are reflected back into the denser medium (see Figure 4-16). Such reflection inside an optically dense medium at angles of incidence that are greater than the critical angle is called **total internal reflection.**

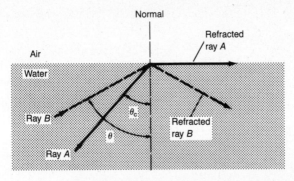

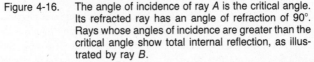

Figure 4-16.   The angle of incidence of ray *A* is the critical angle.
                Its refracted ray has an angle of refraction of 90°.
                Rays whose angles of incidence are greater than the
                critical angle show total internal reflection, as illus-
                trated by ray *B*.

CAN YOU EXPLAIN THIS?

Telephone communication can be carried by laser beams through glass fibers.

A fiber-optic communication system consists of a transducer that converts electrical signals to light signals, an optical fiber that guides the light signals, and a
different kind of transducer that receives the light signals at the other end of the
fiber and converts them back to electrical signals. The light source in the transmitter may be a laser or a light-emitting diode. Thousands of telephone conver-
sations can be transmitted via one or two flexible, hair-thin optical fibers. In
these fibers, the light signals are "piped" from transmission point to reception
point by a series of total internal reflections. A good communication system will
accomplish this without distortion of the signal's waveform.

Dispersive and Nondispersive Media

Most light-wave sources produce waves of different frequencies at the same
time (called **polychromatic waves**). In certain kinds of media, called **dispersive media,** waves of differing frequencies travel with different speeds and have
different indices of refraction. For example, light waves in glass travel at speeds
that depend on the frequency of the light; the higher-frequency waves travel
more slowly than do those of lower frequency. Glass is therefore a dispersive
medium for light waves. **Dispersion,** or separation of polychromatic waves into
their components, can occur if the waves pass through glass. Figure 4-17, which
is on the next page, illustrates the separation of a mixture of red, green, and blue
light into its component frequencies (colors) by a glass **prism.**

In media called **nondispersive media,** waves of all frequencies travel at the
same speed. For example, polyphonic sound waves, such as those of the voice,
all travel at the same speed in air. Air is therefore a nondispersive medium for
sound. A vacuum is a nondispersive medium for light.

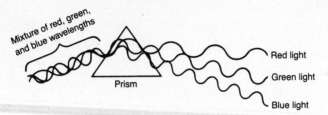

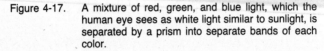

Figure 4-17.   A mixture of red, green, and blue light, which the human eye sees as white light similar to sunlight, is separated by a prism into separate bands of each color.

PRACTICAL APPLICATION

The fact that light can experience total internal reflection in glass has been widely used in the design of binoculars and periscopes. It is also applied in diamond cutting. A diamond is cut in a precise manner, so that light that enters it is internally reflected many times before emerging from the upper facets. This occurs because the absolute index of refraction of diamond is greater than that of any other transparent material. Its critical angle is 24°, as compared with a critical angle of about 42° for glass. In addition, each facet acts as a separate prism to disperse white light as it emerges from the diamond, producing vivid "rainbows." ■

CAN YOU EXPLAIN THIS?

Red, blue, and green light make white.

Although the human visual system can perceive thousands of different colors, any color sensation can be produced by combining red, blue, and green light in proper proportions. These are called the primary colors of light. Any two colors that add together to produce white are called complementary colors. If beams of the three primary light colors are projected on a white screen, it can be shown that green and blue lights combine to produce cyan, the complement of red; green and red lights combine to produce yellow, the complement of blue; and red and blue lights combine to produce magenta, the complement of green. Thus, two primary light colors combine to produce the complement of the third primary color. If appropriate intensities of red, green, and blue light are mixed together, the result is interpreted by the eye as white. The display on the screens of color TV sets makes use of this kind of color mixing.

Wave Nature of Light

Much of the behavior of light can best be explained if light is assumed to travel in the form of waves. In the wave model of light, spherical waves (or circular waves in a plane) travel outward from any point source of light. In the year 1678, Christian Huygens proposed a model of light waves (now called

Huygens' principle) in which each point on a circular wave front is itself a source of circular waves, and each point on these wave fronts is also a source of circular waves. Although all these infinite sets of tiny waves are hard to imagine, Huygens showed that they all cancel out by destructive interference except along a line normal to the original wave front. This line is the direction of propagation of the wave and can be represented by a light ray. That is why such phenomena as reflection and refraction can be described by ray diagrams.

Diffraction. When circular wave fronts have traveled far from their source, the circles are so large that the wave fronts are practically straight lines, and the light rays are all parallel. When these wave fronts reach an opaque barrier with a small opening, you might expect a narrow beam of light to pass through the opening and travel in a straight line behind the barrier. This is not what happens, however. If the opening is very small, it is found that the light spreads out behind the barrier, as shown in Figure 4-18. This spreading of light behind a barrier is called **diffraction.** It can be explained by Huygens' principle, because waves on each side of the beam that would ordinarily cause destructive interference are missing when the light passes through the opening. Diffraction also occurs when light passes the edge of an obstacle, but the effect is usually too small to be noticeable.

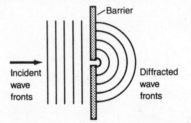

Figure 4-18   Diffraction of parallel wave fronts by a small opening in a barrier.

If the light passing through a small hole or narrow slit in a barrier is allowed to strike a screen, a pattern of light and dark regions appears on the screen. This pattern is called an *interference pattern,* because it is caused by interference between light waves from different parts of the beam passing through the opening. The formation of interference patterns by diffraction is easier to understand in the case of light passing through *two* openings close together.

Double-Slit Diffraction. Two light sources from which the waves always have a constant phase relationship can be produced by passing the light through a double-slit arrangement. Such light of constant phase relationship is said to be **coherent** and is more readily produced today by means of a laser. When two such sources emit waves of the same frequency, amplitude, and phase, and these waves meet at the same point after traveling different paths, they will interfere with one another—that is, they will produce an interference pattern. If the paths from the two sources (or slits) to a point on a screen differ in length by one half-wavelength, then the two beams will produce a dark spot, because the crest of one wave coincides with the trough of the other. Light must be assumed to have wave properties in order to explain this kind of complete destructive interference.

If the paths from a point on the screen to the two sources differ in length by an even number of half-wavelengths, the crest of a wave from one source coincides with the crest of a wave from the other source, producing a bright spot on the screen at that point. If the paths differ by an odd number of half-wavelengths, the crest of a wave from one source coincides with the trough of a wave from the other source, producing a dark spot on the screen. The double-slit experiment, first carried out by Thomas Young in 1801, produces a series of dark and bright regions on the screen, demonstrating constructive and destructive interference, as shown in Figure 4-19. From the geometric arrangement of the experiment, the relationship between wavelength of the light, λ, the distance from source to screen, L, the separation between the slits, d, and the distance from the first bright line to the central bright line, x, has been found to be given by

$$\frac{\lambda}{d} = \frac{x}{L}$$

(Eq. 4-7)

where all measurements are expressed in the same unit of length—usually in meters.

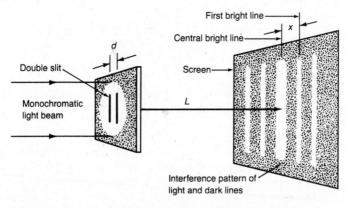

Figure 4-19.   The interference pattern produced by diffraction of a monochromatic beam by two slits in a barrier.

Polarization

As illustrated in Figure 4-3 (page 112), if the end of a horizontal rope is moved rapidly up and down, a wave train moves along the rope. As the wave moves along the rope, the vibrations of the particles of the rope occur in a vertical plane at right angles to the direction of motion of the waves. If the end of the rope is moved from side to side, the vibrations of the particles of the rope move in a horizontal plane at right angles to the direction of motion of the waves. By changing the angle of the motion that produces the waves, the vibrations can be made to occur in any plane around the rope.

A light wave consists of varying electric and magnetic fields. Like the displacement of the particles in a rope wave, the intensities of these fields are continuously changing in magnitude and direction at right angles to the direction of the light wave. The vibration, or *oscillation,* of the fields can occur in a horizontal plane, a vertical plane, or in any other plane around the line of propagation of the light wave.

Ordinarily, a source of light emits waves in which the vibrations are occurring in all possible planes. It is possible, however, to use various means to separate components of a light beam so that all the vibrations are in the same plane. A beam of light in which all the vibrations are in the same plane is called **polarized light,** and the process of producing polarized light is called **polarization.** One method of polarizing a light beam is to pass it through a polarizing filter, which transmits waves vibrating in one plane best, and blocks all others more or less completely (see Figure 4-20). Only transverse waves may be polarized, because longitudinal waves have only one possible direction of vibration: back and forth in the same direction as the direction of wave travel.

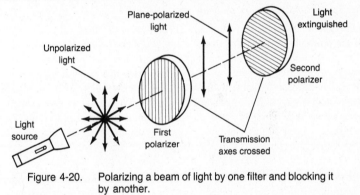

Figure 4-20. Polarizing a beam of light by one filter and blocking it by another.

PRACTICAL APPLICATION

Glare is bright light that reflects off surfaces such as water, snow, and polished metal. Light that shines on these surfaces is reflected, primarily, as waves that are polarized in a horizontal plane. To eliminate this annoying and sometimes blinding glare, sunglasses made with vertically polarizing filters can be worn. The filters act as though having very closely spaced vertical slits. Horizontally polarized light is blocked by the filters, thus eliminating most of the glare. Most of the nonpolarized light from other objects passes through the filters, permitting normal vision of the surroundings. ■

The Electromagnetic Spectrum

Visible light is just one small category of electromagnetic waves. Electromagnetic waves may have frequencies that cover a broad range, from those that are very low (near zero) to those that are extremely high, with corresponding wavelengths from very long to extremely short. The complete range of frequencies and wavelengths of electromagnetic waves is called the **electromagnetic spectrum.** As shown in Figure 4-21, it is divided, for convenience, into a number of generally overlapping sections, each with its own approximate range of frequencies and wavelengths. There are no sharp boundaries between the various ranges; they are classified according to the methods by which they are generated or received. That is, the various frequencies of electromagnetic waves have different effects on receivers. The best known of the electromagnetic waves, **visible light** waves, are caused by the motion of electrons within atoms. The frequency range of visible light waves is a narrow band compared to the total frequency range of the whole electromagnetic spectrum. The other bands in the spectrum are made up of radio waves, infrared waves, ultraviolet waves, x-ray waves, and gamma-ray waves.

CAN YOU EXPLAIN THIS?

You can get a sunburn on a cloudy day.

Ultraviolet radiation is the part of sunlight that causes sunburn. The ozone layer of the atmosphere filters practically all of the high-frequency components of ultraviolet radiation from the sun, but the atmosphere readily transmits the remaining lower-frequency ultraviolet radiation. Although water vapor and droplets in clouds absorb visible light waves, they transmit most of the ultraviolet radiation in sunlight. Thus, even on a cloudy day you should take care to apply a commercial skin lotion in order to prevent sunburn. These preparations are designed to absorb ultraviolet rays, preventing the rays from reaching the skin.

PRACTICAL APPLICATION

Electromagnetic waves other than visible light, which makes up approximately 1% of the spectrum, are important in our lives. Microwaves are used in transmitting long-distance telephone communications in outer space. Microwaves can also be used to cook food, because a natural rotational frequency of water molecules is in the microwave range. The microwaves create resonance in the water molecules of the food and the resulting internal energy due to vibration heats the food. The microwaves also affect the molecules of fats, oils, and sugars.

Radar emitted intermittently to allow for reception of reflected pulses from an object whose motion is being studied is very important in air-traffic control. If the time lapse between the transmission of the wave and the reception of its echo is known, then the distance of the object from the source can be readily calculated. ■

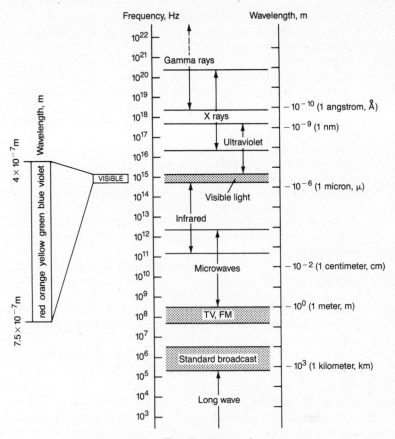

Figure 4-21.   The electromagnetic spectrum.

QUESTIONS

1. If the speed of light in a vacuum is c, the speed of light in a medium with an index of refraction of 2 is (1) $c/2$ (2) $2c$ (3) $c/4$ (4) $4c$

2. A ray of light traveling through water strikes the water-air boundary with an angle of incidence equal to the critical angle. The angle of refraction is (1) 180.° (2) 90.° (3) 45° (4) 30.°

3. The frequency of infrared waves is generally greater than that of (1) visible light rays (2) radio waves (3) ultraviolet waves (4) x rays

4. If a ray of monochromatic yellow light ($\lambda = 5.9 \times 10^{-7}$ m) traveling through the air is incident to a refractive medium at an angle of 30°, the material that would produce the largest angle of refraction is (1) alcohol (2) water (3) glycerol (4) lucite

5. If the speed of light in a medium is 1.5×10^8 meters per second, the index of refraction of the medium is (1) 0.67 (2) 2.0 (3) 3.0 (4) 2.5

6. The critical angle for light passing from a special glass into air is 41°. When the angle of incidence equals the critical angle, the angle of refraction will be (1) between 0° and 41° (2) 41° (3) between 41° and 90.° (4) 90.°

7. A beam of light traveling in air is incident upon a glass block. If the angle of refraction is 30.°, the angle of incidence is (1) 0° (2) between 0° and 30.° (3) between 30.° and 90.° (4) 90.°

8. Which type of electromagnetic wave has the highest frequency? (1) radio (2) infrared (3) x ray (4) visible

9. The separation of white light into component colors as it passes through a triangular glass prism is (1) dispersion (2) diffraction (3) diffusion (4) interference

10. Patterns that are produced on a screen by passing coherent light through a double slit can be explained in terms of which of the following phenomena of light? (1) refraction and dispersion (2) diffraction and dispersion (3) diffraction and refraction (4) diffraction and interference

11. When a beam of white light passes obliquely from air into glass, which component experiences the greatest change in direction? (1) red (2) yellow (3) green (4) blue

12. To form a diffraction (interference) pattern from two light sources, the sources must (1) have different frequencies (2) have different intensities (3) be coherent (4) be incoherent

13. The speed of light in a transparent medium is three-fourths that in a vacuum. The index of refraction of the medium is

(1) $\dfrac{3}{4}$ (2) $\dfrac{4}{3}$ (3) $\dfrac{\sqrt{3}}{2}$ (4) $\dfrac{\sqrt{2}}{3}$

14. Maximum destructive interference occurs when the phase difference between two waves traveling in the same medium is (1) 0° (2) 90° (3) 180° (4) 270°

15. The critical angle is that angle of incidence that produces an angle of refraction of (1) 0° (2) 45° (3) 60.° (4) 90.°

16. What is the color of light with a wavelength of 6.9×10^{-7} meter? (1) blue (2) green (3) yellow (4) red

17. An object resting on the bottom of a tank of water as shown in the diagram is being observed. To the observer, the object will appear to be located at point

(1) A   (3) C

(2) B   (4) D

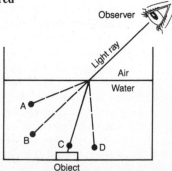

18. A light ray traveling through glass strikes a glass-air surface. The angle of incidence equals the critical angle of 42°. The angle that the refracted ray makes with the normal is (1) 0° (2) 42° (3) 48° (4) 90.°

19. The diagram at the right represents straight wave fronts passing through an opening in a barrier. Which wave phenomenon is exhibited? (1) refraction (2) polarization (3) dispersion (4) diffraction

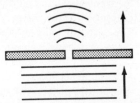

20. Light of a single frequency cannot be (1) dispersed (2) reflected (3) refracted (4) diffracted

21. Which type of wave can be polarized? (1) sound (2) light (3) compression (4) any type

22. A wave passes obliquely from a medium having an index of refraction of 1.3 to a different medium. The wave will bend toward the normal in the second medium if its index of refraction is (1) 1.0 (2) 1.2 (3) 1.3 (4) 1.4

23. Double-slit interference experiments with light were important in establishing the (1) wave theory (2) corpuscular theory (3) quantum theory (4) electromagnetic theory

24. Which diagram shows the path that a monochromatic ray of light will travel as it passes through air, corn oil, lucite, and back into air?

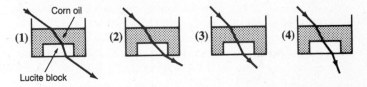

25. As the index of refraction of an alcohol and water mixture increases, the critical angle for the mixture (1) decreases (2) increases (3) remains the same

26. When the index of refraction of a medium increases, the speed of light through the medium (1) decreases (2) increases (3) remains the same

27. A light ray traveling through glass strikes a glass-air surface. As the angle of incidence increases, the critical angle for the glass (1) decreases (2) increases (3) remains the same

28. As the absolute index of refraction of a substance increases, its critical angle (1) decreases (2) increases (3) remains the same

29. As a beam of monochromatic light travels from one medium to another of higher refractive index, the wavelength of the light (1) decreases (2) increases (3) remains the same

30. The speed of light changes when light is (1) polarized (2) refracted (3) reflected (4) diffracted

31. A person standing on a straight railroad track hears the whistle of an approaching train. As the train approaches with a constant velocity, the frequency that the person observes for the whistle, compared to the frequency observed by a person riding on the train, is (1) lower (2) higher (3) the same

32. The speed of monochromatic blue light in glass, compared to the speed of monochromatic red light in the same glass, is (1) less (2) greater (3) the same

33. A ray of monochromatic light passes from air into water. As the angle of incidence of the light ray increases, the index of refraction of the water (1) decreases (2) increases (3) remains the same

34. As the angle of incidence of a light wave entering glass from air increases, the angle of refraction (1) decreases (2) increases (3) remains the same

35. A ray of light is reflected from a plane mirror. If the angle between the incident and reflected rays is 40°, the angle of incidence is (1) 20° (2) 40° (3) 50° (4) 70°

36. Which wave phenomenon best supports the fact that light travels as a transverse wave? (1) reflection (2) refraction (3) dispersion (4) polarization

37. To an observer at B, light rays emitted from point P will appear to originate at point (1) A (2) B (3) C (4) P

38. When a ray of light strikes a mirror perpendicular to its surface, the angle of reflection will be (1) 0° (2) 45° (3) 60° (4) 90°

39. A light beam from the earth is reflected by an object in space. If the round trip for the beam takes 2.0 seconds, then the distance of the object from earth is (1) 6.7×10^7 m (2) 1.5×10^8 m (3) 3.0×10^8 m (4) 6.0×10^8 m

40–43. Base your answers to Questions 40 through 43 on the diagrams below, which show the paths of four rays of monochromatic light as they reach the boundary between two media. N is the normal to the surface.

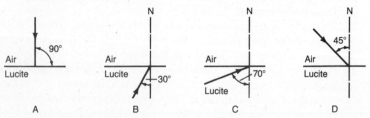

40. The direction of the ray of light will not change as the light enters the other medium in diagram (1) A (2) B (3) C (4) D

41. The ray of light will undergo total internal reflection at the boundary in diagram (1) *A* (2) *B* (3) *C* (4) *D*

42. The angle of refraction of the ray of light will be greater than the angle of incidence in diagram (1) *A* (2) *B* (3) *C* (4) *D*

43. What is the sine of the angle of refraction for the ray of light in diagram *D*? (1) 1.00 (2) 0.71 (3) 0.47 (4) 0.30

44–48. Base your answers to Questions 44 through 48 on the diagram, which shows a glass prism surrounded by air. The dashed line *MN* is a normal and is extended to *A*.

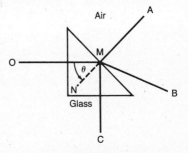

44. Which phenomenon would cause monochromatic light entering the prism along path *OM* to leave along path *MC*? (1) reflection (2) refraction (3) dispersion (4) diffraction

45. If the index of refraction of the prism is 1.5, then the speed of light in this prism is (1) 1.5×10^8 m/s (2) 2.0×10^8 m/s (3) 3.0×10^8 m/s (4) 4.5×10^8 m/s

46. A ray of light striking the prism along path *AM* will follow path (1) *MO* (2) *MN* (3) *MB* (4) *MC*

47. Compared with the index of refraction for blue light, the index of refraction of this glass prism for red light is (1) greater (2) less (3) equal

48. If all the light entering the prism along path *OM* emerges along path *MC*, then angle θ is (1) greater than the critical angle (2) less than the critical angle (3) equal to the critical angle

49–53. Base your answers to Questions 49 through 53 on the diagram, which represents three transparent media arranged one on top of the other. A light ray in air is incident on the upper surface of layer *A*.

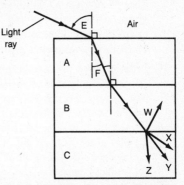

49. If layers *B* and *C* have the same index of refraction, in which direction will the light ray travel after reaching the boundary between layers *B* and *C*? (1) *W* (2) *X* (3) *Y* (4) *Z*

50. If layer *A* were lucite, then layer *B* could be (1) water (2) diamond (3) Canada balsam (4) flint glass

51. If angle *E* is 60° and layer *A* has an index of refraction of 1.61, the sine of angle *F* will be closest to (1) 1.00 (2) 0.866 (3) 0.538 (4) 0.400

52. If angle *E* were increased, then angle *F* would (1) decrease (2) increase (3) remain the same

53. Compared to the apparent speed of light in layer *A*, the apparent speed of light in layer *B* is (1) slower (2) faster (3) the same

54–58. Base your answers to Questions 54 through 58 on the diagram, which shows a narrow beam of monochromatic yellow light passing from lucite into air.

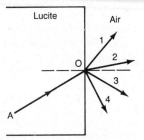

54. Which path will the ray *AO* follow? (1) 1 (2) 2 (3) 3 (4) 4

55. The speed of the light beam in the lucite is (1) 1.0×10^8 m/s (2) 2.0×10^8 m/s (3) 3.0×10^8 m/s (4) 4.5×10^8 m/s

56. As the beam passes from lucite to air, its frequency (1) decreases (2) increases (3) remains the same

57. If the monochromatic yellow beam is replaced by a monochromatic violet beam, the speed of this light in lucite would be (1) slower (2) faster (3) the same

58. If the lucite were replaced by flint glass, the critical angle would be (1) smaller (2) larger (3) the same

59–63. Base your answers to Questions 59 through 63 on the diagram, which shows a ray of monochromatic light as it travels in three transparent media.

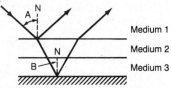

59. What happens to the light incident upon medium *2* from medium *1*? (1) All of the light is refracted. (2) Part of the light is refracted and part is reflected. (3) Part of the light is refracted and part is dispersed. (4) Part of the light is diffracted and part is reflected.

60. If medium *2* is corn oil, then medium *3* could be (1) crown glass (2) flint glass (3) lucite (4) glycerol

61. As the light enters medium *2*, its frequency (1) decreases (2) increases (3) remains the same

62. If angle *A* is increased, angle *B* will (1) decrease (2) increase (3) remain the same

63. If the frequency of the light incident in medium *I* is increased, its wavelength in medium *I* will (1) decrease (2) increase (3) remain the same

64–67. Base your answers to Questions 64 through 67 on the following information.

Two rays of monochromatic yellow light, *A* and *B*, originate in a tank of water as shown. Angle *BON* is the critical angle of water.

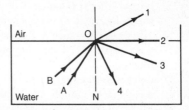

64. Ray *A* will travel along path (1) 1 (2) 2 (3) 3 (4) 4
65. The sine of the critical angle for water is equal to

   (1) $\dfrac{1.33}{1}$ (2) $\dfrac{1}{1.33}$ (3) $\dfrac{3 \times 10^8}{1.33}$ (4) $3 \times 10^8 \times 1.33$

66. As a ray of light in the tank undergoes total internal reflection, its speed will (1) decrease (2) increase (3) remain the same
67. As a ray of light traveling along path *NO* enters the air, its speed will (1) decrease (2) increase (3) remain the same

68–72. Base your answers to Questions 68 through 72 on the diagram, which represents a lucite prism. *HK* is a narrow beam of monochromatic yellow light incident upon the prism at angle θ.

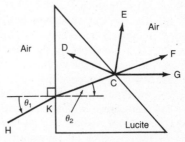

68. Which represents the path of *HK*? (1) *HKCD* (2) *HKCE* (3) *HKCF* (4) *HKCG*
69. The speed of the light beam through the lucite prism is (1) 1.0×10^8 m/s (2) 2.0×10^8 m/s (3) 3.0×10^8 m/s (4) 4.0×10^8 m/s
70. If angle θ_1 is 30°, the sine of angle θ_2 is

   (1) $\dfrac{0.50}{1.5}$ (2) $\dfrac{0.87}{1.5}$ (3) $\dfrac{1.5}{0.50}$ (4) $\dfrac{1.5}{0.87}$

71. If the monochromatic yellow beam is replaced by a monochromatic blue beam, angle θ_2 (1) decreases (2) increases (3) remains the same
72. As angle θ_1 increases from 20° to 30°, angle θ_2 (1) decreases (2) increases (3) remains the same

73. The spreading of a wave front into the region behind an obstruction is known as (1) reflection (2) refraction (3) diffraction (4) dispersion

74. Which phenomenon is evidence of the transverse nature of light?
(1) polarization (2) reflection (3) diffraction (4) interference

75. As a periodic wave passes into a new medium where the wave speed is
greater, the (1) frequency increases (2) frequency decreases (3) wavelength increases (4) wavelength decreases

76. The wave phenomenon that could not be demonstrated with a single
wave pulse is (1) a standing wave (2) diffraction (3) reflection (4) refraction

77. Refraction of a monochromatic light wave is caused by a change in the
wave's (1) amplitude (2) frequency (3) wavelength (4) speed

78. Which phenomenon is associated only with transverse waves? (1) interference (2) dispersion (3) refraction (4) polarization

79. Sources that produce waves with a constant phase relation are said to
be (1) polarized (2) diffused (3) refracted (4) coherent

80. The diagram shows light waves
passing through slit S in barrier
B. This is an example of
(1) reflection
(2) refraction
(3) polarization
(4) diffraction

81. The speed at which light passes through a material medium depends
on the (1) frequency of the light only (2) nature of the medium only
(3) frequency of the light and the nature of the medium (4) angle of
incidence to the medium

82. Which waves require a material medium for transmission? (1) sound
waves (2) radio waves (3) x rays (4) visible light

83. The change in direction that occurs when a wave passes obliquely
from one medium into another is called (1) diffraction (2) interference
(3) refraction (4) superposition

84–87. Base your answers to Questions 84 through 87 on diagrams
A through D, which represent
four interference patterns. The
dark bars indicate areas of *minimum* light intensity.

84. Which phenomenon was primarily responsible for producing all four
interference patterns? (1) polarization (2) dispersion (3) refraction
(4) diffraction

85. If the distance from the slits to the screen upon which pattern B is
displayed is increased, then the most likely pattern to appear would
be (1) A (2) B (3) C (4) D

86. In pattern C, the distance between the central maximum and the first bright line is 2.0×10^{-2} meter. The separation of the double slit is 1.0×10^{-4} meter and the distance from the slits to the screen is 4.0 meters. The wavelength of the source is (1) 2.2×10^{-3} m (2) 8.0×10^{2} m (3) 5.0×10^{-7} m (4) 1.5×10^{-6} m

87. If pattern B is produced by using monochromatic green light and the source is changed to monochromatic red light, then the pattern produced would become like pattern (1) A (2) B (3) C (4) D

88–91. Base your answers to questions 88 through 91 on the following information.

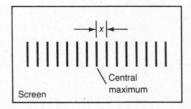

A source of monochromatic light with a wavelength of 6.0×10^{-7} meter is incident upon two slits that are 2.0×10^{-5} meter apart and 2.0 meters from a screen. The dark bars on the screen represent the *bright* areas in the interference pattern produced on the screen.

88. The color of the incident light is (1) green (2) yellow (3) red (4) orange

89. Distance x is equal to (1) 1.7×10^{-2} m (2) 3.0×10^{-2} m (3) 6.0×10^{-2} m (4) 1.2×10^{-1} m

90. If the distance between the slits and the screen is increased, distance x will (1) decrease (2) increase (3) remain the same

91. If the light source is made brighter, distance x will (1) decrease (2) increase (3) remain the same

92–96. Base your answers to Questions 92 through 96 on the diagram, which represents light from a monochromatic source, K, passing through narrow slits S_1 and S_2. A central bright band is observed at C and a first-order bright band is observed at

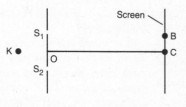

B. The two slits are 1.1×10^{-4} meter apart, distance OC is 2.0 meters and distance CB is 1.0×10^{-2} meter.

92. Light arrives at point B from slit S_2 because of (1) dispersion (2) refraction (3) diffraction (4) polarization

93. Which phenomenon of light causes the bright band at B? (1) interference (2) refraction (3) dispersion (4) polarization

94. What is the color of the light coming from source K? (1) orange (2) yellow (3) blue (4) green

95. If red light had been used, the distance BC would have been (1) shorter (2) longer (3) the same

96. If the two slits are moved closer together, the distance BC will
    (1) decrease (2) increase (3) remain the same

97–101. Base your answers to Questions 97 through 101 on the following information.

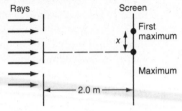

Two parallel slits 2.0×10^{-6} meter apart are illuminated by parallel rays of monochromatic light of wavelength 6.0×10^{-7} meter, as shown. The interference pattern is formed on a screen 2.0 meters from the slits.

97. The distance X is (1) 6.0×10^{-1} m (2) 6.0×10^{-7} m (3) 3.0×10^{-1} m (4) 3.3 m

98. The difference between the distances from each of the slits to the first maximum is (1) λ (2) 2λ (3) $\lambda/2$ (4) 0

99. If the wavelength of the light passing through the slits is doubled, the distance from the central maximum to the first maximum (1) decreases (2) increases (3) remains the same

100. If the screen is moved closer to the slits, the distance between the central maximum and the first maximum (1) decreases (2) increases (3) remains the same

101. If the distance between the slits decreases, the distance between the central maximum and the first maximum (1) decreases (2) increases (3) remains the same

102–106. Base your answers to Questions 102 through 106 on the following information.

Two speakers are arranged as shown so that initially they will emit tones that are in phase, equal in volume, and equal in frequency. A microphone is placed at position A, which is equidistant from both speakers, and then is moved along a line parallel to the line joining the speakers until it reaches a point (position B) at which it picks up no sound. The microphone is then moved to position C, where it again picks up sound.

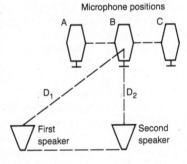

102. Which phenomenon caused the sound to be louder at position C than at position B? (1) reflection (2) dispersion (3) polarization (4) interference

103. Distance D_2 is shorter than distance D_1 by an amount equal to (1) the wavelength of the emitted sound (2) twice the wavelength of the emitted sound (3) one-half the wavelength of the emitted sound (4) the distance between the two speakers

104. If the sound waves emitted by D_1 and D_2 have a frequency of 660 hertz and a speed of 330 meters/second, their wavelength is (1) 1.0 m (2) 2.0 m (3) 0.25 m (4) 0.50 m

105. As the first speaker is adjusted so that the sound that it emits is 180° out of phase with the sound emitted by the second speaker, the loudness of the sound received at A is (1) less (2) greater (3) the same

106. If speaker D_1 were removed and speaker D_2 were accelerated toward microphone B, the frequency of the waves detected at B would (1) decrease (2) increase (3) remain the same

107–111. Base your answers to Questions 107 through 111 on the diagram at right, which shows monochromatic yellow light $(\lambda = 5.9 \times 10^{-7}$ meter) directed upon two narrow slits 1.0×10^{-3} meter apart.

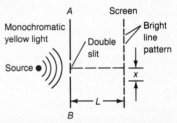

107. The first bright line is 5.9×10^{-3} meter from the central axis of the pattern. The distance (L) between the screen and AB is (1) 1 m (2) 10 m (3) 100 m (4) 1,000 m

108. If the screen is placed 1.0 meter from AB, the separation of the central maximum and the first-order bright line (x) is (1) 5.9×10^{-6} m (2) 2.0×10^{-5} m (3) 2.0×10^{-3} m (4) 5.9×10^{-4} m

109. This double-slit pattern is a result of (1) polarization (2) refraction (3) diffraction (4) dispersion

110. If the separation between the slits is increased, the distance between the bright lines on the screen will (1) decrease (2) increase (3) remain the same

111. If the wavelength of the light incident on the slits is decreased, the separation of the bright lines on the screen will (1) decrease (2) increase (3) remain the same

PROBLEM SOLVING

Sample Problem

Figure A depicts a ray of light ($\lambda = 5.9 \times 10^{-7}$ meter) about to emerge in air from water.

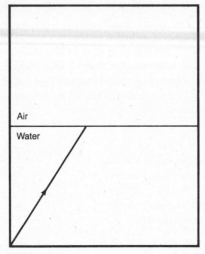

Figure A

(a) On the diagram indicate the angle of incidence by θ_i and label its measure to the nearest degree.

(b) Calculate the corresponding angle of refraction to the nearest degree. Show all work.

(c) On the diagram, draw the refracted light ray, label the angle of refraction $\theta_{r'}$, and indicate its measure to the nearest degree.

(d) At a boundary between two media, *some* of the incident light is always reflected. On the diagram, draw the reflected ray, label the angle of reflection θ_r, and indicate its measure to the nearest degree.

(e) If the angle of incidence is gradually changed from its present value to 55°, what changes if any would occur in the reflected and refracted rays?

Solution

(a) To determine the angle of incidence, a normal to the surface at the point of incidence should be drawn first. The angle of incidence is measured from the normal. See Figure B at the top of the next page.

(b) Snell's law is given by:

$$n_1 \sin \theta_1 = n_2 \sin \theta_2$$

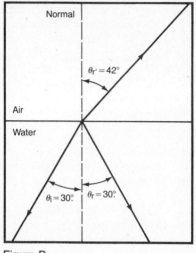

Figure B

Note that the subscript *1* refers to the incident medium and the subscript *2* refers to the refractive medium.

$$\sin \theta_2 = \frac{n_1 \sin \theta_1}{n_2}$$

where $n_1 = 1.33$ (water)
$n_2 = 1.00$ (air)
$\theta_1 = 30.$ degrees

$$\sin \theta_2 = \frac{(1.33)(\sin 30°)}{1.00}$$

$$\sin \theta_2 = \frac{(1.33)(0.500)}{1.00}$$

$$\sin \theta_2 = 0.665$$

$$\theta_2 = 42°$$

(c) The angle of refraction is in air and is measured from the normal, using a protractor. The angle of refraction must be greater than 30 degrees because air is less dense than water, causing the light ray to travel faster in the second medium.

(d) At the interface between the two media, there is a partial reflection of the original ray. According to the law of reflection, the angle of incidence must equal the angle of reflection. Thus, the angle of reflection is 30. degrees, and is measured from the normal.

(e) Increasing the angle of incidence would cause an equal increase in the angle of reflection. However, the angle of refraction would increase only until it reached its maximum value of 90.°, when the angle of incidence is the critical angle for water. As the angle of incidence is made to exceed the critical angle, there would be total internal reflection.

Various skills were needed to solve the above problem. In addition to measuring, applying mathematics, and communicating information, you had to predict what would happen if one of the variables in the problem was changed.

Practice Problems

1. Explain each of the following, using physical principles.
   (a) After a picture is covered with a clear glass plate, the picture cannot be seen as distinctly.
   (b) When a person peers down into a swimming pool filled with water, the bottom appears closer to the person than it actually is.
   (c) As wind blows across the top of a chimney flue when the damper is open, the chimney "sings."
   (d) When a rapidly moving fire engine is coming toward you, the pitch of its siren sounds higher than it does when the fire engine is at rest.
2. Using your knowledge of physics, discuss the path that the light ray travels in the diagram. Be specific. Use the terms *angle of incidence, angle of reflection, angle of refraction, normal,* and *critical angle* in your answer.

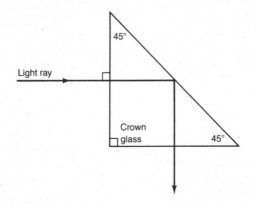

3. A ray of monochromatic light ($\lambda = 5.9 \times 10^{-7}$ meter) is incident upon the triangular lucite plate as shown in the diagram. Draw the ray as it passes into and emerges from the plate. Verify your answer with calculations.

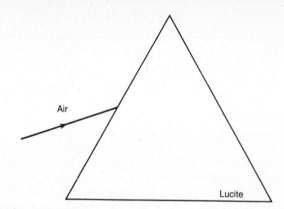

4. Labeling as necessary to ensure understanding, produce sketches of the following wave phenomena.
   (a) reflection
   (b) refraction
   (c) double-slit diffraction
   (d) Doppler effect
   Note: Use standard notation of f for frequency, λ for wavelength, and v for wave speed.
5. A ray of light is incident on the surface of a block of flint glass at an angle of 40. degrees. Part of the light is reflected and part is refracted. Find the angle between the reflected and refracted rays.
6. A light ray ($\lambda = 5.9 \times 10^{-7}$ meter), incident upon an interface of water and an unknown transmitting substance, X, is refracted as shown in the diagram below. Find the speed of light in medium X.

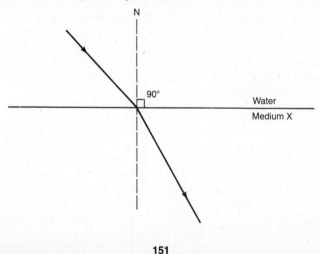

UNIT 5   MODERN PHYSICS

I. DUAL NATURE OF LIGHT

In modern physics, light, or electromagnetic radiation in general, is perceived as acting sometimes like a wave and sometimes like a particle. A wave model provides a better explanation of the observations when light from different sources interact. A particle model gives a better explanation of the observed interactions between light and matter.

In interactions with matter, light acts as though it is made up of particles with kinetic energy and momentum. When light strikes matter, some of its momentum is transferred to the particles of the matter. The effect is similar to the pressure produced by the impact of gas molecules on the walls of a container, and it is referred to as *radiation pressure*. Radiation pressure is one of the causes of the tail of dust and gas driven out of the head of a comet as it passes near the sun.

Wave Phenomena

In the 17th century, Isaac Newton stated his belief that light consists of tiny particles of unknown composition. Other scientists, particularly Christian Huygens, believed that light consists of waves. At that time, it was not possible to perform the kinds of experiments needed to resolve this controversy. Because Newton was so highly regarded in the scientific world, most scientists accepted his particle theory until the beginning of the 19th century. It then became possible to demonstrate and study such phenomena as diffraction, interference, the Doppler effect, and polarization of light—all of which could be explained by a wave model of light but not by a particle model. Eventually, James Clerk Maxwell developed equations that showed how light and other electromagnetic radiation could be described as waves propagated by an interchange of energy between periodically varying electric and magnetic fields. These wave phenomena, together with Maxwell's equations, seemed to establish the wave model as the correct one for light.

Particle Phenomena—The Photoelectric Effect

Near the end of the 19th century, new observations cast doubt on the wave model of light. Among these observations was the discovery that light could cause certain metals to emit electrons, a phenomenon called the **photoelectric effect.** Albert Einstein explained this phenomenon in 1905. Experiments with the photoelectric effect resulted in observations that could not be explained by the wave theory of light.

Figure 5-1a shows an apparatus for investigating the photoelectric effect. The apparatus can be used for measuring the relative number of electrons emitted by a photosensitive metal as the light striking it is varied. The ammeter measures the current flowing in the circuit. Because the current is the rate of flow of charge, and each electron has the same amount of charge, the current measures the rate at which electrons are being emitted. Figure 5-1b is a graph of the current that flows as the brightness, or intensity, of the light is varied. The graphs shows that the current, or number of electrons emitted per unit of time, is proportional to the light intensity, provided the frequency of the light is above a certain minimum value.

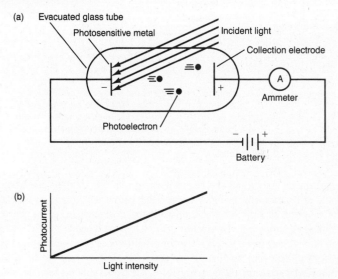

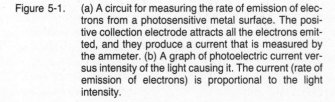

Figure 5-1. (a) A circuit for measuring the rate of emission of electrons from a photosensitive metal surface. The positive collection electrode attracts all the electrons emitted, and they produce a current that is measured by the ammeter. (b) A graph of photoelectric current versus intensity of the light causing it. The current (rate of emission of electrons) is proportional to the light intensity.

This result in itself is not surprising and can be explained by a wave theory of light. However, when the maximum kinetic energy of the emitted electrons is determined, the results are unexpected. A way of measuring the maximum kinetic energy of the emitted electrons is shown in Figure 5-2. The apparatus in Figure 5-2 is similar to that in Figure 5-1a, except that a source of variable potential difference (variable voltage) is substituted for the battery, and this source is connected so that the collection electrode is negative instead of positive, as it was in Figure 5-1a. This electrode, called a stopping electrode when it is positive, now repels electrons that approach it. As the stopping electrode is made more negative, there is a greater force of Coulomb repulsion between it and the electrons emitted from the photosensitive metal. This repulsion causes the slower electrons to stop moving toward the electrode before they reach it.

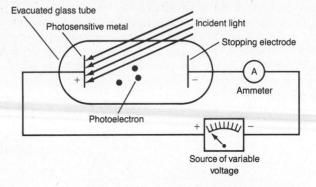

Figure 5-2. The same experimental setup as that shown in Figure 5-1a except that the battery has been replaced by a source of variable voltage and the stopping electrode has been given a negative, rather than positive, charge. The stopping electrode now repels oncoming electrons.

By gradually increasing the negative charge on the stopping electrode, a potential difference will finally be reached that causes the current, as measured by the ammeter, to drop to zero. At this potential difference, even the fastest of the emitted electrons lack the kinetic energy they would need to make it all the way to the stopping electrode. Since potential difference is a measure of energy, the potential difference that causes the current to drop to zero can be used to determine the maximum kinetic energy of the electrons emitted from the photosensitive metal.

Figure 5-3 is a graph showing the maximum kinetic energy of the electrons, for a given metal and a given light source, plotted against the intensity of the light. Contrary to what one might expect, the maximum kinetic energies of the electrons are not affected by the intensity of the light. That is, the maximum kinetic energy is constant as the light intensity is varied. The wave theory of light predicts that the maximum energy should increase as the light intensity increases.

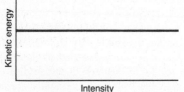

Figure 5-3. A graph of the maximum kinetic energy of the photo-electrons emitted versus intensity of the light causing the emission. The maximum kinetic energy is constant (independent of the light intensity) for a given light source.

Another important observation is that no electrons are emitted by the photosensitive metal, no matter how intense the incident light, unless the *frequency* of the light is greater than a certain lower limit called the **threshold frequency,** f_0. This observation does not agree with the wave theory, which predicts that light

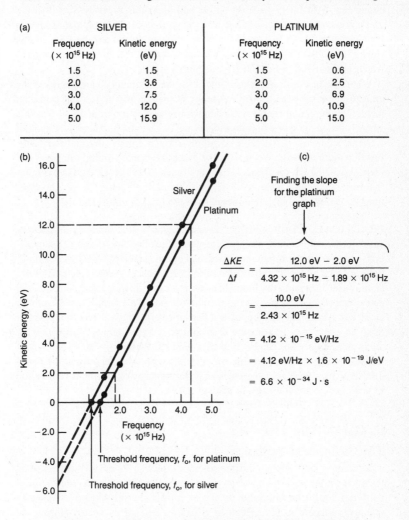

(a)

SILVER		PLATINUM	
Frequency ($\times 10^{15}$ Hz)	Kinetic energy (eV)	Frequency ($\times 10^{15}$ Hz)	Kinetic energy (eV)
1.5	1.5	1.5	0.6
2.0	3.6	2.0	2.5
3.0	7.5	3.0	6.9
4.0	12.0	4.0	10.9
5.0	15.9	5.0	15.0

(b)

(c) Finding the slope for the platinum graph

$$\frac{\Delta KE}{\Delta f} = \frac{12.0 \text{ eV} - 2.0 \text{ eV}}{4.32 \times 10^{15} \text{ Hz} - 1.89 \times 10^{15} \text{ Hz}}$$

$$= \frac{10.0 \text{ eV}}{2.43 \times 10^{15} \text{ Hz}}$$

$$= 4.12 \times 10^{-15} \text{ eV/Hz}$$

$$= 4.12 \text{ eV/Hz} \times 1.6 \times 10^{-19} \text{ J/eV}$$

$$= 6.6 \times 10^{-34} \text{ J} \cdot \text{s}$$

Threshold frequency, f_o, for platinum

Threshold frequency, f_o, for silver

Figure 5-4.   (a) Tables of laboratory data for two photosensitive metals, showing the frequency of incident light and the kinetic energy of electrons emitted from the metals. (b) Graphs plotted from the data. (c) Calculation of the slope of the platinum line. For all metals graphed in this manner, the lines have the same slope: 6.6×10^{-34} J $\cdot$ s

of *any* frequency should cause the emission of at least some electrons, if the intensity is great enough. It is also observed that as the frequency of the incident light increases above f_0, the maximum kinetic energy of the emitted electrons increases. Figure 5-4b is a graph of maximum electron energy versus frequency of incident light for two metals, silver and platinum. It can be seen that the graph in each case is a straight line with the same slope. The graph of maximum kinetic energy versus frequency for any other metal would also be a line of this slope. The slope of the line equals a natural constant called *Planck's constant*, which is discussed in Section II, Quantum Theory.

Where the line crosses the horizontal axis, the maximum kinetic energy of the emitted electrons is zero. The frequency at that point is f_0 for that particular metal. The minimum energy needed to remove an electron from the surface of a metal is called the **work function** of the metal. The graph indicates the light of a frequency below f_0 is unable to supply enough energy to equal that work function and remove an electron. If the graph is extended until it intersects the vertical axis, the intercept equals the work function for that metal. For example, the work function of silver is 4.7 eV, and that of platinum is 5.6 eV. The work function is discussed in greater detail in Section II, Quantum Theory.

PRACTICAL APPLICATION

An "electric eye" makes use of the photoelectric effect for a variety of applications. In these applications, a photosensitive surface is exposed to a beam of light. As long as the light strikes the surface, it produces a small electric current. If an object interrupts the beam, the current stops flowing, and other circuits detect this change and activate some other device. For example, the closing of an elevator door may be stopped if a person entering the car blocks a beam of light; an alarm may be sounded if an intruder enters a home; objects moving along an assembly line can be counted; smoke can cause a fire alarm to sound if it dims the light in a smoke detector. The photoelectric effect can also be used directly to measure light intensity in an exposure meter or automatic camera and to generate electrical energy in a solar cell. ■

II. QUANTUM THEORY

The Quantum of Radiation

Einstein's explanation of the photoelectric effect, given in 1905, depended on the quantum theory, which was proposed in 1900 by Max Planck. Planck originally developed the **quantum theory** to explain the distribution of intensity (energy) observed in the spectra of radiations emitted by heated objects. To explain these observations (which the classical wave theory of light had failed to predict), Planck made the assumption that atoms could not emit electromagnetic radiation in a continuous stream but only in discrete amounts, or packets, of energy. Each such packet of energy is called a **quantum** (plural, *quanta*) of energy. Planck stated that the amount of energy, E, of each quantum is directly proportional to the frequency, f, of the radiation. For example, a quantum of blue (higher frequency) light contains more energy than a quantum of red (lower frequency) light. The constant of proportionality between the energy of the quantum and its frequency is **Planck's constant,** h. Thus the energy of each quantum is given by

$$E = hf \qquad \text{(Eq. 5-1)}$$

where E is the energy of one quantum of electromagnetic radiation of frequency f. If E is given in joules and f in hertz, the unit of h is the joule · second. The value of h is extremely small: 6.6×10^{-34} joule · second. A quantum of visible light (for which f equals approximately 10^{15} Hz) thus has an energy of about 6×10^{-19} J, or about 6 eV.

Photons. Quanta of electromagnetic energy are called **photons.** The photon is thought of as a "particle" of light having energy and momentum. Photon energy can be given by Equation 5-1, but since $f = c/\lambda$ for light in a vacuum, it can also be given as

$$E_{\text{photon}} = \frac{hc}{\lambda} \qquad \text{(Eq. 5-1a)}$$

Thus, the energy of a photon is inversely proportional to its wavelength and directly proportional to its frequency.

In explaining the photoelectric effect, Einstein assumed that electromagnetic radiation is not only *emitted* as photons but is also *received* as separate photons. That is, each photon interacts individually with an atom of the receiving substance. In the interaction, part of the photon's energy is used in releasing an electron from the material; the remainder is converted to kinetic energy of the released electron.

Photoelectric Equation

By applying the law of conservation of energy to the interaction between a photon and the surface on which it is incident, Einstein developed an equation, called the **photoelectric equation,** that relates the maximum kinetic energy, KE_{max}, of the ejected photoelectrons to the energy, hf, of the incoming photons. The equation is

$$KE_{\text{max}} = hf - W_0 \qquad \text{(Eq. 5-2)}$$

where W_0, called the work function, is the minimum energy required to release an electron from the surface of the material and is constant for a given material.

Thus, if the energy, hf, of an incident photon is 5 eV, and the work function, W_0, of the given material is 2 eV, then the maximum kinetic energy of the photoelectron is 5 eV $-$ 2 eV $=$ 3 eV. If the photon energy were greater, 7 eV for example, then the maximum kinetic energy of the photoelectrons would be 7 eV $-$ 2 eV $=$ 5 eV. Illuminated by light of a given frequency, materials with lower work functions produce photoelectrons with higher maximum kinetic energies. For example, if metal A has a work function $W_A = 2$ eV and metal B has a work function $W_B = 3$ eV, then a photon of energy $hf = 6$ eV would release photoelectrons having a $KE_{\text{max}} = 6$ eV $-$ 2 eV $=$ 4 eV from metal A and a $KE_{\text{max}} = 6$ eV $-$ 3 eV $=$ 3 eV from metal B.

Since f_0 is the minimum frequency of radiation that can release an electron from a surface, it follows that

$$W_0 = hf_0 \qquad \text{(Eq. 5-3)}$$

and Equation 5-2 can be written as

$$KE_{max} = hf - hf_0, \quad \text{or}$$

$$KE_{max} = h(f - f_0) \qquad \text{(Eq. 5-4)}$$

Photon-Particle Collisions (The Compton Effect)

In the photoelectric effect, the energy of an incident photon is completely absorbed and transferred to the emitted electron. In 1922, Arthur Compton found that when photons of x rays (which have much higher frequencies and energies than visible light) strike a surface, not only are electrons ejected, but electromagnetic radiation of lower frequency is also given off. Compton interpreted this effect as a collision between an x-ray photon and an electron, in which some of the energy of the photon is transferred to the electron, but the photon then recoils with less energy and therefore as radiation of lower frequency, as illustrated in Figure 5-5. Careful measurements show that both energy (a scalar quantity) and momentum (a vector quantity) are conserved in this interaction, just as they are in collisions of particles. The incident photon loses energy and momentum, while the electron gains energy and momentum.

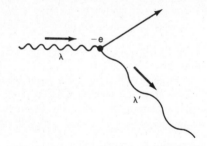

Figure 5-5. The effect of a collision between an x-ray photon of very high energy and an electron in an atom. Besides the electron ejected from the atom, a photon of lower energy (longer wavelength) is also emitted (scattered) by the atom. The energy transferred to the electron equals the difference in energy between the incident photon and the scattered photon. The vector sum of the momentum of the electron and the scattered photon also equals the momentum of the incident photon.

The Momentum of a Photon

Although no particles with mass can travel at the speed of light, c, photons always travel at this speed. Photons are therefore assumed to have zero "rest mass," but they do have energy and momentum at the speed of light. It can be shown that the momentum of a photon is given by the equation

$$p = \frac{E}{c}$$

where E is the photon energy in joules, c is the speed of light in meters/second, and p is the photon momentum in kilogram $\cdot$ meters/second. Since $c = f\lambda$, and $E = hf$, we can write

$$p = \frac{E}{c} = \frac{hf}{f\lambda}, \quad \text{or}$$

$$p = \frac{h}{\lambda} \qquad \textbf{(Eq. 5-5)}$$

and since $\lambda = c/f$,

$$p = \frac{hf}{c} \qquad \text{(Eq. 5-5a)}$$

Because h in Equation 5-5 is a constant, and both h and c are constants in Equation 5-5a, these equations show that the momentum of a photon depends only on its wavelength or frequency.

Matter Waves

Louis de Broglie theorized in 1924 that, just as radiation has both wave and particle characteristics, matter in motion has wave as well as particle characteristics. As shown by Equation 5-5, the momentum of a photon is given by the equation $p = h/\lambda$. The equation for the wavelength of a photon is thus $\lambda = h/p$. The momentum of a particle of mass m traveling at velocity v is given by $p = mv$. By analogy, the de Broglie wavelength of a particle is given by

$$\lambda = \frac{h}{p} \qquad \textbf{(Eq. 5-6)}$$

or

$$\lambda = \frac{h}{mv} \qquad \text{(Eq. 5-6a)}$$

EXAMPLE

Calculate the de Broglie wavelengths of (a) an electron that is traveling at 1.0×10^7 meters per second and (b) a 0.40-kilogram baseball that has a speed of 30. meters per second.

Solution

(a) $\lambda = \dfrac{h}{mv} = \dfrac{6.6 \times 10^{-34} \text{ J} \cdot \text{s}}{(9.1 \times 10^{-31} \text{ kg})(1.0 \times 10^7 \text{ m/s})} = 7.3 \times 10^{-11} \text{ m}$

(This wavelength is in the x-ray range and is detectable.)

(b) $\lambda = \dfrac{h}{mv} = \dfrac{6.6 \times 10^{-34} \text{ J} \cdot \text{s}}{(4.0 \times 10^{-1} \text{ kg})(3.0 \times 10^1 \text{ m/s})} = 5.5 \times 10^{-35} \text{ m}$

(This wavelength is so small that there is no means to detect it.)

As illustrated by the example on the preceding page, the waves associated with the motion of the ordinary objects of daily experience have wavelengths far too small to be noticed, or even detected by experimental means. On the other hand, for particles of atomic or subatomic size, such wave phenomena as diffraction and interference *can* be observed.

The predicted wave properties of electrons were demonstrated in 1927 by Davisson and Germer, who produced interference patterns with beams of electrons. The measured wavelengths agreed with de Broglie's predictions. Since then, the wave properties of other subatomic particles (protons, neutrons, and so on) have also been observed.

PRACTICAL APPLICATION

Optical microscopes can detect details comparable in size to the wavelength of the light used in illuminating an object. In the electron microscope, electrons are accelerated to very high kinetic energies and have wavelengths 100 times shorter than those of visible light used in an ordinary optical microscope. In the electron microscope, a beam of electrons is directed at a slice of material approximately 10^{-8} m thick in a vacuum chamber to minimize scattering of electrons and blurring of the image. The electron beam is focused by a magnetic field on a fluorescent screen to yield magnifications of 100,000 times or more. ∎

QUESTIONS

1. In the photoelectric effect, photoelectrons may be removed from a metallic surface by means of (1) an electron beam (2) electromagnetic radiation (3) alpha particles (4) high temperature

2. During collisions between x-ray photons and electrons, there is conservation of (1) momentum, but not energy (2) energy, but not momentum (3) neither momentum nor energy (4) both momentum and energy

3. Which color of visible light has the greatest quantum energy? (1) blue (2) green (3) yellow (4) orange

4. The maximum kinetic energy of electrons emitted from a photosensitive surface can be increased by increasing the (1) frequency of the incident light (2) intensity of the incident light (3) area of the surface (4) work function of the photosensitive material

5. The photon model of light is more appropriate than the wave model in explaining the phenomenon of (1) interference (2) refraction (3) polarization (4) photoelectric emission

6. The energy of a photon that has a frequency of 3.0×10^{13} hertz is (1) 2.2×10^{-48} J (2) 2.2×10^{-46} J (3) 6.6×10^{-34} J (4) 2.0×10^{-20} J

7. Light falls on a photoelectric material and no electrons are emitted. Electrons may be emitted if the (1) intensity of the light is decreased (2) intensity of the light is increased (3) frequency of the light is decreased (4) frequency of the light is increased

8. What is the frequency of a photon that has 6.6×10^{-19} joule of energy? (1) 3.0×10^{15} Hz (2) 1.0×10^{15} Hz (3) 3.0×10^{-7} Hz (4) 1.0×10^{-5} Hz

9. The energy of a photon that has a frequency of 3.0×10^{14} hertz is approximately (1) 2.0×10^{-48} J (2) 2.0×10^{-19} J (3) 5.0×10^{-19} J (4) 5.0×10^{48} J

10. When photons that have an energy equal to 3.0 electronvolts strike a photoelectric surface, the maximum kinetic energy of the photoelectrons that are emitted is equal to 2.0 electronvolts. What is the value of the work function of the surface? (1) 1.0 eV (2) 0.67 eV (3) 1.5 eV (4) 5.0 eV

11. Interference experiments demonstrate (1) the particle nature of light (2) polarization of light (3) intensity of light (4) the wave nature of light

12. Which property of incident radiation striking a photosensitive surface determines the rate at which the surface emits photoelectrons? (1) frequency (2) intensity (3) velocity (4) wavelength

13. Which graph best represents the energy of a photon as a function of its frequency?

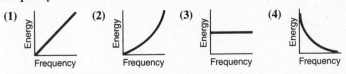

14. Which property of light incident on a photoelectric surface determines the number of electrons emitted per second by the surface? (1) intensity (2) color (3) frequency (4) wavelength

15. Which graph best represents the relationship between the wavelength and the momentum of a photon?

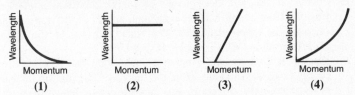

16. As the frequency of a photon increases, its momentum (1) decreases (2) increases (3) remains the same

17. As the intensity of monochromatic light (light consisting of only one wavelength) incident on a photosensitive surface increases, the maximum velocity of the electrons ejected from the surface (1) decreases (2) increases (3) remains the same

18. As the frequency of electromagnetic radiation increases, the energy of the corresponding quanta (1) decreases (2) increases (3) remains the same

19. As the momentum of photons in a vacuum increases, the speed of the photons (1) decreases (2) increases (3) remains the same

20. As the frequency of radiation used to eject photoelectrons from a surface increases, the voltage needed to stop these electrons (1) decreases (2) increases (3) remains the same

21. As the momentum of a particle exhibiting wave properties increases, the wavelength of the particle (1) decreases (2) increases (3) remains the same

22–23. Base your answers to Questions 22 and 23 on the following information.

   Monochromatic light strikes a metal surface that has a work function of 6.7×10^{-19} joule. Each photon has an energy of 8.0×10^{-19} joule.

22. What is the maximum kinetic energy of the photoelectrons emitted by the metal? (1) 1.3×10^{-19} J (2) 2.6×10^{-19} J (3) 6.7×10^{-19} J (4) 8.0×10^{19} J

23. What is the energy of each photon expressed in electronvolts? (1) 5.4×10^{-37} eV (2) 1.6×10^{-19} eV (3) 8.0×10^{-19} eV (4) 5.0 eV

24–28. Base your answers to Questions 24 through 28 on the graph, which represents the relationship between the maximum photoelectron kinetic energy and the frequency of the incident radiation for four target metals A, B, C, and D.

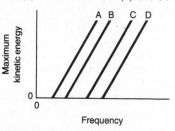

24. Which metal has the highest threshold frequency? (1) A (2) B (3) C (4) D

25. Photons having 4.2 electronvolts of energy produced photoelectric emission from metal B. If the maximum energy of the emitted photoelectrons is 2.5 electronvolts, the work function of the metal is (1) 1.7 eV (2) 3.5 eV (3) 4.2 eV (4) 6.7 eV

26. Metal B is illuminated by monochromatic light that has just enough energy to release electrons from the surface. Compared to the energy of electrons emitted from B, this monochromatic light will cause the emission of electrons from (1) metal A with less energy (2) metal A with more energy (3) metal C with less energy (4) metal D with more energy

27. If the wavelength of the radiation in Question 26 is increased, it may produce photoelectric emission from (1) A, B, C, and D (2) A and B, but not C and D (3) C and D, but not A or B (4) A, but not B, C, or D

28. If a single source of monochromatic light causes photoelectric emission from all four metals, electrons will be emitted with (1) maximum energy from A (2) maximum energy from B (3) maximum energy from C (4) maximum energy from D

29. The energy of a photon that has a frequency of 6×10^{14} hertz is approximately equal to (1) 7×10^{-34} J (2) 1×10^{-24} J (3) 4×10^{-19} J (4) 4×10^{48} J

30. When light shines on a photoelectric surface, the maximum energy of the emitted photoelectrons depends upon the light's (1) intensity (2) frequency (3) speed (4) amplitude

31–35. Base your answers to Questions 31 through 35 on the following information.

Four different sources of electromagnetic radiation, A, B, C, and D, are used successively to illuminate a photoemissive metal. These sources produce photoelectrons whose maximum kinetic energies are 1.0, 2.0, 3.0, and 4.0 electronvolts, respectively.

31. In this experiment, the source that produces the radiation with the longest wavelength is (1) A (2) B (3) C (4) D

32. Each photon from source B has an energy of 3.0 electronvolts. The work function of the metal is (1) 1.0 eV (2) 2.0 eV (3) 3.0 eV (4) 4.0 eV

33. When source C is used, the maximum kinetic energy of the emitted photoelectrons is (1) 1.6×10^{-19} J (2) 3.0×10^{-19} J (3) 4.8×10^{-19} J (4) 5.3×10^{-20} J

34. As the intensity of source A increases, the maximum kinetic energy of the emitted photoelectrons (1) decreases (2) increases (3) remains the same

35. If a metal with a lower work function is used in the experiment, the maximum kinetic energy of the photoelectrons produced by each source will (1) decrease (2) increase (3) remain the same

36–40. Base your answers to Questions 36 through 40 on the following information.

In the diagram, a photon beam is incident on photoemissive surface A. B represents the particle emitted as a photon strikes the surface.

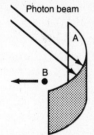
Photon beam
A
B

36. The particle emitted as a result of the photoelectric effect is (1) a proton (2) a photon (3) a neutron (4) an electron

37. If the wavelength of the incident photons is 6.0×10^{-7} meter, the color of the beam is (1) blue (2) green (3) yellow (4) orange

38. If the frequency of the incident photon is 5.0×10^{14} hertz, its energy is (1) 3.3×10^{-19} J (2) 6.0×10^{-7} J (3) 8.0×10^{47} J (4) 3.0×10^{48} J

39. As the frequency of incident photons is increased, the energy of emitted particles (1) decreases (2) increases (3) remains the same

40. As the intensity of incident photons is increased, the rate of emission of particles (1) decreases (2) increases (3) remains the same

41. **At constant photon energies, as the work function of the surface increases, the maximum kinetic energy of emitted photoelectrons** (1) decreases (2) increases (3) remains the same

42. **Which graph best represents the relationship between photon momentum (p) and wavelength (λ)?**

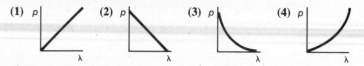

43. **The wave characteristics of a batted ball cannot be observed because** (1) its matter waves are too long (2) its matter waves are too short (3) its speed is too large (4) the ball is made up of matter rather than energy

III. MODELS OF THE ATOM

Rutherford Model of the Atom

At the same time that Planck and Einstein were studying the nature of radiation, other scientists were developing new theories about the nature of matter. In 1897, it was discovered that electrons are relatively low-mass, negatively charged particles present in atoms. This meant that part of the atom must also possess a positive charge equal to that of the electrons, because atoms are electrically neutral. In a model of the atom proposed by J. J. Thomson, the atom consisted of a uniform distribution of positive charge in which electrons were embedded, like raisins in rice pudding. In 1911, from results of scattering experiments involving *alpha particles,* Ernest Rutherford discovered how the positive charge is actually distributed in an atom.

Alpha Particles. Shortly after the discovery of radioactivity in 1895, Rutherford was able to show that radioactive emissions are of three kinds, which he named *alpha, beta,* and *gamma,* the first three letters in the Greek alphabet. **Alpha particles** were later found to be helium atoms with their electrons removed. That is, an alpha particle consists of a helium nucleus, or two protons and two neutrons. Upon emission from such radioactive elements as radium, these relatively massive, positively charged particles travel at approximately $\frac{1}{10}$ the speed of light, and they range in kinetic energy from 4.5 to 9.0 MeV (million electronvolts).

Alpha-Particle Scattering. Rutherford directed a beam of alpha particles at extremely thin gold foil. If the atoms were like those described in Thomson's model, there would be only small forces on an alpha particle passing through or near an atom, because the Coulomb forces of the positive and negative charges acting on the alpha particle would mainly cancel out, as illustrated in Figure 5-6.

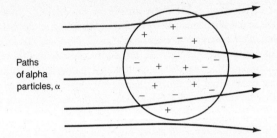

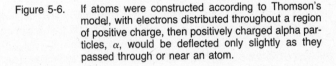

Paths of alpha particles, α

Figure 5-6.   If atoms were constructed according to Thomson's model, with electrons distributed throughout a region of positive charge, then positively charged alpha particles, α, would be deflected only slightly as they passed through or near an atom.

Rutherford observed that only about 1 alpha particle in 5,000 was deflected from its straight-line path. That is, most of the particles were not deflected even by a small amount. A small fraction of the particles, however, were scattered at large angles, some back toward the source at angles of nearly 180°, as shown in Figure 5-7.

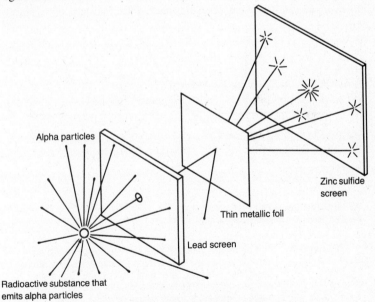

Alpha particles

Zinc sulfide screen

Thin metallic foil

Lead screen

Radioactive substance that emits alpha particles

Figure 5-7.   The large angles of deflection observed for a small fraction of the alpha particles directed toward a thin metal foil in Rutherford's experiments.

From the angles at which the alpha particles were deflected, Rutherford decided that the scattering of such massive and energetic particles must be due to collision with other even more massive particles having a large positive charge. Assuming that atoms are symmetrical, he had to conclude that this concentration of mass and positive charge, which he called the *nucleus,* is located at the center of the atom. From the relative number of alpha particles deflected, he calculated that the nucleus is only about ¹⁄₁₀,₀₀₀ the diameter of the average atom.

Trajectories of Alpha Particles. Since the nucleus of the atom, according to Rutherford's model, occupies an extremely small part of the atom's volume, very few alpha particles will approach a nucleus head-on. Even if one did, the particle would not have enough momentum to reach the nucleus and collide with it. It would be stopped before hitting the nucleus and would then return along the line of its approach. Alpha particles that pass close to a nucleus will be repelled by the Coulomb force because both alpha particles and the nucleus are positively charged. Rutherford calculated the trajectories, or paths, that the alpha particles will follow as their motion is changed by this force. He found that the trajectories will always be curves of the type called *hyperbolas,* as shown in Figure 5-8. The trajectories are therefore described as **hyperbolic.**

The "Solar System" Model of the Atom. Based on the results of his "gold-foil" experiments, Rutherford described atoms as being similar to miniature solar systems. The "sun" was a tiny nucleus that contained all the positive

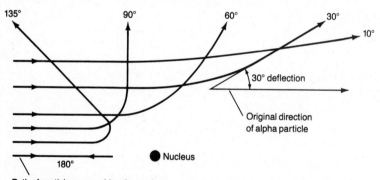

Figure 5-8.   The paths of alpha particles as they pass through an atom in a thin metal foil. Alpha particles, which are positively charged, are repelled by the positively charged nuclei of atoms in the foil. Because atoms are made up mostly of empty space, however, most of the alpha particles pass through the foil at relatively large distances from any of the nuclei in the foil and are scarcely deflected. This illustration depicts those few that pass relatively close to a nucleus and are deflected by relatively large angles.

charge of the atom and virtually all of its mass. This was surrounded by enough electrons to balance the positive charge of the nucleus, thus giving the atom as a whole electric neutrality. In the Rutherford atom, illustrated in Figure 5-9, the electrons were held in the atom by the Coulomb force of attraction that existed between their negative charge and the positive charge of the nucleus. This is essentially the modern view of atomic structure, except that the idea of electrons as particles in orbits has been replaced by a more complex description.

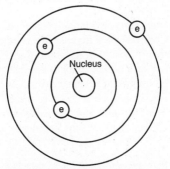

Figure 5-9.   Rutherford's planetary model of the atom. Electrons revolve in orbits around the nucleus, just as the planets revolve around the sun. The model was later modified to allow more than one electron to be present in the same orbit, or shell.

Limitations of Rutherford's Model.   According to the well-established theory of electromagnetic radiation, an accelerating charge should generate an electromagnetic field and radiate energy. In Rutherford's model of the atom, the electrons are traveling around the nucleus, held in their orbits by the Coulomb force of attraction of the positive charge of the nucleus. Their motion is therefore accelerated, since change in direction of motion is an acceleration. These accelerated charges should radiate electromagnetic energy, lose kinetic energy and momentum in the process, and spiral rapidly into the nucleus.

Atoms built according to Rutherford's model could not exist for longer than one hundred-millionth of a second. In addition, the electrons would have to emit a burst of electromagnetic energy of increasing frequency and a continuous spectrum as they were drawn into the nucleus. This conclusion contradicted the observed bright-line spectrum that was characteristic of, and different for, each element. Bright–line spectra are discussed in Section IV, Atomic Spectra.

Bohr Model of the Hydrogen Atom

In 1913, Niels Bohr proposed a model of atomic structure that attempted to explain why atoms are stable—that is, why electrons can maintain their positions outside the nucleus, rather than spiraling into the nucleus and thus causing the atom to collapse. Bohr concentrated his attention on the hydrogen atom— the simplest atom, consisting of a nucleus with a single elementary unit of positive charge and a single electron revolving about it. Bohr assumed, to begin with, that the orbit of the electron is a circle with the nucleus at its center. He then built a model of the hydrogen atom based on these additional assumptions:

1. Just as all electromagnetic energy is quantized, all other forms of energy are also quantized. In particular, an electron can gain or lose kinetic energy only in fixed amounts, that is, in quanta.
2. The electron in the hydrogen atom can occupy only certain specific orbits of fixed radius and no others.
3. The electron can jump from one orbit to a higher one by absorbing a quantum of energy. If it later falls back from the higher orbit to the lower, it gives off the same quantum of energy in the form of a photon.
4. Each allowed orbit in the atom corresponds to a specific amount of energy. The orbit nearest the nucleus represents the smallest amount of energy that the electron can have. Since there is no lower-energy orbit it can go to, the electron can remain in this orbit without losing energy, even though it is being constantly accelerated toward the nucleus by the Coulomb force of attraction.

When the electron is in any particular orbit, it is said to be in a **stationary state.** Each stationary state represents a specific quantity of energy and is therefore also called an **energy level.** The successive energy levels of an atom are assigned integral numbers called **principal quantum numbers,** represented by n, starting with 1 as the principal quantum number of the lowest energy level. When the electron is in its lowest energy level ($n = 1$), it is said to be in the **ground state.** For a hydrogen atom, an electron in any level above the ground state is said to be in an **excited state.**

Energy Levels. It should be noted that a photon's energy will be absorbed by an electron in an atom only if it corresponds exactly to an energy-level difference possible for the electron. The existence of such energy levels in atoms was demonstrated in 1914 by J. Franck and G. Hertz. They projected a beam of electrons of known energy into mercury vapor and found that atoms of mercury interacted with the electrons. The atoms absorbed energy only if the electrons had certain definite amounts of kinetic energy. When the mercury atoms did absorb energy, they then emitted electromagnetic radiation whose photon wavelength corresponded exactly to the energy given up by the electrons during their collisions with the mercury atoms. The energy absorbed by the mercury atoms raised the energy level of the electrons in the atoms.

Any process that raises the energy level of electrons in an atom is called **excitation.** Excitation can be the result of absorbing the energy of colliding particles of matter, such as electrons, or of photons of electromagnetic radiation. Different elements have different excitation energies. Atoms rapidly emit the energy of their various excited states in the form of photons of specific frequencies as their electrons return to the ground state.

Ionization Potential. The energy needed to remove an electron completely from an atom (that is, to form an ion from an atom) is called the **ionization potential.** For example, the ionization potential of a hydrogen atom is

13.60 eV, which means that this much energy will remove an electron completely from a hydrogen atom in its ground state. For an atom in an excited state, a correspondingly smaller amount of energy is required to ionize it.

Figure 5-10 shows some of the energy levels of the hydrogen atom. The energy levels have negative values because the energy level of an electron that has been completely removed from an atom is *defined* to be zero. As an electron moves closer and closer to the nucleus, its energy becomes smaller and smaller. If the energy of an electron that has been completely removed from the atom is zero, then the energies of all electrons within the atom must be negative. Because an electron in the ground state has the least energy of all, its energy has the largest negative value. Similar energy-level diagrams exist for other elements. Compare the energy-level diagram for hydrogen in Figure 5-10 with the energy-level diagram for mercury in Figure 5-11.

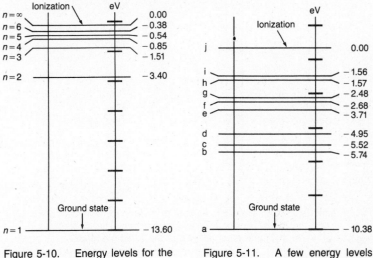

Figure 5-10.   Energy levels for the hydrogen atom.

Figure 5-11.   A few energy levels for the mercury atom.

Standing Waves

While Bohr assumed that an electron in a hydrogen atom could occupy orbits of only certain sizes, it was several years before anyone was able to explain why this should be so. In 1924, de Broglie related his theory of the wave character of particles to the Bohr model by proposing that an electron orbit could be stable only if it contained an integral multiple of electron wavelengths because in other orbits destructive interference would occur. The electron can be located only at specific distances from the nucleus that will yield an orbit that has a circumference corresponding to an integral number of de Broglie wavelengths. An electron in such an orbit is in a standing wave about the nucleus and does not lose energy. Standing-wave patterns for an electron in various stable orbits of hydrogen are shown in Figure 5-12. In each case, the number of de Broglie wavelengths corresponds to the principal quantum number.

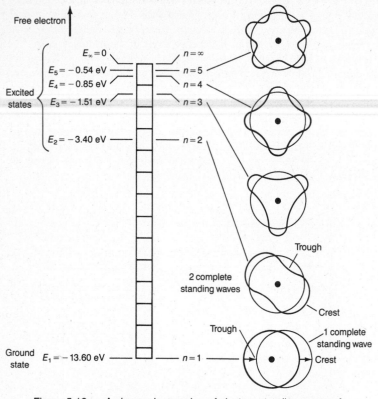

Figure 5-12. An increasing number of electron standing waves of de Broglie wavelengths can occupy successively higher energy levels of the hydrogen atom.

Limitations of the Bohr Model

Although the Bohr model was successful in explaining certain properties of the hydrogen atom, it failed to explain which of the spectral lines of hydrogen should be brightest and which should be dimmest. Bohr's model also did not account for the pairs of very closely spaced spectral lines observed in the hydrogen spectrum. The major weakness of the theory was its inability to predict the spectra or explain the electron orbits of elements having many electrons.

IV. ATOMIC SPECTRA

When the atoms of an element in the gaseous state are excited, they give off a specific series of frequencies of electromagnetic radiation called the **atomic spectrum** of the element. Each element has a characteristic spectrum that is different from those of all other elements. Thus, the spectrum can be used to identify the element, even when the element is mixed with other elements.

CAN YOU EXPLAIN THIS? ===========================

Helium was found in the sun before it was found on the earth.

Evidence of the existence of helium was first obtained by studies of the spectrum of the sun's corona during the solar eclipse of 1868. Spectral lines not previously reported for any known element appeared in the corona. It was assumed that the sun contained an element that had not yet been isolated on the earth. The name *helium* was given to the element (from *helios,* the Greek word for sun). In 1895, an element with spectral lines identical to those observed in 1868 in the sun's corona was isolated from a mineral in the earth's crust. This element was thus shown to be helium, the element previously discovered in the sun.

Emission (Bright-Line) Spectra

The energy levels of the Bohr atom provided an explanation for atomic spectra. Because electrons can have many different energy levels in an atom, a large number of energy differences are possible. When an electron in an atom in an excited state falls to a lower energy level, the emitted photon energy is given by the formula

$$E_{photon} = E_i - E_f \qquad \text{(Eq. 5-7)}$$

where E_i is the initial energy of the electron in its excited state, and E_f is the final energy of the electron at the lower level. Each energy difference between two energy levels corresponds to a photon of specific frequency. Thus, a set of frequencies characteristic of each atom is produced when the electrons of an atom in an excited state fall back to lower states or to the ground state. When viewed in a spectroscope, an **emission spectrum** appears as a series of bright lines against a dark background and is therefore also called a **bright-line spectrum.**

In the visible part of the emission spectrum of hydrogen gas, there is a series of variously spaced, bright, colored lines called the **Balmer series,** in honor of J. Balmer, who in 1885 devised an empirical formula relating their wavelengths. Calculations based on the Bohr atom model were able to give the correct frequencies of these lines, which confirmed Bohr's theory. In addition, the calculations predicted the existence of other series of lines in the infrared and ultraviolet regions. The Balmer series was shown to be due to photons emitted by the transitions of electrons from higher energy states to the $n = 2$ level, which is one level above the ground state. The Balmer series consists of visible spectral lines of red, green, and violet, as well as lines in the ultraviolet region. The other predicted lines are produced when the excited atoms of hydrogen return to either the ground state, producing the *Lyman series* in the ultraviolet, or to the third, fourth, or fifth energy levels, producing three series of infrared lines. These three series are called the *Paschen, Brackett,* and *Pfund series,* respectively. The energy emissions producing the various series of lines are indicated in the energy-level diagram for hydrogen that is shown in Figure 5-13.

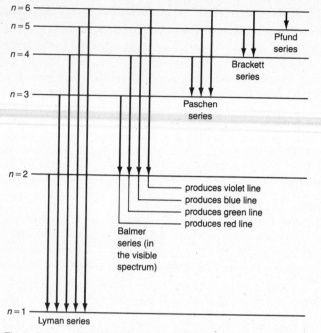

Figure 5-13. The relationship between possible electron energy-state transitions in the hydrogen atom and the observed series of wavelengths in the hydrogen spectrum.

Absorption Spectra

As previously explained, atoms can *absorb* photons whose energies correspond to differences in energy levels in the atom. The frequencies and wavelengths of these photons are exactly the same as those of the photons *emitted* when electrons fall between the same levels. Consequently, under certain conditions, if light of all frequencies (white light) is supplied to an element, the atoms will selectively absorb the same frequencies that they can emit when excited. These absorbed frequencies appear as dark lines in the white-light spectrum. Such a spectrum is therefore called an **absorption spectrum.** Note that an atom will absorb a photon only if the photon energy is *exactly* the amount needed to raise the atom to one of its possible excited states. Photons having intermediate energies will not excite the atom and will not be absorbed by it. (Photons having sufficient energy to ionize the atom by completely removing an electron *will* be absorbed, however. In this case, any excess energy of the photon will appear as kinetic energy of the ejected electron. This is, of course, the photoelectric effect discussed at the start of this unit.)

In both the release of photons that produces an emission spectrum and the absorption of photons that produces a dark-line absorption spectrum, the frequency of the photon emitted or absorbed agrees with Equation 5-1 ($E = hf$).

PRACTICAL APPLICATION

An incandescent light bulb contains a tungsten filament and a mixture of argon and nitrogen. Electricity heats the filament to roughly 2900 K and more than 95% of the resulting radiation is in the form of heat, rather than light. On the other hand, a fluorescent lamp consists of a low-pressure mercury arc within a glass tube having an inner coating of a *phosphor*, whose electrons absorb the energy in ultraviolent rays. As these electrons drop back to lower energy levels, they re-radiate the energy in the visible range of the spectrum, with very little radiated in the infrared or ultraviolet regions. ■

Cloud Model of the Atom

In 1926, E. Schrödinger presented a strict mathematical interpretation of de Broglie's wave concept, called *quantum mechanics* or *wave mechanics*. The waves in Schrödinger's theory represent the *probability* of finding an electron in a particular region of the atom. The electrons are therefore not confined to specific orbits, as in Bohr's original model, but may be considered to be spread out in space in a form called an **electron cloud.**

The electron cloud is densest in regions where the probability of finding the electron is highest. Schrödinger's wave equations describe the shape, location, and density of each electron cloud in an atom. Each cloud corresponds to a particular location for the electrons. These locations are called electron orbitals. Each orbital may have zero, one, or two electrons in it, but not more than two. When an orbital is occupied by two electrons, they have opposite spins.

Figure 5-14 shows a cross section of the electron cloud for the ground level state of the hydrogen atom ($n = 1$). The cloud is actually a sphere with the nucleus at its center. For higher values of n, the electron clouds can have other shapes. For example, some of the electron clouds for $n = 2$ are shaped like a pair of dumbbells with their handles pointing toward the nucleus. There are three such clouds with different directions around the nucleus. The Rutherford-Bohr model, as modified by the ideas of the wave-mechanical model, enables us to construct accurate models of the electron arrangements for all elements.

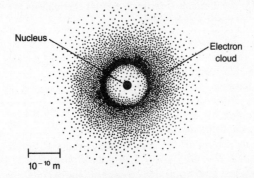

Nucleus

Electron cloud

10^{-10} m

Figure 5-14.   The cloud model of the hydrogen atom, in which the density of the electron cloud represents the probability of finding the electron in that region of the atom.

QUESTIONS

1. The probability of a head-on collision between an alpha particle and a nucleus is (1) extremely small (2) very high (3) about 50% (4) zero

2. If the electron in a hydrogen atom changes from an energy level of $n = 4$ to the ground state in two steps, it can emit a photon whose energy is (1) 2.55 eV (2) 10.00 eV (3) 12.75 eV (4) 13.60 eV

3. The fact that most of the alpha particles directed at a thin metal foil pass through without being deflected indicates that the atom consists mostly of (1) electrons (2) neutrons (3) empty space (4) protons

4. If the electron of a hydrogen atom is in the $n = 5$ energy level, what is the minimum energy needed to ionize the atom? (1) 0.54 eV (2) 13.06 eV (3) 13.60 eV (4) 14.14 eV

5. What is the energy emitted by a hydrogen atom when its electron changes directly from the $n = 5$ state to the $n = 2$ state? (1) 13.60 eV (2) 3.40 eV (3) 2.86 eV (4) 0.54 eV

6. An element will emit its characteristic spectrum as its (1) atoms become ionized (2) nuclei are broken into protons and neutrons (3) electrons in high energy levels go to lower energy levels (4) electrons in low energy levels go to higher energy levels

7. The ionization potential of the mercury atom in the ground state is (1) 4.64 eV (2) 4.86 eV (3) 6.67 eV (4) 10.38 eV

8. Rutherford based his model of the atom on evidence obtained from (1) the photoelectric effect (2) blackbody radiation (3) alpha-particle scattering (4) absorption and emission spectra

9. As an atom absorbs a photon of energy, one of its electrons will (1) exchange energy levels with another of its electrons (2) undergo a transition to a higher energy level (3) undergo a transition to a lower energy level (4) increase its charge

10. The Bohr model of the hydrogen atom contradicts classical physics by assuming that (1) a body can be in orbit without an unbalanced force acting upon it (2) an electron can be accelerated without radiating energy (3) the electron is in orbit around the nucleus (4) the total energy of the electron can change

11–13. Base your answers to Questions 11 through 13 on the diagram, which represents three visible lines in the hydrogen spectrum. Either the energy or the frequency for each of these lines is given below the diagram.

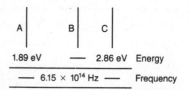

11. What is the energy of the photons that produced line *B*? (1) 3.23 × 10^{-19} J (2) 4.06 × 10^{-19} J (3) 9.28 × 10^{-19} J (4) 9.85 × 10^{-19} J

12. Which energy-level transition produced line *A*? (1) $n = 2$ to $n = 1$ (2) $n = 3$ to $n = 2$ (3) $n = 4$ to $n = 3$ (4) $n = 5$ to $n = 2$

13. If the diagram represented an absorption (dark-line) spectrum, which energy-level transition would have produced line A? (1) $n = 2$ to $n = 3$ (2) $n = 2$ to $n = 2$ (3) $n = 3$ to $n = 2$ (4) $n = 4$ to $n = 2$

14–18. Base your answers to Questions 14 through 18 on the information below and the Physics Reference Tables.

A photon with 14.60 electronvolts of energy collides with a mercury atom in its ground state.

14. What is the energy of the incident photon? (1) 1.5×10^{-18} J (2) 2.3×10^{-18} J (3) 6.3×10^{-18} J (4) 9.1×10^{-18} J

15. If the collision ionizes the atom, what is the maximum energy that the electron removed from the atom can have? (1) 0.0 eV (2) 4.22 eV (3) 10.38 eV (4) 14.60 eV

16. When an electron in a mercury atom changes from energy level c to level b, what is the energy of the emitted photon? (1) 1.00 eV (2) 0.22 eV (3) 4.86 eV (4) 5.52 eV

17. How much energy is required to ionize a mereury atom in the c state? (1) 0.57 eV (2) 1.04 eV (3) 3.96 eV (4) 5.52 eV

18. Which transition in mercury energy levels causes the emission of a photon of highest frequency?   (1) e to d (2) e to c (3) c to b (4) b to a

19. How much energy is required to ionize a hydrogen atom in the ground state? (1) 0.38 eV (2) 1.51 eV (3) 3.40 eV (4) 13.60 eV

20. Of the following, the most energetic photon in the Balmer series is emitted when the electron of a hydrogen atom changes energy directly from (1) $n = 5$ to $n = 2$ (2) $n = 4$ to $n = 2$ (3) $n = 2$ to $n = 4$ (4) $n = 2$ to $n = 5$

21. Which diagram best represents the path of a positively charged particle as it passes near the nucleus of an atom?

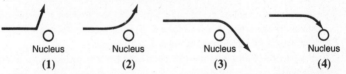

Nucleus   Nucleus   Nucleus   Nucleus
  (1)   (2)   (3)   (4)

22. When an electron in a mercury atom changes from energy level g to energy level b, the expression for the frequency of the emitted photon is

(1) $\dfrac{\lambda}{E_g \times E_b}$ (2) $\dfrac{h}{E_g - E_b}$ (3) $\dfrac{E_g - E_b}{h}$ (4) $\dfrac{\lambda}{2}(E_g - E_b)$

23. Alpha-particle scattering may best be explained by assuming the interacting force is (1) nuclear (2) electrostatic (3) magnetic (4) gravitational

24. When alpha particles are directed toward a thin metal foil, their deflection paths are (1) circular (2) elliptical (3) parabolic (4) hyperbolic

25. Which energy-level transition in a hydrogen atom will emit a photon of the highest frequency? (1) $n = 2$ to $n = 1$ (2) $n = 3$ to $n = 2$ (3) $n = 3$ to $n = 1$ (4) $n = 4$ to $n = 2$

26. The electron in a hydrogen atom can be raised from the $n = 2$ state to the $n = 3$ state by a photon with an energy of (1) 0.22 eV (2) 1.89 eV (3) 10.20 eV (4) 12.09 eV

27. When an atom changes from a higher energy state to a lower energy state, it emits (1) electrons (2) protons (3) neutrons (4) photons

28. A hydrogen atom in the ground state can be ionized by a photon with an energy of (1) 1.89 eV (2) 3.40 eV (3) 10.20 eV (4) 13.60 eV

29. In the Rutherford experiment, a beam of alpha particles was directed at thin gold foil. The deflection pattern of the alpha particles showed that (1) the electrons of gold atoms have waves (2) the nuclear volume is a small part of the atomic volume (3) the energy levels of a gold atom are quantized (4) gold atoms can emit photons under bombardment

30. As an atom goes from the ground state to an excited state, its energy (1) decreases (2) increases (3) remains the same

31. In the Bohr model, as an electron in an atom moves in a circular path of constant radius around the nucleus, the total energy of the atom (1) decreases (2) increases (3) remains the same

32–36. Base your answers to Questions 32 through 36 on the Physics Reference Tables in Appendix II and the following information.

The electron in a hydrogen atom changes energy levels from $n = 1$ to $n = 2$.

32. This energy-level change will occur if the atom (1) emits a 3.40-eV photon (2) emits a 10.20-eV photon (3) absorbs a 10.20-eV photon (4) absorbs a 3.40-eV photon

33. As a result of this transition, there is an increase in the (1) electric charge of the electron (2) electric force on the electron (3) energy of the ground state (4) total energy of the atom

34. The minimum energy required to ionize the atom after the transition is (1) 3.40 eV (2) 10.20 eV (3) 13.60 eV (4) 17.00 eV

35. The photon of greatest frequency would be emitted as a result of a transition from energy level (1) $n = 5$ to $n = 3$ (2) $n = 4$ to $n = 3$ (3) $n = 3$ to $n = 2$ (4) $n = 2$ to $n = 1$

36. The lines in the Balmer series are produced by transitions from higher energy levels to (1) $n = 1$ (2) $n = 2$ (3) $n = 3$ (4) $n = 4$

37. What is the minimum energy needed to ionize a hydrogen atom in the $n = 2$ state? (1) 1.89 eV (2) 3.40 eV (3) 10.20 eV (4) 13.60 eV

38. To excite a ground-state hydrogen atom, a photon must have a minimum energy of (1) 3.40 eV (2) 4.64 eV (3) 10.20 eV (4) 13.22 eV

39–43. Base your answers to Questions 39 through 43 on the diagram, which shows the path of a beam of alpha particles directed at a thin gold foil. The screen is used to detect alpha particles that pass through the foil

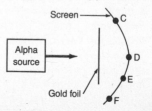

39. Most of the alpha particles that pass through the foil would be detected on the screen in the region of (1) E (2) F (3) C (4) D

40. The maximum angle through which an alpha particle may be deflected is (1) 30° (2) 60° (3) 90° (4) 180°

41. Observed changes in the path of an alpha particle as it approaches a nucleus in the foil can be best explained in terms of (1) the Doppler effect (2) Ohm's law (3) Coulomb's law (4) the Bohr theory

42. Rutherford's experiment with the scattering of alpha particles by a gold foil led him to believe that the positive charge in an atom is (1) concentrated at its center (2) spread uniformly throughout its volume (3) in the form of positive electrons at some distance from its center (4) readily deflected by an incident alpha particle.

43. What kind of path have the alpha particles detected in the region of C followed? (1) linear (2) helical (3) hyperbolic (4) elliptical

44–48. Base your answers to Questions 44 through 48 on the following information.

The Balmer series of the hydrogen bright-line spectrum includes the following lines (refer to Table of Energy Levels for Hydrogen in the Physics Reference Tables in Appendix II):

H_a—which results from an energy-level change from $n = 3$ to $n = 2$
H_b—which results from an energy-level change from $n = 4$ to $n = 2$
H_c—which results from an energy-level change from $n = 5$ to $n = 2$

44. The H_a photon has an energy of (1) 12.09 eV (2) 10.20 eV (3) 2.55 eV (4) 1.89 eV

45. The H_b photon has an energy of (1) 1.6×10^{-19} J (2) 2.55×10^{-19} J (3) 4.1×10^{-19} J (4) 4.6×10^{-19} J

46. The H_a photon has an energy of 3.0×10^{-19} joule. The frequency of this photon is (1) 3.5×10^{14} Hz (2) 4.5×10^{14} Hz (3) 6.2×10^{14} Hz (4) 6.9×10^{14} Hz

47. The H_c photon has an energy of 4.6×10^{-19} joule. What is the color of the H_c line? (1) violet (2) blue (3) green (4) red

48. All the spectral lines of the Lyman series result from changes to the energy level $n = 1$. In which region of the electromagnetic spectrum do these lines belong? (1) radio (2) ultraviolet (3) visible (4) infrared

49. How many different frequencies of light could be emitted from excited hydrogen atoms that have electrons in energy level $n = 4$? (1) 1 (2) 6 (3) 3 (4) 7

PROBLEM SOLVING

Sample Problem

A cesium plate enclosed in an evacuated tube was illuminated with various wavelengths of electromagnetic waves by a student working in the laboratory. The student determined the corresponding maximum kinetic energy of the ejected photoelectrons and recorded the data in the table below. The student wanted to make a graph of maximum kinetic energy versus frequency and thus made a column in the data table to record the light frequencies.

Data Table		
Wavelength ($\times 10^{-7}$ m)	Frequency ( )	Maximum Kinetic Energy (eV)
4.2		1.2
4.6		0.80
5.0		0.58
5.4		0.40
5.9		0.19

(a) Using your knowledge of physics and information in the data table, complete the data table by filling in the column for frequency. Be sure to include appropriate units. (Assume the wavelengths given are for light in a vacuum.)

(b) Identify the region of the electromagnetic spectrum in which these waves are found.

(c) Using the information in the data table, construct a graph of maximum kinetic energy versus frequency. Mark an appropriate scale on each axis. Plot the data on the grid and draw the best-fit line.

(d) Using the graph, determine the threshold frequency for cesium.

(e) Determine the work function of cesium, and indicate its value in joules.

(f) Calculate the slope of the graph. Show all work.

Solution

(a) Since $f = c/\lambda$, where $c = 3.0 \times 10^8$ m/s, the values for λ in the table may be repeatedly substituted into the formula to yield the corresponding values for frequency. See the sample calculation below.

$$f = \frac{c}{\lambda} = \frac{3.0 \times 10^8 \text{ m/s}}{4.2 \times 10^{-7} \text{ m}} = 0.71 \times 10^{15} \text{ Hz}$$

$$f = 7.1 \times 10^{14} \text{ Hz}$$

Data Table		
Wavelength ($\times 10^{-7}$ m)	Frequency ($\times 10^{14}$ Hz)	Maximum Kinetic Energy (eV)
4.2	7.1	1.2
4.6	6.5	0.80
5.0	6.0	0.58
5.4	5.6	0.40
5.9	5.1	0.19

(b) These waves are all found in the visible region of the electromagnetic spectrum. (This information can be obtained from the Physics Reference Tables in Appendix II.)

(c)

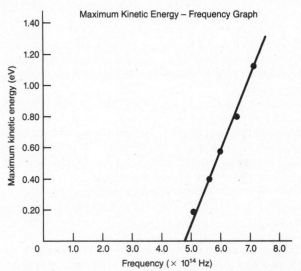

(d) The threshold frequency for cesium, as determined from this best-fit line drawn for this particular set of data, is 4.8×10^{14} Hz. The threshold frequency is always the horizontal intercept of a graph of maximum kinetic energy versus frequency for a photoemissive surface.

(e) The work function, W_0, of cesium can be found either by the extrapolation of the graph to determine the vertical intercept or by the use of the formula $W_0 = hf_0$. Since the answer must be expressed in terms of joules, in the case of extrapolation, a conversion must be made. The use of the formula yields the following result:

$$W_0 = hf_0 = (6.6 \times 10^{-34} \text{ J} \cdot \text{s})(4.8 \times 10^{14} \text{ Hz})$$

$$W_0 = 3.2 \times 10^{-19} \text{ J}$$

(f) The slope of the graph is the ratio of the change in maximum kinetic energy to the corresponding change in frequency. That is,

$$\frac{\Delta KE}{\Delta f} = \frac{1.2 \text{ eV} - 0.40 \text{ eV}}{7.2 \times 10^{14} \text{ Hz} - 5.6 \times 10^{14} \text{ Hz}}$$

$$\frac{\Delta KE}{\Delta f} = \frac{(0.80 \text{ eV}) (1.6 \times 10^{-19} \text{ J/eV})}{1.6 \times 10^{14} \text{ 1/s}}$$

$$\frac{\Delta KE}{\Delta f} = 8.0 \times 10^{-34} \text{ J} \cdot \text{s}$$

(This is a calculated value. It is not the accepted value for Planck's constant.)

Practice Problems

1. Explain each of the following on the basis of physical principles.
   (a) Scientists are able to identify the elements in a star without sending a space probe to it.
   (b) Planck's constant could be written with the unit kilogram · meter squared per second.
   (c) Alpha particles fired at a thin metal foil may pass straight through or be deflected at angles of up to 180 degrees.
   (d) Light of a given frequency is directed at a photoemissive surface, but no photoelectrons are ejected from the surface.
2. Compare and contrast the Rutherford and Bohr models of the atom.
3. Calculate the force of repulsion between an alpha particle and the nucleus of a gold atom having 79 protons, given that the two are 1.0×10^{-10} meter apart.
4. A platinum plate having a work function of 5.6 electronvolts is encased in an evacuated tube. What is the maximum wavelength of light that can be directed at the platinum to produce photoelectrons?
5. A 0.50-kilogram ball is dropped from rest to the ground from a height of 60. meters. Calculate the de Broglie wavelength of the ball just before it strikes the ground.

UNIT 6   MOTION IN A PLANE

I. TWO-DIMENSIONAL MOTION AND TRAJECTORIES

In Unit 1, the motion of an object traveling in a straight line (one-dimensional motion) was discussed in terms of its displacement, velocity, and acceleration. The motion of an object traveling in a two-dimensional plane can be described by separating the motion into the x and y (horizontal and vertical) components of its displacement, velocity, and acceleration.

If air resistance is neglected, an example of two-dimensional motion is the motion of a cannonball projected near the earth's surface at an angle with the vertical. If the only unbalanced force acting on the cannonball is gravity, the vertical component of the cannonball's motion is identical to that of a freely falling body, and the horizontal component is uniform motion. Although the two occur simultaneously, the two components of the motion are independent. Thus, the motion of a projectile in the earth's gravitational field is readily described by the superposition of the two motions, if the object's initial velocity is known.

A Projectile Fired Horizontally

If an object is projected at some initial velocity v_i, its horizontal component of velocity v_{ix} (neglecting air resistance) will remain constant. Although the initial vertical velocity v_{iy} of the projectile is zero, the vertical velocity increases as the projectile accelerates downward due to gravity. Figure 6-1 (on the following page) shows a ball falling straight downward (Figure 6-1a) as well as one having a horizontal component of velocity as it falls downward (Figure 6-1b).

Whether an object is dropped from rest or projected horizontally, the vertical distance fallen by any object is the same at any particular time after the object is dropped or projected. In both Figure 6-1a and Figure 6-1b, the motion of the ball is shown at 1.0-second intervals. The vertical distances of fall were calculated using Equation 1-4 without the deltas, since the initial values are zero:

$$s_y = v_{iy}t + \tfrac{1}{2}gt^2 \qquad \textbf{(Eq. 1–4)}$$

Because $v_{iy} = 0$ and $g = 9.8$ m/s^2, the vertical distances fallen by the object from the rest position after 1, 2, and 3 seconds are given by the following expressions:

$$s_{y_1} = \tfrac{1}{2}(9.8 \text{ m/s}^2)(1.0 \text{ s})^2 = (4.9 \text{ m/s}^2)(1.0 \text{ s}^2) = 4.9 \text{ m}$$

$$s_{y_2} = \tfrac{1}{2}(9.8 \text{ m/s}^2)(2.0 \text{ s})^2 = (4.9 \text{ m/s}^2)(4.0 \text{ s}^2) = 19.6 \text{ m}$$

$$s_{y_3} = \tfrac{1}{2}(9.8 \text{ m/s}^2)(3.0 \text{ s})^2 = (4.9 \text{ m/s}^2)(9.0 \text{ s}^2) = 44.1 \text{ m}$$

These three values for s_y are shown for the vertical displacements of the ball in Figures 6-1a and 6-1b.

In addition to showing the positions of the ball after 1, 2, and 3 seconds have elapsed, Figure 6-1b also shows (using velocity vectors) the vertical and horizontal components of the velocity. At any particular time after the ball is released, the *vertical* component of velocity of an object projected horizontally is the same as the vertical component of velocity of an object dropped from rest.

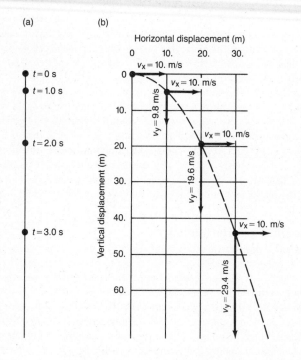

Figure 6-1. (a) Position of a ball at 1.0-second intervals as it falls from rest in a vacuum near the earth's surface. (The vertical scale in drawing (b) applies to (a) as well.) (b) The position of the same ball at 1.0–second intervals after it has been rolled off the edge of a building with an initial horizontal velocity of 10. m/s. The arrows are velocity vectors giving the horizontal and vertical components of the velocity when the ball is at each position. Note that the horizontal component of the ball's velocity is the same after each second but that the vertical component increases with time as the ball is accelerated by gravity. Note also that in both (a) and (b) the vertical distance the ball falls at the end of each second is the same.

For an object being uniformly accelerated from rest, Equation 1-2a gives the velocity of an object being uniformly accelerated from rest after an elapsed time Δt:

$$v = a\Delta t \qquad \text{(Eq. 1-2a)}$$

Therefore, because a is the acceleration of gravity, 9.8 m/s^2, the vertical component of the velocity at the end of each of the first three seconds is

End of 1 second:	$v_{y_1} = (9.8 \text{ m/s}^2)(1.0 \text{ s})$	= 9.8 m/s
End of 2 seconds:	$v_{y_2} = (9.8 \text{ m/s}^2)(2.0 \text{ s})$	= 19.6 m/s
End of 3 seconds:	$v_{y_3} = (9.8 \text{ m/s}^2)(3.0 \text{ s})$	= 29.4 m/s

These are the vertical components of velocity whose vectors are given in Figure 6-1b.

Consider now the horizontal displacement of the ball shown in Figure 6-1b. There is no acceleration (change in velocity) in the horizontal direction, so for an object with a horizontal component of velocity v_x, the horizontal displacement after 1, 2, and 3 seconds is simply found using Equation 1-1a (without the deltas):

$$s = \bar{v}t \qquad \text{(Eq. 1-1a)}$$

After 1 second:	$s_{x_1} = \bar{v}_x(1 \text{ s})$	$= v_x$ m
After 2 seconds:	$s_{x_2} = \bar{v}_x(2 \text{ s})$	$= 2v_x$ m
After 3 seconds:	$s_{x_3} = \bar{v}_x(3 \text{ s})$	$= 3v_x$ m

The greater the value of the horizontal velocity, the greater the horizontal displacement of the object before it strikes the ground. In Figure 6-1b, 10 meters per second was used for the horizontal component of velocity, v_x.

CAN YOU EXPLAIN THIS?

A ball thrown horizontally at 20 meters per second will hit the ground at the same time as another ball dropped from the same height at the same time.

Vertical motion is independent of horizontal motion for a body moving under the action of gravity alone, and the acceleration due to gravity is the same for all bodies near the surface of the earth regardless of their state of motion. Both balls initially have no vertical velocity and both experience the same downward acceleration. Therefore, both balls take the same amount of time to hit the ground when released from the same initial height. If the speed of the thrown ball were increased, its time to hit the ground would remain the same, but its horizontal displacement would increase. If this situation is simulated by dropping a ball from the edge of a table while rolling an identical ball off the edge of the table, the balls can be heard hitting the floor at the same time.

A classic example of an object projected horizontally is a supply drop from an airplane, as illustrated by the following example.

EXAMPLE

A plane flying horizontally at an altitude of 490 meters and a velocity of 200 meters per second east, drops a supply packet to a work crew on the ground. It falls freely without benefit of a parachute. (Assume no wind and negligible air friction.)

(a) How long does it take the packet to fall to the ground?
(b) At what horizontal distance from the target area must the plane drop the packet?

Solution

(a) $\qquad s_y = v_{iy}\Delta t + \tfrac{1}{2}a_y(\Delta t)^2 \qquad$ but $v_{iy} = 0.0$ m/s

so $\qquad s_y = \tfrac{1}{2}a_y t^2$

$$t = \sqrt{\frac{2s_y}{a_y}} \qquad \text{where } a_y = 9.8 \text{ m/s}^2$$

$$t = \sqrt{\frac{2(490 \text{ m})}{9.8 \text{ m/s}^2}}$$

$$t = \sqrt{100 \text{ s}^2}$$

$$t = 10. \ s$$

(b) $\qquad s_x = v_{ix}\Delta t + \tfrac{1}{2}a_x(\Delta t)^2$

However, the horizontal speed of the plane and packet is constant, and $a_x = 0.0$ m/s^2, so

$$s_x = v_{ix}t = (200 \text{ m/s})(10. \text{ s}) = 2{,}000 \text{ m}$$

The plane should release the packet when 2,000 meters west of the target.

A Projectile Fired at an Angle

Many projectiles, such as golf balls and missiles, are launched with an initial velocity directed at an angle to the horizontal. These projectiles rise to some height above the earth and then fall back to the ground. The motion of these objects can be studied by separating the initial velocity into its horizontal and vertical components and then calculating the motions resulting from the two components. As in the case of a projectile launched horizontally, the vertical motion will be accelerated by the force of gravity, while the horizonal motion, if air resistance is ignored, will continue at a constant speed.

Consider a projectile launched from ground level with an initial velocity v_i at an angle θ with the horizontal, as shown in Figure 6-2.

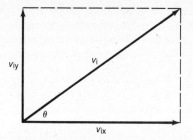

Figure 6-2.   An initial velocity vector separated into horizontal and
vertical components.

Using trigonometry, the velocity vector may be separated into its components:

Horizontal component: $v_{ix} = v_i \cos \theta$ **(Eq. 6-1)**

Vertical component: $v_{iy} = v_i \sin \theta$ **(Eq. 6-2)**

Whereas (neglecting air resistance) the horizontal component of the velocity of
the projectile remains constant during its flight, the vertical component (directed
upward) gradually decreases to zero and then gradually increases downward because of the constant downward acceleration of gravity. When the vertical component of the velocity is zero, all of the velocity is in the horizontal direction and the object is at its highest position above the earth. See Figure 6-3.

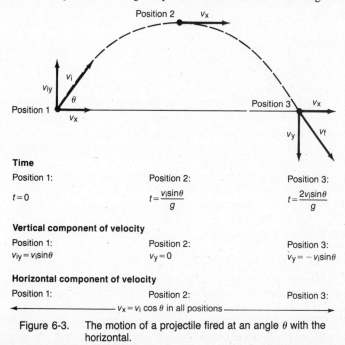

Figure 6-3.   The motion of a projectile fired at an angle θ with the
horizontal.

If the initial velocity of the projectile and the angle at which it is fired are known, appropriate equations for uniformly accelerated motion can be used to calculate two quantities: the maximum height of the projectile and the time required for the projectile to reach the maximum height. To find the time t_u to reach the highest point, you can use the equation

$$v_{fy} = v_{iy} + at_u$$

where v_{iy} is the initial vertical component of the velocity, v_{fy} is the final vertical component of the velocity at the end of time t_u, and $a = g$. If upward velocity is considered the positive direction, then g, a downward acceleration, is negative. Since v_{fy} at the highest point is zero, and $v_{iy} = v_i \sin \theta$, then

$$0 = v_i \sin \theta - gt_u$$

from which

$$t_u = \frac{v_i \sin \theta}{g} \qquad \text{(Equation A)}$$

To find the height s_y to which the projectile rises, the simplest method is to use the equation

$$s_y = \bar{v}_y t_u$$

where the average velocity of the vertical component of velocity $\bar{v}_y = (v_{iy} + v_{fy})/2$. Since $v_{fy} = 0$, and $v_{iy} = v_i \sin \theta$, then

$$\bar{v}_y = \tfrac{1}{2} v_i \sin \theta$$

and therefore

$$s_y = \tfrac{1}{2}(v_i \sin \theta)t_u \qquad \text{(Equation B)}$$

(You could also use the equation $s_y = v_{iy}t_u - \tfrac{1}{2}gt_u^2$ to find the maximum height, but the calculation involves more arithmetic and gives the same result. You may want to try this method in the example on the next page.)

It can be shown that the time for the projectile to reach its maximum height is the same as the time to fall back to the ground from that height. Therefore, the total time of travel T equals $2t_u$.

For the horizontal motion, we use the equation for uniform motion, since there is no acceleration in that direction:

$$s_x = v_x t_x$$

In this case, $v_x = v_i \cos \theta$, and $t_x = 2t_u$. Therefore,

$$s_x = (v_i \cos \theta) \cdot 2t_u \qquad \text{(Equation C)}$$

The horizontal distance traveled by the projectile is called its *range*. It can be shown that for any given initial velocity, the range is a maximum when $\theta = 45°$.

EXAMPLE

A rifle bullet is fired with a muzzle velocity of 300. meters per second at an angle of 30.° with the horizontal. Determine the (a) time of flight, (b) maximum height, and (c) horizontal range for the bullet.

Solution

(a) Use Equation A to find the time to reach the maximum height:

$$t_u = \frac{v_i \sin \theta}{g}$$

$v_i = 300.$ m/s, and $\sin \theta = \sin 30.° = 0.500$. Therefore,

$$t_u = \frac{(300.\text{ m/s})(0.500)}{9.80 \text{ m/s}^2} = 15.3 \text{ s}$$

Since the total travel time, T, equals $2t_u$,

$$T = 2(15.3 \text{ s}) = 30.6 \text{ s}$$

(b) Use Equation B to find the maximum height:

$$s_y = \tfrac{1}{2}(v_i \sin \theta)t_u$$

$$s_y = \tfrac{1}{2}(v_i \sin 30.°)t_u$$

$$s_y = \tfrac{1}{2}(300.\text{ m/s})(0.500)(15.3 \text{ s}) = 1,150 \text{ m}$$

(c) Use Equation C to find the range (the horizontal distance traveled):

$$s_x = (v_i \cos \theta)2t_u$$

where $v_i \cos \theta = (300.\text{ m/s})(0.866) = 260.$ m/s, and $2t_u = 30.6$ s.

$$s_x = (260.\text{ m/s})(30.6 \text{ s}) = 7,960 \text{ m}$$

QUESTIONS

1–8. Base your answers to Questions 1 through 8 on the information below.

A ball of mass m is thrown horizontally with speed v from a height h above level ground.

1. If the height above the ground from which the ball is thrown were increased, the initial vertical velocity of the ball would (1) decrease (2) increase (3) remain the same

2. If the height above the ground from which the ball is thrown were increased, the time of flight of the ball would (1) decrease (2) increase (3) remain the same

3. If the initial speed of the ball were increased, the time of flight of the ball would (1) decrease (2) increase (3) remain the same

4. If the initial speed of the ball were increased, the horizontal distance traveled by the ball would (1) decrease (2) increase (3) remain the same

5. If the initial speed of the ball were increased, the vertical acceleration of the ball would (1) decrease (2) increase (3) remain the same

6. If the ball were replaced with a ball of mass $2m$, the horizontal distance traveled by the ball would (1) decrease (2) increase (3) remain the same

7. If the ball were replaced with a ball of mass $2m$, the vertical acceleration of the ball would (1) decrease (2) increase (3) remain the same

8. As time elapses before the ball strikes the ground, the horizontal velocity of the ball (1) decreases (2) increases (3) remains the same

9–10. Base your answers to Questions 9 and 10 on the information below.
    A ball is thrown horizontally at 20. meters per second from a height of 1.0 meter above the level ground.

9. The time of flight of the ball is nearest (1) 1.0 s (2) 0.50 s (3) 9.8 s (4) 20. s

10. The total horizontal distance travelled by the ball before it strikes the ground is (1) 4.9 m (2) 9.8 m (3) 20. m (4) 40. m

11–14. Base your answers to Questions 11 through 14 on the information below.
    A 0.50-kilogram rock is thrown horizontally with a speed of 20. meters per second off a ledge 19.6 meters high.

11. The time of flight of the rock is (1) 1.0 s (2) 2.0 s (3) 9.8 s (4) 20. s

12. The horizontal distance traveled by the rock before striking the ground is (1) 9.8 m (2) 20. m (3) 40. m (4) 400 m

13. The weight of the rock is (1) 0.50 N (2) 4.9 N (3) 9.8 N (4) 20. N

14. The momentum of the rock at the moment it is thrown is
    (1) 10. kg · m/s (2) 50. kg · m/s (3) 100 kg · m/s (4) 200 kg · m/s

15. If the total time of flight of a projectile fired from and returning to the ground is T, the time required for the projectile to reach maximum height is (1) T (2) 2T (3) T/2 (4) T/4

16–23. Base your answers to Questions 16 through 23 on the information below.
    A mortar at an angle of 30.° with the ground fires a shell with a muzzle velocity of 196 meters per second.

16. The initial vertical component of the velocity is (1) 0.0 m/s (2) 98.0 m/s (3) 170. m/s (4) 196 m/s

17. The initial horizontal component of the velocity is (1) 0.0 m/s (2) 98.0 m/s (3) 170. m/s (4) 196 m/s

18. When the mortar shell reaches a maximum height, the vertical component of the velocity is (1) 0.0 m/s (2) 98.0 m/s (3) 170. m/s (4) 196 m/s

19. The time of flight of the shell is (1) 10. s (2) 20. s (3) 30. s (4) 40. s

20. The maximum height of the shell is approximately (1) 500 m (2) 2,000 m (3) 3,000 m (4) 4,000 m
21. The horizontal range of the shell is closest to (1) 2,000 m (2) 3,400 m (3) 3,900 m (4) 6,800 m
22. If the angle of the mortar were increased to 45°, the range of the shell would (1) decrease (2) increase (3) remain the same
23. Compared to the maximum height of the shell when fired at 30.°, the maximum height when fired at 60.° is (1) shorter (2) longer (3) the same

24–28. Base your answers to Questions 24 through 28 on the information below.

A projectile fired from the level ground has an initial vertical velocity component of 49 meters per second and a horizontal velocity component of 70. meters per second.

24. How long is the projectile in the air? (1) 5.0 s (2) 7.0 s (3) 10. s (4) 20. s
25. The horizontal range of the projectile is closest to (1) 250 m (2) 350 m (3) 700 m (4) 1,400 m
26. The magnitude of the initial velocity of the projectile is closest to (1) 11 m/s (2) 60. m/s (3) 85 m/s (4) 120 m/s
27. The maximum height of the projectile is closest to (1) 25 m (2) 120 m (3) 350 m (4) 490 m
28. The initial angle the projectile makes with the ground is (1) smaller than 45° (2) larger than 45° (3) 45°

II. UNIFORM CIRCULAR MOTION

According to Newton's first law, an object in motion remains in motion at constant velocity (in a straight line at constant speed) unless acted upon by an unbalanced force. If the force has a component in the direction of motion, the magnitude of the velocity will change. If the force is applied perpendicular to the direction of motion, however, only the *direction* of the velocity will change; its magnitude will remain the same. In both instances the object experiences an acceleration, that is, a time rate of change of velocity. If the force is constant and always acts perpendicular to the direction of the velocity vector, the object will move in a circular path at constant speed, experiencing **uniform circular motion.**

Centripetal Acceleration

The acceleration experienced by an object moving uniformly in a circular path is always directed toward the center of curvature, that is, toward the center of the circle, and is called **centripetal** ("center-seeking") **acceleration.** Like all accelerations, centripetal acceleration is a vector quantity. It can be shown that the magnitude of the centripetal acceleration is directly proportional to the square of the speed of the object and is inversely proportional to the radius of the circular path along which the object moves:

$$a_c = \frac{v^2}{r} \qquad \text{(Eq. 6-3)}$$

where the speed of the object v is in meters per second, the radius of curvature r is in meters, and the centripetal acceleration a_c is in meters per second squared. Note that the centripetal acceleration of an object is independent of its mass.

Centripetal Force

A centripetal acceleration is caused by a **centripetal force,** which is a vector quantity directed toward the center of curvature. The magnitude of a centripetal force F_c is derived from Newton's second law, $F = ma$, by substituting for a the centripetal acceleration $a_c = v^2/r$:

$$F_c = \frac{mv^2}{r} \qquad \text{(Eq. 6-4)}$$

where the mass, m, is in kilograms, the speed, v, is in meters per second, the radius, r, is in meters, and the centripetal force, F_c, is in kilogram · meters per second squared, or newtons. Figure 6-4 represents the relationships between these quantities for an object in uniform circular motion.

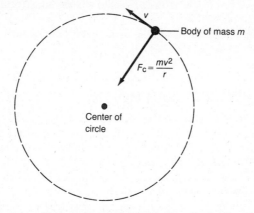

Figure 6-4.   The relationship between the velocity, v, mass, m, radius of curvature, r, and centripetal force, F_c, for a body in uniform circular motion. The velocity vector is tangent to the circle, the centripetal force is directed toward the center of the circle, and the radius of curvature is simply the radius of the circle.

When an object is in uniform circular motion, there is no net force acting on it *in the direction of motion,* that is, tangent to the circular path, so the speed along this path remains constant. However, the body is *not* in equilibrium. There is a net (unbalanced) force acting on the body—the centripetal force directed toward the center of the circle. This force produces a constant acceleration (change of direction) toward the center, and, therefore, the direction of the velocity is constantly changing, as shown in Figure 6-5.

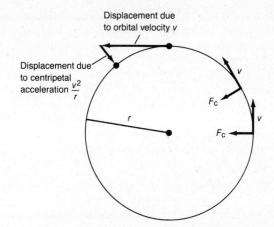

Figure 6-5. The velocity, acceleration, and displacement of a body in uniform circular motion. The velocity vector is always tangent to the circle and perpendicular to the centripetal acceleration. The acceleration causes a continuous change in the direction of the velocity and a continuous displacement to the circular path.

EXAMPLE

A 2.0-kilogram cart moves in a circular path of 10.-meter radius at a constant speed of 20. meters per second. Determine (a) the magnitude of the centripetal acceleration of the cart, and (b) the magnitude of the centripetal force acting on it.

Solution

(a) $$a_c = \frac{v^2}{r} = \frac{(20.\ \text{m/s})^2}{10.\ \text{m}} = \frac{400\ \text{m}^2/\text{s}^2}{10.\ \text{m}} = 40.\ \text{m/s}^2$$

(b) $$F_c = \frac{mv^2}{r} = \frac{(2.0\ \text{kg})(20.\ \text{m/s})^2}{10.\ \text{m}} = \frac{(2.0\ \text{kg})(400\ \text{m}^2/\text{s}^2)}{10.\ \text{m}}$$

$$F_c = 80.\ \text{kg} \cdot \text{m/s}^2 = 80.\ \text{N}$$

Note that the arithmetic in (b) can be simplified by substituting the calculated value of a_c from (a) for v^2/r:

$$F_c = ma_c = (2.0\ \text{kg})(40.\ \text{m/s}^2) = 80.\ \text{kg} \cdot \text{m/s}^2 = 80.\ \text{N}$$

Both the centripetal acceleration and the centripetal force are directed toward the center of curvature.

Many amusement park rides subject riders to the physics of circular motion. Another common type of experience is explained on the next page.

PRACTICAL APPLICATION

As a car rounds a left turn sharply, a passenger in the front seat appears to be thrown against the door on the right. The passenger is not being pushed to the right, however, but is simply obeying Newton's law of inertia and continuing to move in a straight-line path as the car turns. The car is accelerated toward the center of curvature of the road by a centripetal force provided by the frictional force between the tires and the road. If the frictional force between the passenger and the car seat is not sufficient to accelerate the person along the curved path, the person slides to the right. Then the passenger slides up against the car door, which supplies the required centripetal force. ■

The effects of centripetal force may be felt in space as well as on the earth.

CAN YOU EXPLAIN THIS?

A rotating space station may have artificial gravity.

A large cylindrical space station rotating about its axis could give the effect of gravity. As in the case of a car rounding a curve, the occupants of the space station would experience a central force by the walls of the cylinder causing them to follow circular paths around its axis. The people inside would have the sensation of having their feet being pressed or pulled toward the walls of the station just as people on earth have the sensation of having their feet pulled toward the ground beneath them. The people inside would interpret this sensation as the effect of an artificial gravity. Objects released by the occupants would also appear to "fall" toward the outside walls.

If the persons could not look outside their cylindrical home, it would be difficult for them to determine whether the apparent gravity is a real force or the result of rotation. Calculations show that to produce artificial gravity about equal to gravity on the earth, a space station rotating once per minute would have to be two kilometers in diameter. Such large space environments are not likely to be provided in the near future.

QUESTIONS

1–10. Base your answers to Questions 1 through 10 on the information below.

A 2.0-kilogram cart travels in a horizontal circle of radius 3.0 meters at a constant speed of 6.0 meters per second, as shown at the right.

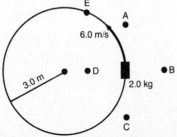

1. The magnitude of the centripetal acceleration of the cart is (1) 0.0 m/s^2 (2) 2.0 m/s^2 (3) 12 m/s^2 (4) 24 m/s^2

2. The magnitude of the centripetal force acting on the cart is (1) 1.0 N (2) 12 N (3) 24 N (4) 36 N

3. If the mass of the cart were doubled, the centripetal force on the cart would be (1) halved (2) doubled (3) quartered (4) quadrupled

4. If the radius of curvature of the path were doubled, the centripetal acceleration of the cart would be (1) halved (2) doubled (3) quartered (4) quadrupled

5. If the speed of the cart were doubled, the centripetal force on the cart would be (1) halved (2) doubled (3) quartered (4) quadrupled

6. If the mass of the cart were halved, the centripetal acceleration of the cart would (1) decrease (2) increase (3) remain the same

7. The centripetal force acting on the cart is directed toward point (1) A (2) B (3) C (4) D

8. In the position shown in the diagram, the velocity of the cart is directed toward point (1) A (2) B (c) D (4) E

9. As the cart in the diagram travels about the circle at constant speed, the magnitude of the momentum of the cart (1) decreases (2) increases (3) remains the same

10. As the cart travels about the circle, the kinetic energy of the cart (1) decreases (2) increases (3) remains the same

11-13. Base your answers to Questions 11 through 13 on the following information.

A car is traveling around the track shown in the drawing below at a constant speed of 20.0 meters per second. Arcs *GHA* and *CDEF* are circular. *AC* and *FG* are tangent to both circles.

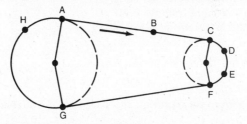

11. If the total length of the track is 700. meters, the time required for the car to make a complete circuit is (1) 17.5 s (2) 35.0 s (3) 7,000 s (4) 14,000 s

12. The acceleration of the car is zero at point (1) E (2) B (3) H (4) D

13. As the car travels from point C to point D at constant speed, the centripetal force on the car is (1) constant in magnitude, but changing in direction (2) constant in both magnitude and direction (3) changing in magnitude, but constant in direction (4) changing in both magnitude and direction

14–18. Base your answers to Questions 14 through 18 on the following information.

The diagram at right represents a flat (unbanked) circular racetrack with a radius of 250. meters. Racing car R is moving around the track at a uniform speed of 40.0 meters per second. The mass of the car is 2.00×10^3 kilograms.

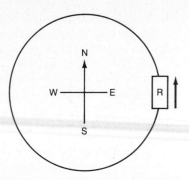

14. At the instant shown in the diagram, the car's acceleration is directed toward the (1) north (2) south (3) east (4) west

15. The magnitude of the car's acceleration is (1) 0.0250 m/s² (2) 1.60 m/s² (3) 6.40 m/s² (4) 12.8 m/s²

16. The centripetal force necessary to keep the car in its circular path is provided by (1) the engine (2) the brakes (3) friction (4) the stability of the car

17. The kinetic energy of the car is (1) 2.50×10^5 J (2) 1.60×10^6 J (3) 6.40×10^6 J (4) 1.30×10^7 J

18. If the speed of the car were 50.0 meters per second, the magnitude of the centripetal force would be (1) 4.00×10^2 N (2) 1.00×10^1 N (3) 2.00×10^4 N (4) 4.00×10^4 N

19–23. Base your answers to Questions 19 through 23 on the diagram at right, which represents a satellite orbiting the earth. The satellite's distance from the center of the earth equals 4 earth radii.

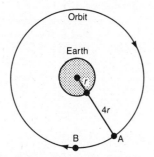

19. Which vector best represents the velocity of the satellite at B?

(1) ↑   (2) ↓   (3) ←   (4) →

20. The original satellite is replaced by one with twice the mass, but the orbit speed and radius are unchanged. Compared to the magnitude of the acceleration of the original satellite, the magnitude of the acceleration of the new satellite is (1) one-half as great (2) the same (3) twice as great (4) four times as great

21. **Which vector best represents the acceleration of the satellite at point A in its orbit?**

(1) 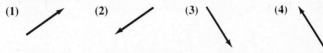 (2)   (3)   (4)

22. **As the satellite moves from point A to point B, its potential energy with respect to the earth will (1) decrease (2) increase (3) remain the same**

23. **If the satellite's distance from the center of the earth were increased to 5 earth radii, the centripetal force on the satellite would (1) decrease (2) increase (3) remain the same**

III. KEPLER'S LAWS

As discussed earlier in this text, the current model of the atom was developed over many years and involved the work of many scientists. In a similar manner, the model of the universe evolved in the past and will continue to change in the future.

In the second century, the Greek astronomer Ptolemy proposed a *geocentric* (earth-centered) model of the universe. This model was the accepted one for the next 1,400 years. In 1543, the Polish astronomer Copernicus published a *heliocentric* (sun-centered) model that placed the earth and the planets in circular orbits around the sun. Copernicus accounted for the apparent daily circling of the sun, the stars, and other celestial bodies from east to west by assuming that the earth is rotating on its axis once a day from west to east, as well as revolving about the sun once a year.

Tycho Brahe, observing the heavens in the second half of the 16th century, before the invention of the telescope, made thousands of measurements of the apparent positions of the visible planets. His assistant, Johannes Kepler, inherited Brahe's data and spent many years trying to find the precise motions of the planets that would agree with these observations. No arrangement of circular orbits could be made to fit the data, and Kepler eventually looked for other possible types of orbits.

Kepler's First Law

In 1609, Kepler announced the first of three laws that govern the motion of the planets around the sun. Kepler did not propose a theory to account for these laws. He arrived at them by trial-and-error with Brahe's data. Newton's laws of motion, combined with the law of gravitation, later explained why the laws are true.

Kepler's first law states that the orbits of all the planets are mathematical curves called *ellipses*. As shown in Figure 6-6, an **ellipse** is a closed curve in which the sum of the distances from any point P on the curve to two fixed points F_1 and F_2, called *foci* (singular, **focus**), is a constant. In the case of the planetary orbits, the sun is located at one of the foci of the ellipse.

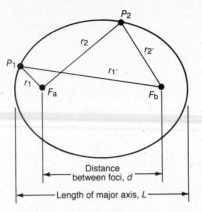

Figure 6-6.   The properties of an ellipse. An ellipse is the path of a
point that moves so that the sum of its distances from
two fixed points (called foci) is constant. Points F_a and
F_b are foci. The definition is illustrated by the fact that
$r_1 + r_1' = r_2 + r_2'$. By definition, the eccentricity of an
ellipse equals d divided by L.

An ellipse looks like a flattened circle. The greater the distance d between the
two foci, the flatter, or more *eccentric,* the ellipse becomes. On the other hand,
as the foci become closer together, the ellipse becomes closer to being a circle.
In fact, a circle is simply a special case of an ellipse in which the distance
between the foci is zero. The line drawn through the foci with its ends on the
ellipse is called the *major axis.* The *eccentricity* of an ellipse is the ratio of the
distance between the foci to the length of the major axis. The eccentricity of an
ellipse is always less than 1. A circle is an ellipse in which the eccentricity is
zero. Except for Mercury and Pluto, the eccentricities of the orbits of the planets
are quite small, and the orbits are nearly circular.

CAN YOU EXPLAIN THIS?

Neptune is sometimes farther from the Sun than Pluto is.

Of the known planets, Pluto has an orbit with the largest mean radius, and
Neptune has the second largest mean radius. We would therefore expect Pluto to
be farther from the Sun than Neptune at all times. The eccentricity of Pluto's
orbit is 0.25, however, while that of Neptune is only 0.009. The Sun is practically at the center of Neptune's orbit, and Neptune is always just about the same
distance from the Sun. Although Pluto's orbit is still so nearly a circle that the
eye cannot detect the difference, its eccentricity puts the Sun one-quarter of a
radius away from the center of the orbit and therefore much nearer one end of
the major axis than the other. As Figure 6-7 shows, the result is that part of
Pluto's orbit passes closer to the Sun than Neptune's orbit does. When Pluto is
in this part of its orbit, it is nearer to the Sun than Neptune is.

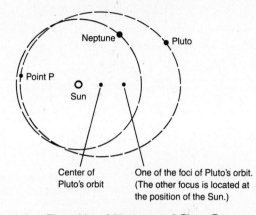

Center of
Pluto's orbit

One of the foci of Pluto's orbit.
(The other focus is located at
the position of the Sun.)

Figure 6-7. The orbits of Neptune and Pluto. Because Pluto's orbit is more elliptical than Neptune's, Pluto is closer to the Sun while traveling over part of its orbit (while at point P, for example) than Neptune is at any point in its orbit.

Kepler's Second Law

Kepler announced his second law at the same time he announced his first law. Imagine a line drawn from the sun to a planet. As the planet moves along its orbit, this line sweeps out an area inside the ellipse. **Kepler's second law** states that the line from the sun to a planet sweeps out equal areas in equal periods of time. The shaded areas in Figure 6-8 illustrate the second law (see the following page). The two areas, which are equal, would be swept out during equal time intervals.

From Kepler's second law certain important conclusions can be drawn about the speed and energy of a planet at different parts of its orbit. When the planet is at point p in Figure 6-8, the point on the orbit closest to the sun, the planet is said to be at **perihelion.** At point a, the point farthest from the sun, the planet is at **aphelion.** Suppose the planet at perihelion moves along its orbit for a short time, Δt. If its speed at perihelion is v_p, it will move a distance $v_p\Delta t$ during that time interval. If Δt is very short, the distance along the orbit is practically a straight line. The radius R_p will sweep out a triangle with an area equal to $\frac{1}{2}R_p(v_p\Delta t)$. If the planet moves along its orbit at aphelion for the same time interval, the distance moved will be $v_a\Delta t$, and the radius R_a will sweep out a triangle with an area equal to $\frac{1}{2}R_a(v_a\Delta t)$.

Kepler's second law states that these two triangles must have the same area, since the motion occurs for the same time interval in both cases. Therefore,

$$\tfrac{1}{2}R_p(v_p\Delta t) = \tfrac{1}{2}R_a(v_a\Delta t), \quad \text{and}$$

$$\frac{v_p}{v_a} = \frac{R_a}{R_p}$$

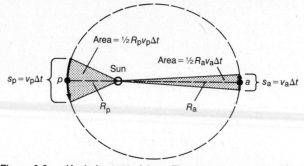

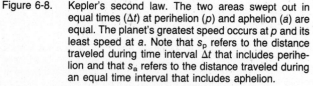

Figure 6-8.   Kepler's second law. The two areas swept out in equal times (Δt) at perihelion (p) and aphelion (a) are equal. The planet's greatest speed occurs at p and its least speed at a. Note that s_p refers to the distance traveled during time interval Δt that includes perihelion and that s_a refers to the distance traveled during an equal time interval that includes aphelion.

We see that by Kepler's second law, the speed of the planet is inversely proportional to its distance from the sun. As a planet moves farther from the sun, its speed decreases, and as a planet moves nearer, its speed increases. The speed of a planet is greatest at perihelion and least at aphelion.

From Equation 2-6, $KE = \frac{1}{2}mv^2$, you can see that the kinetic energy of a planet is proportional to the square of its speed. A planet therefore has a greater kinetic energy at perihelion than at aphelion. Where does this additional kinetic energy come from? At aphelion, the planet is farther from the sun than at perihelion. It therefore has a greater gravitational potential energy, relative to the sun, at aphelion. As the planet moves along its orbit from aphelion to perihelion, it is actually falling toward the sun. As the planet falls closer to the sun, its potential energy decreases, and its kinetic energy increases. As the planet "climbs" back from perihelion to aphelion, its kinetic energy decreases and its potential energy increases. At all points along the orbit, the total mechanical energy (the sum of the potential and kinetic energy) is the same. Since the planets move without friction, none of their mechanical energy is lost as heat, so they have been able to continue circling the sun along the same orbits for billions of years.

Kepler's Third Law

Ten years after announcing his first two laws, Kepler published a third law concerning a relationship he had found between the distance of a planet from the sun and its **period,** or the time required to make one complete circuit of its orbit. **Kepler's third law** states that the **mean** (average) **radius,** R_p, of a planet's orbit and its period of revolution, T_p, are related as follows:

$$\frac{R_p{}^3}{T_p{}^2} = K$$

where K is a constant that has the same value for all the sun's planets.

Kepler's third law can be derived from Newton's laws as follows. Suppose a planet is in a nearly circular orbit around the sun with a mean radius of R_p and an orbital speed of v_p. By Equation 1-7 (Newton's universal law of gravitation), the gravitational force on the planet is:

$$F = \frac{Gm_sm_p}{R_p{}^2}$$

where G is the universal gravitational constant, m_s is the mass of the sun, m_p is the mass of the planet, and R_p is the distance between the sun and the planet.

F is directed toward the sun and is the only force acting on the planet. It is therefore the centripetal force that is keeping the planet in its orbit. By Equation 6-4, this force equals mv^2/r. We can therefore write

$$F = \frac{m_pv_p{}^2}{R_p}, \quad \text{or}$$

$$\frac{Gm_sm_p}{R_p{}^2} = \frac{m_pv_p{}^2}{R_p}, \quad \text{and} \quad \frac{Gm_s}{R_p{}^2} = \frac{v_p{}^2}{R_p}$$

The circumference of the orbit, or distance the planet travels in time T_p, equals $2\pi R_p$. The speed of the planet, v_p, therefore equals $2\pi R_p/T_p$, and you can substitute this value for v_p in the equation above:

$$\frac{Gm_s}{R_p{}^2} = \frac{(2\pi R_p/T_p)^2}{R_p}$$

$$\frac{Gm_s}{R_p{}^2} = \frac{4\pi^2 R_p}{T_p{}^2}$$

$$\frac{R_p{}^3}{T_p{}^2} = \frac{Gm_s}{4\pi^2}$$

On the right side of the last equation, all of the quantities (G, m_s, $4\pi^2$) are constants that can be combined into a single constant, K_{sun}.

$$\frac{R_p{}^3}{T_p{}^2} = \frac{Gm_s}{4\pi^2} = K_{sun}$$

Notice that K_{sun} is independent of the mass of the planet but it does depend on the mass of the sun, m_s. For planets (or any other objects) revolving about a body of different mass, the value of K would be different from K_{sun}. It would, however, be the same for all the objects in orbit around that particular body.

CAN YOU EXPLAIN THIS?

The sun is closest to the earth in January, the middle of the Northern Hemisphere's winter, and furthest away in July, the middle of its summer.

The earth's orbit around the sun is not a perfect circle, but an ellipse. On January 3, the earth is at perihelion. On that date, the earth is 147 million kilometers from the sun. On July 4, aphelion, the earth is 152 million kilometers from the sun. The earth's axis is tilted 23.5° to a perpendicular to the plane of its orbit. This angle of tilt is maintained throughout the earth's revolution about the sun. In the Northern Hemisphere, the axis is tilted *toward* the sun in July and *away from* the sun in January, as shown in Figure 6-9.

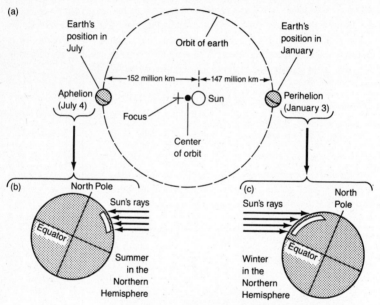

Figure 6-9.   (a) One focus of the earth's elliptical orbit is at the position of the sun. The location of the other focus is marked with a + sign. Its elliptical orbit puts the earth at the greatest distance from the sun in July. (b) and (c) Because of the earth's inclination, a given quantity of sunlight (here depicted by four rays) is concentrated on a smaller area of the Northern Hemisphere in July than in January, making July in that region of earth a warm time of the year.

It is the angle at which the sun's rays strike the earth, rather than the distance they travel, that is important in determining the earth's seasonal changes in temperature. A beam of sunlight that strikes a surface at an angle of 90° delivers twice as much energy per square meter as does the same beam of light striking at an angle of 30°. In the Northern Hemisphere, the sun's rays come closest to hitting the earth's surface at right angles on June 21. That is why we have summer at that time, even though the sun is farther away than it is in our winter. (In the Southern Hemisphere, the seasons are reversed because the sun's rays come closest to hitting its surface at right angles in January.)

QUESTIONS

1. The foci of the elliptical orbit of Pluto are (1) the sun and the earth (2) the earth and the moon (3) the sun and an empty focus (4) the earth and an empty focus

2. The shape of Mars' orbit is (1) elliptical (2) parabolic (3) hyperbolic (4) circular

3. The centripetal force that holds Mars in its orbit is directed toward (1) the earth (2) the sun (3) the moon (4) Mars

4. If the two foci of an ellipse coincide, the figure formed is a (1) straight line (2) hyperbola (3) parabola (4) circle

5. The diagram at the right shows a planet P traveling in an elliptical orbit. A and B are any two points on the orbit. Which of the following is true?
   (1) $\overline{AF_1} = \overline{AF_2}$
   (2) $\overline{AF_1} = \overline{BF_1}$
   (3) $\overline{AF_1} + \overline{AF_2}$ is greater than $\overline{BF_1} + \overline{BF_2}$
   (4) $\overline{AF_1} + \overline{AF_2} = \overline{BF_1} + \overline{BF_2}$

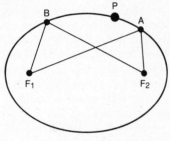

6–10. Base your answers to Questions 6 through 10 on the diagram at the right, which shows a planet in its orbit about the sun.

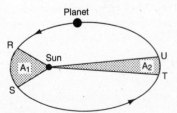

6. If area A_1 equals area A_2, the time required for the planet to travel distance RS compared to the time required to travel distance TU is (1) shorter (2) longer (3) the same

7. As the planet moves from U to R, its potential energy (1) decreases (2) increases (3) remains the same

8. As the planet moves from U to R, its kinetic energy (1) decreases (2) increases (3) remains the same

9. As the planet moves from S to T, its total energy (1) decreases (2) increases (3) remains the same

10. As the planet moves from U to R, its orbital speed (1) decreases (2) increases (3) remains the same

11–12. Base your answers to Questions 11 and 12 on the information below.

The ratio of the mean radius of orbit cubed to the orbital period squared is the same for all planets; that is, $R^3/T^2 = K$.

11. This law is attributed to (1) Newton (2) Doppler (3) Kepler (4) Rutherford

12. If R is measured in meters and T is measured in seconds, the units for K are (1) $N \cdot m^2/C^2$ (2) $N \cdot m^2/kg^2$ (3) m^3/s^2 (4) s^2/m^3

13. The nature of the force that holds the planets in their orbits is (1) gravitational (2) electrical (3) magnetic (4) nuclear

14. The time required for a planet to orbit the sun is called its (1) period (2) day (3) mean radius (4) focus

IV. SATELLITE MOTION

A smaller body that revolves about a larger body is called a **satellite.** The planets, including the earth, are natural satellites of the sun. These satellites of the sun can have satellites of their own. The earth has one natural satellite, the moon, and numerous human-made satellites that have been placed in orbits around the earth for various purposes. These human-made satellites have many uses, including long-distance communications across continents and oceans, weather observations, studies of the earth's surface and its resources, and military surveillance.

As you will recall from the study of projectiles fired horizontally from some height, the greater the initial speed of the projectile, the farther the body will travel before reaching the ground. Newton realized that if a projectile were fired with sufficient speed, and there were no air friction, it would circle about the earth without ever landing. The reason for this is that the earth's surface is curved. As the projectile falls toward the earth along its curved trajectory, at some certain launching speed, the earth's surface will curve away just as rapidly as the object falls toward it. The projectile will then remain in a circular orbit, always accelerating toward the earth, but never getting any closer to it.

Satellite Speeds

The speed necessary to launch a satellite into orbit around the earth, and the altitude needed to avoid significant air friction, are technological feats that have been possible only during this century following the development of powerful rocket engines. However, the laws of Newton, published more than 300 years ago (in 1687), can be used to calculate the orbital speed needed to keep a satellite in a circular orbit around the earth.

To begin this calculation, note that if the mass of a satellite is m, then its weight, w, is equal to mg, where g is the acceleration due to gravity at the altitude of the satellite. The weight, w, is the centripetal force acting on the satellite, and it must be equal to mv^2/r, where v is the velocity of the satellite and r is the radius of the orbit measured from the center of the earth. Thus

$$mg = mv^2/r, \quad \text{and} \quad v = \sqrt{rg}$$

For orbits near the earth's surface (within 50,000 m of the earth's surface), r is approximately the same as the earth's radius, 6.4×10^6 m, and g is approximately 9.8 m/s^2. Then,

$$v = \sqrt{(6.4 \times 10^6 \text{ m})(9.8 \text{ m/s}^2)}$$

$$v = \sqrt{63 \times 10^6 \text{ m}^2/\text{s}^2}$$

$$v = 7.9 \times 10^3 \text{ m/s}$$

The circumference of an orbit with a radius of 6.4×10^6 m is

$$C = 2\pi(6.4 \times 10^6 \text{ m}) = 40. \times 10^6 \text{ m} = 4.0 \times 10^7 \text{ m}$$

At an orbital speed of 7.9×10^3 m/s, the period of the satellite will be

$$T = \frac{40. \times 10^6 \text{ m}}{7.9 \times 10^3 \text{ m/s}} = 5{,}100 \text{ s} = 85 \text{ minutes}$$

All earth satellites in low circular orbits (altitudes of about 300 km) have periods between 80 and 90 minutes.

CAN YOU EXPLAIN THIS?

Satellites are falling around the earth.

Figure 6-10 (see the following page) is a vector diagram of the components of the displacement of an earth satellite in a circular orbit at low altitude. The motion of the satellite tangent to the orbit is not accelerated. At an orbital speed of 7,900 meters per second, its displacement along the tangent, Δs_T, is 7,900 meters in 1 second. Its acceleration toward the earth is $g = 9.8$ meters per second squared. Its displacement in this direction, Δs_C, equals $\frac{1}{2}gt^2$. In 1.0 second,

$$\Delta s_C = \frac{1}{2}(9.8 \text{ m/s}^2)(1.0 \text{ s})^2 = 4.9 \text{ m}$$

Thus, the satellite falls 4.9 meters toward the earth each second.

The radius of the earth is 6.4×10^6 meters. If a tangent 7,900 meters long is drawn to the earth's surface from any point, the end of the tangent will be 4.9 meters above the earth's surface. In other words, as the satellite falls toward the earth, the earth's surface drops by the same distance. The satellite therefore remains at the same distance from the earth at all times. The same thing happens to a satellite in a circular orbit at any distance from the earth.

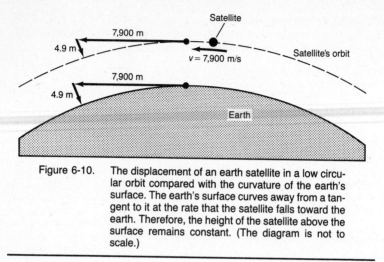

Figure 6-10. The displacement of an earth satellite in a low circular orbit compared with the curvature of the earth's surface. The earth's surface curves away from a tangent to it at the rate that the satellite falls toward the earth. Therefore, the height of the satellite above the surface remains constant. (The diagram is not to scale.)

Escape Velocity

A satellite in a low earth orbit is subject to frictional drag of the atmosphere. This friction force opposes the motion of the satellite and causes its orbital speed to decrease. As its speed drops below 7,900 meters per second, the centripetal force, mg, becomes greater than v^2/r, and the satellite cannot remain in its circular orbit. The satellite drops nearer the earth. The atmospheric drag then increases, and the satellite drops further. It therefore gradually spirals down toward the surface. It may land on the earth, or it may be destroyed by the heat generated by air friction.

If a satellite is launched near the earth's surface with an initial speed *greater* than 7,900 meters per second, it will be moving too fast to drop into a circular orbit. It will begin to rise higher above the earth. As it does so, its potential energy will increase, and its kinetic energy and speed will decrease. Eventually, it will stop rising and start to fall back toward the earth. A satellite launched at an initial speed greater than 7,900 m/s will go into an elliptical, rather than a circular, orbit.

As the launching speed is increased, the orbit becomes more and more eccentric, and the satellite moves farther and farther from the earth before returning. At some sufficiently high speed, the object (no longer a satellite) will continue to travel away from the earth into space and never return. This happens because the gravitational field at a sufficiently large distance from the earth becomes too weak to stop the rise of the object. The speed at which objects escape the gravitational field of the earth is called the **escape velocity.** For the earth, the escape velocity from the surface is 11,200 meters per second. The escape velocity from any other large body, such as another planet or the moon, depends on its mass and radius. Although the escape velocity is different for each of these bodies, it is the same for all objects launched from the surface of the same body.

Absolute Temperature

The molecules of any body of matter are in continuous random motion. As the temperature of a body changes, the average kinetic energy of this random motion also changes. If two bodies have different temperatures, the particles of the warmer body will have more kinetic energy, on the average, than those of the cooler body. Suppose that the two bodies are brought close to each other. *Heat,* or *thermal energy,* is always spontaneously transferred from a warmer body to a colder body. Hence, the warmer body will cool off and the cooler body will warm up as heat transfer takes place between the two bodies.

The temperature of a body is related to the average kinetic energy of random motion of its molecules. As a body is cooled, the average kinetic energy of the molecules of the body decreases along with the temperature of the body. **Absolute zero** is the lowest possible temperature of any material. At absolute zero, no thermal energy can be transferred from a body because no other body can have a lower temperature. The **absolute temperature** of a gas is the temperature of the gas measured on the Kelvin scale (described later in this section).

Temperature Scales

Although many different temperature scales have been developed, the *Celsius* and *Kelvin* scales are those used most often in the laboratory. A temperature scale can be constructed by determining the temperature of two conditions that can be reproduced in the laboratory. These two temperatures are called fixed points, and they can be assigned any two values desired. The interval between the two fixed points is then divided into any number of equal parts, called *degrees.* The symbol for degrees is °.

Celsius Scale. The two fixed points that have been selected for the **Celsius scale** are the point at which a mixture of ice and water is in equilibrium at standard pressure (that is, the freezing point of water) and the point at which a mixture of steam and water is in equilibrium at standard pressure (the boiling point of water). On the Celsius scale, the freezing point of water is 0°C and the boiling point of water is 100°C at a standard pressure of one atmosphere. The interval between the fixed points is divided into 100 equal degrees. Room temperature is about 20°C and normal body temperature is 37°C.

Kelvin Scale. When a fixed quantity of a gas is cooled in a container of constant volume, a graph of the pressure versus the temperature of the gas is a straight line (as long as the gas does not change to a liquid). According to the kinetic theory of gases, the pressure of a gas at constant volume is proportional to the average kinetic energy of its molecules. A pressure-temperature graph is therefore a graph of average kinetic energy versus temperature. Experiments show that if the graphs for different gases are extrapolated (extended) below the temperature at which the gas changes to a liquid, all the graphs reach zero pressure (zero energy) at the same temperature, −273.16°C. This temperature is therefore absolute zero, and it has been designated as the zero point, 0 K, on the Kelvin scale. (Note that the ° symbol is not used with Kelvin temperatures.) The size of a unit on the Kelvin scale is equal to a Celsius degree. It is called the

PRACTICAL APPLICATION

The terms "weightlessness" and "zero gravity" are misleading descriptions of the condition experienced by astronauts as they "float" in an orbiting spacecraft. The astronauts do, in fact, have weight in the spacecraft, since the force of the earth's gravity is acting on them. This force provides the centripetal force necessary to maintain them, as well as the spacecraft and everything in it, in orbit around the earth. On the earth's surface, a person is prevented from falling toward the center of the earth by the reaction force of the ground or the floor. It is this reaction force that is felt and that provides the sensation of weight. In the orbiting spacecraft, everything is actually falling freely. There is no reaction force opposing this falling motion, and so no "weight" is felt. An object released from a hand seems to be weightless because it does not fall relative to the person. It is falling, however, but with the same acceleration as the person, the spacecraft, and everything in it. (If you were to jump off a diving board while holding a bowling ball, you would find that the ball becomes "weightless" during the descent for the same reasons.) ∎

Geosynchronous Orbits

It was mentioned earlier that satellites in circular orbits around the earth at low altitudes have periods of about 85 minutes. For certain purposes, it is desirable to have a satellite traveling around the earth from west to east with a period of exactly one day (24.0 hours, or 8.64×10^4 seconds). If the satellite is located over the earth's equator and moving parallel to it, it will remain over the same point on the equator, since the earth is rotating with the satellite with the same period. An orbit in which a satellite remains over the same point on the earth is called a **geosynchronous orbit,** and the satellite is called *geostationary.* Geostationary satellites are used in communication networks to relay radio and television signals around the world.

The simplest way to find the radius of a geosynchronous orbit is to use Kepler's third law together with the known radius and period of any earth satellite. For example, the mean radius of the orbit of the moon and its period can be used.

The mean radius, R_m, of the moon's orbit is 3.84×10^8 meters, and its period of revolution, T_m, around the earth is 2.36×10^6 seconds (about 27 days). By Kepler's third law, the ratio $R_m{}^3/T_m{}^2$ is a constant for any earth satellite. If R_s is the radius of a satellite's orbit, and T_s is its period, we can write

$$\frac{R_s{}^3}{T_s{}^2} = \frac{R_m{}^3}{T_m{}^2}$$

For a geosynchronous orbit, $T_s = 8.64 \times 10^4$ seconds (1 day). Substituting the known values into the equation above gives

$$R_s{}^3 = \frac{(8.64 \times 10^4 \text{ s})^2(3.84 \times 10^8 \text{ m})^3}{(2.36 \times 10^6 \text{ m})^2}$$

If you carry out this calculation, you will find that $R_s = 4.23 \times 10^7$ meters. Since this is the distance of the orbit's radius from the earth's center, the radius of the earth, 6.38×10^6 meters, must be subtracted to find the altitude of the orbit above the earth's surface:

$$4.23 \times 10^7 \text{ m} - 0.64 \times 10^7 \text{ m} = 3.59 \times 10^7 \text{ m}$$

or about 36,000 kilometers. (In the Regents Examination in Physics, you will not be expected to make arithmetic calculations of this kind, but you will be expected to understand the principles involved.)

QUESTIONS

1. The orbits of satellites about the earth are (1) never circular (2) never elliptical (3) always circular (4) always either elliptical or circular
2. A satellite in a geosynchronous orbit has a period of one (1) minute (2) hour (3) day (4) year
3. If a satellite is in a geosynchronous orbit, it is always located (1) at the same point relative to the sun (2) above the North Pole (3) at 45° north latitude (4) above the same point on the equator
4. As the speed of a human-made satellite decreases, it (1) escapes earth orbit (2) goes into orbit about the moon (3) spirals into the sun (4) spirals down toward the earth
5. Atmospheric friction causes the speed of a satellite to (1) decrease (2) increase (3) remain the same
6. The radius of the orbit of a human-made satellite orbiting Earth may be determined by equating R^3/T^2 to the Kepler constant calculated for the (1) satellite and the Moon (2) satellite and Earth (3) Earth and Mars (4) satellite and the Sun

UNIT 7   INTERNAL ENERGY

I. TEMPERATURE

A student touching a wooden desk with one hand and a metal file cabin the other may believe that the cabinet is colder than the desk. In fact, th cabinet only *feels* colder. Metal is a better conductor of heat than wood so it conducts heat away from the student's hand at a faster rate than th does, causing the sensation of lower temperature. The sense of touch pr relative indication of temperature that is not reliable or reproducible in measurement. **Temperature,** a scalar quantity, is a measure of how ho a body is with respect to a standard. Quantitative measurements of ten are made with a **thermometer.**

PRACTICAL APPLICATION

Nearly all materials expand when heated but not at the same rate. A *strip,* consisting of two securely bonded and very thin metals having coefficients (rates) of expansion, operates according to this principle temperature, both metals have the same length. As the temperature the two metals expand by different amounts and the bimetallic strip example, brass expands 50% faster per unit length than iron does wh experience the same temperature change, as shown in Figure 7-1.

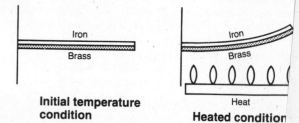

Initial temperature condition   **Heated condition**

Figure 7-1.   Because a unit length of brass expands more unit length of iron when the two metals experien same temperature change, a bimetallic strip m the two metals bends in the direction shown.

The "degree of bend" of the strip can be calibrated for a rang tures, and the bimetallic strip can be used as a thermometer or the oven thermometer, a bimetallic strip is wound into a coil, and its to temperature changes moves the dial on a calibrated scale. ■

kelvin, K, and is the fundamental *SI* unit of temperature. Therefore, a temperature change of 5 Celsius degrees equals a temperature change of 5 kelvins. As shown in Figure 7-2, a temperature of 0°C is the same as 273.16 K. For convenience, this value is usually rounded to 273, and the Kelvin temperature equals the sum of the Celsius temperature plus 273:

$$T_K = T_C + 273$$

where T_K is the Kelvin temperature and T_C is the Celsius temperature.

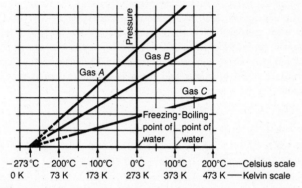

Figure 7-2.   Graphs of the pressure of three gases at constant volume plotted against the Celsius and Kelvin temperature scales. The point at which an unbroken line changes to a dashed line represents the temperature at which the gas changes to a liquid. Hence, the dashed lines are extrapolations of the unbroken lines. The temperature at which the three dashed lines converge at zero pressure is the coldest possible temperature, absolute zero.

QUESTIONS

1. **Which of the following are equivalent temperatures? (1) 0°C and 0 K (2) 0°C and −273 K (3) −273°C and 0 K (4) −273°C and 273 K**
2. **On the Kelvin scale, the zero point is (1) absolute zero (2) the boiling point of water (3) the freezing point of water (4) the triple point of water**
3. **The *SI* unit of temperature is the (1) Celsius degree (2) joule (3) kelvin (4) kilojoule**
4. **Which of the following is a fundamental *SI* unit? (1) Celsius degree (2) kelvin (3) kilojoule (4) kilojoule per kilogram · Celsius degree**
5. **An indication of how hot or cold something is with respect to a chosen standard is called (1) heat (2) specific heat (3) temperature (4) thermodynamics**

6. The temperature at which no thermal energy can be transferred to another object is called (1) absolute temperature (2) absolute zero (3) triple point (4) zero point

7. A change of 10 kelvins compared to a change of 10 Celsius degrees is (1) less (2) greater (3) the same

8. A temperature of 50°C is the same as a temperature of (1) −223 K (2) 223 K (3) 273 K (4) 323 K

9. Temperature is a measure of an object's (1) average molecular kinetic energy (2) average molecular potential energy (3) total molecular kinetic energy (4) total molecular potential energy

10. At what temperature is the internal energy of a body at a minimum? (1) 0°C (2) −273°C (3) 272°C (4) 373°C

11. Which graph best represents the relationship between the Celsius temperature of an ideal gas and the average kinetic energy of its molecules?

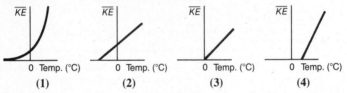

(1)   (2)   (3)   (4)

12. An increase in temperature of 54 Celsius degrees is equal to an increase of (1) 54 K (2) 219 K (3) 327 K (4) 454 K

13. The lowest possible temperature of a body is (1) −273 K (2) 0 K (3) 100 K (4) 273 K

14. The number of kelvins between the freezing point and boiling point of pure water at standard pressure is (1) 0 (2) 100 (3) 180 (4) 273

15. A graph of pressure versus temperature is drawn for a sample of an ideal gas in a closed container. The graph intercepts the temperature axis at (1) 0°C (2) 273 K (3) −273 K (4) −273°C

16. As the kinetic energy of the molecules of an ideal gas increases, its absolute temperature (1) decreases (2) increases (3) remains the same

17. As the temperature of a substance approaches absolute zero, the random motion of its molecules (1) decreases (2) increases (3) remains the same

18. If only the potential energy of the molecules of a substance increases, the absolute temperature of the substance (1) decreases (2) increases (3) remains the same

II. INTERNAL ENERGY AND HEAT

The sum of the kinetic and potential energies possessed by the molecules of an object due to their motions and positions relative to each other is called the **internal energy** of the object. It does not include the kinetic or potential energy of the object as a whole. The internal energy of a substance depends on its temperature, mass, phase (solid, liquid, or gas), and nature. For example, one kilogram of water at 40.°C has more internal energy than an equal mass of water at 20.°C. At a higher temperature, the kinetic energy of the water molecules on the average is greater. Thus, the sum of these molecular kinetic energies is greater.

If the temperature of two samples of water is the same, but the first has twice the mass of the second, the first sample has more internal energy than the second. This is the case because the first sample has twice as many particles as the second sample; since each particle possesses the same kinetic energy on the average, the more massive sample has the greater sum of kinetic energies, and, thus the greater internal energy.

Consider the internal energies of two samples of a substance identical in all respects except phase—for example, 10. grams of water at 0 degrees Celsius and standard pressure and 10. grams of ice at the same temperature and pressure. Clearly the water has more internal energy than the ice because heat would have to be added to the ice to change it to 10. grams of water at that temperature and pressure. Although it can often be stated that one body has a greater internal energy than another, the actual internal energy of a body cannot be calculated. However, the amount of *change* in internal energy of a body can be determined when certain conditions change (such as the body's phase or temperature).

Heat is the name given to energy that is transferred from a warmer body to a colder body because the bodies have different temperatures. The heat content of a body is the total of the kinetic energies of its individual particles. Like all types of energy, heat is a scalar quantity. Since heat is a form of energy, the *SI* unit for heat is the joule, J. As heat enters a body, the body's temperature usually increases.

Mechanical energy is often converted to heat as the result of friction. The heat generated raises the temperature of the bodies in the immediate surroundings. For example, as a hammer drives a nail into wood, some of the work done by the hammer forces the nail into the wood, against friction, and this work is converted to heat. The nail, hammerhead, and immediately surrounding wood become hotter as a result.

CAN YOU EXPLAIN THIS? ==============

There is more heat energy in the Arctic Ocean during the winter than there is in a cup of boiling water.

From mechanics, it is known that the kinetic energy of a particle is directly proportional to its mass and the square of its velocity, that is, $KE = \frac{1}{2}mv^2$. Temperature is a measure of the average kinetic energies of the particles of a substance. The temperature of the Arctic Ocean is generally below 0°C and the temperature of the cup of boiling water is 100°C at standard pressure. Thus, the kinetic energy of an individual particle in the cup would be greater, on average, than that of one in the ocean. Heat, however, is a measure of the *total* kinetic energy of the particles of a substance. The Arctic Ocean is vastly more massive than the cup of water. Therefore, the sum of the kinetic energies of all the particles in the ocean is much greater than the sum of the kinetic energies of the molecules in the cup of water, and the ocean has more heat than the cup of water.

Specific Heat

When heat is added to a substance, the substance will usually experience an increase in temperature as a result of an increase in the kinetic energies of its particles. The amount of heat required to produce a temperature change of one Celsius degree in one kilogram of a substance is called the **specific heat,** c, of the substance. That is,

$$c = \frac{Q}{m\Delta T_C}$$

where Q is the amount of heat in joules added to a mass, m, in kilograms, and ΔT_C is the temperature change produced in Celsius degrees. Rearranged, this equation becomes:

$$Q = mc\Delta T_C \qquad \text{(Eq. 7-1)}$$

Every substance has a unique specific heat. One kilogram of water requires 4,190 joules of heat to increase in temperature by one Celsius degree. (When measuring heat energies, it is often more convenient to use the **kilojoule,** kJ, where 1 kJ = 1,000 J. Thus, the specific heat, c, of water is 4.19 kJ/kg · C°.) Liquid water has one of the highest known specific heats. Other common substances, including water in the forms of ice and steam, have considerably lower specific heats. In fact, the specific heats of ice and steam are about half that of liquid water. A table of heat constants is included in the Reference Tables for Physics (see Appendix II).

PRACTICAL APPLICATION

Although a slice of pizza may not be too hot to handle, you could burn your mouth when taking a bite of it. The specific heat of the cheese that you put into your mouth is greater than the specific heat of the crust that makes contact with your hand, because the cheese has a higher water content. Therefore, the cheese has a greater ability to store heat than the drier crust does and thus takes longer to cool. ■

Equation 7-1 applies to both increases and decreases in heat and temperature. If ΔT_C is positive, then Q is positive and heat has been added to the body. If ΔT_C is negative, then Q is negative and heat has been given up by the body. Equation 7-1 can be used to solve problems involving heat transfer and temperature change.

EXAMPLE

How much heat is required to raise the temperature of 5.0 kilograms of copper from 40.°C to 120.°C?

Solution

$$c = 0.39 \text{ kJ/kg} \cdot \text{C}° \text{ (from the Reference Tables)}$$

$$m = 5.0 \text{ kg}$$

$$\Delta T_C = 120.°C - 40.°C = 80. \text{ C}°$$

$$Q = mc\Delta T_C = (5.0 \text{ kg})(0.39 \text{ kJ/kg} \cdot \text{C}°)(80. \text{ C}°)$$

$$Q = 160 \text{ kJ}$$

When heat absorbed by a substance causes an increase in temperature, or when the release of heat causes a decrease in temperature, a change in the average kinetic energy of the molecules occurs. However, no change in phase of the substance occurs.

Exchange of Internal Energy

Conservation of Internal Energy. In an isolated system in which there is no conversion of energy from one form to another, the total internal energy of the system is constant. This follows from the law of conservation of energy, and it implies that heat removed from one object in the system must appear as heat absorbed by other objects in the system. For example, if a hot object placed in cold water loses 10. kilojoules of heat to the water, then the water must gain 10. kilojoules of heat. The exchange will result in internal changes of average molecular kinetic energy—a decrease for the hot object and an increase for the previously colder water. The transfer of heat continues until all parts of the system have the same temperature.

EXAMPLE

A 1.00-kilogram iron block at 80.0°C is placed in 2.00 kilograms of water at 20.0°C. What is the final temperature of the iron?

Solution

The final temperature of the iron is the same as the final temperature of the water. Let that temperature, in degrees Celsius, be denoted by the letter T.

For the iron: $\quad m = 1.00 \text{ kg} \quad c = 0.45 \text{ kJ/kg} \cdot \text{C}° \quad \Delta T_C = 80.0°C - T$

For the water: $\quad m = 2.00 \text{ kg} \quad c = 4.19 \text{ kJ/kg} \cdot \text{C}° \quad \Delta T_C = T - 20.0°C$

Since heat energy must be conserved,

$$Q \text{ lost} = Q \text{ gained}$$

$$mc\Delta T_C \text{ (iron)} = mc\Delta T_C \text{ (water)}$$

$$(1.00 \text{ kg})(0.45 \text{ kJ/kg} \cdot C°)(80.0°C - T) =$$
$$(2.00 \text{ kg})(4.19 \text{ kJ/kg} \cdot C°)(T - 20.0°C)$$

$$36 \text{ kJ} - (0.45 \text{ kJ/C°})T = (8.38 \text{ kJ/C°})T - 168 \text{ kJ}$$

$$(8.83 \text{ kJ/C°})T = 204 \text{ kJ}$$

$$T = 23.1°C$$

Change of Phase. Each crystalline substance has two particular temperatures at which it can absorb heat and experience an increase in its internal energy without experiencing an increase in temperature. At these temperatures, the internal *kinetic* energy of the substance remains unchanged, because the absorbed energy produces only an increase in the molecular *potential* energies of the particles, as work is done against the attractive molecular forces. The absorbed heat produces a change of phase for the substance—solid to liquid (**melting**) or liquid to gas (**boiling**)—with no change in temperature. If the process is reversed and heat is extracted, phase changes from gas to liquid (condensation) and liquid to solid (freezing) occur with no change in temperature during the phase changes.

The amount of heat required to change one kilogram of a substance at its melting point from the solid to the liquid phase with no change in temperature is called the **heat of fusion**, H_f. The same amount of heat is liberated when one kilogram of the liquid substance at its freezing point freezes. (The freezing point and the melting point of a given substance are the same temperature.) The amount of heat required to melt a given sample is determined by the mass of the sample and its heat of fusion, which is a constant for a particular substance. That is,

$$Q_f = mH_f \qquad \text{(Eq. 7-2)}$$

where Q_f is heat in kilojoules, m is mass in kilograms, and H_f is the heat of fusion in kilojoules per kilogram. Various heats of fusion are listed in the table of heat constants in the Reference Tables for Physics in Appendix II.

The amount of heat required to change one kilogram of a substance at its boiling point from the liquid to the gaseous phase with no change in temperature is called the **heat of vaporization**, H_v. The same amount of heat is liberated if one kilogram of the gaseous substance at its condensation point condenses. (The boiling point and the condensation point of a given substance are the same temperature.)

The average separation of particles in the gaseous phase is much greater than in the solid or liquid phase, so more work is required to vaporize (change to the gaseous phase) a given mass of a substance than to melt it. Therefore, for a given substance, the heat of vaporization is greater than the heat of fusion. Since the mass of a sample and its heat of vaporization determine the amount of heat required to vaporize the sample, it follows that

$$Q_v = mH_v \qquad \text{(Eq. 7-3)}$$

where Q_v is heat in kilojoules, m is mass in kilograms, and H_v is the heat of vaporization in kilojoules per kilogram. Various heats of vaporization are listed in the table of heat constants in Appendix II.

(Liquids *evaporate*, or change to the gaseous or vapor phase, at their surface at any temperature. A liquid *boils* when bubbles of vapor form in the liquid below the surface. At standard atmospheric pressure, the boiling point of a given liquid is a fixed temperature. The heat of vaporization for a liquid refers to vaporization at the boiling point.)

The graph in Figure 7-3 shows what happens when heat is added at a constant rate to 1.0 kg of ice initially at $-20.°C$ until the sample becomes steam (gaseous water) at $120.°C$. When the sample experiences a phase change (melting or boiling), the temperature remains constant because the added heat is being stored as internal potential energy of the molecules.

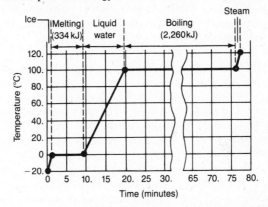

Figure 7-3.   A temperature-versus-time graph for 1.0 kilogram of water, initially ice at $-20.°C$, to which heat is added at a constant rate of 40. kilojoules per minute.

Factors Affecting the Boiling and Freezing Points of Water. A dissolved salt lowers the freezing point of water (melting point of ice). Salt is put on icy roads and sidewalks to cause the ice to melt. If the salt lowers the freezing point below the air temperature, the ice will melt.

A dissolved salt also raises the boiling point of water. This is why adding salt to boiling water causes the boiling to stop. If the water is heated further (with salt now dissolved in it), the water will begin to boil again after it reaches a higher temperature. This behavior of a salt-water solution follows from the definition of the boiling point. The boiling point of a liquid is the temperature at which the vapor pressure of the liquid equals atmospheric pressure. The vapor pressure of a liquid increases as the temperature of the liquid increases. When salt is dissolved in boiling water, the boiling point of the water is immediately increased because the salt-water solution has a lower vapor pressure than pure water. A higher temperature is needed to increase the vapor pressure of the solution to atmospheric pressure.

Pressure is a factor that affects the freezing point of water. (Note that the freezing point of a substance is the same temperature as its melting point.) The effect of pressure on the freezing point of water comes into play when a person ice skates. A skater actually glides on a thin film of water when ice skating. The skater's weight is exerted on the ice along the thin blades of the skates. Thus, the pressure on the ice beneath the blades is considerably greater than the normal air pressure on the ice, and this greater pressure causes the ice beneath the blades to melt. After the blades pass over the region, the water refreezes because of the reduction to normal pressure.

Another factor that has an effect on the boiling point of water is the pressure exerted by the gas over the water. In most situations, the gas over the water is simply air, in which case it is the air pressure that affects the boiling point of the water. Increased air pressure raises the boiling point of water, because it is more difficult for vapor bubbles to form. Decreased air pressure lowers the boiling point. The effect of gas pressure on the boiling point of water is described in the following features.

PRACTICAL APPLICATION

A pressure cooker is a tightly closed container in which food to be cooked is placed with a quantity of water. When the pressure cooker is heated, the water boils at first at its normal boiling point. The steam produced cannot escape, however, and its pressure increases inside the container. As the pressure of the steam increases, the boiling point of the water rises because a higher temperature is required for the vapor pressure of the water to equal the gas pressure exerted by the mixture of air and steam above the water. At the higher temperature, foods cook more quickly than at the normal boiling point of water because chemical changes occur faster at higher temperatures. A safety valve limits the pressure in the cooker to a safe level by opening and allowing steam to escape when the safe pressure is exceeded. ∎

CAN YOU EXPLAIN THIS?

You can hold a flask of boiling water in your bare hand.

Boiling is a state of vaporization occurring within a liquid as well as at its surface. In the process of boiling water, bubbles of gas form within the water and then rise to the surface and escape. The speeds of the water molecules forming the gas bubbles must be sufficient to exert as much pressure within the bubble as the air is exerting on the water. That is, the *vapor pressure* of the water must equal atmospheric pressure. If the air pressure above the water is decreased, molecules of water moving with lower speed will be able to form gas bubbles that will not collapse.

It would be unsafe to hold a flask of water boiling at its normal point, 100°C. If, however, the air pressure inside the flask is reduced below normal air pressure (760. mm of mercury), the water can boil at a lower temperature. The air pressure inside the flask can be reduced substantially by removing air with a vacuum pump. The boiling point can thus be lowered enough to permit safe handling with the bare hand. For example, the boiling point of water at a pressure of 50. mm of mercury (6.6 kilopascals) is less than 40°C.

QUESTIONS

To answer some of the following questions, you may want to refer to information contained in the New York State Regents Reference Tables. See Appendix II.

1. In order for heat to be transferred between two bodies in contact, the bodies must have different (1) heats of fusion (2) masses (3) specific heats (4) temperatures
2. The quantity of heat required to raise the temperature of a kilogram of a substance one Celsius degree is called its (1) absolute heat (2) heat of fusion (3) heat of vaporization (4) specific heat
3. Compared to the heat required to warm 2.0 kilograms of water from 20.°C to 40.°C, the heat required to warm 2.0 kilograms of lead from 40.°C to 60.°C is (1) less (2) greater (3) the same
4. As a melted crystalline substance boils, its temperature (1) decreases (2) increases (3) remains the same
5. As heat is added to a crystalline solid that is beginning to melt, its temperature (1) decreases (2) increases (3) remains the same
6. As heat is added to a crystalline solid below its melting point, the average kinetic energy of its particles (1) decreases (2) increases (3) remains the same
7. As more salt is dissolved in a sample of water, the boiling point of the solution (1) decreases (2) increases (3) remains the same
8. Compared to the freezing point of pure water, the freezing point of a salt-water solution is (1) lower (2) higher (3) the same
9. If the pressure of the air above water in a flask is decreased, the boiling point of the water (1) decreases (2) increases (3) remains the same
10. Compared to the specific heat of water in the gaseous phase, the specific heat of water in the solid phase is (1) less (2) greater (3) the same
11. Which of the following is a liquid over the greatest temperature range? (1) mercury (2) water (3) ethyl alcohol (4) ammonia
12. Equal masses of mercury, platinum, ammonia, and lead are at their respective boiling points. Which requires the least amount of heat to change from the liquid to the gaseous phase? (1) mercury (2) platinum (3) ethyl alcohol (4) ammonia
13. Equal masses of lead and tungsten are at 20.°C and each absorbs one kilojoule of heat. Compared to the temperature change of the lead, the temperature change of the tungsten is (1) less (2) greater (3) the same

14. The amount of heat required to melt one kilogram of silver at its melting point is (1) 0.24 kJ (2) 105 kJ (3) 962 kJ (4) 2,370 kJ

15. When a substance changes from the solid phase to the liquid phase with no change in average internal kinetic energy, it is said to (1) sublimate (2) evaporate (3) melt (4) freeze

16. How much heat is required to raise the temperature of 0.20 kilogram of lead from 10.°C to 20.°C? (1) 0.026 kJ (2) 0.26 kJ (3) 2.6 kJ (4) 26 kJ

17. How much heat is required to melt 0.50 kilogram of tungsten at its melting point? (1) 0.065 kJ (2) 96 kJ (3) 190 kJ (4) 1,700 kJ

18–22. Base your answers to Questions 18 through 22 on the information given below.

The temperature of 1.00 kilogram of mercury is changed from −73°C to 727°C by the addition of heat energy at the rate of 5.00 kilojoules per minute. (Assume normal atmospheric pressure and no heat exchange with the surroundings.)

18. At which temperature can the mercury exist both as a liquid and as a gas? (1) 357°C (2) 396°C (3) 457°C (4) 1000°C

19. What is the total range of temperature in which mercury can exist as a liquid? (1) 39°C (2) 318°C (3) 357°C (4) 396°C

20. What amount of heat is necessary to melt completely the mercury at its melting point? (1) 11 kJ (2) 39 kJ (3) 290 kJ (4) 430 kJ

21. What amount of heat is necessary to raise the temperature of the mercury from −1.0°C to 1°C? (1) 0.14 kJ (2) 0.28 kJ (3) 4.4 kJ (4) 340 kJ

22. How long will it take the mercury to change completely into a gas after it reaches its boiling point of 357°C? (1) 39 min (2) 59 min (3) 295 min (4) 357 min

23–27. Base your answers to Questions 23 through 27 on the following information.

Two kilograms of aluminum at a temperature of 300.°C are placed on a block of ice whose temperature is 0.00°C. The ice melts until the system achieves equilibrium at 0.00°C.

23. What is the equilibrium temperature on the Kelvin scale? (1) 0.00 K (2) 100. K (3) 273 K (4) 573 K

24. How much heat is lost by the block of aluminum? (1) 270 kJ (2) 540 kJ (3) 600 kJ (4) 792 kJ

25. While the system is approaching equilibrium, the average kinetic energy of the molecules of ice (1) decreases (2) increases (3) remains the same

26. As the ice melts, the potential energy of its molecules (1) decreases (2) increases (3) remains the same

27. As the aluminum cools, the average kinetic energy of its molecules (1) decreases (2) increases (3) remains the same

28–34. Base your answers to Questions 28 through 34 on the following information.

The graph shows the temperature for 10. kilograms of an unknown substance as heat is added at a constant rate of 60. kilojoules per minute. The substance is a solid at 0°C.

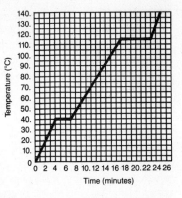

28. How much heat is added to the substance from the time that it stops melting to the time it begins to boil? (1) 10. kJ (2) 60. kJ (3) 320 kJ (4) 600 kJ

29. What is the total heat necessary to change the substance at its melting point from a solid to a liquid? (1) 40. kJ (2) 180 kJ (3) 3.0 kJ (4) 360 kJ

30. From the 17th minute to the 23rd minute, the average kinetic energy of the molecules of the substance (1) decreases (2) increases (3) remains the same

31. As the temperature of the solid increases from 0.°C to 40.°C, its specific heat (1) decreases (2) increases (3) remains the same

32. The melting point of the substance is (1) 0.°C (2) 40.°C (3) 100.°C (4) 115°C

33. Compared to the heat of fusion of the substance, the heat of vaporization of the substance is (1) less (2) greater (3) the same

34. What is the phase of the substance during the 5th minute? (1) solid only (2) liquid only (3) part solid and part liquid (4) solid, liquid, and gas

35–36. Base your answers to Questions 35 and 36 on the information given below.

A 1.0-kilogram sample of ice at 0.°C is added to 1.0 kilogram of water at 20.°C, and the mixture is allowed to reach equilibrium. (Assume that the ice and water are perfectly insulated from the surroundings so that heat is exchanged only between the ice and water.)

35. Compared to the heat lost by the water, the heat gained by the ice is (1) less (2) greater (3) the same

36. The final temperature of the mixture is (1) 0.°C (2) 5.0°C (3) 10.°C (4) 20.°C

37. If 54 kilojoules of heat are added to 1.5 kilograms of aluminum at 20.°C, what will be the final temperature of the aluminum? (1) 20.°C (2) 24°C (3) 40.°C (4) 60.°C

38. A mass of 2.0 kilograms of ethyl alcohol at 20.°C is mixed with 2.0 kilograms of ethyl alcohol at 30.°C, and the mixture is allowed to reach equilibrium. (Assume that no heat exchange with the surroundings occurs.) What is the final temperature of the mixture? (1) 20.°C (2) 22°C (3) 25°C (4) 30.°C

III. KINETIC THEORY OF GASES

To explain the observed relationships between temperature, pressure, and volume for a fixed mass of a gas, scientists have developed the **kinetic theory of gases.** In this theory, it is assumed that gases are composed of large numbers of small individual molecules. In gases at ordinary pressures—that is, when the molecules are relatively far apart—the force of attraction between molecules is assumed to be negligible. The only interactions between molecules are elastic collisions in which kinetic energy and momentum are conserved. Although the molecules are in constant random motion, they do not escape into space because they are either confined by the walls of a container or held by the earth's gravitational field.

In gases of low density, the molecules are separated on the average by distances that are large relative to their diameters. Consequently, the total volume of the gas molecules themselves is much less than the total volume occupied by the gas. Because of the random motion of the molecules and their great average separation, a gas spreads to fill any container in which it is placed. You can also easily compress it or allow it to expand by changing the volume of the container.

Pressure

The force exerted on a unit area is called **pressure,** a scalar quantity. The *SI* unit of pressure is the **pascal,** Pa, a derived unit equal to one newton per square meter. This is a rather small unit, and the **kilopascal,** kPa, is often used for measuring ordinary pressures. There are other units of pressure in common use, and it is helpful to be familiar with them. For example, the average pressure exerted by the earth's atmosphere at sea level is called one atmosphere:

$$\text{one atmosphere} = 1.01 \times 10^5 \text{ Pa} = 101 \text{ kPa}$$

Another common unit of pressure is the *millimeter of mercury* (mm of Hg), also called one *torr*. This unit is derived from the height of a column of mercury that can be supported by a given pressure.

$$\text{one atmosphere} = 760 \text{ mm of Hg} = 760 \text{ torr}$$

Standard pressure is defined as one atmosphere (101 kPa or 760 torr).

A liquid exerts pressure on the bottom of a container because of its weight. The pressure equals the weight of a column of the liquid divided by the area of the base of the column. Because a liquid flows freely, it exerts pressure not only downward but equally in all directions at any given depth. A gas confined in a container exerts pressure on the walls of the container because of the repeated impacts of its randomly moving molecules. The pressure of a confined gas is the same in all directions everywhere inside the container. The earth's atmosphere exerts pressure because of its weight in a manner similar to that of a liquid. Atmospheric pressure decreases with an increase in altitude because of the decreased weight of the column of air above.

CAN YOU EXPLAIN THIS?

Air can cause a sealed metal can to collapse.

If a small amount of water is placed in a metal can and heated until it boils, the air in the can will be driven out and the can will fill with steam at atmospheric pressure. If the can is then sealed by screwing on a cap and the can is allowed to cool, the steam inside the can will condense to water. There will be very few gas molecules left inside the can to produce a pressure. The pressure inside the can will be much less than the outside air pressure, and the outside pressure will cause the walls of the can to collapse inward.

The situation described above is a particularly dramatic demonstration of air pressure. There are, however, many common occurrences of air pressure at work in our lives.

PRACTICAL APPLICATION

If a straw is placed in a glass of water, the level of the water in the straw is the same as in the glass. When a person inhales through the straw, the air pressure inside the straw becomes less than the atmospheric pressure on the water in the glass. The air pushing on the surface of the water forces water up the straw. In a similar manner, the pressure inside the canister of an operating vacuum cleaner is less than atmospheric pressure. The air in the room, at higher pressure than the air in the canister, forces dirt into the canister's porous bag. ∎

Gas Laws

According to the kinetic theory of gases, a gas in a container consists of a very large number of molecules in random motion with an average kinetic energy that depends on the temperature of the gas. When the molecules collide with the walls of the container, their momentum is reversed. The impulse due to this change in momentum results in a force that produces pressure on the walls.

Suppose that the volume of a container of gas is increased, for example, by moving a piston in a cylinder or by stretching a rubber balloon. If the gas temperature remains the same, the molecules will have the same velocity and momentum, on the average, as before. However, they will now have to travel a greater distance, on the average, between collisions, so the collisions will occur less frequently. The collisions with the walls will also be spread out over a larger area. For both of these reasons, the pressure of the gas will be reduced.

By similar reasoning, it can be seen that increasing the temperature of the gas but keeping the volume constant will increase the pressure. The molecules will be traveling faster, on the average, so they will strike the walls with more momentum. They will also strike the walls more frequently. Both of these factors have the effect of increasing the pressure.

Scientists have conducted rigorous mathematical analysis of the mechanics of large numbers of molecules moving randomly. The results indicate that the following equation should describe the relationship between the pressure, volume, and temperature of a fixed mass of gas:

$$PV = nRT$$

where P is the pressure, V is the volume, n is the number of molecules, T is the absolute (Kelvin) temperature, and R is a constant that is the same for all gases. By dividing both sides of the above equation by the temperature T, the equation can be rewritten as

$$\frac{PV}{T} = nR$$

Because n and R are both constants for a given sample of gas, this equation tells us that if a given mass of a gas has a certain initial pressure, volume, and temperature, and these values change, then

$$\frac{P_iV_i}{T_i} = \frac{P_fV_f}{T_f}$$

where i indicates the initial conditions and f indicates the final conditions.

The equation

$$PV = nRT$$

is called the *ideal gas law*. An **ideal gas** is one for which the assumptions of the kinetic theory of gases stated at the beginning of this section (page 220) are true. An ideal gas would obey the ideal gas law under all conditions. No real gas behaves exactly like an ideal gas, but the behavior of a real gas is close to that of an ideal gas if its density is low and its temperature is well above its boiling point.

Three simple relationships can be obtained from the ideal gas law by considering each of the variables to be constant in turn.

Boyle's Law. If the temperature of a given mass of gas is constant, it follows that:

$$PV = \text{a constant}, \quad \text{and}$$

$$P_iV_i = P_fV_f$$

This relationship is called **Boyle's law.**

Charles' Law. If the pressure of the gas is kept constant,

$$\frac{V}{T} = \text{a constant, and}$$

$$\frac{V_i}{T_i} = \frac{V_f}{T_f}$$

This relationship is called **Charles' law.**

The Pressure-Temperature Relationship. If the volume of the gas is kept constant,

$$\frac{P}{T} = \text{a constant, and}$$

$$\frac{P_i}{T_i} = \frac{P_f}{T_f}$$

This last relationship is the one that was used to arrive at the value of absolute zero and to establish the Kelvin temperature scale. Charles' law can be used in the same way, since all graphs of temperature versus volume reach absolute zero when the graph is extrapolated to zero volume.

The three gas law relationships given above are illustrated graphically in Figure 7-4.

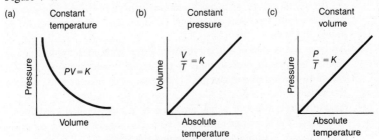

Figure 7-4.   Graphs of three relationships between the pressure, volume, and absolute temperature of a fixed mass of any gas, derived from the ideal gas law. (a) Graph representing Boyle's law. (b) Graph representing Charles' law. (c) The relationship between pressure and absolute temperature at constant volume is not named for a person.

QUESTIONS

1. **Doubling the absolute temperature of an ideal gas will affect the molecules by doubling their average (1) kinetic energy (2) velocity (3) momentum (4) potential energy**

2. **Which graph shows the variation of pressure with absolute temperature for a fixed mass and volume of an ideal gas?**

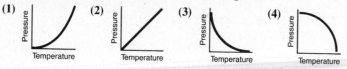

3. **Which graph best represents the relationship between pressure and volume for a fixed mass of an ideal gas at constant temperature?**

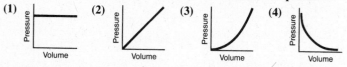

4. **Which graph best represents the relationship between volume and absolute temperature for a fixed mass of an ideal gas at constant pressure?**

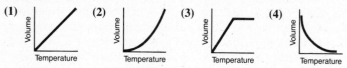

5. As the temperature of a gas enclosed in a rigid-walled container is increased, the pressure of the gas (1) decreases (2) increases (3) remains the same

6. An ideal gas is enclosed in a cyclinder fitted with a frictionless piston. As the temperature of the gas is increased, while pressure remains constant, the volume of the gas (1) decreases (2) increases (3) remains the same

7. As the temperature of a gas enclosed in a rigid-walled container is decreased, the force per unit area exerted on the walls of the container (1) decreases (2) increases (3) remains the same

8. An ideal gas occupies 60.0 cubic meters at a temperature of 600. K. If the temperature is lowered to 300. K at constant pressure, the new volume of the gas will be (1) 30.0 m^3 (2) 60.0 m^3 (3) 120. m^3 (4) 240. m^3

9. If the absolute temperature of a fixed mass of an ideal gas is doubled, while its volume remains constant, the pressure of the gas will be (1) halved (2) doubled (3) quartered (4) quadrupled

10. A fixed mass of an ideal gas is enclosed in a rigid-walled container. If the velocity of the gas molecules colliding with the walls of the container decreases, the (1) pressure of the gas decreases (2) density of the gas decreases (3) temperature of the gas increases (4) volume of the gas increases

11. An ideal gas occupies 20.0 cubic meters at 293 K and standard pressure. If the pressure on the gas is doubled with temperature remaining

constant, the volume of the gas will be (1) 10.0 m³ (2) 20.0 m³ (3) 80.0 m³ (4) 40.0 m³

12. A gas enclosed in a rigid-walled container is heated. Which of the following is true of the gas? (1) Temperature increases and volume decreases. (2) Pressure increases and volume remains the same. (3) Temperature remains the same and pressure increases. (4) Pressure increases and volume increases.

13. An assumption of the kinetic theory of gases is that the actual volume of the gas molecules compared to the volume occupied by the gas is (1) much less (2) much greater (3) exactly the same

14. According to the kinetic theory of gases, molecules of an ideal gas (1) never touch the walls of a container (2) have inelastic collisions with the walls of the container (3) collide only with the walls of the container, never with each other (4) are in constant random motion

15. According to the kinetic theory of gases, the force of attraction between the molecules of an ideal gas (1) may be ignored (2) depends on their average kinetic energy (3) causes gas pressure (4) is proportional to the absolute temperature of the gas

IV. LAWS OF THERMODYNAMICS

First Law of Thermodynamics

The **first law of thermodynamics** states that

$$E = Q - W$$

where E is the change in internal energy of a system, Q is the heat entering or leaving a system, and W is the work done on or by the system. Sign conventions apply to the quantities in the above equation. The quantity E is positive when there is an increase and negative when there is a decrease in the internal energy of the system. The quantity Q is positive when heat enters the system and is negative when heat leaves the system. The quantity W is positive when the system does work on the surroundings and is negative when the surroundings do work on the system.

To illustrate the first law, consider a system of an ideal gas in a cylinder fitted with a movable piston. If heat is added to the system, there are three possible outcomes:

• The heat added to the system causes the gas to expand and do work in moving the piston. If all the heat is changed to work done in this way, there is no change in the internal energy of the system.

• The piston is prevented from moving, so the gas cannot expand and do work. All the heat added increases the internal energy of the system by increasing the average kinetic energy of the molecules, thus raising the temperature.

• The gas expands and does work in moving the piston, but only some of the heat added becomes work done. The rest of the heat increases the internal energy and raises the temperature of the gas.

PRACTICAL APPLICATION

Most internal-combustion engines operate in a sequence of four strokes of a piston in a cylinder, as shown in Figure 7-5.

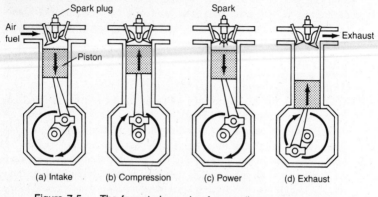

Figure 7-5.   The four-stroke cycle of a gasoline engine.

In the first stroke (Figure 7-5a), a mixture of gasoline and air from the carburetor is drawn into the cylinder through the open intake valve, as the piston moves down. In the second stroke (Figure 7-5b), the intake valve closes and the piston moves up, compressing the gasoline and air mixture, which now has no means of escape. In this stroke, work is done by the piston on the gas, increasing the internal energy and temperature of the gas. In the third stroke (Figure 7-5c), an electric spark from the spark plug ignites the mixture causing it to burn rapidly and add heat to the system. The heated gases expand and do work on the piston. This work is transferred to rotary motion of the crankshaft, which does work in moving the vehicle. Finally, in the fourth stroke (Figure 7-5d), the exhaust valve opens and the piston moves up, expelling the burned gases from the cylinder. ■

Second Law of Thermodynamics

The **second law of thermodynamics** may be expressed in a variety of ways. Among them is the statement that the *entropy* of the universe is increasing. **Entropy** is a quantitative measure of the disorder of a system. All physical systems have a natural tendency toward increasing disorder. Although it is possible for a given system to experience a decrease in entropy, this occurs at the expense of an increase in entropy of another system. When all systems are considered, there is a net increase in entropy.

The concept of entropy is based on the observation that, in a natural state, a disorderly arrangement is much more probable than an orderly arrangement. Consider the examples at the top of the next page.

- Falling leaves do not collect in neat piles, but, rather, are scattered about the ground.

- It is easier to shatter a dish than it is to reassemble the broken pieces.

- It is possible for a block of ice to melt completely when it strikes the ground if the ice has been dropped from a sufficient height above the ground. However, the resulting puddle of water will not, in turn, rise from the ground and be transformed into a block of ice again.

- When a hammer is used to drive a nail into a board, part of the "ordered" energy that drives the nail is converted into "disordered" energy of the motion of the molecules of the system (heat), reducing the ability of the system to do work.

Another expression of the second law of thermodynamics is the statement that heat will not flow spontaneously from a cold object or region to a hotter object or region. Real processes have a preferred direction. The natural direction of heat flow is from a reservoir at high temperature to a reservoir at low temperature, regardless of the total heat content of each. To reverse the natural flow of heat, work must be done. For example, energy is needed for a refrigerator to absorb heat from a low-temperature region (the inside of the refrigerator) and expel it into a high-temperature environment (the room in which the refrigerator is located).

A *heat engine* is a device that absorbs heat from a reservoir at high temperature, converts some of the heat to work done by the engine, and expels heat to a reservoir at lower temperature. In fact, the greater the difference between the temperature of the heat source of a heat engine and the reservoir to which it exhausts heat, the greater the efficiency of the engine. It is impossible, however, to convert all of the heat that leaves a reservoir into work; some of the heat leaving the hotter reservoir must flow into a cold reservoir. Thus, it is impossible to have a heat engine that is 100% efficient.

CAN YOU EXPLAIN THIS?

Even at 0°C, outside air can be used to heat your home.

A heat pump is a device that transfers heat from a low-temperature reservoir to a high-temperature reservoir. Heat can be absorbed from the cold outside air by a refrigerant, a low-pressure vapor circulating in the outside coils of the heat pump. The refrigerant is usually Freon, which has a boiling point of −28°C, and thus boils at the operating temperature. Using electrical energy, a compressor increases the pressure of the gas, which is sent to the indoor coils. Once inside, the Freon condenses to a liquid, releasing stored heat in the process. Air at any temperature, even 0°C, has internal energy and can be used to heat a home. A heat pump can be used as an air conditioner in the summer by reversal of the above cycle.

Third Law of Thermodynamics

According to the **third law of thermodynamics,** it is impossible to reduce the temperature of an actual system to absolute zero by any set of operations. Although a temperature less than 1×10^{-6} kelvin has been achieved in the laboratory, absolute zero itself has never been reached.

If the temperature of a system *could* be reduced to absolute zero, the particles would have no kinetic energy. Recall that $KE = \frac{1}{2}mv^2$. Because each particle would have mass, its velocity would have to be zero in order for its kinetic energy to be zero. A particle having zero velocity would have zero momentum because momentum is equal to the product of mass and velocity ($p = mv$). The matter wavelength (see Unit 5) given by the formula

$$\lambda = \frac{h}{p}$$

would have to be infinite, an impossible situation. Thus, scientists believe it is physically impossible to reach a temperature of absolute zero.

QUESTIONS

1. The first law of thermodynamics expresses the conservation of (1) charge (2) energy (3) entropy (4) momentum
2. A quantitative measure of the disorder of a system is called (1) absolute temperature (2) energy (3) entropy (4) specific heat
3. The entropy of the universe is (1) decreasing (2) increasing (3) remaining the same
4. The direction of heat flow between two bodies in contact is determined by their relative (1) masses (2) specific heats (3) temperatures (4) volumes
5. The disorder of a system has a natural tendency to (1) decrease (2) increase (3) remain the same
6. One thousand joules of heat is added to a system consisting of an insulated cylinder fitted with a piston and containing an ideal gas. If the internal energy of the system increases by 700 joules, the work done by the gas on the piston is (1) 300 J (2) 700 J (3) 1,000 J (4) 1,700 J

7–11. Base your answers to Questions 7 through 11 on the following information.

The diagram at right shows a frictionless piston that weighs 100 newtons fitted into an insulated cylinder containing an ideal gas at 290 K. As 25 joules of heat energy are supplied by a heater, the piston rises 0.10 meter.

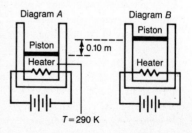

7. What was the Celsius temperature of the gas before the heat energy was added? (1) 563°C (2) 290°C (3) 17°C (4) 0°C

8. How much work is done by the gas as it raises the piston 0.10 meter? (1) 1.0 J (2) 10. J (3) 100 J (4) 1,000 J

9. As heat is supplied to the cylinder, the internal energy of the gas (1) decreases (2) remains constant (3) increases by the same amount (4) increases by a smaller amount

10. As the heat energy is supplied to the cylinder, the temperature of the gas (1) decreases (2) increases (3) remains the same

11. Compared to the pressure in diagram *A*, the pressure of the gas in diagram *B* is (1) less (2) greater (3) the same

UNIT 8   ELECTROMAGNETIC
           APPLICATIONS

I. TORQUE ON A CURRENT-CARRYING LOOP

The explanation of the torque on a current-carrying loop is based on concepts from Unit 3 concerning the electric and magnetic fields. The magnetic field in the space between two opposite magnetic poles (for example, the poles of a horseshoe magnet) is basically uniform, with lines of flux parallel to each other and directed toward the south pole. If electrons travel in a straight conductor, a magnetic field is produced around the conductor, with the lines of flux forming concentric circles in a plane perpendicular to the conductor.

If a conductor is placed between two opposite magnetic poles, and a current passes through the conductor, the two magnetic fields interact. In Figure 8-1a, the cross section of a conductor having electrons traveling *into* the page is shown between the poles of a horseshoe magnet. Above the wire, the magnetic field is weakened, because the circular lines of force due to the current in the conductor are directed opposite to the lines of force of the magnet. On the other hand, below this wire, the magnetic field is strengthened, because both sets of

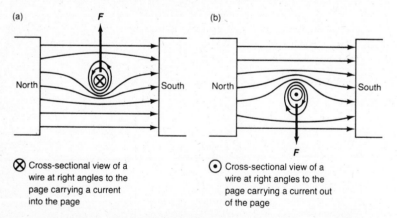

(a)   *F*

North   South

(b)

North   South

                                                                    F

⊗ Cross-sectional view of a
  wire at right angles to the
  page carrying a current
  into the page

⊙ Cross-sectional view of a
  wire at right angles to the
  page carrying a current out
  of the page

Figure 8-1.   The interaction between an existing magnetic field
               and the magnetic field generated by a current moving
               in the existing field at right angles to the existing
               field. (a) When the existing magnetic field is from left to
               right and the current is into the page, an upward force
               is exerted on the conductor. (b) When the current is
               out of the page, a downward force is exerted on the
               conductor.

lines of force are in the same direction. The resultant magnetic force on the wire is directed from the stronger to the weaker field (upward in the diagram). In Figure 8-1b, the direction of the electron flow is reversed—that is, the electron flow is traveling *out* of the page. The force on the conductor is now downward.

If the individual wires were replaced with a loop of wire in the magnetic field, and electrons traveled as indicated in Figure 8-2, the forces acting on the wire loop would cause it to turn clockwise. Any force that tends to cause a body to rotate is called **torque.** Torque is usually produced by a force acting at a distance from an axis of rotation. The current-carrying loop in Figure 8-2 experiences a clockwise torque when it is in the field of the magnet in the position shown in the illustration. Increasing either the current, I, in the loop or the strength of the magnetic field, B, causes the magnitude of the torque, F, to increase. Reversing the direction of either the current or the field causes the torque to be reversed, which makes the coil turn in the opposite direction (counterclockwise, in this case). The torque on a current-carrying coil in a magnetic field is the basis of operation for electric meters and electric motors.

Recall from Unit 3 (page 103) that the force on a moving charge or electric current in a magnetic field is at right angles to both the direction of the current and the direction of the field. In the position of Figure 8-2, the forces on opposite sides of the loop produce a maximum torque. Figure 8-3a (see the following page) shows the field inside the loop produced by the current when the loop is in the position shown. Note that the field of the loop (pointing up at the center of the loop) is at right angles to the field of the magnet (pointing to the right). In Figure 8-3b, the loop has rotated 90°. When the loop is in this position, the field inside the loop produced by the current is *parallel* to the field of the magnet. In this position, the torque on the loop is zero. Whenever a current flows through a loop in a magnetic field, the torque tends to rotate the loop until its magnetic field is parallel to that of the existing field.

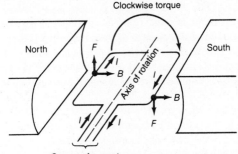

Figure 8-2.   The torque on a current-carrying loop when the loop is in a magnetic field in the position shown. The magnetic force F exerted on the moving electrons in the current I causes the loop to rotate in the direction shown.

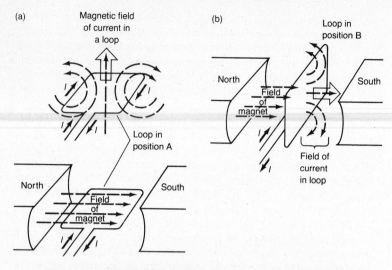

Figure 8-3. Field relationships of a current-carrying loop in a magnetic field. (a) When the loop is in the position shown (position *A*), the current in the loop produces a field that is directed upward in the center of the loop. When the loop is placed in a magnetic field directed to the right, the field in the current-carrying loop is at right angles to the field of the magnet. (b) The torque on the loop tends to rotate the loop to position *B*, where the magnetic field of the loop is parallel to the field of the magnet and is in the same direction.

Meters

Galvanometer. A very sensitive meter designed to detect and measure weak electric currents (as little as 10^{-7} ampere) is called a **galvanometer.** A galvanometer makes use of the fact that a current-carrying loop experiences a torque in a magnetic field (unless the plane of the loop is perpendicular to the magnetic field). Figure 8-4 is a diagram of a typical galvanometer. A permanent horseshoe magnet produces a magnetic field. Between the poles of the magnet, there is a small coil of fine, insulated wire wound on an iron core and mounted on an axle. When the current to be measured passes through the coil, the torque produced causes the coil to rotate in the magnetic field. Since iron is highly *permeable* to magnetic flux, it concentrates the magnetic field produced in the coil and thereby greatly increases the torque produced.

The current to be measured is carried to the coil by a pair of hairsprings attached to the axle. As the coil rotates, these hairsprings exert a mechanical torque that opposes the rotation. This opposing torque is proportional to the amount of rotation. When the opposing torque of the springs equals the magnetic torque of the coil, the coil stops turning and the pointer attached to it comes to rest at some particular angle. Since the magnetic torque of the coil is proportional to the current in it, a larger current will turn the coil through a

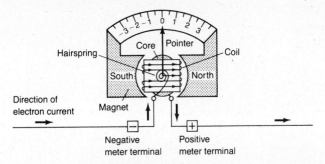

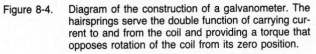

Figure 8-4.   Diagram of the construction of a galvanometer. The hairsprings serve the double function of carrying current to and from the coil and providing a torque that opposes rotation of the coil from its zero position.

larger angle before the spring torque becomes large enough to stop it. As a result, the deflection of the pointer is proportional to the current in the coil. When there is no current in the coil, there is no magnetic torque, and the hairsprings return the pointer to its zero position. The zero point on a galvanometer scale is usually in the center. A current flow through the coil in one direction causes the pointer to move to one side of zero. If the current flows in the other direction, the torque will be reversed and the pointer will move to the other side of zero.

A galvanometer is designed to measure very small currents. For example, a typical galvanometer may be deflected to its maximum scale reading by a current of only 1×10^{-4} ampere (0.0001 A). It also operates on very small potential differences. For example, if the resistance of the coil is 50 ohms (a typical value), the potential difference needed to produce a full-scale current of 1×10^{-4} ampere is:

$$V = IR = (1 \times 10^{-4} \text{ A})(50 \ \Omega) = 5 \times 10^{-3} \text{ V}, \quad \text{or} \quad 0.005 \text{ V}$$

Any current much larger than 0.0001 ampere would damage the meter by either the excessive torque or the heating effect of the current. Likewise, any potential difference applied to the meter much larger than 0.005 volt would damage it by driving much more than 0.0001 ampere through it. Yet a sensitive galvanometer of this type can be used to measure currents of many amperes and potential differences of hundreds of volts by connecting suitable resistances to it, as explained below.

Ammeter. An ammeter, which is used to measure currents that are larger than the very weak currents measured by a galvanometer, is made by connecting a conductor of very low resistance, called a **shunt,** in parallel with a galvanometer, as shown in Figure 8-5a (see the following page). When this parallel combination is inserted in series with a circuit carrying a current, as shown in Figure 8-5b, nearly all the current will flow through the low-resistance shunt, and only a small fraction will flow through the galvanometer coil. Yet, the

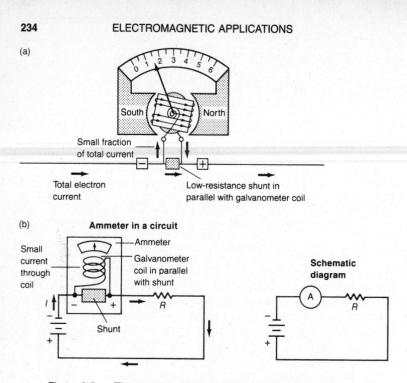

(a)

South North

Small fraction of total current

Total electron current

Low-resistance shunt in parallel with galvanometer coil

(b) **Ammeter in a circuit**

Small current through coil

Ammeter

Galvanometer coil in parallel with shunt

Schematic diagram

I

R

A

R

Shunt

Figure 8-5. The ammeter. (a) A low-resistance shunt is connected in parallel with a galvanometer coil to convert it to an ammeter. The coil is rotated from its zero position by the small fraction of the current that flows through it. (b) An ammeter is connected in series in a circuit to measure the current flowing through the circuit.

current that flows through the coil is a constant fraction of the total, since the currents in the branches of a parallel circuit are inversely proportional to their resistances (see Unit 3, pages 89–90). If the current increases, the currents in the shunt and in the coil increase in the same proportion.

For example, suppose a shunt with a resistance of 5.0×10^{-3} ohm is connected in parallel with a galvanometer that has a coil resistance of 50. ohms and a current of 1.0 ampere flows through the combination. Practically all the current flows through the shunt. The potential difference across the shunt is

$$V = IR = (1.0 \text{ A})(5.0 \times 10^{-3} \text{ } \Omega) = 5.0 \times 10^{-3} \text{ V}$$

Since the galvanometer coil is in parallel with the shunt, this same potential difference exists across its 50.-ohm resistance. The current that will flow in the coil is

$$I = V/R = (5.0 \times 10^{-3} \text{ V})/(50. \text{ } \Omega) = 1.0 \times 10^{-4} \text{ A}$$

Thus, a current of 1.0 ampere passing through the circuit results in a current through the galvanometer coil of 1.0×10^{-4} ampere, just enough to cause a full-scale deflection of the pointer. If the current is reduced to 0.5 ampere, the current through the coil becomes 0.5×10^{-4} ampere, and the pointer will stop halfway up the scale. The scale can therefore be marked, or *calibrated,* to read amperes of total current. Unlike the galvanometer, the zero point of an ammeter scale is usually at the left end of the scale. To use the ammeter, it must be connected into a circuit with the correct *polarity* so that the current through it will be in the correct direction to move the pointer up the scale. The ammeter terminal marked + must always be connected to the part of the circuit that leads to the positive (+) terminal of the current source.

Note that the resistance of the ammeter is so low that it has no noticeable effect on the current in the circuit when the ammeter is added to the circuit. Practically the same current will flow in the circuit whether the ammeter is connected or not. The low potential difference across the ammeter also has no noticeable effect on the other potential differences around the circuit.

The range of currents that an ammeter can measure is easily changed by changing the resistance of the shunt. For example, if the resistance of the shunt is decreased, a smaller fraction of the current will pass through the galvanometer coil. The maximum current the ammeter can measure is thus increased, since a larger total current is needed to produce a full-scale deflection.

Voltmeter. A voltmeter is used to measure the potential difference, or potential drop, across a circuit element by connecting the voltmeter in parallel with the element. The potential difference applied to the meter is then the same as that across the element. The type of galvanometer described on page 232 can be made into a voltmeter by connecting a high resistance in series with the galvanometer coil, as shown in Figure 8-6a (see the following page). When this combination is connected in parallel with a circuit element, as shown in Figure 8-6b, only a small current will flow through the meter circuit. The amount of resistance used depends on the maximum potential difference to be measured. For example, if the maximum potential difference to be measured is 100 volts, and the coil current for maximum deflection is 1.0×10^{-4} ampere, the resistance of the meter should be

$$R = V/I = (100 \text{ V})/(1.0 \times 10^{-4} \text{ A}) = 1.0 \times 10^6 \ \Omega, \quad \text{or} \quad 1,000,000 \text{ ohms}$$

Therefore, a resistance of 1.0×10^6 ohms would be connected in series with the galvanometer to make a 100-volt voltmeter. To measure a maximum potential difference 1/10 as large (10 volts), a resistance of 1.0×10^5 ohms (100,000 ohms) would be used.

Like the scale of an ammeter, the zero point of a voltmeter scale is at one end of the scale, so a voltmeter must also be connected with the correct polarity. As in the case of the ammeter, using a voltmeter usually has no noticeable effect on the current and potential difference being measured. In ordinary circuits, the current in the voltmeter is too small to make any significant difference.

Meters often have a switch that can be turned to change the resistance of the shunt (in an ammeter) or the resistance of the series resistor (in a voltmeter). Turning this switch changes the range of current or potential difference the meter can measure.

(a)

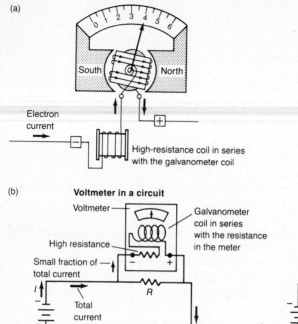

(b) **Voltmeter in a circuit**

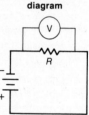

Figure 8-6. The voltmeter. (a) A high resistance is connected in series with a galvanometer coil to convert it to a voltmeter. (b) A voltmeter is connected in parallel with a circuit element to measure the potential difference across it.

Motors

A device that converts electrical energy into rotational mechanical energy is called an **electric motor.** Its operation is based on the principle that a current-carrying coil experiences a torque in a magnetic field.

Consider a rectangular loop of wire mounted on an axle and positioned so that the plane of the loop is parallel to the field produced by a stationary magnet, as shown in Figure 8-7a. If the electron flow is as indicated from point X toward point Y, the loop will experience a torque that will cause it to rotate clockwise. As the loop moves through the vertical position (where the torque on it is zero) toward the position shown in Figure 8-7b, the torque reverses. The loop therefore slows down, stops, and starts to rotate counterclockwise toward the vertical position. As the loop passes the vertical position in this direction, the torque will again reverse. The loop will thus oscillate a few times back and forth around the vertical position and will finally be brought to rest in that position by friction.

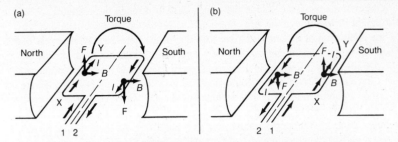

Figure 8-7. (a) A clockwise torque on a current-carrying loop in a magnetic field. (b) The counterclockwise torque on the same loop when it is rotated 180° and the current continues to flow in the same direction (in at 1 and out at 2).

If the direction of the current were reversed every time the loop passed through the vertical position, however, the direction of the torque on the loop would be reversed and the loop would continue to rotate in the same direction— clockwise. This continuous rotation would provide useful mechanical energy. In a motor designed to operate on direct current, this is exactly what does happen.

The basic parts of a direct-current (DC) motor are shown in Figure 8-8. A coil, called the *armature,* consisting of many turns of wire around an iron core, is mounted on an axle in the field between the opposite poles of a magnet, called the *field magnet.* The field magnet may be a permanent magnet, but in most motors it is an electromagnet. Current for the *field coil* of the electromagnet

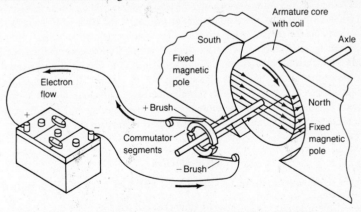

Figure 8-8. Diagram of a simple direct-current motor. The commutator reverses the direction of the current through the coil every 180° of rotation, thereby maintaining the torque in the same direction.

comes from the same source that sends current through the armature. When current flows through the armature, a torque is exerted on the armature coil by the interaction of its magnetic field with that of the field magnet. As explained in the discussion of meters, the iron core of the armature concentrates and strengthens its magnetic field and thus greatly increases the torque produced.

Each end of the armature coil is attached to one of the halves of a split ring, called a **commutator,** which is mounted on the axle and rotates with the armature. Two graphite or copper *brushes* connected to the direct-current source make contact with opposite halves of the commutator. As the armature rotates, each half of the commutator makes contact alternately with each brush. As a result, the current in the armature coil reverses every half-turn (180°) of rotation. This reversal of the current maintains the direction of the torque on the armature, causing it to rotate continually in the same direction.

In Unit 3 (page 105) it was stated that when a moving conductor cuts across the flux lines of a magnetic field, a potential difference, or voltage, is induced in the conductor. When an electric motor is operating, the conductors of its armature cut across the flux lines of the field magnet, and therefore a potential difference is induced in the armature coil. The direction of this induced potential difference is always opposite to the applied potential difference that is driving the armature. A term used for a generated potential difference or voltage is *electromotive force,* or **EMF.** The induced potential difference in the armature of a motor is called **back EMF.** (Induced potential difference is treated in greater detail in the discussion of the electric generator in Section III, Induced Voltage.)

Since the back EMF opposes the applied potential difference, it acts to reduce the current flowing through the armature and the torque on it. When a motor is first turned on, the current drawn and the torque are very high, because there is no back EMF. As the speed of the motor increases, the back EMF increases, thus reducing the current in the armature. The motor eventually reaches a speed at which the difference between the applied potential difference and the back EMF sends just enough current through the armature to keep it turning against the resistance of the "load" device to which it is attached. If the load on the motor (that is, the resistance to its turning) increases, the motor will be slowed down. The back EMF will therefore decrease, more current will flow through the armature, and the torque will increase until it matches the new load.

QUESTIONS

1–4. Base your answers to Questions 1 through 4 on the information below.

An ammeter and a voltmeter are connected properly in a simple circuit to determine the resistance of a lamp in the circuit.

1. How are the meters connected in the circuit with the lamp? (1) Both meters are in parallel. (2) Both meters are in series. (3) The ammeter is in parallel, and the voltmeter is in series. (4) The ammeter is in series, and the voltmeter is in parallel.

2. Compared to the potential drop across the ammeter, the potential drop across the voltmeter is (1) less (2) greater (3) the same

3. Compared to the current through the ammeter, the current through the voltmeter is (1) less (2) greater (3) the same

4. Compared to the internal resistance of the ammeter, the internal resistance of the voltmeter is (1) less (2) greater (3) the same

5. An ammeter is a galvanometer with (1) a low resistance in series with it (2) a low resistance in parallel with it (3) a high resistance in series with it (4) a high resistance in parallel with it

6. A voltmeter is a galvanometer with (1) a low resistance in series with it (2) a low resistance in parallel with it (3) a high resistance in series with it (4) a high resistance in parallel with it

7. If the shunt resistance of an ammeter is decreased, the maximum possible reading on the meter (1) decreases (2) increases (3) remains the same

8. If the internal resistance of a voltmeter is increased, the maximum possible reading on the meter (1) decreases (2) increases (3) remains the same

9. The function of the iron core in a galvanometer is to (1) increase the resistance of the meter (2) decrease the sensitivity of the meter (3) strengthen the magnetic field of the coil (4) reduce the torque of the coil

10. If the current in a conducting loop in a magnetic field is doubled, the torque on the loop is (1) halved (2) doubled (3) quartered (4) quadrupled

11. When a permeable substance is inserted into a current-carrying coil of wire, the strength of the magnetic field of the coil (1) decreases (2) increases (3) remains the same

12. Compared to the resistance of the shunt in an ammeter, the resistance of the ammeter's galvanometer coil is (1) less (2) greater (3) the same

13. As the current passing through the coil of a galvanometer decreases, the degree of deflection of the coil (1) decreases (2) increases (3) remains the same

14. The function of the shunt in an ammeter is to (1) increase the internal resistance of the meter (2) provide a permanent magnetic field (3) permit rotation of the galvanometer coil (4) provide a low-resistance path for the current

15. A device that converts electrical energy into rotational mechanical energy is a (1) generator (2) laser (3) motor (4) transformer

16. The function of the split-ring commutator in a motor is to (1) reduce the effects of the back EMF (2) provide a permanent magnetic field (3) increase the magnitude of the torque on the coil (4) reverse the direction of the current in the coil each half-rotation

17. As the armature of an operating electric motor rotates, a back EMF is induced in the armature. Compared to the applied EMF, the net EMF in the armature is (1) less (2) greater (3) the same

18. In an operating electric motor, the direction of rotation of the armature (1) reverses every 45° (2) reverses every 90° (3) reverses every 180° (4) remains the same

19. The function of the iron core in an electric motor is to (1) decrease the torque on the armature (2) increase the torque on the armature (3) eliminate back EMF in the armature (4) reverse current direction in the armature

20–23. Base your answers to Questions 20 through 23 on the diagram at the right, which shows a current-carrying loop positioned horizontally in a horizontal magnetic field. A point *P* is marked on the loop.

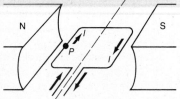

20. The magnetic force on the loop at *P* is directed (1) vertically downward (2) vertically upward (3) in the same direction as the current (4) in a direction opposite to that of the current

21. If the current in the loop is increased, the magnetic force on the loop at *P* will (1) decrease (2) increase (3) remain the same

22. If the field magnet is replaced with a stronger magnet, the magnetic force on the loop at *P* will (1) decrease (2) increase (3) remain the same

23. If the direction of the current is reversed, the magnitude of the magnetic force at *P* (1) decreases (2) increases (3) remains the same

24. A device used to detect and measure weak electric currents in a circuit is the (1) compass (2) electroscope (3) voltmeter (4) galvanometer

II. ELECTRON BEAMS

Thermionic Emission

As a material is heated, the average kinetic energy of its particles increases. Some of this kinetic energy may be transferred to the electrons in the atoms of the material. When the temperature is high enough, some electrons may acquire enough energy to escape from the surface of the material. The ejection of electrons (or other charged particles) from the surface of a heated body is called **thermionic emission.**

Thermionic emission of electrons is most easily produced by using an electric current to heat a wire filament in an evacuated tube, or *vacuum tube*. A vacuum tube is one from which most of the gas has been removed. Electrons are then emitted from the heated filament or from a surface heated by it. This source of electrons is called a **cathode.** The emitted electrons surround the cathode, producing a negative charge in the space around it. Since the cathode is left with a net positive charge, the emitted electrons are attracted back toward it. An equilibrium develops between the number of electrons being emitted from the cathode and the number falling back into it. If the temperature of the cathode is increased, the rate of electron emission increases, and a new equilibrium is established with a larger negative charge around the cathode. The rate of electron emission and the amount of charge around the cathode can therefore be controlled by regulating the filament temperature.

Electron Beams in an Electric Field

In Unit 3 (page 73), it was stated that a uniform electric field exists between a pair of oppositely charged parallel plates whose separation is small compared to their dimensions. If an electron is present at some point between these plates, the particle will be acted on by a constant electric force from the negative plate toward the positive plate in a direction perpendicular to the plates (see Figure 8-9). This force will produce a constant acceleration of the electron toward the positive plate.

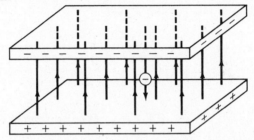

Figure 8-9.   The force on an electron in the uniform electric field between a pair of oppositely charged plates.

From Equation 3-2 (page 72), the force F exerted on the electron by the electric field is given by

$$F = Eq$$

where E is the electric field intensity and q is the charge on the electron. If the separation of the plates is d and the potential difference between the plates is V, then the electric field intensity E is given by Equation 3-4 (page 75):

$$E = V/d$$

Thus, the force exerted by the electric field on the electron is given by $F = Vq/d$. As a result of this constant unbalanced force, the particle experiences uniform acceleration as it moves in the electric field between the charged plates. If the potential difference between the plates is increased, the unbalanced force on the electron increases, increasing the electron's acceleration.

Control of Electron Beams

By placing positively charged **anodes** near the cathode of a vacuum tube, the emitted electrons can be accelerated to a high velocity and formed into a narrow beam. The electrodes that form such a beam are called an **electron gun.** Electron beams from an electron gun can be controlled by passing them through electric and magnetic fields.

Electrostatic Control. If an electron beam enters the uniform electric field between two oppositely charged parallel plates, the beam will be deflected toward the positive plate in a plane parallel to the field. For example, if the plates are horizontal, so that the field lines are vertical, the electron beam will be deflected in a vertical plane and will curve toward the positive plate, as shown in Figure 8-10. If your have studied Unit 6, you can see that the curved trajectory of the electrons will have the same shape as that of a projectile fired horizontally in the earth's gravitational field. The component of velocity at right angles to the field will remain constant, while the component of velocity parallel to the field will increase uniformly toward the positive plate.

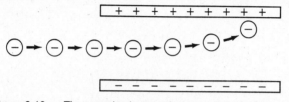

Figure 8-10.   The curved trajectory of a beam of electrons moving across a uniform electric field.

Magnetic Control. Recall from Unit 3 (page 103) that a charged particle moving through a magnetic field at an angle to the lines of force is acted on by a force. The force is perpendicular to both the direction of motion of the particle and the direction of the field. If a particle with a negative charge, such as an electron, is moving across a magnetic field, the direction of the magnetic force on the particle can be found by using the left-hand rule shown in Figure 8-11. If the fingers of the left hand point in the direction of the magnetic field, and the thumb points in the direction of motion perpendicular to the field, the palm faces in the direction of the force on the negatively charged particle. If an electron beam crosses a magnetic field, it will be deflected in accordance with this rule. A particle with a positive charge would be deflected in the opposite direction.

If a charged particle moves at right angles to a magnetic field, the *magnitude* of the magnetic force on the particle is directly proportional to the charge on the particle, the velocity of the particle, and the strength of the magnetic field:

$$F = qvB \qquad \text{(Eq. 8-1)}$$

where q is the charge in coulombs, v is the velocity at right angles to the field in meters per second, B is the magnetic field strength in teslas, and F is the force on the particle in newtons. (To check the units, recall that 1 tesla equals 1 newton per ampere · meter, and 1 ampere equals 1 coulomb per second.) In Equation 8-1, v is the component of the velocity perpendicular to the field. If the particle is moving parallel to the field, this component is zero, and there is no magnetic force on the particle.

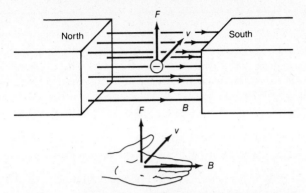

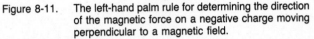

Figure 8-11. The left-hand palm rule for determining the direction of the magnetic force on a negative charge moving perpendicular to a magnetic field.

When a charged particle moves across a uniform *electric* field, the direction of the force on the particle does not change as it moves along its curved path. The trajectory in this case is a mathematical curve called a *parabola*. In the case of a particle moving across a uniform *magnetic* field, the direction of the force is always at right angles to the direction of motion. That is, the direction is continuously changing as the particle moves. If you have studied Unit 6, you know that the path of a particle in this case is a circle. Figure 8-12 shows the paths of a negatively charged particle and a positively charged particle moving at right angles to a magnetic field directed into the page. If the particles have the same charge and velocity, the radius of each path depends only on the mass of the particle.

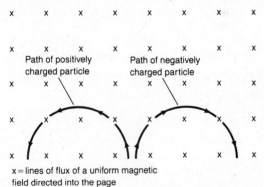

Figure 8-12. The circular paths of positively charged and negatively charged particles of the same mass moving at the same speed and perpendicular to a magnetic field.

EXAMPLE

An electron traveling at a constant speed of 2.0×10^7 meters per second enters a uniform magnetic field of 1.0×10^{-4} tesla. Find the magnitude of the magnetic force on the electron, assuming that the electron enters perpendicular to the field.

Solution

$$q = 1.6 \times 10^{-19} \text{ C}$$

$$v = 2.0 \times 10^7 \text{ m/s}$$

$$B = 1.0 \times 10^{-4} \text{ tesla} = 1.0 \times 10^{-4} \text{ N/A} \cdot \text{m}$$

$$F = qvB$$

$$F = (1.6 \times 10^{-19} \text{ C})(2.0 \times 10^7 \text{ m/s})(1.0 \times 10^{-4} \text{ N/A} \cdot \text{m})$$

$$F = 3.2 \times 10^{-16} \text{ N}$$

Cathode-Ray Tube. Electron beams, originally called "cathode rays," were produced and studied in "cathode-ray tubes" before the electron was discovered and the nature of the cathode rays was understood. The term "cathode-ray tube" is still used today. A modern **cathode-ray tube** is an evacuated glass tube in which a beam of electrons is produced by thermionic emission from a cathode at one end, and then electric fields in the tube accelerate and deflect the beam to produce an image on a fluorescent screen at the other end. The beam of electrons is produced by an electron gun located in the neck of the tube, as shown in Figure 8-13.

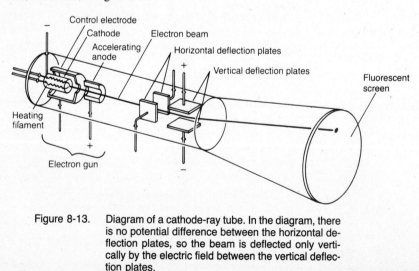

Figure 8-13.   Diagram of a cathode-ray tube. In the diagram, there is no potential difference between the horizontal deflection plates, so the beam is deflected only vertically by the electric field between the vertical deflection plates.

A *control electrode* near the cathode regulates the number of electrons in the beam and, consequently, the brightness of the image produced on the screen. If the deflection plates are not used, a spot appears in the center of the screen. A *phosphor* coating on the inside of the screen absorbs the energy from the high-speed electrons and converts it to visible light. The phosphor continues to glow for a short time after the electron beam has been extinguished or moved to another position.

There are two pairs of deflection plates in the neck of the tube. The two plates of each pair are parallel to each other, and the two pairs are perpendicular to each other. Each pair of deflection plates is connected to an external circuit that controls the potential difference between the plates and thus the direction and intensity of the electric field between them.

As the electron beam passes between the plates, it is deflected to the left or right by the horizontal pair, and up or down by the vertical pair. The amount of deflection in each case is determined by the intensity of the field between the plates. By changing the potential difference between the plates of each pair, the electron beam can be moved to any desired point on the screen. In this way, images of various kinds, such as the shape of an alternating current, can be traced on the screen.

PRACTICAL APPLICATION

The picture tube of a television receiver is a cathode-ray tube in which the electron beam is controlled by magnetic, rather than electric, fields. The controlling fields are produced by pairs of electromagnets placed around the outside of the neck of the tube. Electromagnetic waves from the television transmitter carry information about the brightness of each point of the image being transmitted. This information controls the intensity of the electron beam as the controlling magnets cause it to sweep across the screen in horizontal lines.

In a color television broadcast, the waves also carry information about the intensity of three *primary* colors—red, green, and blue—at each point of the image. Combinations of these three colors can produce any color that the human eye can see. The screen of a color television picture tube has sets of three different phosphors that emit red, green, and blue light, respectively. The tube also has three electron guns—one for each primary color. The electron beams are controlled by the magnets so that the beam from each gun strikes only the dots for the color assigned to that gun. As the three beams sweep across the screen, the signal from the broadcast waves controls the intensity of each beam to produce the correct combination of primary colors at each point. ∎

Other Charged Particle Beams

Mass Spectrometer. A **mass spectrometer** is a device used to determine the masses of individual atoms by studying the paths of their ions in a magnetic field. Figure 8-14 (see the following page) illustrates a mass spectrometer. A sample of the element being studied is vaporized. The gas is then exposed to an electric discharge, which removes electrons from the gas atoms, producing positive ions of the element. A beam of these positive ions is then passed through a *velocity selector*, which consists of uniform electric and magnetic fields perpendicular to each other. The electric field exerts a force on each positive ion toward the negative plate (to the right in the diagram). The magnitude of this force is $F_e = Eq$, where E is the electric field intensity and q is the charge on the ion. The magnetic field is directed upward from the page so that it exerts a magnetic force on the ions in the opposite direction (to the left). The magnitude of the magnetic force on each ion is $F_m = Bqv$, where B is the magnetic field strength and v is the velocity of the ion perpendicular to the field.

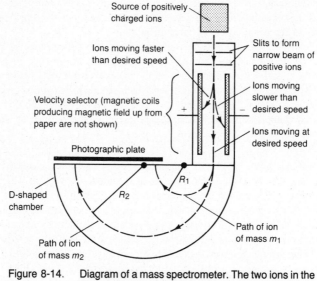

Figure 8-14.   Diagram of a mass spectrometer. The two ions in the D-shaped chamber have the same charge and velocity, but mass m_2 is greater than mass m_1.

If $F_e = F_m$, the net force on the ion is zero, since F_e and F_m act in opposite directions. The two forces are equal when $Eq = Bqv$, or $v = E/B$. An ion with this velocity will travel through the velocity selector in a straight line and leave through the slit at the end. Ions moving with less velocity will experience a smaller magnetic force and will be deflected to the right by the excess electric force. Ions moving with greater velocity will be deflected to the left by the excess magnetic force. Thus, only ions with the particular velocity equal to E/B will pass through the slit and enter the D-shaped chamber. In this chamber, they pass through another uniform magnetic field directed upward from the page.

As explained previously (page 243), the charged ions will follow circular paths in the magnetic field. If the ions all have the same charge and velocity, the radius of each path will depend only on the mass of the ion following that path. When ions strike the photographic plate, they produce a line that is visible when the plate is developed. The radius, r, of the path of the ion can be determined from the position of the line on the plate. The magnetic force exerted on an ion of charge, q, traveling with velocity, v, perpendicular to a uniform magnetic field of strength, B, is given by the equation $F = Bqv$. Because the force causes the ion to travel in a circle, it is a centripetal force and therefore equals $\dfrac{mv^2}{r}$ (a relationship discussed in Unit 6). Hence,

$$Bqv = \frac{mv^2}{r}$$

where Bqv and r are all easily measured. Therefore, m can be calculated. The mass spectrometer can thus be used to separate the isotopes of an element and determine their masses.

The Mass of the Electron. Soon after the discovery of the electron, the ratio of its charge to its mass was determined by passing a beam of electrons of the same velocity through electric and magnetic fields and comparing the deflections produced. However, there was no simple way to measure either the mass or the charge of the electron separately. The problem was solved by Robert Millikan in his famous "oil-drop" experiment.

As shown in the diagram of the Millikan apparatus in Figure 8-15, an atomizer is used to produce a fine spray of oil droplets. Some of the droplets fall slowly into the space between the two oppositely charged parallel plates through a hole in the upper plate. A burst of x rays (from a source not shown in the diagram) then ionizes the air between the plates by removing electrons from the gas atoms, thus producing ions with a positive charge equal in magnitude to the negative charge of the electrons removed. One or more of these positive ions become attached to the oil droplets, giving them a positive charge. The droplets can be observed through the telescopic eyepiece.

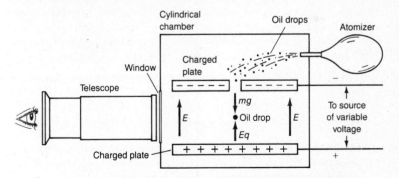

Figure 8-15   Millikan's oil-drop experiment. The oil drop, charged by friction, remains suspended between the charged plates when the upward electric force Eq equals the downward force mg, where E is the electric field intensity, q is the charge on the drop, m is the drop's mass, and g is the acceleration due to gravity. From the values of E, m, and g, q can be calculated for each observed drop.

The weight of an oil droplet acts downward on the droplet. The electric field acts upward on the positively charged droplet. The potential difference between the parallel plates can be adjusted until the drop remains suspended in the lower chamber. This condition of static equilibrium exists when the electric force Eq on the charged droplet is equal in magnitude but opposite in direction to the gravitational force mg on the droplet.

Millikan knew the intensity, E, of the electric field and was able to measure the mass of a droplet by observing its rate of fall against air friction when the electric field was turned off. He could therefore calculate the charge q on each droplet he observed. After accumulating data on thousands of oil droplets, Millikan concluded that the charge on any droplet is an integral multiple of an indivisible unit of charge now called the *elementary charge,* and he was able to determine its value from his data. Since the ratio of charge to mass of the electron was known, it was then easy to calculate the mass.

Particle Accelerators. Particle accelerators are devices that use electric and magnetic fields to accelerate electrons, protons, or other charged particles to speeds near that of light. At such speeds, the particles have tremendous kinetic energies and are used to bombard atomic nuclei, or to collide with each other, under controlled conditions. The products of these collisions often consist of unusual, high-energy, short-lived particles that do not normally exist. Studies of their modes of decay have greatly increased understanding of the fundamental nature of matter.

The *Van de Graaff generator,* the earliest type of particle accelerator, builds up very high potential differences between two spheres. Charged particles injected into the electric field are then accelerated to high velocities in a single large potential drop. In the *cyclotron,* and its later version, the *synchrotron,* charged particles travel in circular orbits in a magnetic field and are accelerated by means of repeated small potential drops in an electric field. After many orbits and accelerating pulses, the particles achieve the required high velocity and kinetic energy and are released as projectiles. There is also a group of devices, called *linear accelerators,* that give the particles a series of energizing pulses as they move in a straight path.

QUESTIONS

1. **Electrons are ejected from a hot metal surface. As the temperature of the surface increases, the rate of electron emission (1) decreases (2) increases (3) remains the same**

2. **As an electron between a pair of oppositely charged parallel plates approaches the positive plate, the force on the electron (1) decreases (2) increases (3) remains the same**

3. **As a proton between a pair of oppositely charged parallel plates approaches the negative plate, the acceleration of the proton (1) decreases (2) increases (3) remains the same**

4. An electron is located between two oppositely charged parallel plates. As the potential difference between the plates is decreased, the acceleration of the electron (1) decreases (2) increases (3) remains the same

5. To direct an electron beam in a cathode-ray tube to any point on the screen, the number of deflection plates needed is (1) 1 (2) 2 (3) 3 (4) 4

6. As the intensity of the electron beam in a cathode-ray tube increases, the brightness of the fluorescent spot on the screen (1) decreases (2) increases (3) remains the same

7. A device used to separate isotopes of the same element is a (1) laser (2) mass spectrometer (3) split-ring commutator (4) transformer

8. In a mass spectrometer, the element being analyzed must be in the form of (1) atoms in the solid phase (2) ions in the solid phase (3) atoms in the gas phase (4) ions in the gas phase

9. Mass spectrometers are used to determine the (1) masses of isotopes (2) half-lives of elements (3) gravitational field strength (4) electric field intensity

10. In a mass spectrometer, the direction of the ion beam is controlled by (1) an electric field only (2) a magnetic field only (3) both an electric and a magnetic field (4) neither an electric nor a magnetic field

11. The charge on the electron was determined by (1) Rutherford (2) Thomson (3) Chadwick (4) Millikan

12. Which of the following was proved by the Millikan oil-drop experiment? (1) Electric charge is always an integral multiple of 1.6×10^{-19} coulomb. (2) Gravitational field strength near the surface of the earth is always 9.8 newtons per kilogram. (3) The speed of light is always 3.00×10^8 meters per second. (4) The gravitational constant is 6.7×10^{-11} newton · meter squared per kilogram squared.

13. An electron is moving perpendicular to the lines of force of a uniform magnetic field. As the speed of the electron increases, the magnetic force on the electron (1) decreases (2) increases (3) remains the same

14. As the charge on a particle traveling at constant speed perpendicular to a magnetic field is increased, the deflecting force on the particle (1) decreases (2) increases (3) remains the same

15–19. Base your answers to Questions 15 through 19 on the following information.

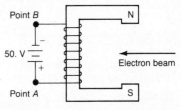

The current in the electromagnet shown is 5.0 amperes. The magnitude of the flux density, B, of the magnet is 1.0×10^{-2} newton per ampere · meter. A beam of electrons passes from right to left between the poles of the magnet at a speed of 3.0×10^6 meters per second.

15. The resistance of the magnet's coil is (1) 5.0 Ω (2) 10. Ω (3) 15 Ω (4) 250 Ω

16. **Which point has the most positive electric potential?** (1) *A* (2) *B* (3) *S* (4) *N*

17. **The rate at which electrical energy conversion occurs in the circuit is** (1) 0.010 J/s (2) 0.050 J/s (3) 10. J/s (4) 250 J/s

18. **As the electron beam passes between the poles of the electromagnet, it will be deflected** (1) toward pole N (2) toward pole S (3) into the page (4) out of the page

19. **The magnitude of the force exerted on each electron by the magnetic field is** (1) 4.8×10^{-15} N (2) 4.0×10^{-2} N (3) 3.0×10^{4} N (4) 1.5×10^{5} N

20–24. **Base your answers to Questions 20 through 24 on the diagram, which shows a beam of electrons moving perpendicular to a uniform magnetic field.**

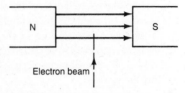

Electron beam

20. **The magnetic field deflects the electron beam** (1) to the right (2) to the left (3) out of the page (4) into the page

21. **Which will occur if only the direction of the magnetic field is reversed?** (1) The magnitude of the force exerted on the beam of electrons will decrease. (2) The magnitude of the force exerted on the beam of electrons will increase. (3) The direction of the force exerted on the beam of electrons will change. (4) The speed of the electron beam will change.

22. **If the magnetic flux density is 1.0 tesla and the speed of the electrons is 2.0×10^{7} meters per second, what force is exerted by the magnetic field on an electron?** (1) 3.0×10^{11} N (2) 3.2×10^{-12} N (3) 4.0×10^{-5} N (4) 6.4×10^{-5} N

23. **If the speed of the electrons is decreased, the magnetic force exerted on the beam will** (1) decrease (2) increase (3) remain the same

24. **Compared to the magnitude of the magnetic force on the electron, the magnitude of the magnetic force on a proton traveling with the same velocity in this field is** (1) less (2) greater (3) the same

III. INDUCED VOLTAGE

Any change in a magnetic field relative to a conductor will induce a potential difference (voltage or electromotive force) in the conductor. One way that this can happen is for a conductor, such as a wire, to move in such a way as to cut across the lines of flux of a magnetic field.

Magnitude and Direction of an Induced Potential Difference

When a straight conductor moves across a magnetic field, the magnitude of the induced potential difference depends partly on the rate at which the conductor cuts the lines of flux. This rate is a maximum when the conductor moves in a direction that is perpendicular to both itself and the field. For example, if a horizontal straight conductor is perpendicular to a horizontal field, as shown in Figure 8-16a, it will cut the field at a maximum rate by moving vertically. In this case, the magnitude of the induced potential difference is directly proportional to the magnetic field strength (or flux density), the length of the conductor in the magnetic field, and the velocity of the conductor relative to the flux:

$$V = Blv \qquad \text{(Eq. 8-2)}$$

where B is the magnetic field strength in teslas (or newtons per ampere · meter), l is the length of the conductor in meters, v is the velocity of the conductor perpendicular to the flux in meters per second, and V is the induced potential difference in volts. If the conductor is moving at some angle to the flux less than 90°, v in Equation 8-2 is the component of the velocity perpendicular to the flux. If the conductor moves parallel to the flux (at an angle of 0° to it), v is zero and there is no induced potential difference.

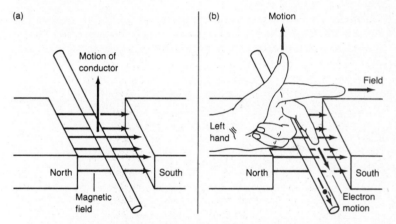

Figure 8-16   (a) The direction of motion of a straight conductor relative to a magnetic field that produces a maximum induced potential difference in the conductor. (b) The left-hand rule for finding the direction of the induced electron current.

If a conductor with an induced potential difference in it is part of a complete circuit, the induced potential difference will cause a current to flow in the circuit. The direction of this induced current (and of the potential difference causing it) can be determined by applying a rule called *Lenz's law,* which is derived from the law of conservation of energy. Lenz's law states that the direction of an induced current must be such that its magnetic effects oppose the forces that are inducing the current. This means that the force on the conductor that results from the flow of current in the magnetic field must tend to oppose the motion of the conductor or tend to reduce the rate of change of the field that is causing the current flow.

A convenient way to find the direction of the induced current is by using a hand rule. To find the direction in which electrons will move, the *left-hand generator rule* can by used. This rule is illustrated in Figure 8-16b. The thumb, forefinger, and middle finger of the left hand are extended at right angles to each other. If the forefinger points in the direction of the magnetic field and the thumb points in the direction of motion of the conductor, the middle finger points in the direction of the induced electron motion. This is also the direction of the induced potential difference *from negative to positive*.

Generator Principle

Electromagnetic induction is the basis of the electric generator. In a generator, a source of mechanical energy causes a coil of wire to rotate in a uniform magnetic field so that the flux linked (enclosed) by the coil continually changes. The resulting induced potential difference across the ends of the coil causes a current to flow in a complete external circuit. In this way, mechanical energy is converted to electrical energy.

Consider a wire loop positioned in a uniform magnetic field as shown in Figure 8-17a. If the loop is rotated clockwise, the side between points 1 and 2 moves upward across the lines of flux. The left-hand generator rule says that a

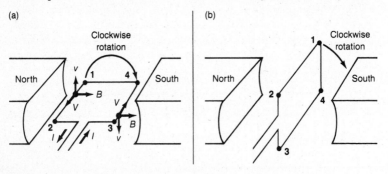

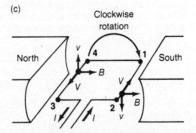

Figure 8-17. The principle of an alternating-current generator. (a) The induced potential difference is a maximum and tends to drive electrons through the coil from 1 to 2 and from 3 to 4. (b) The induced potential difference is zero. (c) The induced potential difference is again a maximum but in the opposite direction.

potential difference will be induced in this side of the loop that tends to drive electrons in the direction shown by the vector, V (from point 1 to point 2). At the same time, the side of the loop between points 3 and 4 moves downward across the flux, and a potential difference is induced in this side tending to drive electrons in the direction of vector, V, on that side of the loop (from point 3 to point 4). Note that the two potential differences tend to drive electrons in the same direction through the conductor of the loop.

In the position of the loop shown in Figure 8-17a, each side of the loop is moving *perpendicular* to the lines of flux. Therefore, the induced potential difference is a maximum. Notice also that although the loop does not link (enclose) any flux in this position, it encloses an increasing amount as it rotates to the position shown in Figure 8-17b. The *rate of change* of the flux linked by the loop is a maximum when the loop is in the position shown in Figure 8-17a.

After rotating 90°, the plane of the loop is perpendicular to the magnetic field, as shown in Figure 8-17b. The velocity of each side of the loop is parallel to the flux. The flux linked by the loop in this position is a maximum and for the moment is not changing. Therefore, there is no induced potential difference in the loop.

When the loop reaches the position shown in Figure 8-17c (180° from its original position), the side between points 1 and 2 is moving downward, and the side between points 3 and 4 is moving upward. The induced potential difference in each side is again a maximum, but it tends to drive electrons in the opposite direction around the loop (from point 2 to point 1 and from point 4 to point 3). When the loop rotates an additional 90°, the loop's plane is again perpendicular to the magnetic field, and again there is no induced potential difference.

Figure 8-18 is a graph of induced potential difference plotted against the angular position of the loop in the magnetic field. If the loop is rotating at

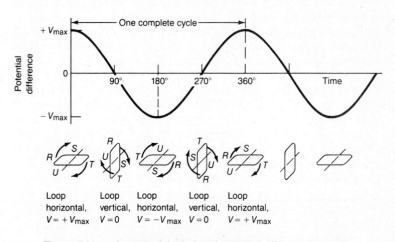

Figure 8-18.   A graph of the induced potential difference in a generator coil rotating at constant speed as its angular position changes.

constant speed, the horizontal axis of the graph also represents time. Note that the potential difference in the loop is changing direction, or *alternating,* with a regular frequency. If the loop is connected to an external circuit, this alternating potential difference will produce an **alternating current** in the circuit, that is, a current that reverses its direction with a regular frequency.

Figure 8-19 is a diagram of an alternating-current generator. A coil of wire consisting of many loops in series is wound on a permeable iron core and is rotated in a uniform magnetic field by a source of mechanical energy, such as a steam engine or turbine. Each end of the coil is connected to an external circuit through a slip ring that rotates with the coil and a brush that is always in contact with it. The alternating potential difference induced in the coil drives an alternating current of the same frequency through the external circuit. The current carries electrical energy that can do work or produce heat. Generators that supply electric power for commercial use in the United States operate at a frequency of 60 hertz (60 complete cycles of current change per second).

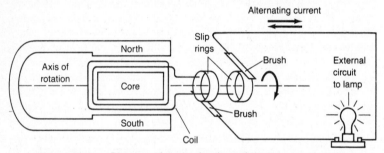

Figure 8-19.   Diagram of a simple alternating-current generator.

Transformers

A **transformer** is a device that changes the potential difference (voltage) of an alternating current to a smaller or larger alternating potential difference of the same frequency. The operation of the transformer is based upon the principles that a changing current in a conductor produces a changing magnetic field, and a changing magnetic field can induce a potential difference in a conductor. As a result of these changes, the transformer can transfer electrical energy from one alternating-current circuit to another without a direct connection between them.

Figure 8-20 is a diagram of a transformer. As shown in the diagram, coils of wire are wound around a common iron core. The highly permeable iron core concentrates the magnetic lines of flux. The coil that is connected to the alternating-current source is called the **primary coil,** and the coil in which an alternating potential difference is induced is called the **secondary coil.**

Potential Difference (Voltage) Relationships in a Transformer. The ratio of the number of turns on the primary coil, N_p, to the number of turns on the

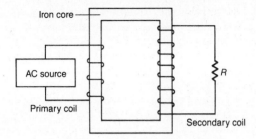

Figure 8-20.   Diagram of a transformer.

secondary coil, N_s, is equal to the ratio of the potential difference across the primary coil, V_p, to the potential difference induced in the secondary coil, V_s:

$$\frac{N_p}{N_s} = \frac{V_p}{V_s} \qquad \text{(Eq. 8-3)}$$

When N_s is greater than N_p, V_s is greater than V_p, and the device is called a *step-up transformer*. Step-up transformers are used in the operation of neon and fluorescent lights. On the other hand, if N_s is less than N_p, then V_s is less than V_p, and the device is a *step-down transformer*. Step-down transformers are commonly used in the design of toy trains, toy electric cars, and doorbells.

Power Relationships in a Transformer. If the secondary coil is connected to a complete circuit, as in Figure 8-20, the transformer will transfer energy from the primary coil to the secondary coil. Since energy must be conserved in any system, the power output from the secondary coil can never exceed the power input to the primary coil. In an *ideal transformer*—one in which there are no energy losses between the primary and secondary coils—the power input to the primary coil equals the power output from the secondary coil. Recall from Unit 3 (page 93) that the power in an electrical circuit is given by

$$P = VI$$

where P is power in watts, V is potential difference in volts, and I is current in amperes. In an alternating-current circuit, the instantaneous values of potential difference and current are changing continuously. The values of V and I in alternating-current relationships are the *effective* (average) values over the course of a complete cycle. With this understanding of the meaning of V and I, we can write the following relationship for an ideal transformer, in which power input equals power output:

$$V_p I_p = V_s I_s \qquad \text{(Eq. 8-4)}$$

where V_p and I_p are the potential difference and current in the primary coil, and V_s and I_s are the corresponding values in the secondary coil.

Efficiency of a Transformer. The **efficiency** of a transformer is the actual ratio of the power output from the secondary coil to the power input to the primary coil, expressed as a percent:

$$\% \text{ efficiency} = \frac{V_s I_s}{V_p I_p} \times 100 \qquad \text{(Eq. 8-5)}$$

No real transformer has an efficiency of 100%, but transformer efficiencies are much higher than those of most other power devices. They range from about 90% to as high as 99%. The chief sources of energy loss in a transformer are heat losses caused by the resistance of the coils and the rapid alternation of the flux in the iron core.

EXAMPLE

An ideal transformer that has 200. turns in its primary coil and 50. turns in its secondary coil is connected to a 120-volt alternating-current power line. The secondary current is 3.0 amperes. Find (a) the potential difference induced in the secondary coil, (b) the current in the primary coil, and (c) the power input and output of the transformer.

Solution

(a) $\qquad N_p = 200. \quad N_s = 50. \quad V_p = 120 \text{ V} \quad I_s = 3.0 \text{ A}$

$$\frac{N_p}{N_s} = \frac{V_p}{V_s} \quad \text{or} \quad V_s = \frac{N_s V_p}{N_p} = \frac{(50.)(120 \text{ V})}{200.} = 30. \text{ V}$$

(b) $\qquad V_p I_p = V_s I_s \quad \text{or} \quad I_p = \frac{V_s I_s}{V_p} = \frac{(30. \text{ V})(3.0 \text{ A})}{120. \text{ V}} = 0.75 \text{ A}$

(c) $\qquad P_p = V_p I_p = (120 \text{ V})(0.75 \text{ A}) = 90. \text{ W}$

$$P_s = V_s I_s = (30. \text{ W})(3.0 \text{ A}) = 90. \text{ W}$$

PRACTICAL APPLICATION

Commercial alternating current is transmitted long distances through high-voltage power lines usually made of aluminum, rather than copper, to reduce weight. Although aluminum is a good conductor of electricity, over long distances its resistance is significant, and much power ($P = I^2 R$) is lost to heating of the transmission lines. Since the power loss is directly proportional to the square of current, electricity is most efficiently transmitted from its point of generation at very low currents and, consequently, very high voltages. In a typical case, an output voltage of 24,000 V from the generators at the power plant may be stepped up by transformers to 230,000 V for long-distance transmission. The current needed to transmit a given amount of power is correspondingly reduced. Since controlling such large voltages presents problems, the voltage is stepped down by transformers several times before it finally reaches a home or factory. For example, it may be stepped down to 100,000 V at a regional substation, and further stepped down to 7,200 V at a local substation for transmission to the utility poles on the street. A pole transformer finally steps the voltage down to 240 V for delivery to the consumer. ∎

Induction Coils

If a direct (unvarying) current flows through the primary coil of a transformer, there is no induced potential difference or current in the secondary coil, since the magnetic flux in the core remains constant. It is possible, however, to obtain a varying potential difference from the secondary coil by rapidly turning on and off the direct current in the primary coil. This can be done automatically by means of an electromechanical switch or a solid-state circuit device. Each time the current starts to flow, the magnetic flux builds up in the core, and each time the current stops, the magnetic flux collapses. These repeated changes in the flux will induce potential differences in the secondary coil. An **induction coil** is a transformer that operates in this way from a direct-current source.

PRACTICAL APPLICATION ▬▬▬▬▬▬▬

In the cylinders of most automobile engines and small gasoline engines, power is obtained by igniting a mixture of gasoline vapor and air by means of an electric spark. To produce the spark, a potential difference of about 20,000 V must be applied across the terminals of a spark plug. An induction coil is often used to supply this high voltage from the car's 12-volt battery, a direct-current source. ∎

QUESTIONS

1. **Lenz's law is an application of the law of conservation of (1) charge (2) energy (3) mass (4) momentum**

2–6. **Base your answers to Questions 2 through 6 on the diagram, which shows a conducting loop being rotated at a constant speed in a uniform magnetic field of 5.6×10^{-2} tesla.**

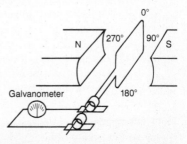

2. **As the loop is rotated clockwise through 360°, the galvanometer needle will (1) deflect only to the left (2) deflect only to the right (3) deflect first in one direction and then in the other (4) not deflect in either direction**

3. During one cycle, the potential difference induced in the rotating loop will be a maximum at (1) 0° and 90° only (2) 0° and 180° only (3) 90° and 270° only (4) 0°, 90°, 180°, and 270°

4. If the loop is made smaller, the maximum induced potential difference will (1) decrease (2) increase (3) remain the same

5. If the speed of rotation of the loop is increased, the induced potential difference will (1) decrease (2) increase (3) remain the same

6. If the north and south poles of the magnet are reversed, the induced potential difference will (1) decrease (2) increase (3) remain the same

7–10. Base your answers to Questions 7 through 10 on the diagram shown, which represents the end view of a closed rectangular loop of wire rotating at a constant speed in a uniform magnetic field.

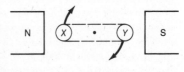

7. If the flux density between the two poles is increased, the magnitude of the maximum induced potential difference will (1) decrease (2) increase (3) remain the same

8. During one complete rotation of the loop, the induced potential difference in the X side of the loop will be (1) out of the page only (2) into the page only (3) both out of and into the page (4) neither into nor out of the page

9. If the loop is connected to an external circuit, the current in the loop will produce a magnetic field inside the loop directed (1) upward (2) downward (3) to the right (4) to the left

10. As the loop rotates through an angle of 90° from the position shown, the magnitude of the induced potential difference will (1) decrease (2) increase (3) remain the same

11–15. Base your answers to Questions 11 through 15 on the diagram at right, which represents a straight conductor perpendicular to the page, moving in a circular path at constant speed in a uniform magnetic field. Points A, B, C, and D represent different positions of the wire as it moves.

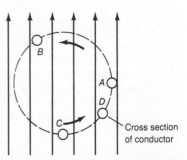

Cross section of conductor

11. The largest potential difference will be induced in the conductor as it moves through position (1) A (2) B (3) C (4) D

12. When the conductor is moving through position B, the direction of the force on the electrons in the conductor will be (1) into the page (2) out of the page (3) toward the top of the page (4) toward the bottom of the page

13. If the strength of the magnetic field is increased, then the maximum potential difference induced in the conductor will (1) decrease (2) increase (3) remain the same

14. If the speed of the conductor is decreased and the magnetic field strength is kept constant, the maximum potential difference induced in the conductor will (1) decrease (2) increase (3) remain the same

15. If the ends of the conductor are connected to a light bulb, the force needed to continue to move the conductor at the same speed will (1) decrease (2) increase (3) remain the same

16–20. Base your answers to Questions 16 through 20 on the following information.

The diagram represents a rectangular wire loop, *ABCD*, rotating between two magnetic poles. Sides *AB* and *CD* move at a constant speed of 1.0 meter per second. The strength of the uniform magnetic field between the magnetic poles is 5.0 teslas. Side *AB* is 0.30 meter long.

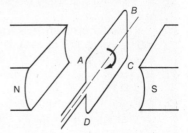

16. The maximum potential difference induced in side *AB* is (1) 1.5 V (2) 2.0 V (3) 3.0 V (4) 6.0 V

17. The induced potential difference will be a maximum when the angle between the plane of the loop and the direction of the magnetic field is (1) 0° (2) 30° (3) 45° (4) 90°

18. If two loops are joined to form a coil of two turns, the maximum potential difference induced in the coil, compared to that induced in the single loop, will be (1) less (2) greater (3) the same

19. If the strength of the magnetic field is decreased, and the rate at which the coil rotates remains constant, the maximum induced potential difference will (1) decrease (2) increase (3) remain the same

20. If the loop's direction of rotation is reversed, the maximum induced potential difference will (1) decrease (2) increase (3) remain the same

21. An alternating potential difference is induced in the secondary coil of a transformer if (1) there is no current in the primary coil (2) there is an alternating current in the primary coil (3) there is a constant magnetic flux in the core (4) the magnetic field is constant

22. Compared to the power input of a real transformer, the power output is always (1) less (2) greater (3) the same

23–25. Base your answers to Questions 23 through 25 on the information below.

The primary coil of a transformer with an efficiency of 100% has 200. turns and its secondary coil has 50. turns. The primary coil is connected to a 120-volt alternating-current power supply and develops 600 watts of power.

23. The potential difference across the secondary coil is (1) 30. V (2) 60. V (3) 3.0 V (4) 480 V

24. The current in the primary coil is (1) 5.0 A (2) 12 A (3) 3.0 A (4) 20. A

25. The power developed in the secondary coil is (1) 0.0 W (2) 150 W (3) 600 W (4) 2,400 W

26. The primary coil of a transformer has 50. turns and its secondary coil has 200 turns. If the current in the primary coil is 40. amperes, the current in the secondary coil is (1) 10. A (2) 50. A (3) 160 A (4) 200 A

27–28. Base your answers to questions 27 and 28 on the information below.

A transformer with an efficiency of 100% has 100. turns in its primary coil and 300. turns in its secondary coil. The power input to the transformer is 60. watts.

27. The power output of the transformer is (1) 0.0 W (2) 20. W (3) 60. W (4) 180 W

28. The ratio of the potential difference in the primary coil to that in the secondary coil is (1) 1/3 (2) 1/5 (3) 3/1 (4) 6/1

IV. THE LASER

The term **laser** is an acronym (a word formed from initial letters of a name) for *light amplification by stimulated emission of radiation*. The light beam produced by a laser is an extremely intense, narrow beam of light of a single frequency in which all the waves are in phase. In other words, a laser beam is *monochromatic* and *coherent*. Such a light beam spreads very little as it travels away from its source. It can concentrate a large amount of radiant energy on a microscopic spot, or it can be sent to the moon and be reflected back to the earth by a small mirror.

CAN YOU EXPLAIN THIS?

A beam of light may replace the scalpel used in surgery.

Muscle tissue can be cut through by heating and evaporating the water contained in cells, using infrared radiation from a carbon-dioxide laser. There is less blood loss than there is when a scalpel is used, because the laser cuts tissue and coagulates blood at the same time. It is also possible to cauterize bleeding tissues by means of a laser beam trapped in a fiber-optic tool that is introduced through a patient's mouth and moved through the body to a specific location.

Recall from Unit 5 (page 68) that when the atoms of a substance are subjected to a source of energy, such as heat or an electric discharge, electrons absorb quanta of energy and are excited to higher energy levels in the atoms. An excited electron almost immediately drops back to a lower energy level, emitting a photon of the frequency corresponding to the change in energy of the electron. This process, called *spontaneous emission,* usually occurs at random, and the excited atoms emit light and other types of electromagnetic radiation at many different frequencies, in all directions, and in all possible phases. Thus the light emitted from ordinary sources is neither monochromatic nor coherent.

In a laser, the emission of photons by excited atoms is not random. The atoms of the laser material are first raised to an excited state that is much more stable than is usually the case. This process is called *pumping.* An electron in this excited state does not drop back to a lower lever immediately. It does so only when *stimulated* by a photon with energy exactly equal to the energy the electron will lose. The atom then emits two identical photons at exactly the same time—the original stimulating photon and the one emitted by the electron. This process is called *stimulated emission.* The two photons can now produce stimulated emission in two other atoms, thus producing four photons of exactly the same frequency and phase. This multiplication of photons, or amplification of light, can be repeated many times, resulting in a burst of monochromatic, coherent light.

The material in a laser is usually in the shape of a long, narrow cylinder, and the multiplication of photons proceeds from one end of the cylinder to the other. The cylinder also has silvered ends, so that the photons are reflected back through the cylinder from each end, thus continuing the amplification in each reflection. One of the ends is only partly silvered, so that some of the photons reaching this end pass through. As the stimulated emission reaches a peak in the laser material, an intense pulse of light is emitted through the partly silvered end. The material is then pumped again, and the process is repeated.

In some lasers, there are two active substances. One substance is continuously pumped to an excited state, and it transfers energy to the second substance by collision, exciting it to a similar energy level. The stimulated emission then occurs in the second substance. The advantage of this method is that the laser then produces a continuous beam, rather than a series of pulses, because the pumping and emission processes occur in different atoms. The helium-neon gas laser is this type of laser.

PRACTICAL APPLICATION

Many supermarkets use a low-power helium-neon laser to "read" the Universal Product Code (bar code) that is generally printed on items for sale. The laser beam is focused by a lens, and is then reflected from a mirror that oscillates to produce a rapidly moving small-dot image. This dot is scanned over the barcode label, whose dark areas absorb the light and whose light areas reflect it. The reflected light is "read" by a light-sensitive detector, which transmits the information to a central computer. There, the product is identified by name and price, and the information is relayed back to the cash register. ∎

QUESTIONS

1. The light emitted by a laser is (1) both monochromatic and coherent (2) neither monochromatic nor coherent (3) monochromatic, but not coherent (4) coherent, but not monochromatic

2. In stimulated emission of radiation, a photon entering an atom (1) excites an electron to a lower energy level (2) passes through without producing any change in the atom (3) changes the atom to one of a different element (4) causes the release of a second photon of the same frequency and phase

3. In the helium-neon laser, coherent light is produced by (1) an electric discharge (2) the neon atoms only (3) the helium atoms only (4) both the helium and the neon atoms

UNIT 9   GEOMETRICAL OPTICS

I. IMAGES

Light rays travel in straight lines if the transmitting medium is of uniform optical density and the rays do not strike a reflecting surface. If the light rays from an object are affected by a change in the optical density of the transmitting medium or by reflection from a surface, an observer may see an image of the object that is at a different position or has a different size from that of the actual object. An **image** is formed where light rays originating from the same point on an object intersect on a surface or appear to intersect for the observer.

Real Image

A **real image** is formed when light rays from a common point pass through an optical system that causes them to converge and intersect at a point. A real image can be projected on a surface placed where the image is formed. The image may then be seen by diffuse reflection from the surface. Lenses in a slide projector produce a real image of a slide on a screen. The lenses in a camera produce a real image of an object on light-sensitive film inside the camera.

Virtual Image

Unlike a real image, a *virtual image* cannot be projected on a screen, because no light from the object actually reaches the point where the image appears to be located. A **virtual image** is formed when light rays from a common point pass through or are reflected by an optical system that causes the rays to diverge in such a way that they appear to come from a different point. The reflection of an object in a plane mirror is an example of a virtual image. The rays reaching an observer's eyes actually come from the object. They are reflected by the mirror in such a way that they appear to come from the image, as explained in the next section.

II. IMAGES FORMED BY REFLECTIONS

Images Formed by a Plane Mirror

Any light ray incident on a plane mirror will be reflected in accordance with the law of reflection stated in Unit 4 (page 125). The angle between the incident ray and the normal, $\angle i$, always equals the angle between the reflected ray and the normal, $\angle r$.

Figure 9-1a shows several rays of light from the same point P_o being reflected by a plane mirror. Note that the ray perpendicular to the mirror is reflected back upon itself. All the reflected rays appear to be coming from a single point P_i behind the mirror. Point P_i is the virtual image of P_o, because the light rays only *appear* to be originating there. Point P_i could not be projected on a screen located at P_i since no light rays actually converge at P_i. By the geometry of the diagram, it can be shown that P_i is the same distance behind the mirror as P_o is in front of it.

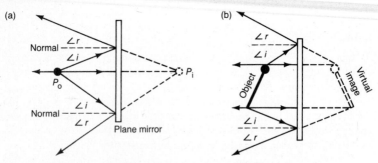

Figure 9-1.   Image formation by a plane mirror. (a) All rays from a point source, P_o, are reflected as though coming from an image point, P_i, as far behind the mirror as P_o is in front of it. (b) Any two reflected rays that originate from a point on a object are sufficient to locate the virtual image of that point by extending the reflected rays until they intersect behind the mirror.

The image of an object placed in front of a plane mirror can be constructed as shown in Figure 9-1b. The image point corresponding to any given point on the object can be located by tracing the path of any two rays originating from the given point on the object. For example, one ray can be the ray perpendicular to the mirror. The other ray can be drawn at any other angle to the mirror. By geometry, it can be shown that the image is the same distance behind the mirror as the object is in front of it, and the image and the object are also the same size. Although the image formed by a vertical mirror is erect with respect to the object, it is reversed from left to right. For example, the top of the image of a printed page is the top of the page, but the print reads backward.

CAN YOU EXPLAIN THIS?

To view the entire body of a person, a mirror that is half the person's height is all that is needed.

The law of reflection states that the angle of incidence is equal to the angle of reflection. Looking straight ahead into a plane mirror, positioned in front of you and perpendicular to the floor, you see your eyes. If you look halfway down the mirror, you see your toes. If you raise your eyes and look at the mirror at a distance halfway between your eyes and the top of your head, you see the top of your head. Thus, the minimum size of a plane mirror for viewing the entire body is one-half the viewer's height, as illustrated in Figure 9-2.

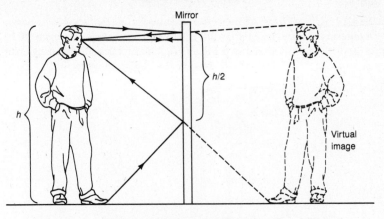

Figure 9-2. Seeing your image in a vertical mirror. The portions of the mirror outside the length marked $h/2$ are unnecessary for seeing your full image.

The rays that are reflected by one mirror can be reflected by a second mirror, as shown in Figure 9-3. Note that image 1 is the image in mirror 1 of the object. However, image 1 also serves as the object of the image that is reflected by mirror 2. Therefore, the distance from image 1 to mirror 2 must be the same as the distance from image 2 to mirror 2.

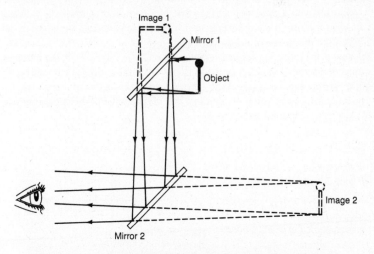

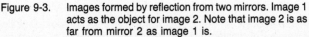

Figure 9-3. Images formed by reflection from two mirrors. Image 1 acts as the object for image 2. Note that image 2 is as far from mirror 2 as image 1 is.

PRACTICAL APPLICATION

A toy periscope uses two mirrors that enable an observer to see the image of an object behind a wall, as shown in Figure 9-4. (One mirror would be enough, but the observer would then have to look up at an awkward angle.)

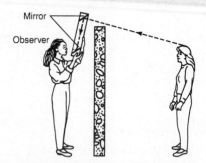

Mirror

Observer

Figure 9-4.   Using a toy periscope to observe a person standing behind a wall.

A submarine periscope and many other optical devices use total internal reflection from prisms, rather than from plane mirrors, to produce images. The light reflected by a plane mirror is not as bright as that reflected by a prism, because more light energy is lost by absorption at a mirror surface than is lost by total internal reflection in a prism. ■

Images Formed by a Spherical Mirror

A mirror with a reflecting surface that is a portion of a sphere is called a **spherical mirror.** If the reflecting surface curves inward from the edges to the center (like the inside of a bowl), as in Figure 9-5a, the mirror is a **concave mirror.** If the reflecting surface curves outward, as in Figure 9-5b, the mirror is a **convex mirror.** The radius of the sphere is called the **radius of curvature,** R, of the mirror, and the center of the sphere is called the **center of curvature,** C. The line through the center of curvature and the midpoint of the curved surface is called the **principal axis.**

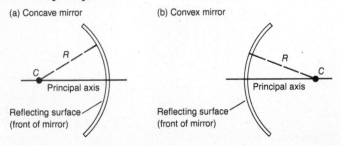

(a) Concave mirror

(b) Convex mirror

Principal axis

Reflecting surface
(front of mirror)

Principal axis

Reflecting surface
(front of mirror)

Figure 9-5.   The two kinds of spherical mirrors. In each, C is the center of curvature and R is the radius of curvature.

Images Formed by Concave Mirrors. As with any reflecting surface, the angle of incidence of a light ray incident on the surface of a concave mirror equals the angle of reflection of the reflected ray. As shown in Figure 9-6a, when the arc of a concave spherical mirror is small compared to the radius of curvature, an incident ray parallel to the principal axis is reflected so that it passes through a point on the principal axis that is halfway between the center of curvature and the mirror. This point is called the **principal focus, F,** of the mirror. The distance from F to the mirror is called the **focal length,** f. Since F is halfway between C and the mirror, the radius of curvature R equals twice the focal length f. A concave mirror is called a **converging mirror** because all rays parallel to the principal axis are reflected so that they come together, or converge, at the principal focus, as shown in Figure 9-6b. A converging mirror can concentrate the parallel rays of the sun to a point at its principal focus, producing enough heat to ignite a piece of paper held at that point.

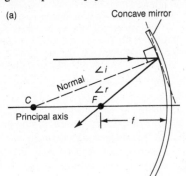

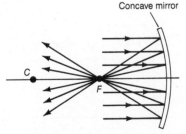

Figure 9-6.   Reflection of rays parallel to the principal axis of a concave (converging) mirror. (a) Any radius drawn from C is normal to the surface, because it is perpendicular to the tangent at the point of intersection. (b) All of the rays parallel to the principal axis are reflected through the principal focus F (provided that the arc of the mirror is small compared to the radius of curvature).

To construct the image formed by a concave lens of any point, P_o, on an object, draw any two reflected rays from that point. There are three rays whose paths are easily traced if the position of C, the center of curvature, and F, the principal focus, are known. These three rays are shown in Figure 9-7.

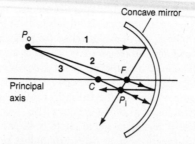

Figure 9-7.　Three rays from Point P_o for which the positions of the reflected rays from a concave mirror are known. (1) The ray parallel to the principal axis is reflected through F. (2) The ray through F is reflected parallel to the principal axis. (3) The ray through C is reflected back upon itself. A real image of the point is formed at P_i.

Ray 1, parallel to the principal axis, is reflected through F, the principal focus. Ray 2, directed through F, is reflected parallel to the principal axis. Ray 3, directed through C, strikes the mirror along a normal to the mirror surface and is reflected back along the same normal. It therefore is reflected back upon itself. The three reflected rays intersect at a point that is the image of the point from which the rays originated. To draw the image of an object, use any two of these three rays from representative points of the object. Figure 9-8 shows how the image of an object formed by a concave mirror can be constructed.

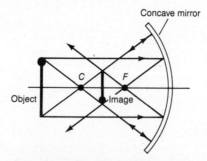

Figure 9-8.　Image formation by a concave (converging) mirror. Rays 1 and 3 in Figure 9-7 have been used to find the image points of the top and bottom of the object. Ray 2, through F, could also have been used. When the object is beyond C, the image is real, inverted, smaller than the object, and between C and F.

The image formed by a concave mirror is a real image when the reflected rays meet at and pass through the image, which is what happens for most positions of the object. An observer looking toward the mirror will see the real image when the reflected rays continue on past the image and enter the observer's eyes. Note also that the image is inverted. Real images produced by optical devices are usually inverted.

Figure 9-9 shows how the image changes as an object is moved closer to a concave mirror. When the object is beyond C (Figure 9-9a), the real image is between C and the principal focus, F, and it is smaller than the object. As the object approaches C, the real image moves closer to C and becomes larger (but remains smaller than the object). When the object is at C (Figure 9-9b), the real image is also at C and is the same size as the object.

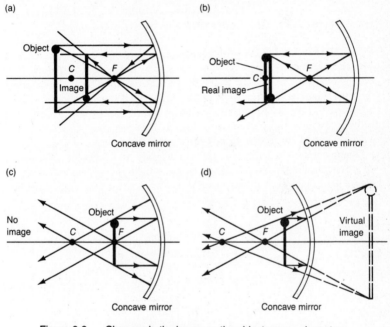

Figure 9-9.   Changes in the image as the object moves closer to a concave mirror.

As the object moves past C toward F, the real image moves beyond C and becomes larger than the object. When the object reaches F (as shown in Figure 9-9c), however, no image is formed because all the rays from any point on the object are reflected parallel to each other. When the object passes F and is between F and the mirror (as shown in Figure 9-9d), the reflected rays diverge and form a virtual image. This virtual image is behind the mirror, erect, and larger than the object. Table 9-1 (see the following page) summarizes the characteristics of the images produced by a concave mirror.

Table 9-1. The relationship between the object and the image formed by a
concave mirror.

Figure	Position	Position	Type	Orientation	Size*
	OBJECT	IMAGE			
9-9a	Beyond C	Between C and F	Real	Inverted	Smaller
9-9b	At C	At C	Real	Inverted	Same size
9-9c	At F	--------(no image)----			--------
9-9d	Between F and mirror	Behind the mirror	Virtual	Erect	Larger

*Note that the size of the image is relative to the size of the object.

PRACTICAL APPLICATION

The concave mirror is used in many devices in and around the home. In a
flashlight or car headlight, the bulb is placed at the principal focus of a spherical
reflector. Light reflected from the mirror surface produces a concentrated, parallel beam of light rays. A magnifying mirror is used with the object (your face)
between the principal focus and the mirror. You therefore see an erect and
enlarged virtual image that appears to be behind the mirror.

Concave mirrors as large as 6 meters in diameter are used in the construction
of astronomical telescopes to collect as much light as possible. As shown in
Figure 9-10, light from an astronomical object enters the tube of the telescope

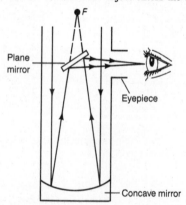

Figure 9-10.   Simplified diagram of a reflecting telescope. Without
the plane mirror, the essentially parallel rays from a
distant star would be reflected to a real focus at F.
The plane mirror is small compared to the concave
light-gathering mirror, and therefore blocks only a
small portion of the incident light.

and strikes the concave mirror at the base of the telescope. Since the rays from distant objects are essentially parallel, all the light received by the mirror is reflected toward its principal focus, where a point image would normally be formed. The light rays are intercepted, however, by a small plane mirror that is placed at an angle just in front of the principal focus. The mirror reflects the rays to an eyepiece for direct observation or to a camera for making a photographic image.

The principles of a concave mirror are also evident in the satellite dishes that many people use to obtain better television reception. The satellite dish itself acts as a spherical "mirror" that reflects the waves of the television signal and causes the waves to converge at the focal point of the dish, where a receptor is located. ∎

An analysis of the geometry of image formation by a concave mirror gives the following relationship:

$$\frac{1}{d_o} + \frac{1}{d_i} = \frac{1}{f}$$
(Eq. 9-1)

where d_o is the distance of the object from the mirror, d_i is the distance of the image from the mirror, and f is the focal length. When using this equation, remember that distances in front of the mirror have positive values, but distances behind the mirror have negative values. The focal length, f, of a concave mirror is therefore positive.

Equation 9-1 can be rewritten as follows:

$$\frac{1}{d_i} = \frac{1}{f} - \frac{1}{d_o}$$
(Eq. 9-1a)

When d_o is greater than f, $1/d_o$ is smaller than $1/f$, and d_i is a positive value. A positive value of d_i means that the image is located in front of the mirror and is real. When d_o is smaller than f, $1/d_o$ is larger than $1/f$, and d_i is a negative value. A negative value of d_i indicates that the image is behind the mirror and is virtual.

The size of the object and the image are related to their distances as shown in the following equations:

$$\frac{S_o}{S_i} = \frac{d_o}{d_i}$$
(Eq. 9-2)

and

$$S_i = \frac{S_o d_i}{d_o}$$
(Eq. 9-2a)

where S_o is the object size and S_i is the image size. A negative value for S_i indicates that the image is virtual and erect.

EXAMPLE

An object 0.050 meter tall is located 0.30 meter from a concave mirror having a focal length of 0.20 meter. Find (a) the location of the image and (b) the height of the image.

Solution

$$d_o = 0.30 \text{ m} \qquad f = 0.20 \text{ m} \qquad S_o = 0.050 \text{ m}$$

(a) Solve for d_i. By Equation 9-1a,

$$\frac{1}{d_i} = \frac{1}{f} - \frac{1}{d_o}$$

Giving the two fractions to the right of the equals sign a common denominator yields

$$\frac{1}{d_i} = \frac{d_o - f}{d_o f}$$

Solving for d_i:

$$d_i = \frac{d_o f}{d_o - f}$$

$$d_i = \frac{(0.30 \text{ m})(0.20 \text{ m})}{0.30 \text{ m} - 0.20 \text{ m}}$$

$$d_i = \frac{0.060 \text{ m}^2}{0.10 \text{ m}}$$

$$d_i = 0.60 \text{ m}$$

(b) Using Equation 9-2a, solve for S_i:

$$S_i = \frac{S_o d_i}{d_o}$$

$$S_i = \frac{(0.050 \text{ m})(0.60 \text{ m})}{0.30 \text{ m}}$$

$$S_i = \frac{0.030 \text{ m}^2}{0.30 \text{ m}}$$

$$S_i = 0.10 \text{ m}$$

Note that the image is real, larger than the object, and inverted, as is to be expected when the object is between C and F.

Compare the results obtained in the problem above with those obtained in the following example.

EXAMPLE

An object 0.050 meter tall is located 0.10 meter from a concave mirror having a focal length of 0.20 meter. Find (a) the location of the image and (b) the height of the image.

Solution

$$d_o = 0.10 \text{ m} \qquad f = 0.20 \text{ m} \qquad S_o = 0.050 \text{ m}$$

(a) Solve for d_i, using the equation found in Part (a) of the preceding example:

$$d_i = \frac{d_o f}{d_o - f}$$

$$d_i = \frac{(0.10 \text{ m})(0.20 \text{ m})}{0.10 \text{ m} - 0.20 \text{ m}}$$

$$d_i = \frac{0.020 \text{ m}^2}{-0.10 \text{ m}}$$

$$d_i = -0.20 \text{ m}$$

The negative sign indicates that the image is located behind the mirror and is therefore virtual.

(b) Using Equation 9-2a, Solve for S_i:

$$S_i = \frac{S_o d_i}{d_o}$$

$$S_i = \frac{(0.050 \text{ m})(-0.20 \text{ m})}{(0.10 \text{ m})}$$

$$S_i = \frac{0.010 \text{ m}^2}{0.10 \text{ m}}$$

$$S_i = -0.10 \text{ m}$$

The negative sign indicates that the image is erect and virtual.

In the example on this page, the object is located between the principal focus and the concave mirror. As a result, the image is located behind the mirror and is a virtual image. This example contrasts with the one on page 272, where the image is a real image located in front of the mirror because the object is *beyond* the principal focus (that is, its object distance is greater than f).

Images Formed by Convex Mirrors. In the case of a convex mirror, incident rays parallel to the principal axis are reflected as though coming from a principal focus, F, behind the mirror, as shown in Figure 9-11. A focus behind the mirror is called a **virtual focus**. Since these reflected rays spread apart, or diverge, a convex mirror is called a **diverging mirror**. As in the case of a concave mirror, you can draw three rays from a point on an object, P_o, as shown in Figure 9-12.

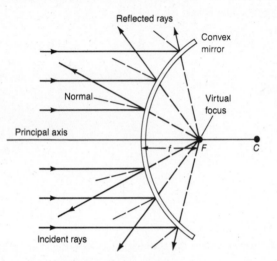

Figure 9-11.   Reflection of rays parallel to the principal axis of a convex mirror. The reflected rays diverge as though coming from the virtual focus, F, behind the mirror.

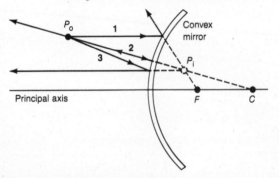

Figure 9-12.   Three rays from Point P_o for which the positions of the reflected rays from a convex mirror are known. (1) The ray parallel to the principal axis is reflected as though coming from F. (2) The ray directed toward C is reflected back upon itself. (3) The ray directed toward F is reflected parallel to the principal axis. A virtual image of the point appears at P_i.

Ray 1, parallel to the principal axis, is reflected as though coming from the virtual focus, *F*. Ray 2, directed toward the center of curvature *C*, is reflected back on itself. Ray 3, directed toward the virtual focus *F*, is reflected parallel to the principal axis. All of these reflected rays seem to be coming from a virtual image point, P_i, behind the mirror. Figure 9-13 shows how any two of these rays can be used to construct the image formed by a convex mirror. The image is always virtual (behind the mirror), erect, and smaller than the object.

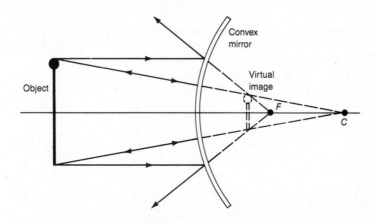

Figure 9-13.   Image formation by a convex mirror. The image is always virtual, behind the mirror, erect, and smaller than the object.

Equations 9-1 and 9-1a can be applied to convex mirrors if you remember that *f*, the focal length, is negative, because *F* is behind the mirror. The effect of a negative value for *f* on the value of the image distance can be determined from Equation 9-1a:

$$\frac{1}{d_i} = \frac{1}{f} - \frac{1}{d_o}$$ (Eq. 9-1a)

The first term to the right of the equals sign, $\frac{1}{f}$, is negative because *f* is negative for a convex mirror. The second term, $\frac{1}{d_o}$, is positive because d_o is always positive, but the minus sign preceding the term has the effect of making it negative. When these two negative quantities are added, they produce a negative sum that is equal to the term $\frac{1}{d_i}$ to the left of the equals sign. If $\frac{1}{d_i}$ is negative, then d_i, the image-to-mirror distance, must be negative, too. The negative sign indicates that the image is always behind the mirror and is therefore virtual.

When Equation 9-2a

$$S_i = \frac{S_o d_i}{d_o} \qquad \text{(Eq. 9-2a)}$$

is applied to a convex mirror, it can be seen that the negative value for d_i makes S_i negative. For a convex mirror, a negative value for S_i indicates that the image is erect.

EXAMPLE

An approaching car is viewed in a convex side-view mirror that has a focal length of 5.0 meters. The height of the car is 2.0 meters, and it is 20. meters from the mirror. How tall does the image of the car appear to be?

Solution

$$d_o = 20. \text{ m} \qquad f = -5.0 \text{ m} \qquad S_o = 2.0 \text{ m}$$

As in the previous examples, first find d_i from Equation 9-1a:

$$d_i = \frac{d_o f}{d_o - f}$$

$$d_i = \frac{(20. \text{ m})(-5.0 \text{ m})}{20. \text{ m} - (-5.0 \text{ m})}$$

$$d_i = -4.0 \text{ m}$$

Now find S_i by using Equation 9-2a:

$$S_i = \frac{S_o d_i}{d_o}$$

$$S_i = \frac{(2.0 \text{ m})(-4.0 \text{ m})}{20. \text{ m}}$$

$$S_i = -0.40 \text{ m}$$

The negative sign indicates that the image is erect and virtual.

CAN YOU EXPLAIN THIS?

When viewed through automobile side-view mirrors, objects appear to be farther away than they actually are.

Some side-view mirrors are convex mirrors. They provide a wider range of vision behind a car than a plane mirror does, but the images in a convex mirror always appear smaller than the objects they reflect. The images in a plane mirror always appear the same size as the objects. An observer judges the distance of familiar objects, such as cars, by their apparent size. Since the image of a car seen in a convex mirror looks smaller than the image would look in a plane mirror, people tend to assume the car is farther away than it actually is.

Spherical Aberration. Although it has been stated that rays parallel to the principal axis of a concave spherical mirror are reflected through the principal focus, this is only approximately true. Parallel rays reflected from the outer areas of the mirror cross the principal axis closer to the mirror than rays reflected from the central portion. As a result, the images produced by spherical mirrors are not in sharp focus. This phenomenon is called **spherical aberration.** It is minimized by making the size of the mirror small compared to its radius of curvature, so that only a small portion of the complete sphere is used.

Spherical aberration can be completely eliminated in a concave mirror if the mirror is made in the shape of a parabola. A parabolic mirror reflects parallel rays precisely to a single focus. Parabolic mirrors are used in technical instruments such as astronomical telescopes. Spherical mirrors are used for less technical applications, because they are much easier and cheaper to manufacture, and they produce satisfactory images for most ordinary uses.

QUESTIONS

1. The image produced by a plane mirror is always (1) virtual and erect (2) virtual and inverted (3) real and erect (4) real and inverted

2. A student 1.8 meters tall stands 1.0 meter in front of a plane mirror. The height of the image is (1) 1.0 m (2) 1.8 m (3) 2.8 m (4) 0.20 m

3. As a student approaches a plane mirror, the size of her image (1) decreases (2) increases (3) remains the same

4. The image seen in a vertical plane mirror is always (1) inverted and reversed (2) inverted and real (3) erect and reversed (4) erect and real

5. A light ray incident perpendicular to a plane mirror will be reflected at an angle to the mirror of (1) 0° (2) 30° (3) 45° (4) 90°

6. Compared to the focal length of a spherical mirror, the radius of curvature of a spherical mirror is (1) one-half as long (2) twice as long (3) the same length (4) four times as long

7. Incident rays parallel to the principal axis of a spherical concave mirror are reflected (1) through the center of curvature (2) through the principal focus (3) perpendicular to the principal axis (4) through a point midway between the principal focus and the center of curvature

8. Light rays directed toward the center of curvature of a spherical mirror strike the mirror at an angle to the normal of (1) 0° (2) 30° (3) 60° (4) 90°

9. The measure of the angle between an incident light ray directed toward the center of curvature of a spherical mirror and its reflected ray is (1) 0° (2) 45° (3) 90° (4) 180°

10. Which of the following will cause parallel light rays to converge? (1) concave lens (2) plane mirror (3) concave mirror (4) convex mirror

11–14. Base your answers to Questions 12 through 15 on the information below.

An object is located at the center of curvature C of a concave mirror with principal focus F.

11. Compared to the size of the object, the size of the image is (1) smaller (2) larger (3) the same

12. As the object is moved farther away from the mirror, the size of its image (1) decreases (2) increases (3) remains the same

13. If the object is located beyond C, the image is located (1) beyond C (2) between C and F (3) at F (4) between F and the mirror

14. If the object is moved inside of F, the resulting image is (1) virtual and larger than the object (2) virtual and smaller than the object (3) real and larger than the object (4) real and smaller than the object

15. Which of the following will *always* cause parallel light rays to diverge? (1) concave mirror (2) convex mirror (3) plane mirror (4) convex lens

16. Which of the following is true of the focal length and image distance for a convex mirror? (1) Both are negative. (2) Both are positive. (3) Focal length is negative and image distance is positive. (4) Focal length is positive and image distance is negative.

17. An image formed by a convex mirror is always (1) real and larger than the object (2) real and smaller than the object (3) virtual and larger than the object (4) virtual and smaller than the object

18. Not all of the parallel light rays incident on a concave mirror converge at the principal focus. This phenomenon is called (1) spherical aberration (2) chromatic aberration (3) diffraction (4) refraction

19. Which of the following produce only virtual images? (1) convex lens and convex mirror (2) convex lens and concave mirror (3) concave lens and convex mirror (4) concave lens and concave mirror.

20–26. Base your answers to Questions 21 through 25 on the information below.

An object 0.10 meter tall is placed 0.60 meter in front of a concave mirror having a focal length of 0.40 meter.

20. The radius of curvature of the mirror is (1) 0.20 m (2) 0.40 m (3) 0.80 m (4) 1.2 m

21. The image distance is (1) 1.0 m (2) 1.2 m (3) 0.83 m (4) 0.24 m

22. The size of the image is (1) 0.10 m (2) 0.14 m (3) 0.20 m (4) 0.50 m

23. The image produced is (1) real and inverted (2) real and erect (3) virtual and inverted (4) virtual and erect

24. If the object were moved to 0.80 meter from the mirror, the size of the image would be (1) 0.050 m (2) 0.10 m (3) 0.20 m (4) 0.80 m

25. Compared to the size of the object at a distance of 0.80 m from the mirror, the size of the image is (1) less (2) greater (3) the same

26. The object is moved to 0.20 meter from the mirror. Compared to the size of the object, the size of the image is (1) less (2) greater (3) the same

27–29. Base your answers to Questions 27 through 29 on the information below.

An object 0.10 meter tall is placed 0.60 meter in front of a convex mirror having a focal length of 0.40 meter.

27. The image distance is (1) 0.040 m (2) 0.24 m (3) 0.60 m (4) 1.2 m
28. The size of the image is (1) 0.020 m (2) 0.040 m (3) 0.060 m (4) 0.10 m
29. The image produced is (1) real and inverted (2) real and erect (3) virtual and inverted (4) virtual and erect

III. IMAGES FORMED BY REFRACTIONS

A disk of a transparent material, such as glass or plastic, with curved surfaces is called a **lens.** When rays of light from an object pass through a lens, the rays are refracted to form an image, somewhat the way a curved mirror forms an image.

Converging Lenses

Recall that the principal axis is the line that passes through the center of curvature and the midpoint of the curved surface. When rays parallel to the principal axis pass through a lens that is thicker at the center than at the edges, the rays converge toward a point on the other side of the lens. Such a lens is therefore called a **converging lens.** Because of its shape, it is also called a **convex lens.** As in a concave mirror, the point where the rays meet on the principal axis is called the **principal focus,** F. Figure 9-14 shows how a converging lens causes parallel rays to meet at the principal focus. Each ray is refracted twice—once as it enters the lens and again as it leaves. Because of the shape of the lens, each ray is refracted *toward* the principal axis. (The thickness of the lens has been exaggerated to show how refraction takes place.)

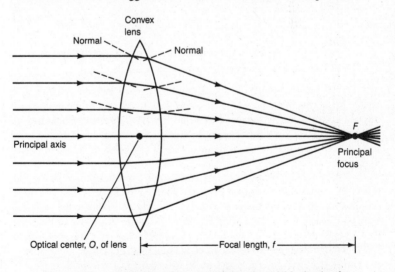

Figure 9-14.   Refraction of rays parallel to the principal axis of a converging (convex) lens. The incident rays are converged by the lens to a real focus at F on the other side of the lens.

Since light can pass through a lens from either side, there is a principal focus on each side of the lens. The center of a lens is called its **optical center,** O. The distance from O to the principal focus on either side is the **focal length,** f, of the lens. For a lens of a given shape, the focal length depends on the absolute index of refraction of the lens material. As the absolute index of refraction is made greater, the focal length becomes shorter.

In the laboratory the focal length of a converging lens can be determined by focusing light from the sun (the object) on a screen. Since the sun is in effect at an infinite distance from the lens, the incident rays are parallel to each other and converge to the principal focus of the lens, forming a bright point of light on the screen. The distance from the lens to the principal focus can then be measured to find the focal length.

Remember that a light ray is represented by an arrow perpendicular to the wave front, showing its direction of travel. Parallel rays represent a series of parallel wave fronts perpendicular to the rays. Figure 9-15 shows the refracted wave fronts after parallel waves pass through a converging lens.

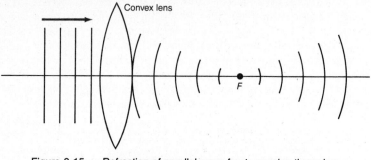

Figure 9-15.   Refraction of parallel wave fronts passing through a converging lens.

A ray that passes through the optical center of a lens is refracted slightly as it enters and leaves the lens, and in this case the two refractions are in opposite directions. As a result, the ray leaves the lens in a direction parallel to its original direction. For a thin lens, a ray that passes through the optical center can be drawn as a straight line without any significant error, as shown in Figure 9-16.

The image formed by a converging lens can be constructed by drawing any two rays whose paths are known from any point on the object. There are three rays that can be used, as shown in Figure 9-17. Ray 1, parallel to the principal axis, is refracted through the principal focus, F, on the other side of the lens. Ray 2 passes through the optical center, O, with no change of direction. Ray 3 passes through the principal focus, F, on the same side of the lens as the object, P_o. This ray is refracted to emerge parallel to the principal axis on the other side of the lens.

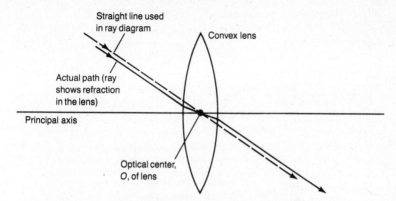

*Note that the thickness of the lens has been exaggerated in this drawing in order to show the refraction that takes place as the ray enters and leaves the lens.

Figure 9-16.   Refraction of a ray passing through the optical center of a converging lens. For practical purposes, the ray may be drawn as a straight line through the optical center.

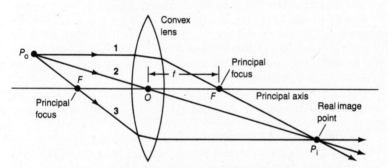

Figure 9-17.   The three rays from a point P_o whose paths through a converging lens are known. (1) The ray parallel to the principal axis is refracted through F on the other side of the lens. (2) The ray through the optical center is a straight line. (3) The ray through F on the same side of the lens is refracted parallel to the principal axis. All three refracted rays intersect at the real image P_i (provided that P_o is beyond the principal focus on the same side of the lens).

Figure 9-18 (see the next page) shows the formation of an image by a converging lens when the object is more than twice the focal length from the lens (beyond $2F$). The image is real, inverted, and smaller than the object. The image of a flat surface, such as a map, would be reversed as well as inverted.

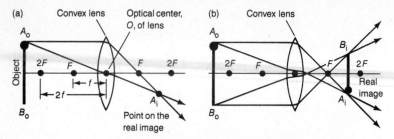

Figure 9-18.   Real image formation by a converging lens. (a) Two
rays that meet to form the image, A_i, of the head of
the object, A_o. (b) The image completed by drawing
two rays that form the image of the bottom of the
object. When the object is beyond $2F$, the image is
real, inverted, smaller than the object, and between
F and $2F$ on the opposite side of the lens.

Consider how the size and position of the real image change as an object is
moved closer to the lens from beyond $2F$. As long as the object distance is
beyond $2F$ (Figure 9-18), the image is between F and $2F$, and the image is
smaller than the object. This is the way a converging lens is used in a camera.

Figure 9-19 shows how the size and position of the real image change as the
object is moved closer to the lens than it is in Figure 9-18. When the object
distance is exactly $2f$ (as shown in Figure 9-19a), the image distance is also $2f$,
and the image is the same size as the object. This is the way a converging lens is
usually used in a photocopying machine.

When the object distance is between $2f$ and f (as shown in Figure 9-19b), the
image distance is greater than $2f$, and the image is larger than the object. This is
the way a converging lens is used in a projector.

When the object is at F and its distance from the lens is exactly equal to f (as
shown in Figure 9-19c), no image is formed, because all the refracted rays from
any point on the object emerge parallel to one another. They never intersect to
form an image. This is the way a converging lens is used to produce a parallel
beam of light.

When the object distance is less than f (Figure 9-19d), the refracted rays from
any point on the object diverge as though coming from an image on the same
side of the lens as the object. So, the image formed is virtual. The virtual images
formed by a converging lens are always erect and larger than the object. This is
the image seen when a converging lens is used as a magnifier.

These relationships are summarized in Table 9-2. They can be derived by
using Equations 9-1 and 9-2. When applying the equations to a converging lens,
f is positive, and an image distance on the side opposite the object is positive,
since that is where real images are formed. When the image distance, d_i, is
negative, the image is on the same side of the lens as the object and is virtual.

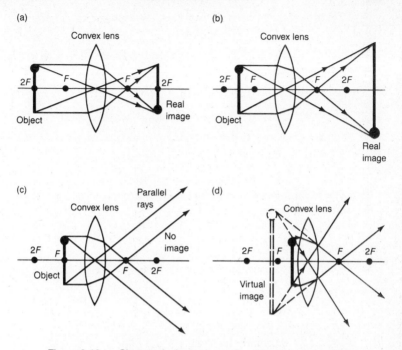

Figure 9-19.   Changes in the image as the object moves nearer to a converging lens.

Table 9-2.   The relationship between the object and the image formed by a convex lens

Figure	OBJECT Position	IMAGE Position	Type	Orientation	Size*
9-18	Beyond $2F$	Between F and $2F$	Real	Inverted	Smaller
9-19a	At $2F$	At $2F$	Real	Inverted	Same size
9-19b	Between F and $2F$	Beyond $2F$	Real	Inverted	Larger
9-19c	At F	----------------- (no image) -----------------			
9-19d	Between F and lens	Same side of lens as object	Virtual	Erect	Larger

*Note that the size of the image is relative to the size of the object.

EXAMPLE

An object 0.030 meter tall is placed 0.050 meter in front of a converging lens having a focal length of 0.040 meter. Find (a) the image distance and (b) the image size.

Solution

$$d_o = 0.050 \text{ m} \qquad f = 0.040 \text{ m} \qquad S_o = 0.030 \text{ m}$$

(a) As in the previous examples, first find d_i from Equation 9-1a:

$$\frac{1}{d_i} = \frac{1}{f} - \frac{1}{d_o}$$

Giving the two fractions to the right of the equals sign a common denominator yields

$$\frac{1}{d_i} = \frac{d_o - f}{d_o f}$$

Solving for d_i:

$$d_i = \frac{d_o f}{d_o - f}$$

$$d_i = \frac{(0.040 \text{ m})(0.050 \text{ m})}{0.050 \text{ m} - 0.040 \text{ m}}$$

$$d_i = \frac{0.0020 \text{ m}^2}{0.010 \text{ m}}$$

$$d_i = 0.20 \text{ m}$$

(b) Using Equation 9-2a, solve for S_i:

$$S_i = \frac{S_o d_i}{d_o}$$

$$S_i = \frac{(0.030 \text{ m})(0.20 \text{ m})}{0.050 \text{ m}}$$

$$S_i = 0.12 \text{ m}$$

CAN YOU EXPLAIN THIS?

Slides are put into a projector upside down and backward.

In a slide projector, the slide is located slightly more than one focal length from a converging lens. A bright beam of light is sent through the slide, and the lens produces an enlarged image of the slide on the screen. Since this is a real image, it is inverted and reversed with respect to the slide. For the image to be right side up and have the same orientation from left to right as the original scene, the slide has to be upside down and backward in the projector.

PRACTICAL APPLICATION ═══════════

A camera uses a converging lens to form a real image of a scene on photosensitive film behind the lens. To produce a sharp image on the film, the object and image distances must satisfy Equation 9-1. For a particular object distance, the image distance must be adjusted to bring it into agreement with the equation. This is usually done by moving the lens closer to or farther from the film. If you observe the lens of a camera with manual focusing, you can see it move as you change the focus of the camera. As you know from Equation 9-1, when the object distance is reduced, the image distance must increase. The amount by which you can increase the lens-to-film distance is limited by the design of the camera. Therefore, there is a limit to how close you can get to the object being photographed and still be able to focus for a sharp image. You can get closer if you reduce the focal length of the lens, either by replacing the lens or attaching a "closeup" lens. ■

Diverging Lenses

When rays parallel to the principal axis pass through a lens that is thinner at the center than at the edges, the rays are refracted so that they spread apart, or diverge, as shown in Figure 9-20a. Such a lens is therefore called a **diverging lens** and, because of its shape, is also called a **concave lens.** The diverging rays appear to be coming from a virtual focus on the same side of the lens as the incident parallel rays. Figure 9-20b shows the effect of refraction by a diverging lens on parallel wave fronts.

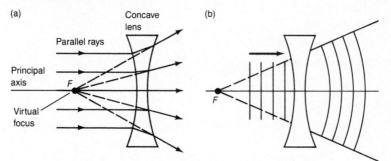

Figure 9-20.   Refraction of rays parallel to the principal axis of a diverging (concave) lens. (a) The refracted rays appear to be coming from a virtual focus on the same side of the lens as the incident rays. (b) The refraction of parallel wave fronts as they pass through a diverging lens.

The image formed by a diverging lens can be constructed as shown in Figure 9-21 on the following page. From any point on the object, the ray parallel to the principal axis is combined with the ray passing through the optical center. A virtual image is formed on the same side of the lens as the object. The virtual image formed by a diverging lens is always erect, smaller than the object, and between the principal focus and the lens. When applying Equation 9-1 to a diverging lens, f and d_i are negative, because the principal focus and the image are on the same side of the lens as the object.

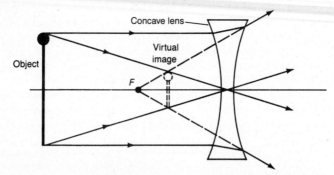

Figure 9-21.   Image formation by a diverging lens. The image is virtual, erect, smaller than the object, and between F and the lens on the same side as the object.

EXAMPLE

An object 0.030 meter tall is placed 0.050 meter in front of a diverging lens having a focal length of 0.040 meter. Find (a) the image distance and (b) the image size.

Solution

$$d_o = 0.050 \text{ m} \qquad f = -0.040 \text{ m} \qquad S_o = 0.030 \text{ m}$$

(a) As in the previous examples, first find d_i from Equation 9-1a:

$$\frac{1}{d_i} = \frac{1}{f} - \frac{1}{d_o}$$

Giving the two fractions to the right of the equals sign a common denominator yields

$$\frac{1}{d_i} = \frac{d_o - f}{d_o f}$$

Solving for d_i:

$$d_i = \frac{d_o f}{d_o - f}$$

$$d_i = \frac{(0.050 \text{ m})(-0.040 \text{ m})}{0.050 \text{ m} - (-0.040 \text{ m})}$$

$$d_i = \frac{-0.0020 \text{ m}^2}{0.090 \text{ m}}$$

$$d_i = -0.022 \text{ m}$$

(b) Using Equation 9-2a, solve for S_i:

$$S_i = \frac{S_o d_i}{d_o}$$

$$S_i = \frac{(0.030 \text{ m})(-0.022 \text{ m})}{0.050 \text{ m}}$$

$$S_i = -0.013 \text{ m}$$

The negative sign indicates the image is erect and virtual.

PRACTICAL APPLICATION

The human eye has a lens that produces an image on a light-sensitive tissue, called the *retina*, at the rear of the eyeball. For a person to see clearly, this image must be in focus, which means that Equation 9-1 must be satisfied in the eye just as it is in a camera. The human eye focuses the image for different object distances not by changing the image distance (as in a camera) but by changing the focal length of the lens. This is accomplished by muscles that change the shape of the lens as needed. For seeing distant objects, the muscles stretch the edges of the lens to flatten it, thus increasing the focal length of the eye lens. For seeing near objects, the muscles relax and let the lens become more convex to decrease the focal length.

In *nearsighted* eyes, the lens is unable to focus distant objects because the focal length of the lens cannot be made large enough. The nearly parallel rays from distant objects are brought to a focus in front of the retina. The image at the retina is blurred. This condition can be corrected by using eyeglasses or contact lenses with diverging lenses that spread the rays from distant objects, as though coming from nearer objects, that the eye lens can bring into focus. (See Figure 9-22.)

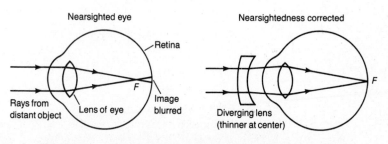

Figure 9-22. The cause and correction of nearsightedness. Nearsightedness is corrected by wearing diverging lenses that spread the rays from distant objects to make them seem nearer.

In *farsighted* eyes, the opposite condition exists. The focal length of the eye lens cannot be made short enough to focus the diverging rays from nearby objects. This condition can be corrected by using converging lenses to make the rays more nearly parallel before they enter the eye. (See Figure 9-23.) ■

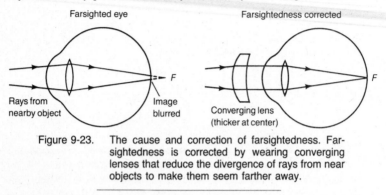

Figure 9-23.　The cause and correction of farsightedness. Farsightedness is corrected by wearing converging lenses that reduce the divergence of rays from near objects to make them seem farther away.

Defects in Lenses

No real lens refracts light exactly as described above. There are two main reasons why the rays from an object do not converge to (or appear to diverge from) a perfect image. The image produced by a lens with spherical surfaces is always blurred to some extent by effects called **aberrations.**

Chromatic Aberration. As discussed in Unit 4, polychromatic light is separated into its component colors if it enters a dispersive medium, such as glass, obliquely. Each frequency of light has a different absolute index of refraction in glass, with violet being refracted more than red light. Consequently, if polychromatic light is passed through a glass lens, all of the component colors do not have the same focal point. As shown in Figure 9-24, violet light is focused

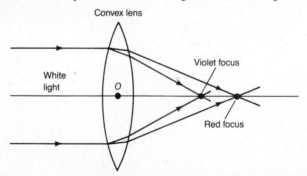

Figure 9-24.　Chromatic aberration. Violet rays are refracted through a larger angle by a glass lens than red rays are, and therefore violet regions of an image are formed closer to a converging lens than red regions are.

closer to a converging lens than red light is, with the other colors of the spectrum in between. (A diverging lens reverses the order of the colors.) The result is that the image of an object illuminated by white light appears to have a fringe of colors around its edges. This phenomenon, called **chromatic aberration,** can be corrected by utilizing a combination of two lenses, one converging and the other diverging. The dispersion caused by one lens is canceled by the other, if the lenses are made of two different types of glass, but the net effect of the combination is either converging or diverging.

CAN YOU EXPLAIN THIS?

When infrared film is used, the focal length of the camera lens must be adjusted.

Infrared light has a smaller absolute index of refraction in glass than red light does. Consequently, infrared light would focus farther from a given lens than would red light or any of the other component colors of white light. To produce a distinct image on infrared film, the focal length of the camera lens would have to be decreased from that used with ordinary photographic film. Infrared photography has many special applications. It can be used, for example, to detect areas of heat loss from the walls of a home. Because infrared radiation is not scattered by tiny water droplets, infrared photographs can be taken through clouds and fog. They can also be taken in the dark.

Spherical Aberration. As in the case of spherical mirrors, rays parallel to the principal axis of a spherical lens do not all come to a focus at exactly the same point. As shown in Figure 9-25, the farther a ray is from the principal axis of a lens, the greater its refraction by the lens. As already stated in connection with curved mirrors, this phenomenon is called **spherical aberration,** and it causes images to be blurred. Spherical aberration, which occurs even with monochromatic light, can be reduced by using the smallest possible area around the optical center of a lens. In a camera, this is accomplished by closing the camera's diaphragm.

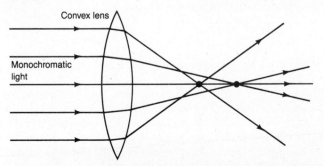

Figure 9-25.   Spherical aberration. Rays passing through the outer portions of a lens are not refracted exactly to the same point on the principal axis as rays through the central portion, causing a blurring of the image.

QUESTIONS

1. A real image can be produced by a (1) plane mirror (2) concave lens (3) convex lens (4) convex mirror

2. Which diagram correctly shows light rays passing through the lens?

　　　　(1)　　　　　　(2)　　　　　　(3)　　　　　　(4)

3. A spectrum is formed on a screen when white light is passing through a converging lens. This phenomenon is caused by (1) interference (2) diffraction (3) reflection (4) dispersion

4–6. Base your answers to Questions 4 through 6 on the diagram, which represents a thin converging lens and its principal axis. *F* represents the principal focus.

4. If the light rays are to be parallel when they leave the lens, the light source must be placed (1) between *F* and the lens (2) at *F* (3) between *F* and 2*F* (4) at 2*F*

5. As an object is moved from point *A* toward point *B*, its image will (1) become erect (2) move toward the lens (3) change from real to virtual (4) become enlarged

6. If the image is located at 2*F'* the object must be located (1) at *F* (2) between *F* and 2*F* (3) at 2*F* (4) beyond 2*F*

7–11. Base your answers to Questions 7 through 11 on the diagram, which shows a lens whose focal length is 0.10 meter.

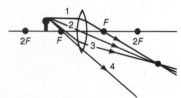

7. Which ray from the head of the object is not drawn correctly? (1) 1 (2) 2 (3) 3 (4) 4

8. If the object is 0.15 meter from the lens, then the distance from the image to the lens is (1) 0.060 m (2) 0.10 m (3) 0.15 m (4) 0.30 m

9. If an object 0.24 meter tall is placed at 2*F*, then the height of the image is (1) 0.060 m (2) 0.12 m (3) 0.24 m (4) 0.48 m

10. As the object is moved from 2*F* toward *F*, the size of the image (1) decreases (2) increases (3) remains the same

11. If the index of refraction of the lens is increased, then the focal length of the lens (1) decreases (2) increases (3) remains the same

12–16. Base your answers to Questions 12 through 16 on the diagram, which represents a converging (convex) lens whose principal focus is at *F*.

12. An object placed at 2*F'* will produce an image at (1) *F* (2) 2*F* (3) *E* (4) *D*

13. If an object is placed at point *C*, the resulting image is (1) real and smaller than the object (2) real and larger than the object (3) virtual and smaller than the object (4) virtual and larger than the object

14. An object placed 0.060 meter to the left of the lens produces an image 0.030 meter to the right of the lens. What is the focal length of the lens? (1) 0.015 m (2) 0.020 m (3) 0.20 m (4) 0.50 m

15. As an object is moved from *A* to *B*, the size of the image (1) decreases (2) increases (3) remains the same

16. As the size of an object placed at point *A* *increases*, the size of the image (1) decreases (2) increases (3) remains the same

17–21. Base your answers to Questions 17 through 21 on the diagram, which represents a thin convex lens and its principal axis. The principal foci are indicated at *F* and *F'*. The focal length of the lens is 0.20 meter.

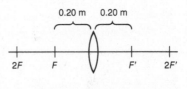

17. If the object is placed 0.30 m from the lens, then the distance from the lens to the image will be (1) 0.10 m (2) 0.12 m (3) 0.50 m (4) 0.60 m

18. A 0.12-meter tall object is placed 0.40 meter from the lens. The size of the image formed is (1) 0.060 m (2) 0.12 m (3) 0.24 m (4) 0.48 m

19. In order to form an image between *F'* and 2*F'*, the object must be placed (1) at *F* (2) between *F* and 2*F* (3) at 2*F* (4) beyond 2*F*

20. Which type of image cannot be formed by this lens? (1) a real image smaller than the object (2) a real image larger than the object (3) a virtual image smaller than the object (4) a virtual image larger than the object

21. For which color is the focal length of this lens greatest? (1) red (2) yellow (3) green (4) blue

22–25. Base your answers to Questions 22 through 25 on the following information.

A converging lens produces an image of a large, distant object. The object distance is 5,000 meters, and the image distance is 0.50 meter.

22. What is the approximate focal length of the lens? (1) 1.0 m (2) 0.75 m (3) 0.50 m (4) 0.25 m

23. If the object size is **1,000 meters**, what is the image size? (1) **0.050 m** (2) **0.10 m** (3) **0.15 m** (4) **0.20 m**

24. If the size of the object were increased, the size of the image would (1) decrease (2) increase (3) remain the same

25. The lens is replaced with another lens having the same curvature but a greater index of refraction. Compared to the focal length of the original lens, the focal length of the new lens is (1) less (2) greater (3) the same

26. It is observed that a spectrum surrounds an object's image produced by white light passing through a converging lens. This phenomenon is (1) diffraction (2) total internal reflection (3) spherical aberration (4) chromatic aberration

27. The phenomenon illustrated in the diagram at the right is
    (1) chromatic aberration
    (2) spherical aberration
    (3) dispersion
    (4) diffraction

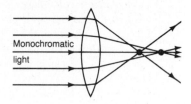

28. Which of the following glass lenses is capable of producing both real and virtual images of an object?

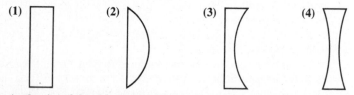

(1)   (2)   (3)   (4)

29. As the size of the object placed before a convex lens decreases, the focal length of the lens (1) decreases (2) increases (3) remains the same

30. An object is located 0.02 meter from a converging lens having a focal length of 0.03 meter. As the object is moved closer to the lens, the size of its image will (1) decrease (2) increase (3) remain the same

31. Which of the following is true of the focal length and image distance of a diverging lens? (1) Both are positive. (2) Both are negative. (3) Focal length is positive and image distance is negative. (4) Focal length is negative and image distance is positive.

32. Which of the following wave-front refraction patterns is possible?

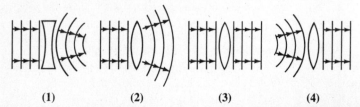

(1)   (2)   (3)   (4)

UNIT 10   SOLID STATE PHYSICS

I. CONDUCTION IN SOLIDS

Resistivity and Conductivity

Experiments with electric circuits show that samples of different materials of the same size and shape produce different currents under identical conditions of applied potential difference and temperature. One property of a substance that determines the current that will flow through it is called its *resistivity*.

If one desires to produce maximum current from a source of potential difference, the connecting wires to the circuit components are made of materials of low resistivity. On the other hand, if a device requires small currents, materials of high resistivity are used. Numerical magnitudes of resistivity are determined by experiment at a specified temperature. If a wire of length L meters and cross-sectional area A square meters is found to have a resistance of R ohms, the **resistivity,** ρ (Greek letter rho), of the material is defined by the equation

$$\rho = \frac{RA}{L} \text{ ohm} \cdot \text{meters}$$

The resistivity of a material, unlike its resistance, is a constant for any given temperature and does not depend on the dimensions of the sample. (The equation for ρ may lead you to believe otherwise—that a change in either A or L will cause a change in ρ. However, whenever either A or L changes at any particular temperature, there is an offsetting change in R that keeps ρ constant.)

It is sometimes useful to refer to the *conductivity* of a substance, which is defined as the reciprocal of its resistivity, $1/\rho$. The unit of conductivity is the $(\text{ohm} \cdot \text{meter})^{-1}$. For example, if a material has a resistivity of 10. ohm · meters, its conductivity is

$$\frac{1}{10. \text{ ohm} \cdot \text{meters}} = 0.10 \text{ (ohm} \cdot \text{meter)}^{-1}$$

or 0.10 per ohm · meter.

Circuit materials are classified as *conductors, insulators,* and *semiconductors.* Materials with very low resistivities are **conductors.** All metals are conductors, with resistivities as low as 1.6×10^{-8} ohm · meter for silver and only slightly higher for copper. Materials with very high resistivities (more than 10^8 ohm · meters) are **insulators.** Most nonmetallic solids, such as sulfur, glass, rubber, and ceramics, are insulators. The resistivity of quartz is as high as 5×10^{17} ohm · meters. Materials with resistivities midway between the extremes of good conductors and good insulators are **semiconductors.** Many of the elements called metalloids, such as germanium and silicon, are semiconductors. The resistivity of pure silicon is about 3×10^4 ohm · meters.

Theories of Conduction in Solids

Electric currents in solids are in most cases movements of electrons through the material. Since all the electrons in an electrically neutral solid are parts of the atoms of the material, a theory of electrical conduction must explain how the electrons become free to move through the material. The following text explores two models that have been proposed to explain electrical conduction in solids— the Electron-sea Model and the Energy Band Model.

Electron-sea Model. An early theory of conduction assumed that in conducting solids there is a mobile cloud of free electrons called an *electron sea.* According to this model, the free electrons that constitute the sea come from the outer or valence electrons of the atoms that make up the solid. Since the valence electrons in metals are loosely bound to the nucleus, there are many of them available to form an electron sea. Consequently, all metals are good conductors. On the other hand, the atomic and molecular structures of insulators are such as to bind all of the electrons, including the valence electrons, tightly to fixed positions. There are no free electrons available to form an electron sea for charge transport. Semiconductors are assumed to be solids that have some free electrons, but they have fewer free electrons than conductors have. The actual properties of semiconductors, however, such as the variation of resistivity with temperature, do not agree well with the Electron-sea Model.

Energy Band Model. The Electron-sea Model of conduction could not predict the behavior of new materials that began to be used as circuit elements, such as the semiconductors. The **Energy Band Model,** based on the quantum theory of atomic structure, has been more successful in explaining and predicting the electrical behavior of semiconductors. It has led to the revolution in electronic technology that has resulted in reasonably priced radio and TV sets, computers and calculators, medical diagnostic and therapeutic instruments, music synthesizers, video cassette recorders, compact disc players, and a long list of other products with capabilities previously unimagined even in science fiction.

The quantum theory of electron energies within the atom states that only a limited number of energy magnitudes, or **energy levels,** are available to electrons in the atom. For example, in an isolated hydrogen atom, only the energy levels indicated in Figure 10-1 are possible for the single electron of that atom. The electron cannot exist in any intermediate energy state between these levels. These other energies are called **forbidden states.**

The situation is entirely different in solid materials consisting of numerous atoms, each with many electrons. The quantum theory predicts that the energy levels of the outer, or valence, electrons of two atoms near each other will interact and merge. According to the *exclusion principle* of the quantum theory, only two electrons, of opposite spin, can occupy the same energy level. Therefore, when two atoms interact, corresponding energy levels in both atoms become two close levels of nearly, but not exactly, the same energy. As more and

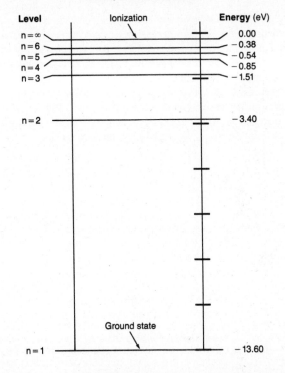

Level	Ionization	Energy (eV)
$n = \infty$		0.00
$n = 6$		-0.38
$n = 5$		-0.54
$n = 4$		-0.85
$n = 3$		-1.51
$n = 2$		-3.40
	Ground state	
$n = 1$		-13.60

Figure 10-1.   The possible energy levels that can be occupied by the valence electron of an isolated hydrogen atom. Within each level there are sublevels (not shown). All other energy levels within the atom are "forbidden" states for the electron.

more atoms interact in this way, each energy level becomes an **energy band** of many closely spaced levels. All the valence electrons of the entire solid then occupy an energy band called the **valence band.**

According to the quantum theory, all electrons in the solid occupy the lowest energy levels that are available. Therefore, for an electron to leave its position and move through the solid, it must first be raised to a higher energy level. If the valence band has unoccupied energy levels, only a small amount of energy is needed to raise a valence electron to the next available level in the band. If, on the other hand, the valence band is filled with all the electrons it can hold, there is no higher energy level within the valence band available for an electron. In that case, an electron may absorb enough energy to leave the valence band and enter a higher energy band called the **conduction band.** Electrons in the conduction band can move freely through the solid and thus transport the charge of an electric current.

In many solids, the lowest energy level of the conduction band is separated from the highest level of the valence band by an "energy gap" called the **forbidden band,** as illustrated in Figure 10-2. An electron may not exist in the forbidden band. To enter the conduction band, an electron must acquire an amount of energy at least equal to the energy gap—that is, at least equal to the difference between E_c (the smallest energy in the conduction band) and E_v (the largest energy in the valence band). See Figure 10-2. The resistivity of any particular material thus depends on the structure of its valence band and the width of its forbidden band, as described in the next section.

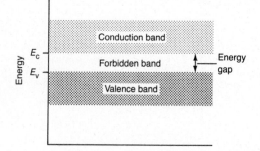

Figure 10-2.   Energy bands in a solid consisting of large numbers of atoms. The valence electrons occupy a band of closely spaced energy levels called the valence band. To leave the valence band and become a free electron in the conduction band, an electron must absorb a quantum of energy at least equal to the difference between the lowest energy level of the conduction band, E_C, and the highest level of the valence band, E_V.

Electron Bands of Conductors

The valence level, or *valence shell,* of every atom can hold a maximum of eight electrons. The atoms of most common metals, such as sodium, calcium, zinc, copper, gold, silver, nickel, and iron, have only one or two valence electrons. None of the metals has more than three valence electrons. (Aluminum is the most familiar example of a metal with three valence electrons.) As a result, the valence band of a metal has plenty of empty energy levels.

It takes very little energy to raise a valence electron to one of these unoccupied levels for the conduction of current. At any temperature above absolute zero, the energy for the transition can come from the thermal energy of random motion or can be absorbed from a photon of radiation. In addition, the valence band of a metal touches or overlaps its conduction band, as shown in Figure 10-3, so that there is no forbidden band between them. For these reasons, at any given moment practically all of the valence electrons of a metal are free and

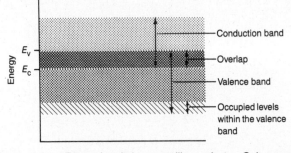

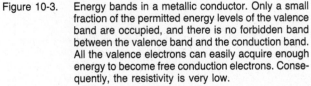

Figure 10-3. Energy bands in a metallic conductor. Only a small fraction of the permitted energy levels of the valence band are occupied, and there is no forbidden band between the valence band and the conduction band. All the valence electrons can easily acquire enough energy to become free conduction electrons. Consequently, the resistivity is very low.

available to carry current. Even a small potential difference across the metal will cause vast numbers of electrons to move through the material in response to the electrostatic force exerted on charged particles in the electric field. In other words, the resistivity of the metal is very low.

Note that both the Energy Band Model and the Electron-sea Model give the same picture of a pool of free electrons in a metal. However, the Energy Band Model gives a more complete explanation of *why* these free electrons are present in such large numbers.

Effect of Temperature on Resistivity. The resistance of a conductor is due mainly to the frictional effect of collisions between the moving electrons and the atoms of the material. These collisions absorb kinetic energy and convert it to energy given off as heat. When the temperature of a metal conductor increases, the average kinetic energy of its particles also increases. Since practically all the valence electrons are already free, this increase in energy does not increase the number of free electrons. However, it does increase the rate of collisions and the energy loss they cause. At the higher temperature, a greater potential difference is needed to move electrons through the conductor at the same rate. As a result, the resistivity of a metallic conductor increases when its temperature increases.

Band Patterns of Insulators

In many substances the atoms are joined to one another by pairs of shared valence electrons that form what is called a covalent bond. The two electrons in a covalent bond occupy the same energy level, or *orbital,* in both atoms. In an insulator, the covalent bond between atoms has the effect of filling the valence band of the material. The valence band has no vacant levels. Furthermore, the

SOLID STATE PHYSICS

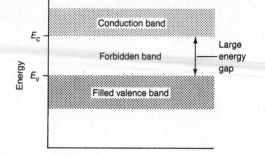

Figure 10-4. Energy bands in an insulator. All permitted energy levels in the valence band are occupied, and the energy gap, or forbidden band, between the valence band and the conduction band is large. Only a few electrons at any moment are present in the conduction band. Consequently, the resistivity is very high.

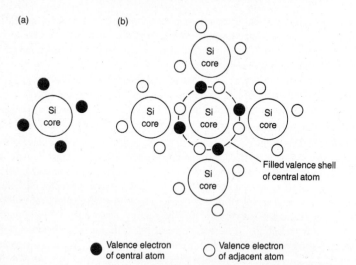

Figure 10-5. Bonding of atoms in a Group 14 element, such as silicon. (a) There are four valence electrons in the valence shell outside the core of a silicon atom. (b) Each silicon atom bonds to four other atoms by sharing one valence electron with each, thus filling its valence shell with eight electrons. Each of the other atoms also bonds to four atoms (not shown) in the same way. The result is a fixed pattern of atoms in a structure called a crystal.

forbidden band is wide, as shown in Figure 10-4. It is almost impossible for an electron to acquire enough energy to leave the valence band and enter the conduction band. There are almost no free electrons available to carry current, and the resistivity is very high.

Band Patterns of Semiconductors

The atoms of semiconductor elements typically have four valence electrons, as shown in Figure 10-5a. Silicon (Si) and germanium (Ge) are examples. If you have studied chemistry, you will recognize these elements as members of Group 14 of the Periodic Table. In a pure sample of one of these elements, each of the valence electrons of one atom forms a covalent bond with a valence electron of an adjacent atom, as shown in Figure 10-5b. With the addition of four electrons to the valence level, each atom is filled with its maximum of eight electrons. As a result of this bonding, the atoms are arranged in a regular pattern called a crystal. The valence band of a pure semiconductor crystal is filled.

At zero K, (absolute zero) a semiconductor is theoretically a perfect insulator—the valence band is completely filled, and no electron has enough energy to leave it. The band pattern resembles that of insulators. Above zero K, some electrons acquire thermal energy, or absorb the energy of a photon of radiation. This thermal energy is greater than the energy gap of the forbidden band. These electrons enter the conduction band, as shown in Figure 10-6, and are available to carry current. A further increase of temperature will produce more electrons with conduction band energy, and therefore the resistivity will decrease.

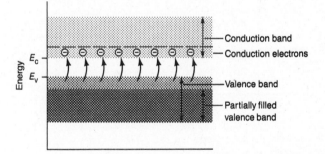

Figure 10-6.   Conduction electrons in a semiconductor. At any temperature above zero K, some electrons acquire enough energy to have magnitudes lying within the conduction band. The higher the temperature, the greater the number of electrons that are present in the conduction band. Consequently, the resistivity of a semiconductor decreases as the temperature increases.

An electron that breaks away from its covalent bond and enters the conduction band leaves a vacancy called a **hole** in the valence band, as shown in Figure 10-7. A hole can be filled by an electron from a nearby atom, leaving a hole in that atom. In effect, the hole has moved in a direction opposite to the electron. Under the influence of a potential difference, electrons in the conduction band move from the negatively charged electrode (from the negative potential) to the positively charged electrode (to the positive potential). This means that in Figure 10-7 electrons move from right to left. At the same time, holes in the valence band move in the opposite direction, acting like positive electrons.

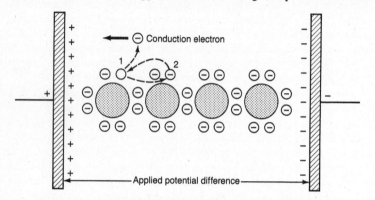

Figure 10-7. Conduction in a semiconductor. The electron that was at position 1 moves up to the conduction band, leaving a vacancy called a hole in the valence band. Under the influence of a potential difference across the material, the electron at position 2 moves to position 1, leaving a hole in its place. Thus, as the electron moves in one direction toward the positive potential, the hole moves in the opposite direction toward the negative potential. At any particular time, there are many electrons and holes in a semiconductor that move in a similar manner. Holes act like positive charge carriers.

Thus, in semiconductors there are two types of charge carriers—electrons and holes—whereas in metallic conductors only electrons carry charge. At the positive terminal of the source of potential difference, electrons in a semiconductor are drawn off from both the conduction band and the valence band. In the valence band, the loss of an electron leaves a new hole, which moves toward the negative terminal. At the negative terminal, electrons flow into the semiconductor, filling (neutralizing) the positive holes in the valence band and replacing the electrons removed from the conduction band (see Figure 10-8). A semiconductor acting in this manner is called an *intrinsic semiconductor*.

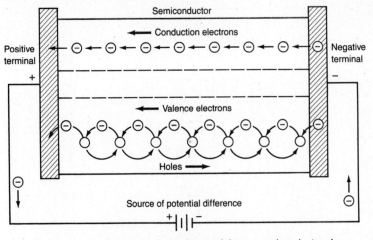

Figure 10-8. Current in a circuit containing a semiconductor. In the valence band, electrons leaving the material at the positive terminal leave holes behind. Holes arriving at the negative terminal are filled by electrons entering the material. Thus, current in the semiconductor consists of electrons moving from the negative to the positive terminal and holes moving in the opposite direction. In the external circuit, only moving electrons carry the current.

PRACTICAL APPLICATION

When an electron in the conduction band loses energy and drops to the valence band, this energy is usually converted into heat. However, the semiconductor made from gallium and phosphorus behaves differently. When an excited electron in the conduction band makes its transition to the valence band, recombining with a hole, the energy is released in the form of light. This process is called *electroluminescence*. The device in which electroluminescence takes place, known as an LED (light–emitting diode), consumes little energy and is inexpensive.

Figure 10-9a (see the following page) shows seven LED segments in a pattern of rectangles. Each segment may be activated by a separate circuit to emit light. By activating a particular set of segments, any digit from 0 to 9 can be displayed. For example, the digit 4 is displayed by activating segments *B, C, F,* and *G,* as shown in Figure 10-9b. If all seven LED segments are activated to emit light, the digit eight is produced.

Because they consume little energy, LEDs are commonly used for displaying numbers in devices powered by batteries. LEDs have been used in digital watches and electronic calculators for some time. More recently, they have been used in lap-top computers.

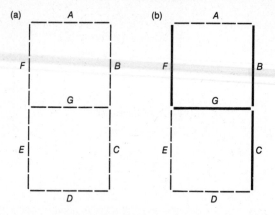

Figure 10-9.   LED segments can be used to display numbers.

Many electronic devices incorporate LED assemblies of the kind shown in Figure 10-9 to display numbers. Digital clocks and pocket calculators are common examples. (Liquid crystal displays, or LCDs, such as those found in quartz watches and other low-power digital displays, do not emit light. They operate by changing their reflectivity under the influence of a potential difference.) ∎

Extrinsic Semiconductors

The manufacture of semiconductor circuit devices begins with the formation of a single large crystal of a semiconductor element, which is usually silicon. The crystal is formed by slowly withdrawing it from a pool of liquid silicon (melted silicon) as the liquid solidifies. Before the crystal is allowed to grow from the liquid, small amounts of another element are mixed into the liquid in precisely controlled proportions. This addition of another element gives the semiconductor useful electrical properties. Because the silicon is no longer pure silicon after the second element has been added, the second element is referred to as the *impurity*. The process of adding a controlled amount of an impurity to silicon is called **doping.** Elements used in this manner are called *dopants*. The type of semiconductor produced by adding the dopant depends on the element used for the dopant.

N-**Type Semiconductors.**   One kind of element used in doping the semiconductor has atoms with five valence electrons. Among these are phosphorus (P), arsenic (As), antimony (Sb), and bismuth (Bi). These elements are members of Group 15 of the Periodic Table. The valence shell structure of these atoms is shown in Figure 10-10.

Atoms of these elements can take the place of a silicon atom in the crystal structure without disturbing its pattern, as shown in Figure 10-11. However, there will be five electrons, rather than four, in the valence shell of the impurity

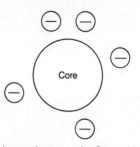

Figure 10-10.   Valence electrons of a Group 15 atom. There are 5 valence electrons in the atom.

atom. Four of these electrons are enough to complete the crystal bonding and fill the valence shell. The fifth electron, not bonded to any atom, enters the conduction band and is available to carry current. The impurity atom, having lost one electron, becomes a fixed positive ion in the crystal. The crystal as a whole, however, is neutral, since the electron is still present in the crystal.

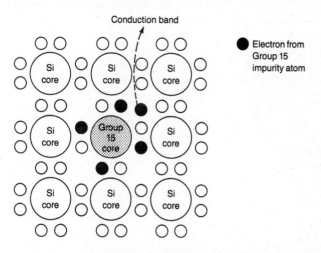

Figure 10-11.   Crystal structure of a Group 14 semiconductor (Si) doped with a Group 15 element. Each impurity atom provides one valence electron for which no energy level in the valence band is possible. This electron therefore enters the conduction band.

This process is repeated for every impurity atom, and the product is called an **extrinsic semiconductor.** Because the crystal has an excess number of electrons compared to a crystal of a pure intrinsic semiconductor, it is called an *N*-type semiconductor, *N* standing for *negative.* Elements whose atoms donate additional electrons as charge carriers are known as **donor materials.**

Remember that the conduction band also contains electrons that have come from silicon atoms, leaving holes behind in the valence band. As a result, the energy band pattern of an *N*-type semiconductor is like the one shown in Figure 10-12.

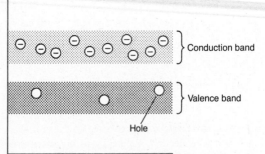

Figure 10-12. Energy bands of an *N*-type semiconductor. The majority carriers are electrons with conduction band energies. Minority carriers are holes. The charge carriers in the external circuit are electrons only.

In an electric circuit, as in Figure 10-13, the electrons in the conduction band will move toward the high-potential region of the field, that is, toward the positive battery terminal, and the holes in the valence band will move toward

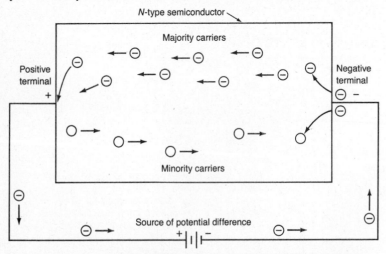

Figure 10-13. Conduction in a circuit containing an *N*-type semi-conductor. The majority carriers are electrons in the conduction band. The minority carriers are holes in the valence band. The current carriers in the external circuit are electrons only.

the low-potential region of the field, the negative terminal. The algebraic sum of these two currents *within* the semiconductor, taking into account both charge and direction, is the total circuit current and is equal to the current in the external circuit. The current in the external circuit, however, is due to electron carriers only. Since there is an excess of electrons over holes in an *N*-type semiconductor, the electrons are called the **majority carriers.** The holes are called the **minority carriers.**

P-Type Semiconductors. Elements from Group 13 of the Periodic Table, whose atoms have three valence electrons, as shown in Figure 10-14, are also used to dope the semiconductor and produce extrinsic semiconductors. When one of these elements is added to the pure intrinsic semiconductor during crystal growth, its atoms also will take the place of original atoms in the crystal.

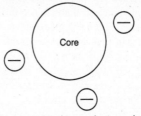

Figure 10-14. There are 3 valence electrons in a Group 13 atom.

Since these atoms have only three valence electrons, they can form only three covalent bonds with adjoining atoms, leaving a vacancy, or hole, in the valence shell, as shown in Figure 10-15. The hole will readily accept an electron to

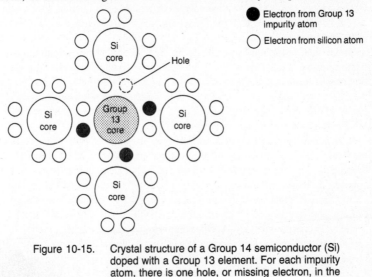

Figure 10-15. Crystal structure of a Group 14 semiconductor (Si) doped with a Group 13 element. For each impurity atom, there is one hole, or missing electron, in the valence shell.

complete the fourth bond. Such impurities are therefore called **acceptor materials.** When an acceptor atom acquires a fourth valence electron, it becomes a negative ion in the crystal structure. The crystal as a whole, however, is neutral because the electron acquired by the acceptor atom has merely moved from one place in the neutral crystal to another.

A hole may be filled by an electron from an adjoining atom, but that atom will then have a hole. Another electron may fill this hole, leaving a hole elsewhere. The holes created by the acceptor atoms can thus act as positive charge carriers, just as those in an intrinsic semiconductor do. This type of extrinsic semiconductor is therefore called a *P*-type, *P* standing for *positive*.

As in all semiconductors at temperatures above zero K, there are some electrons from the original semiconductor atoms that have enough thermal energy to enter the conduction band, leaving holes behind in the valence band. The holes contributed by the acceptor atoms are additional to those normally present in the pure semiconductor material. When a potential difference is applied to a *P*-type semiconductor, a dual current again appears—one due to the electron carriers in the conduction band and the other, in the opposite direction, due to the hole carriers. In the external circuit, only electrons are charge carriers. Since holes outnumber mobile electrons in the *P*-type semiconductor, the majority carriers are holes and the minority carriers are electrons.

CAN YOU EXPLAIN THIS?

Only negative, mobile charge carriers—that is, electrons—were known to exist in solids. How do we know that positive charge carriers are also responsible for currents in some solid materials?

Experiments proving that positive charge carriers do exist in some solids were first performed by E. H. Hall (with the help of J. H. Rowland) about 100 years ago. The basic principle, which is covered in Units 3 and 8, is that when a magnetic field is applied perpendicular to the direction of the current in a conductor, a force is exerted on the charge carriers perpendicular to both the direction of the current and the direction of the magnetic field. Figure 10-16a shows the effect produced when a metal strip is in a magnetic field. The electrons are forced to one side of the strip, creating a potential difference and internal electric field, which can be readily measured.

If the majority charge carriers are positive, as is true of *P*-doped materials, the force is exerted in the same direction on positive carriers, which causes them to move in the same direction but which produces a potential difference in the opposite direction, as shown in Figure 10-16b. Hall concluded that positive charge carriers must exist in some metallic conductors, but it was almost a century later that modern quantum physics identified this charge carrier as the "hole." This experiment also verifies that negative charge carriers moving in a particular direction produce currents similar to positive charge carriers moving in the opposite direction.

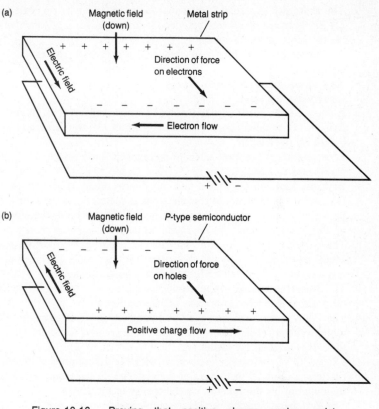

Figure 10-16. Proving that positive charge carriers exist. (a) When a metal strip is placed in a magnetic field, a force is exerted on electrons traveling through the circuit that forces the electrons to one side of the strip. This establishes an electric field in the strip and a potential difference from the positive side of the strip to the negative side. (b) When a P-type semiconductor is substituted for the metal strip, the electric field and the potential difference reverse their direction.

QUESTIONS

1. When a metal is heated, (1) its conductivity increases (2) both its conductivity and resistivity increase (3) its resistivity increases and its conductivity decreases (4) its resistivity decreases and its conductivity increases

2. The resistivity of a solid is (1) equal to 1 divided by its conductivity (2) the negative of its conductivity (3) unrelated to its conductivity (4) the same as its resistance

3. As the temperature of a semiconductor is increased, its resistivity (1) increases (2) decreases (3) remains the same

4. As a metal ribbon is heated, its resistivity (1) increases (2) decreases (3) remains the same

5. A one-meter length of wire is doubled in cross-sectional area. Its resistivity is (1) doubled (2) decreased by one-half (3) decreased by one-fourth (4) unchanged

6. Semiconductors are most often to be found in the Periodic Table in (1) Groups 1 or 2 (2) Group 13 (3) either Group 13 or 15 (4) Group 14

7. Both the Electron-sea Model and the Energy Band Model of solids (1) assume the existence of free electrons in metals (2) explain the behavior of semiconductors (3) have been useful in explaining the effects of temperature change (4) are based on modern quantum theory

8. The existence of holes in semiconductors (1) is part of the Electron-sea Model of solids (2) is purely theoretical (3) has been experimentally demonstrated (4) explains why metals are good conductors

9. The properties of holes resemble most nearly those of (1) negative ions (2) positive electrons (3) protons (4) atomic nuclei

10. The width of the forbidden band or energy gap is (1) the same for all semiconductors (2) is greatest in metals (3) is greatest for semiconductors (4) is greatest for insulators

11. The width of the energy gap varies with (1) the number of charge carriers present (2) the nature of the material (3) the temperature of the material (4) the random kinetic energy of the atoms

12. The two band structures that resemble one another are those of (1) conductors and semiconductors at absolute zero (2) insulators and semiconductors at absolute zero (3) insulators and semiconductors at room temperature (4) conductors and semiconductors at room temperature

13. As the energy gap of the band structure of semiconductors increases, resistivity (1) increases (2) decreases (3) remains the same

14. In the Energy Band Model of conduction, one reason that metals are good conductors is (1) the absence of holes (2) the presence of holes (3) the absence of an energy gap (4) the presence of a large energy gap

15. In the Energy Band Model of conduction, one reason that insulators are poor conductors is (1) the absence of valence electrons (2) the absence of a conduction band (3) the absence of covalent bonds (4) the presence of a large energy gap

16. To produce a P-type semiconductor from a crystal of silicon, the number of electrons in the valence shell of the dopant element should be (1) 0 (2) 5 (3) 3 (4) 4

17. The best choice for the outer covering of electric wires is a substance with (1) maximum resistivity (2) minimum resistivity (3) high conductivity (4) semiconductor properties

18. As the temperature rises, the width of the energy gap in the band structure of semiconductors (1) increases (2) decreases (3) remains the same

19. As the temperature falls, the number of charge carriers in a semiconductor (1) increases (2) decreases (3) remains the same

20. The process of adding impurities to a semiconductor in order to change its electrical properties is called (1) alloying (2) contaminating (3) melting (4) doping

21. Members of Group 13 of the Periodic Table are similar in that each has three (1) vacancies in the outer shell (2) holes in the outer shell (3) electrons in the conduction band (4) electrons in the outer shell

22. The element that may not be used to dope a semiconductor is (1) arsenic (2) silicon (3) gallium (4) antimony

23. The doping process may (1) decrease conductivity (2) decrease the number of charge carriers (3) increase the number of holes present (4) increase resistivity

24. Adding N-type dopant (1) creates a negative charge on the semiconductor mass (2) creates a positive charge on the semiconductor mass (3) creates positive and negative charges at the ends of the semiconductor (4) leaves the semiconductor mass neutral

25. As the amount of dopant in a semiconductor increases, the resistance of the semiconductor (1) increases (2) decreases (3) remains the same

26. The charge carriers that produce a current in a semiconductor are (1) electrons and holes (2) electrons, holes, and ions (3) electrons only (4) holes only

27. An intrinsic semiconductor is a semiconductor that has been injected with (1) donor atoms (2) acceptor atoms (3) either donor or acceptor atoms (4) neither donor nor acceptor atoms

28. The doping of a semiconductor produces (1) an intrinsic semiconductor (2) an extrinsic semiconductor (3) a charged semiconductor (4) a noncrystalline semiconductor

29. When the connections from a semiconductor to a battery are reversed, the current (1) will increase (2) will decrease (3) may increase or decrease (4) will remain the same

30. Compared to the energy of the shared electrons in a semiconductor crystal, the energy of the mobile electrons is (1) greater (2) smaller (3) the same

31. When a potential difference is applied to a semiconductor, the holes will (1) remain fixed (2) move in the direction of lower potential (3) move in the direction of higher potential (4) move in the same direction as the free electrons

32. **Within a *P*-type semiconductor, the majority charge carriers (1) may be holes (2) may be electrons (3) are always electrons (4) are always holes**

33–35. **Base your answers to Questions 33–35 on the following circuit diagrams in which *P* represents a *P*-type semiconductor and *N* represents an *N*-type semiconductor.**

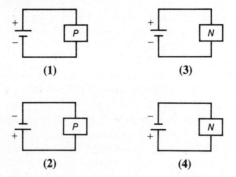

33. **In which circuits is current flowing? (1) 1 and 2 only (2) 1 and 3 only (3) 1 and 4 only (4) 1, 2, 3, and 4**
34. **In which circuits are holes the majority carriers of current in the semiconductor? (1) 1 only (2) 2 only (3) 1 and 2 only (4) 1, 2, 3, and 4**
35. **In which circuits are electrons the carriers of current outside the semiconductor? (1) 3 and 4 only (2) 1, 2, 3, and 4 (3) 3 only (4) 4 only**

II. SEMICONDUCTOR DEVICES

Several kinds of circuit devices can be made by combining *P*-type and *N*-type semiconductors in various arrangements. The modern technology of manufacturing semiconductor crystals makes it possible to produce these devices in the course of the crystal growth or by diffusion of impurities in the gaseous phase into the crystal surface.

The Junction Diode

The simplest type of semiconductor circuit device consists of a *P*-type semiconductor adjoining an *N*-type, as shown in Figure 10-17a. The area of contact is called the **interface,** and the device is called a solid-state **diode.** The diode symbol is shown in Figure 10-17b. The arrowhead represents the *P*-type section and it points in the direction of travel of positive charge carriers. The vertical bar represents the *N*-type portion. In circuit applications, these are sometimes called the *anode* and *cathode,* respectively. The theory of diode operation is important for understanding how all solid-state devices operate.

When there is no external potential difference applied to the diode, free conduction electrons from the *N* side tend to drift across the interface and neutralize

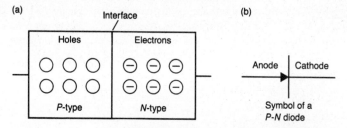

Figure 10-17.   A *P-N* junction diode. (a) The diode consists of an
                 N-type and a *P*-type semiconductor in contact at an
                 interface. (b) The symbol for a *P-N* junction diode.
                 The arrow points from *P* to *N*, the direction in which
                 the positive charge carriers (the holes) move.

some of the holes on the *P* side, converting some of the atoms on the *P* side to
negative ions and leaving positive ions behind on the *N* side. The *P* side thus
acquires a small net negative charge, and the *N* side acquires an equal positive
charge.

This charge difference creates a potential difference, called a *potential barrier,* across the *P-N* junction, as shown in Figure 10-18. The electric field of the
potential barrier acts to prevent further drift of electrons across the junction.

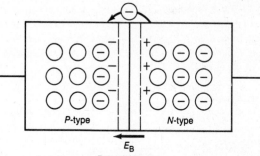

Figure 10-18.   Potential barrier across a *P-N* junction. Electrons
                 drift across the interface from *N* to *P*, filling holes on
                 the *P* side and leaving holes on the *N* side. As a
                 result, a layer of negatively charged ions is formed
                 on the *P* side and a layer of positively charged ions
                 is formed on the *N* side. The potential difference
                 between these layers is called a potential barrier.
                 Its electric field prevents further drift of electrons
                 across the interface.

Conduction in the *P-N* Diode. Diodes in circuits may be connected to
sources of potential difference in two ways. In one case, the *P* portion (anode) is
connected to the positive terminal of the source of potential difference, and the

N portion (cathode) is connected to the negative terminal (Figure 10-19a). The diode is then said to be **forward biased.** When the connections are reversed, with the anode connected to the negative terminal and the cathode to the positive terminal, as in Figure 10-19b, the diode is said to be **reverse biased.**

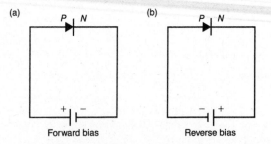

Figure 10-19.   Forward and reverse bias in junction-diode circuits. In forward bias, the positive terminal of a source of potential difference is connected to the P side and the negative terminal to the N side. The potentials are the opposite direction in reverse bias.

The field established in the forward-biased diode by the source of potential difference is in a direction opposite to that of the potential barrier across the junction, as shown in Figure 10-20a. When the potential difference across the junction due to the source is greater than the potential barrier, a net electric field is established from P to N. Conduction electrons will then flow across the junction from N to P and holes will flow from P to N, thus establishing a current through the diode circuit.

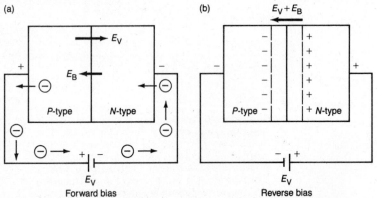

Figure 10-20.   Conduction in the P-N diode. (a) Current exists when the forward bias, E_V, is greater than the potential barrier, E_R. (b) No current exists under reverse bias. The potential barrier is increased, and the separation between the layers of oppositely charged ions becomes wider.

The field established in the reverse-biased diode is in the same direction as that of the potential barrier, as shown in Figure 10-20b. It reinforces the opposition to current and actually widens the separation between the positively and negatively charged surfaces that produce the barrier field. Under these conditions, almost no current flows through the diode. Only a small reverse current, from P to N, flows because of the few conduction electrons that are always present in the P-type semiconductor and the few holes in the N-type.

The graph of Figure 10-21 shows the electron current that flows through a P-N junction diode as the applied potential difference varies. On the graph, the vertical axis above the origin represents the electron current whose direction is from N to P when the diode is forward biased. The vertical axis below the origin represents the reverse current during reverse bias. The horizontal axis to the right of the origin represents the potential difference during forward bias that causes the electrons to move from N to P. The horizontal axis to the left of the origin represents the opposite potential difference.

The potential difference across the diode is normally kept within a moderate range (usually less than 1 volt). However, if the reverse bias becomes very large (200 to 300 volts), the covalent bonds of the crystal are suddenly disrupted and a very large reverse current flows. The diode is said to break down, or "avalanche," under these conditions of large reverse potential difference. The potential difference that produces avalanching is called the **breakdown voltage.** The greater the extent of doping, the lower the breakdown voltage.

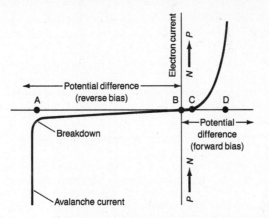

Figure 10-21.   Actual electron current in a P-N diode as the applied potential difference varies. When the potential difference is negative (reverse bias), a small reverse current flows unless the potential difference equals the breakdown voltage, when a very large reverse current (avalanche current) is produced. The graph is not drawn to the same scale on both sides of zero. The breakdown voltage is usually about 200–300 volts. The range of normal operation (from B to D) on the right side is usually less than 1 volt.

Point *A* in Figure 10-21 represents the reverse voltage that will cause a breakdown of the diode. From *A* to *B*, there is a small reverse current. From *B* to *C*, the current is practically zero. From *C* to *D*, there is an increase in forward current as the potential difference increases. The graph is curved because a diode does not obey Ohm's law. (If a device obeys Ohm's law, its graph of current versus potential difference is a straight line through the origin and the device is said to be *linear*.) All semiconductor devices are nonlinear.

Rectification of AC by a Junction Diode. If an alternating potential difference is applied across a junction diode, the electron current will be from *N* to *P* (the forward direction) when the potential difference in that direction is negative. When the potential difference reverses, the current becomes nearly zero. As a result, an applied alternating potential difference produces a pulsating direct current through the diode circuit (Figure 10-22a). Because the diode is nonlinear, the output current pulse has a different shape from the input wave form. If the alternating potential-difference input has a square wave form, as in Figure 10-22b, the output current will consist of a series of square-wave pulses, all in the same direction. The *P-N* junction diode can thus act as a *rectifier*—a device that changes an AC (alternating current) input to a DC output.

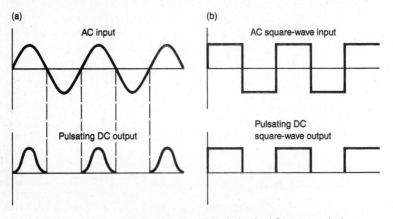

Figure 10-22. Rectification by a *P-N* diode. An AC input results in a pulsating DC output. (a) The result when the input is normal AC. (b) The result when the input is a square wave.

CAN YOU EXPLAIN THIS?

AC may enter a diode, but only DC will leave the diode.

Since current can flow through a diode only in one direction, only a direct current can flow through its external circuit. The AC "entering" the diode is actually an alternating potential difference, not an alternating current. The current that enters the diode must be the same as the current that leaves, since the circuit is a series circuit with just one path for electrons.

PRACTICAL APPLICATION

Distribution of electrical energy is usually in the form of alternating current (AC). However, direct current (DC) is needed for certain uses. In those cases, a diode rectifier can often be used to convert AC to DC. The output of a diode, however, is *pulsating* DC, and pure DC of constant amplitude may be needed. Pulsating DC can be smoothed to pure DC by using a series of capacitors and resistors, called filters. The pulsations are smoothed out by the action of the capacitors, which store charge during the half-cycle of current flow and release it during the other half-cycle when current would normally be zero. ∎

QUESTIONS

1. A diode may be constructed (1) by connecting a P-type semiconductor to an N-type semiconductor (2) by injecting one end of an intrinsic semiconductor with N-type and the other end with P-type dopant (3) by mixing N-type and P-type semiconductors (4) by creating a crystal containing a layer of N-type semiconductor adjoining a layer of P-type semiconductor

2. The arrow in the symbol for a diode indicates the direction of flow of (1) all charges carriers (2) electrons only (3) holes only (4) positive ions

3. The N and P regions of an isolated diode have (1) zero net charge (2) the same number of electrons (3) the same number of holes (4) equal and opposite net charges

4. The origin of the potential barrier in a P-N diode is the (1) application of an external potential difference (2) recombination of holes and electrons (3) presence of positive ions in the P-region of the semiconductor (4) existence of static electric charges on opposite sides of the interface

5. The potential barrier of a P-N diode most nearly resembles (1) a source of potential difference (2) a resistor (3) a capacitor (4) an insulator

6. When a P-N diode is reverse biased, the potential barrier width (1) increases (2) decreases (3) remains the same

7. As the potential barrier in a diode increases, the forward bias required to overcome it (1) increases (2) decreases (3) remains the same

8. A diode connected to a battery as shown in Figure (a) has a resistance of R_1 ohms. When connected as in Figure (b), the resistance is R_2 ohms. Which of the following is true?
   (1) $R_1 = R_2$
   (2) $R_1 > R_2$
   (3) $R_1 < R_2$
   (4) $R_1 + R_2 = 0$

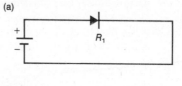

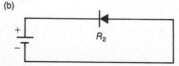

9. Two diodes are connected to a source of potential difference and to two light bulbs, *A* and *B*, as shown in the diagram. Which of the following statements is true?

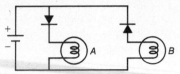

(1) Both bulbs will be on. (2) Both bulbs will be off. (3) *A* will be on and *B* will be off. (4) *A* will be off and *B* will be on.

10. In which circuit element will the resistance change when the connections to a battery are reversed? (1) a diode (2) an intrinsic semiconductor (3) an extrinsic semiconductor (4) a resistor

11. When electrons interact with holes, the energy of the electrons (1) increases (2) decreases (3) remains the same

12. A diode is connected to a source of alternating potential difference. The diode will be (1) forward biased all the time (2) reverse biased all the time (3) alternately forward and reverse biased (4) not biased

13. When reverse bias beyond certain limits is applied to a diode, (1) a large reverse current is produced (2) the resistance of the diode suddenly increases (3) the diode becomes a rectifier (4) the forward direction is reversed

14. Because a diode does not obey Ohm's law (1) it has limited utility (2) its resistance is independent of the applied potential difference (3) the current is independent of the applied potential difference (4) the relation between potential difference and current is not a direct proportion

15–16. Base your answers to Questions 15 and 16 on the following diagrams, which show a diode connected to a house lamp and an AC source in a home outlet.

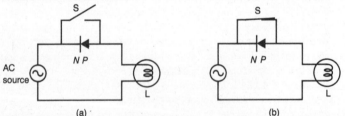

(a)   (b)

15. When the switch is open, the diode will conduct (1) only when the potential difference is positive from *P* to *N* (2) only when the potential difference is negative from *P* to *N* (3) at all times (4) at no time

16. When the switch is closed (1) there will be no change (2) the lamp will dim (3) the lamp will brighten (4) the lamp will go out

17–19. Base your answers to Questions 17–19 on this diagram, which shows a semiconductor device connected to a battery.

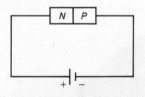

17. The semiconductor device is (1) a transistor (2) an intrinsic semiconductor (3) a dopant (4) a junction diode

18. The semiconductor device is (1) forward biased (2) reverse biased (3) not biased (4) both forward and reverse biased

19. If the battery is disconnected, the potential barrier of the device will (1) increase (2) decrease (3) become zero (4) remain the same

20. Two diodes are connected to an ammeter and a battery as shown in the diagram. The ammeter will show a current flowing if (1) no change in the circuit is made (2) the connections to diode A are reversed (3) the connections to diode B are reversed (4) the connections to both A and B are reversed

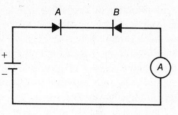

Transistors

In the manufacture of semiconductor crystals, it is possible to create a thin layer of one type of semiconductor between two layers of the other type. The circuit device produced in this way is called a **transistor.** There can be a layer of *P*-type between two layers of *N*-type, forming an *N-P-N* transistor (Figure 10-23a), or a layer of *N*-type between two layers of *P*-type, forming a *P-N-P* transistor (Figure 10-23b). Since every transistor has two *P-N* junctions, a transistor looks like two junction diodes sharing the same semiconductor material.

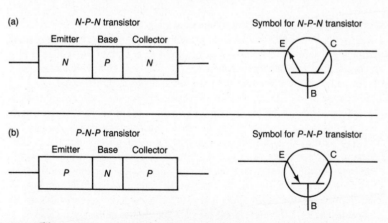

Figure 10-23.   (a) The *N-P-N* transistor and its symbol. (b) The *P-N-P* transistor and its symbol. The arrow in each symbol shows the direction of flow of positive charge carriers (holes) in the transistor.

The middle layer of the transistor is called the **base.** One of the outer layers is heavily doped with charge carriers—conduction electrons in an N-type or holes in a P-type. This layer is called the **emitter.** The other outer layer is less heavily doped with the same type of charge carrier. This layer is called the collector. An arrow between the base and the emitter shows the direction of flow of positive charge carriers (holes). Electron flow is in the opposite direction.

Conduction in Transistors.   A transistor is used in a circuit by connecting it to sources of potential difference. The emitter-base junction is always connected so that it is forward biased. In an N-P-N transistor, this means that the emitter is connected to the negative terminal of the source, and the base is connected to the positive terminal (Figure 10-24). The base-collector junction is reverse biased; the base is connected to the negative terminal, and the collector is connected to the positive terminal. The potential difference across the base-collector junction is usually much larger than that across the emitter-base junction.

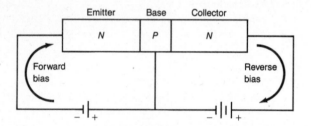

Figure 10-24.   Circuit connections for an *N-P-N* transistor. The emitter-base junction is forward biased. The base-collector junction is reverse biased by a much larger potential difference.

Since the emitter-base junction is forward biased, electrons will flow from the negative terminal of the source into the emitter, through the base, to the positive terminal, as shown in Figure 10-25a. Electrons entering the base will neutralize its holes, and electrons leaving the base will leave new holes behind them. The holes will thus move through the base in the opposite direction.

Since the base-collector junction is reverse-biased, electrons cannot flow in the forward direction of this junction—from the collector to the base. However, electrons entering the base from the emitter can easily continue on into the collector and produce a reverse current in the base-collector circuit. In fact, because the base is very thin and contains relatively few holes, while the emitter has been doped to supply large numbers of conduction electrons, most of the electrons leaving the emitter do continue on through the collector circuit, as shown in Figure 10-25b. If I_b in Figure 10-25b is the base current, and I_c is the collector current, I_c is much larger than I_b. The emitter current, I_e, equals $I_b + I_c$, since charge must be conserved. Thus, I_c is only slightly less than I_e.

In a P-N-P transistor circuit, the potential differences and currents are all reversed, as shown in Figure 10-26, but the operation is similar to that of the N-P-N transistor. The majority carriers are holes rather than electrons.

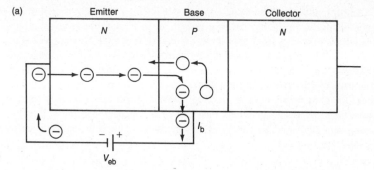

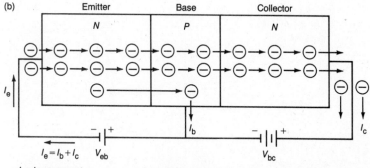

Figure 10-25. The *N-P-N* transistor circuit. (a) Charge carrier flow through the base circuit. Charge carriers in the base are electrons and holes. The symbol V_{eb} refers to the potential difference across the emitter-base circuit. (b) Current through the collector circuit. The collector current is made up of many electrons that pass across the base. The symbol V_{bc} refers to the potential difference across the base-collector circuit.

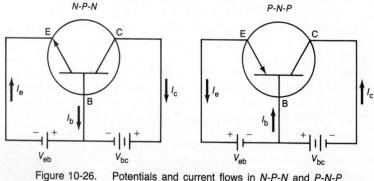

Figure 10-26. Potentials and current flows in *N-P-N* and *P-N-P* transistor circuits compared.

Amplification by Transistors. If a source of small varying potential difference is applied to the emitter-base circuit, as in Figure 10-27, an amplified replica of this wave form appears at the collector output. This amplification results because the ratio of the collector current to the base current is large and constant. Small varying base currents produce large varying collector currents. The transistor is able to function in this manner because of the doping procedure, the extremely thin base structure, and the proper bias voltages. Thus, a wave form of greater amplitude than that of the input is generated, drawing energy from the collector battery or voltage source. This is the basic transistor action.

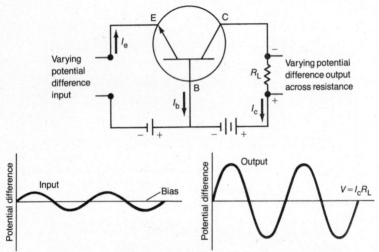

Figure 10-27.   Amplification by a transistor. A small variation of potential difference in the emitter-base circuit produces a corresponding variation, of much larger amplitude, across the load resistance, R_L, in the collector circuit. The varying potential difference across this resistance may be amplified in turn by becoming the input to the emitter-base circuit of a second transistor.

A single transistor can produce an amplification of several hundred times the input. If there is a resistance in the collector circuit, as shown in Figure 10-27, the potential difference across this resistance can be made the input to the base of a second transistor and be amplified again. By means of a series of transistors, a very small potential difference or current can be amplified to millions of times its initial value. That is how transistors in a radio receiver use the tiny amount of power input from a broadcast signal to produce a similar, but much more powerful, output signal in a speaker.

One of the earliest uses of transistors was as a replacement for triode vacuum tubes in radios and other electronic devices. A triode vacuum tube, as shown in Figure 10-28, is an evacuated bulb containing three electrodes: (1) a heated *cathode* that releases electrons and corresponds to the emitter of a transistor,

(2) a sheet of metal, called the *plate,* that is given a large positive potential with respect to the cathode and corresponds to the collector, and (3) a wire screen between the cathode and the plate, called the *grid,* that corresponds to the base; a varying potential applied to the grid as an input signal controls the electron current from the cathode to the plate. Transistors are much smaller and more reliable than vacuum tubes, and they do not need the relatively large amount of power that must be supplied to heat a vacuum-tube cathode.

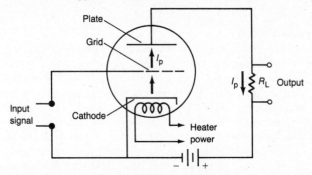

Figure 10-28.   Diagram of a triode vacuum (electron) tube. The cathode corresponds to the emitter of a transistor; the grid corresponds to the base; the plate, to the collector. An important difference is that the vacuum tube requires power to heat the cathode.

PRACTICAL APPLICATION

The transistor amplifier circuit can be modified to produce alternating currents of any desired frequency without the need for a separate AC input. Such a circuit is called an *oscillator* and is the basis for many devices, including radio, radar, TV transmitters, music synthesizers, medical diagnostic and therapeutic instruments, and sophisticated laboratory instruments.

To convert an amplifier to an oscillator, part of the output becomes the input to the same circuit, as shown in Figure 10-29. This process is called feedback.

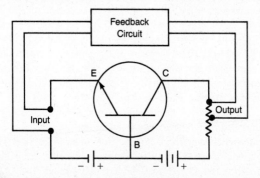

Figure 10-29.   A transistor amplifier circuit with a feedback circuit to convert it to an oscillator.

If the feedback has the correct phase, the circuit will amplify its own currents repeatedly, first building up to a peak value, and then dropping down to a low value. Any slight random fluctuation in the circuit initially will start the oscillation. It will then continue at a frequency that depends on the characteristics of the feedback circuit and may range from just a fraction of 1 hertz to billions of hertz. ∎

Integrated Circuits.

The term **integrated circuit** is the name for any number of tiny devices that control electric signals in computers, television sets, and other types of electronic equipment. Integrated circuits can contain thousands of electronic parts on an extremely thin layer of silicon. The parts that make up an integrated circuit can include individual capacitors, diodes, resistors, and transistors along with the connecting leads, all etched onto a surface as small as a few square millimeters. Integrated circuits are known colloquially as *chips*. An integrated circuit can do the same kinds of jobs as conventional circuits (large-scale circuits) that are made up of many separate parts. However, because the conductors in integrated circuits are so tiny, they can handle only very small currents. Because these chips require little space, use little energy to operate, release little waste heat, and are inexpensive to make in mass production, they have replaced the electron tube almost completely. They have had a considerable impact on our standard of living and, by bringing electronics to the masses, have been a force in producing social changes in the way people work, spend leisure time, and interact with each other.

PRACTICAL APPLICATION ▬▬▬▬▬▬▬▬▬▬▬▬▬

Computers store and process information in the form of numbers expressed in the binary system, which uses only two digits—0 and 1. All numbers, words, and even instructions are expressed as a string of 0's and 1's, called *bits*. Transistors are ideally suited to represent bits, since a transistor can be made conducting or nonconducting by a positive or negative potential applied to its base. It thus has two states, one of which can stand for a 0 and the other for a 1.

Integrated circuits on a silicon chip are ideally suited to handle millions of bits, since thousands of transistors and their connections can be etched onto a single, tiny semiconductor area. Transistors can also carry out the steps of a logical procedure, which are usually "yes" or "no" decisions. Transistors connected for this purpose make up *logic circuits*.

The heart of a computer is its *microprocessor,* a semiconductor chip that has the instructions and logic circuits for carrying out millions of operations each second on information supplied to it in the form of strings of bits. Thus, transistors and integrated circuits have made today's powerful computers not only possible but also reasonable in cost and extremely reliable. ∎

QUESTIONS

1. In the circuit shown, with the collector circuit open, the transistor (1) may be destroyed (2) will function as a diode (3) cannot function at all (4) will act as an amplifier

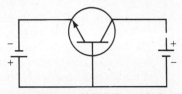

2. An isolated transistor always has equal numbers of (1) holes and electrons (2) positive and negative ions (3) positive and negative charge carriers (4) atoms of donor and acceptor dopants

3. As the magnitude of the emitter-base current increases, the magnitude of the emitter-collector current (1) increases (2) decreases (3) remains the same

4. Which of these symbols correctly represents a *P-N-P* transistor?

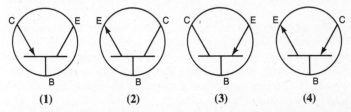

    (1)   (2)   (3)   (4)

5. The current through the collector in a transistor circuit is 24 mA and the current through the emitter is 26 mA. The current through the base is (1) 24 mA (2) 2.0 mA (3) 26 mA (4) 28 mA

6. In *N-P-N* circuits, the base bias should be (1) negative with respect to emitter and negative with respect to collector (2) negative with respect to emitter and positive with respect to collector (3) positive with respect to emitter and positive with respect to collector (4) positive with respect to emitter and negative with respect to collector

7–8. Base your answers to Questions 7 and 8 on this diagram of a semiconductor device.

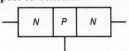

7. The device represented is (1) a transistor (2) a diode (3) an amplifier (4) an intrinsic semiconductor crystal

8. The number of *P-N* junctions in the device is (1) 1 (2) 2 (3) 3 (4) 0

9–14. Base your answers to Questions 9–14 on this diagram of a semiconductor circuit.

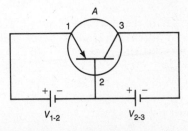

9. The device represented by the symbol labeled *A* is (1) a diode (2) a triode vacuum tube (3) a *P-N-P* transistor (4) an *N-P-N* transistor

10. The emitter, base, and collector are numbered, respectively, (1) 3, 2, 1 (2) 1, 2, 3, (3) 1, 3, 2, (4) 2, 1, 3,

11. The arrowhead in the symbol indicates (1) the flow of an electron current (2) a reverse bias on the base (3) the direction of the electric field of the potential barrier (4) the flow of positive charge carriers.

12. Holes are moving from (1) 2 to 1 (2) 1 to 3 (3) 3 to 2 (4) 2 to 3

13. If V_{1-2} is decreased, the current in the collector circuit will (1) increase (2) decrease (3) remain the same

14. The symbol labeled *A* could also be represented by which of these illustrations?

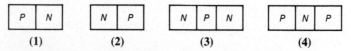

| P | N | | N | P | | N | P | N | | P | N | P |
(1)   (2)   (3)   (4)

15. The particles that exist in the greatest number in a transistor are (1) holes (2) ions (3) mobile electrons (4) neutral atoms

16. In an isolated *N-P-N* transistor, there will be more holes than mobile electrons in (1) the emitter and base only (2) the emitter and collector only (3) the base only (4) all segments of the transistor

17. As the potential difference of battery *B* in the diagram is increased, the current will increase in (1) the emitter only (2) the base only (3) the collector only (4) the emitter, base, and collector

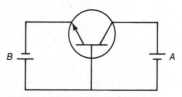

18. In a transistor circuit, charge carriers travel the least distance through the (1) emitter (2) base (3) collector (4) external circuit

19. The majority carriers in the *N-P-N* transistor are (1) electrons in emitter and holes in collector (2) electrons in both emitter and collector (3) holes in emitter and electrons in collector (4) holes in both emitter and collector.

20. The minority carriers in the bases of *N-P-N* and *P-N-P* transistors are (1) electrons in *N-P-N* and holes in *P-N-P* (2) holes in *N-P-N* and electrons in *P-N-P* (3) electrons in both *N-P-N* and *P-N-P* (4) holes in both *N-P-N* and *P-N-P*

21. In the operation of an *N-P-N* transistor, recombination of holes and electrons occurs (1) in the emitter only (2) in the base only (3) in the collector only (4) in each part of the transistor

UNIT 11   NUCLEAR ENERGY

I. THE NUCLEUS

In 1911, Ernest Rutherford conducted experiments that let him observe the paths taken by alpha particles fired at a thin gold foil. As explained in Unit 5, Rutherford concluded that there is a concentrated positive charge at the center of the atom and that almost all the mass of the atom is also concentrated there. Rutherford coined the term *nucleus* for the core of the atom; the nucleus contains all of the atom's positive charge and nearly all of its mass.

Nucleons

The positive charge of the atomic nucleus is due to the protons in it. A *proton* is a particle with one positive elementary charge—a charge exactly equal in magnitude to the negative charge of an electron but opposite in sign. In addition to its protons, the atomic nucleus contains neutral particles called neutrons. A *neutron* has almost the same mass as a proton but has no charge. It is electrically neutral. The protons and neutrons that make up nuclei are called **nucleons.**

Atomic Number

The number of protons in the nucleus of an atom is called its **atomic number** and is represented by the symbol Z. Since each proton has a charge of $+1e$, Z equals the total positive charge of the nucleus. Each element has a different number of protons in its atoms. For example, every hydrogen atom has 1 proton, every helium atom has 2, and every carbon atom has 6. Thus, these elements have atomic numbers of 1, 2, and 6, respectively.

An atom is normally electrically neutral because the positive charge of the protons in its nucleus is balanced by the negative charge of an equal number of electrons in the space around the nucleus. Thus, a neutral hydrogen atom has 1 proton and 1 electron, a neutral helium atom has 2 protons and 2 electrons, and a neutral carbon atom has 6 protons and 6 electrons. The chemical properties of an element are determined by the number of electrons in its neutral atom. The number of electrons in a neutral atom equals the number of protons in that atom. Therefore, the scientist who knows the number of protons in the nucleus of an atom also knows (or can look up) the element the atom represents and the chemical properties of the atom.

Mass Number

The total number of protons and neutrons in the nucleus of an atom is called the **mass number** of the atom and is denoted by the symbol A. The mass number of an atom equals the number of nucleons in its nucleus. With the exception of the hydrogen atom, the nucleus of every atom has at least one neutron. If the atomic number Z and the mass number A for any atom are known, the number of neutrons in its nucleus can be found by subtracting Z from A.

The general form of the symbol for a nucleus is ^A_ZSy, where Sy is the symbol of the element, the superscript A is the mass number, and the subscript Z is the atomic number. For example, $^{14}_6$C represents an atom of carbon that has 6 protons and 14 nucleons. It therefore has $14 - 6$, or 8, neutrons. The symbol $^{226}_{88}$Ra represents an atom of radium that has 88 protons, 226 nucleons, and $226 - 88$, or 138, neutrons.

This notation for describing an atomic nucleus is also used to describe the particles in the atom. The electron is represented as $_{-1}^0$e, because its charge is $-1e$ and its mass is practically zero compared to that of a proton or a neutron. The neutron is represented as $^1_0$n, since its mass number is 1 and its charge is zero. The proton, which is actually the entire nucleus of a hydrogen atom with no neutrons, is represented as $^1_1$H, since its mass number is 1 and its charge is $+1e$.

Nuclear Force

In any nucleus that contains more than one proton, the protons are separated by a distance of only 10^{-15} meter and therefore experience large repulsive Coulomb forces. The gravitational force of attraction between protons is far too weak to counterbalance the electrostatic force of repulsion. Since it is known that protons are concentrated in the nucleus of the atom in spite of the electrostatic repulsion, a very strong attractive nuclear force must hold the protons together. This **nuclear force** acts not only between protons and protons but also between neutrons and neutrons and between protons and neutrons. The nuclear force accounts for the stability of the atomic nucleus.

The nuclear force of attraction between two protons in a nucleus is about 100 times stronger than the electrostatic force of repulsion. At distances greater than a few nucleon diameters, however, the nuclear force diminishes rapidly and becomes much less than the gravitational or electrostatic forces. So, although nuclear forces are the strongest forces known to exist, they have a very short range.

Atomic Mass Unit

Because the masses of single atoms are such small fractions of a kilogram, scientists use a smaller unit to express such masses. The **atomic mass unit,** u, is defined as $\frac{1}{12}$ the mass of an atom of $^{12}_6$C, that is, an atom of carbon with a mass number of 12. This means that the mass of an atom of $^{12}_6$C (also written C-12, or carbon-12) is exactly 12 u (12.0000 . . . u). Since an atom of carbon-12 has 12 nucleons, and its mass is 12.0000 u, it follows that each nucleon has a mass of about 1 u. Actually, the mass of the proton is 1.0073 u and the mass of the neutron is 1.0087 u. The mass of the electron is 0.0005 u. In *SI* units, a mass of one atomic mass unit, or 1 u, equals 1.66×10^{-27} kg.

Mass-Energy Relationship

In his theory of relativity, Albert Einstein showed that mass and energy are different forms of the same thing and are equivalent. The energy equivalent of mass is proportional to the mass and the speed of light squared. That is,

$$E = mc^2 \qquad \text{(Eq. 11-1)}$$

where E is the energy is joules, m is the mass in kilograms, and c is the speed of light in a vacuum, 3.00×10^8 meters per second. For example, if the mass in a one-kilogram mass were converted to energy, that energy would equal 9.00×10^{16} joules. In many experiments in nuclear physics, charged particles are accelerated by electric fields. It is therefore convenient to express the energy gained by the particles in units of electronvolts, eV, rather than in joules. The masses of subatomic particles are also expressed as their energy equivalent in electronvolts. Larger units, such as the megaelectronvolt (1 million electronvolts), MeV, are often used.

EXAMPLE

Given that one atomic mass unit (1 u) equals 1.66×10^{-27} kg and one electronvolt (1 eV) equals 1.60×10^{-19} J, find the energy equivalent of one atomic mass unit in megaelectronvolts (MeV). (Since one megaelectronvolt equals 1 million electron volts, then 1 MeV = 10^6 eV.)

Solution

$$E = mc^2$$

$$E = (1.66 \times 10^{-27} \text{ kg})(3.00 \times 10^8 \text{ m/s})^2$$

$$E = 1.49 \times 10^{-10} \text{ J}$$

But, as given in the statement of the problem,

$$1 \text{ eV} = 1.60 \times 10^{-19} \text{ J}$$

Dividing both sides of the above equality by 1.60×10^{-19} gives:

$$1 \text{ J} = \frac{1 \text{ eV}}{1.60 \times 10^{-19}} = 6.25 \times 10^{18} \text{ eV}$$

Therefore,

$$E = (1.49 \times 10^{-10} \text{ J})(6.25 \times 10^{18} \text{ eV/J})$$

$$E = 9.31 \times 10^8 \text{ eV}$$

$$E = 931 \times 10^6 \text{ eV} = 931 \text{ MeV}$$

According to Einstein's theory, any change in energy results in an equivalent change in mass. For example, when 1 kilogram of carbon burns and combines with oxygen to form carbon dioxide, the chemical reaction gives off about 33×10^6 joules of energy. While this amount of energy may seem large, it is equivalent to only about 4×10^{-10} kilogram of mass. Thus the mass of the carbon dioxide formed in this reaction is theoretically 4×10^{-10} kg less than the total mass of the carbon and oxygen before they reacted. Compared to the mass of material involved, this change in mass is far too small to detect or measure. This is true of all chemical reactions and other ordinary energy changes. In *nuclear* reactions, however, the changes in energy relative to the masses involved are very much larger, and the corresponding changes in mass *can* be measured.

Nuclear Mass and Binding Energy

The measured mass of a proton is 1.0073 u, and the mass of a neutron is 1.0087 u. Thus, the total mass of two protons and two neutrons is 2(1.0073 u + 1.0087 u), or 4.0320 u. However, a helium-4 nucleus, which consists of two protons and two neutrons, has a measured mass of only 4.0016 u. Thus, the mass of this atomic nucleus is less than the sum of the masses of its individual nucleons when measured separately. With the exception of hydrogen-1, which has only one nucleon, there is always a difference between the mass of an atomic nucleus and the total mass of its separate nucleons. This difference is called the **mass defect** of the nucleus.

The reason that the mass defect of every nucleus exists can be understood by recognizing that work would have to be done against the strong nuclear force of attraction to separate the nucleons. The energy that would have to be supplied to make this separation is called the **binding energy** of the nucleus. The energy supplied to the nucleons to separate them from the nucleus appears as an equivalent increase in their total mass. When these nucleons come together to form the nucleus, the same amount of energy is released, and they lose the same amount of mass. Thus the binding energy of a nucleus and its mass defect are really the same quantity. Each is the equivalent of the other in accordance with Einstein's equation.

EXAMPLE

Find the binding energy of the helium-4 nucleus in megaelectronvolts.

Solution

The mass of 2 protons and 2 neutrons = 4.0320 u (a measurement)

The mass of the helium-4 nucleus = 4.0016 u (a measurement)

The mass defect = 4.0320 u − 4.0016 u = 0.0304 u

The energy equivalent of 1 u = 931 MeV (obtained from the example on page 327)

The binding energy = (0.0304 u)(931 MeV/u) = 28.3 MeV

The stability of a nucleus is related to its *binding energy per nucleon,* that is, its total binding energy divided by its mass number. For example, the binding energy per nucleon for helium-4 equals 28.3 MeV/4 = 7.08 MeV. If the binding energy per nucleon of all known nuclei is plotted against mass number, the graph of Figure 11-1 is obtained. The graph has a maximum value for a mass number of about 60. However, the actual values for individual nuclei do not lie exactly on the curve. The nucleus with the largest binding energy per nucleon (8.8 MeV) is iron-56, which lies slightly above the smoothed curve. The binding energy per nucleon for helium-4 is also exceptionally high for its mass.

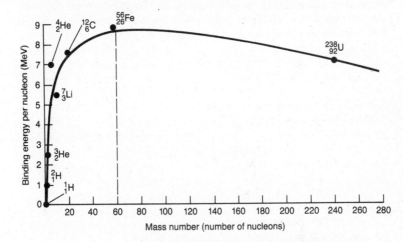

Figure 11-1.   The relationship between binding energy per nucleon and the mass number of a nucleus. Since the nucleus of hydrogen-1 is a single proton, there are no nucleons to be separated, and its binding energy is zero. The smoothed curve has a maximum for a mass number of about 60, but the nucleus of iron-56 actually has the largest binding energy per nucleon. The binding energy per nucleon of helium-4 is exceptionally large.

Isotopes

Although all atoms of a particular element must have the same number of protons, or atomic number, these atoms may differ in the number of neutrons and, therefore, have different mass numbers. Nuclei that have the same atomic number but different mass numbers are called **isotopes** of the same element. All elements have isotopes. For example, oxygen (atomic number 8) has three common isotopes: oxygen-16 ($^{16}_{8}O$), oxygen-17 ($^{17}_{8}O$), and oxygen-18 ($^{18}_{8}O$), which have 8, 9, and 10 neutrons, respectively. Each of these three isotopes can combine with hydrogen to form water, but the masses of the resulting water molecules will be different.

Hydrogen also has three isotopes. Most of the hydrogen atoms in natural samples of matter containing hydrogen are **protium,** the isotope whose nucleus consists of a single proton. In these same samples, there is one atom of the isotope **deuterium** for about every 6,000 atoms of protium. The nucleus of deuterium consists of one proton and one neutron. The nucleus of the third isotope of hydrogen, **tritium,** has one proton and two neutrons. Tritium is not found in natural samples of hydrogen. It must be made by artificial means.

All nuclei that have the same number of protons and the same number of neutrons are considered to be a single **nuclear species,** or **nuclide.** Each nuclide is a nucleus of a particular element with a particular mass number. Different nuclides of the same element (the same atomic number but different mass numbers) are isotopes of that element. Note that nuclides of different atomic number (nuclides of different elements) can have the same mass number. For example, $^{14}_{6}C$ and $^{14}_{7}N$ are nuclides of different elements (atomic numbers 6 and 7) with the same mass number (14).

Methods of Studying Atomic Nuclei

Particle Accelerators. The structure of the atomic nucleus and the basic nature of matter have been investigated chiefly by means of *particle accelerators,* such as cyclotrons, synchrotrons, and linear accelerators. A **particle accelerator** uses electric and magnetic fields to increase the kinetic energy of charged particles, such as electrons and protons, and project them at high speeds (often close to that of light) into samples of matter. Collisions between the high-speed particles and atomic nuclei may disrupt the nuclei and release new particles. The study of these ejected particles can give useful information about the structure and forces within the nucleus.

Detection Devices. Particles ejected from atoms by natural processes or produced by collisions in particle accelerators are called *subatomic particles*. Charged subatomic particles can be detected by photographic film and by means of various devices, such as the *Geiger counter, ionization chamber, bubble chamber, cloud chamber, spark chamber,* and *scintillation counter*. Many of the devices are designed on the principle that charged particles ionize the material through which they pass.

A *Geiger counter* includes a thin-walled glass tube that contains very little air. Inside the tube, and insulated from each other, are a metal cylinder and a thin central wire, between which a very high potential difference is maintained. This potential difference is only slightly lower than that needed to cause a discharge through the gas in the tube. When charged particles pass through the tube, some gas molecules inside are ionized, and the resulting ions are accelerated by the electric field. Consequently, the tube briefly conducts electricity, which is used to activate a counting device.

A *cloud chamber* contains air saturated with water or alcohol vapor. Charged subatomic particles introduced into the chamber ionize the air molecules in their paths. These ions act as *condensation nuclei,* attracting molecules of the vapor, which condense to form visible droplets. A charged particle leaves a vapor trail that is easily seen by the naked eye and that can be photographed, although the particle itself cannot be seen. The path of a charged particle can be curved by means of a magnetic field. The mass, charge, and other properties of the particle can be determined by an analysis of its path. The presence of uncharged particles can also be inferred from gaps in the tracks where ionization did not occur.

PRACTICAL APPLICATION

A *dosimeter* consists of photographic film encased in a badge. Dosimeters are worn by workers in nuclear power plants or nuclear research facilities. Charged subatomic particles absorbed by the dosimeter film ionize the emulsion on the film. The greater the number of charged particles absorbed, the greater is the exposure of the film. When the film is developed, the degree of film exposure is compared to a known standard to determine whether the person wearing the badge has encountered dangerous levels of charged particles. ■

Kinds of Subatomic Particles. Besides the proton, neutron, and electron that are present in existing atoms, there are a great many other subatomic particles that have been produced and observed as a result of natural or artificially induced processes. Among these are the *antiparticles* of the three atomic constituents. The *antiproton,* or negative proton, has the same mass as the proton but has a negative charge. The *positron,* the antiparticle of the electron, has the same mass as an electron but has a positive charge. The *antineutron,* the antiparticle of the neutron, has the same mass as the neutron and is also electrically neutral; it differs from the neutron in its spin and the direction of its magnetic field. When a particle collides with its antiparticle, they may annihilate each other. All their mass may then be converted to the energy of photons.

The existence of a particle called the **neutrino** has been proven. The neutrino is necessary to explain the process called *beta decay* (which will be discussed later in this text). The neutrino has no charge and little, if any, mass, but it does possess both energy and momentum. Its existence allows the conservation principles of energy and momentum to hold for beta decay. An antiparticle exists for the neutrino; the two are identical except for their direction of spin.

Hundreds of other kinds of elementary particles, all very unstable, are known to exist. The lifetimes of these unstable particles vary from 10^{-6} to 10^{-23} second. The particles are placed in categories such as *bosons* (which include photons), *leptons* (which include neutrinos and electrons), *mesons,* and *baryons* (which include protons and neutrons). Some of the bosons are particles that account for the fundamental forces between other particles of matter. The **leptons** are particles of small mass, **mesons** have intermediate masses, and **baryons** have the largest masses. Baryons and mesons are believed to be composed of elementary particles called **quarks.** Quarks are the only particles with charges that are a fraction of the elementary charge e, some having charges of $\frac{1}{3}e$ and others having charges of $\frac{2}{3}e$. These charges may be positive or negative. When quarks combine to form baryons, their charges add algebraically to 0, $+1$, or -1. Quarks have not yet been isolated. Some physicists believe it is impossible to observe them as separate particles and thus prove their existence.

QUESTIONS

1. A neutral atom has 24 neutrons and 20 protons. The number of electrons in the atom is (1) 24 (2) 20 (3) 44 (4) 4

2. Which nucleus has the largest number of neutrons? (1) ^3_1A (2) ^5_2B (3) ^7_3C (4) ^8_5D

3. Which could not be accelerated by a particle accelerator? (1) a proton (2) an electron (3) a neutron (4) an alpha particle

4. An atom of a certain element contains 12 protons and 13 neutrons. An atom of an isotope of this element must contain (1) 12 neutrons (2) 13 neutrons (3) 12 protons (4) 13 electrons

5. The rest mass of a proton is approximately the same as the rest mass of (1) an electron (2) a neutron (3) an alpha particle (4) a deuteron

6. Nuclei of isotopes of the same element contain different numbers of (1) electrons (2) neutrons (3) protons (4) positrons

7. A tritium nucleus contains 1 proton and 2 neutrons. What is the mass number of the nucleus? (1) 1 (2) 2 (3) 3 (4) 0

8. Isotopes of the same element have the same number of (1) neutrons (2) neutrons and electrons only (3) protons and electrons only (4) electrons, protons, and neutrons

9. What is the relationship between the atomic number Z, the mass number A, and the number of neutrons N in a nucleus? (1) $A = Z + N$ (2) $A = Z - N$ (3) $A = N/Z$ (4) $A = NZ$

10. One atomic mass unit is defined as (1) the mass of an electron (2) the mass of a proton (3) the mass of an atom of $^{12}_6C$ (4) $\frac{1}{12}$ the mass of an atom of $^{12}_6C$

11. It is difficult for a proton to approach the nucleus of an atom because of the (1) gravitational field (2) electrostatic field (3) magnetic field (4) nuclear force

12. In the equation $E = mc^2$, E may be expressed in (1) watts (2) coulombs (3) electronvolts (4) joules per second

13. A platinum atom consists of 78 protons, 78 electrons, and 116 neutrons. Its mass number is (1) 78 (2) 116 (3) 194 (4) 272

14. The isotopes $^{235}_{92}U$ and $^{238}_{92}U$ have the same (1) mass number (2) atomic number (3) binding energy (4) number of neutrons

15. As the mass of the isotopes of a given element increases, the number of protons in their nuclei (1) decreases (2) increases (3) remains the same

16. If nucleus A has more nucleons than nucleus B, A *must* have (1) a greater mass number than B (2) a greater atomic number than B (3) fewer protons than B (4) more neutrons than B

17. As the mass defect of nuclei increases, the binding energy of the nuclei (1) decreases (2) increases (3) remains the same

18. If the mass defect created in forming a nucleus is 0.010 atomic mass unit, its binding energy equals (1) 9.3 MeV (2) 9.0×10^{14} J (3) 1.6×10^{-21} J (4) 0.010 eV

19. **A proton and an antiproton, which have identical mass, interact and annihilate each other. The amount of energy released equals (1) 1.5 × 10^{-10} J (2) 3.0 × 10^{-10} J (3) 1.8 × 10^{17} J (4) 9.3 × 10^{8} eV**

20. **A Geiger counter is a device that (1) measures the charge of subatomic particles (2) captures subatomic particles (3) detects subatomic particles (4) accelerates subatomic particles**

II. NUCLEAR REACTIONS

Natural Radioactivity

A nucleus of a naturally occurring atom that disintegrates spontaneously, without any external influence, to form a nucleus of different atomic number or mass number or both is said to be *naturally radioactive,* and the process is called **natural radioactivity.** Another term for radioactivity is **radioactive decay.** The rate of disintegration for a particular radioactive nuclide cannot be altered by heat or chemical action. All the isotopes of the elements that have an atomic number greater than 83 are naturally radioactive, but every element has at least one radioactive isotope. For example, hydrogen-3, or tritium, is naturally radioactive.

In all nuclear reactions, the sum of the mass numbers of the reactants equals the sum of the mass numbers of the products. Also, the sum of the charges of the reactants equals the sum of the charges of the products. The examples of radioactive decay given in the following sections will illustrate these rules.

Alpha Decay. A nucleus that is unstable may experience **alpha decay,** the spontaneous emission of an alpha particle. An **alpha particle** consists of two protons and two neutrons and is identical to the nucleus of a helium-4 atom. Thus, the alpha particle can be denoted as $^{4}_{2}\text{He}$, since it has an atomic number of 2 (which indicates that it has two protons) and a mass number of 4 (which indicates that it has four nucleons). Alpha particles, which have relatively weak penetrating power, can be stopped by a single sheet of paper. When an alpha particle is emitted from an unstable nucleus, the mass number of the nucleus decreases by 4 and the atomic number decreases by 2, as illustrated in the nuclear equations below:

$$\text{radium-226} \longrightarrow \text{radon-222} + \text{alpha particle}$$

$$^{226}_{88}\text{Ra} \longrightarrow {}^{222}_{86}\text{Rn} + {}^{4}_{2}\text{He}$$

Note the conservation of mass number and charge in this reaction:

$$\text{Conservation of mass number:} \quad 226 = 222 + 4$$

$$\text{Conservation of charge:} \quad 88 = 86 + 2$$

Although mass *number* is conserved in all radioactive processes, the exact masses do change slightly. The total mass of the products is less than the mass of the original nucleus. The difference in mass appears as kinetic energy of the products. Since momentum must also be conserved, the products of small mass are ejected at very high velocities and carry off most of the energy released.

Beta Decay (Negative). The spontaneous emission of an electron from a nucleus is called **beta decay,** and the emitted electrons are called **beta particles.** Negative beta decay occurs naturally in nuclei that have a relatively large number of neutrons compared to the number of protons. Beta particles, which have greater penetrating power than alpha particles, can be stopped by a thin sheet of aluminum. In negative beta decay, one of the excess neutrons emits an electron and is itself transformed into a proton. As a result of beta decay, the number of neutrons in the nucleus decreases by 1, and the number of protons increases by 1, but the number of nucleons remains constant. Therefore, the atomic number of the nucleus increases by 1, but its mass number remains the same, as illustrated in the following example:

$$\text{lead-210} \longrightarrow \text{bismuth-210} + \text{beta particle}$$

$$^{210}_{82}\text{Pb} \longrightarrow {}^{210}_{83}\text{Bi} + {}^{0}_{-1}\text{e}$$

Note again the conservation of charge and mass number.

The process by which a neutron emits an electron and changes to a proton can be represented by the following equation:

$$^{1}_{0}\text{n} \longrightarrow {}^{1}_{1}\text{p} + {}^{0}_{-1}\text{e}$$

If the proton, $^{1}_{1}\text{p}$, had been emitted as a free particle, it would be represented as $^{1}_{1}\text{H}$. The $^{1}_{1}\text{p}$ notation indicates that it remains in the nucleus. Note the conservation of charge and mass number.

Studies of the energy of the electrons emitted in beta decay led to the assumption that a neutrino is usually produced in addition to the proton and the electron. The neutrino has no charge, and its mass is either zero or extremely small (scientists have not yet resolved this issue). The neutrino carries off some of the energy released in beta decay and helps to conserve momentum.

Gamma Radiation. Often a nucleus is left with its nucleons in an excited state after emitting an alpha or beta particle. The protons and neutrons in the nucleus release energy as they "fall" from an excited energy state to a more stable energy state. The energy released is emitted as **gamma radiation,** which consists of photons of very high energy compared to that of visible light. Gamma radiation has high penetrating power. It takes several centimeters of lead to stop it. The emission of gamma radiation does not change the atomic number or the mass number of the nucleus.

CAN YOU EXPLAIN THIS?

One element can become another naturally.

The identity of an element is determined by the number of protons in the nucleus of its atoms—that is, by its atomic number. If a particular isotope of an element is naturally radioactive and emits an alpha particle, a new nuclide with atomic number that is 2 less than that of the original isotope is produced. If it undergoes beta decay, a neutron is transformed into a proton, thus increasing its atomic number by 1. In each instance, the atomic number changes, so there is a change in the identity of the element.

Half-Life

The time required for one-half of the nuclei of a sample of a radioactive nuclide to disintegrate is called the **half-life** of the nuclide. For example, suppose the initial mass of a sample of phosphorus-32 is 0.060 kilogram. After 14 days, only 0.030 kilogram of phosphorus-32 (one-half the initial mass) will remain. (The other 0.030 kilogram of the original mass does *not* disappear. It is merely transformed into matter of a different kind.) This period of 14 days is the half-life of this particular radioactive isotope of phosphorus. After an additional 14 days, half of the 0.030 kg, or 0.015 kg, of phosphorus-32 will remain. That is, after two half-life periods, only ¼ of the mass of the original isotope remains, ¾ of the nuclei having decayed. If the initial mass of a radioactive isotope is represented by m_i, and the final mass after n half-life periods is represented by m_f, then

$$m_f = \frac{m_i}{2^n} \qquad \text{(Eq. 11-2)}$$

Each isotope has a specific half-life. Half-lives range from less than 10^{-22} second to more than 10^{17} years.

PRACTICAL APPLICATION

Cosmic rays from outer space consist primarily of extremely energetic protons. These particles strike the nuclei of atoms, producing various secondary particles, including neutrons. Neutrons react with nitrogen in the atmosphere to create carbon-14 by the following reaction:

$$^{14}_{7}\text{N} + ^{1}_{0}\text{n} \longrightarrow ^{14}_{6}\text{C} + ^{1}_{1}\text{H}$$

The resulting proton is transformed to a hydrogen atom as it acquires a stray electron. The carbon-14 nuclide is unstable because of its excess of neutrons. It changes back to nitrogen-14 by negative beta decay, with a half-life of 5,760 years:

$$^{14}_{6}\text{C} \longrightarrow ^{14}_{7}\text{N} + ^{0}_{-1}\text{e}$$

In carbon dioxide molecules in the atmosphere, the ratio of carbon-14 to carbon-12 is constant, because the rate at which new atoms of carbon-14 are being formed equals the rate of their decay. All green plants convert water and carbon dioxide into carbohydrates that contain carbon-14. Animals, in turn, eat such plants. The result is that all living organisms have the same ratio of carbon-14 to carbon-12 in their tissues, because they continually exchange carbon dioxide with their environment. When an organism dies, it stops absorbing carbon-14, and the ratio of carbon-14 to carbon-12 in its remains decreases, as the existing carbon-14 experiences beta decay. The age of the remains of an organism can be calculated by measuring the present ratio of carbon-14 to carbon-12 in the material. One typical use of this dating method is to determine the age of ashes or bones in a prehistoric human campsite. The method is accurate for ages from about 1,000 to 25,000 years. For ages greater than that, the percentage of carbon-14 remaining in the sample becomes increasingly difficult to measure with precision. ∎

The Uranium Disintegration Series

It has already been stated that there are no stable isotopes with atomic numbers greater than 83 (the element bismuth). The element with the largest atomic number that occurs naturally on the earth is uranium, whose atomic number is 92. More than 99% of the uranium on the earth is the isotope of mass number 238 ($^{238}_{92}U$). By alpha decay, the nucleus of $^{238}_{92}U$ changes to a nucleus of thorium-234 ($^{234}_{90}Th$), with an atomic number that is 2 less and a mass number that is 4 less:

$$^{238}_{92}U \longrightarrow {}^{234}_{90}Th + {}^4_2He$$

By beta decay, thorium-234 changes to $^{234}_{91}Pa$, and $^{234}_{91}Pa$ in turn changes to $^{234}_{92}U$:

$$^{234}_{90}Th \longrightarrow {}^{234}_{91}Pa + {}^{\ 0}_{-1}e$$

$$^{234}_{91}Pa \longrightarrow {}^{234}_{92}U + {}^{\ 0}_{-1}e$$

Other alpha and beta decays occur in turn until radioactive decay ends with the production of a stable isotope of lead, $^{206}_{82}Pb$.

The complete sequence of "daughter" isotopes produced from the "parent" uranium-238 is called the **uranium disintegration series.** It is shown graphically in Figure 11-2. In this graph, each arrow pointing diagonally downward to the left is an alpha decay, which reduces the atomic number by 2 and the mass number by 4. Each horizontal arrow pointing to the right is a negative beta decay, which increases the atomic number by 1 and leaves the mass number unchanged.

The half-life of uranium-238 is 4.15×10^9 years. The age of the earth is estimated to be between 5×10^9 and 6×10^9 years. Therefore, somewhat more than one half-life of uranium-238 has decayed since the earth and its rocks were formed, and somewhat less than half of the original mass of the element still remains. The radioactive daughter elements of the uranium series have half-lives much shorter than that of their parent and would by themselves have decayed to undetectable amounts by now. The decay of uranium, however, continues to produce fresh supplies. As long as there is still some uranium-238 on the earth, these other radioactive isotopes will also be present.

Conservation of Mass-Energy

As mentioned previously, the conservation of total mass number in a nuclear equation does not mean that actual mass is exactly conserved. Some mass is

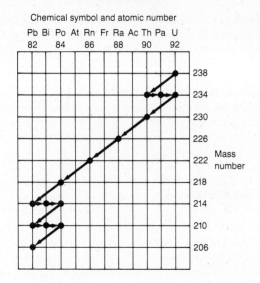

Figure 11-2. The uranium-238 disintegration series. Each alpha decay produces a nuclide with an atomic number that is 2 less and a mass number that is 4 less. Each negative beta decay produces a nuclide with an atomic number that is greater by 1 and that has the same mass number. The series ends with the stable isotope lead-206

always converted to an equivalent amount of energy. However, the total of the mass and energy equivalents remains constant during all changes. This fact is usually expressed as the **conservation of mass-energy,** where the term ''mass-energy'' means the total of the mass and energy expressed in the same units. In nuclear physics, the unit most frequently used for both mass and energy is the electronvolt.

Artificial Transmutation

For centuries, scientists attempted to change elements into one another, but the task was impossible until the discovery of radioactivity. Radioactivity is an example of natural transmutation, or change of one nuclide to another, as the nucleus gains or loses protons and/or neutrons. Artificial transmutations are produced by bombardment of nuclei with such particles as protons, neutrons, alpha particles, and deuterons (nuclei of hydrogen-2). With the exception of neutrons, these particles must have kinetic energy large enough to overcome repulsive electrostatic forces in order to penetrate nuclei. Particle accelerators may be used to produce such energetic particles.

High-energy photons may also cause the ejection of a proton or a neutron from a nucleus, or the nucleus may become unstable and disintegrate, producing a new nuclide. This is another type of artificial transmutation.

The first artificial transmutation was accomplished by Rutherford in 1919. By bombarding nitrogen-14 with alpha particles, he was able to produce nuclei of oxygen-17 and protons. The equation for the reaction is

$$\ce{^{14}_{7}N + ^{4}_{2}He -> ^{17}_{8}O + ^{1}_{1}H}$$

The isotopes produced by artificial transmutation are often radioactive. The first artificially radioactive nuclide was produced in 1934 by the Joliet-Curies by bombardment of aluminum-27 with alpha particles. The products of this reaction are phosphorus-30 and a neutron. The equation for the reaction is

$$\ce{^{27}_{13}Al + ^{4}_{2}He -> ^{30}_{15}P + ^{1}_{0}n}$$

Phosphorus-30 is radioactive and decays to a stable isotope of silicon by the emission of a positive electron:

$$\ce{^{30}_{15}P -> ^{30}_{14}Si + ^{0}_{+1}e}$$

Positron Emission. If a nucleus has too many protons relative to its number of neutrons, it may eject a positively charged electron, which is called a **positron.** A positron is produced when a nuclear proton changes to a neutron, as shown in the equation below:

$$\ce{^{1}_{1}p -> ^{1}_{0}n + ^{0}_{+1}e}$$

This process is called **positron emission,** or **positive beta decay.** In artificial transmutations, both positive and negative beta decay are possible.

The emission of a positron decreases the atomic number of the nucleus by 1 and leaves the mass number unchanged. The positive beta decay of $\ce{^{30}_{15}P}$ to $\ce{^{30}_{14}Si}$ described above is an example. Another is the positive beta decay of copper-64 to nickel-64, as illustrated by the following nuclear equation:

$$\ce{^{64}_{29}Cu -> ^{64}_{28}Ni + ^{0}_{+1}e}$$

In contrast, the emission of a negative electron in radioactive decay *increases* the atomic number of the nucleus by 1, with the mass number remaining unchanged. The negative beta decay of sodium-24 produces magnesium-24 and is given by the following equation:

$$\ce{^{24}_{11}Na -> ^{24}_{12}Mg + ^{0}_{-1}e}$$

Electron Capture (K-capture). If a nucleus has too many protons relative to its number of neutrons, it may experience **electron capture.** Since the electron captured by the nucleus generally comes from the innermost electron shell, or K shell, of the same atom, this phenomenon is often referred to as **K-capture.** The electron is absorbed by a proton, which is thereby converted into a neutron, as shown in the equation below:

$$\ce{^{1}_{1}p + {}_{-1}^{0}e -> ^{1}_{0}n}$$

Electron capture decreases the atomic number of the nucleus by 1 and leaves the mass number unchanged. Potassium-40 can experience electron capture, to produce argon-40, as illustrated by the following nuclear equation:

$$^{40}_{19}K + {^{0}_{-1}e} \longrightarrow {^{40}_{18}Ar}$$

The Neutron. James Chadwick discovered the neutron in 1932 by bombarding beryllium-9 with alpha particles, to produce carbon-12, as illustrated below.

$$^{9}_{4}Be + {^{4}_{2}He} \longrightarrow {^{12}_{6}C} + {^{1}_{0}n}$$

Note the conservation of charge and mass number in the equation.

Because they have no charge, neutrons are not repelled by positively charged nuclei, and, therefore, they require relatively little energy to enter into nuclear reactions. When a neutron is very close to a nucleus, the neutron is, in fact, attracted to the nucleus by the nuclear force.

Outside a nucleus, a neutron is unstable, having a half-life of about 10^3 seconds. The decay of the neutron produces a proton and an electron:

$$^{1}_{0}n \longrightarrow {^{1}_{1}p} + {^{0}_{-1}e}, \quad or$$

$$^{1}_{0}n \longrightarrow {^{1}_{1}H} + {^{0}_{-1}e}$$

Nuclear Fission

Some very heavy nuclei can be split into two nearly equal parts by absorbing a neutron. This splitting process is called **fission.** Although fission can also occur as a result of absorption of a highly energetic gamma ray by a heavy nucleus, only certain nuclides of high atomic number, such as uranium-235 and plutonium-239, can be made to undergo fission. The smaller nuclei, called **fission fragments,** that are produced by fission have too many neutrons relative to their number of protons and immediately emit one or two neutrons each. In addition to a variety of fission fragments and the neutrons produced by fission, a tremendous amount of energy is released. The energy release results from the fact that the binding energy per nucleon of the fission fragments is greater than the binding energy per nucleon of the fissionable nuclide, as can be seen from the graph of Figure 11-1. A typical fission reaction is illustrated by the following equations:

$$^{235}_{92}U + {^{1}_{0}n} \longrightarrow {^{236}_{92}U} \longrightarrow {^{140}_{54}Xe} + {^{94}_{38}Sr} + 2{^{1}_{0}n} + Q$$

where Q represents the energy released (which in this reaction is about 200 MeV). In a nuclear power plant, this type of reaction is controlled; in an atomic bomb, the reaction is uncontrolled.

Nuclear Fuels. Only certain nuclides of high atomic number are fissionable. A fissionable nuclide, such as uranium-235 or plutonium-239, that is used to produce energy on a commercial scale is called a **nuclear fuel.** Mined uranium is about 99.3% uranium-238, which is not fissionable, and 0.7% uranium-235, which is fissionable. The uranium is usually enriched to about 3% uranium-235 by adding uranium-235 to it. The nuclear fuel is formed into pellets that are stacked into long rods. These **fuel rods** are then placed in the **core** of a **nuclear reactor,** a device in which fission reactions produce energy for commercial purposes under controlled conditions.

CAN YOU EXPLAIN THIS?

A uranium fuel pellet (3 cubic centimeters) has as much energy as a ton of coal.

The energy released in nuclear reactions per unit of mass is very much greater than that released in chemical reactions. One ton of good-quality bituminous coal releases about 3×10^{10} joules of energy when burned. If all the atoms in a uranium pellet were to undergo fission, 6×10^{12} joules of energy would be released—about 200 times as much as can be obtained by burning a ton of coal.

Thermal Neutrons. Neutrons that have kinetic energies approximately equal to those of the molecules of a substance at ordinary temperatures are called **thermal neutrons.** Thermal neutrons, with kinetic energies of about 0.04 electronvolt, are more likely to be absorbed by a nucleus and cause fission reactions than are the fast-moving neutrons that are themselves products of fission.

Moderators. The neutrons produced by the fission of uranium-235 move at high speeds. These neutrons must be slowed down to produce efficient nuclear fission. Therefore, uranium fuel in a reactor is surrounded by a **moderator,** a material that has the ability to slow down neutrons quickly but that has little tendency to absorb them. A fast neutron is most effectively slowed by a head-on collision with a particle of comparable mass, because the nearer the masses of two particles are to being equal, the greater is the energy that is transferred.

Hydrogen-1 and hydrogen-2 (deuterium), which have small masses, are therefore effective moderators when present in the form of water, whose molecules contain two hydrogen atoms. A reactor that uses ordinary water formed from hydrogen-1 is called a *light-water reactor*. If the water is formed from hydrogen-2, whose atoms have twice the mass of hydrogen-1, it is called a *heavy-water reactor*. Carbon in the form of graphite is also used as a moderator, because the atomic mass of carbon is relatively small, graphite is inexpensive, and graphite slows neutrons without absorbing them or reacting with them.

Chain Reactions. The neutrons produced by the fission of a uranium-235 nucleus can be used to produce fission of other uranium-235 nuclei by absorption. Such a fission reaction can thus be self-sustaining, because the reaction, once begun, produces the required energy and enough neutrons for the reaction to spread to other fissionable atoms. Such a self-sustaining reaction is called a **chain reaction.** In a nuclear reactor, the fission chain reaction is controlled. In an atomic bomb, the chain reaction is not controlled. A chain reaction that begins with fission of a single atom of uranium-235 can produce 2×10^{13} J of energy, primarily in the form of heat, in less than 10^{-6} s. The minimum amount of fissionable nuclide required for a chain reaction to occur is called the **critical mass.**

Control Rods. The rate of a chain reaction is controlled by adjusting the number of neutrons available for absorption in the fission process. **Control rods** made of cadmium or boron, two materials that have an affinity for slow-moving neutrons, are used to absorb neutrons in a nuclear reactor, as shown in Figure 11-3. If the rate of the fission reaction in the reactor becomes too great, the control rods are lowered into the reactor to slow the reaction and reduce the amount of heat generated. If the control rods are inserted to their maximum depth, the reactor "shuts down," since neutrons become unavailable for absorption by the fuel.

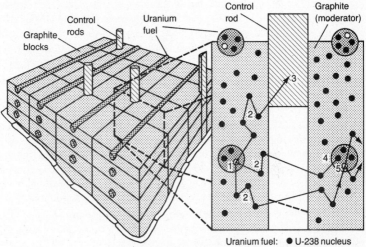

Uranium fuel: ● U-238 nucleus
              ○ U-235 nucleus

Figure 11-3.   A section of a nuclear reactor. One of the uranium-235 nuclei in the uranium fuel, like that at (1), undergoes fission, releasing energy and several high-speed neutrons. Several things can happen to the neutrons. Most of them are slowed by colliding with the atoms of the moderator (2). Some of them are then absorbed by the atoms of the control rods (3). Still others, like that at (4), are captured by atoms of uranium-238, producing uranium-239, which decays by beta emission to plutonium-239, a fissionable plutonium isotope also usable as a reactor fuel. Finally, in the most essential step for continuing the reaction, some neutrons, like that at (5), are captured by other atoms of uranium-235, resulting in fissions and a repetition of the steps described.

Coolants. In a nuclear reactor, the heat generated by fission is kept at reasonable levels and transported to heat exchangers and turbines by a substance called the **coolant.** The coolant must be circulated continuously through the reactor. Water and heavy water are common coolants that can also serve as moderators at the same time. Helium, carbon dioxide, and molten sodium are sometimes used as coolants in reactors that operate at high temperatures.

If the radioactively "hot" coolant mixes with the water in the secondary system in the heat exchanger, the leaking of radiation to the environment is likely. If there were a loss of coolant or a failure of the coolant to circulate to the heat exchanger, heat buildup in the core of the reactor could cause the fuel rods to melt and burn through the reactor vessel. This phenomenon, called "meltdown," would leak radioactive material into the environment.

Shielding. A steel lining is used for **internal shielding** of the containment vessel to protect the walls of the reactor from radiation damage. High-density concrete is utilized in the walls, ceiling, and floor as **external shielding** to protect personnel from radiation. Windows through which the reactor may be viewed directly are made of very thick glass that contains lead salts, which absorb dangerous radiation.

Radioactive Wastes. The products of a fission reaction are highly radioactive and have half-lives up to tens of thousands of years. Thus, these fission products cannot be disposed of by conventional means. Solid and liquid wastes are stored in special double-walled containers that are buried in the ground in isolated areas, so there is low risk of contamination of ground water. Plans exist to use underground caves in rock or salt formations for permanent underground burial. The radioactively "hot" material would be placed in special containment vessels or solidified in glass to prevent dissolving and corrosion.

Low-level radioactive wastes are currently diluted and released directly into the environment. (This is especially true of radioactive material used for medical diagnosis.) Gaseous radioactive wastes, such as radon-222, krypton-85, and nitrogen-16, are stored until a sufficient amount has decayed to stable nuclides and the level of radiation is safe enough for the material to be dispersed into the air.

Production of Plutonium. Uranium-238 does not undergo fission when exposed to thermal neutrons. This isotope is therefore not directly useful in conventional fission reactors, which generally rely on uranium-235 for energy production. However, uranium-238, as described in the next paragraph, can be used in **breeder reactors** to produce the fissionable isotope plutonium-239. Breeder reactors can produce more fissionable fuel than they consume.

When uranium-238 captures a fast neutron, it becomes uranium-239, which is radioactive and decays by beta emission. The neptunium-239 that results from the beta decay goes on to decay to plutonium-239 by beta emission, as shown in the nuclear equations below. Because this plutonium is an isotope that can be made to undergo fission and produce energy, it can be considered to be a fuel rather than a waste:

$$^{238}_{92}U + ^{1}_{0}n \longrightarrow ^{239}_{92}U \longrightarrow ^{239}_{93}Np + ^{0}_{-1}e$$

$$^{239}_{93}Np \longrightarrow ^{239}_{94}Pu + ^{0}_{-1}e$$

Fusion Reactions

The process of combining two light nuclei to form a heavier nucleus is called **fusion.** The mass of the nucleus formed is less than the sum of the masses of the original nuclei. The difference represents mass that has been converted to energy. The new, more stable nucleus formed has a greater binding energy per nucleon than the original nuclei did. As can be seen from Figure 11-1 (page 329), this is particularly true if a nucleus of helium-4 is formed by fusion of hydrogen nuclei. The energy released per nucleon in a fusion reaction is considerably greater than the energy released per nucleon in a fission reaction.

Only nuclei that have the smallest number of protons—and therefore minimal internuclear electrostatic repulsion—can be considered for use as fusion fuels. Therefore, isotopes of hydrogen are most likely to be used for this purpose. The probability is low that hydrogen-1 will fuse, and so hydrogen-2 (deuterium) and radioactive hydrogen-3 (tritium) are the isotopes currently being explored as energy sources. The nuclear equations for the reactions they undergo are as follows:

$$^{2}_{1}H + ^{2}_{1}H \longrightarrow ^{3}_{1}H + ^{1}_{1}H + 4.0 \text{ MeV}, \quad \text{and}$$

$$^{2}_{1}H + ^{3}_{1}H \longrightarrow ^{4}_{2}He + ^{1}_{0}n + 17.6 \text{ MeV}$$

In order to fuse, these nuclei must have kinetic energies large enough to overcome the electrostatic repulsion they exert on one another. The necessary kinetic energies can be achieved at temperatures of 10^8 K, but this very high temperature *(thermonuclear)* condition must be maintained for about one second, and the fuel must be at very high density to promote frequent collisions and the production of a substantial amount of energy. At present, these conditions have existed only during detonation of hydrogen bombs. If the required temperature, density, and containment time can be achieved by other means, fusion can be controlled. Then water in the world's oceans can serve as a cheap, nearly limitless supply of deuterium. Furthermore, fusion, unlike fission, produces little radioactive waste.

QUESTIONS

1. The mass number of an alpha particle is (1) 1 (2) 2 (3) 0 (4) 4
2. The emission of an alpha particle from a radioactive nucleus (1) decreases the atomic number by 2 (2) increases the atomic number by 2 (3) decreases the atomic number by 4 (4) increases the atomic number by 4

3. If a negative beta particle is emitted by a radioactive nucleus, the mass number of the nucleus (1) decreases (2) increases (3) remains the same

4. A beta particle is identical to (1) a helium nucleus (2) a hydrogen nucleus (3) a deuteron (4) an electron

5. If gamma radiation is emitted from a radioactive nucleus, the atomic number of the nucleus (1) decreases (2) increases (3) remains the same

6. When gamma radiation is emitted from a radioactive nucleus, (1) the nucleus goes to a more stable state (2) the nucleus goes to an excited state (3) an electron goes to the ground state (4) an electron goes to an excited state

7. If a positron is emitted from a radioactive nucleus, the atomic number of the nucleus (1) decreases (2) increases (3) remains the same

8. As a result of electron capture by a nucleus, the atomic number of the nucleus (1) decreases (2) increases (3) remains the same

9. K-capture is another name for (1) gamma radiation (2) beta decay (3) electron capture (4) positron emission

10. Fission occurs primarily as the result of a nucleus absorbing (1) a neutron (2) a proton (3) an electron (4) an alpha particle

11. The function of a moderator in a nuclear reactor is to (1) absorb neutrons (2) produce neutrons (3) slow down neutrons (4) speed up neutrons

12. The minimum amount of fissionable material necessary for a chain reaction to occur is called (1) critical mass (2) rest mass (3) relative mass (4) atomic mass

13. A neutron is most effectively slowed down by a head-on collision with a particle whose mass, compared to that of the neutron, is (1) less (2) greater (3) the same

14. When uranium-238 absorbs a neutron, the resulting reactions produce (1) lead (2) plutonium (3) radium (4) uranium-235

15. Compared to the energy released per nucleon in a fusion reaction, the energy released per nucleon in a fission reaction is generally (1) less (2) greater (3) the same

16. The binding energy per nucleon in a nucleus created by fusion, compared to the binding energy per nucleon of its constituent nuclei, is (1) less (2) greater (3) the same

17. If all of the following particles were traveling at the same velocity, which would have the greatest energy? (1) alpha particle (2) beta particle (3) neutron (4) proton

18. If the half-life of $^{234}_{90}$Th is 24 days, the amount of a 12.00-gram sample remaining after 96 days is (1) 1.00 g (2) 0.75 g (3) 6.00 g (4) 1.50 g

19. Given the equation $^{27}_{13}$Al + $^{4}_{2}$He → $^{30}_{15}$P + X, the correct symbol for X is (1) $^{0}_{+1}$e (2) $^{0}_{-1}$e (3) $^{4}_{2}$He (4) $^{1}_{0}$n

20. When lead $^{214}_{82}$Pb emits a beta particle, the resultant nucleus will be (1) $^{214}_{81}$Tl (2) $^{213}_{82}$Pb (3) $^{214}_{83}$Bi (4) $^{211}_{84}$Po

21. In the equation $^{239}_{92}$U → $^{239}_{93}$Np + X, particle X is (1) a proton (2) a neutron (3) an alpha particle (4) a beta particle

22. When the nucleus $^{238}_{92}U$ emits an alpha particle, the resulting nucleus is (1) $^{230}_{90}Th$ (2) $^{234}_{90}Th$ (3) $^{234}_{91}Pa$ (4) $^{234}_{92}U$

23. As the original mass of a radioactive substance decreases, its half-life (1) decreases (2) increases (3) remains the same

24. A certain radioactive isotope has a half-life of 400 years. To be sure that less than $\frac{1}{32}$ of the isotope's present mass remains, it is necessary to wait at least (1) 80 years (2) 2,000 years (3) 3,200 years (4) 12,800 years

25–30. Base your answers to Questions 25 through 30 on the following information.

A sample of pure radon gas ($^{222}_{86}Rn$) is sealed in a glass ampule. The half-life of radon is 4 days.

25. Which is an isotope of radon? (1) $^{222}_{88}X$ (2) $^{220}_{84}X$ (3) $^{220}_{86}X$ (4) $^{222}_{89}X$

26. If the pressure inside the glass ampule were doubled, the half-life of the radon would (1) be halved (2) remain the same (3) be doubled (4) be quadrupled

27. Twelve days after the radon gas is sealed in the glass ampule, the fraction of radon gas remaining will be (1) $\frac{1}{2}$ (2) $\frac{1}{4}$ (3) $\frac{1}{8}$ (4) $\frac{1}{16}$

28. The number of neutrons in the nucleus of $^{222}_{86}Rn$ is (1) 86 (2) 136 (3) 222 (4) 308

29. Several days later, an analysis shows that there is a second gas in the sealed ampule. This second gas is most likely (1) hydrogen (2) helium (3) oxygen (4) nitrogen

30. The gas referred to in Question 29 is probably the result of (1) transmutation of the radon nucleus (2) a chemical reaction (3) alpha decay (4) beta decay

31–35. Base your answers to Questions 31 through 35 on the uranium-238 disintegration series in Figure 11-2 on page 337.

31. An example of alpha decay is the change of (1) $^{238}_{92}U$ into $^{234}_{90}Th$ (2) $^{234}_{90}Th$ into $^{234}_{91}Pa$ (3) $^{234}_{91}Pa$ into $^{234}_{92}U$ (4) $^{214}_{82}Pb$ into $^{214}_{83}Bi$

32. Which isotope is not formed during the decay of $^{238}_{92}U$? (1) $^{234}_{90}Th$ (2) $^{230}_{90}Th$ (3) $^{226}_{84}Po$ (4) $^{218}_{84}Po$

33. Which will be emitted when $^{210}_{83}Bi$ changes to $^{206}_{82}Pb$? (1) 1 alpha particle only (2) 1 beta particle only (3) 2 alpha particles only (4) 1 alpha particle and 1 beta particle

34. Which stable isotope is formed when $^{238}_{92}U$ decays? (1) $^{214}_{83}Bi$ (2) $^{214}_{84}Po$ (3) $^{214}_{82}Pb$ (4) $^{206}_{82}Pb$

35. What is the total number of alpha particles emitted as an atom of $^{238}_{92}U$ decays to $^{206}_{82}Pb$? (1) 6 (2) 7 (3) 8 (4) 13

36–37. Base your answers to Questions 36 and 37 on the following information.

When aluminum is bombarded with alpha particles, the following reaction occurs: $^{27}_{13}Al + ^{4}_{2}He \rightarrow ^{30}_{15}P + X$

36. The atomic number of particle X is (1) 1 (2) 11 (3) 23 (4) 0

37. The mass number of particle X is (1) 1 (2) 0 (3) 11 (4) 23

38–41. Base your answers to Questions 38 through 41 on the following four equations.

(1) $^{234}_{90}\text{Th} \longrightarrow {}^{234}_{91}\text{Pa} + {}^{0}_{-1}\text{e}$

(2) $^{14}_{7}\text{N} + {}^{4}_{2}\text{He} \longrightarrow {}^{17}_{8}\text{O} + {}^{1}_{1}\text{H}$

(3) $^{3}_{1}\text{H} + {}^{1}_{1}\text{H} \longrightarrow {}^{4}_{2}\text{He} + Q$

(4) $^{1}_{0}\text{n} + {}^{235}_{92}\text{U} \longrightarrow {}^{92}_{36}\text{Kr} + {}^{141}_{56}\text{Ba} + 3{}^{1}_{0}\text{n} + Q$

38. Which equation represents an artificial transmutation by alpha-particle bombardment? (1) 1 (2) 2 (3) 3 (4) 4

39. Which equation is a fusion reaction? (1) 1 (2) 2 (3) 3 (4) 4

40. Which equation could be the basis of a fission chain reaction? (1) 1 (2) 2 (3) 3 (4) 4

41. Which equation is an example of negative beta decay? (1) 1 (2) 2 (3) 3 (4) 4

42. The reaction $^{40}_{19}\text{K} + {}^{0}_{-1}\text{e} \longrightarrow {}^{40}_{18}\text{Ar}$ is an example of (1) negative beta decay (2) positive beta decay (3) artificial transmutation (4) K-electron capture

43. The equation $^{1}_{0}\text{n} \rightarrow {}^{1}_{1}\text{p} + {}^{0}_{-1}\text{e}$ represents (1) electron capture (2) a fission reaction (3) neutron decay by positive beta emission (4) neutron decay by negative beta emission

44. When a nucleus in an excited state changes to a more stable state, the nucleus normally emits (1) visible light (2) infrared waves (3) gamma radiation (4) long radio waves

45. Silver-108 has a half-life of 2.4 minutes. If the initial mass is M, the mass remaining after 7.2 minutes is (1) $M/2$ (2) $M/4$ (3) $M/6$ (4) $M/8$

46. Materials for slowing neutrons are called (1) coolants (2) shielding (3) controls (4) moderators

47. In the reaction $^{24}_{11}\text{N} \rightarrow {}^{24}_{12}\text{Mg} + X$, the letter X represents (1) a neutron (2) a proton (3) an electron (4) a positron

48. In the reaction $^{30}_{15}\text{P} \rightarrow {}^{30}_{14}\text{Si} + {}^{0}_{+1}\text{e}$, the atoms $^{30}_{15}\text{P}$ and $^{30}_{14}\text{Si}$ have the same (1) mass number (2) atomic number (3) number of neutrons (4) number of electrons

49. In nuclear fusion, the total mass–energy of the system before fusion, compared to the total mass–energy of the system after fusion, is (1) smaller (2) larger (3) the same

50. When fast neutrons are slowed down, their effectiveness in producing fission is (1) decreased (2) increased (3) not changed

51. Base your answer to this question on the following information.

> The mass of a radium-226 nucleus is 226.0244 u.
> The mass of a radon-222 nucleus is 222.0165 u.
> The mass of an alpha particle is 4.0026 u.

In the reaction $^{226}_{88}\text{Ra} \rightarrow {}^{222}_{86}\text{Rn} + {}^{4}_{2}\text{He} + Q$, the energy Q is equivalent to a mass of (1) 0 u (2) 0.0026 u (3) 0.0053 u (4) 0.0079 u

Appendix I   Measurement and Mathematics

Measurement

Measurement is a comparison of an unknown quantity with a known quantity. All physical measurements are subject to errors.

Errors may be the result of the method used, environmental fluctuation, instrumental limitations, and personal error. Systematic errors tend to be in one direction. Random errors tend to fluctuate in both directions. The random error may be reduced by increasing the number of observations.

When using common measuring devices, such as metersticks, stopwatches, and graduated cylinders, you should be aware of the devices' limitations. You should also develop an appreciation for the size of the unit you are using. For example, a reasonable walking speed is 1 m/sec and the range of masses for your classmates is about 40 to 120 kg.

Significant Figures

You are expected to understand significant figures in terms of the degree of precision to which a common measuring device can be used. This is subject to testing. Performing operations with significant figures is not subject to testing.

A significant figure is one that is known to be reasonably reliable. In expressing the results of a measurement, one estimated figure is considered significant; for example, in measuring temperature, if the thermometer is calibrated in degrees, the reading may be *estimated* to the tenth of a degree. In this case, in reading 20.3°, the figure "3" is considered significant.

Zeros that appear *in front* of a number are not significant figures. The number 0.083 contains two significant figures.

Zeros that appear *between* numbers are always significant. The number 803 contains three significant figures.

Zeros that appear *after* a number are significant *only* (1) if followed by a decimal point or (2) if to the right of a decimal point. The number 1,800 contains two significant figures, but the numbers 1,800. and 18.00 contain four significant figures.

For whole numbers ending in two or more zeros, there is no way of indicating that some, but not all, of the zeros are significant; for example, the number 186,000 would indicate three significant figures if no decimal point is expressed, and six significant figures if the decimal point is expressed. There is no way of indicating its accuracy to four or five significant figures except by the use of scientific notation.

The information in this Appendix is taken from Appendix E of the Regents Physics Syllabus published by the State Education Department of New York.

The following rules will assist you when rounding off a number:

- When the number dropped is less than 5, the preceding number remains unchanged; for example, changing 5.3634 to three significant figures becomes 5.36.

- When the number dropped is 5 or more, the preceding number is increased by 1; for example, changing 2.4179 to three significant figures becomes 2.42.

Please note that there are other conventions for rounding off a number.

- When adding or subtracting, the answer should be rounded off to contain the least accurately known figure as the final one; for example:

$$
\begin{array}{r}
32.6 \\
431.33 \\
+6144.212 \\
\hline
6608.142 = 6{,}608.1
\end{array}
\qquad
\begin{array}{r}
531.46 \\
-86.3 \\
\hline
445.16 = 445.2
\end{array}
$$

- When multiplying or dividing, the answer should be rounded off to contain only as many significant figures as are contained in the least accurate number; for example:

$$
\begin{array}{r}
1.36 \\
\times\ 4.2 \\
\hline
272 \\
544 \\
\hline
5.712 = 5.7
\end{array}
\qquad
\begin{array}{r}
5.1 \div 2.13 \\
2.39 = 2.4 \\
2.13\overline{)5.1000} \\
4\ 26 \\
\hline
840 \\
639 \\
\hline
2010
\end{array}
$$

- When adding, subtracting, multiplying, or dividing, numbers may be rounded off to one more than the number of significant figures to be carried in the answer *before* the manipulation is carried out; for example $2.7468 \times 3.2 = 2.75 \times 3.2 = 8.8$.

Scientific Notation (Standard or Exponential Notation)

Scientific notation should be used to indicate the number of significant figures and to facilitate mathematical operations with large and small numbers.

Any number can be expressed in the form $A \times 10^n$, where A is any number with one digit to the left of the decimal point and n is an integer. All the digits in A are significant. The value of n is determined by counting the number of places the decimal was moved. If the decimal was moved to the left, n is positive. If it was moved to the right, n is negative. For example, 186,000 becomes 1.86×10^5, and 0.0000520 becomes 5.20×10^{-5}. In scientific notation it is possible to indicate any desired number of significant figures. For example, if 186,000 were known to four significant figures, it would be written 1.860×10^5.

Multiplication and Division in Standard Notation. To multiply or divide numbers in scientific notation, multiply or divide the significant figure factors to obtain the new values of A, retaining the correct number of significant figures (see examples below), and then add or subtract the powers of 10 to obtain the new value of n. Adjust the decimal point if the new A has more or less than one non-zero digit to the left of the decimal point. Examples:

$$2.2 \times 10^4 \times 3.01 \times 10^2 = 6.6 \times 10^6$$

$$2.2 \times 10^{-4} \times 3.01 \times 10^2 = 6.6 \times 10^{-2}$$

$$6.0 \times 10^3 \times 3.01 \times 10^4 = 18 \times 10^7 = 1.8 \times 10^8$$

$$6.0 \times 10^5 \div 3.0 \times 10^2 = 2.0 \times 10^3$$

$$6.0 \times 10^5 \div 3.0 \times 10^{-2} = 2.0 \times 10^7$$

$$3.0 \times 10^2 \div 6.0 \times 10^5 = 0.50 \times 10^{-3} = 5.0 \times 10^{-4}$$

Addition and Subtraction in Scientific Notation. To add or subtract numbers in standard notation, the powers of 10 must be the same; for example, $5 \times 10^3 + 2 \times 10^3 = (5 + 2) \times 10^3 = 7 \times 10^3$. If the numbers to be added or subtracted have different powers of 10, then the powers must be equalized. For example, $2 \times 10^2 + 3 \times 10^3 = 2 \times 10^2 + 30 \times 10^2 = 32 \times 10^2 = 3.2 \times 10^3$.

Estimation

The technique of estimating answers will enable you to quickly verify the procedures you are using for solving a problem and to determine the reasonableness of an answer before performing tedious calculations.

For example: What is the gravitational force between the earth and the moon?

$$F = \frac{Gm_1m_2}{r^2}$$

$$F = \frac{6.7 \times 10^{-11} \text{ N} \cdot \text{m}^2/\text{kg}^2 \times 7.4 \times 10^{22} \text{ kg} \times 6.0 \times 10^{24} \text{ kg}}{(3.8 \times 10^8 \text{ m})^2}$$

estimating: $$F = \frac{7 \times 10^{-11}(7 \times 10^{22})(6 \times 10^{24}) \text{ N}}{16 \times 10^{16}}$$

$$F = \frac{300 \times 10^{35} \text{ N}}{16 \times 10^{16}}$$

$$F = 20 \times 10^{19} \text{ N} = 2 \times 10^{20} \text{ N}$$

exactly: $$F = \frac{297.5 \times 10^{35} \text{ N}}{14.4 \times 10^{16}}$$

$$F = 20.6 \times 10^{19} \text{ N} = 2.1 \times 10^{20} \text{ N}$$

Estimating answers using orders of magnitude is a skill that should be developed. For example, as the Voyager spacecraft flew by Uranus, it sent signals back to Earth. How many seconds did it take such signals to reach Earth?

$$\text{Distance from Uranus to Earth} = 2.71 \times 10^{12} \text{ m}$$
$$= 3 \times 10^{12} \text{ m}$$

$$\text{Speed of light} = 3.00 \times 10^8 \text{ m/s}$$

Therefore,

$$\Delta t = \frac{\Delta s}{\bar{v}} = \frac{3 \times 10^{12} \text{ m}}{3 \times 10^8 \text{ m/s}} = 10^4 \text{ seconds}$$

Order of magnitude: 10^4 seconds

Units and Equations

In mathematical manipulations, units behave like algebraic quantities. In any physical equation, the units on each side must be equivalent.

A proportionality represents a ratio and can be written as an equation by inserting the proper proportionality constant, k. Care should be taken to associate the proper units with the proportionality constant, so that the units on each side of the equation will be equivalent.

Relationships and equations:

(1) direct linear relations, $y = kx$;
(2) direct square relations, $y = kx^2$;
(3) inverse relations, $y = k/x$; and
(4) inverse square relations, $y = k/x^2$.

Graphing

Graphs should be used to illustrate physical relationships. A line representing the relationship should be smooth and probably will not pass through all measured points. Error bars may be used to indicate their uncertainty. The dependent variable is generally placed on the vertical axis coordinate.

Appendix II — Physics Reference Tables and Summary of Physics Equations

Reference Tables for Physics

LIST OF PHYSICAL CONSTANTS		
Name	Symbol	Value(s)
Gravitational constant	G	6.7×10^{-11} N · m²/kg²
Acceleration due to gravity (up to 16 km altitude)	g	9.8 m/s²
Speed of light in a vacuum	c	3.0×10^8 m/s
Speed of sound at STP		3.3×10^2 m/s
Mass-energy relationship		1 u (amu) = 9.3×10^2 MeV
Mass of the earth		6.0×10^{24} kg
Mass of the moon		7.4×10^{22} kg
Mean radius of the earth		6.4×10^6 m
Mean radius of the moon		1.7×10^6 m
Mean distance from earth to moon		3.8×10^8 m
Electrostatic constant	k	9.0×10^9 N · m²/C²
Charge of the electron (1 elementary charge)		1.6×10^{-19} C
One coulomb	C	6.3×10^{18} elementary charges
Electronvolt	eV	1.6×10^{-19} J
Planck's constant	h	6.6×10^{-34} J · s
Rest mass of the electron	m_e	9.1×10^{-31} kg
Rest mass of the proton	m_p	1.7×10^{-27} kg
Rest mass of the neutron	m_n	1.7×10^{-27} kg

ABSOLUTE INDICES OF REFRACTION	
($\lambda = 5.9 \times 10^{-7}$ m)	
Air	1.00
Alcohol	1.36
Canada Balsam	1.53
Corn Oil	1.47
Diamond	2.42
Glass, Crown	1.52
Glass, Flint	1.61
Glycerol	1.47
Lucite	1.50
Quartz, Fused	1.46
Water	1.33

WAVELENGTHS OF LIGHT IN A VACUUM	
Violet	$4.0 - 4.2 \times 10^{-7}$ m
Blue	$4.2 - 4.9 \times 10^{-7}$ m
Green	$4.9 - 5.7 \times 10^{-7}$ m
Yellow	$5.7 - 5.9 \times 10^{-7}$ m
Orange	$5.9 - 6.5 \times 10^{-7}$ m
Red	$6.5 - 7.0 \times 10^{-7}$ m

HEAT CONSTANTS

	Specific Heat (average) (kJ/kg · C°)	Melting Point (°C)	Boiling Point (°C)	Heat of Fusion (kJ/kg)	Heat of Vaporization (kJ/kg)
Alcohol (ethyl)	2.43 (liq.)	−117	79	109	855
Aluminum	0.90 (sol.)	660	2467	396	10500
Ammonia	4.71 (liq.)	−78	−33	332	1370
Copper	0.39 (sol.)	1083	2567	205	4790
Iron	0.45 (sol.)	1535	2750	267	6290
Lead	0.13 (sol.)	328	1740	25	866
Mercury	0.14 (liq.)	−39	357	11	295
Platinum	0.13 (sol.)	1772	3827	101	229
Silver	0.24 (sol.)	962	2212	105	2370
Tungsten	0.13 (sol.)	3410	5660	192	4350
Water ice	2.05 (sol.)	0	—	334	—
Water water	4.19 (liq.)	—	100	—	2260
Water steam	2.01 (gas)	—	—	—	—
Zinc	0.39 (sol.)	420	907	113	1770

VALUES OF TRIGONOMETRIC FUNCTIONS

Angle	Sine	Cosine	Angle	Sine	Cosine
1°	.0175	.9998	46°	.7193	.6947
2°	.0349	.9994	47°	.7314	.6820
3°	.0523	.9986	48°	.7431	.6691
4°	.0698	.9976	49°	.7547	.6561
5°	.0872	.9962	50°	.7660	.6428
6°	.1045	.9945	51°	.7771	.6293
7°	.1219	.9925	52°	.7880	.6157
8°	.1392	.9903	53°	.7986	.6018
9°	.1564	.9877	54°	.8090	.5878
10°	.1736	.9848	55°	.8192	.5736
11°	.1908	.9816	56°	.8290	.5592
12°	.2079	.9781	57°	.8387	.5446
13°	.2250	.9744	58°	.8480	.5299
14°	.2419	.9703	59°	.8572	.5150
15°	.2588	.9659	60°	.8660	.5000
16°	.2756	.9613	61°	.8746	.4848
17°	.2924	.9563	62°	.8829	.4695
18°	.3090	.9511	63°	.8910	.4540
19°	.3256	.9455	64°	.8988	.4384
20°	.3420	.9397	65°	.9063	.4226
21°	.3584	.9336	66°	.9135	.4067
22°	.3746	.9272	67°	.9205	.3907
23°	.3907	.9205	68°	.9272	.3746
24°	.4067	.9135	69°	.9336	.3584
25°	.4226	.9063	70°	.9397	.3420
26°	.4384	.8988	71°	.9455	.3256
27°	.4540	.8910	72°	.9511	.3090
28°	.4695	.8829	73°	.9563	.2924
29°	.4848	.8746	74°	.9613	.2756
30°	.5000	.8660	75°	.9659	.2588
31°	.5150	.8572	76°	.9703	.2419
32°	.5299	.8480	77°	.9744	.2250
33°	.5446	.8387	78°	.9781	.2079
34°	.5592	.8290	79°	.9816	.1908
35°	.5736	.8192	80°	.9848	.1736
36°	.5878	.8090	81°	.9877	.1564
37°	.6018	.7986	82°	.9903	.1392
38°	.6157	.7880	83°	.9925	.1219
39°	.6293	.7771	84°	.9945	.1045
40°	.6428	.7660	85°	.9962	.0872
41°	.6561	.7547	86°	.9976	.0698
42°	.6691	.7431	87°	.9986	.0523
43°	.6820	.7314	88°	.9994	.0349
44°	.6947	.7193	89°	.9998	.0175
45°	.7071	.7071	90°	1.0000	.0000

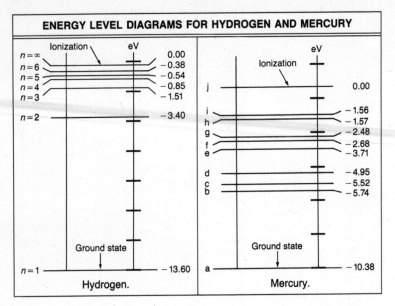

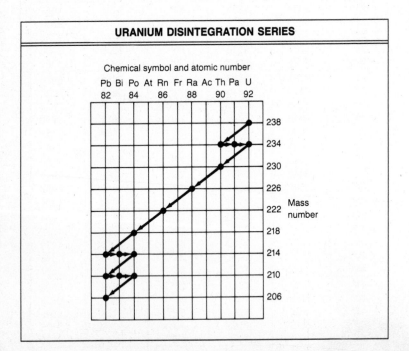

Summary of Equations

MECHANICS	
$\bar{v} = \dfrac{\Delta s}{\Delta t}$	a = acceleration
	F = force
$\bar{a} = \dfrac{\Delta v}{\Delta t}$	g = acceleration due to gravity
	G = universal gravitation constant
	J = impulse
$\bar{v} = \dfrac{v_f + v_i}{2}$	m = mass
	p = momentum
	r = distance between centers
$\Delta s = v_i \Delta t + \frac{1}{2} a (\Delta t)^2$	Δs = displacement
$v_f^2 = v_i^2 + 2a\Delta s$	t = time
	v = velocity
$F = ma$	w = weight
$F = \dfrac{G m_1 m_2}{r^2}$	
$w = mg$	
$p = mv$	
$J = F\Delta t$	
$F\Delta t = m\Delta v$	

ENERGY	
$W = F\Delta s$	F = force
	g = acceleration due to gravity
$P = \dfrac{W}{\Delta t} = \dfrac{F\Delta s}{\Delta t} = F\bar{v}$	h = height
	k = spring constant
$\Delta PE = mg\Delta h$	KE = kinetic energy
	m = mass
$F = kx$	P = power
$PE_s = \frac{1}{2}kx^2$	PE = potential energy
	PE_s = potential energy stored in a spring
$KE = \frac{1}{2}mv^2$	Δs = displacement
	t = time
	v = velocity
	W = work
	x = change in spring length from the equilibrium position

ELECTRICITY AND MAGNETISM

$$F = k\frac{q_1 q_2}{r^2}$$

$$E = \frac{F}{q}$$

$$V = \frac{W}{q}$$

$$E = \frac{V}{d}$$

$$I = \frac{\Delta q}{\Delta t}$$

$$R = \frac{V}{I}$$

$$P = VI = I^2 R = \frac{V^2}{R}$$

$$W = Pt = VIt = I^2 Rt$$

d = separation of parallel plates
E = electric field intensity
F = force
I = current
k = electrostatic constant
P = power
q = charge
r = distance between centers
R = resistance
t = time
V = electric potential difference
W = energy

Series Circuits:

$$I_t = I_1 = I_2 = I_3 = \cdots$$

$$V_t = V_1 + V_2 + V_3 + \cdots$$

$$R_t = R_1 + R_2 + R_3 + \cdots$$

Parallel Circuits:

$$I_t = I_1 + I_2 + I_3 + \cdots$$

$$V_t = V_1 = V_2 = V_3 = \cdots$$

$$\frac{1}{R_t} = \frac{1}{R_1} + \frac{1}{R_2} + \frac{1}{R_3} + \cdots$$

WAVE PHENOMENA

$$T = \frac{1}{f}$$

$$v = f\lambda$$

$$n = \frac{c}{v}$$

$$n_1 v_1 = n_2 v_2$$

$$n_1 \sin \theta_1 = n_2 \sin \theta_2$$

$$\sin \theta_c = \frac{1}{n}$$

$$\frac{\lambda}{d} = \frac{x}{L}$$

c = speed of light in a vacuum
d = distance between slits
f = frequency
L = distance from slit to screen
n = index of absolute refraction
T = period
v = speed
x = distance from central maximum to first-order maximum
λ = wavelength
θ = angle
θ_c = critical angle of incidence relative to air

MODERN PHYSICS

$$E_{photon} = hf$$

$$KE_{max} = hf - W_o$$

$$W_o = hf_o$$

$$p = \frac{h}{\lambda}$$

$$E_{photon} = E_i - E_f$$

E = energy
f = frequency
f_o = threshold frequency
h = Planck's constant
KE = kinetic energy
p = momentum
W_o = work function
λ = wavelength

MOTION IN A PLANE

$$v_{ix} = v_i \cos \theta$$

$$v_{iy} = v_i \sin \theta$$

$$a_c = \frac{v^2}{r}$$

$$F_c = \frac{mv^2}{r}$$

a_c = centripetal acceleration
F_c = centripetal force
m = mass
r = radius
v = velocity
θ = angle

INTERNAL ENERGY

$Q = mc\Delta T_C$

$Q_f = mH_f$

$Q_v = mH_v$

c = specific heat
H_f = heat of fusion
H_v = heat of vaporization

m = mass
Q = amount of heat
T_C = Celsius temperature

ELECTROMAGNETIC APPLICATIONS

$F = qvB$

$V = B\ell v$

$\dfrac{N_p}{N_s} = \dfrac{V_p}{V_s}$

$V_p I_p = V_s I_s$
(ideal)

% efficiency $= \dfrac{V_s I_s}{V_p I_p} \times 100$

B = flux density
F = force
I_p = current in primary coil
I_s = current in secondary coil
ℓ = length of conductor
N_p = number of turns of
      primary coil
N_s = number of turns of
      secondary coil
q = charge
v = velocity
V_p = voltage of primary coil
V_s = voltage of secondary coil
V = electric potential

GEOMETRIC OPTICS

$\dfrac{1}{d_o} + \dfrac{1}{d_i} = \dfrac{1}{f}$

$\dfrac{S_o}{S_i} = \dfrac{d_o}{d_i}$

d_i = image distance
d_o = object distance
f = focal length
S_i = image size
S_o = object size

NUCLEAR ENERGY

$E = mc^2$

$m_f = \dfrac{m_i}{2^n}$

c = speed of light in a vacuum
E = energy
m = mass
n = number of half-lives

Appendix III   Problem Solving

Problem solving is one of the major themes of Regents physics. Learning how to organize information is an important first step in acquiring this skill. The following procedure may prove helpful in solving free-response questions:

1. Read the problem carefully.

2. Re-read the problem to make certain you understand what is being asked.

3. Make a sketch of the situation described in the problem.

4. Include on the sketch all values of quantities given in the statement of the problem. To save time and space, use symbols to represent quantities and be sure to include the correct units with numbers. (A speed of 10.0 meters per second can be written as $v = 10.0$ m/s.)

5. Include on your sketch quantities that can be inferred from the statement of the problem. (If the problem states that "an object falls freely from rest near the surface of the earth," it can be inferred that $a = 9.8$ m/s^2 and $v_i = 0$ m/s.)

6. Use the proper symbol for the quantity being sought.

7. Refer to the Reference Tables for Physics to help decide which formulas are relevant to solving the problem.

8. Solve the appropriate formula(s) for the variable in question before substituting in values.

9. Substitute into the formula(s) known values along with their correct units. Expressing derived units in terms of fundamental units will help you determine if the answer has the correct unit.

10. Do the calculations and simplify the units, paying particular attention to exponents. Show all your work so that you can go back over the work as a final check.

11. Check the accuracy of your work and the reasonableness of your answer. Be on the lookout for answers that are not physically possible. (For example, a particle cannot have a velocity greater than 3.0×10^8 m/s.)

The College Board Physics
Achievement Test

Description of the Achievement Test

The Achievement Test in Physics is a carefully prepared test designed to evaluate student mastery of content of the typical high school physics course. The test takes one hour and consists of 75 questions that represent a sample of the many concepts covered in high school physics.

All of the questions are multiple-choice questions. You should read all of the choices carefully, for although one choice may be correct, another choice may be better since it may include additional correct choices. The maximum "raw score" is 75 if all questions are answered correctly. If 60 questions are answered correctly and you do not answer any of the other 15, your score will be 60. However, there is a ¼-point penalty for wrong answers. The formula used to calculate the "raw score" is:

$$\text{"raw score"} = \text{number correct} - \frac{\text{number wrong}}{4}$$

For example, if you answer 60 questions correctly, leave 11 unanswered, and answer 4 incorrectly, your raw score will be

$$60 - \frac{4}{4} = 60 - 1 = 59$$

There is no penalty for unanswered questions. Therefore, if you have NO knowledge of any of the choices offered, DO NOT GUESS. However, if you are certain that one or more choices can be eliminated, then it is worth guessing at one of the other choices.

The "raw score" is converted to a College Board score, ranging from 200 to 800, which is the score reported to you and to colleges. Conversion formulas vary from test to test. A typical conversion table published by the test preparers shows some of the conversions: raw scores 71 to 75 were all graded as 800; 56 and 57 were 710; 34 and 35 were 580; 16 and 17 were 470; 1 and 2 were graded as 380. These College Board scores are based on the mathematical theory of statistics and are interpreted on the basis of distribution of abilities among large populations.

The topics covered and the percentage of questions allotted to each are: Mechanics, 40%; Electricity and Magnetism, 20%; Optics and Waves, 20%; Heat, Kinetic Theory, and Thermodynamics, 10%; Modern Physics, 10%. Some questions overlap and require knowledge of several of these topics. Questions may also be classified as information recall, 20–33%; single concept, 40–53%; multiple concept, 20–33%.

The questions are not grouped according to any topical arrangement, but follow an irregular sequence. They also vary in degree of difficulty. It is a good idea to scan the questions rapidly and answer first those that seem easy. You might also wish to answer questions covering one topic at a time. That is, answer all mechanics questions first, then all electricity and magnetism, and so on. Remember not to be upset if you leave some questions unanswered; the scoring methods compensate for that.

In the preparation of test items, the College Board committee expects the student to have the ability to: (a) apply physical principles to specific situations, (b) answer questions based on laboratory data, (c) interpret results obtained by experimentation or observation, (d) answer word problems, and (e) analyze data displayed in the form of graphs. To answer the questions, only simple algebraic and trigonometric relations are required, and numerical calculations are limited to simple arithmetic.

Preparing for the Achievement Test

The listing of the content for the College Board Achievement Test includes some areas of physics that are lightly covered in schools in various parts of the country. This section will review and summarize those areas of physics and supply typical questions.

Satellite Orbits

All types of orbital paths obey Newton's laws of motion and the law of universal gravitation, but usually only circular paths are considered. Satellites in such orbit have constant speed, but since they are always changing their direction, they are accelerating. The accelerating force and direction are always at right angles to the velocity direction, which is tangent to the orbit at the point where the satellite is located at that instant.

The magnitude of the accelerating force is inversely proportional to the square of the satellite distance from the earth's center:

$$F = \frac{k}{r^2}$$

F is the gravitational force exerted by the earth on the satellite and r is the distance of the satellite from the earth's center. The constant k may be calculated from the mass of the earth and G, the universal gravitational constant.

Similarly, the acceleration magnitude is

$$a = \frac{k'}{r^2}$$

On the surface of the earth, a is the same as g. Thus, the magnitude of the gravitational acceleration is inversely proportional to the square of the distance of the earth's center to the object in space. Figure 1 (see the following page) illustrates this.

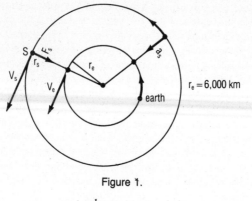

Figure 1.

$$a_s = \frac{k}{r_s^2}$$

$$F_s = m_s a_s = m_s g_s$$

a_s or g_s = gravitational acceleration

For a satellite at distance r_s,

$$\frac{g_s}{g} = \frac{r_e^2}{r_s^2} = \left(\frac{r_e}{r_s}\right)^2$$

A satellite may orbit the earth yet seem to be stationary. This occurs if the satellite's orbit is in the plane of the earth's equator and if its period of revolution about the earth is the same as the earth's rotation about its axis—23 hours and 56.07 minutes. Communication satellites for network television broadcasts are one such application of so-called "stationary" orbits. Calculation of r_s is not difficult and may be obtained by using the formulas of kinematics together with the above dynamics.

Inside a manned satellite, the astronauts are not weightless. They are under the same acceleration as the satellite itself and their weight is ma_s or mg_s, which may be found from their mass and the acceleration of the satellite. They are said to be "weightless" because they are falling to earth with the same acceleration as the satellite, and they also are in free fall. Similarly, a person standing on a scale in a free-falling elevator has zero weight if the acceleration of the elevator and of the person and scale are all equal to the downward acceleration, g, of objects on the earth.

Planetary motions of the celestial bodies are analogous to those of the satellite orbits, but in these cases the sun, not the earth, is the source of the gravitational forces.

SAMPLE QUESTIONS

1. An astronaut weighs 800 newtons on earth. What is the astronaut's weight (not apparent weight) in a satellite 12,000 kilometers from the earth's center? (The earth's center is 6,000 kilometers from the sur-

face.) (A) **3,200 newtons** (B) **1,600 newtons** (C) **800 newtons** (D) **400 newtons** (E) **200 newtons**

2. **A person on the surface of the earth is moving about the earth's center as it turns. An astronaut in stationary orbit has (A) the same speed (B) the same period of revolution (C) the same acceleration (D) the same gravitational force (E) the same distance traveled per day**

3. **Two stars in space isolated from other masses have masses m and $2m$. The force on the greater mass is F when they are s meters apart. If the separation distance increases to $2s$, the force on the greater mass will be (A) $F/2$ (B) $F/4$ (C) $F/8$ (D) $F/16$ (E) $F/32$**

Simple Harmonic Motion

A body is said to be in simple harmonic motion if the following are true:

• It moves in a straight line.
• A variable force acts on it.
• The magnitude of the force is proportional to the displacement of the mass.
• The force is always opposite in direction to the displacement direction.
• The motion is repetitive and a round trip, back and forth, is always made in equal time periods.

An example of such motion is that of a mass attached to a fixed spring on a frictionless surface moving after the spring is compressed and then released, as shown in Figure 2.

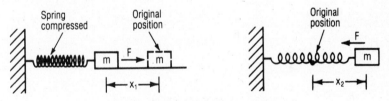

$x_1 = x_2 = $ maximum displacement = amplitude

Figure 2.

The equation describing the magnitude and direction of the force is

$$F = -kx$$

where x is the displacement vector and k is a constant for the particular spring, obtained experimentally in terms of newtons per meter. The negative sign indicates the opposing directions of force and displacement. The time it takes to complete a passage from starting point back to starting point, T, is called the *period*. T is proportional to the square root of the mass in motion under the influence of the forces; it is also inversely proportional to the square root of the force constant k. The complete equation for the period T is:

$$T = 2\pi\sqrt{\frac{m}{k}}$$

From examination of the two equations, the following inferences may be made:

- If the displacement is changed by a factor n, then the forces change by the same factor n.
- The period T is independent of the maximum displacement, since x does not appear in the formula for T.
- Since acceleration is proportional to force, the magnitude of the acceleration is a maximum when the displacement is a maximum, and the acceleration is zero when the object is located at its initial equilibrium position (midway between extremes of position).
- Speed is maximum when $a = 0$ and minimum when a is maximum.

The to and fro motion of a mass suspended by a string is an additional example of simple harmonic motion (if the maximum displacement is small compared to the length of the string). Figure 3 illustrates some terms associated with the pendulum.

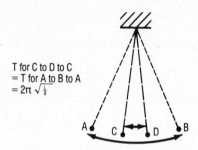

T for C to D to C
= T for A to B to A
= $2\pi \sqrt{\frac{L}{g}}$

Figure 3.

The equation for the period T is:

$$T = 2\pi\sqrt{\frac{L}{g}}$$

where L represents the length of the pendulum and g is the magnitude of gravitational acceleration at the place where the experiment is performed. Since neither the mass of the pendulum bob nor the magnitude of displacement appears in the equation for T, the period is independent of these.

The motion of particles that make up the wave form of a wave is also simple harmonic motion. Figure 4 illustrates the relationship between the different particles, their individual displacements from the horizontal equilibrium position, and how they vary in position at various times. The forces that are responsible for the motion are those generated in the medium.

The unbroken line shows the wave in an initial position. An instant later, the crest of the wave is at the right, particle c has moved to c', and particle b has moved down to b'. The whole wave has been displaced to the right, but each particle has moved up or down.

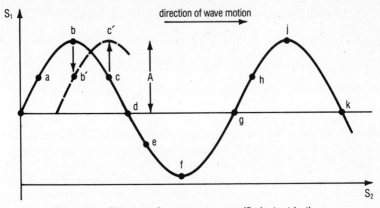

Figure 4.   Diagram of a wave at a specific instant in time.

SAMPLE QUESTIONS

1. A particular pendulum has a period of 1.000 second at sea level. When taken down into a deep valley, the period is found to be different from 1.000 second. In its new location, the period can be made 1.000 second again by (A) increasing the mass of the bob (B) decreasing the mass of the bob (C) changing the amplitude of the swing (D) increasing the length of the string (E) decreasing the length of the string

2. The wave shown in Figure 4 on page 365 is moving toward the right. Which pair of points on the wave form have vertical displacements that are the same but are moving in opposite directions? (A) a, c (B) a, h (C) b, f (D) b, g (E) e, c

3. A mass, m, of a spring-mass system is moving in simple harmonic motion with a period of t seconds. A different mass equal to $9m$ is substituted for mass m. The new period is (A) unchanged (B) $9t$ (C) $3t$ (D) $t/3$ (E) $t/9$

Summary of Gas Laws

Experimental study of the relations between the volume V, pressure P, and absolute temperature (Kelvin scale) of gases resulted in this general gas law: $PV = kT$. The symbol k represents a constant that depends on the mass of gas used. If one of the three variables is held constant then this law may be rewritten as three relations: (A) PV = constant, providing the temperature is unchanged. (B) $V = k_1T$, provided the pressure is unchanged. (C) $P = k_2T$, provided the volume is unchanged. The constants in each equation are different. These relations may be expressed as proportions, according to the usual mathematical procedures. They may then be rewritten as:

$$A': \quad P_1V_1 = P_2V_2 \quad \text{at constant } T$$

B′: $\dfrac{P_1}{T_1} = \dfrac{P_2}{T_2}$ at constant V

C′: $\dfrac{V_1}{T_1} = \dfrac{V_2}{T_2}$ at constant pressure

Only the Kelvin scale may be used in the above formulas ($K° = C° + 273$). The Kinetic Molecular Theory further clarifies the concept of temperature. The molecules of a gas are in random motion with various average speeds. However, if one determines the average of all the individual molecular speeds and converts these to an average molecular kinetic energy, the average molecular kinetic energy is directly proportional to the Kelvin temperature of the gas: *Average $E_k \propto T$*. The theory further indicates that the sum of all the average kinetic energies of all of the molecules is equal to the total internal energy that is transferable as heat under appropriate conditions. Since some of the molecular energies are not due to kinetic energy, not all of the internal energy may be transferred as heat. The pressure of a gas is due to the cumulative effect of molecular collisions against the walls of the container.

First and Second Laws of Thermodynamics

The First Law of Thermodynamics. This is a restatement of the law of conservation of energy. It includes thermal energy as part of the total internal energy of a system. It states that the change in internal energy of a system must be equal to the algebraic sum of the changes in work and in heat energy. Thus, if X joules of work are added to a system and Y joules of heat are removed from the system, then $X - Y$ joules of energy is the internal energy change. If E is the change in internal energy of a system, Q is the heat energy change, and W is the work done by the system, then $E = Q - W$.

The Second Law of Thermodynamics. When two containers at different temperatures are in contact and the hotter one loses 10 joules of energy, then the colder one will have gained 10 joules of energy. This is in harmony with the energy conservation law. On the other hand, if the colder container spontaneously transferred 10 joules of energy to the hotter one, the latter would gain 10 joules and become hotter. This is not a violation of the law of conservation of energy, but it never happens.

The second law of thermodynamics covers such phenomena. The law may be stated in many forms, but it is presented here in one of its readily understandable forms. The second law states that isolated systems tend to arrange themselves spontaneously so as to manifest the greatest state of disorder. The mathematics of random motion proves that for the same average speed of a system of molecules there may exist many velocity ranges between minimum and maximum speeds. The most probable distribution, however, is that range with the greatest difference between least and greatest speeds. This is also the greatest disorderly arrangement. It turns out that the transfer of kinetic energies from a hot mass to a cold one involves a final state of greater disorder than the converse energy transfer. That is the reason for the unidirectional nature of spontaneous heat transfer. It also explains the many changes that occur in nature, such as disintegration of structures, and the difficulty in keeping one's room neat.

SAMPLE QUESTIONS

1. Two identical gases are in two cylinders at the same temperature, pressure, and volume. Cylinder A has a piston free to move and cylinder B has a fixed piston. Q joules of heat energy are transferred to each. The piston of cylinder A rises; the piston of cylinder B is stationary. Which of the following statements is true? (A) The pressure of gas A is the greater. (B) The internal energy and volume of B are greater. (C) The pressure of gas A equals the pressure of gas B. (D) The internal energy and temperature of A are greater. (E) The pressure, internal energy, and temperature of B are greater.

2. A container with unknown contents has 20 joules of energy supplied to it during a compression and simultaneously 5 joules of energy leaves it as heat. The change of internal energy of the system is (A) indeterminate (B) 25 joules (C) 20 joules (D) 15 joules (E) 5 joules

3. Five samples of a gas are at the same temperature, with the average speed of their molecules being $10v$. They are isolated so that no temperature change occurs. The velocity ranges of the individual molecules vary between the following ranges: Gas 1, $9v$ to $11v$; Gas 2, $8v$ to $12v$; Gas 3, $7v$ to $13v$; Gas 4, $6v$ to $14v$; Gas 5, $5v$ to $15v$. After a lapse of time, which range of speeds will all 5 samples most likely resemble? (A) $9v$ to $11v$ (B) $8v$ to $12v$ (C) $7v$ to $13v$ (D) $6v$ to $14v$ (E) $5v$ to $15v$

Relativity Theory

Albert Einstein developed the relativity theory because of limitations of the older Newtonian classical laws. The newer theory has changed our way of thinking about time, energy, mass, velocity, and field theory. The most dramatic changes, that everyone has been exposed to, deal with mass, energy and velocity relations.

It had been observed experimentally, even by engineers unacquainted with the theory, that calculations involving predicted times of arrival of electrons from one point to another in a vacuum did not agree with experimental times. The calculations do agree, however, if increase of mass with velocity is taken into account. The change of mass is due to conversion of kinetic energy to mass. The relation deduced by Einstein established a direct proportion between mass and energy in the form of the constant c^2, where c represents the known speed of light in a vacuum. Algebraically the formula is

$$\Delta E = c^2 \Delta m$$

where E is expressed in joules, m is expressed in kilograms, and c equals 10^8 meters per second.

In ordinary experiments the change in mass that occurs when bodies are accelerated is too small to be measured. However, when velocities are approaching about 10% that of light, the effects become appreciable. This is especially true of electrons in vacuum tubes, such as in television picture tubes, oscilloscopes, and particle accelerators. The older mechanics is still valid for small velocities and is considered a limiting case.

In problems involving velocities where the relativity theory must be used, we must differentiate between the mass of a body at rest, m_0, and its variable mass when in motion, m. The relativistic equation relating the two is

$$m = \frac{m_0}{\sqrt{1 - \dfrac{v^2}{c^2}}}$$

At ordinary speeds, v is small, v^2/c^2 is practically zero, and m is the same as m_0.

Similarly, kinetic energy has to be redefined. KE is not $mv^2/2$ at high speeds, but

$$KE = (m - m_0)\, c^2 \text{ or } KE = c^2\, \Delta m$$

where m is calculated by the relativistic equation given above. At small velocities, the kinetic equation approaches the Newtonian equation:

$$KE = \frac{1}{2}\, mv^2$$

The concept of energy transformation into mass includes forms of energy other than kinetic energy. The transfer of heat, magnetic, or electric energy to a mass will also increase the mass of the body, but these increases are generally too small to have any perceptible effect under ordinary conditions. The laws of energy conservation and mass conservation must now be modified and combined into a statement that covers the relativistic changes. The relations must include the changes in mass and energy involved by making use of the energy-mass conversion factor, $\Delta E = c^2 \Delta m$.

SAMPLE QUESTIONS

1. **Three different masses—I, II, and III—are each moving with the same speed at 90% of the speed of light. The kinetic energy of I is 100 J, of II is 1,000 J, and of III is 10,000 J. Each receives an increase in energy so they are now traveling with kinetic energies of 110 J, 1,010 J and 10,010 J. The change in mass had which of the following relationships? (A) III greater than II greater than I (B) I greater than II greater than III (C) I = II smaller than III (D) I smaller than II = III (E) I = II = III**

2. **The photon is considered a particle of varying discrete energies having zero mass and traveling at the speed of light. When a photon passes close to a huge celestial mass, which of the following may occur? (A) It**

will be attracted. (B) It will be captured. (C) It will be repelled. (D) It will not be affected. (E) It will be slowed down.

3. Base your answer to this question on the relation between the mass of a moving particle and its rest mass:

$$m = \frac{m_0}{\sqrt{1 - \dfrac{v^2}{c^2}}}$$

As a particle approaches the speed of light c, (A) m is constant (B) m becomes equal to m_0 (C) m becomes smaller than m_0 (D) m approaches infinity (E) m may take on negative values

Practice Test for the College Board Physics Achievement Test

Directions: For each of questions 1 to 75, choose one of the letters (A) to (E) as the answer. You are allowed 75 minutes for the test.

1. Which of these fields may be used to accelerate a charged particle that is initially at rest?

(I) electric field
(II) magnetic field
(III) gravitational field

The correct answer is (A) I (B) II (C) III (D) I and II (E) I and III

2. Which of the following is known to exist in the form of a minimum unit magnitude?

(I) mass
(II) electric charge
(III) energy

The correct answer is (A) I (B) II (C) III (D) I and II (E) I, II, and III

3. An astronaut who weighs 700 newtons on earth steps on a scale while in circular orbit in a satellite. Select the correct statement. (A) The scale reads zero because there is no gravitational force acting on the astronaut. (B) The scale reads zero because both scale and astronaut travel with the same speed. (C) The scale reads zero because both satellite and astronaut are traveling with the same acceleration. (D) The scale reads zero because the scale and astronaut have equal forces acting on them. (E) The scale displays a non-zero reading.

4. Any of the following is evidence that an unbalanced force is acting on a mass EXCEPT a change of (A) momentum (B) kinetic energy (C) velocity (D) position (E) direction of motion

5. Which of these particles has the greatest mass? (A) alpha particle (B) beta particle (C) proton (D) photon (E) hydrogen molecule

Questions 6–8 refer to the graphs below, showing speed versus time. For each question, choose an answer from the following list.

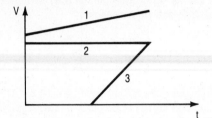

(A) Graph 1
(B) Graph 2
(C) Graph 3
(D) Graphs 1 and 2
(E) Graphs 1 and 3

6. Which show(s) acceleration?
7. Which show(s) a condition of rest at some time?
8. Which show(s) the greatest distance traveled?
9. A person weighing 800 newtons steps on a platform scale, picks up a cane weighing 10 newtons, and presses the cane down on the platform of the scale with a force of 20 newtons. The scale will read (A) 790 newtons (B) 800 newtons (C) 810 newtons (D) 820 newtons (E) 830 newtons
10. Ionized atoms often become neutral atoms by means of the
 (I) capture of a proton
 (II) loss of a proton
(III) capture of an electron.
The correct answer is (A) I (B) II (C) III (D) either I or II (E) either I or III
11. In the circuit diagram below, voltmeter V reads 6 volts and the resistance of R is 2 ohms. The power is (A) 6 watts (B) 18 watts (C) 30 watts (D) 60 watts (E) 120 watts

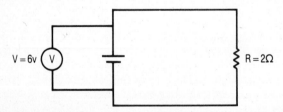

12. A wave has a length of 0.5 meter. It passes a given point at a speed of 40 meters per second. The frequency of the wave, in hertz, is (A) ⅟₈₀ (B) 2 (C) 20 (D) 40 (E) 80
13. The index of refraction of a medium provides information about a wave's (A) frequency (B) amplitude (C) speed (D) frequency and amplitude (E) frequency and speed
14. Each of the following is an energy unit EXCEPT (A) kilogram-meter (B) newton-meter (C) kilowatt-hour (D) kilocalorie (E) electronvolt

15. Three vectors are shown representing the forces on a mass. Which set(s) indicate that the mass is being accelerated? (A) I (B) II (C) III (D) I and II (E) I, II, and III

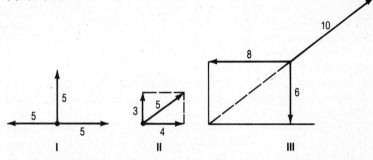

16. In the study of mechanics the symbol G bears the same relation to mass as the symbol k in electricity relates to (A) current (B) voltage (C) electric field (D) charge (E) resistance

17. Which of the elementary particles cannot be accelerated? (A) ion (B) photon (C) proton (D) electron (E) neutron

Questions 18 and 19 refer to the diagram below, which indicates a positively charged particle suspended motionless in a vacuum between two charged plates.

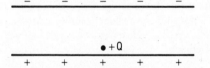

18. From this diagram, one may conclude that (A) a magnetic force must also be present (B) the gravitational field strength is equal to the electric field strength (C) the gravitational force is equal and opposite to the electric force on the particle (D) there is neither a gravitational force nor an electric force acting (E) the positive charge of the particle equals the magnitude of the mass of the particle

19. The identical experiment is repeated on a distant planet. The result will be (A) the particle will remain suspended (B) the particle will move up toward the negative plate (C) the particle will move down toward the positive plate (D) the particle will move down if the gravitational acceleration on the planet is smaller than that of the earth (E) the particle will move up if the gravitational acceleration on the planet is smaller than that of the earth

20. A proton in the region of a positive point charge will experience a force that is (A) constant and away from the source (B) constant and toward the source (C) variable and toward the source (D) variable and away from the source (E) perpendicular to the line joining proton and source

21. A mass has a positive charge of 20 coulombs. It is separated into two parts. The charges on the spheres may be which one of the following pairs? (A) 15+ and 5+ (B) 15− and 5− (C) 10− and 10− (D) 25− and 5+ (E) 20− and 0

22. Two identical spheres are in contact. The total charge on the pair is 20 coulombs positive. They are then separated. The pair that will experience the greatest force will be the pair that have the charges (A) 5+ and 5+ (B) 4+ and 6+ (C) 3− and 13+ (D) 2+ and 8+ (E) 12+ and 2−

23. A closed container contains a mass of ice floating in water, both at the same temperature. Some time later it is observed that the mass of ice has increased. The room temperature must have been (A) greater than 0°C (B) equal to 0°C (C) less than 0°C (D) less than 4°C (E) less than −4°C

24. All of the following are electromagnetic radiations. The longest waves are (A) radio waves (B) infrared rays (C) ultraviolet rays (D) gamma rays (E) neon sign illumination

25. Each of the following is a unit of power EXCEPT (A) joules per second (B) watt-seconds (C) volt-amperes (D) calories per second (E) newton-meters per second

26. An electron in an energy level about the nucleus of an atom has been raised to a higher energy level. The atom has (A) been ionized (B) been accelerated (C) released energy (D) undergone a nuclear reaction (E) been excited

27. When a photon strikes a metal surface, which one of the following occurs? (A) a possible emission of an ion (B) always an emission of an electron (C) sometimes an emission of a proton (D) sometimes an emission of an electron (E) capture of a photon by the nucleus of the atom

The following statement applies to questions 28 and 29.
The time, T, that it takes for a pendulum to make a complete oscillation is given by the formula $T = 2\pi\sqrt{L/g}$, where L is the length of the pendulum and g is the gravitational acceleration.

28. From this equation we may conclude that
 (I) doubling the length of the pendulum will double the oscillation time
 (II) the oscillation time T depends upon the mass of the pendulum
 (III) the oscillation time T will differ when the experiment is performed at street level compared to the same experiment performed at the top of a skyscraper
Select the correct answer. (A) I (B) II (C) III (D) I and II (E) I and III

29. The equation indicates that there is an inverse square relation between (A) T and L (B) T and g (C) L and g (D) T and L/g (E) T and $\sqrt{L/g}$

30. The circuit in the diagram below consists of a battery connected to two resistors—a resistor of r ohms and another resistor of R ohms. The combined resistance of the circuit is R_t. This may be calculated from (A) $R_t = r + R$ (B) $R_t = R − r$ (C) $R_t = r − R$ (D) $\dfrac{1}{R_t} = \dfrac{1}{r} + \dfrac{1}{R}$ (E) $R_t = \dfrac{1}{r} + \dfrac{1}{R}$

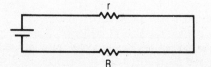

31. The greatest change in internal energy occurs when (A) ice becomes water (B) water becomes steam (C) steam becomes water (D) steam becomes ice (E) water becomes ice

32. A virtual image is produced by a lens. The lens (A) must be concave (B) must be convex (C) must be plane (D) may be either plane or concave (E) may be either plane, convex, or concave

33. In order to produce an exact dimensional duplicate of a postage stamp by means of a camera with a lens of two centimeters focal length, the distance of the object from the lens must be (A) greater than 2 centimeters (B) at 4 centimeters (C) at 2 centimeters (D) between 2 and 3 centimeters (E) less than 2 centimeters

34. The graph shown is that of a hyperbola. Which pair of variables will produce this curve? (A) speed versus time at constant acceleration (B) temperature versus time as ice melts (C) frequency versus wavelength of a light wave (D) force versus acceleration of a falling body (E) energy versus mass at speeds close to that of light

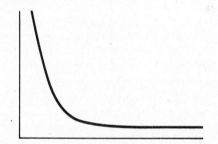

35. The graph indicates the displacement of a particle as time proceeds. The time scale is indicated in tenths of a second.

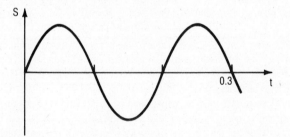

The frequency of the wave in hertz is (A) ½ (B) 1 (C) 2 (D) 5 (E) 10

36. The following are three physical relations between variables

$$\text{(I) } m = \frac{E}{c^2} \quad \text{(II) } V = IR \quad \text{(III) } F = k\,\frac{q_1 q_2}{r^2}$$

Which expresses an inverse square law? (A) I (B) II (C) III (D) I and II (E) I and III

37. An isolated system of charged particles in motion in a closed container is examined at different intervals. The only change that may be observed is in the total (A) mass (B) number of particles (C) charge (D) momentum (E) energy

38. The nucleus of an atom consists of 8 protons and 8 neutrons. It is converted into a nucleus with 9 protons and 7 neutrons. The new nucleus

 (I) is that of a different element

 (II) has a different atomic number

(III) is an isotope of the original element

The correct answer is (A) I (B) II (C) III (D) I and II (E) II and III

39. The circuit diagram below consists of two batteries and three resistors. There is a current of 4 amperes through one of them and a current of 1 ampere through the other in the directions shown. What is the current through the resistor R? (A) 1 ampere right to left (B) 3 amperes right to left (C) 3 amperes left to right (D) 5 amperes left to right (E) 5 amperes right to left

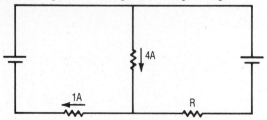

40. The excited atoms of a gas exist only in the third energy level above zero level, as shown in the diagram. How many possible radiation frequencies may be observed in the spectrum when the electrons return to the ground or zero state? (A) 1 (B) 3 (C) 5 (D) 6 (E) 7

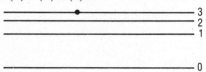

41. Two positive ions are r meters apart. One bears a charge of q and the other a charge of $3q$. The force on the smaller charged ion is F newtons. The force on the other is (A) $3F/r$ newtons (B) $3F/r^2$ newtons (C) $3F^2/r$ newtons (D) F newtons (E) r newtons

42. A car is seen in motion at point A and again at point C. Between A and C it is out of sight, but it is known that it has dropped a blob of paint every 5 seconds, illustrated in the diagram. From these markings one may conclude that (A) it travels at constant speed (B) it speeds up and then slows down (C) it slows down and then speeds up (D) it is accelerating at all times (E) it has stopped at some point between A and C

A • •• • • •   •   •   •   C

43. Which of these graphs describe the same motion?

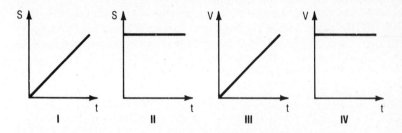

I   II   III   IV

(A) I and II (B) I and III (C) I and IV (D) II and III (E) II and IV

Questions 44 and 45 refer to the diagram below, which shows two tanks of water of unequal size but containing the same quantity of water. They are connected by means of a pipe with valve closed.

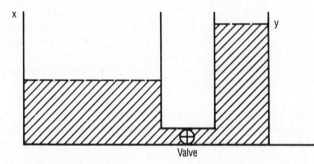

Valve

44. The valve is opened.
 (I) Water will flow from tank x to tank y.
 (II) Water will flow from tank y to tank x.
(III) No water will flow.
(IV) Water will flow until the weight of water is the same in each tank.
 (V) Water will flow until the level of water in each tank is the same.
Select the correct answer. (A) III (B) I and V (C) II and V (D) II and IV (E) III and V

45. After the valve has been opened and equilibrium has occurred
 (I) the potential energy of the system will have decreased
 (II) the potential energy of the system will have increased
(III) no change in potential energy will have occurred
(IV) there has been a small increase in temperature
 (V) there has been a small decrease in temperature
The correct answer is (A) I (B) II (C) III (D) I and IV (E) II and V

46. The graph is a plot of voltage across a resistor as the current is varied. The coordinates of the point *P* are known.

(I) The resistance may be calculated from the slope of the line.
(II) The power may be calculated from the area of the triangle formed.
(III) The temperature of the resistor did not affect the electrical characteristics of the circuit.

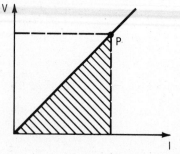

Select the correct answer. (A) I (B) II (C) III (D) I and II (E) I, II, and III

47. A sound wave and a radio wave have the same frequency and amplitude. They move together in the same direction. The effect will be (A) an interference pattern will be produced (B) only the sound wave will be changed in form (C) only the radio wave will be changed in form (D) they will interfere with one another only when traveling in the opposite directions (E) they will not affect one another

48. A single electrical component is sealed in a box with only the terminals exposed. It is found that a difference of potential of several volts exists between the terminals. The box most probably contains (A) a motor (B) a generator (C) a resistor (D) a capacitor (E) a coil of wire

49. The diagram shows two conductors near one another but not touching. One has a current of 2 amperes and the other a current of 3 amperes, in the directions shown. Select the true statement. (A) There is a force on *A* only. (B) There is a force on *B* only. (C) There is a force on each, but the force on *A* is greater. (D) There is a force on each, but the force on *B* is greater. (E) There is force on each of equal magnitude but in opposite directions.

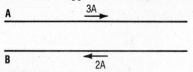

50. Electromagnetic radiation may be produced by

(I) an accelerating proton
(II) an electron having constant velocity
(III) an accelerating neutron

Select the correct answer. (A) I (B) II (C) III (D) I and II (E) I and III

51. A beam of light consisting of one color only strikes a metallic surface that then emits electrons. Which characteristic of the beam determines the maximum

kinetic energy of the emitted electrons? (A) brightness (B) photon velocity (C) wave amplitude (D) frequency (E) beam diameter

52. A gas is heated in a closed container. Which graph shows the correct relation between pressure and absolute temperature?

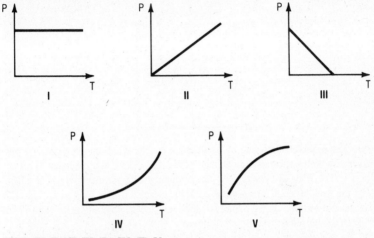

(A) I (B) II (C) III (D) IV (E) V

Questions 53–55 refer to the following information.

A marble from a spring gun is shot vertically from a rooftop while simultaneously an identical marble is shot horizontally from the same point with the same speed. Air resistance is negligible and g is constant. Select your answer from these statements. The same answer may be used in more than one response. (A) the marble that is shot vertically (B) the marble that is shot horizontally (C) they are the same (D) it depends on the magnitude of g (E) it depends upon the height of the roof

53. Which marble has the greater speed as it strikes the ground?

54. If the mass of each is doubled, which will strike the ground with greater kinetic energy?

55. Which will undergo a greater change in potential energy from the time it is shot until the time it strikes the ground?

56. A soloist performs in a concert hall. Sometimes a person farther away from the stage hears the sound louder than a person nearer the stage. This effect is caused by (A) sound velocity variations (B) effects of refraction (C) inverse square law of wave propagation (D) interference between incident and reflected waves (E) sound frequency variations

57. The half-life of a radioactive substance is 3 days. After 9 days the amount of radioactive material remaining from an original sample of 12 grams is (A) 3 grams (B) 4 grams (C) 6 grams (D) 1.5 grams (E) 0 grams

58. A source of monochromatic light is (A) the sun (B) a tungsten house lamp (C) a laser beam (D) an ultraviolet lamp (E) a neon sign

59. The diagram shows four positively charged masses situated at the corners of a square. q_1 has a charge of 1 micro-coulomb; q_2, two micro-coulombs; q_3, three micro-coulombs; and q_4, four micro-coulombs. The greatest resultant force will be experienced by (A) q_1 (B) q_2 (C) q_3 (D) q_4 (E) each will experience equal forces

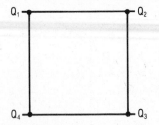

60. The index of refraction of a substance is 1.5. When an experiment is performed with the substance on another planet, it is found that the index of refraction is 1.4. This is because (A) the frequency of light changed at the planet (B) the gravitational forces were different there (C) there existed an optically denser atmosphere on the planet (D) there existed an optically rarer atmosphere there (E) the planet had no atmosphere

61. It is commonly observed that it is much easier to take apart a toy or an appliance than it is to put it together. This observation is made understandable by (A) the law of conservation of energy (B) the laws of motion (C) the law of universal gravitation (D) the second law of thermodynamics (E) the law of conservation of mass-energy

62. The diagram shows ray 1 incident perpendicularly to one side of an isosceles right-angled prism.

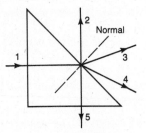

The ray or rays that can possibly emerge from the prism are (A) 2 and 3 (B) 2 and 4 (C) 2 and 5 (D) 3 and 4 (E) 4 and 5

63. A 10-kilogram mass is pulled along a horizontal rough surface by means of a force of 60 newtons acting horizontally. The acceleration produced is 5 meters per second squared. What is the force of friction? (A) 2 newtons (B) 6 newtons (C) 10 newtons (D) 12 newtons (E) 50 newtons

64. The potential difference between two points in an electric field is 3 volts. A mass with 0.5 coulombs of charge is transferred from one point to the other. The

energy change involved in the transfer is (A) 0.75 joules (B) 1.5 joules (C) 3.5 joules (D) 4.5 joules (E) 0.5/81 joules

65. Which of the following may be used to increase the frequency of vibration of a taut string? Increasing (A) the diameter of the string (B) the length of the string (C) the amplitude of displacement in plucking the string (D) the tension of the string (E) the mass of the string

Questions 66 and 67 refer to the diagram, which shows a capacitor, a switch, and a resistor connected in series. There is potential difference of V volts across the capacitor plates, switch S is open, and the resistance is R ohms.

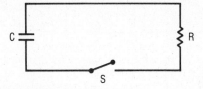

66.   (I) The voltage across R is zero.
   (II) The voltage across the switch terminals is zero.
   (III) The current is zero.
Select the correct answer. (A) I (B) II (C) III (D) I and II (E) I and III

67. Switch S is now closed until there is no charge on either plate of the capacitor. Select the correct statement. (A) A steady direct current will be present. (B) The temperature of R will increase slightly. (C) There will exist a potential difference between the plates of the capacitor. (D) No energy transfer has occurred. (E) There will be a potential difference between the terminals of the resistor.

68. An airplane is in level flight at constant velocity. Which set of vectors represents the forces acting on the plane?

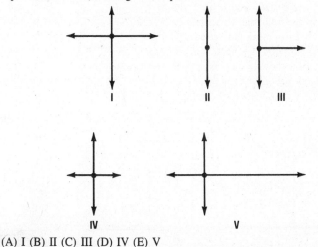

(A) I (B) II (C) III (D) IV (E) V

69. A force of constant magnitude is applied to a mass in uniform circular motion. There will be no change in any of the following EXCEPT (A) kinetic energy (B) speed (C) radius of orbit (D) magnitude of acceleration (E) momentum

70. A car is racing around a track, as shown, at constant speed.

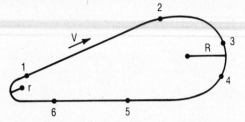

Between which two points is there the greatest acceleration? (A) 1 and 2 (B) 2 and 3 (C) 4 and 5 (D) 5 and 6 (E) 6 and 1

Questions 71 and 72 refer to the diagram, which shows a transverse wave moving to the right. Vertical displacement is plotted against horizontal distance.

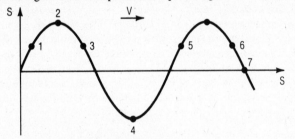

71. The pair of points on the waveform that are in phase are (A) 1 and 3 (B) 2 and 4 (C) 3 and 5 (D) 3 and 6 (E) 1 and 6

72. Which of the following statements is correct? (A) 3 and 5 are rising. (B) 7 is at rest. (C) 2 has maximum speed. (D) 1 and 5 move down with the same velocity. (E) No point is at rest.

73. The diagram shows a mass M, moving with constant speed v_1 over a frictionless mound, with speed v at the top and reaching the ground with speed v_2.

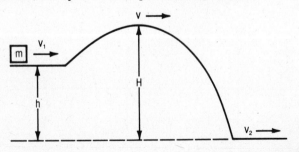

Select the correct answer. (A) ½ mv_1^2 is greater than ½ mv_2^2 (B) v is smaller than either v_1 or v_2 (C) $mgH = $ ½ mv_2^2 (D) ½ $v_1^2 + gh = $ ½ v_2^2 (E) both statements B and D

74. The half-life of a radioactive element (A) is constant (B) increases with increase in temperature (C) decreases with time (D) increases with pressure (E) changes when chemically combined with another radioactive element

75. Masses I and II are identical trapezoidal solids of the same uniform material in different positions. Each is then placed into position III.

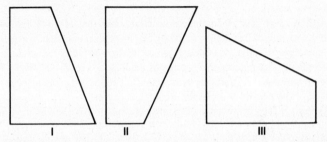

Which statement is correct? (A) There is no change of potential energy for either mass. (B) The decrease in potential energy of one mass equals the increase in potential energy of the other. (C) Each mass has the same decrease in potential energy. (D) Mass II has a greater decrease in potential energy than mass I has. (E) Mass I has a greater increase in potential energy than mass II has.

Glossary

absolute index of refraction: A property of optical substances equal to the ratio of the speed of light in a vacuum to the speed of light in the substance.

absolute temperature: A measure of the average kinetic energy of the molecules of a body.

absolute zero: The theoretical lower limit of temperature designated as 0 on the Kelvin scale.

absorption spectrum: A continuous spectrum, like that of white light, interrupted by dark lines that are produced by the absorption of certain wavelengths by a substance (often a gas) through which the light or other radiation passes.

acceleration: The time rate of change of velocity; a vector quantity.

acceptor material: A substance used as an additive to a semiconductor in order to increase the density of holes in the semiconductor.

alpha decay: The phenomenon of spontaneous ejection of a helium ion from an atomic nucleus.

alpha particle: A helium nucleus—a particle consisting of two protons and two neutrons.

alternating current: An electron flow in a circuit that changes rapidly many times per second in direction or magnitude.

ammeter: A device designed to measure electric current when connected in series in an electric circuit; a galvanometer with a low resistance connected in parallel with the galvanometer coil.

ampere: The fundamental *SI* unit of current, which is equal to one coulomb per second.

amplifier: Any device that increases the amplitude of a signal without appreciably changing its wave form.

amplitude: The magnitude of the maximum displacement of a vibrating field or maximum displacement of a particle from its rest position.

angle of incidence: The angle between a ray of light and the normal to the surface at the point where the ray strikes the surface.

angle of reflection: The angle between a ray of light that is reflected from a surface and the normal to that surface at the point where the ray is reflected.

angle of refraction: The angle between a ray emerging from the interface of two media and the normal to that interface at the point where the ray emerges.

anode: A terminal in an electric circuit that is connected to the positive terminal of a battery or other source of potential difference.

antinodal lines: A region of maximum displacement of a medium in which waves are interacting.

aphelion: The point in a planet's orbit that is farthest from the sun; the point in the orbit where the planet has the smallest speed and the largest gravitational potential energy relative to the sun.

atomic mass unit: A unit of mass in particle physics defined as $\frac{1}{12}$ the mass of a carbon-12 nucleus.

atomic number: A number indicating the number of protons in the nucleus of an atom of a specific element.

atomic spectrum: The characteristic frequencies of electromagnetic radiation produced by each element.

average speed: The total distance traveled by an object divided by the time of its travel; a scalar quantity.

back EMF: The potential difference induced in the armature of an operating motor that opposes the applied potential difference.

Balmer series: The visible red, green, and violet spectral lines produced by electrons of hydrogen falling from a higher energy state to the lower state designated $n = 2$.

baryons: In an atom, subatomic particles of the largest masses (including protons and neutrons).

base: The middle layer in a transistor.

battery: A combination of two or more electric cells.

beta decay: The process of spontaneous emission of an electron from the nucleus of an atom; alternatively, the emission of positrons during induced radioactivity.

beta particle: An electron emitted spontaneously from a radioactive atomic nucleus.

binding energy: The energy required to break up the nucleus of an atom into the individual protons and neutrons of which the nucleus is composed; the energy equivalent of the mass defect.

boiling: The condition in which the liquid and gaseous phases of matter are in equilibrium, usually at atmospheric pressure.

Boyle's law: The volume of a sample of gas is inversely proportional to the pressure, provided the temperature is constant.

breakdown voltage: A reverse potential difference that causes a large reverse current in a diode.

breeder reactor: A nuclear reactor designed to produce more fissionable fuel than is consumed.

bright-line spectrum: A display of bright individual lines on a plate or other surface, indicating the radiation of energy at specific frequencies by a heated gas at low pressure.

cathode: The negative terminal of a battery or some other source of potential difference.

cathode ray tube: An evacuated glass tube in which a beam of electrons, accelerated and deflected by electric fields or magnetic fields or both, produces an image on a fluorescent screen.

Celsius scale: The temperature scale on which the freezing point of water is $0°$ and the boiling point of water is $100°$ at standard pressure.

center of curvature: The point that is equidistant from every point on the surface of a spherical mirror.

centripetal acceleration: The acceleration of a body moving along a circular path at constant speed; a vector quantity.

centripetal force: The force needed to keep an object moving in a circular path; a vector quantity directed toward the center of the circular path.

chain reaction: A fission reaction producing sufficient energy and neutrons to be self-sustaining once the reaction has begun.

Charles' law: This law states that the volume occupied by a sample of gas is directly proportional to the Kelvin temperature, provided the pressure exerted by the sample is constant.

chromatic aberration: The inability of a single lens to refract all the different colors of light to the same focus.

coefficient of friction: The ratio of the force needed to overcome friction to the normal force pressing two surfaces together.

coherent: A term applied to a beam of waves, all of which possess an identical wavelength and an identical constant phase relationship.

collector: One of the two outer layers in a transistor; the layer less heavily doped.

commutator: A split ring in a DC motor, the segments of which are connected to the armature coil in such a way that the current in the coil reverses direction every half turn.

component: One of the two or more forces into which a given vector may be resolved.

concave lens: A diverging lens that causes incident parallel rays to emerge from the lens as if the rays diverged from a point.

concave mirror: A spherical mirror whose reflecting surface curves inward from the edges to the center.

concurrent forces: Two or more forces acting on the same body at the same time.

conduction band: In a semiconductor, the energy band that defines the magnitudes of those electrons that can readily move and transport electric charge.

conductor: A substance, usually a metal, in which electric charge moves easily.

conservation of mass-energy: During a change in which mass is converted into energy, the total of the mass and energy remains constant.

conservative force: A force whose work performed on a system can be recovered without loss.

constructive interference: The effect produced by the interaction of two waves that are in phase with each other as they pass through a medium.

control rod: A device used to regulate the rate of a nuclear chain reaction.

converging lens: A lens capable of refracting incident light rays so as to form an image on a screen; a lens that is thicker at the center than at the edges.

converging mirror: A concave mirror.

convex lens: A converging lens.

convex mirror: A spherical mirror whose reflecting surface curves outward from the edges to the center.

coolant: A fluid circulated through a nuclear reactor to remove heat generated by fission.

core: The part of a nuclear reactor where the fuel rods are placed and where fission occurs.

coulomb: The *SI* unit of electric charge equal to one ampere of current passing through a given area in one second; a derived unit.

Coulomb's law: The electrostatic force between two point charges is directly proportional to the product of the charges and inversely proportional to the square of the distance between the charges.

critical angle: The angle an incident ray makes with the normal when the refracted ray is at a right angle to the normal.

critical mass: The minimum amount of a fissionable nuclide needed to sustain a chain reaction.

current: The rate at which electric charge is transferred in an electric circuit; a scalar quantity.

current element: A theoretical unit for testing the strength of a magnetic field, consisting of a specific length of conductor carrying a standard current.

cycle: One of a complete sequence of repetitive events, vibrations, or oscillations that constitute a wave.

derived unit: A combination of two or more fundamental units of measure.

destructive interference: The effect produced by the interaction of two waves out of phase with one another as they pass simultaneously through a medium.

deuterium: An isotope of hydrogen that has one proton and one neutron in the nucleus.

diffraction: The movement of waves around corners and obstacles in their paths.

diffuse reflection: The reflection of parallel light rays incident on unpolished or irregular surfaces.

diode: A device that conducts electric current more readily in one direction than in another.

direct current: An electric current that flows in a circuit in one direction at a steady rate.

dispersion: The separation of light consisting of more than one wavelength into its spectrum.

dispersive medium: An optical medium that produces the effect of dispersion.

displacement: The change of position of an object described by the vector that begins at the initial position of the object and ends at its final position.

distance: The total length of a path; a scalar quantity.

diverging lens: A lens that refracts incident light rays so that no image can be produced on a screen; a lens that is thinner at the center than at the edges.

diverging mirror: A convex mirror.

donor material: A substance containing impurities that increase the number of electrons available; the *N*-type semiconductor in a transistor.

doping: A process of adding atoms having three or five valence electrons to a semiconducting material to increase its conductivity.

Doppler effect: An apparent change in frequency and wavelength when a wave source and observer are in relative motion with respect to each other; the effect is observed for sound and light waves.

dynamics: The branch of physics dealing with the motion of masses as various forces are applied to them; the study of how forces acting on a object affect its motion.

efficiency: The ratio of the power from the secondary coil of a transformer to the power input to the primary coil.

elastic potential energy: The energy stored in a spring when work is done in compressing or stretching it; a scalar quantity.

electric cell: A device for generating electricity by chemical action.

electric circuit: The complete path taken by electrons during their passage through various interconnected wires and components.

electric current: The flow of electric charge between two points in an electric circuit due to a potential difference between the points.

electric field: A region in which electrical force acts on a charged particle.

electric field intensity: The force on a unit charge at a point in an electric field; a vector quantity.

electric motor: A current-carrying coil, which, as a result of experiencing a torque in a magnetic field, converts electrical energy into rotational mechanical energy.

electrical ground: An arbitrary zero potential reference point, from which potential difference may be measured, very often the earth itself or a negative terminal of a battery.

electromagnet: A coil of wire wound around a soft iron core whose magnetic field may be controlled by passing an electric current through the coil.

electromagnetic induction: The production of an electrical potential or current in a conductor due to the relative motion of the conductor in a magnetic field or a change in magnetic field relative to the conductor; the process of inducing a potential difference in a conductor that occurs when there is a change in the number of lines of magnetic flux linked by the conductor.

electromagnetic spectrum: The range of frequencies of electromagnetic waves that encompass subsonic waves, radio and television waves, microwaves, visible and invisible light, x rays, gamma rays, and rays of still higher frequency.

electromagnetic wave: A wave generated by an oscillating charge producing interacting electric and magnetic fields that propagate into space.

electron: A subatomic particle bearing a negative electric charge and having negligible mass compared to a proton.

electron capture: The process whereby an orbital electron is absorbed by a proton in a nucleus possessing too many protons compared to the number of neutrons.

electron cloud: The region inside an atom where the negative electrons are most likely to be found.

electron gun: A device consisting of a cathode for producing electrons by thermionic emission and a cylindrical anode for accelerating the electrons and forming them into an electron beam.

electronvolt: A unit of energy equal to the work done moving an elementary charge through a potential difference of one volt.

electroscope: An instrument used to detect the nature of electrostatic charge on a mass.

elementary charge: The charge on the electron.

elementary unit of charge: A charge equal to the negative charge on an electron or the positive charge on a proton.

ellipse: A closed curve in which the sum of the distances from any point on the curve to two fixed points (the foci) inside the curve is constant; an oval-shaped curve.

EMF: The potential difference produced as a result of the conversion of other forms of energy into electrical energy.

emission spectrum: The set of electromagnetic frequencies emitted by any source when energized.

emitter: One of the two outer layers in a transistor; the layer that is heavily doped.

energy: The capacity to perform work; a scalar quantity.

energy band: A group of many energy levels in a semiconductor having nearly, but not exactly, the same energy.

Energy Band Model: A theory—replacing the cloud or Electron-sea Model of conduction—that explains the electrical behavior of semiconductors.

energy level: One of a series of regions about the nucleus of an atom in which an electron may move; each region is associated with a specific energy value.

entropy: A quantitative measure of a physical system's natural tendency toward increasing disorder.

equilibrant: A force that is equal in magnitude and opposite in direction to the resultant of two or more concurrent forces.

escape velocity: The velocity a body must have to escape from the earth's gravitational pull.

excitation: The process in which an atom absorbs energy as electrons are raised to a higher energy state.

excited state: The condition of an atom whose electrons, or a nuclide whose particles, have temporarily changed their positions to positions of higher potential energy in response to the absorption of energy.

external shielding: Material, such as high-density concrete, used to protect people from radiation at a nuclear reactor.

extrinsic semiconductor: A semiconducting material to which impurities, such as silicon or germanium, have been added.

ferromagnetic materials: Substances such as iron, nickel, and cobalt that are attracted by magnets.

field: A region that is characterized by the appearance of a force on an appropriate test body, such as a unit mass in a gravitational field or a unit charge in an electric field.

field intensity: The force exerted on an appropriate test body at a particular point in a field; a vector quantity.

field line: A line in a field that indicates the direction of the force on an appropriate test element in that field.

first law of thermodynamics: The law of conservation of energy applied to systems involving heat energy and work.

fission: The splitting apart of an atomic nucleus by neutron absorption with an accompanying release of energy.

fission fragments: The smaller nuclei produced by the splitting of certain heavy nuclei.

fluid friction: The force opposing the motion of a body through a fluid (a gas or liquid); a vector quantity.

flux density: A quantitative measure of the field intensity per unit area, expressed in terms pertinent to the nature of the field; a vector quantity.

focal length: The distance along the principle axis between the principle focus and the center of a lens or curved mirror.

focus: Either of the two fixed points within an ellipse used in determining the shape of the ellipse.

forbidden band: The energy band between the highest level of a valence band and the lowest level of a conduction band.

forbidden states: In quantum theory, any energy level in an atom between the particular levels in which an electron can exist.

force: A push or pull on a mass; a vector quantity.

forward bias: A voltage applied to a P-N junction in a direction that increases both the electron and hole currents across the junction.

free-body diagram: A representation of all the forces acting concurrently on a body.

frequency: The number of cycles per unit time of an oscillating particle or field; a scalar quantity.

friction: A retarding force that acts parallel to surfaces in contact when a body moves or attempts to move relative to another body; a vector quantity.

fuel rods: Rods packed with nuclear fuel pellets that are placed in the core of a nuclear reactor.

fundamental unit: An arbitrary unit in physics defined by describing a set of operations and measurements.

fusion: The combination of two or more light nuclei accompanied by a release of energy.

galvanometer: A meter designed to measure weak electric currents when connected in series in an electric circuit.

gamma radiation: High energy photons emitted spontaneously from a radioactive atomic nucleus.

geosynchronous orbit: The path of a satellite that always remains over the same point on the earth.

gravitation: The mutual force of attraction between masses.

gravitational field strength: The force on a unit mass due to a gravitational field; a vector quantity.

gravitational field strength: The force on a unit mass due to a gravitational field.

gravitational force: *See* gravitation.

gravitational potential energy: The energy of a system due to the relative positions of the masses within the system.

gravity: Gravitation, usually referring to the force that exists between the mass of the earth and the mass of a body in the vicinity of the earth.

ground state: The lowest energy state of a particle when it is neither absorbing nor radiating energy.

half-life: The average time it takes a sample of a radioactive nuclide to disintegrate to one-half of its original mass.

heat: A manifestation of energy transfer by particle collision in a material medium; a scalar quantity.

heat of fusion: The energy required to melt one unit mass of a solid at its normal melting point.

heat of vaporization: The energy required to change one unit mass of a liquid to a gas at its normal boiling point.

hertz: The derived *SI* unit of frequency equivalent to one cycle per second.

hyperbolic: The shape of the graph that is produced when the values for two quantities that are inversely proportional to each other are plotted on Cartesian coordinates.

ideal gas: A gas for which the assumptions of the kinetic theory of gases are valid.

image: An optical reproduction of an object by means of a lens or mirror; a display by means of an electron beam.

impulse: The product of an average applied force and the time during which it acts; a vector quantity.

incident ray: A ray of light impinging upon a surface.

induced potential difference: A difference of potential created in a conductor due to its relative motion in a magnetic field.

induction: *See* electromagnetic induction.

induction coil: A transformer in which a varying potential difference in the secondary coil is produced when a direct current in the primary coil is turned on and off.

inertia: The resistance of a body to a change of motion, directly proportional to its mass.

instantaneous speed: The speed of a body at any particular instant in time; a scalar quantity.

insulator: A substance, usually a compound or a nonmetallic element, in which electric charge flows poorly because of the absence of free electrons.

integrated circuit: A miniaturized semiconductor circuit of many components etched on a small silicon chip.

interface: A surface that forms a boundary between two materials.

interference: The superposition of one wave on another.

interference pattern: The pattern produced by the constructive and destructive interference of waves generated in a medium by two point sources.

internal energy: The sum of the potential and kinetic energies of a system due to the relative motion and positions of the particles of the system.

internal shielding: A steel lining placed in the containment vessel of a nuclear reactor.

ion: A positively or negatively charged particle produced when a neutral atom loses or gains one or more electrons.

ionization potential: The work required to remove an electron from an atom.

isolated system: A group of bodies not being acted upon by any external force.

isotopes: Atoms of the same element that differ from each other in the number of neutrons in their nuclei.

joule: The *SI* unit of energy equal to the work done by a force of one newton causing a displacement of one meter; a derived unit that is equivalent to one kilogram · meter squared per second squared.

K-capture: Electron capture.

kelvin: The fundamental *SI* unit of temperature.

Kelvin scale: The temperature scale on which the freezing point of water at standard pressure is 273 K, the boiling point of water is 373 K, and the coldest possible temperature is 0 K.

Kepler's first law: The orbits of all the planets are elliptical.

Kepler's second law: A line from the sun to a planet sweeps out equal areas in equal periods of time.

Kepler's third law: The ratio of the cube of the mean radius of a planet's orbit to the square of its period of revolution about the sun is the same for all planets in the solar system.

kilogram: The *SI* unit of mass; a fundamental unit.

kilojoule: A unit of energy equal to 1,000 joules.

kilopascal: A unit of pressure equal to 1,000 pascals.

kinematics: The branch of physics concerned with the mathematics of motion.

kinetic energy: The energy of a body due to its rotational or translational motion.

kinetic (sliding) friction: The force opposing the motion of one body sliding over another; a vector quantity.

kinetic theory of gases: The universally accepted postulate that the molecules of all matter are in a perpetual state of motion.

laser: A device that produces a monochromatic, coherent beam of electromagnetic radiation of great energy per unit area.

law of conservation of charge: In a system that neither receives nor transmits charge, the total net charge is constant, no matter what internal changes occur.

law of conservation of energy: In a system that neither receives nor delivers energy external to itself, the total energy of the system is constant, no matter what changes occur within the system.

law of conservation of mass and energy: The total quantity of mass and energy in the universe remains constant.

law of conservation of momentum: The momentum of a system remains unchanged if no external force interacts with the system, regardless of collisions within the system.

law of reflection: The incident ray, the refracted ray, and the normal at the point of incidence lie in the same plane, and the angle of reflection is always equal to the angle of incidence.

lens: A transparent object with one or two curved surfaces used to direct light rays by refraction.

leptons: Subatomic particles of relatively small mass, including electrons, neutrinos, and muons.

line of force: An imaginary line drawn in a gravitational, magnetic, or electric field so that its tangent at any point is in the direction of the force on a test element in the field.

longitudinal wave: A wave in which the oscillating particles composing the wave vibrate parallel to the direction of wave travel.

magnet: An object that can exert a force on ferrous materials.

magnetic field: A region in which a moving charged particle will experience a force due to its motion.

magnetic field strength: The force on a unit current element at a point in a magnetic field; a vector quantity.

magnetic flux density: The total number of magnetic lines of flux per unit area.

magnetic flux lines: Imaginary lines used to indicate the direction and strength of a magnetic field.

magnetic force: The force exerted on charged particles in motion in a magnetic field; a vector quantity.

magnetic pole: A region on a magnet where the magnetic effects are most pronounced.

majority carriers: The term describing the electrons in an N-type semiconductor or the holes in a P-type semiconductor.

mass: The property of an object defined by Newton's second law of motion; colloquially, the amount of matter composing an object.

mass defect: The difference in mass between the mass of a nucleus and the sum of the masses of the protons and neutrons that constitute the nucleus.

mass number: The sum of all the neutrons and protons within the nucleus of an atom.

mass spectrometer: A device used to determine the mass of ionized particles.

mean radius: The average distance between the sun and a planet in its orbit.

mechanics: The study of how forces affect the motions of bodies.

melting: The condition in which the solid and liquid phases of a substance are in equilibrium.

mesons: Subatomic particles whose masses are intermediate between the masses of an electron and a proton.

meter: The *SI* unit of length; a fundamental unit.

minority carriers: The term describing the holes in an *N*-type semiconductor or the electrons in a *P*-type seminconductor.

mirror image: The image of an object produced by regular reflection of light from a smooth, plane surface.

moderator: A material surrounding the fuel in a nuclear reactor that slows down neutrons but has little tendency to absorb them.

momentum: The product of the mass and velocity of an object in motion; a vector quantity.

natural frequency: The particular frequency with which an elastic body will vibrate if disturbed.

natural radioactivity: Radioactivity occurring in nature without the intervention of humans.

negative charge: One of two types of charge; opposite to positive charge.

net force: The single force that is equivalent to the combined effect of concurrent forces acting on a body.

neutrino: An illusive subatomic particle of zero mass and zero charge.

neutron: A subatomic particle having no charge and a mass approximately equal to that of a proton.

newton: The derived *SI* unit of force; the force that imparts an acceleration of one meter per second squared to a one-kilogram mass.

nodal line: A region in a medium where the interference of waves produces a zero displacement.

nodal point: A point of zero displacement where two waves interact.

non-conservative force: A force, such as friction, that performs work on a system, but from which system only a lesser amount of work can be recovered.

nondispersive medium: A medium in which waves of differing frequencies have the same speed.

normal: A line perpendicular to a surface.

normal force: The force pressing together two surfaces that are in contact; on a horizontal surface, the normal force is equal in magnitude but opposite in direction to the weight of an object resting on the surface; a vector quantity.

north magnetic pole: The magnetic pole from which the magnetic flux of a magnet is considered to emerge.

nuclear force: The attractive force between particles in an atomic nucleus responsible for the stability of the nucleus; the strongest force known.

nuclear fuel: A radioactive material whose fissionable nuclides are used to produce energy on a commercial scale.

nuclear reactor: A device in which controlled fission reactions produce energy.

nuclear species: A nuclide.

nucleon: A proton or a neutron in a nucleus of an atom.

nucleus: The positively charged core of an atom made up of one or more protons and (except for one of the isotopes of hydrogen) one or more neutrons.

nuclide: An atomic nucleus specified by its atomic number, atomic mass, and energy state.

ohm: The derived *SI* unit of electrical resistance equivalent to one volt per ampere.

Ohm's law: At constant temperature, the ratio of the potential difference across a resistor to the current flowing in the resistor is constant.

optical center: The center of a converging or diverging lens.

parallel circuit: A circuit in which the ends of two or more devices are connected to the same points so as to provide two or more paths for the flow of current.

particle accelerator: A device that uses electric and electromagnetic fields to increase the speed of atomic or nuclear particles.

pascal: The *SI* unit of pressure equal to one newton per square meter; a derived unit.

perihelion: The point in a planet's orbit that is closest to the sun and at which the planet has the greatest speed and smallest gravitational potential energy.

period: The time taken for an oscillating body or wave to complete one cycle; the time required for a body to make one complete revolution in its orbit; a scalar quantity.

periodic waves: A series of regularly repeated disturbances of a field or medium.

phase: The relative position of a point on a wave with respect to another point on the same wave.

photoelectric effect: The phenomenon in which electromagnetic radiation interacts with a substance with a subsequent emission of electrons.

photoelectric equation: $KE_{max} = hf - hf_0$, where KE_{max} is the maximum kinetic energy of a electron ejected from a photoelectric surface when light of frequency f is incident upon the surface, h is Planck's constant, and f_0 is the threshold frequency of the photoelectric surface.

photon: The basic unit of electromagnetic energy.

Planck's constant: A universal constant relating the energy of a photon to the frequency of the radiation from which it comes.

polarization: The condition of light or radiant energy in which all vibrations are confined to a single plane perpendicular to the direction of the wave's motion.

polarized light: A beam of light in which all the wave oscillations are in one plane only.

pole: A region on the surface of a mass where there is a great concentration of magnetic or electric lines of force.

polychromatic waves: Light having many frequencies.

positive beta decay: The emission of positrons from an atomic nucleus.

positive charge: One of two types of charge; opposite to negative charge.

positron: A particle whose mass is equal to the mass of the electron, and whose positive electric charge is equal in magnitude to the negative charge of the electron.

positron emission: The spontaneous ejection of a positively charged electron from the nucleus of an atom that occurs when a proton in the nucleus changes to a neutron.

potential difference: The difference in potential energy per unit charge between two points in an electric field.

potential energy: The stored energy of a body in terms of its condition or position with respect to other bodies; a scalar quantity.

power: The time rate of utilization of energy; the time rate of doing work; a scalar quantity.

pressure: The force exerted on one unit of area; a scalar quantity.

primary coil: In a transformer, the wire coil connected to a source of alternating current.

principal axis: An imaginary line passing through the center of curvature and the center of a curved mirror or lens.

principal focus: A point to which rays parallel to the principal axis of a lens or mirror converge, or from which they diverge, after reflection or refraction.

principal quantum numbers: The integers, beginning with one, that are assigned to successive energy levels of an atom.

prism: A transparent optical device having two identical triangles as sides and three rectangular faces; used for dispersion or refraction of light.

protium: An isotope of hydrogen whose nucleus is composed of one proton (and no neutrons).

proton: A positively charged subatomic particle with a charge equal in magnitude to that of the electron and a mass number of 1.

pulse: An abrupt nonperiodic disturbance of a field or medium.

quantum: An individual discrete packet of energy radiated and absorbed as a unit.

quantum theory: The modern theory, extensively verified, that radiant energy is emitted from and absorbed by matter in discrete packets of energy (quanta).

quark: A particle deduced to exist, not yet isolated, but for which there is now evidence of its existence; it possesses a fractional elementary charge.

radioactive decay: The spontaneous disintegration of the nuclei of atoms causing the formation of new nuclei.

radius of curvature: The distance from the center of curvature to the curved surface of a spherical mirror.

ray: A straight line indicating the direction of travel of a wave.

real image: An image formed by an optical system that can be focused on a screen.

reflected ray: The ray appearing from a surface when an incident ray strikes the interface between two media of different optical densities.

refraction: The bending of the path of a ray when it passes obliquely from one medium to another of different optical density.

regular reflection: The reflection produced when light rays are incident upon a smooth plane surface.

resistance: The opposition of a circuit or part of a circuit to the flow of current; the ratio of applied potential difference to current through a circuit element; a scalar quantity.

resistivity: A quantity property of a material, independent of the material's physical shape, that is closely related to its resistance; can be calculated from a sample of uniform composition by multiplying the resistance of the sample by the ratio of its area to length.

resolution of forces: The process of determining the magnitude and direction of the components of a force.

resonance: Sympathetic vibrations in a body at its natural vibrational frequency set up by another vibrating force at the same frequency.

reverse bias: A voltage applied to a *P-N* junction that reduces the electron current across the junction.

rolling friction: The force opposing the motion of one body rolling over another body; a vector quantity.

satellite: A natural or human-made body that revolves about a larger body.

scalar: A physical quantity, such as length and mass, characterized by magnitude only.

second: The *SI* unit of time; a fundamental unit.

second law of thermodynamics: Heat will not flow from a cold body to a warm body unless work is done; the entropy of the universe is increasing.

secondary coil: In a transformer, the wire coil in which an alternating potential difference is induced.

semiconductor: A material whose resistivity lies between that of insulators and conductors.

series circuit: An electrical circuit connected so that there is only one path for electron flow.

shunt: A low resistance in an ammeter that has been placed in parallel with a galvanometer coil.

sliding friction: A force that resists the relative motion of objects that are in contact with each other; a vector quantity.

Snell's law: For a ray passing from one medium to another, the ratio of the sine of the angle of incidence to the sine of the angle of refraction is constant for all angles of incidence.

solenoid: A coil of wire of one or more layers wound on a solid or air core; used as a component in electrical circuits.

south magnetic pole: That pole of a magnet into which the magnetic lines of flux flow.

specific heat: The heat energy required to raise the temperature of a unit mass of a substance one Celsius degree.

speed: The time rate at which a body travels distance; a scalar quantity.

spherical aberration: The failure of mirrors and lenses with spherical surfaces to bring parallel light rays striking all parts of the mirror or lens to the same focus.

spherical mirror: A mirror having a reflecting surface that is a portion of a sphere.

spring constant: The ratio of the force required to stretch or compress a particular spring to the distance of stretch or compression.

standard pressure: A pressure of 101.3 kilopascals.

standing wave: A stationary wave pattern formed in a medium when two sets of waves of equal wavelength and amplitude pass through the medium in opposite directions.

starting friction: When two bodies are in contact, the minimum force required to begin moving one body relative to the other; a vector quantity.

static electricity: Stationary electric charges.

static equilibrium: The condition of a body when it has a net force of zero acting on it; the condition of a body at rest or moving with a constant velocity.

static friction: The force preventing the motion of one body relative to another when they are at rest with respect to each other; a vector quantity.

statics: The study of the forces acting on a body when it is at rest or is moving so that its center of mass has a constant velocity.

stationary state: The energy condition of an electron in an atom in which it neither absorbs nor radiates energy.

superposition: The process of determining the resultant wave of two or more interfering waves.

temperature: The measure of a substance's warmth or coldness with respect to a standard; a scalar quantity.

tesla: The *SI* unit of flux density equal to one weber per square meter and equivalent to a magnetic field strength of one newton per ampere · meter; a derived unit.

test charge: A small positively charged mass used to detect an electric field.

test mass: A hypothetical small mass used to detect a gravitational field.

thermal neutrons: Neutrons likely to cause fission because they have kinetic energies close to those of the molecules of a substance at ordinary temperatures.

thermionic emission: The emission of electrons at high temperatures when metallic filaments or cores are heated.

thermometer: A device that is used to make quantitative measurements of temperature.

third law of thermodynamics: The temperature of a system cannot be reduced to absolute zero by a finite number of operations.

threshold frequency: The frequency below which electromagnetic radiation will not eject electrons from the surface of a given metal.

torque: A force applied perpendicular to a designated line that tends to produce circular motion.

total internal reflection: The reflection of a ray in a denser medium from the surface of a less dense medium that occurs when the angle of incidence exceeds the critical angle.

total mechanical energy: The sum of the potential and kinetic energies of a mechanical system.

transformer: Two coils used to change the potential difference of an alternating current to a larger or smaller alternating potential difference.

transistor: A semiconductor device, used in the place of the vacuum tube, that is able to control current and to generate, shape, and amplify wave forms of a wide range of frequencies with such efficiency that it has formed the basis for the current advances in electrical technology.

transmutation: The conversion of an atomic nucleus of one element into that of another element by a loss or gain of protons.

transverse wave: A wave whose oscillating particles or oscillating field vibrates perpendicular to the direction of wave travel.

tritium: An isotope of hydrogen whose nucleus is composed of one proton and two neutrons.

uniform circular motion: Constant speed in a circular path.

uniform motion: Straight-line motion at constant speed.

unit: A standard value for a quantity used for comparing other values of the same quantity.

universal law of gravitation: Any two bodies in the universe are attracted to each other with a force that is directly proportional to their masses and inversely proportional to the square of the distance between them.

uranium disintegration series: The sequence of nuclides formed as uranium-238 decays by alpha and beta particle emissions to the stable nuclide lead-206.

valence band: The band of energy that encompasses the energy magnitudes of the outermost electrons of the atoms of a solid material.

vector: A quantity, such as velocity and force, described by both magnitude and direction; often depicted graphically by a directed line segment.

velocity: The time rate of change of displacement; a vector whose magnitude is speed and whose direction is the direction of motion.

virtual focus: The point at which rays diverging from a lens would meet if extended in straight lines back through the lens.

virtual image: An image formed by an optical system that cannot be focused on a screen.

visible light: The portion of the electromagnetic spectrum whose frequencies produce the sensation of color when viewed.

volt: The derived *SI* unit of electric potential difference, equal to one joule per coulomb.

volt per meter: The *SI* unit of electric field intensity equal to a newton per coulomb; a derived unit.

voltmeter: An electrical device used to measure the potential difference across an element when connected in parallel with it in an electric circuit; a galvanometer with a high resistance connected in series with the galvanometer coil.

watt: The derived *SI* unit of power, equal to one joule per second.

wave: A series of periodic oscillations of a particle or a field in time and space.

wave front: All points on a three-dimensional wave that are in phase with each other.

wavelength: The distance between any two corresponding points on adjacent cycles of a wave that are in the same phase.

weber: The derived *SI* unit of magnetic flux.

weight: The gravitational force of attraction of the earth on a body, or in space the attraction of one celestial body for another; a vector quantity.

work: For a force whose magnitude and direction are constant while applied to a body, the product of the magnitude of the body's displacement during the time the force acts times the component of the force in the direction of the displacement; a scalar quantity.

work function: The minimum energy required to remove an electron from the surface of a metal.

Index

PHYSICS

June 17, 1993

PART I

Answer all 55 questions in this part. [65]

Directions (1–55): For *each* statement or question, select the word or expression that, of those given, best completes the statement or answers the question.

1. A car travels a distance of 98 meters in 10. seconds. What is the average speed of the car during this 10.-second interval?
   (1) 4.9m/s
   (2) 9.8 m/s
   (3) 49 m/s
   (4) 98 m/s

2. Which measurement of an average classroom door is closest to 1 meter?
   (1) thickness
   (2) width
   (3) height
   (4) surface area

3. A boat initially traveling at 10. meters per second accelerates uniformly at the rate of 5.0 meters per second^2 for 10. seconds. How far does the boat travel during this time?
   (1) 50. m
   (2) 250 m
   (3) 350 m
   (4) 500 m

4. The graph below represents the relationship between distance and time for an object.

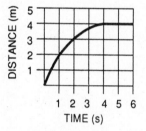

What is the instantaneous speed of the object at t = 5.0 seconds?
   (1) 0 m/s
   (2) 2.0 m/s
   (3) 5.0 m/s
   (4) 4.0 m/s

5. An object accelerates uniformly from rest to a speed of 50. meters per second in 5.0 seconds. The average speed of the object during the 5.0-second interval is
   (1) 5.0 m/s
   (2) 10. m/s
   (3) 25 m/s
   (4) 50. m/s

6. A 5-newton ball and a 10-newton ball are released simultaneously from a point 50 meters above the surface of the Earth. Neglecting air resistance, which statement is true?
   (1) The 5-N ball will have a greater acceleration than the 10-N ball.
   (2) The 10-N ball will have a greater acceleration than the 5-N ball.
   (3) At the end of 3 seconds of free-fall, the 10-N ball will have a greater momentum than the 5-N ball.
   (4) At the end of 3 seconds of free-fall, the 5-N ball will have a greater momentum than the 10-N ball.

7. In the diagram below, the weight of a box on a plane inclined at 30.° is represented by the vector W.

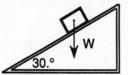

What is the magnitude of the component of the weight (W) that acts parallel to the incline?
(1) W
(2) 0.50W
(3) 0.87W
(4) 1.5W

8. The diagram at the right represents a force acting at point P. Which pair of concurrent forces would produce equilibrium when added to the force acting at point P?

P • ↗ — FORCE

P → ↓   (1)   P → ↑   (2)   ↑ ← P   (3)   ← P ↓   (4)

(1)   (2)   (3)   (4)

9. A boat heads directly eastward across a river at 12 meters per second. If the current in the river is flowing at 5.0 meters per second due south, what is the magnitude of the boat's resultant velocity?
(1) 7.0 m/s
(2) 8.5 m/s
(3) 13 m/s
(4) 17 m/s

10. A bird feeder with two birds has a total mass of 2.0 kilograms and is supported by wire as shown in the diagram below.

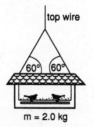

top wire

60°   60°

m = 2.0 kg

The force in the top wire is approximately
(1) 10. N
(2) 14 N
(3) 20. N
(4) 39 N

11. A 50.-kilogram woman wearing a seat belt is traveling in a car that is moving with a velocity of +10. meters per second. In an emergency, the car is brought to a stop in 0.50 second. What force does the seat belt exert on the woman so that she remains in her seat?
(1) -1.0×10^3 N
(2) -5.0×10^2 N
(3) -5.0×10^1 N
(4) -2.5×10^1 N

12. A 0.10-kilogram ball dropped vertically from a height of 1.0 meter above the floor bounces back to a height of 0.80 meter. The mechanical energy lost by the ball as it bounces is approximately
(1) 0.080 J
(2) 0.20 J
(3) 0.30 J
(4) 0.78 J

13. A student rides a bicycle up a 30.° hill at a constant speed of 6.00 meters per second. The combined mass of the student and bicycle is 70.0 kilograms. What is the kinetic energy of the student-bicycle system during this ride?
    (1) 210. J
    (2) 420. J
    (3) 1,260 J
    (4) 2,520 J

Base your answers to questions 14 and 15 on the information and diagram below.

Spacecraft S is traveling from planet P_1 toward planet P_2. At the position shown, the magnitude of the gravitational force of planet P_1 on the spacecraft is equal to the magnitude of the gravitational force of planet P_2 on the spacecraft.

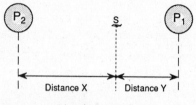

Distance X   Distance Y

(not drawn to scale)

Note that questions 14 and 15 have only three choices.

14. If distance X is greater than distance Y, then the mass of P_1 must be
    (1) less than the mass of P_2
    (2) greater than the mass of P_2
    (3) equal to the mass of P_2

15. As the spacecraft moves from the position shown toward planet P_2, the ratio of the gravitational force of P_2 on the spacecraft to the gravitational force of P_1 on the spacecraft will
    (1) decrease
    (2) increase
    (3) remain the same

16. The graph at the right shows the relationship between weight and mass for a series of objects. The slope of this graph represents
    (1) change of position
    (2) normal force
    (3) momentum
    (4) acceleration due to gravity

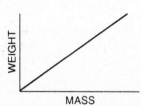

17. Each diagram below shows a different block being pushed by a force across a surface at a constant velocity.

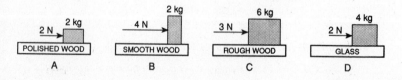

In which two diagrams is the force of friction the same?
    (1) A and B
    (2) B and D
    (3) A and D
    (4) C and D

18. A student running up a flight of stairs increases her speed at a constant rate. Which graph best represents the relationship between work and time for the student's run up the stairs?

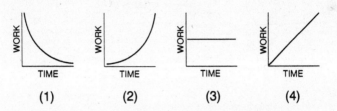

(1)   (2)   (3)   (4)

19. A net force of 5.0 newtons moves a 2.0-kilogram object a distance of 3.0 meters in 3.0 seconds. How much work is done on the object?
    (1) 1.0 J   (3) 15 J
    (2) 10. J   (4) 30. J

20. Which graph best represents the relationship between the elongation of a spring whose elastic limit has not been reached and the force applied to it?

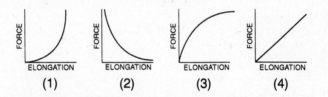

(1)   (2)   (3)   (4)

21. If a positively charged rod is brought near the knob of a positively charged electroscope, the leaves of the electroscope will
    (1) converge, only
    (2) diverge, only
    (3) first diverge, then converge
    (4) first converge, then diverge

22. The diagram below shows four charged metal spheres suspended by strings. The charge of each sphere is indicated.

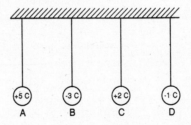

If spheres *A, B, C,* and *D* simultaneously come into contact, the net charge on the four spheres will be
    (1) +1 C   (3) +3 C
    (2) +2 C   (4) +4 C

23. The diagram below represents the electric field lines in the vicinity of two isolated electrical charges, A and B.

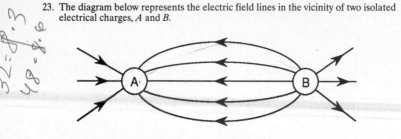

Which statement identifies the charges of A and B?
(1) A is negative and B is positive.
(2) A is positive and B is negative.
(3) A and B are both positive.
(4) A and B are both negative.

Base your answers to questions 24 through 26 on the diagram below which represents a frictionless track. A 10-kilogram block starts from rest at point A and slides along the track.

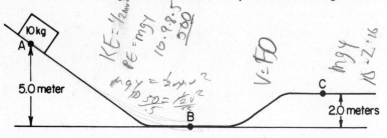

24. As the block moves from point A to point B, the total amount of gravitational potential energy changed to kinetic energy is approximately
(1) 5 J   (3) 50 J
(2) 20 J   (4) 500 J

25. What is the approximate speed of the block at point B?
(1) 1 m/s   (3) 50 m/s
(2) 10 m/s   (4) 100 m/s

26. What is the approximate potential energy of the block at point C?
(1) 20 J   (3) 300 J
(2) 200 J   (4) 500 J

27. If the potential difference between two oppositely charged parallel metal plates is doubled, the electrical field intensity at a point between them is
(1) halved   (3) doubled
(2) unchanged   (4) quadrupled

28. Moving a point charge of 3.2×10^{-19} coulomb between points A and B in an electric field requires 4.8×10^{-19} joule of energy. What is the potential difference between these two points?
(1) 0.67 V   (3) 3.0 V
(2) 2.0 V   (4) 1.5 V

29. The slope of the line on the graph at the right represents
(1) resistance of a material
(2) electrical field intensity
(3) power dissipated in a resistor
(4) electrical energy

30. In the diagrams below, ℓ represents a unit length of copper wire and A represents a unit cross-sectional area. Which copper wire has the *smallest* resistance at room temperature?

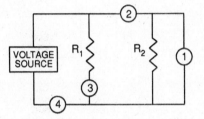

31. Two resistors are connected to a source of voltage as shown in the diagram below.

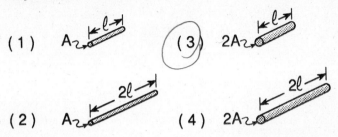

At which position should an ammeter be placed to measure the current passing only through resistor R_1?
(1) 1   (3) 3
(2) 2   (4) 4

32. A toaster dissipates 1,500 watts of power in 90. seconds. The amount of electric energy used by the toaster is approximately
(1) 1.4×10^5 J   (3) 5.2×10^8 J
(2) 1.7×10^1 J   (4) 6.0×10^{-2} J

33. In the diagram below, a steel paper clip is attached to a string, which is attached to a table. The clip remains suspended beneath a magnet.

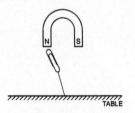

As the magnet is lifted, the paper clip begins to fall as a result of
(1) an increase in the potential energy of the clip
(2) an increase in the gravitational field strength near the magnet
(3) a decrease in the magnetic properties of the clip
(4) a decrease in the magnetic field strength near the clip

34. The diagram below shows the magnetic field that results when a piece of iron is placed between unlike magnetic poles.

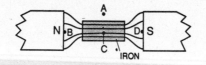

At which point is the magnetic field strength greatest?
(1) *A*   (3) *C*
(2) *B*   (4) *D*

35. A wire carrying an electron current (e⁻) is placed between the poles of a magnet, as shown in the diagram below.

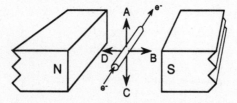

Which arrow represents the direction of the magnetic force on the current?
(1) *A*   (3) *C*
(2) *B*   (4) *D*

36. The diagram below shows a coil of wire connected to a battery.

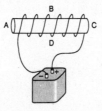

The *N*-pole of this coil is closest to
(1) *A*   (3) *C*
(2) *B*   (4) *D*

37. The diagram below shows radar waves being emitted from a stationary police car and reflected by a moving car back to the police car.

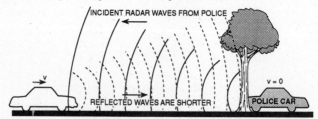

The difference in apparent frequency between the incident and reflected waves is an example of
(1) constructive interference   (3) the Doppler effect
(2) refraction   (4) total internal reflection

38. The diagram below shows a transverse pulse moving to the right in a string.

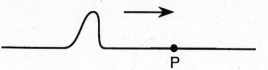

Which diagram best represents the motion of point *P* as the pulse passes point *P*?

(1)   (2)   (3)   (4)

39. Light is to brightness as sound is to
    (1) color
    (2) loudness
    (3) period
    (4) speed

40. The periodic wave in the diagram below has a frequency of 40. hertz.

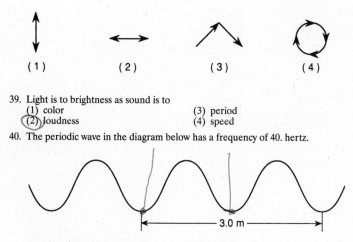

|←——————— 3.0 m ———————→|

What is the speed of the wave?
    (1) 13 m/s
    (2) 27 m/s
    (3) 60. m/s
    (4) 120 m/s

41. Two waves have the same frequency. Which wave characteristic must also be identical for both waves?
    (1) phase
    (2) amplitude
    (3) intensity
    (4) period

42. A typical microwave oven produces radiation at a frequency of 1.0×10^{10} hertz. What is the wavelength of this microwave radiation?
    (1) 3.0×10^{-1} m
    (2) 3.0×10^{-2} m
    (3) 3.0×10^{10} m
    (4) 3.0×10^{18} m

43. Two wave sources operating in phase in the same medium produce the circular wave patterns shown in the diagram below. The solid lines represent wave crests and the dashed lines represent wave troughs.

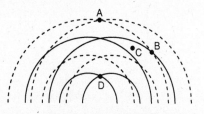

Which point is at a position of maximum destructive interference?
    (1) *A*
    (2) *B*
    (3) *C*
    (4) *D*

44. The distance between successive antinodes in the standing wave pattern shown at the right is equal to
    (1) 1 wavelength
    (2) 2 wavelengths
    (3) $\frac{1}{2}$ wavelength
    (4) $\frac{1}{3}$ wavelength

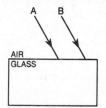

45. The diagram below shows a ray of light passing from medium X into air.

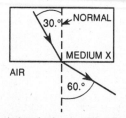

What is the absolute index of refraction of medium X?
(1) 0.50   (3) 1.7
(2) 2.0   (4) 0.58

46. In the diagram below, a ray of monochromatic light (A) and a ray of polychromatic light (B) are both incident upon an air-glass interface.

Which phenomenon could occur with ray B, but *not* with ray A?
(1) dispersion   (3) polarization
(2) reflection   (4) refraction

47. If the critical angle for a substance is 44°, the index of refraction of the substance is equal to
(1) 1.0   (3) 1.4
(2) 0.69   (4) 0.023

48. The diagram below shows a beam of light entering and leaving a "black box."

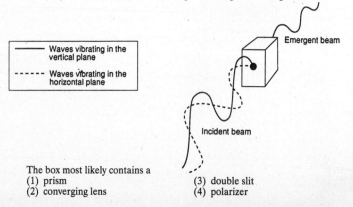

The box most likely contains a
(1) prism   (3) double slit
(2) converging lens   (4) polarizer

49. Which graph best represents the relationship between the intensity of light that falls on a photoemissive surface and the number of photoelectrons that the surface emits?

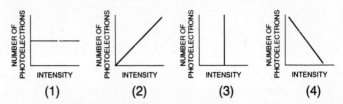

50. The work function of a certain photoemissive material is 2.0 electronvolts. If 5.0-electronvolt photons are incident on the material, the maximum kinetic energy of the ejected photoelectrons will be
    (1) 7.0 eV
    (2) 5.0 eV
    (3) 3.0 eV
    (4) 2.5 eV

51. Alpha particles fired at thin metal foil are scattered in hyperbolic paths due to the
    (1) attraction between the electrons and alpha particles
    (2) magnetic repulsion between the electrons and alpha particles
    (3) gravitational attraction between the nuclei and alpha particles
    (4) repulsive forces between the nuclei and alpha particles

52. The momentum of a photon with a wavelength of 5.9×10^{-7} meter is
    (1) 8.9×10^{26} kg·m/s
    (2) 1.6×10^{-19} kg·m/s
    (3) 1.1×10^{-27} kg·m/s
    (4) 3.9×10^{-40} kg·m/s

Note that questions 53 through 55 have only three choices.

53. As the resistance of a lamp operating at a constant voltage increases, the power dissipated by the lamp
    (1) decreases
    (2) increases
    (3) remains the same

54. Circuit A and circuit B are shown below.

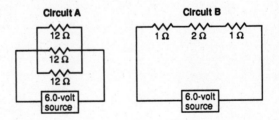

Compared to the total resistance of circuit A, the total resistance of circuit B is
    (1) less
    (2) greater
    (3) the same

55. The diagram at the right represents the path of periodic waves passing from medium *A* into medium *B*. As the waves enter medium *B*, their speed
    (1) decreases
    (2) increases
    (3) remains the same

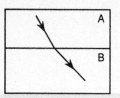

PART II

This part consists of six groups, each containing ten questions. Each group tests an optional area of the course. Choose two of these six groups. Be sure that you answer all ten questions in each group chosen. [20]

Group 1—Motion in a Plane

If you choose this group, be sure to answer questions 56–65.

56. A ball is thrown horizontally at a speed of 20. meters per second from the top of a cliff. How long does the ball take to fall 19.6 meters to the ground?
    (1) 1.0 s   (3) 9.8 s
    (2) 2.0 s   (4) 4.0 s

57. A book is pushed with an initial horizontal velocity of 5.0 meters per second off the top of a desk. What is the initial vertical velocity of the book?
    (1) 0 m/s   (3) 5.0 m/s
    (2) 2.5 m/s   (4) 10. m/s

58. The diagram below shows a baseball being hit with a bat. Angle θ represents the angle between the horizontal and the ball's initial direction of motion.

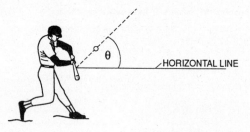

Which value of θ would result in the ball traveling the longest horizontal distance? [Neglect air resistance.]
    (1) 25°   (3) 60°
    (2) 45°   (4) 90°

59. The diagram below represents a bicycle and rider traveling to the right at a constant speed. A ball is dropped from the hand of the cyclist.

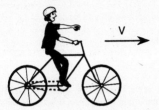

Which set of graphs best represents the horizontal motion of the ball relative to the ground? [Neglect air resistance.]

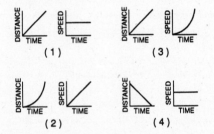

60. Pluto is sometimes closer to the Sun than Neptune is. Which statement is the best explanation for this phenomenon?
   (1) Neptune's orbit is elliptical and Pluto's orbit is circular.
   (2) Pluto's orbit is elliptical and Neptune's orbit is circular.
   (3) Pluto and Neptune have circular orbits that overlap.
   (4) Pluto and Neptune have elliptical orbits that overlap.

Base your answers to questions 61 through 63 on the diagram below which shows a 2.0-kilogram model airplane attached to a wire. The airplane is flying clockwise in a horizontal circle of radius 20. meters at 30. meters per second.

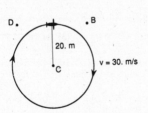

61. The centripetal force acting on the airplane at the position shown is directed toward point
   (1) A   (3) C
   (2) B   (4) D

62. What is the magnitude of the centripetal acceleration of the airplane?
   (1) 0 m/s^2 (3) 45 m/s^2
   (2) 1.5 m/s^2 (4) 90. m/s^2

63. If the wire breaks when the airplane is at the position shown, the airplane will move toward point
    (1) A
    (2) B
    (3) C
    (4) D

Note that questions 64 and 65 have only three choices.

64. A motorcycle travels around a flat circular track. If the speed of the motorcycle is increased, the force required to keep it in the same circular path
    (1) decreases
    (2) increases
    (3) remains the same

65. The diagram represents the path taken by planet P as it moves in an elliptical orbit around sun S. The time it takes to go from point A to point B is t_1, and from point C to point D is t_2.

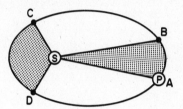

If the two shaded areas are equal, then t_1 is
    (1) less than t_2
    (2) greater than t_2
    (3) the same as t_2

Group 2—Internal Energy

If you choose this group, be sure to answer questions 66–75.

66. What is the difference between the melting point and boiling point of ethyl alcohol on the Kelvin scale?
    (1) 38
    (2) 196
    (3) 352
    (4) 469

67. A kilogram of each of the substances below is condensed from a gas to a liquid. Which substance releases the most energy?
    (1) alcohol
    (2) mercury
    (3) water
    (4) silver

68. Which sample of metal will gain net internal energy when placed in contact with a block of lead at 100°C?
    (1) platinum at 60°C
    (2) iron at 100°C
    (3) lead at 125°C
    (4) silver at 200°C

69. Which graph best represents the relationship between absolute temperature (T) and the product of pressure and volume ($P \cdot V$) for a given mass of ideal gas?

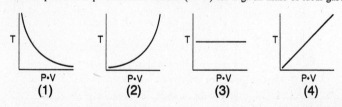

Base your answers to questions 70 through 72 on the information below.

Ten kilograms of water initially at 20°C is heated to its boiling point (100°C). Then 5.0 kilograms of the water is converted into steam at 100°C.

70. What was the approximate amount of heat energy needed to raise the temperature of the water to its boiling point?
    (1) 840 kJ
    (2) 3,400 kJ
    (3) 4,200 kJ
    (4) 6,300 kJ

71. The amount of heat energy needed to convert the 5.0 kilograms of water at 100°C into steam at 100°C is approximately
    (1) 1,700 kJ
    (2) 2,100 kJ
    (3) 5,500 kJ
    (4) 11,000 kJ

Note that question 72 has only three choices.

72. If salt is added to the water, the temperature at which the water boils will
    (1) decrease
    (2) increase
    (3) remain the same

73. The graph below shows temperature versus time for 1.0 kilogram of a substance at constant pressure as heat is added at a constant rate of 100 kilojoules per minute. The substance is a solid at 20°C.

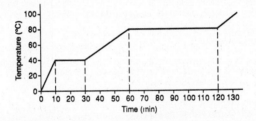

How much heat was added to change the substance from a liquid at its melting point to a vapor at its boiling point?
    (1) 3,000 kJ
    (2) 6,000 kJ
    (3) 9,000 kJ
    (4) 11,000 kJ

Note that questions 74 and 75 have only three choices.

74. As pressure is applied to a snowball, the melting point of the snow
    (1) decreases
    (2) increases
    (3) remains the same

75. Oxygen molecules are about 16 times more massive than hydrogen molecules. An oxygen gas sample is in a closed container and a hydrogen gas sample is in a second closed container of different size. Both samples are at room temperature. Compared to the average speed of the oxygen molecules, the average speed of the hydrogen molecules will be
    (1) less
    (2) greater
    (3) the same

Group 3—Electromagnetic Applications

If you choose this group, be sure to answer questions 76–85.

Base your answers to questions 76 through 78 on the information and data table below.

During a laboratory investigation of transformers, a group of students obtained the following data during four trials, using a different pair of coils in each trial.

	Primary Coil		Secondary Coil	
	V_p (volts)	I_p (amperes)	V_s (volts)	I_s (amperes)
Trial 1	3.0	12.0	16.0	2.0
Trial 2	6.0	3.0	8.0	2.2
Trial 3	9.0	4.3	54.0	0.7
Trial 4	12.0	2.5	5.0	9.0

76. What is the efficiency of the transformer in trial 1?
   (1) 75%   (3) 100%
   (2) 89%   (4) 113%

77. What is the ratio of the number of turns in the primary coil to the number of turns in the secondary coil in trial 3?
   (1) 1:6   (3) 6:1
   (2) 1:9   (4) 9:1

78. In which trial was an error most likely made in recording the data?
   (1) 1   (3) 3
   (2) 2   (4) 4

79. A wire of 0.50 meter long cuts across a magnetic field with a magnetic flux density of 20. teslas. The wire moves at a speed of 4.0 meters per second and travels in a direction perpendicular to the magnetic flux lines. What is the maximum potential difference induced between the ends of the wire?
   (1) 2.5 V   (3) 40. V
   (2) 10. V   (4) 160 V

80. Compared to the resistance of the circuit being measured, the internal resistance of a voltmeter is designed to be very high so that the meter will draw
   (1) no current from the circuit
   (2) little current from the circuit
   (3) most of the current from the circuit
   (4) all the current from the circuit

81. A proton and an electron traveling with the same velocity enter a uniform electric field. Compared to the acceleration of the proton, the acceleration of the electron is
   (1) less, and in the same direction
   (2) less, but in the opposite direction
   (3) greater, and in the same direction
   (4) greater, but in the opposite direction

82. The diagram below shows an end view of a straight conducting wire, W, moving with constant speed in uniform magnetic field B.

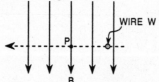

   As the conductor moves through position P, the electron current induced in the wire is directed
   (1) toward the bottom of the page   (3) into the page
   (2) toward the top of the page   (4) out of the page

83. An electron moves at 3.0×10^7 meters per second perpendicularly to a magnetic field that has a flux density of 2.0 teslas. What is the magnitude of the force on the electron?
   (1) 9.6×10^{-19} N   (3) 9.6×10^{-12} N
   (2) 3.2×10^{-19} N   (4) 4.8×10^{-12} N

84. In each diagram below, an electron travels to the right between points *A* and *B*. In which diagram would the electron be deflected toward the bottom of the page?

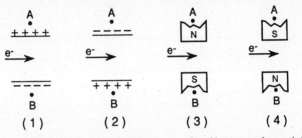

85. What is one characteristic of a light beam produced by a monochromatic laser?
    (1) It consists of coherent waves.
    (2) It can be dispersed into a complete continuous spectrum.
    (3) It cannot be reflected or refracted.
    (4) It does not exhibit any wave properties.

Group 4—Geometric Optics

If you choose this group, be sure to answer questions 86–95.

86. An object is placed in front of a plane mirror as shown in the diagram at the right. Which diagram below best represents the image that is formed?

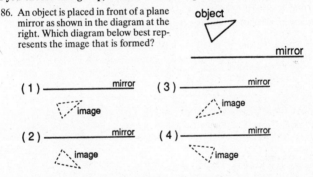

87. The diagram below shows light ray *R* parallel to the principal axis of a spherical concave (converging) mirror. Point *F* is the focal point of the mirror and *C* is the center of curvature.

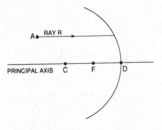

After reflecting, the light ray will pass through point

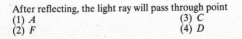

(1) *A*   (3) *C*
(2) *F*   (4) *D*

88. The tip of a person's nose is 12 centimeters from a concave (converging) spherical mirror that has a radius of curvature of 16 centimeters. What is the distance from the mirror to the image of the tip of the person's nose?
    (1) 8.0 cm
    (2) 12 cm
    (3) 16 cm
    (4) 24 cm

89. The image of a shoplifter in a department store is viewed in a convex (diverging) mirror. The image is
    (1) real and smaller than the shoplifter
    (2) real and larger than the shoplifter
    (3) virtual and smaller than the shoplifter
    (4) virtual and larger than the shoplifter

90. When light rays pass through the film in a movie projector, an image of the film is produced on a screen. In order to produce the image on the screen, what type of lens does the projector use and how far from the lens must the film be placed?
    (1) converging lens, at a distance greater than the focal length
    (2) converging lens, at a distance less than the focal length
    (3) diverging lens, at a distance greater than the focal length
    (4) diverging lens, at a distance less than the focal length

91. Two light rays from a common point are refracted by a lens. A real image is formed when these two refracted rays
    (1) converge to a single point
    (2) diverge and appear to come from a single point
    (3) travel in parallel paths
    (4) totally reflect inside the lens

92. The diagram below represents a convex (converging) lens with focal point *F*.

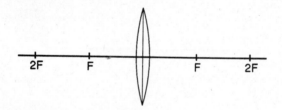

If an object is placed at 2*F*, the image will be
    (1) virtual, erect, and smaller than the object
    (2) real, inverted, and the same size as the object
    (3) real, inverted, and larger than the object
    (4) virtual, erect, and the same size as the object

93. The diagram below shows the refraction of the blue and red components of a white light beam.

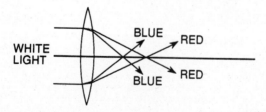

Which phenomenon does the diagram illustrate?
    (1) total internal reflection
    (2) critical angle reflection
    (3) spherical aberration
    (4) chromatic aberration

94. When a 2.0-meter-tall object is placed 4.0 meters in front of a lens, an image is formed on a screen located 0.050 meter behind the lens. What is the size of the image?
(1) 0.10 m   (3) 2.5 m
(2) 0.025 m   (4) 0.40 m

Note that question 95 has only three choices.

95. As the distance between a man and a plane mirror increases, the size of the image of the man produced by the mirror
(1) decreases
(2) increases
(3) remains the same

Group 5—Solid State

If you choose this group, be sure to answer questions 96–105.

96. A particular solid has a small energy gap between its valence and conduction bands. This solid is most likely classified as
(1) a good conductor   (3) a type of glass
(2) a semiconductor   (4) an insulator

97. The diagram below shows an electron moving through a semiconductor.

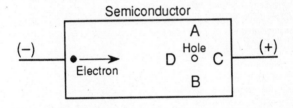

Toward which letter will the hole move?
(1) A   (3) C
(2) B   (4) D

98. Diagram A represents the wave form of an electron current entering a semiconductor device, and diagram B represents the wave form as the current leaves the device.

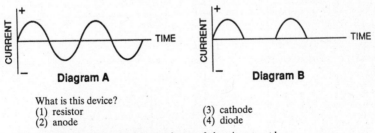

What is this device?
(1) resistor   (3) cathode
(2) anode   (4) diode

99. Compared to an insulator, a conductor of electric current has
(1) more free electrons per unit volume
(2) fewer free electrons per unit volume
(3) more free atoms per unit volume
(4) fewer free atoms per unit volume

Base your answers to questions 100 through 102 on the diagram below which represents a diode.

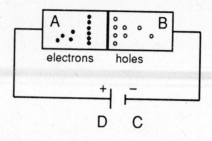

100. The *P-N* junction in the diagram is biased
    (1) reverse
    (2) forward
    (3) *B* to *C*
    (4) *A* to *D*

101. In the diagram, *B* represents the
    (1) *N*-type silicon
    (2) *P*-type silicon
    (3) cathode
    (4) diode

Note that question 102 has only three choices.

102. If the positive and negative wires of the circuit in the diagram were reversed, the current would
    (1) decrease
    (2) increase
    (3) remain the same

103. The graph at the right represents the alternating current signal input to a transistor amplifier. Which graph below best represents the amplified output signal from this transistor?

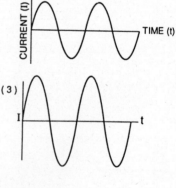

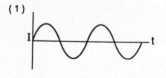

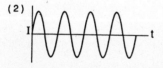

104. Which device contains a large number of transistors on a single block of silicon?
    (1) junction diode
    (2) conductor
    (3) integrated circuit
    (4) *N*-type semiconductor

Note that question 105 has only three choices.

105. The diagram below represents an operating N-P-N transistor circuit. Ammeter A_c reads the collector current and ammeter A_b reads the base current.

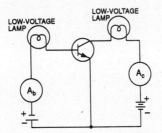

Compared to the reading of ammeter A_c, the reading of ammeter A_b is
(1) less
(2) greater
(3) the same

Group 6—Nuclear Energy

If you choose this group, be sure to answer questions 106–115.

106. An element has an atomic number of 63 and a mass number of 155. How many protons are in the nucleus of the element?
(1) 63   (3) 155
(2) 92   (4) 218

107. Which particle would generate the greatest amount of energy if its entire mass were converted into energy?
(1) electron   (3) alpha particle
(2) proton   (4) neutron

108. Which particles can be accelerated by a linear accelerator?
(1) protons and gamma rays   (3) electrons and protons
(2) neutrons and electrons   (4) neutrons and alpha particles

109. The equation below represents an unstable radioactive nucleus that is transmuted into another isotope (X) by the emission of a beta particle.

$$^{234}_{90}\text{Th} \rightarrow X + {}^{0}_{-1}e$$

Which new isotope is formed?
(1) $^{234}_{91}\text{Pa}$ (3) $^{235}_{90}\text{Pa}$

(2) $^{234}_{91}\text{Th}$ (4) $^{235}_{90}\text{Th}$

110. In 4.0 years, 40.0 kilograms of element A decays to 5.0 kilograms. The half-life of element A is
(1) 1.3 years   (3) 0.7 year
(2) 2.0 years   (4) 4.0 years

111. The subatomic particles that make up both protons and neutrons are known as
(1) electrons   (3) positrons
(2) nuclides   (4) quarks

112. Which equation is an example of positron emission?

(1) $^{226}_{88}\text{Ra} \rightarrow {}^{222}_{86}\text{Rn} + {}^{4}_{2}\text{He}$ (3) $^{64}_{29}\text{Cu} \rightarrow {}^{64}_{28}\text{Ni} + {}^{0}_{+1}e$

(2) $^{210}_{82}\text{Pb} \rightarrow {}^{210}_{83}\text{Bi} + {}^{0}_{-1}e$ (4) $^{14}_{7}\text{N} + {}^{4}_{2}\text{He} \rightarrow {}^{17}_{8}\text{O} + {}^{1}_{1}\text{H}$

113. Which process occurs during nuclear fission?
    (1) Light nuclei are forced together to form a heavier nucleus.
    (2) A heavy nucleus splits into lighter nuclei.
    (3) An atom is converted to a different isotope of the same element.
    (4) Transmutation is produced by the emission of alpha particles.

114. In order to increase the likelihood that a neutron emitted from a nucleus will be captured by another nucleus, the neutron should be
    (1) accelerated through a potential difference
    (2) heated to a higher temperature
    (3) slowed down to decrease its kinetic energy
    (4) absorbed by a control rod

115. The energy emitted by the Sun originates from the process of
    (1) fission
    (2) fusion
    (3) alpha decay
    (4) beta decay

PART III

You must answer *all* questions in this part. [15]

116. Base your answers to parts *a* through *c* on the information below.

   A newspaper carrier on her delivery route travels 200. meters due north and then turns and walks 300. meters due east.

   a *On your answer paper*, draw a vector diagram following the directions below.

   (1) Using a ruler and protractor and starting at point *P*, construct the sequence of two displacement vectors for the newspaper carrier's route. Use a scale of 1.0 centimeter = 50. meters. Label the vectors. [3]
   (2) Construct and label the vector that represents the carrier's resultant displacement from point *P*. [1]

   b What is the magnitude of the carrier's resultant displacement? [1]

   c What is the angle (in degrees) between north and the carrier's resultant displacement? [1]

117. The diagram below shows a spring compressed by a force of 6.0 newtons from its rest position to its compressed position.

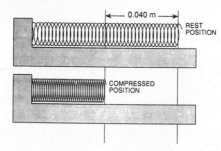

   Calculate the spring constant for this spring. [Show all calculations, including equations and substitutions with units.] [2]

118. Base your answers to parts *a* through *c* on the diagram and information below.

Monochromatic light is incident on a two-slit apparatus. The distance between the slits is 1.0×10^{-3} meter, and the distance from the two-slit apparatus to a screen displaying the interference pattern is 4.0 meters. The distance between the central maximum and the first-order maximum is 2.4×10^{-3} meter.

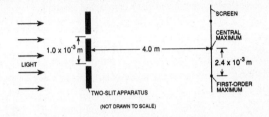

a What is the wavelength of the monochromatic light? [Show all calculations, including equations and substitutions with units.] [2]
b What is the color of the monochromatic light? [1]
c List *two* ways the variables could be changed that would cause the distance between the central maximum and the first-order maximum to increase [2]

119. Infrared electromagnetic radiation incident on a material produces no photoelectrons. When red light of equal intensity is shone on the same material, photoelectrons are emitted from the surface.

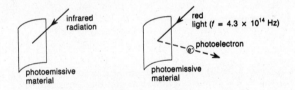

Using one or more complete sentences, explain why the visible red light causes photoelectric emission, but the infrared radiation does not. [2]

PHYSICS

June 16, 1994

PART I

Answer all 55 questions in this part. [65]

Directions (1–55): For *each* statement or question, select the word or expression that, of those given, best completes the statement or answers the question.

1. A car travels 20. meters east in 1.0 second. The displacement of the car at the end of this 1.0-second interval is
   (1) 20. m
   (2) 20. m/s
   (3) 20. m east
   (4) 20. m/s east

2. Which two graphs represent the motion of an object on which the net force is zero?

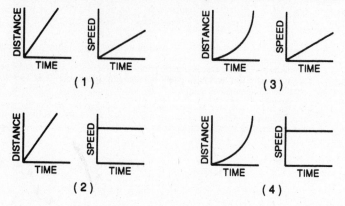

3. As shown in the diagram below, an astronaut on the Moon is holding a baseball and a balloon. The astronaut releases both objects at the same time.

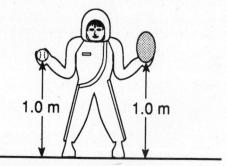

   What does the astronaut observe? [Note: The Moon has no atmosphere.]
   (1) The baseball falls slower than the balloon.
   (2) The baseball falls faster than the balloon.
   (3) The baseball and balloon fall at the same rate.
   (4) The baseball and balloon remain suspended and do not fall.

4. Which is a vector quantity?
   (1) distance
   (2) time
   (3) speed
   (4) acceleration

5. A 3.0-newton force and a 4.0-newton force act concurrently on a point. In which diagram below would the orientation of these forces produce the greatest net force on the point?

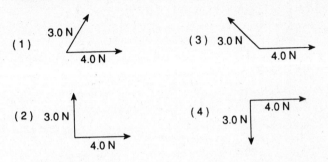

(1)   3.0 N
          4.0 N

(3)   3.0 N
          4.0 N

(2)   3.0 N
          4.0 N

(4)   4.0 N
         3.0 N

6. A rock falls freely from rest near the surface of a planet where the acceleration due to gravity is 4.0 meters per second^2. What is the speed of this rock after it falls 32 meters?
   (1) 8.0 m/s
   (2) 16 m/s
   (3) 25 m/s
   (4) 32 m/s

7. The diagram below represents a 10.-newton block sliding down a 30.° incline at a constant speed.

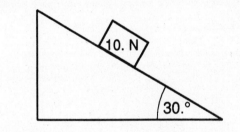

10. N

30.°

The force of friction on the block is approximately
   (1) 5.0 N
   (2) 10. N
   (3) 49 N
   (4) 98 N

8. The graph below shows speed as a function of time for four cars, A, B, C, and D, in straight-line motion.

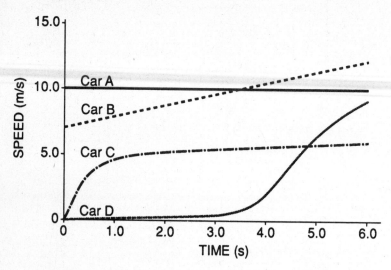

Which car experienced the greatest average acceleration during this 6.0-second interval?
(1) car A
(2) car B
(3) car C
(4) car D

Base your answers to questions 9 and 10 on the information and diagram below.

A car is traveling at a constant speed of 14 meters per second along a straight highway. A tree and a speed limit sign are beside the highway. As it passes the tree, the car starts to accelerate. The car is accelerated uniformly at 2.0 meters per second² until it reaches the speed limit sign, 5.0 seconds later.

Note that question 9 has only three choices.

9. When the car reaches the sign, the car's speed is
   (1) less than the speed limit
   (2) greater than the speed limit
   (3) equal to the speed limit

10. What is the distance between the tree and the sign?
    (1) 10. m
    (2) 25 m
    (3) 70. m
    (4) 95 m

11. The approximate mass of a nickel is
    (1) 0.0005 kg
    (2) 0.005 kg
    (3) 0.5 kg
    (4) 5 kg

12. A net force of 5.0×10^2 newtons causes an object to accelerate at a rate of 5.0 meters per second^2. What is the mass of the object?
    (1) 1.0×10^2 kg
    (2) 2.0×10^{-1} kg
    (3) 6.0×10^2 kg
    (4) 2.5×10^3 kg

13. The magnitude of the gravitational force between two objects is 20. newtons. If the mass of each object were doubled, the magnitude of the gravitational force between the objects would be
    (1) 5.0 N
    (2) 10. N
    (3) 20. N
    (4) 80. N

14. The mass of a space shuttle is approximately 2.0×10^6 kilograms. During lift-off, the net force on the shuttle is 1.0×10^7 newtons directed upward. What is the speed of the shuttle 10. seconds after lift-off? [Neglect air resistance and the mass change of the shuttle.]
    (1) 5.0×10^0 m/s
    (2) 5.0×10^1 m/s
    (3) 5.0×10^2 m/s
    (4) 5.0×10^3 m/s

15. A 2.0-kilogram toy cannon is at rest on a frictionless surface. A remote triggering device causes a 0.005-kilogram projectile to be fired from the cannon. Which equation describes this system after the cannon is fired?
    (1) mass of cannon + mass of projectile = 0
    (2) speed of cannon + speed of projectile = 0
    (3) momentum of cannon + momentum of projectile = 0
    (4) velocity of cannon + velocity of projectile = 0

16. Which statement explains why a book resting on a table is in equilibrium?
    (1) There is a net force acting downward on the book.
    (2) The weight of the book equals the weight of the table.
    (3) The acceleration due to gravity is 9.8 m/s^2 for both the book and the table.
    (4) The weight of the book and the table's upward force on the book are equal in magnitude, but opposite in direction.

17. A student pulls a block 3.0 meters along a horizontal surface at constant velocity. The diagram below shows the components of the force exerted on the block by the student.

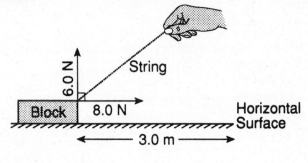

How much work is done against friction?
    (1) 18 J
    (2) 24 J
    (3) 30. J
    (4) 42 J

18. The diagram below shows a 1.0×10^3-newton crate to be lifted at constant speed from the ground to a loading dock 1.5 meters high in 5.0 seconds.

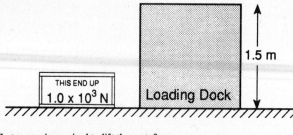

What power is required to lift the crate?
(1) 1.5×10^3 W   (3) 3.0×10^2 W
(2) 2.0×10^2 W   (4) 7.5×10^3 W

19. Graphs A and B below represent the results of applying an increasing force to stretch a spring which did not exceed its elastic limit.

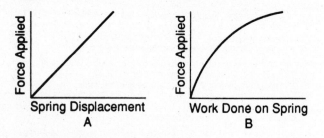

The spring constant can be represented by the
(1) slope of graph A
(2) slope of graph B
(3) reciprocal of the slope of graph A
(4) reciprocal of the slope of graph B

20. A force of 0.2 newton is needed to compress a spring a distance of 0.02 meter. The potential energy stored in this compressed spring is
(1) 8×10^{-5} J   (3) 2×10^{-5} J
(2) 2×10^{-3} J   (4) 4×10^{-5} J

21. An object with a speed of 20. meters per second has a kinetic energy of 400. joules. The mass of the object is
(1) 1.0 kg   (3) 0.50 kg
(2) 2.0 kg   (4) 40. kg

22. In the diagram below, an ideal pendulum released from point *A* swings freely through point *B*.

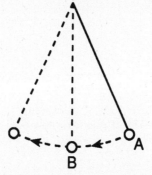

Compared to the pendulum's kinetic energy at A, its potential energy at *B* is
(1) half as great   (3) the same
(2) twice as great   (4) four times as great

23. As shown in the diagram below, a neutral pith ball suspended on a string is attracted to a positively charged rod.

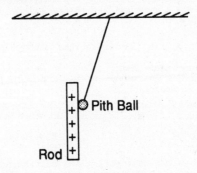

During contact with the rod, the pith ball
(1) loses electrons   (3) loses protons
(2) gains electrons   (4) gains protons

24. The electrostatic force between two positive point charges is *F* when the charges are 0.1 meter apart. When these point charges are placed 0.05 meter apart, the electrostatic force between them is
(1) 4*F*, and attracting
(2) $\frac{F}{4}$, and attracting
(3) 4*F*, and repelling
(4) $\frac{F}{4}$, and repelling

25. An electron is located 1.0 meter from a +2.0-coulomb charge, as shown in the diagram below.

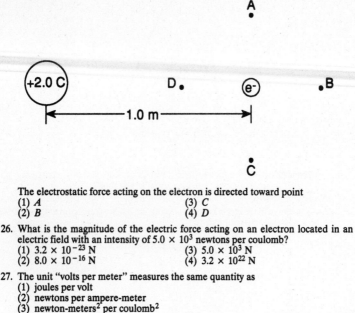

The electrostatic force acting on the electron is directed toward point
(1) *A*
(2) *B*
(3) *C*
(4) *D*

26. What is the magnitude of the electric force acting on an electron located in an electric field with an intensity of 5.0×10^3 newtons per coulomb?
(1) 3.2×10^{-23} N
(2) 8.0×10^{-16} N
(3) 5.0×10^3 N
(4) 3.2×10^{22} N

27. The unit "volts per meter" measures the same quantity as
(1) joules per volt
(2) newtons per ampere-meter
(3) newton-meters^2 per coulomb^2
(4) newtons per coulomb

28. A series circuit has a total resistance of 1.00×10^2 ohms and an applied potential difference of 2.00×10^2 volts. The amount of charge passing any point in the circuit in 2.00 seconds is
(1) 1.26×10^{19} C
(2) 2.00 C
(3) 2.52×10^{19} C
(4) 4.00 C

29. A copper wire is connected across a constant voltage source. The current flowing in the wire can be increased by increasing the wire's
(1) cross-sectional area
(2) length
(3) resistance
(4) temperature

30. Which two of the resistor arrangements shown below have equivalent resistance?

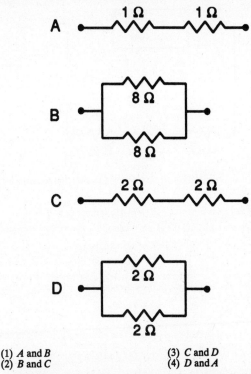

A   1 Ω   1 Ω

B   8 Ω   8 Ω

C   2 Ω   2 Ω

D   2 Ω   2 Ω

(1) A and B   (3) C and D
(2) B and C   (4) D and A

31. A clothes dryer connected to a 240-volt line draws 30. amperes of current for 20. minutes (1,200 seconds). Approximately how much electrical energy is consumed by the dryer?
(1) 4.8×10^3 J   (3) 1.4×10^5 J
(2) 7.2×10^3 J   (4) 8.6×10^6 J

32. Electrons are flowing in a conductor as shown in the diagram at the right. What is the direction of the magnetic field at point P?
(1) toward the top of the page
(2) toward the bottom of the page
(3) into the page
(4) out of the page

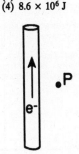

33. The diagram below shows a circuit with two resistors.

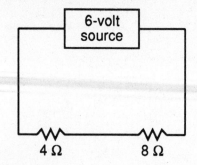

Compared to the potential drop across the 8-ohm resistor, the potential drop across the 4-ohm resistor is
(1) the same
(2) twice as great
(3) one-half as great
(4) four times as great

34. An electromagnet would have the greatest strength if its wire were wrapped around a core made of
(1) wood
(2) iron
(3) aluminum
(4) copper

35. An electron moving in an uniform magnetic field experiences the maximum magnetic force when the angle between the direction of the electron's motion and the direction of the magnetic field is
(1) 0°
(2) 45°
(3) 90°
(4) 180°

36. An accelerating particle that does *not* generate electromagnetic waves could be
(1) a neutron
(2) a proton
(3) an electron
(4) an alpha particle

37. A characteristic common to sound waves and light waves is that they
(1) are longitudinal
(2) are transverse
(3) transfer energy
(4) travel in a vacuum

38. As a longitudinal wave passes through a medium, the particles of the medium move
(1) in circles
(2) in ellipses
(3) parallel to the direction of wave travel
(4) perpendicular to the direction of wave travel

Base your answers to questions 39 through 41 on the diagram below which shows a parked police car with a siren on top. The siren is producing a sound with a frequency of 680 hertz, which travels first through point *A* and then through point *B*, as shown. The speed of the sound is 340 meters per second.

POLICE

A   B

(not drawn to scale)

39. If the sound waves are in phase at points A and B, the distance between the points could be
   (1) 1λ
   (2) $\frac{1}{2}\lambda$
   (3) $\frac{3}{2}\lambda$
   (4) $\frac{1}{4}\lambda$

40. What is the wavelength of the sound produced by the car's siren?
   (1) 0.50 m
   (2) 2.0 m
   (3) 2.3×10^5 m
   (4) 2.3×10^{-6} m

Note that question 41 has only three choices.

41. If the car were to accelerate toward point A, the frequency of the sound heard by an observer at point A would
   (1) decrease
   (2) increase
   (3) remain the same

42. The diagram below shows two pulses, each of length λ, traveling toward each other at equal speed in a rope.

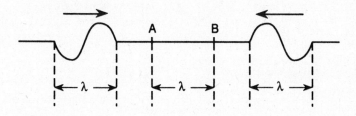

Which diagram best represents the shape of the rope when both pulses are in region AB?

43. The diagram below shows two waves traveling in the same medium for the same length of time.

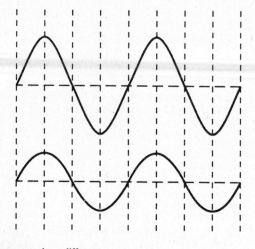

The two waves have different
(1) amplitudes
(2) frequencies
(3) speeds
(4) wavelengths

44. The distance from the Moon to Earth is 3.9×10^8 meters. What is the time required for a light ray to travel from the Moon to Earth?
(1) 0.65 s
(2) 1.3 s
(3) 2.6 s
(4) 3.9 s

45. Parallel light rays are incident on the surface of a plane mirror. Upon reflection from the mirror, the light rays will
(1) converge
(2) diverge
(3) be parallel
(4) be scattered

46. In the diagram below, a ray of monochromatic light ($\lambda = 5.9 \times 10^{-7}$ meter) reaches the boundary between medium X and air and follows the path shown.

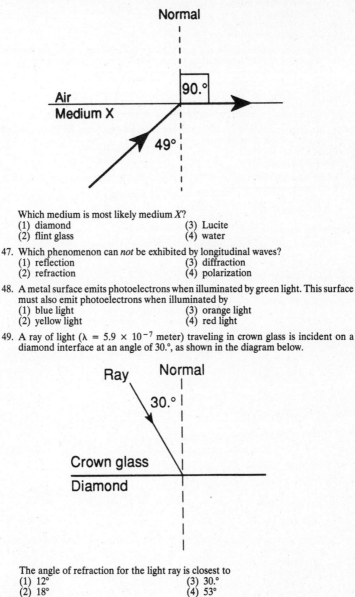

Which medium is most likely medium X?
(1) diamond
(2) flint glass
(3) Lucite
(4) water

47. Which phenomenon can *not* be exhibited by longitudinal waves?
(1) reflection
(2) refraction
(3) diffraction
(4) polarization

48. A metal surface emits photoelectrons when illuminated by green light. This surface must also emit photoelectrons when illuminated by
(1) blue light
(2) yellow light
(3) orange light
(4) red light

49. A ray of light ($\lambda = 5.9 \times 10^{-7}$ meter) traveling in crown glass is incident on a diamond interface at an angle of 30.°, as shown in the diagram below.

The angle of refraction for the light ray is closest to
(1) 12°
(2) 18°
(3) 30.°
(4) 53°

50. An x-ray photon collides with an electron in an atom, ejecting the electron and emitting another photon. During the collision, there is conservation of
    (1) momentum, only
    (2) energy, only
    (3) both momentum and energy
    (4) neither momentum nor energy

51. After Rutherford bombarded gold foil with alpha particles, he concluded that the volume of an atom is mostly empty space. Which observation led Rutherford to this conclusion?
    (1) Some of the alpha particles were deflected 180°.
    (2) The paths of deflected alpha particles were hyperbolic.
    (3) Many alpha particles were absorbed by gold nuclei.
    (4) Most of the alpha particles were not deflected.

52. The threshold frequency for a photoemissive surface is 1.0×10^{14} hertz. What is the work function of the surface?
    (1) 1.0×10^{-14} J
    (2) 6.6×10^{-20} J
    (3) 6.6×10^{-48} J
    (4) 2.2×10^{-28} J

53. What is the *minimum* amount of energy needed to ionize a mercury electron in the c energy level?
    (1) 0.57 eV
    (2) 4.86 eV
    (3) 5.52 eV
    (4) 10.38 eV

Note that questions 54 and 55 have only three choices.

54. As the color of light changes from red to yellow, the frequency of the light
    (1) decreases
    (2) increases
    (3) remains the same

55. A car is driven from Buffalo to Albany and on to New York City, as shown in the diagram below.

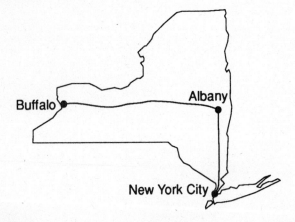

Compared to the magnitude of the car's total displacement, the distance driven is
(1) shorter
(2) longer
(3) the same

PART II

This part consists of six groups, each containing ten questions. Each group tests an optional area of the course. Choose two of these six groups. Be sure that you answer all ten questions in each group chosen. [20]

Group 1 — Motion in a Plane

If you choose this group, be sure to answer questions 56–65.

Base your answers to questions 56 and 57 on the information and diagram below.

A vehicle travels at a constant speed of 6.0 meters per second around a horizontal circular curve with a radius of 24 meters. The mass of the vehicle is 4.4×10^3 kilograms. An icy patch is located at P on the curve.

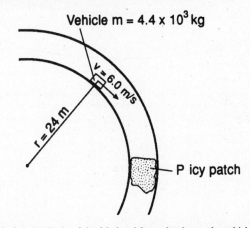

56. What is the magnitude of the frictional force that keeps the vehicle on its circular path?
    (1) 1.1×10^3 N (3) 4.3×10^4 N
    (2) 6.6×10^3 N (4) 6.5×10^4 N

57. On the icy patch of pavement, the frictional force on the vehicle is zero. Which arrow best represents the direction of the vehicle's velocity when it reaches icy patch P?

(1) $\longrightarrow$ (3) $\uparrow$

(2) $\longleftarrow$ (4) $\downarrow$

Base your answers to questions 58 and 59 on the information and diagram below.

A 60.-kilogram adult and a 30.-kilogram child are passengers on a rotor ride at an amusement park. When the rotating hollow cylinder reaches a certain constant speed, v, the floor moves downward. Both passengers stay "pinned" against the wall of the rotor, as shown in the diagram below.

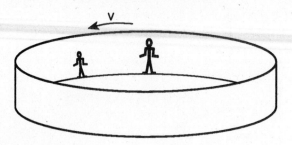

58. The magnitude of the frictional force between the adult and the wall of the spinning rotor is F. What is the magnitude of the frictional force between the child and the wall of the spinning rotor?
   (1) F (3) $\frac{F}{2}$

   (2) $2F$ (4) $\frac{F}{4}$

Note that question 59 has only three choices.

59. Compared to the magnitude of the acceleration of the adult, the magnitude of the acceleration of the child is
   (1) less
   (2) greater
   (3) the same

60. A satellite is moving at constant speed in a circular orbit about the Earth, as shown in the diagram below.

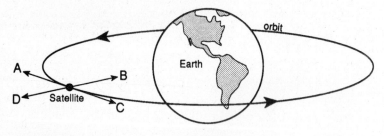

The net force acting on the satellite is directed toward point
   (1) A   (3) C
   (2) B   (4) D

61. Which diagram best represents the orbit of the planet Pluto around the Sun?

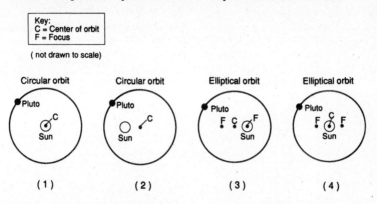

Key:
C = Center of orbit
F = Focus

(not drawn to scale)

Circular orbit   Circular orbit   Elliptical orbit   Elliptical orbit

(1)   (2)   (3)   (4)

Base your answers to question 62 and 63 on the diagram below which shows a ball projected horizontally with an initial velocity of 20. meters per second east, off a cliff 100. meters high. [Neglect air resistance.]

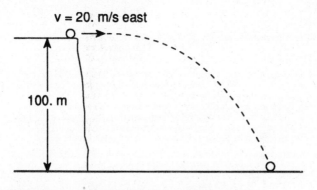

v = 20. m/s east

100. m

62. How many seconds does the ball take to reach the ground?
    (1) 4.5 s   (3) 9.8 s
    (2) 20. s   (4) 2.0 s

63. During the flight of the ball, what is the direction of its acceleration?
    (1) downward   (3) westward
    (2) upward   (4) eastward

64. A projectile is fired at an angle of 53° to the horizontal with a speed of 80. meters per second. What is the vertical component of the projectile's initial velocity?
    (1) 130 m/s   (3) 64 m/s
    (2) 100 m/s   (4) 48 m/s

Note that question 65 has only three choices.

65. As the distance between the Moon and Earth increases, the Moon's orbital speed
    (1) decreases
    (2) increases
    (3) remains the same

Group 2—Internal Energy

If you choose this group, be sure to answer questions 66–75.

66. Which line on the graph below best represents the relationship between the average kinetic energy of the molecules of an ideal gas and absolute temperature?

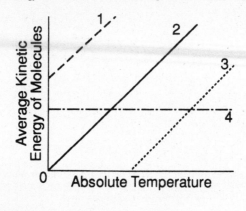

(1) 1   (3) 3
(2) 2   (4) 4

67. The difference between the boiling point of lead and the freezing point of lead is
(1) 328 K   (3) 1658 K
(2) 1412 K   (4) 1740 K

68. Equal masses of aluminum and copper, both at 0°C, are placed in the same insulated can of hot water. Which statement describes this system at equilibrium (the next exchange of internal energy is zero)?
(1) The water has a higher temperature than the aluminum and copper.
(2) The aluminum has a higher temperature than the copper and water.
(3) The copper has a higher temperature than the aluminum and water.
(4) The aluminum, copper, and water have the same temperature.

69. An unknown liquid with a mass of 0.010 kilogram absorbs 0.032 kilojoule of heat. Its temperature rises 8.0 C°, with no change in phase. What is the specific heat of the unknown liquid?
(1) 0.0040 kJ/kg•C°   (3) 26 kJ/kg•C°
(2) 0.40 kJ/kg•C°   (4) 260 kJ/kg•C°

70. On the graph below, the four lines show the relationship between temperature and heat added to equal masses of aluminum, copper, iron, and platinum in the solid phase.

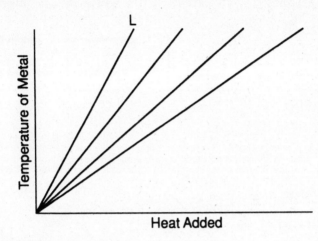

Which metal is represented by line L?
(1) aluminum   (3) iron
(2) copper   (4) platinum

71. How much heat is required to change 3.0 kilograms of ice at 0.0°C to water at 0.0°C?
(1) 1.0×10^3 kJ   (3) 2.3×10^3 kJ
(2) 3.3×10^2 kJ   (4) 6.8×10^3 kJ

72. According to the second law of thermodynamics, as time passes, the total entropy in the universe
(1) decreases, only
(2) increases, only
(3) remains the same
(4) cyclically increases and decreases

Note that question 73 has only three choices.

73. As the number of gas molecules in a rigid container at constant temperature is increased, the pressure on the walls of the container
(1) decreases
(2) increases
(3) remains the same

74. In which diagram below does the water have the highest boiling point?

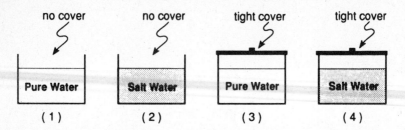

(1)   (2)   (3)   (4)

75. A crystalline solid at a temperature below its melting point is heated at a constant rate to a temperature above its melting point. Which graph best represents the average internal kinetic energy ($\overline{KE}$) of the substance as a function of heat added?

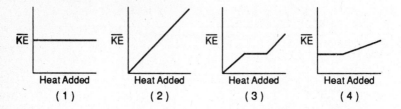

(1)   (2)   (3)   (4)

Group 3—Electromagnetic Applications

If you choose this group, be sure to answer questions 76–85.

76. A beam of particles is produced in a cathode-ray tube. The beam may be deflected by a magnetic field because each particle in the beam
   (1) possesses a charge
   (2) is at rest
   (3) has a rest mass greater than 9.1×10^{-31} kilogram
   (4) has a speed of 3.0×10^8 meters per second

77. Which device does *not* operate by means of torque exerted on a current-carrying loop of wire in a magnetic field?
   (1) ammeter   (3) transformer
   (2) electric motor   (4) voltmeter

Base your answers to questions 78 and 79 on the diagram below which represents an electron about to enter uniform magnetic field B. The velocity of the electron (v) is 6.0×10^7 meters per second to the right. The flux density of the magnetic field is 4.0×10^{-2} tesla, directed into the page.

$$
\begin{array}{cccc}
\text{X} & \text{X} & \text{X} & \text{X} \ \text{B} \\
\text{X} & \text{X} & \text{X} & \text{X} \\
\text{(e}^-\text{)} \xrightarrow{v} \quad \text{X} & \text{X} & \text{X} & \text{X} \\
\text{X} & \text{X} & \text{X} & \text{X} \\
\text{X} & \text{X} & \text{X} & \text{X}
\end{array}
$$

78. When the electron first enters the magnetic field, the electron experiences a magnetic force directed toward the
    (1) top of the page
    (2) bottom of the page
    (3) left of the page
    (4) right of the page

79. The magnitude of the magnetic force acting on the electron in the field is approximately
    (1) 2.4×10^{-11} N
    (2) 3.8×10^{-13} N
    (3) 1.6×10^{-18} N
    (4) 2.2×10^{-24} N

80. In the diagram below, an electron moving with speed v enters the space between two oppositely charged parallel plates.

Which diagram best represents the path the electron follows as it passes between the plates?

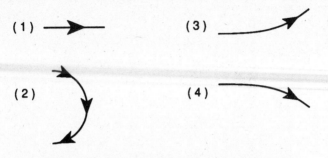

81. After Millikan performed his oil drop experiment, he concluded that
    (1) there is a minimum amount of charge that particles can acquire
    (2) oil drops exhibit gravitational attraction for other oil drops
    (3) oil drops are largely empty space
    (4) there is a minimum amount of mass that particles can require

82. When a 12-volt potential difference is applied to the primary coil of a transformer, an 8.0-volt potential difference is induced in the secondary coil. If the primary coil has 24 turns, how many turns does the secondary coil have? [Assume 100% efficiency.]
    (1) 36   (3) 3
    (2) 16   (4) 4

Base your answers to questions 83 through 85 on the diagram below which shows a loop of wire being rotated at a constant rate about an axis in a uniform magnetic field.

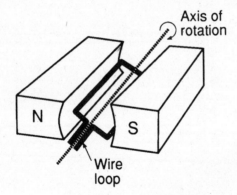

83. Which graph best represents the relationship between induced potential difference across the ends of the loop and time, for one complete rotation?

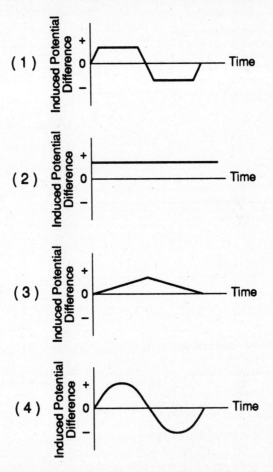

(1)

(2)

(3)

(4)

84. Which procedure would enable a current to flow in the loop, due to the induced potential difference?
   (1) turning the loop in the opposite direction at the same rate of rotation
   (2) increasing the distance between the ends of the loop
   (3) connecting the ends of the loop to each other with an insulating material
   (4) connecting the ends of the loop to each other with a conducting material

Note that question 85 has only three choices.

85. As the speed of rotation of the wire loop is increased, the maximum electromotive force induced in the loop
   (1) decreases
   (2) increases
   (3) remains the same

Group 4—Geometric Optics

If you choose this group, be sure to answer questions 86–95.

86. A plane mirror produces an image of an object. Compared to the object, the image appears
    (1) inverted and the same size
    (2) reversed and the same size
    (3) inverted and larger
    (4) reversed and larger

87. A candle is located beyond the center of curvature, C, of a concave spherical mirror having principal focus F, as shown in the diagram below.

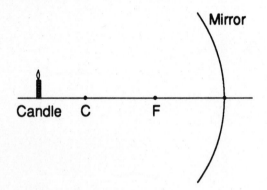

    Where is the candle's image located?
    (1) beyond C
    (2) between C and F
    (3) between F and the mirror
    (4) behind the mirror

88. The convex spherical mirror found on the passenger side of many cars contains the warning: "Objects are closer than they appear." Which phrase best describes the image of an object viewed in this mirror?
    (1) real and smaller than the object
    (2) real and larger than the object
    (3) virtual and smaller than the object
    (4) virtual and larger than the object

Base your answers to questions 89 and 90 on the information below.
    A concave mirror with a focal length of 20. centimeters is used to examine a 0.50-centimeter-wide freckle on a person's face. The person's face is located 10. centimeters from the mirror.

89. The image of the freckle produced by the mirror is
    (1) real and inverted   (3) virtual and inverted
    (2) real and erect   (4) virtual and erect

90. What is the width of the image of the freckle?
    (1) 1.0 cm   (3) 0.50 cm
    (2) 2.0 cm   (4) 1.5 cm

91. In the diagram below, a crown glass converging lens has foci F and F'. An object is placed at a distance slightly less than the focal length from the lens, and a virtual image is produced.

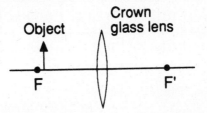

The object remains in the same position and the crown glass lens is replaced with another lens of identical shape. If the new lens produces a real image of the object, the new lens is most likely made of

(1) water
(2) Lucite

(3) fused quartz
(4) flint glass

92. Which diagram below shows the path of light rays as they pass from an object at $2F$ through a converging lens to the image formed at $2F'$?

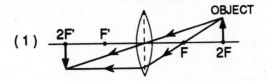

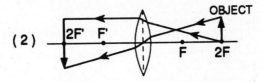

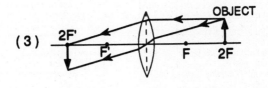

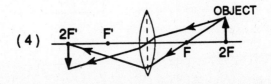

93. A student placed an object at various distances (d_o) from a converging lens. The corresponding image distance (d_i) was measured and recorded in the data table below.

d_o	0.15 m	0.20 m	0.30 m
d_i	0.30 m	0.20 m	0.15 m

What is the focal length of the lens?
(1) 0.10 m
(2) 0.15 m
(3) 0.20 m
(4) 0.30 m

94. A lens forms a real image three times the size of the object when the image is 0.12 meter from the lens. How far from the lens is the object?
(1) 0.36 m
(2) 0.09 m
(3) 0.03 m
(4) 0.04 m

95. What causes chromatic aberration in a crown glass lens?
(1) Each wavelength of light reflects from the surface of the lens.
(2) Each wavelength of light is refracted a different amount by the lens.
(3) White light waves interfere inside the lens.
(4) White light waves diffract around the edge of the lens.

Group 5—Solid State

If you choose this group, be sure to answer questions 96–105.

96. Which quantity is equal to the reciprocal of resistivity?
(1) conductivity
(2) current
(3) resistance
(4) voltage

97. A solid is determined to be a conductor, an insulator, or a semiconductor on the basis of
(1) its melting point and boiling point
(2) its atomic number and mass number
(3) the number of electrons in the conduction band and the energy gap between bands
(4) the number of electrons per square meter of cross-sectional area of the material

98. P-type semiconducting material functions primarily as
(1) an acceptor of protons
(2) an acceptor of electrons
(3) a donor of protons
(4) a donor of electrons

99. What permits current to flow through a semiconductor when it is connected to a battery, as shown in the diagram at the right?
(1) holes moving toward the right, only
(2) electrons moving toward the left, only
(3) both electrons and holes moving toward the left
(4) electrons moving left and holes moving right

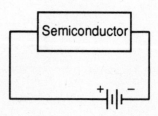

100. The diagram below shows the alternating current input signal to a diode.

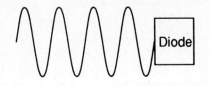

Which diagram below best represents the output signal?

(1)

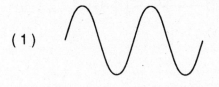

(2)

(3)

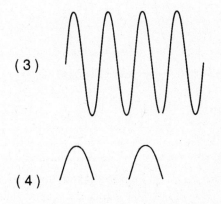

(4)

101. What is a basic difference between a transistor and a diode?
   (1) the number of junctions between *P*-type and *N*-type material
   (2) the size of the single junction between the *P*-type and *N*-type material
   (3) the nature of the donor material used in the *N*-type semiconductor
   (4) the amount of current applied to the semiconductor material

102. In the diagram below, which part of the operating *N-P-N* transistor is the collector?

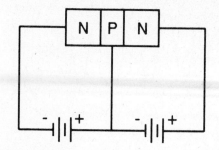

    (1) the left *N*-type section
    (2) the right *N*-type section
    (3) the left *P-N* junction
    (4) the right *P-N* junction

103. A small change in the emitter-base current in a transistor brings about a large change in the collector current. This current-increasing property of a transistor is called
    (1) amplification   (3) Ohm's law
    (2) biasing   (4) rectification

Base your answers to questions 104 and 105 on the graph below of current versus potential difference for a diode.

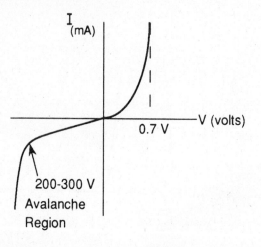

104. The "avalanche" occurs only if the diode circuit is
    (1) open   (3) reverse biased
    (2) closed   (4) forward biased

Note that question 105 has only three choices.

105. As the amount of doping material in the semiconductor increases, the magnitude of the voltage required for the "avalanche" to occur
    (1) decreases
    (2) increases
    (3) remains the same

Group 6—Nuclear Energy

If you choose this group, be sure to answer questions 106–115.

106. How many neutrons are in an atom of $^{222}_{86}\text{Rn}$?

    (1) 84   (3) 136
    (2) 86   (4) 222

107. The chart below shows the masses of selected particles.

Particle	Mass
$^{235}_{92}\text{U}$	235.0 u
$^{138}_{56}\text{Ba}$	137.9 u
$^{95}_{36}\text{Kr}$	94.9 u
$^{1}_{0}\text{n}$	1.0 u

In the equation

$$^{235}_{92}\text{U} + ^{1}_{0}\text{n} \rightarrow ^{138}_{56}\text{Ba} + ^{95}_{36}\text{Kr} + 3^{1}_{0}\text{n} + E,$$

the energy E is equivalent to a mass of
    (1) 0.2 u   (3) 2.2 u
    (2) 2.0 u   (4) 0.0 u

108. Isotopes of the same element have nuclei with identical
    (1) mass numbers
    (2) binding energies
    (3) numbers of neutrons
    (4) numbers of protons

109. Which subatomic particle can *not* be accelerated by an electromagnetic field?
    (1) alpha   (3) electron
    (2) neutron   (4) positron

110. According to the Uranium Disintegration Series, the immediate decay product of $^{234}_{90}\text{Th}$ is

    (1) $^{230}_{92}\text{U}$ (3) $^{238}_{92}\text{U}$

    (2) $^{230}_{89}\text{Ac}$ (4) $^{234}_{91}\text{Pa}$

111. In the reaction $^{27}_{13}\text{Al} + {}^{4}_{2}\text{He} \rightarrow {}^{30}_{15}\text{P} + {}^{1}_{0}\text{n} + X$, what could X represent?
    (1) proton
    (2) gamma radiation
    (3) alpha particle
    (4) beta particle

112. A radioactive isotope has a half-life of 3 minutes. If 10 kilograms of this isotope remains after 15 minutes, the original mass of the isotope must have been
    (1) 50 kg
    (2) 160 kg
    (3) 250 kg
    (4) 320 kg

113. When an atomic nucleus captures an electron, the atomic number of that nucleus
    (1) decreases by 1
    (2) decreases by 2
    (3) increases by 1
    (4) increases by 2

114. The equation $^{3}_{1}\text{H} + {}^{1}_{1}\text{H} \rightarrow {}^{4}_{2}\text{He}$ + energy is an example of
    (1) alpha decay
    (2) positron capture
    (3) fusion
    (4) fission

115. Which equation represents nuclear fission?
    (1) $^{214}_{82}\text{Pb} \rightarrow {}^{214}_{83}\text{Bi} + {}_{-1}^{0}\text{e}$
    (2) $4{}^{1}_{1}\text{H} \rightarrow {}^{4}_{2}\text{He} + 2{}_{+1}^{0}\text{e}$
    (3) $^{235}_{92}\text{U} + {}^{1}_{0}\text{n} = {}^{138}_{56}\text{Ba} + {}^{95}_{36}\text{Kr} + 3{}^{1}_{0}\text{n}$
    (4) $^{238}_{92}\text{U} \rightarrow {}^{234}_{90}\text{Th} + {}^{4}_{2}\text{He}$

PART III

You must answer *all* questions in this part. [15]

116. Base your answers to part *a* through *c* on the information and data table below.

A resistor was held at constant temperature in an operating electric circuit. A student measured the current through the resistor and the potential difference across it. The measurements are shown in data table below.

Data Table

Current (A)	Potential Difference (V)
0.010	2.3
0.020	5.2
0.030	7.4
0.040	9.9
0.050	12.7

a Using the information in the data table, construct a graph on the grid provided on your answer paper, following the directions below.
 (1) Mark an appropriate scale on the axis labeled "Current (A)."   [1]
 (2) Plot the data points for potential difference versus current.   [1]
 (3) Draw the best-fit line.   [1]

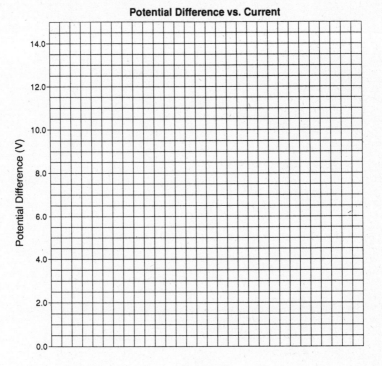

Potential Difference vs. Current

Current (A)

b Using your graph, find the slope of the best-fit line. [Show all calculations, including the equation and substitution with units.]   [2]
c What physical quantity does the slope of the graph represent?   [1]

117. Base your answers to part *a* through *d* on the information below.

A 6.0-kilogram concrete block is dropped from the top of a tall building. The block has fallen a distance of 55 meters and has a speed of 30. meters per second when it hits the ground.

a At the instant the block was released, what was its gravitational potential energy with respect to the ground? [Show all calculations, including the equation and substitution with units.]   [2]
b Calculate the kinetic energy of the block at the point of impact. [Show all calculations, including the equation and substitution with units.]   [2]
c How much mechanical energy was "lost" by the block as it fell?   [1]
d Using one or more complete sentences, explain what happened to the mechanical energy that was "lost" by the block.   [1]

118. Base your answers to parts *a* through *c* on the information and diagram below.
A ray of light *AO* is incident on a plane mirror as shown.

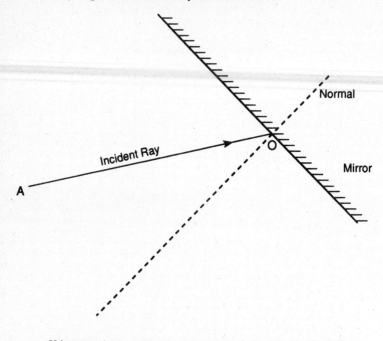

a Using a protractor, measure the angle of incidence for light ray *AO* and record the value on your answer sheet.   [1]
b What is the angle of reflection of the light ray?   [1]
c Using a protractor and straightedge, construct the reflected ray on the diagram *on your answer paper*.   [1]

PHYSICS

June 16, 1995

PART I

Answer all 55 questions in this part. [65]

Directions (1–55): For *each* statement or question, select the word or expression that, of those given, best completes the statement or answers the question.

1. The thickness of a dollar bill is closest to
   (1) 10^{-4} m
   (2) 10^{-2} m
   (3) 10^{-1} m
   (4) 10^{1} m

2. A jogger accelerates at a constant rate as she travels 5.0 meters along a straight track from point A to point B, as shown in the diagram below.

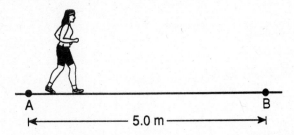

   If her speed was 2.0 meters per second at point A and will be 3.0 meters per second at point B, how long will it take her to go from A to B?
   (1) 1.0 s
   (2) 2.0 s
   (3) 3.3 s
   (4) 4.2 s

3. Which graph best represents the motion of an object falling from rest near the Earth's surface? [Neglect friction.]

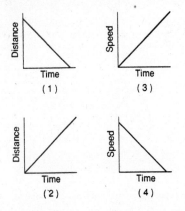

4. An object falls freely from rest near the surface of the Earth. What is the speed of the object when it has fallen 4.9 meters from its rest position?
   (1) 4.9 m/s
   (2) 9.8 m/s
   (3) 24 m/s
   (4) 96 m/s

5. Which term represents a vector quantity?
   (1) work
   (2) power
   (3) force
   (4) distance

6. A river flows due east at 1.5 meters per second. A motorboat leaves the north shore of the river and heads due south at 2.0 meters per second, as shown in the diagram below.

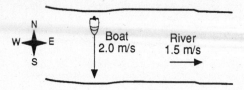

Which vector best represents the resultant velocity of the boat relative to the riverbank?

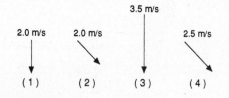

7. Which combination of concurrent forces could *not* produce equilibrium?
   (1) 10. N, 20. N, and 50. N
   (2) 20. N, 30. N, and 50. N
   (3) 30. N, 40. N, and 50. N
   (4) 40. N, 40. N, and 50. N

8. A 60.-kilogram astronaut weighs 96 newtons on the surface of the Moon. The acceleration due to gravity on the Moon is
   (1) 0.0 m/s^2
   (2) 1.6 m/s^2
   (3) 4.9 m/s^2
   (4) 9.8 m/s^2

9. The handle of a lawn roller is held at 45° from the horizontal. A force, F, of 28.0 newtons is applied to the handle as the roller is pushed across a level lawn, as shown in the diagram below.

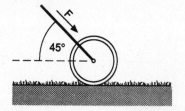

What is the magnitude of the force moving the roller forward?
   (1) 7.00 N
   (2) 14.0 N
   (3) 19.8 N
   (4) 39.0 N

10. A 1.0×10^2-kilogram box rests on the bed of a truck that is accelerating at 2.0 meters per second². What is the magnitude of the force of friction on the box as it moves with the truck without slipping?
   (1) $1.0 \times 10^3 \text{ N}$
   (2) $2.0 \times 10^2 \text{ N}$
   (3) $5.0 \times 10^2 \text{ N}$
   (4) 0.0 N

11. A student weighing 500. newtons stands on a spring scale in an elevator. If the scale reads 520. newtons, the elevator must be
    (1) accelerating upward
    (2) accelerating downward
    (3) moving upward at constant speed
    (4) moving downward at constant speed

12. A box decelerates as it moves to the right along a horizontal surface, as shown in the diagram at the right. Which vector best represents the force of friction on the box?

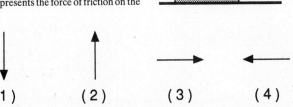

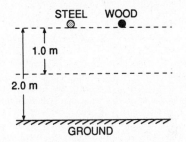

13. If a net force of 10. newtons acts on a 6.0-kilogram mass for 8.0 seconds, the total change of momentum of the mass is
    (1) 48 kg•m/s
    (2) 60. kg•m/s
    (3) 80. kg•m/s
    (4) 480 kg•m/s

14. In the diagram below, a 0.4-kilogram steel sphere and a 0.1-kilogram wooden sphere are located 2.0 meters above the ground. Both spheres are allowed to fall from rest.

STEEL   WOOD

1.0 m

2.0 m

GROUND

Which statement best describes the spheres after they have fallen 1.0 meter? [Neglect air resistance.]
    (1) Both spheres have the same speed and momentum.
    (2) Both spheres have the same speed and the steel sphere has more momentum than the wooden sphere.
    (3) The steel sphere has greater speed and has less momentum than the wooden sphere.
    (4) The steel sphere has greater speed than the wooden sphere and both spheres have the same momentum.

15. A constant force of 2.0 newtons is used to push a 3.0-kilogram mass 4.0 meters across the floor. How much work is done on the mass?
    (1) 6.0 J
    (2) 8.0 J
    (3) 12 J
    (4) 24 J

16. A 4.0×10^3-watt motor applies a force of 8.0×10^2 newtons to move a boat at constant speed. How far does the boat move in 16 seconds?
    (1) 3.2 m
    (2) 5.0 m
    (3) 32 m
    (4) 80. m

17. When a spring is stretched 0.200 meter from its equilibrium position, it possesses a potential energy of 10.0 joules. What is the spring constant for this spring?
    (1) 100. N/m
    (2) 125 N/m
    (3) 250. N/m
    (4) 500. N/m

18. A 1.0×10^3-kilogram car is moving at a constant speed of 4.0 meters per second. What is the kinetic energy of the car?
    (1) 1.6×10^3 J
    (2) 2.0×10^4 J
    (3) 8.0×10^3 J
    (4) 4.0×10^3 J

19. A force is applied to a block, causing it to accelerate along a horizontal, frictionless surface. The energy gained by the block is equal to the
    (1) work done on the block
    (2) power applied to the block
    (3) impulse applied to the block
    (4) momentum given to the block

20. A 1.0-kilogram mass gains kinetic energy as it falls freely from rest a vertical distance, d. How far would a 2.0-kilogram mass have to fall freely from rest to gain the same amount of kinetic energy?

    (1) d

    (2) $2d$

    (3) $\dfrac{d}{2}$

    (4) $\dfrac{d}{4}$

21. The diagram below shows the arrangement of three charged hollow metal spheres, $A, B,$ and C. The arrows indicate the direction of the electric forces acting between the spheres. At least two of the spheres are positively charged.

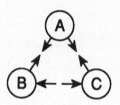

Which sphere, if any, could be negatively charged?
    (1) sphere A
    (2) sphere B
    (3) sphere C
    (4) no sphere

22. The diagram below shows the initial charge and position of three identical metal spheres, $X, Y,$ and Z, which have been placed on insulating stands.

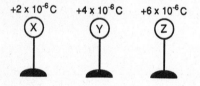

All three spheres are simultaneously brought into contact with each other and then returned to their original positions. Which statement best describes the charge of the spheres after this procedure is completed?
    (1) All the spheres are neutral.
    (2) Each sphere has a net charge of $+4 \times 10^{-6}$ coulomb.
    (3) Each sphere retains the same charge that it had originally.
    (4) Sphere Y has a greater charge than spheres X or Z.

23. Which diagram best represents the electric field of a point charge?

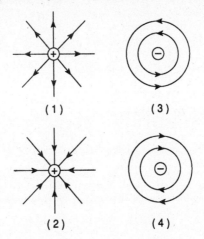

(1) (3)

(2) (4)

24. If 20. joules of work is done in transferring 5.0 coulombs of charge between two points, the potential difference between these two points is
    (1) 100 V (3) 0.25 V
    (2) 50. V (4) 4.0 V

25. A neutral atom must contain equal numbers of
    (1) protons and neutrons, only (3) electrons and neutrons, only
    (2) protons and electrons, only (4) protons, neutrons, and electrons

26. A 20.-ohm resistor has 40. coulombs passing through it in 5.0 seconds. The potential difference across the resistor is
    (1) 8.0 V (3) 160 V
    (2) 100 V (4) 200 V

27. The diagram below shows a circuit in which a copper wire connects points A and B.

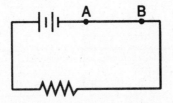

The electrical resistance between points A and B can be decreased by
    (1) replacing the wire with a thicker copper wire of the same length
    (2) replacing the wire with a longer copper wire of the same thickness
    (3) increasing the temperature of the copper wire
    (4) increasing the potential difference supplied by the battery

28. In the circuit diagram below, ammeter A measures the current supplied by the 10.-volt battery.

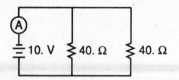

The current measured by ammeter A is
(1) 0.13 A
(2) 2.0 A
(3) 0.50 A
(4) 4.0 A

29. Which unit is equivalent to a watt, the SI unit of power?
(1) joule/second
(2) joule/volt
(3) joule/ohm
(4) joule/coulomb

30. An electric fan draws 1.7 amperes of current when operated at a potential difference of 120 volts. How much electrical energy is needed to run this fan for 1 hour? [1 hour = 3600 seconds]
(1) 7.1×10^1 J
(2) 2.0×10^2 J
(3) 2.5×10^5 J
(4) 7.3×10^5 J

31. Two solenoids are wound on soft iron cores and connected to batteries, as shown in the diagram below.

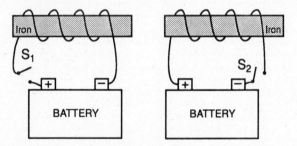

When switches S_1 and S_2 are closed, the solenoids
(1) repel because of adjacent north poles
(2) repel because of adjacent south poles
(3) attract because of adjacent north and south poles
(4) neither attract nor repel

32. Which diagram below best represents the magnetic field near a bar magnet?

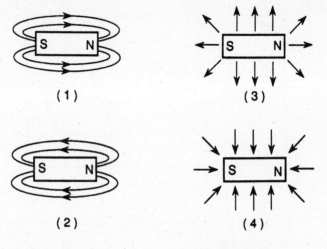

33. In a nondispersive medium, the speed of a light wave depends on
    (1) its wavelength
    (2) its amplitude
    (3) its frequency
    (4) the nature of the medium

34. The diagram below shows a piston being moved back and forth to generate a wave. The piston produces a compression, C, every 0.50 second.

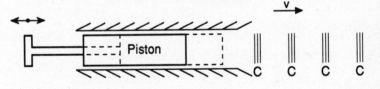

The frequency of this wave is
    (1) 1.0 Hz
    (2) 2.0 Hz
    (3) 5.0×10^{-1} Hz
    (4) 3.3×10^{2} Hz

35. The diagram below represents lines of magnetic flux within a region of space.

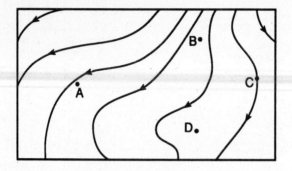

The magnetic field strength is greatest at point
(1) *A*   (3) *C*
(2) *B*   (4) *D*

36. The diagram below shows a current-carrying wire located in a magnetic field which is directed toward the top of the page. The electromagnetic force on the wire is directed out of the page.

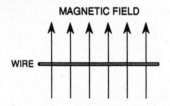

In the wire, the electron flow is directed toward the
(1) left   (3) top of the page
(2) right   (4) bottom of the page

37. What is the angle between the direction of propagation of a transverse wave and the direction in which the amplitude of the wave is measured?
(1) 0°   (3) 90°
(2) 45°   (4) 180°

38. The diagram below represents wave movement.

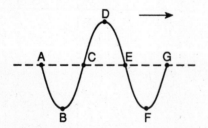

Which two points are in phase?
(1) *A* and *G*   (3) *C* and *E*
(2) *B* and *F*   (4) *D* and *F*

39. In the diagram below, the distance between points A and B on a wave is 0.10 meter.

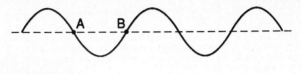

This wave must have
(1) an amplitude of 0.10 m
(2) an amplitude of 0.20 m
(3) a wavelength of 0.10 m
(4) a wavelength of 0.20 m

40. Which diagram best represents the reflection of light from an irregular surface?

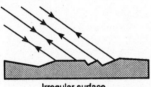

Irregular surface
(1)

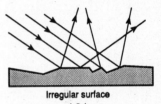

Irregular surface
(3)

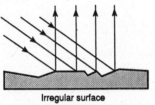

Irregular surface
(2)

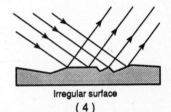

Irregular surface
(4)

41. A stationary radar gun can determine the speed of a pitched baseball by measuring the difference in frequency between incident and reflected radar waves. This process illustrates
(1) the Doppler effect
(2) standing waves
(3) the critical angle
(4) diffraction

42. The diagram below represents a rope along which two pulses of equal amplitude, A, approach point P.

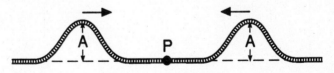

When the two pulses meet at P, the vertical displacement of the rope at point P will be
(1) A
(2) $2A$
(3) 0
(4) $\frac{A}{2}$

43. In a vacuum, a monochromatic beam of light has a frequency of 6.3×10^{14} hertz. What color is the light?
    (1) red
    (2) yellow
    (3) green
    (4) blue

44. When an opera singer hits a high-pitch note, a glass on the opposite side of the opera hall shatters. Which statement best explains this phenomenon?
    (1) The frequency of the note and natural vibration frequency of the glass are equal.
    (2) The vibrations of the note are polarized by the shape of the opera hall.
    (3) The amplitude of the note increases before it reaches the glass.
    (4) The singer and glass are separated by an integral number of wavelengths.

45. A beam of light crosses a boundary between two different media. Refraction can occur if
    (1) the angle of incidence is 0°
    (2) there is no change in the speed of the wave
    (3) the media have different indices of refraction
    (4) all of the light is reflected

46. What is the energy of a photon with a frequency of 5.0×10^{14} hertz?
    (1) 3.3 eV
    (2) 3.2×10^{-6} eV
    (3) 3.0×10^{48} J
    (4) 3.3×10^{-19} J

47. The diagram below shows white light being dispersed as it passes from air into a glass prism.

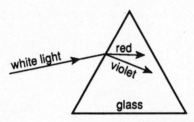

This phenomenon occurs because, in glass, each frequency of light has a different
    (1) intensity
    (2) amplitude
    (3) angle of incidence
    (4) absolute index of refraction

48. Which graph below best represents the relationship between the frequency of a light source causing photoemission and the maximum kinetic energy of the photo-electrons produced?

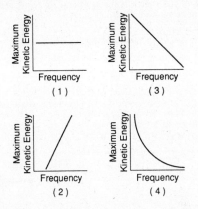

49. Which observation was made by Rutherford when he bombarded gold foil with alpha particles?
    (1) Alpha particles were deflected toward a positive electrode.
    (2) Some alpha particles were deflected by the gold foil.
    (3) Most alpha particles were scattered 180° by the gold foil.
    (4) Gold foil had no effect on the path of alpha particles.

50. Which electron transition in the hydrogen atom results in the emission of a photon of greatest energy?
    (1) $n = 2$ to $n = 1$ (3) $n = 4$ to $n = 2$
    (2) $n = 3$ to $n = 2$ (4) $n = 5$ to $n = 3$

51. The term "electron cloud" refers to the
    (1) electron plasma surrounding a hot wire
    (2) cathode rays in a gas discharge tube
    (3) high-probability region for an electron in an atom
    (4) negatively charged cloud that can produce a lightning strike

Note that questions 52 through 55 have only three choices.

52. As the angle between a force and level ground decreases from 60° to 30°, the vertical component of the force
    (1) decreases   (3) remains the same
    (2) increases

53. In a baseball game, a batter hits a ball for a home run. Compared to the magnitude of the impulse imparted to the ball, the magnitude of the impulse imparted to the bat is
    (1) less   (3) the same
    (2) greater

54. As the mass of a body increases, its gravitational force of attraction on the Earth
    (1) decreases   (3) remains the same
    (2) increases

55. An interference pattern is observed as light passes through two closely spaced slits. As the distance between the two slits is decreased, the distance between adjacent bright bands in the interference pattern
    (1) decreases   (3) remains the same
    (2) increases

PART II

This part consists of six groups, each containing ten questions. Each group tests an optional area of the course. Choose two of these six groups. Be sure that you answer all ten questions in each group chosen.   [20]

Group 1—Motion in a Plane

If you choose this group, be sure to answer questions 56–65.

Base your answers to questions 56 through 58 on the information and diagram below.

In the diagram below, a 10.-kilogram sphere, A, is projected horizontally with a velocity of 30. meters per second due east from a height of 20. meters above level ground. At the same instant, a 20.-kilogram sphere, B, is projected horizontally with a velocity of 10. meters per second due west from a height of 80. meters above level ground. [Neglect air friction.]

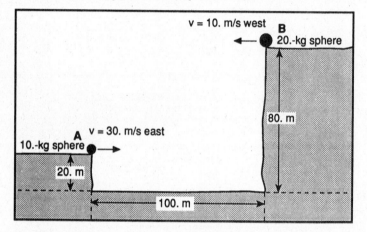

56. Initially, the spheres are separated by a horizontal distance of 100. meters. What is the horizontal separation of the spheres at the end of 1.5 seconds?
    (1) 15 m   (3) 40. m
    (2) 30. m   (4) 45 m

57. The magnitude of the horizontal acceleration of sphere A is
    (1) 0.0 m/s^2 (3) 9.8 m/s^2
    (2) 2.0 m/s^2 (4) 15 m/s^2

58. Compared to the vertical acceleration of sphere A, the vertical acceleration of sphere B is
    (1) the same   (3) one-half as great
    (2) twice as great   (4) four times as great

Base your answers to questions 59 through 62 on the information and diagram below.

The diagram shows a 5.0-kilogram cart traveling clockwise in a horizontal circle of radius 2.0 meters at a constant speed of 4.0 meters per second.

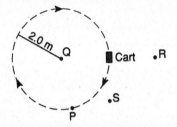

59. At the position shown, the velocity of the cart is directed toward point
    (1) P   (3) R
    (2) Q   (4) S

60. At the position shown, the centripetal acceleration of the cart is directed toward point
    (1) P   (3) R
    (2) Q   (4) S

61. If the mass of the cart was doubled, the magnitude of the centripetal acceleration of the cart would be
    (1) unchanged   (3) halved
    (2) doubled   (4) quadrupled

62. What is the magnitude of the centripetal force acting on the cart?
    (1) 8.0 N   (3) 40. N
    (2) 20. N   (4) 50. N

63. What would occur as a result of the frictional drag of the atmosphere on an artificial satellite orbiting the Earth?
    (1) The satellite would increase in speed and escape the gravitational field of the Earth.
    (2) The satellite would increase in speed and spiral toward the Earth.
    (3) The satellite would decrease in speed and escape the gravitational field of the Earth.
    (4) The satellite would decrease in speed and spiral toward the Earth.

64. A cannon with a muzzle velocity of 500. meters per second fires a cannonball at an angle of 30.° above the horizontal. What is the vertical component of the cannonball's velocity as it leaves the cannon?
    (1) 0.0 m/s   (3) 433 m/s
    (2) 250. m/s   (4) 500. m/s

Note that question 65 has only three choices.

65. Satellites A and B are orbiting the Earth in circular orbits as shown below. The mass of satellite A is twice as great as the mass of satellite B. Earth has radius R.

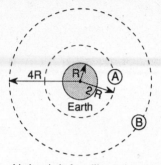

Compared to the orbital period of satellite A, the orbital period of satellite B is
(1) shorter
(2) longer
(3) the same

Group 2—Internal Energy

If you choose this group, be sure to answer questions 66–75.

66. Absolute zero represents a substance's minimum
    (1) internal molecular energy
    (2) gravitational potential energy
    (3) specific heat
    (4) heat of fusion

67. At 1.0 atmosphere of pressure, which substance is a solid at $-51°C$ and a liquid at $-33°C$?
    (1) ammonia
    (2) ethyl alcohol
    (3) mercury
    (4) lead

68. Equal masses of four different solids, $A, B, C,$ and D, are heated at a constant rate. The graph below represents the temperature of each solid as a function of the heat added to the solid.

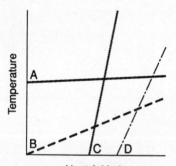

Which solid has the greatest specific heat?
(1) A
(2) B
(3) C
(4) D

69. A change of 10. Celsius degrees is produced by adding 2.4 kilojoules of heat to 1.0 kilogram of a substance. The substance could be
    (1) silver
    (2) lead
    (3) platinum
    (4) aluminum

70. The amount of heat required to melt 0.50 kilogram of iron at its melting point is approximately
    (1) 0.23 kJ
    (2) 0.90 kJ
    (3) 13 kJ
    (4) 130 kJ

71. Increasing the external pressure on a sample of water will
    (1) increase its boiling point and increase its freezing point
    (2) increase its boiling point and decrease its freezing point
    (3) decrease its boiling point and increase its freezing point
    (4) decrease its boiling point and decrease its freezing point

72. According to the kinetic theory of gases, an ideal gas of low density has relatively large
    (1) molecules
    (2) energy loss in molecular collisions
    (3) forces between molecules
    (4) distances between molecules

73. If the pressure on a fixed mass of an ideal gas is doubled at a constant temperature, the volume of this gas sample will be
    (1) the same
    (2) doubled
    (3) halved
    (4) quartered

74. According to the second law of thermodynamics, which phenomenon will most likely occur?
    (1) The entropy of the universe will steadily decrease.
    (2) The universe will steadily become more disordered.
    (3) The universe will eventually reach equilibrium at absolute zero.
    (4) Within the universe, more heat will flow from colder to warmer regions than from warmer to colder regions.

Note that question 75 has only three choices.

75. A sample of liquid ethyl alcohol is boiling. As more heat is added, the temperature of the liquid alcohol will
    (1) decrease
    (2) increase
    (3) remain the same

Group 3—Electromagnetic Applications

If you choose this group, be sure to answer questions 76–85.

76. Which graph best represents the relationship between the degree of deflection of a galvanometer needle and the current passing through its coil?

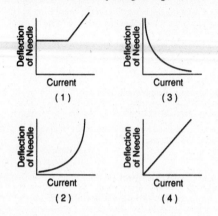

77. The torque on the armature of an operating electric motor may be increased by
    (1) decreasing the current in the armature
    (2) decreasing the magnetic field strength of the field poles
    (3) increasing the potential difference applied to the armature
    (4) increasing the distance between the armature and the field poles

78. In an operating practical motor, the magnetic field produced by the current-carrying coil is strengthened and concentrated by the
    (1) split-ring commutator   (3) field pole
    (2) back emf   (4) iron core

79. The diagram below represents an electron beam entering the region between two oppositely charged parallel plates.

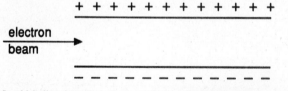

In which direction will the beam of electrons be deflected?
(1) out of the page   (3) toward the top of the page
(2) into the page   (4) toward the bottom of the page

80. A proton having a velocity of 1.5×10^6 meters per second to the right is projected into a magnetic field having a flux density of 3.0 teslas directed out of the page, as shown in the diagram below.

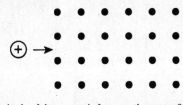

What is the magnitude of the magnetic force on the proton?
(1) 4.1×10^{-24} N   (3) 4.5×10^6 N
(2) 7.2×10^{-13} N   (4) 7.2×10^6 N

Base your answers to questions 81 and 82 on the information and diagram below.

Four electron beams, $A, B, C,$ and D, are projected into a magnetic field directed out of the page.

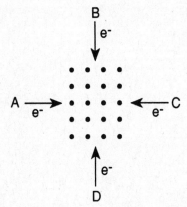

81. Which beam of electrons will initially be deflected toward the top of the page by the magnetic field?
(1) A (3) C
(2) B (4) D

82. If the speed of the electrons in beam B is doubled and the magnetic field strength is halved, the magnitude of the deflecting force on the electrons will be
(1) unchanged   (3) halved
(2) doubled   (4) quadrupled

83. The charge-to-mass ratio of an electron is
(1) 9.1×10^{-31} C/kg   (3) 5.7×10^{-12} C/kg
(2) 1.6×10^{-19} C/kg   (4) 1.8×10^{11} C/kg

84. A potential difference of 10. volts is induced in a wire as it is moved at a constant speed of 5.0 meters per second perpendicular to a magnetic field having a flux density of 4.0 newtons per ampere-meter. What is the length of the wire in the field?
(1) 0.50 m   (3) 8.0 m
(2) 2.0 m   (4) 200 m

85. The primary coil of an operating transformer has 200 turns and the secondary coil has 40 turns. This transformer is being used to
    (1) decrease voltage and decrease current
    (2) decrease voltage and increase current
    (3) increase voltage and decrease current
    (4) increase voltage and increase current

Group 4—Geometric Optics

If you choose this group, be sure to answer questions 86–95.

86. A truck has the letters OWOW painted on the front of its hood. A person in a car driving ahead of the truck views these letters in the rear-view mirror. How do the letters appear?
    (1) WOWO   (3) OMOM
    (2) OWOW   (4) MOMO

87. A concave mirror has a radius of curvature of 0.60 meter. When an object is placed 0.40 meter from the reflecting surface, the image distance will be
    (1) 0.10 m   (3) 0.83 m
    (2) 0.20 m   (4) 1.2 m

88. The diagram below shows parallel monochromatic incident light rays being reflected from a concave mirror.

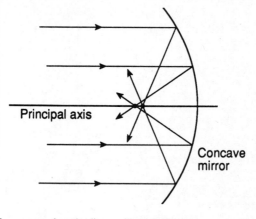

Which phenomenon does the diagram illustrate?
    (1) chromatic aberration   (3) refraction
    (2) spherical aberration   (4) dispersion

89. Which piece of glass could be used to focus parallel rays of sunlight to a small spot of light?

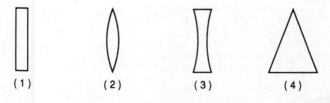

90. In the diagram below, a lamp 0.4 meter tall is placed 0.6 meter in front of a convex mirror.

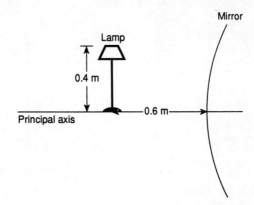

Which diagram best represents an image of the lamp that could be formed by this mirror?

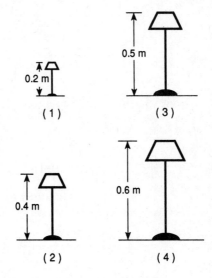

91. Which type of images can be formed by a converging lens?
   (1) real images, only
   (2) virtual images, only
   (3) both real and virtual images
   (4) neither real nor virtual images

92. A converging lens is used to produce an image of an object. The object distance is twice the image distance. If the object is 0.050 meter tall, the height of its image is
   (1) 0.010 m
   (2) 0.020 m
   (3) 0.025 m
   (4) 0.050 m

93. When an object is placed 0.40 meter from a diverging lens with a focal length of -0.10 meter, the image produced will be
    (1) virtual and smaller than the object
    (2) virtual and larger than the object
    (3) real and smaller than the object
    (4) real and larger than the object

94. Photographers sometimes use colored filters to restrict the light entering a lens to a single wavelength. The filters are used to eliminate
    (1) diffusion
    (2) diffraction
    (3) polarization effects
    (4) chromatic aberration

Note that question 95 has only three choices.

95. As an object is moved from 0.2 meter to 0.3 meter away from a plane mirror, the image distance
    (1) decreases
    (2) increases
    (3) remains the same

Group 5—Solid State

If you choose this group, be sure to answer questions 96–105.

96. The circuit diagram below shows a *P*-type semiconductor in series with a lamp, a resistor, and a battery.

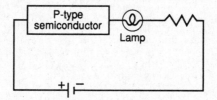

What would increase the current in the circuit?
    (1) increasing the resistance of the resistor
    (2) reversing the battery polarity
    (3) reversing the connections to the semiconductor
    (4) increasing the temperature of the semiconductor

97. According to the energy band model, in which material is the energy gap between the conduction band and the valence band greatest?
    (1) a conductor
    (2) an insulator
    (3) an extrinsic semiconductor
    (4) an intrinsic semiconductor

98. The diagram below shows a circuit connecting a battery to semiconductor *A*.

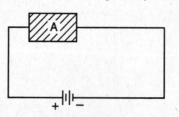

If the battery connection is reversed, the current in the circuit will
    (1) decrease only if *A* is *N*-type
    (2) decrease only if *A* is *P*-type
    (3) increase if *A* is either *N*-type or *P*-type
    (4) remain the same if *A* is either *N*-type or *P*-type

99. The majority charge carriers in a *P*-type semiconductor are holes. When a section of *P*-type semiconductor is connected across the terminals of a battery, where do the holes flow?
    (1) toward the negative terminal, only
    (2) toward the positive terminal, only
    (3) equally toward both the negative and positive terminals
    (4) toward neither terminal

100. The simplest circuit element that will allow electric current to pass through a circuit in only one direction is
    (1) a transistor
    (2) a diode
    (3) an *N*-type semiconductor
    (4) a *P*-type semiconductor

101. The graph below shows the relationship between current and applied potential difference for an electrical device.

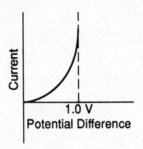

This device is most likely a
    (1) forward-biased *P*-type semiconductor
    (2) reverse-biased *P*-type semiconductor
    (3) forward-biased *P-N* junction
    (4) reverse-biased *P-N* junction

102. The symbol 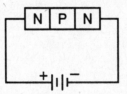 is to a *P-N* junction as the symbol is to
    (1) an *N-P-N* transistor
    (2) a *P-N-P* transistor
    (3) a zener diode
    (4) an integrated circuit

103. The diagram below shows an *N-P-N* semiconductor device.

The base in the semiconductor shown is the
    (1) right *N*
    (2) left *N*
    (3) *P*
    (4) *P-N* junction

104. A student is designing a circuit to amplify a small voltage change into a larger voltage change. The electric circuit element best suited to this task is
    (1) a transistor
    (2) a diode
    (3) an *N*-type semiconductor
    (4) a *P*-type semiconductor

105. What is the name for a large group of electronic components that are interconnected on a single block of silicon inside a computer?
    (1) a thermistor
    (2) an integrated circuit
    (3) a transistor
    (4) a collector

Group 6—Nuclear Energy

If you choose this group, be sure to answer questions 106–115.

106. Which atom has the same number of neutrons as $^{16}_{8}O$?
    (1) $^{16}_{7}N$
    (2) $^{17}_{8}O$
    (3) $^{15}_{7}N$
    (4) $^{15}_{8}O$

107. The force that holds the nucleons of an atom together is
    (1) weak and short-ranged
    (2) weak and long-ranged
    (3) strong and short-ranged
    (4) strong and long-ranged

108. Approximately how much energy is produced when 0.50 atomic mass unit of matter is completely converted into energy?
    (1) 9.3 MeV
    (2) 9.3×10^2 MeV
    (3) 4.7 MeV
    (4) 4.7×10^2 MeV

109. Atoms of different isotopes of the same element contain the same number of
    (1) neutrons, but a different number of protons
    (2) neutrons, but a different number of electrons
    (3) electrons, but a different number of protons
    (4) protons, but a different number of neutrons

110. The disintegration of the nucleus of an atom of a naturally occurring radioactive element may produce more
    (1) neutrons in the nucleus
    (2) electrons in the nucleus
    (3) protons in the nucleus
    (4) atomic mass

111. In the nuclear equation $^{14}_{6}C \rightarrow \,^{14}_{7}N + X$, the X represents a
    (1) beta particle
    (2) gamma ray
    (3) neutron
    (4) positron

112. The half-life of a radium isotope is 1,600 years. After 4,800 years, approximately how much of an original 10.0-kilogram sample of this isotope will remain?
    (1) 0.125 kg
    (2) 1.25 kg
    (3) 1.67 kg
    (4) 3.33 kg

113. In nuclear reactors, neutrons are slowed down by
    (1) moderators
    (2) control rods
    (3) fuel rods
    (4) accelerators

114. For nuclear fusion to occur, the reacting nuclei must
    (1) absorb thermal neutrons
    (2) have large kinetic energies
    (3) be fissionable
    (4) have a critical mass

Note that question 115 has only three choices.

115. If the mass defect for nucleus X is larger than the mass defect for nucleus Y, then nucleus X has
    (1) a smaller binding energy than nucleus Y
    (2) a larger binding energy than nucleus Y
    (3) the same binding energy as nucleus Y

PART III

You must answer *all* questions in this part. **[15]**

Base your answers to questions 116 through 118 on the speed-time graph below, which represents the linear motion of a cart.

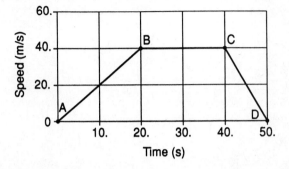

116. Determine the magnitude of the acceleration of the cart during interval *AB*. [Show all calculations, including the equation and substitution with units.]   **[2]**

117. Calculate the distance traveled by the cart during interval *BC*. [Show all calculations, including the equation and substitution with units.]   **[2]**

118. What is the average speed of the cart during interval *CD*?   **[1]**

Base your answers to questions 119 and 120 on the information and diagram below. [The same diagram appears on your answer paper.]

Two parallel plates separated by a distance of 2.0×10^{-2} meter are charged to a potential difference of 1.0×10^2 volts. Points *A*, *B*, and *C* are located in the region between the plates.

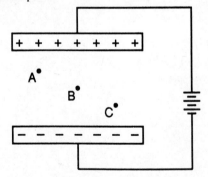

119. *On the diagram on your answer paper,* sketch the electric field lines between the oppositely charged parallel plates through points *A*, *B*, and *C*. [Draw lines with arrowheads in the proper direction.]   **[2]**

120. Calculate the magnitude of the electric field strength between the plates. [Show all calculations, including the equation and substitutions with units.]   **[2]**

Base your answers to questions 121 through 123 on the diagram below, which shows light ray *AO* in Lucite. The light ray strikes the boundary between Lucite and air at point *O* with an angle of incidence of 30°. The dotted line represents the normal to the boundary at point *O*. [The same diagram appears on your answer paper.]

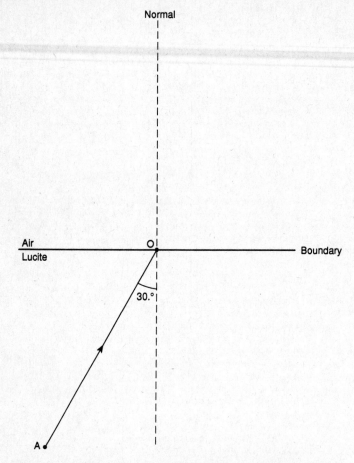

121. Calculate the angle of refraction for incident ray *AO*. [Show all calculations, including the equation and substitution with units.]   **[2]**

122. *On the diagram on your answer paper*, using your answer from question 121, construct an arrow with a protractor and straightedge, to represent the refracted ray.   **[2]**

123. Calculate the critical angle for a Lucite-air boundary. [Show all calculations, including the equation and substitution with units.]   **[2]**

PHYSICS

June 14, 1996

PART I

Answer all 55 questions in this part. [65]

Directions (1–55): For *each* statement or question, select the word or expression that, of those given, best completes the statement or answers the question.

1. A car travels between the 100.-meter and 250.-meter highway markers in 10. seconds. The average speed of the car during this interval is
   (1) 10. m/s
   (2) 15 m/s
   (3) 25 m/s
   (4) 35 m/s

2. A student walks 40. meters along a hallway that heads due north, then turns and walks 30. meters along another hallway that heads due east. What is the magnitude of the student's resultant displacement?
   (1) 10. m
   (2) 35 m
   (3) 50. m
   (4) 70. m

3. The graph below represents the relationship between speed and time for a car moving in a straight line.

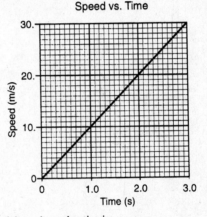

Speed vs. Time

The magnitude of the car's acceleration is
   (1) 1.0 m/s^2
   (2) 0.10 m/s^2
   (3) 10. m/s^2
   (4) 0.0 m/s^2

4. Oil drips at 0.4-second intervals from a car that has an oil leak. Which pattern best represents the spacing of oil drops as the car accelerates uniformly from rest?

(1) .   .   .   .

(2) . .   .   .

(3) . . . .

(4) .   ..   .

5. In an experiment that measures how fast a student reacts, a meter stick dropped from rest falls 0.20 meter before the student catches it. The reaction time of the student is approximately
   (1) 0.10 s
   (2) 0.20 s
   (3) 0.30 s
   (4) 0.40 s

6. A race car traveling at 10. meters per second accelerates at the rate of 1.5 meters per second^2 while traveling a distance of 600. meters. The final speed of the race car is approximately
   (1) 1900 m/s
   (2) 910 m/s
   (3) 150 m/s
   (4) 44 m/s

7. A 4.0-kilogram rock and a 1.0-kilogram stone fall freely from rest from a height of 100. meters. After they fall for 2.0 seconds, the ratio of the rock's speed to the stone's speed is
   (1) 1:1
   (2) 2:1
   (3) 1:2
   (4) 4:1

8. Which pair of concurrent forces could produce a resultant force having a magnitude of 10. newtons?
   (1) 10. N, 10. N
   (2) 10. N, 30. N
   (3) 4.7 N, 4.7 N
   (4) 4.7 N, 5.0 N

9. The diagram below shows a person exerting a 300.-newton force on the handle of a shovel that makes an angle of 60.° with the horizontal ground.

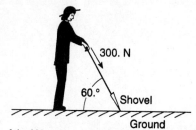

The component of the 300.-newton force that acts perpendicular to the ground is approximately
   (1) 150. N
   (2) 260. N
   (3) 300. N
   (4) 350. N

10. Which graph best represents the motion of an object that has *no* unbalanced force acting on it?

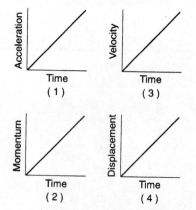

11. The weight of an apple is closest to
    (1) 10^{-2} N
    (2) 10^0 N
    (3) 10^2 N
    (4) 10^4 N

12. Two forces are applied to a 2.0-kilogram block on a frictionless, horizontal surface, as shown in the diagram below.

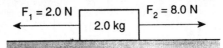

Frictionless Surface

The acceleration of the block is
    (1) 5.0 m/s² to the right
    (2) 5.0 m/s² to the left
    (3) 3.0 m/s² to the right
    (4) 3.0 m/s² to the left

13. Compared to the inertia of a 0.10-kilogram steel ball, the inertia of a 0.20-kilogram Styrofoam ball is
    (1) one-half as great
    (2) twice as great
    (3) the same
    (4) four times as great

14. A 3.0-kilogram mass weighs 15 newtons at a given point in the Earth's gravitational field. What is the magnitude of the acceleration due to the gravity at this point?
    (1) 45 m/s²
    (2) 9.8 m/s²
    (3) 5.0 m/s²
    (4) 0.20 m/s²

15. As shown in the diagram below, an inflated balloon released from rest moves horizontally with velocity v.

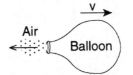

The velocity of the balloon is most likely caused by
    (1) action-reaction
    (2) centripetal force
    (3) gravitational attraction
    (4) rolling friction

16. A horizontal force is used to pull a 5.0-kilogram cart at a constant speed of 5.0 meters per second across the floor, as shown in the diagram below.

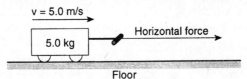

Floor

If the force of friction between the cart and the floor is 10. newtons, the magnitude of the horizontal force along the handle of the car is
    (1) 5.0 N
    (2) 10. N
    (3) 25 N
    (4) 50. N

17. A bullet traveling at 5.0×10^2 meters per second is brought to rest by an impulse of 50. newton-seconds. What is the mass of the bullet?
    (1) 2.5×10^4 kg
    (2) 1.0×10^1 kg
    (3) 1.0×10^{-1} kg
    (4) 1.0×10^{-2} kg

18. A box weighing 1.0×10^2 newtons is dragged to the top of an incline, as shown in the diagram below.

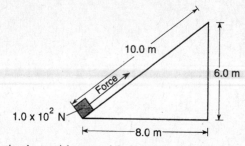

The gravitational potential energy of the box at the top of the incline is approximately

(1) 1.0×10^2 J

(2) 6.0×10^2 J

(3) 8.0×10^2 J

(4) 1.0×10^3 J

19. A 10.-newton force is required to move a 3.0-kilogram box at constant speed. How much power is required to move the box 8.0 meters in 2.0 seconds?

(1) 40. W

(2) 20. W

(3) 15 W

(4) 12 W

20. A 20.-newton weight is attached to a spring, causing it to stretch, as shown in the diagram below.

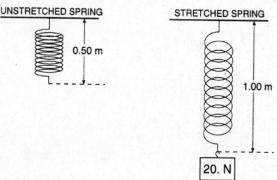

What is the spring constant of this spring?

(1) 0.050 N/m

(2) 0.25 N/m

(3) 20. N/m

(4) 40. N/m

21. Spring A has a spring constant of 140 newtons per meter, and spring B has a spring constant of 280 newtons per meter. Both springs are stretched the same distance. Compared to the potential energy stored in spring A, the potential energy stored in spring B is

(1) the same

(2) twice as great

(3) half as great

(4) four times as great

22. A cart of mass m traveling at speed v has kinetic energy KE. If the mass of the cart is doubled and its speed is halved, the kinetic energy of the cart will be

(1) half as great

(2) twice as great

(3) one-fourth as great

(4) four times as great

23. A repulsive electrostatic force of magnitude F exists between two metal spheres having identical charge q. The distance between their centers is r. Which combination of changes would produce *no* change in the electrostatic force between the spheres?
    (1) doubling q on one sphere while doubling r
    (2) doubling q on both spheres while doubling r
    (3) doubling q on one sphere while halving r
    (4) doubling q on both spheres while halving r

24. An inflated balloon which has been rubbed against a person's hair is touched to a neutral wall and remains attracted to it. Which diagram best represents the charge distribution on the balloon and wall?

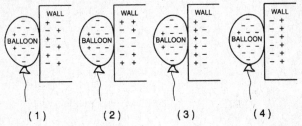

    (1)   (2)   (3)   (4)

25. Two metal spheres having charges of $+4.0 \times 10^{-6}$ coulomb and $+2.0 \times 10^{-5}$ coulomb, respectively, are brought into contact and then separated. After separation, the charge on each sphere is
    (1) 8.0×10^{-11} C
    (2) 8.0×10^{-6} C
    (3) 2.1×10^{6} C
    (4) 1.2×10^{-5} C

26. Which graph best represents the relationship between electric field intensity and distance from a point charge?

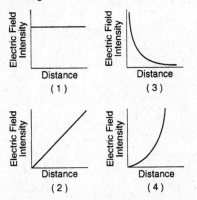

27. Moving $+2.0$ coulombs of charge from infinity to point P in an electric field requires 8.0 joules of work. What is the electric potential at point P?
    (1) 0.25 V
    (2) 8.0 V
    (3) 16 V
    (4) 4.0 V

28. What is the magnitude of the electrostatic force experienced by one elementary charge at a point in an electric field where the electric field intensity is 3.0×10^3 newtons per coulomb?
    (1) 1.0×10^3 N
    (2) 1.6×10^{-19} N
    (3) 3.0×10^3 N
    (4) 4.8×10^{-16} N

29. A metal conductor is used in an electric circuit. The electrical resistance provided by the conductor could be increased by
    (1) decreasing the length of the conductor
    (2) decreasing the applied voltage in the circuit
    (3) increasing the temperature of the conductor
    (4) increasing the cross-sectional area of the conductor

30. In the circuit shown below, voltmeter V_2 reads 80. volts.

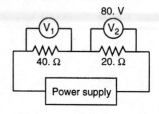

What is the reading of voltmeter V_1?
    (1) 160 V   (3) 40. V
    (2) 80. V   (4) 20. V

31. In a lightning strike, a charge of 18 coulombs is transferred between a cloud and the ground in 2.0×10^{-2} second at a potential difference of 1.5×10^6 volts. What is the average current produced by this strike?
    (1) 3.6×10^{-1} A   (3) 3.0×10^4 A
    (2) 9.0×10^2 A   (4) 7.5×10^7 A

32. The diagram below shows the current in a segment of a direct current circuit.

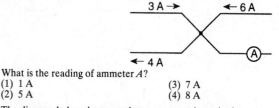

What is the reading of ammeter A?
    (1) 1 A   (3) 7 A
    (2) 5 A   (4) 8 A

33. The diagram below shows an electron current in a wire loop.

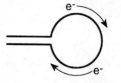

What is the direction of the magnetic field at the center of the loop?
    (1) out of the page   (3) clockwise
    (2) into the page   (4) counterclockwise

34. A charged particle is moving with a constant velocity. On entering a uniform magnetic field, the particle
    (1) must decrease in speed
    (2) must change the magnitude of its momentum
    (3) may change its direction of motion
    (4) may increase in kinetic energy

35. Electromagnetic waves can be generated by accelerating
    (1) a hydrogen atom   (3) a neutron
    (2) a photon   (4) an electron

36. If the potential drop across an operating 300.-watt floodlight is 120 volts, what is the current through the floodlight?
    (1) 0.40 A   (2) 2.5 A   (3) 7.5 A   (4) 4.8 A

37. Which diagram correctly shows a magnetic field configuration?

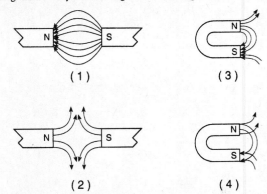

(1)   (3)

(2)   (4)

38. Two points on a transverse wave that have the same magnitude of displacement from equilibrium are in phase if the points also have the
    (1) same direction of displacement and the same direction of motion
    (2) same direction of displacement and the opposite direction of motion
    (3) opposite direction of displacement and the same direction of motion
    (4) opposite direction of displacement and the opposite direction of motion

39. A periodic wave travels through a rope, as shown in the diagram below.

As the wave travels, what is transferred between points A and B?
    (1) mass, only   (3) both mass and energy
    (2) energy, only   (4) neither mass nor energy

40. Which graph best represents the relationship between the frequency and period of a wave?

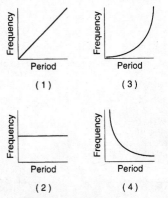

(1)   (3)

(2)   (4)

41. A beam of monochromatic light ($\lambda = 5.9 \times 10^{-7}$ meter) crosses a boundary from air into Lucite at an angle of incidence of 45°. The angle of refraction is approximately
    (1) 63° (2) 56° (3) 37° (4) 28°

42. The diagram below represents shallow water waves of wavelength λ passing through two small openings, A and B, in a barrier.

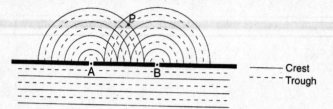

Compared to the length of path BP, the length of path AP is
(1) 1λ longer (2) 2λ longer (3) ½λ longer (4) the same

43. The speed of light in a material is 2.5×10^8 meters per second. What is the absolute index of refraction of the material?
    (1) 1.2 (2) 2.5 (3) 7.5 (4) 0.83

44. The diagram below represents wave fronts traveling from medium X into medium Y.

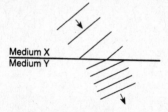

Medium X
Medium Y

All points on any one wave front shown must be
(1) traveling with the same speed (3) in phase
(2) traveling in the same medium (4) superposed

45. A laser beam does *not* disperse as it passes through a prism because the laser beam is
(1) monochromatic (3) polarized
(2) polychromatic (4) longitudinal

46. The diagram below shows a wave phenomenon.

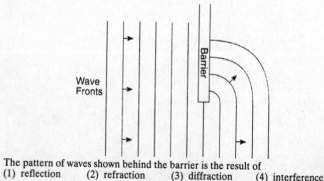

The pattern of waves shown behind the barrier is the result of
(1) reflection (2) refraction (3) diffraction (4) interference

47. In the diagram below, monochromatic light ($\lambda = 5.9 \times 10^{-7}$ meter) in air is about to travel through crown glass, water, and diamond.

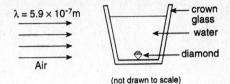

$\lambda = 5.9 \times 10^{-7}$m

Air

crown glass

water

diamond

(not drawn to scale)

In which substance does the light travel the slowest?
(1) air   (2) diamond   (3) water   (4) crown glass

48. Which phenomenon is most easily explained by the particle theory of light?
(1) photoelectric effect   (3) polarization
(2) constructive interference   (4) diffraction

49. The work function for a copper surface is 7.3×10^{-19} joule. If photons with an energy of 9.9×10^{-19} joule are incident on the copper surface, the maximum kinetic energy of the ejected photoelectrons is
(1) 2.6×10^{-19} J   (3) 9.9×10^{-19} J
(2) 7.3×10^{-19} J   (4) 1.7×10^{30} J

50. The diagram below shows sunglasses being used to eliminate glare.

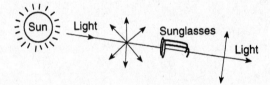

Sun   Light   Sunglasses   Light

Which phenomenon of light is represented in the diagram?
(1) dispersion   (3) internal reflection
(2) diffraction   (4) polarization

51. What is the minimum energy required to ionize a hydrogen atom in the $n = 3$ state?
(1) 13.60 eV   (3) 5.52 eV
(2) 12.09 eV   (4) 1.51 eV

52. When a source of dim orange light shines on a photosensitive metal, no photoelectrons are ejected from its surface. What could be done to increase the likelihood of producing photoelectrons?
(1) Replace the orange light source with a red light source.
(2) Replace the orange light source with a higher frequency light source.
(3) Increase the brightness of the orange light source.
(4) Increase the angle at which the photons of orange light strike the metal.

53. In Rutherford's model of the atom, the positive charge
(1) is distributed throughout the atom's volume
(2) revolves about the nucleus in specific orbits
(3) is concentrated at the center of the atom
(4) occupies most of the space in the atom

Note that questions 54 and 55 have only three choices.

54. Light ($\lambda = 5.9 \times 10^{-7}$ meter) travels through a solution. If the absolute index of refraction of the solution is increased, the critical angle will
(1) decrease   (2) increase   (3) remain the same

55. An astronomer on Earth studying light coming from a star notes that the observed light frequencies are lower than the actual emitted frequencies. The astronomer concludes that the distance between the star and Earth is
(1) decreasing   (2) increasing   (3) not changing

PART II

This part consists of six groups, each containing ten questions. Each group tests an optional area of the course. Choose two of these six groups. Be sure that you answer all ten questions in each group chosen. [20]

Group I—Motion in a Plane

If you choose this group, be sure to answer questions 56–65.

Base your answers to questions 56 through 58 on the information and diagram below.

A cannon elevated at an angle of 35° to the horizontal fires a cannonball, which travels the path shown in the diagram below. [Neglect air resistance and assume the ball lands at the same height above the ground from which it was launched.]

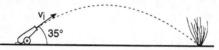

56. If the ball lands 7.0×10^2 meters from the cannon 10. seconds after it was fired, what is the horizontal component of its initial velocity?
    (1) 70. m/s   (2) 49 m/s   (3) 35 m/s   (4) 7.0 m/s

57. If the ball's time of light is 10. seconds, what is the vertical component of its initial velocity?
    (1) 9.8 m/s   (2) 49 m/s   (3) 70. m/s   (4) 98 m/s

58. If the angle of elevation of the cannon is decreased from 35° to 30.°, the vertical component of the ball's initial velocity will
    (1) decrease and its horizontal component will decrease
    (2) decrease and its horizontal component will increase
    (3) increase and its horizontal component will decrease
    (4) increase and its horizontal component will increase

Base your answers to questions 59 through 61 on the diagram below. The diagram shows a student spinning a 0.10-kilogram ball at the end of a 0.50-meter string in a horizontal circle at a constant speed of 10. meters per second. [Neglect air resistance.]

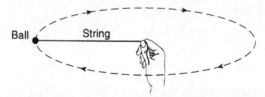

Note that question 59 has only three choices.

59. If the magnitude of the force applied to the string by the student's hand is increased, the magnitude of the acceleration of the ball in its circular path will
    (1) decrease
    (2) increase
    (3) remain the same

60. The magnitude of the centripetal force required to keep the ball in this circular path is
    (1) 5.0 N   (3) 20. N
    (2) 10. N   (4) 200 N

61. Which is the best description of the force keeping the ball in the circular path?
    (1) perpendicular to the circle and directed toward the center of the circle
    (2) perpendicular to the circle and directed away from the center of the circle
    (3) tangent to the circle and directed in the same direction that the ball is moving
    (4) tangent to the circle and directed opposite to the direction that the ball is moving

62. A convertible car with its top down is traveling at constant speed around a circular track, as shown in the diagram below.

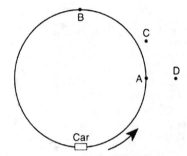

When the car is at point *A*, if a passenger in the car throws a ball straight up, the ball could land at point
    (1) *A*   (3) *C*
    (2) *B*   (4) *D*

63. The comet Hyakutake, seen in the Earth's sky this year, will take more than 10,000 years to complete its orbit. Which object is at a focus of the comet's orbit?
    (1) Earth   (3) Moon
    (2) Sun   (4) Jupiter

64. The diagram below represents the path of a planet moving in an elliptical orbit around a star. The orbital period of the planet is 1,000 days.

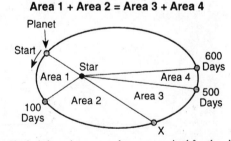

According to Kepler's laws, how many days are required for the planet to travel from the starting point to point *X*?
    (1) 400   (3) 300
    (2) 350   (4) 250

65. A ball is projected horizontally to the right from a height of 50. meters, as shown in the diagram below.

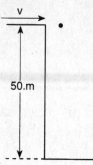

50.m

Which diagram best represents the position of the ball at 1.0-second intervals? [Neglect air resistance.]

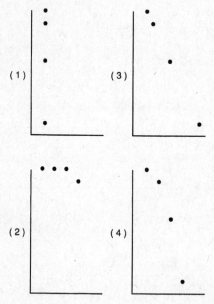

(1)   (3)

(2)   (4)

Group 2—Internal Energy

If you choose this group, be sure to answer questions 66–75.

66. If the temperature of 1 liter of an ideal gas is increased from 4 K to 16 K, the average kinetic energy of the molecules of the gas will be
    (1) half as great
    (2) twice as great
    (3) one-fourth as great
    (4) four times as great

Base your answers to questions 67 through 70 on the graph below which shows the relationship between the temperature of 1.0 kilogram of a pure substance and the heat energy added to the substance.

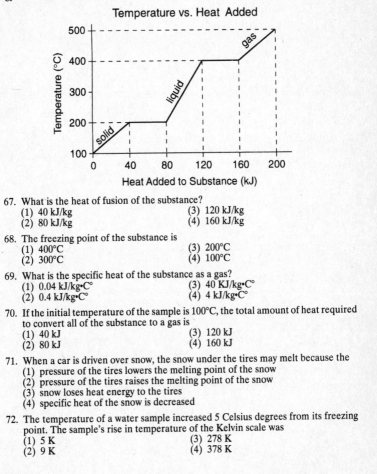

Temperature vs. Heat Added

67. What is the heat of fusion of the substance?
    (1) 40 kJ/kg
    (2) 80 kJ/kg
    (3) 120 kJ/kg
    (4) 160 kJ/kg

68. The freezing point of the substance is
    (1) 400°C
    (2) 300°C
    (3) 200°C
    (4) 100°C

69. What is the specific heat of the substance as a gas?
    (1) 0.04 kJ/kg•C°
    (2) 0.4 kJ/kg•C°
    (3) 40 KJ/kg•C°
    (4) 4 kJ/kg•C°

70. If the initial temperature of the sample is 100°C, the total amount of heat required to convert all of the substance to a gas is
    (1) 40 kJ
    (2) 80 kJ
    (3) 120 kJ
    (4) 160 kJ

71. When a car is driven over snow, the snow under the tires may melt because the
    (1) pressure of the tires lowers the melting point of the snow
    (2) pressure of the tires raises the melting point of the snow
    (3) snow loses heat energy to the tires
    (4) specific heat of the snow is decreased

72. The temperature of a water sample increased 5 Celsius degrees from its freezing point. The sample's rise in temperature of the Kelvin scale was
    (1) 5 K
    (2) 9 K
    (3) 278 K
    (4) 378 K

73. Which graph best represents the relationship between pressure (P) and absolute temperature (T) for a fixed mass of an ideal gas in a rigid container?

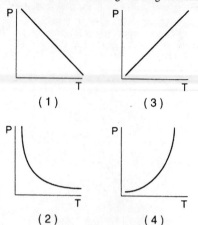

(1)   (3)

(2)   (4)

74. Which characteristic of a gas sample results from the collision of gas molecules with the walls of its container?
    (1) specific heat   (3) temperature
    (2) condensation point   (4) pressure

Note that question 75 has only three choices.

75. As the absolute temperature of a fixed mass of an ideal gas is increased at constant pressure, the volume occupied by the gas
    (1) decreases
    (2) increases
    (3) remains the same

Group 3—Electromagnetic Applications

If you choose this group, be sure to answer questions 76–85.

76. Which diagram best represents how galvanometer G can be modified to make it a voltmeter? [In the diagrams, R represents resistance.]

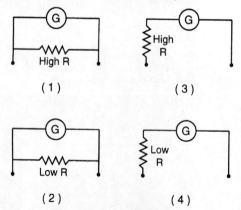

(1)   (3)

(2)   (4)

77. A motor is to rotational mechanical energy as a generator is to
    (1) chemical potential energy
    (2) induced electrical energy
    (3) thermal internal energy
    (4) elastic potential energy

78. A split-ring commutator is used to
    (1) reduce the voltage in a transformer
    (2) reduce the resistance of the shunt in an ammeter
    (3) make the light waves coherent in a laser
    (4) keep the torque acting in the same direction in a motor

79. A straight conductor 1.0 meter long is moved at a constant speed of 10. meters per second perpendicular to a magnetic field. If the flux density of the field is 5.0×10^{-3} tesla, what is the magnitude of the electromotive force induced in the conductor?
    (1) 0.0 V
    (2) 2.0×10^3 V
    (3) 5.0×10^{-2} V
    (4) 5.0×10^{-4} V

Base your answers to questions 80 and 81 on the diagram below which represents an electron being projected between two oppositely charged parallel plates.

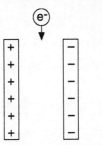

80. In which direction will the electric field deflect the electron?
    (1) into the page
    (2) out of the page
    (3) to the right
    (4) to the left

Note that question 81 has only three choices.

81. As the electron moves through the electric field, the magnitude of the electric force on the electron
    (1) decreases
    (2) increases
    (3) remains the same

82. The diagram below represents a negatively charged oil drop between two oppositely charged parallel plates. The forces acting on the oil drop are in equilibrium.

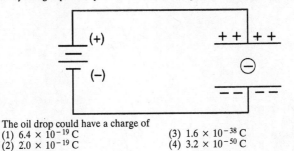

The oil drop could have a charge of
    (1) 6.4×10^{-19} C
    (2) 2.0×10^{-19} C
    (3) 1.6×10^{-38} C
    (4) 3.2×10^{-50} C

83. As a charged particle moves through a magnetic field, the particle is deflected. The magnitude of the magnetic force acting on the particle is directly proportional to the
    (1) mass of the particle
    (2) electric charge on the particle
    (3) polarity of the magnetic field
    (4) work done on the charge by the magnetic field

84. The 100% efficient transformer in the diagram below has three turns in its primary coil and nine turns in its secondary coil. When a 12-volt alternating current source is connected to the primary coil, 3.0 amperes flows in the primary coil.

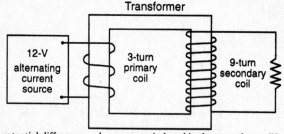

Transformer

What potential difference and current are induced in the secondary coil?
(1) 36 V and 1.0 A   (3) 4.0 V and 1.0 A
(2) 36 V and 9.0 A   (4) 4.0 V and 9.0 A

85. The diagram below shows particles produced by thermionic emission at the end of a heater element about to enter a magnetic field directed into the page.

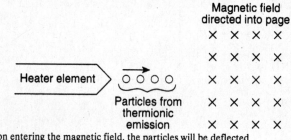

Upon entering the magnetic field, the particles will be deflected
(1) toward the top of the page   (3) into the page
(2) toward the bottom of the page   (4) out of the page

Group 4—Geometric Optics

If you choose this group, be sure to answer questions 86–95.

86. A plane mirror will form an image that is
    (1) virtual and erect   (3) virtual and inverted
    (2) real and inverted   (4) real and erect

87. Which graph best represents the relationship between image distance (d_i) and object distance (d_o) for a plane mirror?

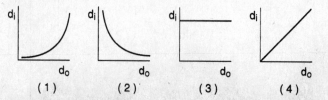

88. Which lens defect is correctly paired with its cause?
    (1) chromatic aberration, caused by refraction
    (2) chromatic aberration, caused by diffraction
    (3) spherical aberration, caused by wave interference
    (4) spherical aberration, caused by wave polarization

Base your answers to questions 89 and 90 on the information and diagram below. The diagram shows a concave (converging) spherical mirror having principal focus F and center of curvature C. Point A lies on the principal axis.

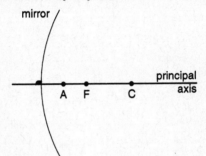

89. When an object is placed at point A, its image is observed
    (1) at F (3) to the right of C
    (2) between F and C (4) to the left of the mirror

90. If an object is located at point A, its image is
    (1) virtual and inverted   (3) real and inverted
    (2) virtual and erect   (4) real and erect

91. Which phenomenon allows a lens to focus light?
    (1) diffraction   (3) interference
    (2) refraction   (4) polarization

92. The diagram below represents an object placed two focal lengths from a converging lens.

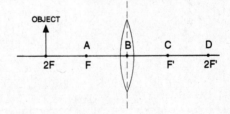

At which point will the image be located?
    (1) A (3) C
    (2) B (4) D

93. An image that is 1.0×10^{-2} meter tall is formed on a screen behind a converging lens when an object 2.0 meters tall is placed 8.0 meters in front of the lens. What is the distance from the lens to the screen?
    (1) 2.5×10^{-3} m   (3) 4.0×10^{-2} m
    (2) 2.5×10^{-1} m   (4) 4.0×10^{-1} m

94. A student uses a magnifying glass to examine the crystals in a mineral specimen. The magnifying glass contains a
    (1) convex (diverging) mirror   (3) concave (diverging) lens
    (2) convex (converging) lens   (4) plane mirror

95. The focal length of a lens is *not* dependent on the
    (1) material from which the lens is made
    (2) color of the light incident on the lens
    (3) distance of an object from the lens
    (4) shape or curvature of the lens

Group 5—Solid State

If you choose this group, be sure to answer questions 96–105.

96. Copper is to conductor as germanium is to
    (1) insulator
    (2) fuse
    (3) resistor
    (4) semiconductor

97. The diagram at the right shows the valence and conduction bands of an intrinsic semiconductor. Some of the electrons in the valence band have been promoted to the conduction band.

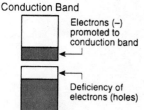

Which diagram below best represents the valence and conduction bands of the intrinsic semiconductor when its temperature is increased?

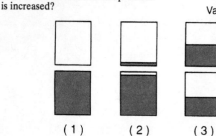

(1)　　　　(2)　　　　(3)　　　　(4)

98. What does the diagram below represent?

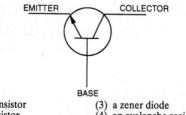

    (1) an *N-P-N* transistor
    (2) a *P-N-P* transistor
    (3) a zener diode
    (4) an avalanche region

Base your answers to questions 99 and 100 on the diagram below which represents an *N*-type silicon semiconductor connected to a battery.

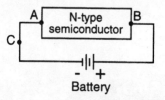

99. A very small amount of antimony, which has 5 valence electrons, had previously been added to the silicon crystal. This process produced
    (1) an excess of free electrons
    (2) an excess of free protons
    (3) more resistance
    (4) a higher emf

100. Which statement best describes the flow of charge through the conducting wire between points *A* and *C*?
    (1) Electrons flow from *A* to *C*.
    (2) Electrons flow from *C* to *A*.
    (3) Holes flow from *A* to *C*.
    (4) Holes flow from *C* to *A*.

101. Which diagram below represents a *P-N* junction with a forward bias?

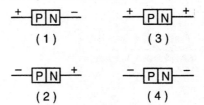

102. Materials such as indium that provide "holes" to semiconductors are often referred to as
    (1) holistic
    (2) donors
    (3) acceptors
    (4) *N*-types

103. The diagram below shows alternating current input to a black box containing diodes.

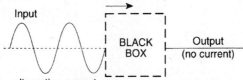

Which diode configuration in the black box accounts for the output (no current)?

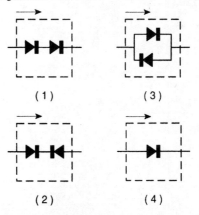

104. As a result of transistor amplification, small increases in the emitter-base current will bring about large
    (1) decreases in the emitter-base voltage
    (2) decreases in the collector current
    (3) increases in the emitter-base voltage
    (4) increases in the collector current

Note that question 105 has only three choices.

105. A source of alternating current, a junction diode, and a lamp are connected, as shown in the diagram below.

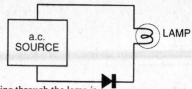

The current passing through the lamp is
(1) alternating current, only
(2) direct current, only
(3) both alternating and direct current

Group 6—Nuclear Energy

If you choose this group, be sure to answer questions 106–115.

Base your answers to questions 106 through 109 on the information in the chart below.

Particle	Rest Mass
proton	1.0073 u
neutron	1.0087 u

106. The energy equivalent of the rest mass of a proton is approximately
(1) 9.4×10^2 MeV
(2) 1.9×10^3 MeV
(3) 9.1×10^{16} MeV
(4) 6.4×10^{18} MeV

107. A tritium nucleus consists of one proton and two neutrons and has a total mass of 3.0170 atomic mass units. What is the mass defect of the tritium nucleus?
(1) 0.0014 u
(2) 0.0077 u
(3) 1.0010 u
(4) 2.0160 u

108. Which force between the proton and neutrons in a tritium atom has the greatest magnitude?
(1) electrostatic force
(2) gravitational force
(3) magnetic force
(4) nuclear force

109. Tritium would most likely be used as a
(1) fuel in a fusion reaction
(2) fuel in a fission reaction
(3) coolant in a nuclear reactor
(4) moderator in a nuclear reactor

110. A nucleus having an odd number of protons and an odd number of neutrons is likely to be radioactive. Which nuclide matches this description?

(1) $^{29}_{14}\text{Si}$

(2) $^{32}_{15}\text{P}$

(3) $^{32}_{16}\text{S}$

(4) $^{35}_{17}\text{Cl}$

111. How do cloud chambers, spark chambers, and Geiger counters aid in the study of the nucleus?
(1) They detect subatomic particles that exit the nucleus.
(2) They detect the presence of a magnetic field around the nucleus.
(3) They accelerate the nucleus before it collides with the particle beam.
(4) They accelerate subatomic particles that exit the nucleus.

112. Which nuclear particle is emitted as an atom of $^{238}_{92}\text{U}$ decays to $^{234}_{90}\text{Th}$?

(1) neutron
(2) positron
(3) alpha particle
(4) beta particle

113. In the equation below, what is particle X?

$$^{9}_{4}Be + {}^{4}_{2}He \longrightarrow {}^{12}_{6}C + X$$

    (1) an electron   (3) a positron
    (2) a proton   (4) a neutron

114. In a nuclear reactor, the function of a control rod is to
    (1) slow down neutrons   (3) absorb neutrons
    (2) speed up neutrons   (4) produce neutrons

115. The radioactive waste strontium-90 has a half-life of 28 years. How long must a sample of strontium-90 be stored to insure that only $\frac{1}{16}$ of the original sample remains as radioactive strontium-90?
    (1) 28 years   (3) 84 years
    (2) 56 years   (4) 112 years

PART III

You must answer *all* questions in this part. Record your answers in the spaces provided on the separate answer paper. Pen or pencil may be used. [15]

Base your answers to questions 116 through 118 on the diagram and data table below. The diagram shows a worker moving a 50.0-kilogram safe up a ramp by applying a constant force of 300. newtons parallel to the ramp. The data table shows the position of the safe as a function of time.

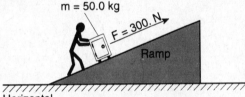

m = 50.0 kg

F = 300. N

Ramp

Horizontal

Time (s)	Distance Moved up the Ramp (m)
0.0	0.0
1.0	2.2
2.0	4.6
3.0	6.6
4.0	8.6
5.0	11.0

116. Using the information in the data table, construct a line graph on the grid provided *on your answer paper*. Plot the data points *and* draw the best-fit line. [2]

The grid on the next page is provided for practice purposes only. Be sure your final answer appears *on your answer paper*.

Distance vs. Time

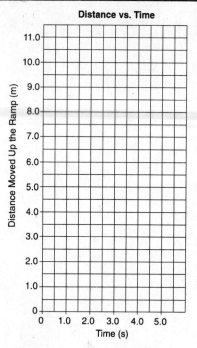

117. Using one or more complete sentences, explain the physical significance of the slope of the graph. [1]

118. Calculate the work done by the worker in the first 3.0 seconds. [Show all calculations, including the equation and substitution with units.] [2]

Base your answers to questions 119 and 120 on the information below.

An electron is accelerated from the rest to a speed of 2.0×10^6 meters per second.

119. How much kinetic energy is gained by the electron as it is accelerated from rest to this speed? [Show all calculations, including the equation and substitution with units.] [2]

120. What is the matter wavelength of the electron after it is accelerated to this speed? [Show all calculations, including the equations and substitution with units.] [3]

$$E = hf = \frac{hc}{\lambda}$$

$$\text{KEmax} = hf - W_0$$

$$E = mc^2$$

$$\uparrow \quad \nwarrow \text{speed}$$
mass $\qquad$ of light

$$E = pc \quad \boxed{p} = mc \quad \nearrow \text{momentum}$$

$$\cdot \; hf = pc$$

$$p = \frac{h}{\lambda}$$

Base your answers to questions 121 through 124 on the information and diagram below. The diagram represents a wave generator having a constant frequency of 12 hertz producing parallel wave fronts in a ripple tank. The velocity of the waves is *v*.

RIPPLE TANK

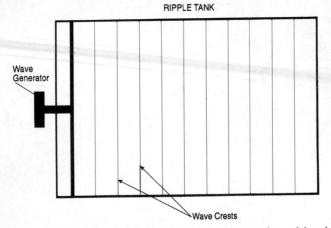

121. Using a ruler, measure the wavelength of the waves shown and record the value *on your answer paper to the nearest tenth of a centimeter.* [1]

122. Determine the speed of the waves in the ripple tank. [Show all calculations, including the equation and substitution with units.] [2]

123. A barrier is placed in the ripple tank as shown in the diagram below. [The same diagram appears on your answer paper.]

RIPPLE TANK

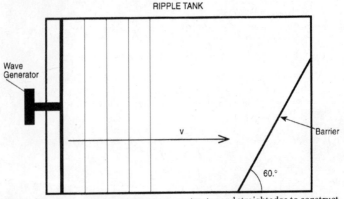

On the diagram on your answer paper, use a protractor and straightedge to construct an arrow to represent the direction of the velocity of the reflected waves. [1]

124. Using one or more complete sentences, state the Law of Reflection. [1]